BOB DYLAN LIVE IN CANADA

A CONCERT HISTORY, 1962-2005

by BRADY J. LEYSER
and OLOF BJÖRNER

Front and back cover photo: Bob Dylan in Kitchener, Ontario on October 31, 1981. Reproduced with permission of the Kitchener-Waterloo Record Photographic Negative Collection, University of Waterloo Library. All rights reserved.

Note for Librarians: A cataloguing record for this book is available from Library and Archives Canada at www.collectionscanada.ca/amicus/index-e.html
ISBN 1-4120-8372-9

Printed in Victoria, BC, Canada. Printed on paper with minimum 30% recycled fibre.
Trafford's print shop runs on "green energy" from solar, wind and other environmentally-friendly power sources.

Offices in Canada, USA, Ireland and UK

Book sales for North America and international:
Trafford Publishing, 6E–2333 Government St.,
Victoria, BC V8T 4P4 CANADA
phone 250 383 6864 (toll-free 1 888 232 4444)
fax 250 383 6804; email to orders@trafford.com
Book sales in Europe:
Trafford Publishing (UK) Limited, 9 Park End Street, 2nd Floor
Oxford, UK OX1 1HH UNITED KINGDOM
phone 44 (0)1865 722 113 (local rate 0845 230 9601)
facsimile 44 (0)1865 722 868; info.uk@trafford.com
Order online at:
trafford.com/06-0127

10 9 8 7 6 5 4 3 2

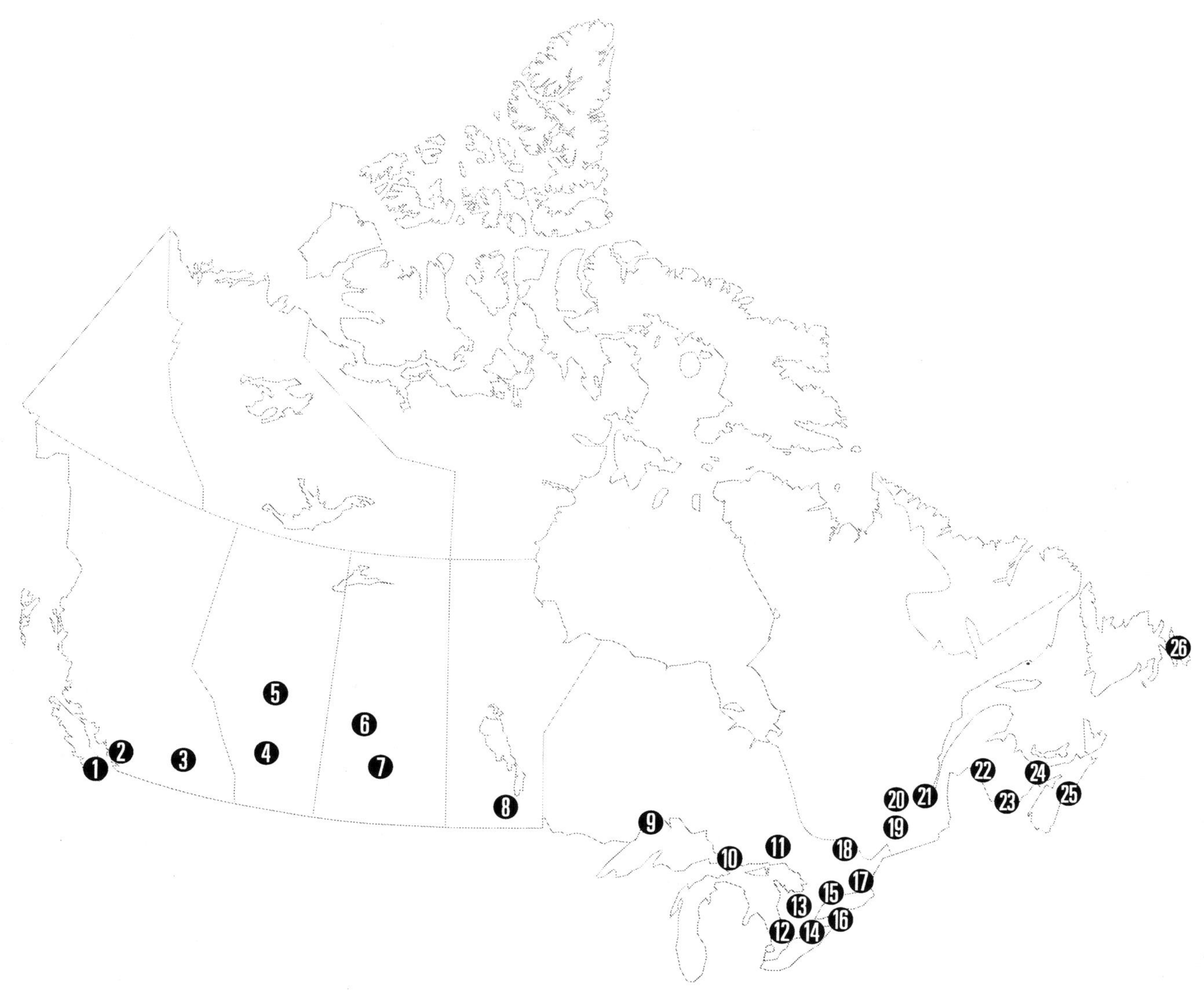

Canadian Cities Where Bob Dylan Has Performed

1. Victoria, BC
2. Vancouver, BC
3. Kelowna, BC
4. Calgary, AB
5. Edmonton, AB
6. Saskatoon, SK
7. Regina, SK
8. Winnipeg, MB
9. Thunder Bay, ON
10. Sault Ste. Marie, ON
11. Sudbury, ON
12. London, ON
13. Kitchener, ON
14. Hamilton, ON
15. Toronto, ON
16. Niagara Falls, ON
17. Kingston, ON
18. Ottawa, ON
19. Montreal, QC
20. Joliette, QC
21. Quebec City, QC
22. Saint John, NB
23. Fredericton, NB
24. Moncton, NB
25. Halifax, NS
26. St. John's, NL

Contents

Introduction

Bob Dylan has performed 119 concerts in Canada. This book is a concert-by-concert, song-by-song, exploration of those concerts.

A concert experience elicits many emotions. From the pre-show anticipation – to the adrenaline rush of the concert – to the excitement of the post show analysis – to reading the reviews in the morning newspapers.

As well, a concert experience ultimately evokes many memories. The stage set-up, the band, the songs, the venue, who you went to the show with, what was happening in your life at the time and many other incidentals, perhaps meaningful only to you.

In essence one could say this book is jam packed with memories. The memories of the concerts you were at and/or the ones you wish you had been at.

And while this book is definitely a historic record of Bob Dylan concerts in Canada, I don't see it as a time capsule but rather a recurring evolution.

It is common knowledge that Mr. Dylan certainly does not look back. Iconic figures tend to do that.

However, fans are different and this book is for the fans, both old and new alike. Hopefully, it will bring back some wonderful memories, give you new or renewed appreciation and most definitely make you wait in anticipation for Bob Dylan's next concert in Canada.

So this is the story so far.

Bob Dylan has:

- Performed 119 concerts in Canada. The debut concert was in Montreal (1962) and the most recent show was in Calgary (2005).
- Played in twenty-six Canadian cities from coast-to-coast. He has performed in Toronto the most times followed by Montreal and Vancouver.
- Performed 1,923 songs in Canada that have been documented. He has played 241 different songs.
- Played seventy-seven songs only once in Canada.
- Performed eleven songs that made their worldwide live debut in Canada.
- Played the songs All Along the Watchtower, Like a Rolling Stone and Highway 61 Revisited the most times in Canada.
- Performed 181 individual songs from thirty-five different albums. In total, these songs have been performed 1,796 times.
- Played songs from the albums Highway 61 Revisited, Bringing It All Back Home and The Freewheelin' Bob Dylan more times than any other album.
- Performed 8 unreleased songs. In total, these songs have been performed twenty-five times.
- Played 52 cover and/or traditional songs. In total, these songs have been played 102 times.
- Opened his Canadian concerts with thirty different songs and closed them with twenty-one different songs.
- Performed Gotta Serve Somebody as the opening song at the most concerts and All Along the Watchtower as the closing song at the most concerts.
- Toured and performed with 65 different band members at his 119 concerts in Canada. Current and long time band member Tony Garnier has played more concerts with Dylan in Canada than any other musician.
- Toured in Canada with 26 different acts, be it opening acts or bands on a shared bill. He has not toured in Canada with an opening act since 1998 or been on a shared bill since 2000.
- Performed at sixty-two different venues in Canada. He has played Massey Hall in Toronto the most times followed by Maple Leaf Gardens in Toronto and the Montreal Forum.
- Played more shows in Canada in 1990 than any other year. There were sixteen concerts in 1990.
- Performed in Canada the most times in the month of August.
- Played in Canada the most times on the 29th day of the month.
- Performed in Canada the most times on a Friday night.
- Played in nine Canadian provinces.

About the Set Lists

The set lists are complete from 1974 through 2005. Set lists are not available for five concerts and are incomplete for seven concerts.

- 1962 (three unknown set lists and two incomplete set lists)
- 1964 (one incomplete set list)
- 1965 (two unknown set lists and one incomplete set list)
- 1966 (three incomplete set lists)

About the Reviews

There are 229 concert reviews included in the book. They have been placed in the order that enabled the text to flow from page to page, regardless of their source or their content. All reviews have been reprinted exactly the way they were originally written.

I don't necessarily agree with a few of the reviews (at least for the concerts I have attended) and judging from the number of "Letters to the Editor" we found, many fans have also expressed their mixed opinions. But that is often the case with a concert review. No "Letters to the Editor" have been included in the book.

The majority of the reviews are from newspapers. There are also citations to another 17 concert reviews that appeared in newspapers we could not reprint for one reason or another.

We have also included a number of fan reviews found on various Dylan web sites including, Bob Links, The Dylan Pool, rec.music.dylan and Bobchronicles.com. The fan reviews make for a nice mix. In fact, we would have included more of them had we been able to track down the authors for reprint permission.

About Other Appearances

In addition to the concerts there is a brief section on Bob Dylan's other significant appearances in Canada, including one of the defining moments in the history of rock. It happened in 1965 when Bob Dylan officially hooked up with Levon and the Hawks, later to be called The Band. They began rehearsals for the 1965 Electric Tour at the Friar's Tavern, now the site of the Hard Rock Café in Toronto.

About the Indexes

There are eighteen special indexes of statistical analysis included in the book. They encompass a wide range of data including; Songs Performed, Songs Performed by Album, Musicians on Tour, Concerts by City and Concerts by Venue.

All indexes related to songs performed are based on the set list data that is known (see above). That means the totals in some indexes are obviously not going to be exact since we do not have the complete information necessary to make such a calculation and/or statement. But that's okay. They are also meant to be fun and engaging.

About the Ticket Stubs

There are copies of 82 tickets stubs included in the book. The earliest stub dates back to 1974 and the most recent one is from 2005. There are no ticket stubs for any of Bob Dylan's Canadian concerts in the 1960's.

About the Book

We have made no attempt to contact Mr. Dylan or his management regarding this book. However, we do plan to send him a copy.

The authors welcome any comments or suggestions about the book or any additional information to be added to the book.

It has been a truly amazing experience compiling this book. I sincerely hope you enjoy it!

Brady J. Leyser

April 2006.

Acknowledgements

I would like to take this opportunity to acknowledge the hundreds of people whose participation and contributions helped make this book possible. As well as the numerous newspapers, magazines, wire services, and web sites that played an integral role in the process.

First and foremost, I would like to thank Bob Dylan for providing Canadians with so many enjoyable concerts. We all look forward to your next visit to Canada.

This book is based on the incredibly detailed research of Olof Björner. It's safe to say that even the most casual Dylan fan has probably surfed Olof's wonderful web site "I Happen To Be A Swede Myself" (http://www.bjorner.com). Even Dylan's official site calls it "The best online source of sheer data on Bob Dylan's recording and touring history." When I first contacted Olof about using his set list data for this book, he embraced the project immediately. It is an honour for me to co-author this book with him. Thanks Olof.

I would especially like to thank Patty and Mishka for their loving support and encouragement from the very beginning.

A book of this nature takes a dedicated team. I was fortunate to have Nick Aspinall as my research assistant. Nick spent many hours combing through microfilms, tracking down ticket stubs, transcribing reviews and proofreading. Thanks Nick.

I would like to thank Kal Bedder for his front and back cover design, as well as his guidance throughout the book.

Thanks also to Christina Ogrodnick for her layout of the ticket stubs.

I would also like to thank my talented trio of typists – Jennifer Ball, Lesley Mills and Nicole Steep.

Special thanks go out to Angeles Devesa, Veronica Dimofski and all of the goods folks at Trafford Publishing.

I am very grateful to the Kitchener-Waterloo Record Photographic Negative Collection at the University of Waterloo Library for permission to reproduce the photo on the front and back covers.

I would especially like to thank the 148 writers whose reviews appear in this book. The list reads like a who's who of Canadian music critics, past and present.

James Adams
Denis Armstrong
John Bachusky
Ira Band
Greg Barr
Ron Base
Pierre Beaulieu
Mike Bell
Christiane Berthiaume
Susan Beyer
Bruce Blackadar
Mike Blanchfield
Alain Brunet
Greg Burliuk
Paul Cantin
Allan Casey
Adrian Chamberlain
Elizabeth Chorney-Booth
Charles Cicirella
Chris Cobb
Alan Cochrane
Sylvain Cormier
Chris Dafoe
Daisy DeBolt
Michel Defoy
Helene des Rosiers
Marq DeSouza
Mike Devlin
Mary Dickie
Mike Doherty
T'cha Dunlevy
Bruce Erskine
Robert Everett-Green
Antony Ferry
Robert Fulford
Denis Foley
Cam Fuller
Dale Gago
Patrick Gauthier
Katherine Gilday
John Goddard
Peter Goddard
Kerry Gold
Paul-Henri Goulet
Kieran Grant
Lisa Gregoire
Carole Grenier
John Griffin
Fish Griwkowsky
Jonathan Gross
Barrie Hale
David Hanley
Tom Harrison
Cory Hawley
Gary Hebbard
Don Helling
Nate Hendley
Ralph Hicklin
Peter Howell
Marc André Joanisse
Robert Johnston
Urjo Kareda
John Kendle
John Kiely
Bartley Kives
Alan Kollins
Nick Krewen
Gerry Krochak
Richard Labbé
Liam Lacey
Wilfred Langmaid
Dane Lanken
Denis Lavoie
Kathleen Lavoie
Bruce Lawson
Marthe Lemery
Brady J. Leyser
William Littler
Sandy MacDonald
John Mackie
Alix MacLean
Mariloup Malboeuf
Robert Martin
Joe Matyas
Alison Mayes
Heath McCoy
Paul McGrath
Helen Metella
Nick Miliokas
Jason Mitchell
Tony Montague
Wayne Moriarty
James Muretich
Pierre O. Nadeau
Shirley Newhook
Alan Niester
Peter North
Martin O'Malley
Finbarr O'Reilly
Stephen Ostick
Rick Overall
Vaughn Palmer
Ian Pattison
Stephen Pedersen
Yvon Pellerin
Wilder Penfield III
Colette Perron
Nathalie Petrowski
Chisholm Pothier
Mitch Potter
Betsy Powell
Bill Provick
Shawn Pulver
Greg Quill
Robert Reguly
Philippe Renaud
Bill Reynolds
Philippe Rezzonico
Hans Rollmann
Mike Ross
Paul Roux
Mario Roy
John Sakamoto
Lynn Saxberg
Marvin Schiff
Robert Guy Scully
Jean Sébastien
Derek Shelly
David Sherman
Martin Smith
Sandra Sperounes
Darryl Sterdan
Jane Stevenson
Jerry Tenenbaum
Mike Tenszen
Bob Thompson
Marcus Thunich
Derek Tse
Kyle Valanne
Lucretia van den Berg
David Veitch
Vit Wagner
Morley Walker
Bruce Ward
Neil Watson
Andre Wetjen
Angela Wierzbicki
Lisa Wilton

I would also like to thank the 53 different newspapers, magazines, wire services and web sites where the reviews appeared.

Bob Links
Bobchronicles.com
The Calgary Herald
The Calgary Sun
CanWest News Service
The Charlottetown Guardian
Chartattack.com
Le Devoir
LeDroit
The Dylan Pool
The Edmonton Journal
The Edmonton Sun
The Fredericton Daily Gleaner
fRoots
The Georgia Straight
The Globe and Mail
The Halifax Chronicle-Herald
The Halifax Daily News
The Hamilton Spectator
Jam! Music
Le Journal de Montréal
Le Journal de Québec
The Kelowna Daily Courier
The Kingston Whig-Standard
The Kitchener-Waterloo Record
The London Free Press
The Moncton Times & Transcript
The Montreal Gazette
The Nanaimo Daily News
The National Post
The New Brunswick Telegraph-Journal
The Ottawa Citizen
The Ottawa Sun
La Presse
rec.music.dylan
The Regina Leader Post
The Saint John Telegraph-Journal
The St. John's Telegram
The Saskatoon StarPhoenix
The Sault Star
Le Soleil
The Sudbury Star
The Thunder Bay Chronicle-Journal
The Toronto Star
The Toronto Sun
The Toronto Telegram
The Vancouver Express
The Vancouver Province
The Vancouver Sun
The Victoria Times Colonist
The Winnipeg Free Press
The Winnipeg Sun
Y&R Daily Reading

Every single review appearing in this book is copyrighted. I would like to thank all the individuals responsible for granting reprint permission.

Ian Anderson
Lynne Bazinet
Phylis Beaulieu
Claudette Béliveau
Francine Bellefeuille
Alain Brunet
Hélène Caron
Roger Cazabon
Charles Cicirella
Caron Court
Marie-Hélène D'André
Marq DeSouza
Kathy Dilts
Mike Doherty
Brian Dryden
Howard M. Elliott
Catherine Flegg
Carl Fleming
Dale Gago
Jillian Goddard
John Halucha
David Hanley
Cory Hawley
Don Helling
Nate Hendley
Louise Higgs
Al Hogan
Mary Hogan
Robert Johnston
Alan Kollins
Richard Labbé
Wilfred Langmaid
Dane Lanken
Nada Laskovski
Brady J. Leyser
William Littler
Joanne MacDonald
Gary MacDougall
Alix MacLean
Anita McCallum
Don McCurdy
Tony Montague
Pierre O. Nadeau
Alan Niester
Peter North
Shawn Pulver
Philippe Renaud
Bill Reynolds
Kelsey Robins
Hans Rollmann
John C. Sullivan
Leann Swalwell
Jerry Tenenbaum
June Thompson
Marcus Thunich
Mark Tunney
Christina Spencer
Kyle Valanne
Lucretia van den Berg
Danièle Viger
Russell Wangersky
Andre Wetjen
Bill Witcomb

The majority of ticket stubs reproduced in this book have been downloaded from Mark Scalise's The Bob Dylan Ticket Stub Archive at Dylanstubs.com. Additional tickets stubs are from my own collection, my friend's collections and the individuals who graciously answered the classified ads we ran seeking specific stubs. I want to thank the people listed below. Unfortunately we do not have all the names of the Dylanstubs.com contributors.

Dag Braathen
Michael Cakebread
David Clarance
Kevin Gohm
Dusty Harloff
Hiroshi Hemmi
Jim & Gail
Marty Greenberg
Frank Mroz
Michel Jacques
Robert Lawson
Brent Nimilowich
Kevin Norman
Tom Paul
Gord Robertson
Doug Schnurr
Tracy Schnurr
Mark Scalise
David Soltys

The following web sites proved to be an invaluable source of information. I would like to thank all the people who maintain and contribute to these sites.

- The Official Bob Dylan site – http://www.bobdylan.com
- Bill Pagel's excellent Bob Links – http://my.execpc.com/~billp61/boblink.html
- Karl Erik Andersen's fantastic Expecting Rain – http://www.expectingrain.com
- Mark Scalise's wonderful Dylanstubs.com – http://www.dylanstubs.com
- Arthur Louie's fun filled The Dylan Pool – http://pool.dylantree.com
- The always interesting rec.music.dylan – http://groups.google.com/group/rec.music.dylan
- Bobchronicles.com – http://www.bobchronicles.com

Acknowledgements

In "The Yearly Chronicles" section of Olof's web site he lists his sources for each year. I would like to acknowledge the work of these prior Dylan researchers.

Watt Alexander
Sven Erick Alm
John Baldwin
Derek Barker
Tracy Barker
Paul Cable
William J. Clinton
Glen Dundas
Tim Dunn
Alan Fraser
Sandy Gant
Clinton Heylin
John Howells
Michael Krogsgaard
Craig Pinkerton
Ray Stravou
Ian Woodward
John Wraith
Mike Wyvill

Thanks also go to The Dylan Stockholm Society and all the individuals involved with the following Dylan specific magazines/newsletters.

- The Bridge – http://www.two-riders.co.uk
- Isis Magazine – http://www.bobdylanisis.com
- Judas! – http://www.judasmagazine.com
- On the Tracks: The Unauthorized Bob Dylan Magazine – http://www.b-dylan.com/pages/magazine.shtml
- Series of Dreams – http://www.b-dylan.com/pages/newsletter.shtml
- The Telegraph.
- The Wicked Messenger Newsletter (now part of Isis Magazine)

Thank you to the following librarian's for their assistance; Stephanie Furrow, Sarah Gladwell, Cathy MacDonald, Dianne Seager and Rita.

As well I would like to thank to the following libraries.

The Calgary Public Library
The Fredericton Public Library
The Metropolitan Toronto Reference Library
The Moncton Public Library
The National Library of Canada
The Saint John Free Public Library
The University of Concordia, Webster Library
The University of Toronto, Robarts Library
The University of Waterloo, Dana Porter Library

Special thanks go out to:

Kevin Au
Michelle Au
Janet Dean
Kevin Francois
Blair Hoffman
Daniela Hoffman
Julia Hoffman
Matthew Meagher
Elizabeth P. Rentschler
Grace P. Rentschler
Peter Rentschler
Peter R. Rentschler Jr.
Peter R. Rentschler III
Jessika Rousseau
Gary Smith
The Boyz Club

I would also like to thank my family, as well as Bill & Desi Benet, Gints Bruveris, Dave Collis, Tammy Ezer, Mona Goldstein, David Gordon, John & Lynne Gould, Linda Gross, Olivia Leyser, Gary Marsh, Chris McGroarty, Ian Mirlin, Susan Murray, Ken Nicholson, Norm Oliveira, Heidi Prange, Jennifer Reid, Shawn Sage, Ken Solmon, Marilyn Stewart, Sean & Laura Wakfer, Shawn Wright, and my colleagues at Young & Rubicam Brands.

This book is dedicated to all the Bob Dylan fans from coast-to-coast across Canada.

1962

Introduction

Bob Dylan made his Canadian live debut in 1962. Although virtually unknown outside of New York's Greenwich Village at the time, his first album released only a few months earlier, Mr. Dylan played five-straight nights in Montreal.

These shows would mark Bob Dylan's debut concert, 2nd, 3rd, 4th & 5th concert in Canada.

The Dates

Montreal, QC	Thurs., June 28, 1962
Montreal, QC	Fri., June 29, 1962
Montreal, QC	Sat., June 30, 1962
Montreal, QC	Sunday, July 1, 1962
Montreal, QC	Mon., July 2, 1962

The shows would be Dylan's debut concert, 2nd, 3rd, 4th, & 5th concert in Montreal.

On Stage

Bob Dylan (vocal, guitar & harmonica).

The Songs

Only thirteen of the songs Bob Dylan performed are known. Of those, 6 were from albums, 2 were unreleased songs and 5 were cover and/or traditional songs.

Thirteen songs made their Canadian live debut. (Obviously, many other songs would have made their Canadian live debut).

Freight Train Blues	Quit Your Low Down Ways
Baby, Let Me Follow You Down	He Was a Friend of Mine
The Death of Emmett Till	Let Me Die in My Footsteps
Stealin'	Two Trains Runnin'
Hiram Hubbard	Ramblin' On My Mind
Blowin' in the Wind	Muleskinner Blues
Rocks and Gravel	–

Eleven songs have been played only once in Canada.

Freight Train Blues	He Was a Friend of Mine
The Death of Emmett Till	Let Me Die in My Footsteps
Stealin'	Two Trains Runnin'
Hiram Hubbard	Ramblin' On My Mind
Rocks and Gravel	Muleskinner Blues
Quit Your Low Down Ways	–

Bob Dylan performed songs from 3 different albums.

Album	Released	# of Songs Performed by Album
Bob Dylan	March 19, 1962	2
The Freewheelin' Bob Dylan	May, 27, 1963	1
The Bootleg Series Volumes 1-3	March 26, 1991	3

The Venues

It was Bob Dylan's debut concert and 2nd, 3rd, & 4th time playing at The Pot-pourri in Montreal and debut concert at The Finjan Club in Montreal.

Opening Act

Derek Lamb opened at least one of the four shows at The Pot-pourri.

Thursday, June 28, 1962 --- The Pot-pourri
Montreal, QC

Set List

	Song	From The Album	Released
1.	Freight Train Blues (trad. arranged by Bob Dylan)	Bob Dylan	March 19, 1962
2.	Baby, Let Me Follow You Down	Bob Dylan	March 19, 1962

On Stage

Bob Dylan (vocal, guitar & harmonica).

Notes

- Debut Bob Dylan concert in Canada; Debut Bob Dylan concert in Montreal.
- Canadian live debut of songs 1 & 2.
- Song 1 has been performed only once in Canada.
- The set list is incomplete and the exact order the songs were played is unknown.

Friday, June 29, 1962 --- The Pot-pourri
Montreal, QC

On Stage

Bob Dylan (vocal, guitar & harmonica).

Notes

- 2nd Bob Dylan concert in Canada; 2nd Bob Dylan concert in Montreal.
- The set list is unknown.

Saturday, June 30, 1962 --- The Pot-pourri
Montreal, QC

On Stage

Bob Dylan (vocal, guitar & harmonica).

Notes

- 3rd Bob Dylan concert in Canada; 3rd Bob Dylan concert in Montreal.
- The set list is unknown.

Sunday, July 1, 1962 --- The Pot-pourri
Montreal, QC

On Stage

Bob Dylan (vocal, guitar & harmonica).

Notes

- 4th Bob Dylan concert in Canada; 4th Bob Dylan concert in Montreal.
- The set list is unknown.

Monday, July 2, 1962 --- The Finjan Club
Montreal, QC

Set List

	Song	From The Album	Released
1.	The Death of Emmett Till	Unreleased	–
2.	Stealin' (trad. Arr. Memphis Jug Band)	–	–
3.	Hiram Hubbard (trad.)	–	–
4.	Blowin' in the Wind	The Freewheelin' Bob Dylan	May 27, 1963
5.	Rocks and Gravel	Unreleased	–
6.	Quit Your Low Down Ways	The Bootleg Series Volumes 1-3	March 26, 1991
7.	He Was a Friend of Mine (arr. by Bob Dylan)	The Bootleg Series Volumes 1-3	March 26, 1991
8.	Let Me Die in My Footsteps	The Bootleg Series Volumes 1-3	March 26, 1991
9.	Two Trains Runnin' (McKinley Morganfield)	–	–
10.	Ramblin' On My Mind (Robert Johnson)	–	–
11.	Muleskinner Blues (Jimmie Rodgers & George Vaughan)	–	–

On Stage

Bob Dylan (vocal, guitar & harmonica).

Notes

- 5th Bob Dylan concert in Canada; 5th Bob Dylan concert in Montreal
- Canadian live debut of songs 1, 2, 3, 4, 5, 6, 7, 8, 9, 10 & 11.
- Songs 1, 2, 3, 5, 6, 7, 8, 9, 10 & 11 have been performed only once in Canada.
- A fragment of Blowin' in the Wind was released on the Interactive Music CD-ROM, Bob Dylan: Highway 61 Interactive in Feb. 1995.
- The set list is incomplete and the exact order the songs were played is unknown.

Review

'He was crazy but I was impressed'

By Dane Lanken, of The Gazette.

"I think it will be something I can tell people about," said Kermit Lawson, 27, an executive with a Chicago paper company who managed to get his hands on two tickets to the opening concert.

"Five years from now I can say that I was there." – Associated Press, Chicago, January 3, 1974.

When Bob Dylan finishes his 21-city tour next month, 650,000 people will be able to say that they were there.

Close to 40,000 of those people will be able to say they saw Dylan at the Montreal Forum.

That's a lot of people. A lot more than can say they were among the 3,000 who saw Dylan at his 1966 concert at Place des Arts.

And an awful lot more than the few dozen who saw a very young and unknown Bob Dylan the first time he played in Montreal.

That was back in June 1962, at a coffee house called the Pot-pourri on Stanley Street, where the Rainbow Bar & Grill is now. Dylan spent a week in Montreal, pleased the handful of people who already liked him, annoyed most of the rest – and took away $200 for his efforts.

Just for fun, I looked up some of the people who went to see Mr. D on his first visit here, to see what (if anything) they remembered. Of course they all remembered him well, whether because he made a terrific impression at the time, or because he just happened to become the most important figure in mid-20th century music-poetry.

Peter Weldon was one of those Dylan-watchers, as were his sister, now Phyllis Birks, Anna McGarrigle, Jack Nissenson, Bob Presner, Moishe Feinberg, who owned the Pot-pourri, and Shimon Ash, who ran Montreal's 'other' coffee house of the time, the Finjan up on Victoria Ave.

Some were more 'sold' on Dylan than others back then, but all followed his career. Some went to New York to see his first concert performances, at Town Hall in early '63 and at Carnegie Hall a little later. And most watched when Darryl Duke (who went on to make the fine film Payday) brought him to Toronto for the CBC-TV special at about the same time.

WAY BACK WHEN

Ahhh, Montreal in 1962. Fawzia Amir was the queen of belly-dancing, and her crown princess "the breath-taking Lila Gamel," was in residence in Lou Black's Living Room. When Dylan came here, Bo Diddley was making one of his regular visits to the Esquire Show Bar, and a controversial, "sick" comic named Lenny Bruce was about to open at the LaSalle Hotel.

The airwaves were full of Chubby Checker, Mr. Acker Bilk, Joey Dee and the Starliters, and Little Eva – not to mention the Kingston Trio and the Limeliters. Even the warblings of Joan Baez, were beginning to be noticed.

Perhaps it wasn't the most exciting of musical times, perhaps it was the lull before the storm of the Beatles, the Rolling Stones and Dylan himself.

Down in Greenwich Village, the storm was brewing. Two years before Time magazine recognized it, a "promising young hobo named Bob Dylan" was gathering a fanship that would grow bigger than anyone could have imagined. And one of the careful listeners was John Hammond, director of "talent acquisition" for Columbia Records.

Hammond has a rather remarkable record in acquiring talent. Back in the '30s he initiated the boogie-woogie craze by rediscovering its originator, Meade Lux Lewis, in a Chicago carwash. He went on to organize the Benny Goodman Orchestra, and brought another bandleader named Count Basie from Kansas City obscurity to New York renown.

He recorded Bessie Smith and Billie Holliday, and later gave Aretha Franklin her first recording contract. And in 1961 he signed Bob Dylan and produced his first record.

FIRST ALBUM

The release of Dylan's first LP, early in 1962, was an exciting moment in Greenwich Village. One of the people who got excited was a Montreal girl named Adele Suhl, who at that time, was traveling in the same circles as young Bob.

The first thing she did with her new record was send it to her friends in Montreal.

"It was amazing," recalls Peter Weldon, who like most of the early Dylan-watchers, is a musician himself.

"The first time I heard the record I thought Dylan was crazy – but I was terrifically impressed. On songs like See That My Grave Is Kept Clean or In My Time of Dyin', I had never heard anybody sing with that kind of freedom. Other singers at that time sounded like they were singing an arrangement, but he sang as if he were speaking.

"He had a contrived inflection, but it sounded completely natural.

"His guitar was not as sophisticated as someone like Robert Johnson, but it was far from ordinary. Perhaps he wasn't as technically adept, but he could do so much with a three or four note bass-run as opposed to a fancy arrangement. I had heard nobody with anything like that kind of ability."

Peter's reaction to the record was shared by the few others who heard it.

"It was shocking," says Anna, "but pleasantly so. I thought he was really daring. He didn't sound like anybody else, the standard folk act then being a trio with a guitar and a banjo and a lot of arrangements."

"We were all impressed," says Phyllis. "He sang songs so it seemed they belonged to him. Other people could play fancier stuff, but there was a nice drive to his music, rhythm and good phrasing.

"He sounded a lot like Woody Guthrie, but not like anyone else at the time. His talking blues were humorous and very good.

"It was also the first time," adds Phyllis, "that any of us had seen a harmonica holder. When my brother Christopher saw it (there was a picture on the back of the first LP) he took a coat hanger down to the basement, fiddled around, and came up with something that kind of held a harmonica.

"Adele took it to Dylan in New York, and when he saw it he said, 'hey, I could make a great coat hanger out of this'."

Everybody who went to Greenwich Village in those days, or anybody who came to Montreal from there, brought back stories about this great new talent named Bob Dylan. The singers who played at Moishe's Pot-pourri all talked about him.

"There was a guy named Barry Cornfield, a protégé of Rev. Gary Davis, who used to keep me abreast of up and coming talent," Moishe remembers. "He told me about Bob Dylan playing at Gerde's Folk City and he said why not try him out? So I did.

"There was no background to him, just the in-people in the Village said he was good.

"So when he came up, we were all surprised. He was very young, he looked scruffy, he had his railroad cap on. He was quiet, reserved, he wouldn't talk, and when he sang he sounded like the inheritor of Woody Guthrie's style.

"He played Thursday through Sunday. He got $200 and had to pay his own transportation up and back.

"There were some people there who liked him, but on the whole, he did not go over. The name meant nothing then, he was a poor draw. And personally, I was not that impressed."

Bob Presner, who used to run hootenannies at the Pot-pourri, was impressed.

"Hearing him was a sensual experience," Bob says, "like tasting a good piece of cake. But you got the feeling watching him that he was completely in his own world; nothing else existed except what he was doing himself. Just the same, he was so good, so innately talented, you couldn't be offended.

"As I remember, he used to go to the tavern next door to drink between sets.

"One other thing," Bob adds. "After he was here, it seemed anybody who sang, performers who came to the club or little guys like me, used to do a lot of Dylan songs. I can remember trying to hold that note as long as he did on Freight Train Blues."

SLOPPY LOOKING

"He was very sloppy looking," Anna recalls. "He was very pale and he was wearing a white shirt. He looked like a white worm.

"I asked him to sing Baby, Let Me Follow You Down, and he got excited and wanted to know where we'd heard the song. He said he'd sing it, but that he was drunk, having just come back from watching Bo Diddley down at the Esquire.

"So he did it – with his guitar in one key and his harmonica in another He knew he was doing it, and even if there'd been a hundred people in the audience – there were only four people there that night – he would have done it anyway. He carried it off.

Shimon Ash, who ran the Finjan, went up to the Pot-pourri one night to see what all the excitement was about. He was surprised.

"I'd been down in New York just before that," Shimon says, "watching Jack Elliott at Gerde's. At the end of a set Jack said 'I'd like you to hear a friend of mine', and on came this kid who started singing a lot of songs which nobody listened to. After a while the emcee came out and told him that was enough, and this kid, who was a cocky little guy, says 'no, lemme finish what I'm doing.'

'So then I go down to the Pot-pourri and walk in and see this same kid and my god, that was Bob Dylan!

GUEST SET

"He came up to the Finjan on the Monday night after he finished at the Pot-pourri and did a guest set. He sang for a long time, maybe an hour and a half-two hours, and I remember the place was empty when he finished.

"He told me then that he didn't want to play coffee houses anymore, he only wanted to do concerts. I remember thinking he won't make it.

"I was down in New York shortly after that, and I happened to hear Dylan say he wouldn't mind coming back to play Shimon's coffee house. I pretended not to hear him – I mean, I was in business and he wasn't a draw. Now they introduce me as the ass who turned down Bob Dylan at $250 a week.

"Incidentally," Shimon adds, "he always gave the impression then of drifting, never knowing what he was doing. He stayed at my house a couple of days, and never seemed to know where he was going – until one morning he's up at seven o'clock, says he has to catch a plane. I realized he knew exactly where he was going."

Jack Nissenson was a fan of traditional music and Bob Dylan (in that order) when he went to see Dylan at both coffee houses.

"I liked him," Jack says, "but I have the impression that most other people were mystified.

STORY-TELLER

"He was always an incredible story-teller. He was distant up onstage, very into his own thing; but he could do these long, long monologues, with no point and no punchline – except they kept you in hysterics.

"Same when you talked to him. He either told you a story, or he said 'yeah? Is that right?', as if what you were telling him was the most amazing thing he'd ever heard. But you could never get an opinion out of him, about politics or anything.

"One thing about him," Jack adds, "is that he is clearly very well educated in English literature and especially traditional music. All you have to do is check the songs he took his songs from – and they're songs nobody has ever heard!"

Jack had the presence to bring a tape recorder to that long guest set at the Finjan, and somewhere floating around Montreal today is a two-hour tape of a very young, unknown, but already idolized Bob Dylan.

As appeared in The Montreal Gazette. Sat., Jan. 12, 1974. Reprinted with permission of Dane Lanken.

1964

Introduction

Bob Dylan performed two concerts in Canada in 1964.

These shows would mark Bob Dylan's 6th & 7th concert in Canada.

The Dates

Toronto, ON	Sat., Feb. 1, 1964
Toronto, ON	Fri., Nov. 13, 1964

The shows would be Dylan's debut concert in Toronto and his 2nd concert in the city.

On Stage

Bob Dylan (vocal, guitar & harmonica).

The Songs

Only sixteen of the songs Bob Dylan performed are known. Of those, 13 were different songs.

Thirteen songs made their Canadian live debut.

The Times They Are A-Changin'	With God on Our Side
Talkin' World War III Blues	Gates of Eden
The Lonesome Death of Hattie Carroll	Don't Think Twice, It's All Right
Girl of the North Country	If You Gotta Go, Go Now
A Hard Rain's A-Gonna Fall	To Ramona
Restless Farewell	All I Really Want to Do
It's Alright, Ma (I'm Only Bleeding)	–

Three songs have been played only once in Canada.

Restless Farewell	If You Gotta Go, Go Now
With God on Our Side	–

Bob Dylan performed songs from 5 different albums.

Album	**Released**	**# of Songs Performed by Album**
The Freewheelin' Bob Dylan	May, 27, 1963	4
The Times They Are A-Changin'	Feb., 10, 1964	4
Another Side of Bob Dylan	Aug. 8, 1964	2
Bringing It All Back Home	March 22, 1965	2
The Bootleg Series Volumes 1-3	March 26, 1991	2

The Venues

It was Bob Dylan's debut concert at the CBC TV Studios in Toronto and debut concert at Massey Hall in Toronto.

Saturday, February 1, 1964 --- CBC TV Studios
Toronto, ON

Set List

	Song	From The Album	Released
1.	The Times They Are A-Changin'	The Times They Are A-Changin'	Feb. 10, 1964
2.	Talkin' World War III Blues	The Freewheelin' Bob Dylan	May 27, 1963
3.	The Lonesome Death of Hattie Carroll	The Times They Are A-Changin'	Feb. 10, 1964
4.	Girl of the North Country	The Freewheelin' Bob Dylan	May 27, 1963
5.	A Hard Rain's A-Gonna Fall	The Freewheelin' Bob Dylan	May 27, 1963
6.	Restless Farewell	The Times They Are A-Changin'	Feb. 10, 1964

On Stage

Bob Dylan (vocal, guitar & harmonica).

Notes

- 6th Bob Dylan concert in Canada; Debut Bob Dylan concert in Toronto.
- Canadian live debut of songs 1, 2, 3, 4, 5 & 6.
- Song 6 has been performed only once in Canada.
- Recorded by The Canadian Broadcasting Corporation (CBC) on Feb. 1, 1964 and broadcast on March 10, 1964 on the last episode of the CBC series Quest produced by Darryl Duke.

Press

Citybilly Bob Dylan prefers 'cerebral, visceral' songs

Folksinger no more, he says

By Robert Reguly.

Folksinger Bob Dylan ain't one no more.

Dylan, a skinny, fluffy-haired balladeer who looks like an unmade army cot, says he has graduated from that sort of innocuity.

'Got No Use for Your Red Apple Juice' doesn't talk to me anymore.

"Songs have to be more cerebral and visceral. Like: 'You who philosophize, disgrace and criticize old fears, take the mask away from your face. Now ain't the time for tears."

That's a line from one of his own compositions he'll sing on CBC's "Quest" March 10.

As he says, "My singing style is a conglomeration of contradictions."

NOT ARTISTIC THING

So is he. For a non folksinger, he could have fooled anyone.

In Toronto recently for the "Quest" taping, he wore cowboy boots, blue jeans, rumpled green twill shirt.

"It's not an artistic kind of thing," he explained, "I'm a lazy cat. I never shop for clothes and I'm too lazy even to clean up the place."

A citybilly from "the company town" of Hibbing, Minn. (he used to play hockey against Fort Francis teams) he is literate and articulate, yet can turn on quickly hillbilly accent and mannerisms.

He is acclaimed as the hottest folksinger in the U.S. today by such practitioners of the art as Joan Baez and Peter Yarrow, of Peter, Paul and Mary.

"The people never hear me," he says. "I'm known only through the people who sing my songs – Pete Seeger, Joanie Baez, Peter, Paul and Mary, Marlene Dietrich,"

'NO IDEA'

Then why do the faithful dig his style? "I have no idea. Any reason I would give would be bull, man."

His voice is reedy, but to the aficionados he is an original. His guitar a worthy descendant of Hank Williams, "Big Joe" Williams and Woody Guthrie – his big hero.

His song, "Blowin' In The Wind," has sold 1,000,000 records performed by others.

Most of his share goes to the SNVCC (pronounced "snick") the Student Non-Violent Co-ordinating Committee. It's bent on trying to get Southern U.S. Negroes over the vote barriers and into the polls.

"Rumors say I have illegitimate kids, that I have a $25-a-day junkie habit, that I didn't write Blowin In The Wind." It's all lies spread by people whom he refused to see, he says.

He says he wrote the song two years ago, started singing it around coffee houses and a teenage kid picked it up, appropriating it as his original, but later recanted.

His writing (mainly poetry, but he has now embarked on a play) is a paean to the downtrodden.

"I associate with people who can't picket. I'm writing for the Negro prostitute, for somebody fouled up in love, for somebody who is being stepped on 20 times a day."

He is engaged in the Negro fight for civil rights because "they are my friends before they are Negroes."

He once stomped off the Ed Sullivan show just before going on because they wanted him to cancel "Talking John Birch," losing a $1,000 fee.

He says he's appearing on Quest for a lot less. "But they're letting me sing the songs I want. I could never do it in the U.S."

The Toronto Star. Sat., March 7, 1964. Reprinted with permission - Torstar Syndication Services.

Dylan Is a Writer but Not a Folk Singer

By Ralph Hicklin.

Bob Dylan, a 22-year-old entertainer from New York who rejects the designation of folk singer, has found in Canadian television a freedom to write and sing what he likes, a freedom refused to him in his own country.

He is in Toronto to videotape a half-hour show in the Quest series: the telecast will consist simply of his singing songs of his own composition – songs which have been refused a hearing on such standbys as the Ed Sullivan Show. Sullivan, he explained, approved of the songs, but executives of the Columbia Broadcasting System vetoed the performance.

Dylan – a slight, sensitive-faced man whose wardrobe runs to cowboy boots and denims – gave this reason why U.S. networks shy away from his songs.

"I see no attraction in the topics they sing about on TV or the radio – about I-love-you, or soapsuds. I'll tell you about one of the songs I'll sing on Quest. It's called The Lonesome Death of Hattie Carroll. It's a true story, about this wealthy guy in Maryland, who killed his maid at a big society party.

"Hattie Carroll was like nobody," he continued, "This guy had no reason, he just hit her with a cane and killed her. He got six months.

"I wrote a poem about it, then I sang the poem. About the killing, people cry and say, 'What a tragedy.' About the six months, they say 'Ooh' – and to me, that's the tragedy."

Summing up his aims in composing and singing, he said: "I sing about what's in my mind – about hung-up people, caught up in real things. Why hide it? But they do hide it."

It's two years since Bob Dylan started writing and singing his own songs. Earlier, he had learned and sung folk songs, but that phase, he said, was merely "a stage of learning, about people and things. Folk music gave me a sense of language."

Dylan feels that he is primarily a writer. He has completed 1,000 pages of a novel – "maybe it's half done, maybe a third" – and is working on a play. In addition, Macmillan has contracted to publish three books he is working on in conjunction with a photographer. The first, about Hollywood, will appear this spring.

"The people I identify with," he said, "the people who are trying to do what I try to do, are other writers, like Jimmy Baldwin and Allen Ginsberg.

"But I haven't reached the masses: I'm misunderstood by the masses. I'm not James Dean. People thought he dug culture because he carried a camera and liked poetry. But you never saw any pictures, nor any poems, he'd made. Instead of being a phony idol, I do write and I do things. Idols only make people sad when they break. I break twice a minute.

"I dig beauty, I get images. I gave up folk songs when I discovered Ain't Got No Use For Your Red Apple Juice didn't say anything for me. I didn't want to lose my images."

In the United States, he said, he does not talk with reporters: he always travels with friends to avoid reporters – especially since two national news magazines performed what he considers hatchet jobs on him.

"Reporters try to make what I do political. They want to make me a folk singer, and I'm not a folk singer. They want me to answer questions, and I won't answer questions.

"I'm not a preacher. I'm not a politician. If I didn't write, I'd go insane. I love my guitar: it's a friend. Sometimes I get the feeling I'd like to get inside it, and sing out through the sound hole."

The Globe and Mail. Sat., Feb. 1, 1964. Reprinted with permission from The Globe and Mail.

Friday, November 13, 1964 --- Massey Hall Toronto, ON

Set List

	Song	From The Album	Released
1.	The Times They Are A-Changin'	The Times They Are A-Changin'	Feb. 10, 1964
2.	The Lonesome Death of Hattie Carroll	The Times They Are A-Changin'	Feb. 10, 1964
3.	Talkin' World War III Blues	The Freewheelin' Bob Dylan	May 27, 1963
4.	It's Alright, Ma (I'm Only Bleeding)	Bringing It All Back Home	March 22, 1965

5.	With God on Our Side	The Times They Are A-Changin'	Feb. 10, 1964
6.	Gates of Eden	Bringing It All Back Home	March 22, 1965
7.	Don't Think Twice, It's All Right	The Freewheelin' Bob Dylan	May 27, 1963
8.	If You Gotta Go, Go Now	The Bootleg Series Volumes 1-3	March 26, 1991
9.	To Ramona	Another Side of Bob Dylan	Aug. 8, 1964
10.	All I Really Want to Do	Another Side of Bob Dylan	Aug. 8, 1964

On Stage

Bob Dylan (vocal, guitar & harmonica).

Notes

- 7th Bob Dylan concert in Canada; 2nd Bob Dylan concert in Toronto.
- Canadian live debut of songs 4, 5, 6, 7, 8, 9 & 10.
- Songs 5 & 8 have been performed only once in Canada.
- The set list is incomplete and the exact order the songs were played is unknown.

Reviews

Dedicated audience for Dylan

By Antony Ferry.

Massey Hall was filled to capacity last night by a different kind of audience.

They came to hear folksinger Bob Dylan and they were mainly young people. They filled the place until there seemed to be a spill in the second balcony.

As an audience, they showed Style. They were of a type: the women with Juliette Greco dangling hair and heavily made-up eyes – sporting the kind of female fashion you expect mainly of the girls in Montreal – and young men escorting them who seemed to have even longer hair and who dressed according to fashions that might have been dictated by "The Panic Button."

It was almost like a peace rally, with Dylan singing about the stresses and strains of the 1960's, to his own guitar and harmonica accompaniment, while factions in the audience – pacifists, socialists, beats and Dylanites – exploded in separate bursts of applause, depending on what the verse was about.

But everyone seemed to know everyone else. It was a unique kind of audience for Massey Hall in that the intermission gave no respite. They just stayed close to the stage when the house lights went up, and waved at friends in the second balcony.

Dylan was not up to the same form as his audience. His harmonica holder broke down and the sound system failed him in the second half of the concert. Technical bugs, both. But he also forgot a few lyrics from songs he had written himself, which is less forgivable. And one of his strongest protest songs, about the murder of Hattie Carroll, was done with so much vocal embroidery that it lost most of its punch.

The highlights, for anyone who listens to Dylan, came when he opened the concert with "The Times They Are A Changin" – which he referred to casually as "the new national anthem," and his song about everybody who goes to bed at night and has nightmares about World War III. You pay to tell that dream to a psychiatrist and discover that he's haunted by it too.

Dylan still appeals enough to fill Massey Hall, because he sings with directness but with none of the usual showbiz condescension towards an audience. He brought the whole house down with his last number, yet he coolly played only one encore.

He waved after that. The house lights went up, and the audience left no less committed than they were when they came.

Whether he has an off-night or not, Bob Dylan has a permanent following.

Messiah of the Jet Age

By Marvin Schiff.

It has usually taken men of messianic instincts many years of crying in the wilderness before they have become the consciences of their generations, and then it has often been too late. But Bob Dylan, the 23-year-old folk singer and songsmith, has assumed that august position among hordes of folk music enthusiasts within a couple of years.

The secret of Mr. Dylan's success is not easy to discern unless it is the provocative blend of paradoxical characteristics he displayed last night when he performed to a capacity audience at Massey Hall.

With his harmonica holder harnessed around his neck and his guitar slung over his shoulder, he is the reincarnation of the traditional wandering minstrel of the Deep South who dished out healthy portions of social comment and philosophy in rustic terms.

Yet Mr. Dylan speaks not only to the traditionalists, but to the jet generation, for the poetry of his songs is as avant garde as Ferlinghetti.

As well as being a combination of the traditional and the progressive, Mr. Dylan displays in his poetry-set-to-music frequent flashes of wisdom beyond his years.

Yet at other times his iconoclasm seems sophomoric – the outpourings of a youth turned cynical because the world won't change over night.

Judged strictly as a performer, the poet laureate of the folk world is again a strange combination of opposites. His nasal vocalizing can hardly be called pleasant and he is just as often off key as on.

On the whole, an evening with Bob Dylan, is a rewarding experience. For the young he is a mouthpiece, their world personified. He expresses their hopes, their disappointments, and grinds their axes most articulately.

For the old, he is an explanation. He may rile them with hate and misery that fills the world they made. He may revolt them with his unkept appearance.

But, if they listen to him long enough, they begin to understand, or at least tolerate the young a little more.

To use his own words: "Come, mothers and fathers throughout the land, and don't criticize what you don't understand. The order is rapidly changing."

The Globe and Mail. Sat., Nov. 14, 1964. Reprinted with permission from The Globe and Mail.

They Came To Say Amen

Bob Dylan At Massey Hall

By Barrie Hale.

THE BOB DYLAN concert at Massey Hall last night wasn't so much a concert, but a visitation.

The sell-out, SRO crowd didn't so much come to listen, as to say Amen. Certainly they listened, but they knew the text and had come principally to see the spreader of the gospel and witness to the occasion.

Bob Dylan is 24, and to listen to his songs, he appears to have taken all life and ages for his province. He has taken what he has wanted from American folk music from Leadbelly to Woody Guthrie and affixed to it a kind of Poor Boy In The City social comment. His lyrics derive from an innocent urban underground that is inhabited by the young of all ages who hold to a tinsel-and-tragedy conception of North American Life, and the lyrics go from there to attempt to make Dylan's City all of life.

In a song like It's All Right, Ma, It's Life and Only Life, he will catalogue in a series of shotgun images such things as guns that spark, available for the kiddies, to flesh-colored Christs that glow in dark (for adults).

In a song about a country with God on its side through the changing alliances of the past half dozen wars, he will ask if Judas has god on his side.

And in a song called The Gates Of Eden he will produce a series of charnel house images which convert the East River in New York City into the Styx, to lead the conclusion that "there are no truths outside the gates of Eden."

He assumes a position of innocence that says that everybody was once so gentle, and from it he sings mordant lyrics that ask why we are not still so. His audience is rapt and adoring.

A good percentage of Dylan's audience is 20 or younger, often a good deal younger. Across the border they have been known to react to him the way less innocent innocents respond to the Beatles, but at Massey Hall last night they were quiet as churchmice during every number, thunderous in their approval of each song, quick to quiet when Dylan prepared to deliver another. To depart from the gospel analogy, it was rather like a political convention when the party's choice is a foregone conclusion and everyone there thinks that's fine.

Dylan approaches his audience directly. On the stage there are two mikes, one for him, another one lower-down for his guitar. He is short, slight, with a face like a cherub who's been around, topped with long, curly, taffy-colored hair. He wears well broken-in Levis, a black tee-shirt, a worn brown leather jacket, his guitar, and a harmonica suspended in front of his mouth from a holder that hangs around his neck. He stands feet apart, singing and playing both instruments in wild minor harmonies. As he sings he twists slightly from the waist, the reflection from his harmonica sweeping the audience like a search light.

Aside from songs on the stasis state of life, he sings a number of Dylan Freedom Songs, which have mainly to do with love life. Most of these are as genuinely funny as some of the others are genuinely hurting, and some of them are both.

Last night they ranged from Ramona (a new and saccharine one) through Don't Think Twice (on the royalties of which he could probably retire), a classic put on called If You Got To Go, to another catalogue of things not-to-do called All I Really Want To Do Is Baby Be Friends With You, which ended the concert.

A Dylan concert is a kind of total experience. All the songs are his songs, and there are few that anyone can sing as well as he. And the performance without the presence just wouldn't be the same – like a Bible without a thumper or a party platform without a President.

Last night at Massey Hall, All Anyone Really Wanted To Do Was Bob Be Friends With You.

The Toronto Telegram. Sat. Nov. 14, 1964. Reprinted with permission of The Sun Media Corp.

1965

Introduction

In 1965 Bob Dylan began the year by playing solo concerts. He played one solo concert in Canada in 1965.

This show would mark Bob Dylan's 8th concert in Canada.

In July at the Newport Folk Festival, Bob Dylan went electric and changed the face of popular music forever. His first Electric Tour came to Canada for two concerts in 1965.

These shows would mark Bob Dylan's 9th and 10th concert in Canada.

The Dates

Vancouver, BC	Fri., April 9, 1965
Toronto, ON	Sun., Nov. 14, 1965
Toronto, ON	Mon., Nov. 15, 1965

Bob Dylan performed his last solo concert in Canada in Vancouver. His first electric Tour stopped in Toronto for a two-night stand.

The shows would be Dylan's debut concert in Vancouver and his 3rd & 4th concert in Toronto.

On Stage (Solo Tour)

Bob Dylan (vocal, guitar & harmonica).

The Musicians (Electric Tour)

Bob Dylan (vocal, guitar, piano & harmonica).

On Thursday, September 16, 1965 Dylan began rehearsing for his upcoming Electric Tour with Levon and the Hawks in Toronto at the Friars' Tavern. With the exception of Levon Helm, the rest of the Hawks were born in Canada.

Levon and the Hawks — Robbie Robertson (guitar), Garth Hudson (organ), Richard Manuel (piano), Rick Danko (bass), Levon Helm (drums).

The Songs

Only eleven of the songs Bob Dylan performed are known. Of those, 9 were different songs.

Nine songs made their Canadian live debut.

Just Like Tom Thumb's Blues	Desolation Row
Ballad of a Thin Man	Love Minus Zero/No Limit
Mr. Tambourine Man	It Ain't Me, Babe
It's All Over Now, Baby Blue	I Don't Believe You (She Acts Like We Never Have Met)
She Belongs to Me	–

Bob Dylan performed songs from 4 different albums.

Album	Released	# of Songs Performed by Album
Bob Dylan	March 19, 1962	1
Another Side of Bob Dylan	Aug. 8, 1964	2
Bringing It All Back Home	March 22, 1965	5
Highway 61 Revisited	Aug. 30, 1965	3

The Venues

It was Bob Dylan's debut concert at the Queen Elizabeth Theatre in Vancouver and 2nd & 3rd time playing at Massey Hall in Toronto.

Friday, April 9, 1965 --- Queen Elizabeth Theatre Vancouver, BC

On Stage

Bob Dylan (vocal, guitar & harmonica).

Notes

- 8th Bob Dylan concert in Canada; Debut Bob Dylan concert in Vancouver.
- The set list is unknown.

Review

Bob Dylan keeps his many fans guessing

By Tom Harrison, CanWest News Service.

VANCOUVER – How can you not quote Bob Dylan?

In this case, "You know something's happening, but you don't know what it is, do you Mr. Jones?"

Or, "Don't criticize what you don't understand."

There were a lot of Mr. Jones outside when Bob Dylan came to Vancouver to play the Queen Elizabeth Theatre on April 9, 1965.

The few inside already knew something was happening or they were about to. And they weren't about to criticize. That might come a few months later, when Dylan teamed up with, first, the Paul Butterfield Band and, second, the nucleus of Ronnie Hawkins' Hawks to go electric.

In April '65, though, in the safe haven of the QET, Bob Dylan was what was happening. He was changing perception.

This was evident to two girls from West Vancouver. They'd dressed up neatly, got on the bus, found their seat at the Queen Elizabeth and immediately were aware they were out of place. Here was an audience that was scruffy, casual. Bohemian informal as opposed to West Vancouver proper.

The lights went down, anticipation rose. On the stage was a glass of water on a stool. A curly haired figure walked out and sat at another stool. Bob Dylan.

He strummed guitar rudimentally. He sang in a strangled voice.

The West Van girls didn't get it. Not at first.

They listened. It began to dawn on them. This was about the words. This wasn't about a pitch-perfect tenor rhapsodizing about some enchanted evening. This was about how a hard rain's gonna fall and how the times they are a-changing.

Forty years later, he's still a catalyst. Partly, because he has created such a mystique that whatever is allowed to come out of it has weight. Maybe it will change our perception. And who would criticize what they don't understand?

A few weeks ago, a manager of a rock band asked, 'Where is the next Bob Dylan?' There can't be a next Bob Dylan. Through the years, anybody called the next Bob Dylan – whether John Prine or Loudon Wainwright III or Dan Bern has cast off the tag as quickly as possible. Being called the next Bob Dylan is being cursed.

As appeared in The Nanaimo Daily News. Thur., July 21, 2005.

Additional Review

Dylan Dug by His Own, Not So by 'Out' Critic, by Jack Richards. The Vancouver Sun. Sat., April 10, 1965. p. 11.

Sunday, November 14, 1965 --- Massey Hall Toronto, ON

Set List

	Song	From The Album	Released
1.	Just Like Tom Thumb's Blues	Highway 61 Revisited	Aug. 30, 1965
2.	Baby, Let Me Follow You Down	Bob Dylan	March 19, 1962
3.	Ballad of a Thin Man	Highway 61 Revisited	Aug. 30, 1965
4.	Mr. Tambourine Man	Bringing It All Back Home	March 22, 1965
5.	It's All Over Now, Baby Blue	Bringing It All Back Home	March 22, 1965
6.	Gates of Eden	Bringing It All Back Home	March 22, 1965
7.	She Belongs to Me	Bringing It All Back Home	March 22, 1965

8.	Desolation Row	Highway 61 Revisited	Aug. 30, 1965
9.	Love Minus Zero/No Limit	Bringing It All Back Home	March 22, 1965
10.	It Ain't Me, Babe	Another Side of Bob Dylan	Aug. 8, 1964
11.	I Don't Believe You (She Acts Like We Never Have Met)	Another Side of Bob Dylan	Aug. 8, 1964

The Musicians

Bob Dylan (vocal, guitar, piano & harmonica).

Levon and the Hawks — Robbie Robertson (guitar), Garth Hudson (organ), Richard Manuel (piano), Rick Danko (bass), Levon Helm (drums).

Notes

- 9th Bob Dylan concert in Canada; 3rd Bob Dylan concert in Toronto.
- 3, Bob Dylan solo (piano).
- Canadian live debut of songs 1, 3, 4, 5, 7, 8, 9, 10 & 11.
- The first half of the show Bob Dylan was solo. The second half of the show he was joined by Levon and the Hawks for an electric set.
- The set list is incomplete and the exact order the songs were played is unknown.

Reviews

A changed Bob Dylan booed in Toronto

By Bruce Lawson.

"I'm goin' back to Noo York City, I do be believe I've had enough," wailed Bob Dylan at Massey Hall last night.

"Booo!" shouted somebody in the packed audience. "Sssss!" went somebody else, "Elvis!" spat out a third. There was some weak applause in Dylan's support. Most of the audience appeared to be sitting on their hands, as they did for most of the night.

It was an expression of the mixed feelings folk fans have about the young man who has been their idol. Now he's got a rock beat, and they don't know what to do.

A few people walked out of the concert hall soon after the start of the second (rock) part of the performance.

"He was the greatest writer," said one, emphasizing the past tense. "He's just a cheap imitation of the Beatles," bewailed another.

"He's changed from when he was here last time," one young man said. "It's like he wanted to be somewhere else. I'm going home and play his first records," said another, walking out into the night.

"I'd do anything in this world, if you'd just let me follow you down," Dylan's voice drifted out from inside, as Levon and his Hawks thumped out their backing.

Dylan and his troupe flew into Toronto – in their own plane, so I was told – late yesterday afternoon. Would he be available for an interview before the show? "No," replied a young man called Dan Weiner, who said he "handles all the finance for him".

An interview after the show? "No," Tomorrow some time before his second performance on Monday night? "I don't think so. He doesn't usually talk to the press."

So, sitting in the audience, I conducted my own interview. Just Bob, me and the audience. For the first half, Dylan was on his own, under a hard spotlight: grey suit, pink shirt, guitar, harmonica harnessed close to his mouth. There were touches of vintage Dylan. The only spontaneous applause during a song came as he started Mr. Tambourine Man.

What about the early songs of protest and desolation: are they no more? I asked silently. Back came the answer across the audience: "A vagabond comes rappin' on your door. He's wearing the clothes you once wore," wails Dylan.

What has happened to him? The frail figure flings back through lips that never smiled all night: "... killed him with self-confidence, after poisoning him with words."

Can that be true, Mr. Dylan? "When you asked me how I was doin', was that some kind of joke? ... There's no success like failure and failure's no success at all," he sings mournfully. The audience is silent. Rapt? Bored? Who can tell, but nobody stirs.

He sings of Ezra Pound and T. S. Elliot; he rhymes silence with violence; mixes Ophelia and Noah in the one verse, Cinderella and Romeo in another. The harmonica squeals too close to the microphone. "Hey Mr. Tambourine Man, sing a song to me ... I'm not sleepy and there is no place I'm going to ..."

The first half of the jingle-jangle evening ends, and we know we have seen and heard part of what we used to know as the real Dylan.

The long-distance interview continues with the reticent Mr. Dylan as he comes front and centre with the Hawks for the second half. Why is he shy with the press? "Go 'way from my window," the answer booms back, "I'm not the one you want, baby, I'm not the one you need."

Can you amplify on that? I ask silently. "There oughta be a law 'gainst you comin' round' ... Something; is happ'nin' here, and you don't know what it is – do you Mr. Jones?" comes the multi-decibel reply, reinforced by the Hawk beat and almost every electronic gadget ever invented to boost noise to the unbearable level. Then he sings about a one-eyed dwarf.

One last question, for the interest of the fans, What are you like as a person? "Baby if you want me to, I can be just like you. And pretend that we never touched."

He hurries offstage, and perhaps 30 people – mostly young girls – jump onstage and chase him. None of them gets near him.

Thank you, Mr. Dylan.

Jeers, Cheers For Dylan

By Barrie Hale.

Bob Dylan packed Massey Hall last night, and he will again tonight, with an audience divided against itself.

He is a slim young man with an enormous reputation. One should say, properly, that he has several reputations – as an itinerant folk poet, a maker of diffuse images for these diffuse times; as a composer who has taken from the blues and ballad traditions and given back to them much that is his own; as a spokesman for the young; and, lately, a man who has laid his career on the line by playing rock and roll because he thinks (as many do) that there is more to rock and roll than teen-age corruption of a minor musical form; that there is, in fact, a new framework of musical expression available within it.

It was a curious audience at Massey Hall last night. Some few went because they didn't really believe the early reputation. A great many went because they had heard he'd switched to rock and roll but just couldn't believe their ears.

And some went, as to a Rolling Stones concert, to scream and collect a little piece of The Idol for their altars.

They talked (or shouted) at each other, these various elements of the audience, calling each other names, and showing their regard for Dylan by walking out (a few), throwing sarcastic dimes (very few), or storming the stage (scores of them).

Dylan opened the stage by walking on, unannounced and singing accompanied by himself on guitar and harmonica, the strange and beautiful ballads and (to synthesize several blues ballad-hip traditions) what can only be called Dylan songs…

"She's got everything she needs," he sang "she's an artist, she don't look back. She can take the dark out of the nighttime and paint the daytime black…"

THE BREAK

And he sang The Gates Of Eden and Desolation Row, and Hey, Mr. Tambourine Man, play a song for me…the place was like a church. Not a word from Dylan between the songs, not a sound in Massey Hall except his, and anthems of applause after every number. Then came the break.

Onto the stage to begin the second half, came Levon and The Hawks a powerful rock and roll group consisting of drums, amplified piano, electric organ, electric bass, and an amplified lead guitar. Then Dylan, with amplified guitar, his voice, songs and harmonica.

Together, they played Hard Rock, and often blew hard (playing all Dylan tunes – a Dylan concert is always all Dylan tunes) within the great noise they made, making a new intense, theatrically full-blown kind of music. Baroque, not Roccoco.

The audience split itself during this last half. Where before, during the solo Dylan portion of the concert, they sat rapt, with only a few girls their hair flashing brilliantly through the spotlight, rushed the stage to get an I-was-there photograph, and then retreated, during this last session they packed themselves down in front of the stage, ready to storm it – girls and boys alike.

CHIT-CHAT

The audience began to shout at itself – the cries were directed toward Dylan, but he engrossed with electronic sounds, paid no notice.

"Elvissss?" someone screamed sarcastically.

"Why don't you sing folk?" cried someone else.

"Why don't you mind your own business?" came a female reply, nice and loud (the acoustics at Massey Hall were splendid).

Most of the songs in the second set were met with a combination of applause (heartfelt), boos (ill-organized but real), and screams of transport. The essence of the thing was Dylan singing (at the piano, self-accompanied)…You know something is happening here, but you don't know what it is, do you, Mrs. Jones?

To end the concert, Dylan spoke his first impromptu words: "Thank you very much" and just made it off the stage before he was swept under by the tide of rapturous chicks.

A half-hour after the concert, they were sill there, trying to touch the piano Dylan had played, trying to steal a drumstick, just hanging around for him to come out.

At the height of his career as The New Voice in folk music, Bob Dylan switched to rock and roll. He could stand to lose himself some of the audience that put him where he is. But on the basis of last night's performance at Massey Hall, he is picking up many more where the others left off… they know something is happening there, they don't know just what it is, but they dig it.

The Toronto Telegram. Mon., Nov. 15, 1965. Reprinted with permission of The Sun Media Corp.

Monday, November 15, 1965 --- Massey Hall
Toronto, ON

The Musicians

Bob Dylan (vocal, guitar, piano & harmonica).

Levon and the Hawks — Robbie Robertson (guitar), Garth Hudson (organ), Richard Manuel (piano), Rick Danko (bass), Levon Helm (drums).

Notes

- 10th Bob Dylan concert in Canada; 4th Bob Dylan concert in Toronto.
- The first half of the show Bob Dylan was solo. The second half of the show he was joined by Levon and the Hawks for an electric set.
- The set list is unknown. However, Dylan undoubtedly played some of the same songs as the night before.

Reviews

Let's face an awful truth: Dylan's gone commercial

By Antony Ferry, Star Staff Writer.

A fan of Bob Dylan's came out of Dylan's sold out concert at Massey Hall last night and asked another Dylan fan what he thought of the two-hour program.

"It stank," came the reply, as the fan melted into the cold night.

During the concert itself there were many harsh verdicts. Someone said in the middle of a song, "Stop turning your back to us." As he plugged in an electric guitar, they cried "Let's hear the words, forget the electronics."

A folksong fan walked out crying "Dylan, you're doing it for money," and at the back of the hall came the ultimate insult.

"Elvis," the voice said. "You're another Elvis."

It is hard to explain what this bitterness is all about. I can only say I have been a Dylan fan myself for three years and I went to the concert full of honest anticipation, despite all the rumors that Dylan had sold out to commercialism.

I joined the fan quoted at the top of this story and find it hard to be temperate.

BEATLE ORGY

Here was a Bob Dylan who once was a purist, a folk-poet of America in direct line to Woody Guthrie, now electronically hooked up to a third-rate Yonge St. rock 'n' roll band which he has now contracted. That great voice, a wonderfully clean poet's voice, is buried under the same Big Sound that draws all the Screamies to a Beatle orgy of pubescent kids at Maple Leaf Gardens.

The aforementioned third-rate Yonge St. rock 'n' roll band, called "Levon and the Hawks" does most of the electronic fronting for Dylan, who seems now to be faking his own guitar playing. The Big Sound drowns out all his message, but elicits hysterical squeals from a small segment of young girls who dart to the front of the stage like they dig his sound but are totally deaf to his lyrics and only wish he was the Beatles.

This is apparently what the New Dylan and the makers of his image want.

But in tiers of seats throughout Massey Hall there were serious young kids, university students, and people in their mid-30s and early 40s to whom this is not what they paid out money for.

HAPPENED BEFORE

Their anger at the big sell-out of a talent might be amusing, except that it has happened before to Scott Fitzgerald, and Hemingway, to John dos Passos, Louis Armstrong, Clifford Odets and every other American artist of honest gifts who gave in to the system.

Every disappointed patron at Massey Hall last night should have understood the pressures behind the big Madison Avenue sell-out. But they didn't expect it would ever touch Bob Dylan.

He had even written, a few long years ago, a song which he said "wasn't written in Tin Pan Alley – where most of the folksongs come from now'days. This was written in the United States – ."

Bob Dylan now belongs to Tin Pan Alley.

The Toronto Star. Tues., Nov. 16, 1965. Reprinted with permission - Torstar Syndication Services.

A fresh supply of mistakes

By Robert Fulford, Toronto Star.

When Bob Dylan appeared here for a couple of concerts this week he affronted a few of his fans and at least two newspaper critics by singing half of his program against a rock 'n' roll background.

But to me the new Dylan seems the better Dylan – more expressive and more exciting. Dylan moved on from his old harmonica-and-guitar style because he found it boring. I can see why. The first half of his concert at Massey Hall, in this style, certainly bored me, no matter how much it pleased some of his old fans.

When he began experimenting with rock, Dylan obviously thought he saw tremendous musical possibilities in it. Now he's proving he was right. The second half of the Massey Hall concert, with that wild rock beat coming from Levon and the Hawks, was a remarkable experience – great waves of sound roaring off the stage in marvelously subtle rhythms, a tremendous roaring hurricane of a style. It's not social protest, nor is it New Left, nor is it the bogus Old American of most folk singers. It's Dylan's own new thing. I love it.

The Toronto Star. Fri., Nov. 19, 1965. Reprinted with permission - Torstar Syndication Services.

1966

Introduction

The 1966 World Tour visited Canada for three concerts.

These shows would mark Bob Dylan's 11th, 12th & 13th concert in Canada. It would be almost eight years later before Bob Dylan returned to Canada for a concert.

The Dates

Ottawa, ON	Sat., Feb. 19, 1966
Montreal, QC	Sun., Feb. 20, 1966
Vancouver, BC	Sat., March 26, 1966

The shows would be Dylan's debut concert in Ottawa, 6th concert in Montreal and 2nd concert in Vancouver.

The Musicians

Bob Dylan (vocal, guitar & harmonica).

The Hawks — Robbie Robertson (guitar), Garth Hudson (organ), Richard Manuel (piano), Rick Danko (bass), Sandy Konikoff (drums).

The Songs

Only eleven of the songs Bob Dylan performed are known. Of those, 9 were different songs.

Three songs made their Canadian live debut.

Only a Pawn in Their Game	Positively 4th Street
Leopard-Skin Pill-Box Hat	–

One song has been played only once in Canada.

Only a Pawn in Their Game	–

Bob Dylan performed songs from 5 different albums.

Album	Released	# of Songs Performed by Album
The Times They Are A-Changin'	Feb., 10, 1964	2
Bringing It All Back Home	March 22, 1965	4
Highway 61 Revisited	Aug. 30, 1965	1
Blonde on Blonde	May 16, 1966	1
Bob Dylan's Greatest Hits	March 27, 1967	1

The Venues

It was Bob Dylan's debut concert at the Ottawa Auditorium, debut concert at Place des Arts in Montreal and debut concert at the PNE Agrodome in Vancouver.

Saturday, February 19, 1966 --- Ottawa Auditorium Ottawa, ON

Set List

	Song	From The Album	Released
1.	The Times They Are A-Changin'	The Times They Are A-Changin'	Feb. 10, 1964
2.	Only a Pawn in Their Game	The Times They Are A-Changin'	Feb. 10, 1964

The Musicians

Bob Dylan (vocal, guitar & harmonica).

The Hawks — Robbie Robertson (guitar), Garth Hudson (organ), Richard Manuel (piano), Rick Danko (bass), Sandy Konikoff (drums).

Notes

- 11th Bob Dylan concert in Canada; Debut Bob Dylan concert in Ottawa.
- Canadian live debut of song 2.
- Song 2 has been performed only once in Canada.
- The first half of the show Bob Dylan was solo. The second half of the show he was joined by the Hawks for an electric set.
- The set list is incomplete and the exact order the songs were played is unknown.

Reviews

4,000 fans dig Dylan in folk, rock concert

By Dennis Foley, Citizen Staff Writer.

Bob Dylan, the minstrel from Minnesota with a message, played to 4,000 captive adherents at the Auditorium Saturday night, but the traditionally poor acoustics made reception difficult.

However, perhaps the speakers were not entirely blameworthy.

"If you want to understand Dylan, you have to hear it from others who sing more clearly," said one devotee afterward.

Being the "genius" of the folk-song cult he is hailed to be, it is not unusual that "interpreters" are needed to deliver his message to the uninitiated.

And the bank accounts of Joan Baez, Peter, Paul and Mary, and Pete Seeger serve to attest this.

45-minute solo

The show had the standard format of his recent concerts – a 45-minute solo with acoustic guitar and harmonica followed by a second stint with a rock band.

On stage he moved from one wailing lament to another without benefit of a master of ceremonies or self-introduction.

En route to his dressing room after his first set of songs of protest and affliction, he muttered something to someone about announcing that the concert was not over.

This was not done, but everyone present seemed to know there would be more. They didn't seem to mind the lack of introductions, either.

Refuses interviews

Between halves Dylan rejuvenated himself, an attendant said, with great quantities of tea larded with honey. He consistently refuses to see interviewers, so much so that it is even written into his contracts.

If perception was difficult during the solo stint, it was nigh impossible during the second half with the big sound of the Hawks of Toronto as a backdrop.

It is this deviation and the resulting "folk-rock" sound that has sparked unkind criticism from folk-song purists, who consider this innovation the worst kind of heresy.

The frizzy-haired Dylan, who writes all his own songs and is credited with starting it all, only replies to all this abuse: "It's all music, no more, no less."

Some may wonder about a rights worker being eulogized in Dylan's Only a Pawn in Their Game to a rock-'n-roll beat.

But who's to peg pop culture? As Dylan himself wails: "For the times they are a-changing."

The Ottawa Citizen. Mon., Feb. 21, 1966. Reprinted with permission of The Ottawa Citizen.

Dylan's return to Ottawa revives mid-'60s memories

Ottawa Citizen.

Between bad weather, a cold hall and a 67's hockey game, Bob Dylan and Ottawa haven't enjoyed the best of relationships.

Several months after his last appearance here in February, 1966, Dylan gave an interview to the *Saturday Evening Post*, in which he criticized a Vancouver auditorium by comparing it to Ottawa.

The Vancouver hall, he said was even worse than the one in Ottawa – "and is the worst hole in the Universe."

Dylan was referring to the old Auditorium at Argyle and O'Connor streets (now the site of the YM-YWCA). Dylan's memory of the Auditorium was shared by many of the 4,500 fans who were there for the concert. (The hall was 1,500 short of capacity).

"It was cold," recalls CHEZ FM's Brian Murphy. "It must have been -20 outside and inside the arena everyone was bundled up. The acoustics were appalling and we couldn't hear what was going on at all.

"It was the era when Dylan began going electric and he was being accused of selling out. He played the first set alone and for the second half brought out The Hawks (later to be renamed The Band).

"But everything was against that show and I think a lot of people left disappointed."

Promoter Harvey Glatt, chairman of Treble Clef, recalls Dylan backstage as being "shy, quiet, keeping himself to himself and not very happy."

"It was hard to get people to go to the Auditorium because it wasn't a good place for concerts. The memories of that night aren't very good."

The Citizen's rock reviewer Bill Provick has more positive memories of the show, but agrees it was far from perfect.

"Dylan played a 45-minute solo acoustic set and then broke for an intermission during which he went backstage to sip tea and honey to ward off a sore throat.

"When he returned, carrying an electric guitar, he was backed by Ronnie Hawkins' former band, Levon and the Hawks. Dylan had already shocked the folk world by going electric but by this time he was actually starting to rock.

"However, the Hawks were quite robust in their playing to the point of frequently being too loud. Dylan spent considerable time waving his arms behind his back, signaling to the band to tone it down a bit which resulted in the sight of a charismatic Dylan leaning into the microphone with full facial concentration while his extended arms, in a seemingly detached motion, slowly flapped behind him like some strange bird trying to take off.

"The show featured all of Dylan's material up to that point and was highlighted by the unveiling of some newer material from the *Blonde on Blonde* album.

The incident that may have hardened Dylan's early opinions of Ottawa occurred in January of 1974 when he was already a living legend and the single most important figure in contemporary music.

He agreed to include the Ottawa Civic Centre on his tour that winter, the concert of 1966 either forgotten or chalked up to experience. But alas, the City of Ottawa refused to move the Ottawa 67's out of the arena on Jan. 11, 1974 to accommodate Dylan and his band.

The 67's had already booked the arena and refused to reschedule their game against the Oshawa Generals. Board of control refused to exercise its right to force the move.

Aside from important artistic considerations, Dylan's show that night would have generated more than $10,000 for the Civic Centre. The hockey game made $2,500.

Harvey Glatt recalls the city decision as being "ridiculous and stupid" but despite numerous appeals, letters to the editor and calls from angry Dylan fans, the city wouldn't budge.

Tonight at the Civic Centre, Dylan will be playing some of the songs he played 15 years ago. His program is expected to include the likes of *Blowin' In the Wind, All Along the Watchtower, Mr. Tambourine Man, The Times They Are a-Changing, Ballad of a Thin Man, It Ain't Me Babe* and *I Want You.*

His band will feature Al Kooper on keyboards, former Neil Young bassist Timothy Drummond, Jimmy Keltner on drums, Steve Ripley on guitar and back up singers Regina McCrary, Madelyn Quebec and Clydie King.

All in all, it should be a night when Bob Dylan and Ottawa become friends again.

The Ottawa Citizen. Mon., Nov. 2, 1981. Reprinted with permission of The Ottawa Citizen.

Sunday, February 20, 1966 --- Place des Arts
Montreal, QC

Set List

	Song	**From The Album**	**Released**
1.	She Belongs to Me	Bringing It All Back Home	March 22, 1965
2.	Love Minus Zero/No Limit	Bringing It All Back Home	March 22, 1965

3.	Leopard-Skin Pill-Box Hat	Blonde on Blonde	May 16, 1966
4.	Positively 4th Street	Bob Dylan's Greatest Hits	March 27, 1967
5.	Mr. Tambourine Man	Bringing It All Back Home	March 22, 1965
6.	Desolation Row	Highway 61 Revisited	Aug. 30, 1965

The Musicians

Bob Dylan (vocal, guitar & harmonica).

The Hawks — Robbie Robertson (guitar), Garth Hudson (organ), Richard Manuel (piano), Rick Danko (bass), Sandy Konikoff (drums).

Notes

- 12th Bob Dylan concert in Canada; 6th Bob Dylan concert in Montreal.
- Canadian live debut of songs 3 & 4.
- The first half of the show Bob Dylan was solo. The second half of the show he was joined by the Hawks for an electric set.
- Martin Bronstein of CBC Radio interviewed Bob Dylan at the venue. Referred to as "The Inept Bob Dylan Interview" it was not broadcast until Aug. 24, 1974.
- The set list is incomplete and the exact order the songs were played is unknown.

Reviews

Bob Dylan Makes His Montreal Debut, by Zelda Heller. The Montreal Gazette. Mon., Feb. 21, 1966. p. 11.

Bob Dylan Sings Folk, Pop, Poetry, by Wouter De Wet. The Montreal Star. Mon., Feb. 21, 1966. p. 17.

Saturday, March 26, 1966 --- PNE Agrodome Vancouver, BC

Set List

	Song	From The Album	Released
1.	It's All Over Now, Baby Blue	Bringing It All Back Home	March 22, 1965
2.	Desolation Row	Highway 61 Revisited	Aug. 30, 1965
3.	Mr. Tambourine Man	Bringing It All Back Home	March 22, 1965

The Musicians

Bob Dylan (vocal, guitar & harmonica).

The Hawks — Robbie Robertson (guitar), Garth Hudson (organ), Richard Manuel (piano), Rick Danko (bass), Sandy Konikoff (drums).

Notes

- 13th Bob Dylan concert in Canada; 2nd Bob Dylan concert in Vancouver.
- The first half of the show Bob Dylan was solo. The second half of the show he was joined by the Hawks (minus Levon Helm) for an electric set.
- The set list is incomplete and the exact order the songs were played is unknown.
- This was Bob Dylan's last concert in Canada for almost 8 years.

Reviews

No screams, no riots, no hysteria

Vancouver Province.

The promoters hired nine commissionaires to control expected hysteria and rioting at folk-rock singer Bob Dylan's show in the Agrodome Saturday night.

But the predominately teenaged crowd of 3,100 surprised them – they were orderly and quiet.

"I was very much surprised there was no demonstrating or even individual screaming," said a Famous Artists Ltd. spokesman.

Dylan, who used to sing pure folk songs but switched to the current folk-rock fad, flew here from Seattle in his private plane Saturday afternoon and left for Tacoma Sunday.

The Vancouver Province. Mon., March 28, 1966.

'Electric' Dylan Turns to Banality

By William Littler.

Bob Dylan has me buffaloed.

Until Saturday night, when I joined 3,123 other people in the PNE Agrodome, I had grown to believe that Dylan represented the most creative force in contemporary folk music.

True, it was a force of uneven merit. Not all of his songs conveyed the beauty of Blowin' in the Wind or the raw power of A Hard Rain's A-Gonna Fall.

But at its best, the 24 year old Minnesotan had expressed what today's youth sees in society, what it fears of it and what it wants from it.

He has also shown that the truth of a song's message can stir an audience, even when its writer ignores grammar, rhymes tritely, composes crudely, sings gratingly and plays a rudimentary flat-pick guitar.

All this he still embodies, or rather he did on the first half of his Saturday program.

Standing alone on a raised platform, dressed in a dark suit, his hair resembling an exploding floor mop, he began to sing-talk some of his songs – songs such as: Its All Over Now Baby Blue, Desolation Row and Mr. Tambourine Man.

The songs were not pretty, of course. They weren't meant to be.

They were really musical paragraphs, full of faulty syntax and hip lingo but punctuated with conscience and feeling and delivered with a nasal drawling vocal insistence, searing glissando accents on the harmonica and a monotonous, propulsive guitar rhythm.

They were the kind of songs I could identify with Bob Dylan, spokesman for protest, advocate of personal freedom, poet of mixed-up generation.

But then something happened. Intermission. And after that, nothing seemed quite the same.

Gone was the guitar and in its place Dylan held an electric guitar.

Instead of performing alone, he was joined by two more electric guitar players, a drummer, an organist and a pianist.

Most significant of all, his music had changed. No longer was he singing folk; now it was folk rock, a hybrid uniting some of the simplicity and message of folk with a weakened rock beat.

And in spite of the suddenly increased enthusiasm of his shaggy young audience, I didn't like it.

For one thing I didn't like the way Dylan allowed the sheer sound of his combo to obscure the greatest asset of his songs: their lyrics.

Nor did I like the narrowly personal and sometimes nasty tone of some of these lyrics, the commercial banality of the music and the erratic quality of Dylan's own performances.

It all spelled something I did not want to read or admit – that America's foremost folk voice may have sold out to the jukebox.

As appeared in The Vancouver Sun. Mon., March 28, 1966. Reprinted with permission of William Littler.

1974

Introduction

After almost eight years off the road, Bob Dylan embarked on a North American Tour that stopped in Canada for four concerts.

Tour '74 would mark Bob Dylan's 14th, 15th, 16th & 17th concert in Canada.

The Dates

Toronto, ON	Wed. Jan. 9, 1974
Toronto, ON	Thurs., Jan. 10, 1974
Montreal, QC	Fri., Jan. 11, 1974
Montreal, QC	Sat., Jan 12, 1974

The Tour stopped in both Toronto and Montreal for back-to-back, two-night stands.

The shows would be Dylan's 5th & 6th concert in Toronto and 7th & 8th concert in Montreal.

The Musicians

Bob Dylan (vocal, guitar & harmonica).

Tour '74 featured The Band as Dylan's backing group. Formerly known as the Hawks and prior to that Levon and the Hawks, they had toured with Dylan on his first Electric Tour in 1965 and the 1966 World Tour.

The Band — Robbie Robertson (guitar), Garth Hudson (synthesizer), Richard Manual (keyboards), Rick Danko (bass), Levon Helm (drums).

The Songs

Bob Dylan performed a total of 71 songs. Of those, 25 were different songs (all were from albums).

Fourteen songs made their Canadian live debut.

Rainy Day Women #12 & 35	Nobody 'Cept You
Lay, Lady, Lay	Forever Young
All Along the Watchtower	Something There is About You
Ballad of Hollis Brown	Like A Rolling Stone
It Takes a Lot to Laugh, It Takes a Train to Cry	Most Likely You Go Your Way and I'll Go Mine
Knockin' on Heaven's Door	As I Went Out One Morning
Just Like a Woman	Wedding Song

Two songs have been played only once in Canada.

Wedding Song	As I Went Out One Morning

One song made its worldwide live debut.

As I Went Out One Morning	–

Bob Dylan performed songs from 11 different albums.

Album	Released	# of Songs Performed by Album
The Freewheelin' Bob Dylan	May, 27, 1963	3
The Times They Are A-Changin'	Feb., 10, 1964	2
Another Side of Bob Dylan	Aug. 8, 1964	2
Bringing It All Back Home	March 22, 1965	3
Highway 61 Revisited	Aug. 30, 1965	4
Blonde on Blonde	May 16, 1966	3
John Wesley Harding	Dec. 27, 1967	2
Nashville Skyline	April 9, 1969	1
Pat Garrett and Billy The Kid	July 13, 1973	1
Planet Waves	Jan. 17, 1974	3
The Bootleg Series Volumes 1-3	March 26, 1991	1

The Venues

It was Bob Dylan's debut concert & 2nd time playing at two of Canada's most revered venues — Maple Leaf Gardens in Toronto and the Montreal Forum.

Wednesday, January 9, 1974 --- Maple Leaf Gardens Toronto, ON

Set List

	Song	From The Album	Released
1.	Rainy Day Women #12 & 35	Blonde on Blonde	May 16, 1966
2.	Lay, Lady, Lay	Nashville Skyline	April 9, 1969
3.	Just Like Tom Thumb's Blues	Highway 61 Revisited	Aug. 30, 1965
4.	It Ain't Me, Babe	Another Side of Bob Dylan	Aug. 8, 1964
5.	It Takes a Lot to Laugh, It Takes a Train to Cry	Highway 61 Revisited	Aug. 30, 1965
6.	Ballad of a Thin Man	Highway 61 Revisited	Aug. 30, 1965
7.	All Along the Watchtower	John Wesley Harding	Dec. 27, 1967
8.	Ballad of Hollis Brown	The Times They Are A-Changin'	Feb. 10, 1964
9.	Knockin' on Heaven's Door	Pat Garrett & Billy The Kid	July 13, 1973
10.	Just Like a Woman	Blonde on Blonde	May 16, 1966
11.	Girl of the North Country	The Freewheelin' Bob Dylan	May 27, 1963
12.	Wedding Song	Planet Waves	Jan. 17, 1974
13.	Nobody 'Cept You	The Bootleg Series Volumes 1-3	March 26, 1991
14.	It's Alright, Ma (I'm Only Bleeding)	Bringing It All Back Home	March 22, 1965
15.	Forever Young	Planet Waves	Jan. 17, 1974
16.	Something There is About You	Planet Waves	Jan. 17, 1974
17.	Like a Rolling Stone	Highway 61 Revisited	Aug. 30, 1965
	Encore		
18.	Most Likely You Go Your Way and I'll Go Mine	Blonde on Blonde	May 16, 1966

The Musicians

Bob Dylan (vocal, guitar & harmonica).

The Band — Robbie Robertson (guitar), Garth Hudson (synthesizer), Richard Manual (keyboards), Rick Danko (bass), Levon Helm (drums).

Notes

- 14th Bob Dylan concert in Canada; 5th Bob Dylan concert in Toronto.
- 10-14, Bob Dylan solo (vocal, guitar, & harmonica).
- Canadian live debut of songs 1, 2, 5, 7, 8, 9, 10, 12, 13, 15, 16, 17 & 18.
- Song 12 has been performed only once in Canada.
- The songs The Band performed alone are not included in the set list.

Reviews

Dylan: A fantastic musical evening

By Urjo Kareda, Star Staff Writer.

When the pink-mauve spotlights illuminated the stage of Maple Leaf Gardens at the beginning of the first of Bob Dylan's two Toronto concerts last night, he was spotted instantly, wandering vaguely centre ward with his fellow musicians, The Band.

The 19,000-strong crowd, keyed up for this glimpse (for many, their first) of an authentic myth-figure, sent up a roar. But Dylan, dark-suited and sombre, busied himself with his instruments, his back to the audience, never acknowledging their welcome.

His self-conscious unself-consciousness created a tension, like the people who won't look you in the eye when they speak with you, a feeling of irresolution which didn't dissolve until Dylan, his preparations finished, launched into the first song, Everybody Must Get Stoned.

IMPASSIVE MASK

He is a most extraordinarily enclosed performer, his face an impassive, oblique mask which tells us nothing. His eyes – usually the key to any sort of communication – wield so little that it doesn't really make any difference when he puts on his dark glasses. Except for the throw-away "Thank you, you were great" at the end, he spoke not a word.

What makes this all so unusual is the way the physical presence is at odds with the music. The Dylan stage mask indicates nothing of the experience, perception or wit which has made the songs so much a part of the inner ear of a whole generation. The disparity between the blank personality and the angry, savage, sensual, sardonic temperament in the music is tantalizing, its own kind of come on.

KEEP WAITING

You keep waiting for the spirit which created songs like It Ain't Me Babe, the most aching anti-love song ever written, or Its Alright I'm Only Dying, that contemptuous, accurate condemnation of indifference, to emerge and animate the singer. It never quite does, and the mixture of the ordinary and the uncanny lingers unresolved.

Purely as a concert, this was such, such fantastic music. First of all, the evening's generous length – close to three hours – provided a tellingly cumulative history of Dylan's contribution to contemporary music. It's an achievement in the linking of melody with lyrics which only really becomes apparent and overwhelming when Dylan himself sings his work.

That wonderful incantatory style, challenges and accusations, thrust out like a cross-examination, is still the best Dylan vehicle. He works superbly with The Band, achieving an interplay of instruments and voices which is like chamber music pushed beyond any sensible decibel level. His solo numbers, except for a memorable new song called, I think, Except You, were less complete as experiences. Dylan looked lonely and not a little dubious isolated in the spotlight.

FLOATING VERSION

The Band itself, too, had solo occasions, which they seized to work through most of their best-known material, most beautifully in a floating, transparent version of I Shall Be Released.

Given the exceptional artistic level, then, why did the Dylan concert nevertheless disappoint? I think it's because Bob Dylan is unwilling, or unable, to satisfy us on an emotional level. We respond with such an intensity to his songs, particularly those which we now feel as second nature to ourselves; we want to pay back the debt with our adulation, but Dylan won't have it. A couple of cursory bows were the only indication of our existence.

At times, the audience's need to be acknowledged acquired a manic intensity. Thus, in the finale, when the house lights were turned on as Dylan and The Band took us through the long unwinding melody of Like a Rolling Stone, the audience roared not just because of what Dylan had given to us, but because in the full light he had at last to admit that we were there with him. Dylan's reserve, his disinclination to fulfill a central performer-spectator understanding, may explain why his concert return, for all its musical splendors, nevertheless had a feeling of farewells. We need him to accept our acceptance of him.

A final social historical note: Drink and dope were still much in evidence as props for pop-rock. But they're about to be overtaken by the camera. The lens' eye seems to be the new high. All around me, there was much running to and fro with equipment. The man in front of me actually missed the middle hour of Dylan's concert so that he could go home to get his cameras. Across the aisle, a girl couldn't have heard any of the songs, since she was too busy shrieking "What setting should I make?" She seemed incapable of seeing Dylan except through the eye of her expensive-looking camera.

He just wasn't there except as a potential snapshot. What breed of media mutants have we created?

The Toronto Star. Thurs., Jan. 10, 1974. Reprinted with permission - Torstar Syndication Services.

The sixties' messiah has feet of clay

By Robert Martin.

Bob Dylan, the reluctant pop messiah of the sixties, returned to Toronto last night for the first time in eight years and proved conclusively, as he's claimed all along, that he has feet of clay.

It was, as they say, an off night. Dylan appeared to be totally detached from the proceedings throughout the entire first half of the show at Maple Leaf Gardens. He was technically good, sometimes excellent, but gave the impression that he wasn't really listening to himself sing.

He showed up at his usual starting time, half an hour late, wearing a dark grey suit and light grey vest, strapped on his guitar and harmonica and launched into a lackadaisical rendition of Rainy Day Women No. 12 & 35. Lay Lady Lay was pleasant, Just Like Tom Thumb's Blues was given a perfunctory reading and the show didn't really get started until It Ain't Me Babe.

Dylan's version with The Band backing him up is much more playful than his original. It's bouncy and toe-tapping with lots of syncopation that makes its put-down lyrics all the more cynical. There is no agonizing in this version. Dylan is laughing at the girl.

Or, if you want to interpret it – and many have – as a denial of the leadership of a generation that was imposed upon him, then Dylan is putting down his entire audience by turning a serious statement into a bouncy, frivolous pop song.

Dylan songs, and even entire Dylan concerts invite this sort of interpretation. Each performance becomes another statement on the condition of the universe. If this is true, then Dylan is making an entirely different statement every night because this performance was quite different from the show in Chicago with which he began his tour last Thursday.

Dylan is the only pop act in the business, now that the Beatles are gone, with a repertoire so large and well known that he can change his program at will without losing much of his audience. He can even sing album cuts, traditionally filler between hit singles, with the assurance that the audience will recognize and appreciate them.

Thus he played obscure songs like Down Along the Flood and the Ballad of Hollis Brown. He even improved on the original version of Hollis Brown, a dreary tale of a destitute farmer who, in desperation, shoots his wife and five children and kills himself.

The first half of the show was a safe set, a run-through of old favorites. All Along the Watch Tower was another highlight, thanks to The Band's driving beat, with Richard Manuel's spooky electric piano bridges and Robertson's lead riff that acknowledged Jimi Hendrix' version without imitating it.

The Band did a good job of backing Dylan, but didn't do nearly as good a job playing by itself. Three of its numbers were much slower than they should have been or normally are. The Night They Drove Old Dixie Down and When You Awake were merely dull and turgid, but Rag Mama Rag, one of their best and brightest songs, was utterly destroyed.

This show is much more highly structured than it was in Chicago when Dylan and The Band traded songs, with Dylan playing along when he wasn't singing.

He opened the second half alone, with only his guitar and harmonica. This was classic Dylan and it was the best received section of the concert. He started with a terrible rendition of Just Like a Woman. He completely altered the rhythm of the vocal – which is his prerogative since it's his song – but he played his guitar at still another rhythm, and both differed from the original. It threw the whole song out of kilter.

Dylan then pulled himself together for a sensitive delivery of Girl from the North Country and some of his best harmonica playing of the evening. Finally he got into his new material. He sang one perhaps called Except You, about a man completely isolated from everyone except his woman.

With lyrics like "Everybody wants my attention, everybody's got something to sell, except you" it sounds autobiographical. He concluded his solo mini-set with It's All Right Ma (I'm Only Bleeding) and got a cheer for the line "Even the President of the United States sometimes has to stand naked." It made him look like a prophet, considering that the song was written in 1965.

The Band returned for a few more numbers, including the Shape I'm In and The Weight. Dylan joined in for the finale, two new songs and Like a Rollin' Stone. The new numbers both reveal that Dylan, at 32, is feeling his age.

One of them is a sung prayer, the chorus line of which is "May you stay forever young." The other, Something There Is About You, is a tribute to a woman who reminds him of his youth – "rainy days on the Great Lakes, walking the hills of old Duluth." She "brings back a long forgotten truth" and Dylan has said recently that this song completes a pattern in his life. It probably means he can admit the real facts of his youth as opposed to the romantic fiction he used to claim was his background. He has truly grown up.

Like a Rollin' Stone was accompanied by the gradual raising of the house lights to get the crowd on its feet. It's an old Rolling Stones trick, except that the Stones' audiences are usually already leaping about. Last night it took a while before anyone rose to cheer and when Dylan returned for his encore, Most Likely You Go Your Way (And I'll Go Mine), they quickly sat down again. It just wasn't that exciting.

Notes: Tour manager Bill Graham gets the creep of the year award for his foul-mouthed treatment of press photographers trying to do their jobs. He cursed them, ordering them back to their seats, except for the man from Time magazine, which is doing a cover story on Dylan. And there will be no interviews – except for the one that appeared Tuesday in The New York Times.

The Globe and Mail. Thurs., Jan. 10, 1974. Reprinted with permission from The Globe and Mail.

Look man, I'm not him, said reclusive Mr. Dylan

By Ron Base, Staff Writer.

Two and a half hours before he performed for 18,000 fans at Maple Leaf Gardens last night, Bob Dylan stood leafing through skin magazines in the lobby of the Inn On The Park.

The reclusive poet-singer has said he would give no interviews during his 21-city concert tour with The Band and he decided not to change his mind in the hotel's lobby.

"Aren't you Bob Dylan?" a reporter asked.

Dylan looked up momentarily from the copy of Success magazine he was leafing through. "Ah, no," he replied.

However, he didn't object to Sun photographer Barry Gray snapping pictures. "Did you get enough?" he asked Gray as he wandered away from the newsstand.

Again the reporter approached him. "Look man, I'm not him." Dylan said.

"How are you enjoying your visit to Toronto?"

"Are you talkin' to me?" asked Dylan, staring at the reporter through dark glasses. He stood nervously by a fireplace in the lobby and said nothing else. An unidentified friend hovered nearby.

When photographer Gray began taking more pictures, Dylan seemed to become exasperated. "This guy," he said to his friend. The friend led Dylan away.

Later in the evening, Dylan spoke – but only musically – before a crowd that included Ian and Sylvia Tyson and Ronnie Hawkins who originally brought the Band together.

He wasted no time in giving the audience the old songs they had come to hear – Lay, Lady, Lay, It Ain't Me Babe, Rainy Day Women Nos. 12 and 35.

He sang in red and blue spotlights, rocking back and forth with a yellow Gibson guitar, barely pausing between songs.

It was not until almost intermission that Dylan sang one of the rumored 20 new songs he had written for the tour and new album. The song dealt with death on a South Dakota farm.

After the intermission, The Band had disappeared and there was just Dylan, a guitar and 18,000 people.

He sang two new love songs, a song about youth – five new songs all told throughout the concert – in a disciplined, impassioned voice.

But despite pleas from the crowd to say something, Dylan never spoke a word throughout the more than two hour concert.

The Toronto Sun. Thurs., Jan. 10, 1974. Reprinted with permission of The Sun Media Corp.

Additional Review

Dylan, Band, cheered in Toronto, by Iain MacLeod. The Canadian Press. As appeared in the Montreal Gazette. Fri., Jan. 11, 1974. p. 9.

Thursday, January 10, 1974 --- Maple Leaf Gardens Toronto, ON

Set List

	Song	From The Album	Released
1.	Most Likely You Go Your Way and I'll Go Mine	Blonde on Blonde	May 16, 1966
2.	I Don't Believe You (She Acts Like We Never Have Met)	Another Side of Bob Dylan	Aug. 8, 1964
3.	As I Went Out One Morning	John Wesley Harding	Dec. 27, 1967
4.	Lay, Lady, Lay	Nashville Skyline	April 9, 1969
5.	Just Like Tom Thumb's Blues	Highway 61 Revisited	Aug. 30, 1965
6.	Ballad of a Thin Man	Highway 61 Revisited	Aug. 30, 1965
7.	All Along the Watchtower	John Wesley Harding	Dec. 27, 1967
8.	Ballad of Hollis Brown	The Times They Are A-Changin'	Feb. 10, 1964
9.	Knockin' on Heaven's Door	Pat Garrett & Billy The Kid	July 13, 1973
10.	The Times They Are A-Changin'	The Times They Are A-Changin'	Feb. 10, 1964
11.	Don't Think Twice, It's All Right	The Freewheelin' Bob Dylan	May 27, 1963
12.	Gates of Eden	Bringing It All Back Home	March 22, 1965
13.	Love Minus Zero/No Limit	Bringing It All Back Home	March 22, 1965
14.	It's Alright, Ma (I'm Only Bleeding)	Bringing It All Back Home	March 22, 1965
15.	Forever Young	Planet Waves	Jan. 17, 1974
16.	Something There is About You	Planet Waves	Jan. 17, 1974
17.	Like a Rolling Stone	Highway 61 Revisited	Aug. 30, 1965

The Musicians

Bob Dylan (vocal, guitar & harmonica).

The Band — Robbie Robertson (guitar), Garth Hudson (synthesizer), Richard Manual (keyboards), Rick Danko (bass), Levon Helm (drums).

Notes

- 15th Bob Dylan concert in Canada; 6th Bob Dylan concert in Toronto.
- 10-14, Bob Dylan solo (vocal, guitar & harmonica).
- Canadian live debut of song 3.
- Song 3 has been performed only once in Canada.
- Worldwide live debut of song 3. To date, it has not been played live since.
- The songs The Band performed alone are not included in the set list.

Review

He turned his back on his loving fans

By Robert Martin.

Why do people go to pop concerts?

People do not go to pop concerts to hear music. If all they were interested in was music, they might just as well stay home where they can hear the music much better than they ever will in the acoustic garbage can that is Maple Leaf Gardens.

People go because they want to communicate with their heroes. The hero performs his music, his fans cheer, he smiles, bows, says "thank you" or whatever in appreciation of their appreciation. It is a simple exchange, this pop communion, but a profoundly moving and human one. When a rapport between artist and audience is fully realized it is one of the rare occasions in our emotionally straightjacketed society when people can unabashedly express their admiration, affection, even love for a person they have never met but have much in common with.

That is why Bob Dylan's concerts Wednesday night and last night at the Gardens were such abominations. The feeling of cold didn't come from the boarded-over Gardens ice. It came from just left of centre stage where Dylan stands to sing.

Dylan has taken a vow of silence. He doesn't introduce songs. He doesn't acknowledge applause verbally. Once on Tuesday night he suddenly swivelled on his heel, bowed to the seats behind him, turned back, bowed to the front, and continued.

Once last night he said "thank you." It was at the end of The Times They Are A-Changin' and was really an apology for having forgotten most of the lyrics in the first two verses. Other that that it was a private performance.

But that action got a bigger cheer than any of his songs had. It was the only time he admitted he was not alone. Many people have been waiting eight years to see Dylan. They loved him inordinately, they showed it openly and their hero turned his back to tune his guitar.

It's all part of Dylan's campaign to abdicate from a leadership role he never wanted. But he's going to unnecessary lengths to do this. He doesn't have to alienate his fans in the process. And he appears to be doing just that.

"Say a few words," a fan bellowed repeatedly from the floor. And Dylan, whose sensitivity to audience reaction approaches radar, picked up the cry. After a few bellows, he even answered, that is, his lips moved, but no sound came out. My lip reading at 80 feet is only marginal but I think he mouthed "hello."

Dylan has been saying for years that he's only "a guitar player," not the second coming or any of those other hysterical labels people have pinned on him. But any musician when he mounts a stage becomes more than a player of notes. He becomes a performer. Andres Segovia, another "guitar player," is a magnificent performer. He doesn't speak either but his fatherly smile and kindly eye win audiences everywhere.

As if to make up for the lack of rapport Dylan has with his audiences, the lighting crew on the show has taken to raising the house lights gradually during the final song, Like a Rolling Stone. The Rolling Stones invented this trick. But their audiences are usually already leaping about and cheering when the lights go up and the fact that the audience can now see itself celebrating, heightens the sense of communion and increases the enjoyment.

This ploy didn't work very well in Toronto. Because people, had been sitting quietly in their seats watching a mechanical performance, it took them a while to realize that they were being directed to stand and cheer spontaneously.

The ploy works beautifully for the Rolling Stones because it is the climax of a performance in which Mick Jagger does everything short of cartwheels to get that audience on its feet. A Stones audience knows that Jagger is directing his whole performance at each and every member, that he cares how they react and that he really wants their cheers and applause.

Dylan gives the impression that people who have paid up to $8.80 for an obstructed view are intruding on his privacy. It's as though 18,000 people had stuck their heads through the window of his living room while he was jamming with the Band. He won't close the window, he just turns his back.

Dylan's current tour has, been hailed as the pop event of the year but Dylan is turning it into a non-event, a series of musical evenings in which notes are played and songs are sung from behind an invisible shield by a ghost who purports to be Bob Dylan.

The Globe and Mail. Fri., Jan. 11, 1974. Reprinted with permission from The Globe and Mail.

Friday, January 11, 1974 --- Montreal Forum Montreal, QC

Set List

	Song	From The Album	Released
1.	Most Likely You Go Your Way and I'll Go Mine	Blonde on Blonde	May 16, 1966
2.	Lay, Lady, Lay	Nashville Skyline	April 9, 1969
3.	Just Like Tom Thumb's Blues	Highway 61 Revisited	Aug. 30, 1965
4.	I Don't Believe You (She Acts Like We Never Have Met)	Another Side of Bob Dylan	Aug. 8, 1964
5.	It Ain't Me, Babe	Another Side of Bob Dylan	Aug. 8, 1964
6.	Ballad of a Thin Man	Highway 61 Revisited	Aug. 30, 1965
7.	All Along the Watchtower	John Wesley Harding	Dec. 27, 1967
8.	Ballad of Hollis Brown	The Times They Are A-Changin'	Feb. 10, 1964
9.	Knockin' on Heaven's Door	Pat Garrett & Billy The Kid	July 13, 1973
10.	The Times They Are A-Changin'	The Times They Are A-Changin'	Feb. 10, 1964
11.	Don't Think Twice, It's All Right	The Freewheelin' Bob Dylan	May 27, 1963
12.	Gates of Eden	Bringing It All Back Home	March 22, 1965
13.	Nobody 'Cept You	The Bootleg Series Volumes 1-3	March 26, 1991
14.	It's Alright, Ma (I'm Only Bleeding)	Bringing It All Back Home	March 22, 1965
15.	Forever Young	Planet Waves	Jan. 17, 1974
16.	Something There is About You	Planet Waves	Jan. 17, 1974
17.	Like a Rolling Stone	Highway 61 Revisited	Aug. 30, 1965
	Encore		
18.	Most Likely You Go Your Way and I'll Go Mine	Blonde on Blonde	May 16, 1966

The Musicians

Bob Dylan (vocal, guitar, & harmonica).

The Band — Robbie Robertson (guitar), Garth Hudson (synthesizer), Richard Manual (keyboards), Rick Danko (bass), Levon Helm (drums).

Notes

- 16th Bob Dylan concert in Canada; 7th Bob Dylan concert in Montreal.
- 10-14, Bob Dylan solo (vocal, guitar & harmonica).
- Most Likely You Go Your Way and I'll Go Mine not only opened the show, it was also the encore.
- The songs The Band performed alone are not included in the set list.

Reviews

"Bringin' it all back... here"

par Robert Guy Scully.

Hier soir au Forum, Bob Dylan a fait le contraire de ce qu'il avait fait au Forum il y a huit ans. En 66, la première partie du concert avait été donnée par lui seul, avec sa guitare "sêche": puis pour la deuxième, il s'était fait accompagner d'un orchestre rock et avait pris une guitare électrique. Ces deux parties illustraient les deux Dylan d'alors, le folk et le rock. Amorcée au festival de Newport deux ans plus tôt, cette transformation avait blessé plusieurs milliers de ses fans, les "purs", mais elle avait un sens plus large, dans la mesure où elle symbolisait le passage, chez la jeunesse américaine, d'une vision positive (politique) à une vision plus incertaine, mais plus globale, fondée sur l'émotion et curieuse de Dieu.

Hier personne n'était blessé: on a vu Dylan donner d'abord une excellente heure de musique électrique (assez amplifiée d'ailleurs) avec le groupe The Band, formé de Canadiens anglais, ancêtre de celui, avec lequel il s'était produit ici à la Place des Arts. Puis, après l'entracte, il est revenu tout seul sur scène avec sa guitare d'avant 64. Les spectateurs ont aimé les deux parties, ils ont même goûté à ce long moment où The Band a joué sans son célèbre soliste, interprétant plusieurs hits de dernières années dont une chanson de Dylan, "I shall be released". La réaction était plus chaleureuse que frénétique, contrairement à celle qui avait marqué le passage, par exemple, des Rolling Stones. Il faut dire que D. n'est plus la vedette majeure qu'il a déjà été, qu'il attire surtout ses fidèles de toujours (amateurs de poèsie autant que de sensations musicales) et qu'il n'a jamais encouragé le fla-fla des superspectacles rock.

Le Forum était plein, pas plus. Le climat était bon chaleureux. A noter une bonne proportion de francophones – et d'auditeurs frisant la trentaine. Au début, Dylan a dit une phrase qu'il doit dire dans bien des villes: "It's great to be back in Montreal", mais c'est peut-être le contraire qui était vrai: "It's great to have you back" semblait dire cette foule calme, unie, harmonieuse, toute oreilles.

Certaines chansons de la période rock ont été jouées à la guitare espagnole, telle "It's allright ma (I'm only bleeding)", alors que d'autres de la première périod ont été jouées en "grosse" version électrique, comme "Ballad of Hollis Brown". A chaque concert depuis le début de sa carrière, Dylan a toujours refusé d'être le prisonnier de ses propres succès, des chansons que ses admirateurs aimeraient entendre telles qu'elles ont été endisquées, par une espèce d'idolatrie. Ainsi, il s'efforce presque à frustrer son public, à le secouer, en changeant, immanquablement sa voix, ou la mélodie ou le rythme des chansons connues. Hier soir, pour une version assez fidèle de "Ballad of thin man", ou "All along the Watchtower", on a entendu des classiques tels que "Don't think twice it's allright" ou "I don't believe you" ou "The times they are a'changin' " joués sur des mélodies quasiment méconnaissables, et sur un ton neuf, plus strident.

Notons cependent qu'il n'a pas touché aux paroles de ces chansons. Serait-ce une indication qu'elles renferment l'essentiel, et que la musique n'est en définitive que leur enveloppe. Les spectateurs aussi semblaient y porter une plus grande attention: les multiples harmonies du groupe (deux batteurs, organiste, trois guitares, parfois un piano) étaient agrèables, certes, mais quand leur son couvrait les mots, on aurait dit que vingt mille têtes se penchaient légèrement en avant et que quarante mille lèvres prononcaient en silence des syllabes qu'elles connaissaient déjà...

Le concert a commence avec "Most likely you'll go your way and I'll go mine". Je ne sais pas sur quoi il a fini. Je sais seulement que les réactions sont devenues plus ferventes pendant le performance de ce cryptique chef-d'oeuvre de 1965 "It's allright ma", où il est dit que le président des Etats-Unis doit parfois être nu, que la société n'est qu'une vaste supercherie, et que en définitive. "It's life and life only" qui compte. On a beaucoup applaudi. Après Dylan est sorti pour se reposer et moi, pour écrire ceci de deadline. Maudit!

Le Devoir. Sat., Jan. 12, 1974. Reprinted with permission of Le Devoir.

Vous souvenez-vous de Dylan? Oh! oui ...

par Christiane Berthiaume.

Un des machinistes s'est approché du micro en disant : "Ils sont partis". Avec l'envie peut-être d'ajouter : faut vous faire une raison. Quinze minutes après la fin du concert, les spectateurs n'avaient pas encore quitté leur place et réclamaient à grands cris : "We Want Bob !", en applaudissant à toute rompre.

Quelques minutes auparavant, dans l'amphithéâtre éclairé du Forum, pendant que les projecteurs balayaient la salle, 18,000 personnes debout sur leur siège tapaient dans leur mains et chantaient en choeur (la dernière chanson) "Like A Rolling Stone" avec Bob Dylan. Impressionnant.

C'est le public qui a donné toute sa dimension au spectacle. Le Forum était rempii à craquer de jeunes et de moins jeunes.

Ils ont frénétiquement applaudi presque toutes les chansons, surtout celles qui rappelaient des souvenirs (il y a en avait 27) : "Lay, Lady, Lay", "Don't Think Twice, It's All Right", "It Ain't Me Babe", etc...

Des que Dylan commençait à jouer quelques mesures d'harmonica, les applaudissements doublaient. Ils ne se sont pas interrompus également pendant les longues minutes ou il a enlevé sa guitare et s'est dirigé à l'autre bout de la scène pour s'accompagner au piano.

Dans la noirceur, personne ne pouvait le voir mais sentait sa présence. C'est pourquoi les spectateurs saluaient chacun de ses retours sur scène d'un tonnerre d'applaudissements.

Sur la scène, il y avait les instruments des musiciens, un divan en arrière du piano, une chaise berçante surmontée d'une lampe Tiffany en arrière de la batterie, un tapis persan en avant de la scène, des chandelles un peu partout, sur l'orgue, les boîtes de son, le piano, etc...

Les lumières se sont éteintes. Du fond de la scène sont arrivés six personnages. Les cinq membres de The Band. Dylan devant avec sa tête bouclée, sa guitare, vêtu simplement d'un habit noir, d'une chemise foncée, col ouvert.

Dylan partage la vedette sur scène avec The Band, un groupe canadien qui travaille avec lui depuis les tout débuts, qui l'accompagne pendant tout le spectacle. Il les laisse seuls plusieurs fois interpréter ses chansons.

De tout le spectacle, Dylan n'a dit que trois phrases. L'une pour annoncer l'intermission, les deux autres pour dire qu'il était content d'être à Montreal. Après huit ans d'absence, Bob Dylan a entrepris la semaine dernière une grande tournée nord-américaine.

La fidélité de ses admirateurs était, hier soir, équivalente à l'importance de Dylan dans l'évolution de la chanson contemporaine.

Dylan, ca ne s'oublié pas.

La Presse. Sat., Jan. 12, 1974. Reprinted with permission of La Presse.

DYLAN SE RETIRE ET LE CHAHUT COMMENCE

par Hélène des Rosiers.

Près de vingt mille spectateurs sont là, debout, dans les estrades pleines à craquer, applaudissant, tapant du pied, implorant un rappel. BOB DYLAN, le roi du rock et du folk song, accompagné du très populaire groupe THE BAND, a quitté la scène, après un unique rappel. Et ne reviendra pas. Deux des organisateurs de la soirée tentent de faire accepter cette déception à un public exigeant, et bien réchauffé. En vain... Et pendant plus de dix minutes, les "supplications" se poursuivent, le chahut règne. En vain aussi...

UN CAS FREQUENT

Bob Dylan est reconnu pour se produire très peu souvent en spectacle. Certains ont même prétendu que sa tournée actuelle était en quelque sorte une faveur que l'idole fait à ses "adeptes". Il est donc immanquable qu'à chacune de ses apparitions sur scène, de ville en ville, on tente de lui en demander le plus possible. A plus forte raison dans des endroits (comme Montréal) d'où il a été absent de la scène pendant presque dix ans. Mais la décision d'arrêter son spectacle là où il a choisi de le faire semble tenir de l'irrévocable. Et malgré la très pressante insistance de public, la scène est demeurée vide...

RESIGNATION

Et peu à peu, le Forum a aussi fini par se vider; les fans de Dylan se disant tout de même plus que satisfaits du "show" qu'on venait de leur servir. Quelques-uns ont même expliqué que malgré leur vorace attente, ils avaient été comblés. Alors chacun s'est finalement résigné. Et c'est un public réjoui qu'on a retrouvé ensuite sur les rues environnant le Forum. Des autobus nolisés ont accueilli de gros groupes de jeunes venus peut-être de très loin.

DEUX HEURES INTENSES

Finalement, chacun se retirait satisfait d'avoir en droit à deux heures de musique, particulièrement intenses. Bob Dylan est à la tête d'un courant original auquel de nombreux fidèles se raccrochent depuis longtemps. Sa venue à Montréal était en soi un événement unique.

Lors de ces deux heures (reprises hier soir) qui passeront à l'histoire locale de notre monde du spectacle, Dylan et The Band ont fait revivre des airs du passé sur un mode actuel. Des chansons plus nouvelles étaient aussi inscrites au programme, mais pour plusieurs, les vieilles "tounes" de Dylan demeurent encore les plus attachantes ou du moins les plus évocatrices.

Parmi quelques-uns des titres qu'il a présentés, on a pu reconnaître: "Lay, Lady Lay", "Don't Think Twice, It's All Right", "The Times, They Are Changing", "Ballad of a Thin Man" (pour laquelle Dylan s'est accompagné au piano), "Gates of Ida", "All Along the Watchtower", "Ballad of Hollis Brown", "It's All Right, Ma", "Except For You", "It Ain't Me, Babe", et "Like a Rolling Stone"...

LIKE A ROLLING STONE

Ce dernier hit de Dylan, classable parmi ses airs les plus populaîres, a suscité un enthousiasme débordant. Tous les spectateurs se sont levés d'un même élan, dès les premiers accords et sont restés debout, battant le rythme et se joignant à Dylan et The Band pour entonner le refrain. Une atmosphère quasi religieuse a baigné l'auditoire pendant que de puissants réflecteurs balayaient les estrades.

LE SIGNAL FINAL

C'était un peu là le signal de la fin. Mille petits flambeaux ont jailli de la pénombre aux mains d'autant de spectateurs reconnaissants. Et Dylan n'a pu refuser à ses fidèles un dernier sursaut de plaisir. Et il a offert à nouveau la très belle chanson avec laquelle il était entré en scène: "Most Likely You'll Go Your Way (And I'll Go Mine). Et là, c'ètait vraiment la fin.

Dylan et The Band venaient une fois de plus de se produire en harmonie (ce qu'ils font ensemble à l'occasion, sur scène, depuis leur rencontre, il y a bientôt huit ans, sans jamais avoir enregistré de disque ensemble). Dans une réciproque admiration, dans une égale reconnaissance de leur aptitude commune à faire de la vraie musique, dans leurs apports respectifs à ce qui fait un bon "show"...

Le Journal de Montréal. Sun., Jan. 13, 1974. Reprinted with permission of Le Journal de Montréal.

Additional Reviews

Dylan turns to rock – and the result is dynamite, by Bill Mann. The Montreal Gazette. Sat., Jan. 12, 1974. p. 17.

18,000 stamp and cheer for Dylan, by Juan Rodriguez. The Montreal Star. Sat., Jan. 12, 1974. p. A1 & A2.

Saturday, January 12, 1974 --- Montreal Forum
Montreal, QC

Set List

	Song	From The Album	Released
1.	Most Likely You Go Your Way and I'll Go Mine	Blonde on Blonde	May 16, 1966
2.	Lay, Lady, Lay	Nashville Skyline	April 9, 1969
3.	Just Like Tom Thumb's Blues	Highway 61 Revisited	Aug. 30, 1965
4.	I Don't Believe You (She Acts Like We Never Have Met)	Another Side of Bob Dylan	Aug. 8, 1964
5.	It Ain't Me, Babe	Another Side of Bob Dylan	Aug. 8, 1964
6.	Ballad of a Thin Man	Highway 61 Revisited	Aug. 30, 1965
7.	All Along the Watchtower	John Wesley Harding	Dec. 27, 1967
8.	Ballad of Hollis Brown	The Times They Are A-Changin'	Feb. 10, 1964
9.	Knockin' on Heaven's Door	Pat Garrett & Billy The Kid	July 13, 1973
10.	Blowin' in the Wind	The Freewheelin' Bob Dylan	May 27, 1963
11.	Don't Think Twice, It's All Right	The Freewheelin' Bob Dylan	May 27, 1963
12.	Gates of Eden	Bringing It All Back Home	March 22, 1965
13.	Just Like a Woman	Blonde on Blonde	May 16, 1966
14.	It's Alright, Ma (I'm Only Bleeding)	Bringing It All Back Home	March 22, 1965
15.	Forever Young	Planet Waves	Jan. 17, 1974
16.	Something There is About You	Planet Waves	Jan. 17, 1974
17.	Like a Rolling Stone	Highway 61 Revisited	Aug. 30, 1965
	Encore		
18.	Most Likely You Go Your Way and I'll Go Mine	Blonde on Blonde	May 16, 1966

The Musicians

Bob Dylan (vocal, guitar & harmonica).

The Band — Robbie Robertson (guitar), Garth Hudson (synthesizer), Richard Manual (keyboards), Rick Danko (bass), Levon Helm (drums).

Notes

- 17th Bob Dylan concert in Canada; 8th Bob Dylan concert in Montreal.
- 10-14, Bob Dylan solo (vocal, guitar & harmonica).
- The second time of only two times ever in Canada where a song was played twice in one evening. Most Likely You Go Your Way and I'll Go Mine not only opened the show, it was also the encore.
- The songs The Band performed alone are not included in the set list.

1975

Introduction

The Rolling Thunder Review was conceived by Bob Dylan as a traveling show that was to be on "a forever tour" appearing in small venues without much advertising or marketing hullabaloo. The Revue was to consist of a variable number of performers backed by a core band. If the Revue passed through town and a local artist felt like joining he was always welcome. Well, that was the concept anyway. And it started out pretty much that way, but during the last part of November the venues got bigger and the press coverage got more intense. The Rolling Thunder Review played four concerts in Canada.

These shows would mark Bob Dylan's 18th, 19th, 20th & 21st concert in Canada.

The Dates

Quebec City, QC	Sat., Nov. 29, 1975
Toronto, ON	Mon., Dec. 1, 1975
Montreal, QC	Tues., Dec. 2, 1975
Montreal, QC	Thurs., Dec. 4, 1975

The shows would be Dylan's debut concert in Quebec City, 7th & 8th concert in Toronto and 9th concert in Montreal.

The Musicians

Bob Dylan (vocal, guitar & harmonica).

Guam — Bob Neuwirth (vocal & guitar), T-Bone J. Henry Burnett (guitar), Roger McGuinn (vocal & guitar), Steven Soles (guitar), Mick Ronson (guitar), David Mansfield (steel guitar, violin, mandolin & dobro), Rob Stoner (bass), Howie Wyeth (piano & drums), Luther Rix (drums & percussion), Ronee Blakley (vocal), Joan Baez (vocal & guitar), Scarlet Rivera (violin).

The Songs

Bob Dylan performed a total of 85 songs. Of those, 28 were different songs (24 were from albums and 4 were cover and/or traditional songs).

Seventeen songs made their Canadian live debut.

When I Paint My Masterpiece	Oh, Sister
Tonight I'll Be Staying Here With You	Hurricane
Romance in Durango	One More Cup of Coffee (Valley Below)
Isis	Sara
Dark as a Dungeon	This Land is Your Land
Mama, You Been on My Mind	Never Let Me Go
I Dreamed I Saw St. Augustine	Wild Mountain Thyme
I Shall Be Released	Tangled Up in Blue
Simple Twist of Fate	–

One song has been played only once in Canada.

Wild Mountain Thyme	–

Bob Dylan performed songs from 13 different albums.

Album	Released	# of Songs Performed by Album
The Freewheelin' Bob Dylan	May, 27, 1963	2
The Times They Are A-Changin'	Feb., 10, 1964	2
Another Side of Bob Dylan	Aug. 8, 1964	1
Bringing It All Back Home	March 22, 1965	3
Highway 61 Revisited	Aug. 30, 1965	1
Blonde on Blonde	May 16, 1966	1
John Wesley Harding	Dec. 27, 1967	1
Nashville Skyline	April 9, 1969	1
Bob Dylan's Greatest Hits, Vol. 2	Nov. 17, 1971	2
Pat Garrett and Billy The Kid	July 13, 1973	1
Blood on the Tracks	Jan. 20, 1975	2
Desire	Jan. 5, 1976	6
The Bootleg Series Volumes 1-3	March 26, 1991	1

Special Guests

The four concerts on the 1975 Rolling Thunder Revue Tour featured many special guests that were not part of the core band. Joan Baez played her own music as well as joining in with Dylan on a few songs. Ramblin' Jack Elliott, Cindy Bullens, Joni Mitchell, Gordon

Lightfoot, Ronnie Hawkins, and Jack Scott all played their own songs and joined Dylan on stage for the finale of This Land is Your Land. Some members of the core band (known as Guam) also played a song or two of their own — Bob Neuwirth, T-Bone J. Henry Burnett, Steven Soles, Rob Stoner, Mick Ronson, Ronee Blakley, and Roger McGuinn. Poet Allen Ginsberg also appeared at the shows.

The Venues

It was Bob Dylan's debut concert at the Quebec City Coliseum, 3rd & 4th time playing at Maple Leaf Gardens in Toronto and 3rd time playing at the Montreal Forum.

Saturday, November 29, 1975 --- Quebec City Coliseum Quebec City, QC

Set List

	Song	From The Album	Released
1.	When I Paint My Masterpiece	Bob Dylan's Greatest Hits, Vol. 2	Nov. 17, 1971
2.	It Ain't Me, Babe	Another Side of Bob Dylan	Aug. 8, 1964
3.	The Lonesome Death of Hattie Carroll	The Times They Are A-Changin'	Feb. 10, 1964
4.	Tonight I'll Be Staying Here With You	Nashville Skyline	April 9, 1969
5.	Romance in Durango (Bob Dylan/Jacques Levy)	Desire	Jan. 5, 1976
6.	Isis (Bob Dylan/Jacques Levy)	Desire	Jan. 5, 1976
7.	Blowin' in the Wind	The Freewheelin' Bob Dylan	May 27, 1963
8.	Dark as a Dungeon (Merle Travis)	–	–
9.	Mama, You Been on My Mind	The Bootleg Series Volumes 1-3	March 26, 1991
10.	I Dreamed I Saw St. Augustine	John Wesley Harding	Dec. 27, 1967
11.	I Shall Be Released	Bob Dylan's Greatest Hits, Vol. 2	Nov. 17, 1971

	Song	On Stage
–	Diamonds and Rust (Joan Baez)	Joan Baez
–	Swing Low Sweet Chariot (trad.)	Joan Baez
–	Joe Hill (Earl Robinson)	Joan Baez
–	The Night They Drove Old Dixie Down (Robbie Robertson)	Joan Baez & Roger McGuinn

	Song	From The Album	Released
12.	Love Minus Zero/No Limit	Bringing It All Back Home	March 22, 1965
13.	Simple Twist of Fate	Blood on the Tracks	Jan. 20, 1975
14.	Oh, Sister (Bob Dylan/Jacques Levy)	Desire	Jan. 5, 1976
15.	Hurricane (Bob Dylan/Jacques Levy)	Desire	Jan. 5, 1976
16.	One More Cup of Coffee (Valley Below)	Desire	Jan. 5, 1976
17.	Sara	Desire	Jan. 5, 1976
18.	Just Like a Woman	Blonde on Blonde	May 16, 1966
19.	Knockin' on Heaven's Door	Pat Garrett & Billy The Kid	July 13, 1973
20.	This Land is Your Land (Woody Guthrie)	–	–

The Musicians

Bob Dylan (vocal, guitar & harmonica)

Guam — Bob Neuwirth (vocal & guitar), T-Bone J. Henry Burnett (guitar), Roger McGuinn (vocal & guitar), Steven Soles (guitar), Mick Ronson (guitar), David Mansfield (steel guitar, violin, mandolin & dobro), Rob Stoner (bass), Howie Wyeth (piano & drums), Luther Rix (drums & percussion), Ronee Blakley (vocal), Joan Baez (vocal & guitar), Scarlet Rivera (violin).

Notes

- 18th Bob Dylan concert in Canada; Debut Bob Dylan concert in Quebec City.
- 1, Bob Neuwirth (shared vocal).
- 1-11, 14-20, Bob Dylan (vocal & guitar), Bob Neuwirth (guitar), T-Bone J. Henry Burnett (guitar), Roger McGuinn (guitar), Steven Soles (guitar), Mick Ronson (guitar), David Mansfield (steel guitar, violin, mandolin & dobro), Rob Stoner (bass), Howie Wyeth (piano & drums), Luther Rix (drums & percussion), Ronee Blakley (vocal).
- 2, 12-14, 17, Bob Dylan (harmonica).
- 5-6, 14-20, Scarlet Rivera (violin).
- 7-11, Joan Baez (vocal, guitar).
- 12-13, Bob Dylan solo (vocal, guitar & harmonica).

- 19, Roger McGuinn (shared vocal).
- 20, shared vocal by Bob Dylan and the entire ensemble for the evening.
- Canadian live debut of songs 1, 4, 5, 6, 8, 9, 10, 11, 13, 14, 15, 16, 17 & 20.
- Special guests included; Joni Mitchell, Ramblin' Jack Elliott, & Allen Ginsberg.
- The songs performed by members of Guam are not included in the set list.
- The Joan Baez part of the set list is not complete. She also introduced and sang one or two songs in French.

Reviews

Un spectacle sublime et dècevant

Bob Dylan et la revue Rolling Thunder

par Paul Roux.

La revue ROLLING THUNDER. Principales têtes d'affiche Bob Dylan, Joan Baez, Joni Mitchell, Jack Elliott, Roger Maguinn, Allan Gerber, Roonee Blakley. Au Colisée samedi soir dernier.

Il est difficile de parler dans un même text de la beauté et de la grossièreté, du génie et de la platitude, de l'enthousiasme et de la déception. Deux jours après avoir entendu Bob Dylan et sa revue Rolling Thunder, j'essaie de démêler les impressions contradictoires que le spectacle m'a laissées.

J'étais allé entendre le plus grand des auteurs-interprètes de la chanson américaine. A ce niveau, aucune déception. Dylan était bel et bien là, en chair et en os, avec quelques vieux succès et beaucoup de nouvelles chansons du meilleur cru. L'artiste a changé, laissant une plus grande place à l'orchestre et aux choeurs, mais sans rien perdre de son talent.

Joan Baez aussi était là. Avec la même voix que sur ses disques, et avec une chaleur, une spontanéité, un enthousiasme que seul le contexte du concert peut mettre en relief. Seule ou avec Dylan, elle nous a fait vivre quelques-uns des beaux moments de la soirée.

Comment expliquer, dans ces conditions, qu'il m'ait fallu, comme tant d'autres, autant de temps pour entrer dans la spectacle et me laisser gagner par l'enthousiasme? Comment expliquer que j'en sois sorti presque déçu?

Certaines explications commencent à m'apparaitre. Il y a d'abord le public, ou plus précisément une partie non négligeable du public, dont on se demande, surtout au prix où étaient les billets, ce qu'elle était venue faire là. Tous n'ont pas manifesté, bien sûr, la grossièreté de cet individu qui, pendant un bon quinze minutes, a crié à tue-tête: "Mange de la marde Dylan!". Mais je n'ai jamais ve réunis en un même endroit autant de spectateurs bruyants et peu réceptifs.

Autre explication (qui ne fera pas l'unanimité celle-là), c'est le manque d'homogénéité du spectacle. Pour ceux qui comme moi ont décroché du gros "rock" dont l'originalité est inversement proportionnelle au volume de décibels, la première partie du spectacle était fastidieuse.

Certains invités étaient décevants, mais pour des raisons qui ne tiennent pas à leur orientation musicale. Je pense en particulier à Joni Mitchell, qui possède une voix et un talent exceptionnels, mais qui de toute évidence n'avait pas le qoût d'être là et qui aurait dû se donner la peine d'accorder sa guitare dans la coulisse.

Et puis, surtout, il y a le colisée. Y donner un spectacle c'est comme manger dans sa cave. A plus forte raison si la principale vedette est un poète. Pendant un moment, je me suis plu à imaginer ce qu'aurait été un spectacle de Dylan et de Baez dans une petite salle chaleureuse comme celle de Cartier. C'aurait été sublime, pas seulement par moments, mais de bout en bout!

Je réve, bien sûr. Car Dylan, devenu super-star et millionnaire, ne donne plus que des gros "shows" dans de grosses salles. Ainsi le veut le "système", dit on.

Ce même "système" que dénonce Dylan dans ses chansons.

Le Soleil. Tues., Dec. 2, 1975. Reprinted with permission of Le Soleil.

BOB DYLAN: INOUBLIABLE

par Yvon Pellerin.

Comment décrire cet inoubliable spectacle que fut le "show" de Bob Dylan, au Colisée, samedi, sinon que par l'appellation de chef d'oeuvre?

D'ailleurs comment en aurait-il pu être autrement, quand Joni Mitchell, Jack Elliott, Roger Mcguinn, Joan Baez et Dylan lui-même se retrouvent tour à tour sur la même scène, dans un spectacle admirablement conçu, solide, naturel, envoûtant, au cours duquel il n'y a pas l'ombre d'un temps mort.

Durant trois incroyables heures, plus un demie, ces artistes ont donné ce qu'ils avaient de meilleur dans un cadre style "country-folk-rock", le seul genre qui convenait vraiment pour porter musicalement la poésie contenue dans chaque minute en scène. La base de ce "son" spécial est assurée par un groupe de jeunes musiciens habiles sous la direction du MC, Bob Newirth. Tour à tour "heavy" et rockers, ils pouvaient, l'instant d'après devenir très doux et s'engager tout aussi facilement sur les avenues de la musique "country". Ils pouvaient surtout accompagner d'une façon sensible et intelligente les grands artistes de la revue "Rolling Thunder".

Concept de "party"

Si la tournée de Dylan de 1974 avait été un événement important dans l'histoire de la musique rock, celle que plusieurs milliers de Québécois ont vu samedi est sûrement le "show" de la décennie. Le spectacle est organisé de façon à créer, chez le spectateur, un impression indéfinissable faite des souvenirs de la glorieuse époque du folk des années soixante et de la beauté fraîche des nouvelles compositions des artistes, le tout dans une continuelle atmospère de "jam session" et de party sympathique. Le public, assez âgé pour ce qu'on a l'habitude de voir aux spectacles rock à Québec, a écouté religieusement, fasciné, les deux parties du spectacle également présidées par Dylan, Dylan à la fois dynamique, sarcastique, tendre et attachant, avec un côté comédien que ses disques ne laissaient pas prévoir.

Première partie

Durant la première partie, on accueille Newirth et co. qui nous présentent bientôt Allan Gerber (lui et Zeller qui jouaient au Cabaret de l'Hôtel Victoria, en fin de semaine) Roonee Blakley, jeune chanteuse "country" découverte du film 'Nashville', Joni Mitchell, folk signer de renommée internationale (elle, a entre autres, composé l'hymne "Woodstock") qui a une voix particulièrement pure et hypnotique, et le vétéran "Rambling" Jack Elliot, "folkie" dans la quarantaine, populaire aux Etats-Unis, bien avant Dylan. C'est avec lui que tout a vraiment commencé. Après une couple de chansons enlevantes, Elliot s'est soudainement éclipsé sous une salve d'applaudissements: on croyait le voir revenir, mais c'est Bob Dylan qui apparaît, sa guitare et son harmonica et bandoulière. Et coiffé d'un chapeau orné de plumes et de fleurs naturelles, il démarre avec "It ain't me babe", un de ses premiers succès et poursuit, avec du nouveau "matériel" entrecoupé de morceaux tirés de ses plus récents microsillons, comme "Masterpiece" et "Simple Twist of Fate". Le son est celui du "folk rock" lourd, mais distinct et traditionnel. Dylan ne sourit que peu ou pas, "I don't speak too much french" lance-t-il entre deux chansons, on le savait et on le lui pardonne. Le voir se promener sur scène en imitant Charlie Chaplin, le dos courbé, les jambes en rond et l'oeil par en dessous, a quelque chose de spécial sur une scène de rock, qu'il serait vain d'essayer de décrire.

Si la première partie avait établi le tempo du spectacle, la deuxième devait le porter jusqu'aux plus hauts sommets. Que peut-on demander de plus qu'une ouverture avec "Blowing in the wind" chanté par Dylan et Joan Baez en duo? Ce fut un moment fracassant, que le reste du spectacle n'a pas démenti. "I shall be released" avec Baez, au cou de Dylan, fit le reste pour faire tomber le public dans le pommes, au comble de l'émotion. Joan Baez est un personnage extraordinairement présent sur scène. Simple et joviale, elle est comme le complément de Dylan, son porte-parole, (elle parle français un peu) quand il est avec elle sur scène. Seule pendant un bon moment, elle a ébloui l'assistance, avec ses plus grands succès dont "Joe Hill" et la chanson, sans accompagnement, qui avait emporté tout le monde, à Woodstock.

Puis c'est l'apothéose finale: un invité spécial apparaît. Est-ce possible? Roger Mcguinn, l'âme dirigeante du fameux groupe des Byrds (Turn Turn Turn, M. Tambourine Man). Il enchaîne avec leur grand succès, "Eight Miles High" et tout le monde reconnaît ce "son" si particulier de guitare et monte aussi haute que possible , à ce souvenir encore récent. Efin Dylan revient au milieu de ces retrouvailles et c'est le plus beau de toute l'affaire. Après quelques morceaux très doux et poétiques, dont l'un sans doute dédié à sa femme, "Sarah", le climat rejoint l'intimité voulue, pour terminer avec les deux plus belles pièces de la soirée: "Just Like a woman" admirablement interprété, et "Knock on Heavens door" qui amena à la porte du ciel les derniers retardataires.

C'était trop pour le public qui, spontanément, se leva d'un bond, à la fin du numéro, pour braver les omniprésents placiers et policiers et venir danser en avant, sur les côtés, partout, au son de la dernière piéce avec les choeurs de Dylan, Baez, Mitchell, Mcguinn, Elliott et les autres, tous revenus sur la scène pour entonner ensemble l'hymne de circonstances "This land is your land". On est heureux, on rit, on pleure, on tape du pied, on s'aime, le rêve s'achève, mais on ne veut pas se réveiller...

Le Journal de Québec. Mon., Dec. 1, 1975. Reprinted with permission of Le Journal de Québec.

Monday, December 1, 1975 --- Maple Leaf Gardens Toronto, ON

Set List

	Song	On Stage
–	Good Love Is Hard to Find (N. Albright)	Bob Neuwirth
–	Sleazy (?)	Bob Neuwirth
–	Hula Hoop (John Fleming/J. Henry Burnett & Roscoe West)	T-Bone J. Henry Burnett
–	Laissez-Faire (David Ackles)	Steven Soles
–	Catfish (Bob Dylan/Jacques Levy)	Rob Stoner
–	Is There Life on Mars? (Roscoe West)	Mick Ronson
–	Alabama Dark (Bob Neuwirth)	Bob Neuwirth & Ronee Blakley
–	Need a New Sun Rising (Ronee Blakley)	Ronee Blakley
–	Cindy (When I Get Home) (trad.)	Bob Neuwirth
–	Nowhere to Go (?)	Cindy Bullens
–	Mercedes Benz (Janis Joplin/Michael McClure)	Bob Neuwirth
–	Woman of Heart and Mind (Joni Mitchell)	Joni Mitchell
–	Coyote (Joni Mitchell)	Joni Mitchell
–	Edith and the Kingpin (Joni Mitchell)	Joni Mitchell
–	Don't Interrupt the Sorrow (Joni Mitchell)	Joni Mitchell
–	Ramblin' Jack (Bob Neuwirth)	Bob Neuwirth
–	Muleskinner Blues (Jimmie Rodgers/George Vaughan)	Ramblin' Jack Elliott
–	Pretty Boy Floyd (Woody Guthrie)	Ramblin' Jack Elliott
–	Salt Pork, West Virginia (Moore/Tennyson)	Ramblin' Jack Elliott
–	I'm a Rich and Ramblin' Boy (Derroll Adams)	Ramblin' Jack Elliott

	Song	From The Album	Released
1.	When I Paint My Masterpiece	Bob Dylan's Greatest Hits, Vol. 2	Nov. 17, 1971
2.	It Ain't Me, Babe	Another Side of Bob Dylan	Aug. 8, 1964
3.	The Lonesome Death of Hattie Carroll	The Times They Are A-Changin'	Feb. 10, 1964
4.	Tonight I'll Be Staying Here With You	Nashville Skyline	April 9, 1969
5.	It Takes a Lot to Laugh, It Takes a Train to Cry	Highway 61 Revisited	Aug. 30, 1965
6.	Romance in Durango (Bob Dylan/Jacques Levy)	Desire	Jan. 5, 1976
7.	Isis (Bob Dylan/Jacques Levy)	Desire	Jan. 5, 1976
8.	The Times They Are A-Changin'	The Times They Are A-Changin'	Feb. 10, 1964
9.	Dark as a Dungeon (Merle Travis)	–	–
10.	Never Let Me Go (Joseph C. Scott)	–	–
11.	I Dreamed I Saw St. Augustine	John Wesley Harding	Dec. 27, 1967
12.	I Shall Be Released	Bob Dylan's Greatest Hits, Vol. 2	Nov. 17, 1971

	Song	On Stage
–	Diamonds and Rust (Joan Baez)	Joan Baez
–	Swing Low Sweet Chariot (trad.)	Joan Baez
–	Joe Hill (Earl Robinson)	Joan Baez
–	Love Song to a Stranger (Joan Baez)	Joan Baez
–	Long Black Vail (Danny Dill/Marijohn Wilkin)	Joan Baez
–	Please Come to Boston (Dave Loggins)	Joan Baez
–	The Night They Drove Old Dixie Down (Robbie Robertson)	Joan Baez & Roger McGuinn
–	Eight Miles High (Gene Clark/Roger McGuinn/David Crosby)	Roger McGuinn
–	Chestnut Mare (Roger McGuinn/Jacques Levy)	Roger McGuinn
–	Race Among the Ruins (Gordon Lightfoot)	Gordon Lightfoot
–	The Watchman's Gone (Gordon Lightfoot)	Gordon Lightfoot
–	Sundown (Gordon Lightfoot)	Gordon Lightfoot

	Song	From The Album	Released
13.	It's All Over Now, Baby Blue	Bringing It All Back Home	March 22, 1965
14.	Love Minus Zero/No Limit	Bringing It All Back Home	March 22, 1965
15.	Simple Twist of Fate	Blood on the Tracks	Jan. 20, 1975
16.	Oh, Sister (Bob Dylan/Jacques Levy)	Desire	Jan. 5, 1976
17.	Hurricane (Bob Dylan/Jacques Levy)	Desire	Jan. 5, 1976
18.	One More Cup of Coffee (Valley Below)	Desire	Jan. 5, 1976
19.	Sara	Desire	Jan. 5, 1976
20.	Just Like a Woman	Blonde on Blonde	May 16, 1966
21.	Knockin' on Heaven's Door	Pat Garrett & Billy The Kid	July 13, 1973
22.	This Land is Your Land (Woody Guthrie)	–	–

The Musicians

Bob Dylan (vocal, guitar & harmonica)

Guam — Bob Neuwirth (vocal & guitar), T-Bone J. Henry Burnett (guitar), Roger McGuinn (vocal & guitar), Steven Soles (guitar), Mick Ronson (guitar), David Mansfield (steel guitar, violin, mandolin & dobro), Rob Stoner (bass), Howie Wyeth (piano & drums), Luther Rix (drums & percussion), Ronee Blakley (vocal), Joan Baez (vocal & guitar), Scarlet Rivera (violin).

Notes

- 19th Bob Dylan concert in Canada; 7th Bob Dylan concert in Toronto.
- 1, Bob Neuwirth (shared vocal).
- 1-12, 16-22, Bob Dylan (vocal & guitar), Bob Neuwirth (guitar), T-Bone J. Henry Burnett (guitar), Roger McGuinn (guitar), Steven Soles (guitar), Mick Ronson (guitar), David Mansfield (steel guitar, violin, mandolin & dobro), Rob Stoner (bass), Howie Wyeth (piano & drums), Luther Rix (drums & percussion), Ronee Blakley (vocal).
- 2, 13-16, 19, Bob Dylan (harmonica).
- 6-7 16-22, Scarlet Rivera (violin).
- 8-12, Joan Baez (vocal, guitar).
- 13-15, Bob Dylan solo (vocal, guitar & harmonica).
- 21, Roger McGuinn (shared vocal).
- 22, shared vocal by Bob Dylan and the entire ensemble for the evening.
- Canadian live debut of song 10.
- Special guests included; Cindy Bullens, Joni Mitchell, Ramblin' Jack Elliott, Gordon Lightfoot and Allen Ginsberg.
- Bob Dylan's mother Beatty Zimmerman attended this show and appeared on stage.

Reviews

Most of all, there was Dylan

By Peter Goddard, Star Staff Writer.

His face was smeared with white grease-paint, his lips and nose were red. He was an electric Picasso clown who said every song was a "true story."

"Listen carefully," Bob Dylan told the 16,000 people at last night's four-hour long Maple Leaf Gardens concert, to be repeated tonight.

And who didn't? For his Rolling Thunder Revue, soon to end its two months of wandering in New York, was something of a folk circus in which many of the side shows might have occupied the centre ring.

There were four songs by Joni Mitchell, each an emotional strip without any tease. Then some vintage Woody Guthrie from the equally vintage Ramblin' Jack Elliott, who looked, as if one song ran, as if he had "been lived in too long to tear down."

There was Ronee Blakley, from the film Nashville, looking like an actress playing a part. And Roger McGuinn, Gordon Lightfoot, Bobby Neuwirth and the English guitarist, Mick Ronson, conjuring up letter perfect solos at the drop of a tune.

And there was Joan Baez, a dark angel in duet with Dylan in his gypsy rags, her very dark dignity filling the hall. Elton John was backstage up to intermission. And David Clayton-Thomas dropped by.

But most of all, there was Dylan.

He ended the first half of the concert, his knees and waist bent as he leaned toward the microphone, crackling out new songs like Durango and Isis in his saw-toothed voice.

As he began and ended the second half with his friends, first Baez, then, as the thunder rolled to a close, with everyone on stage.

His last Toronto concert, also at the Gardens but backed by The Band, was a moody affair.

Last night he was caught up in the whirl around him (the excellent band swelled at times to eight members), a jiving, romping Petroushka in baggy blue jeans dancing at his own fair.

Suddenly, it was easy to remember the little rooms you were sitting in when you first heard the warning from the song, "and you who philosophize disgrace." You could remember the people you were with, the hunger and unease you felt and, even stranger, the sense he was saying it all for you.

For he was saying it all again last night.

The Toronto Star. Tues., Dec. 2, 1975. Reprinted with permission - Torstar Syndication Services.

Dylan, Baez, Mitchell... they just kept coming

By Robert Martin.

The Rolling Thunder Revue went on so long and contained so many stars that it almost concealed an important fact: the re-emergence of Bob Dylan as a major creative force in popular music.

Rolling Thunder, as Dylan calls his traveling caravan of folk and rock artists, included performances last night at Maple Leaf Gardens (there'll be another one tonight) by Joan Baez, Joni Mitchell, Ramblin' Jack Eliot, former Byrd Roger McGuinn, and David Bowie's protégé, Mick Ronson. They just kept coming. "Anything can happen with the Rolling Thunder," singer and master of ceremonies Bobby Neuwirth said, and I believed him. It wouldn't have been particularly surprising if the ghost of Woody Guthrie had joined the cast of thousands.

With all those stars, each of them capable of carrying a concert in his own right, the evening was a long one. It started at 8 p.m. and went on past midnight.

Dylan himself didn't appear until the show had been going for an hour and a half. He bounced on to the stage, wearing jeans, a shirt and vest, and the hat he wore in Sam Peckinpah's Pat Garrett and Billy the Kid. He launched into When I Paint My Masterpiece, and the title was significant. It contained the promise that Dylan has not folded up shop as a writer, and the rest of the show fulfilled that promise.

New songs like Isis, and Hurricane, about convicted murderer Ruben Carter, firmly replanted Dylan on his long-abandoned throne as the king of protest singers. Hurricane told the story of a boxer who, Dylan feels, has been unjustly imprisoned for nine years. It showed that he has come full-circle when compared to The Lonesome Death of Hattie Carroll, a song he wrote more than 10 years ago – and sang last night – that also deals with injustice in America. Carroll, a poor woman, was clubbed to death by a cane-wielding aristocrat, William Zanzinger. He received a six-month sentence.

Isis is harder to place. It appeared to combine Greek mythology with the folklore of the American West and is a song that should reward careful analysis. Still, for the first time in years, I'm looking forward to Dylan's next album with anticipation rather than dread.

It also elicited from Dylan the most dramatic delivery I've seen in five performances over the past two years. With his fists clenched he bellowed out the lyrics over the throbbing of the band, especially Scarlet Rivera's screaming violin.

Musically the band was – dare it be said? – better than The Band who used to back Dylan. Mick Ronson, rock-influenced lead solos added fire to even the most mundane Dylan compositions like Tonight I'll Be Staying Here With You. The group also contained three rhythm guitarists, two drummers, a bass-player and a pedal steel guitarist who doubled on violin. Roger McGuinn played banjo and Ronnee Blakely – I knew I'd forget somebody – played piano as well as singing a couple of songs.

The contrast in styles between the performers was enough to leave the mind reeling. Blakely whined out country music. Eliot sang Woody Guthrie's tribute to Pretty Boy Floyd. Mitchell sang a new song that she said she's writing as the tour progresses and a late arrival, Gordon Lightfoot, added Sundown among other songs.

Dylan's return to touring was the pop event of 1974, simply because he hadn't been on tour for eight years. In the hysteria that greeted the return of the pop messiah, many people overlooked the fact the Dylan gave mechanical, disinterested performances during which he sometimes couldn't even remember his own lyrics.

Rolling Thunder is the pop event of 1975 because Dylan is providing the finest performances of his career, singing the best new material he's written in years and has assembled a group of performers the like of which we may never see again.

Dylan & Co. wow fans

By Wilder Penfield III.

The Rolling Thunder Revue began as Bob Dylan and Bobby Neuwirth and a few friends traveling in a stationwagon playing coffee houses. By the time it rolled into Toronto last night, it had expanded to a touring company of about 112, as many as 18 of them performing on stage at the same time. And the audience was a record 16,000 or so at the Gardens.

That was the grateful explanation of Joan Baez for a change which has allowed people like herself and Joni Mitchell and Allen Ginsburg and Ronee Blakely and Mick Ronson to be included in the snowball and do their best to steal the show from the Legend.

Funny thing – Joan Baez almost did it. After a second-half series of mellow duets with Dylan he left her on her own. She aroused the crowd with Diamonds and Rust, her beautiful tribute to Dylan and got them to their feet with Swing Low Sweet Chariot without even her own guitar as accompaniment. Then she made them laugh with her introduction to the Ballad of Joe Hill, a dedication to Canadians supporting the United Farm Workers – "Death shall have no dominion and Dominion shall have no customers."

But it was still Dylan's show. He came on dressed in a long scarf, vest, jeans and flowered grey fedora. Legs wide apart, he tapped both feet, hunched over the microphone and sang, biting off his words, tough and hard like a street punk. When I Paint My Masterpiece. It Ain't Me Babe. Tonight I'll Be Staying Here With You. The old songs had the real Nashville Skyline voice he discovered when he quit smoking. But his lean athletic band brought out the older rock and roll fire in his delivery.

The songs were transformed to suit the relatively smooth melodies of days of old and were cut up into rhythmic chunks. The seven guitars played off each other in the spirit of coordinated anarchy and sounded like a crazy musical banana split fattening and wonderful.

It would have been an excellent show even without the headliners. The first hour proved that to anyone who wasn't here just for the Event. Seven musicians who left their own bands back at their respective homes took turns at the beginning leading original songs. If the spirit of the revue had been better understood they might have won a better reception for they represented a wide variety of styles and gave rise to the possibility of another wave of folk music, new stars for the years ahead.

Leading that band was Bobby Neuwirth, who has had a great deal of background in the backgrounds of other stars. He finally introduced himself with a song he wrote for Janis Joplin (who had given him the guitar he was playing). It was Mercedes Benz and the band sang it joyously as if around a dying campfire. That was the spirit of the review.

So was this line from a Joni Mitchell song, "The times when you impress me the most are the times when you don't even try." Joni Mitchell, who has been on the tour since the Niagara Falls performance, was in great voice last night and she maintained that spirit by not singing any of her hits but presenting a short series of songs you had to listen to like in the old days when folk had Messages.

It may not have been a coffeehouse but you could hear the words and feel the spirit.

A surprise bonus was Gordon Lightfoot who did in fact present an enthusiastically received three-song guest set with his own band.

Also Roger McGuinn, of the late Byrds.

Also a solo set from Bob Dylan.

The Sixties are still alive and well and living in the Seventies.

You have a second chance to catch the Rolling Thunder Revue tonight at 7 p.m. Some seats are still available.

Tuesday, December 2, 1975 --- Maple Leaf Gardens Toronto, ON

Set List

	Song	On Stage
–	Good Love Is Hard to Find (N. Albright)	Bob Neuwirth
–	Sleazy (?)	Bob Neuwirth
–	Werewolves of London (Warren Zevon)	T-Bone J. Henry Burnett
–	Laissez-Faire (David Ackles)	Steven Soles
–	Catfish (Bob Dylan/Jacques Levy)	Rob Stoner
–	Is There Life on Mars? (Roscoe West)	Mick Ronson
–	Alabama Dark (Bob Neuwirth)	Bob Neuwirth & Ronee Blakley
–	Need a New Sun Rising (Ronee Blakley)	Ronee Blakley
–	Cindy (When I Get Home) (trad.)	Bob Neuwirth
–	Mercedes Benz (Janis Joplin/Michael McClure)	Bob Neuwirth
–	Forty Days (Ronnie Hawkins)	Ronnie Hawkins
–	Bo Diddley/Who Do You Love (Ellas McDaniel)	Ronnie Hawkins
–	Woman of Heart and Mind (Joni Mitchell)	Joni Mitchell
–	Coyote (Joni Mitchell)	Joni Mitchell
–	Edith and the Kingpin (Joni Mitchell)	Joni Mitchell
–	Don't Interrupt the Sorrow (Joni Mitchell)	Joni Mitchell
–	Ramblin' Jack (Bob Neuwirth)	Bob Neuwirth
–	San Francisco Bay Blues (Jesse Fuller)	Ramblin' Jack Elliott
–	Talking Fisherman Blues (Woody Guthrie)	Ramblin' Jack Elliott
–	Salt Pork, West Virginia (Moore/Tennyson)	Ramblin' Jack Elliott
–	I'm a Rich and Ramblin' Boy (Derroll Adams)	Ramblin' Jack Elliott

	Song	From The Album	Released
1.	When I Paint My Masterpiece	Bob Dylan's Greatest Hits, Vol. 2	Nov. 17, 1971
2.	It Ain't Me, Babe	Another Side of Bob Dylan	Aug. 8, 1964
3.	The Lonesome Death of Hattie Carroll	The Times They Are A-Changin'	Feb. 10, 1964
4.	A Hard Rain's A-Gonna Fall	The Freewheelin' Bob Dylan	May 27, 1963
5.	Romance in Durango (Bob Dylan/Jacques Levy)	Desire	Jan. 5, 1976
6.	Isis (Bob Dylan/Jacques Levy)	Desire	Jan. 5, 1976
7.	Blowin' in the Wind	The Freewheelin' Bob Dylan	May 27, 1963
8.	Wild Mountain Thyme (trad.)	–	–
9.	Mama, You Been on My Mind	The Bootleg Series Volumes 1-3	March 26, 1991
10	Dark as a Dungeon (Merle Travis)	–	–
11.	I Shall Be Released	Bob Dylan's Greatest Hits, Vol. 2	Nov. 17, 1971

	Song	On Stage
–	Diamonds and Rust (Joan Baez)	Joan Baez
–	Swing Low Sweet Chariot (trad.)	Joan Baez
–	Pastures of Plenty (Woody Guthrie)	Joan Baez
–	Suzanne (Leonard Cohen)	Joan Baez
–	Help Me Make It Through the Night (Kris Kristofferson)	Joan Baez
–	Please Come to Boston (Dave Loggins)	Joan Baez
–	The Night They Drove Old Dixie Down (Robbie Robertson)	Joan Baez & Roger McGuinn
–	Eight Miles High (Gene Clark/Roger McGuinn/David Crosby)	Roger McGuinn
–	Chestnut Mare (Roger McGuinn/Jacques Levy)	Roger McGuinn
–	Race Among the Ruins (Gordon Lightfoot)	Gordon Lightfoot
–	Charokee Bend (Gordon Lightfoot)	Gordon Lightfoot
–	Long Way Back Home (Gordon Lightfoot)	Gordon Lightfoot
–	Sundown (Gordon Lightfoot)	Gordon Lightfoot

	Song	From The Album	Released
12.	Mr. Tambourine Man	Bringing It All Back Home	March 22, 1965
13.	Tangled Up in Blue	Blood on the Tracks	Jan. 20, 1975
14.	Oh, Sister (Bob Dylan/Jacques Levy)	Desire	Jan. 5, 1976
15.	Hurricane (Bob Dylan/Jacques Levy)	Desire	Jan. 5, 1976

16.	One More Cup of Coffee (Valley Below)	Desire	Jan. 5, 1976
17.	Sara	Desire	Jan. 5, 1976
18.	Just Like a Woman	Blonde on Blonde	May 16, 1966
19.	Knockin' on Heaven's Door	Pat Garrett & Billy The Kid	July 13, 1973
20.	This Land is Your Land (Woody Guthrie)	–	–

The Musicians

Bob Dylan (vocal, guitar & harmonica)

Guam — Bob Neuwirth (vocal & guitar), T-Bone J. Henry Burnett (guitar), Roger McGuinn (vocal & guitar), Steven Soles (guitar), Mick Ronson (guitar), David Mansfield (steel guitar, violin, mandolin & dobro), Rob Stoner (bass), Howie Wyeth (piano & drums), Luther Rix (drums & percussion), Ronee Blakley (vocal), Joan Baez (vocal & guitar), Scarlet Rivera (violin).

Notes

- 20th Bob Dylan concert in Canada; 8th Bob Dylan concert in Toronto.
- 1, Bob Neuwirth (shared vocal).
- 1-11, 14-20, Bob Dylan (vocal &guitar), Bob Neuwirth (guitar), T-Bone J. Henry Burnett (guitar), Roger McGuinn (guitar), Steven Soles (guitar), Mick Ronson (guitar), David Mansfield (steel guitar, violin, mandolin & dobro), Rob Stoner (bass), Howie Wyeth (piano & drums), Luther Rix (drums & percussion), Ronee Blakley (vocal).
- 2, 12-14, 17, Bob Dylan (harmonica).
- 4-6 14-20, Scarlet Rivera (violin).
- 7-11, Joan Baez (vocal, guitar).
- 12-13, Bob Dylan solo (vocal, guitar & harmonica).
- 19, Roger McGuinn (shared vocal).
- 20, shared vocal by Bob Dylan and the entire ensemble for the evening.
- Canadian live debut of songs 8 & 13.
- Song 8 has been performed only once in Canada.
- During A Hard Rains A-Gonna Fall (4), Bob Dylan added a line to the second verse: "I met Ronnie Hawkins and Gordon Lightfoot".
- Special guests included; Ronnie Hawkins, Joni Mitchell, Ramblin' Jack Elliott, Gordon Lightfoot and Allen Ginsberg.

Review

The little guy in hat and jeans was Dylan

T'hell with being 'a square hip'

By Martin O'Malley.

It didn't seem right to be worrying about hiring a babysitter so we could go to Maple Leaf Gardens to hear Bob Dylan's Rolling Thunder Revue. It didn't seem right, either, to be going to Barberian's Steak House before the show. It's not something one would have done in the heat of the sixties when the answers were blowin' in the wind.

Ah, but one of the prerequisites of reaching one's mid-thirties is a sublime absence of pretension – t'hell with what's in, t'hell with the gaucheries of middle class, t'hell with being what Tom Wolfe once nastily put down as "a square hip." So we went to Barberian's and had a scotch, then a fine red wine with a filet wrapped in bacon. Then we took a taxi to the Gardens, only five blocks away. T'hell with it.

I never was part of the flower generation anyway. Missed it by three years. Some people miss wars, some depressions: I missed by a hair's breadth the most publicized generation of the century. I didn't even get on to Bob Dylan until four years ago when we bought a new stereo set and just happened to buy a two-record album of Dylan's greatest hits. I was so out of it back then I used to confuse Bob Dylan with Dylan Thomas, the Welsh poet.

After everyone else had swallowed and digested Dylan I sat down one evening in my living room, lighted a candle, put the head set on, and listened for the first time to Memphis Blues Again, and Don't Think Twice, and Watching The River Flow, and Lay Lady Lay. You can imagine the gratuitous disdain I encountered when I asked people, "Hey, didja ever hear Memphis Blues Again?" It was like asking someone in 1960 if they ever heard Blue Suede Shoes.

I got to like Dylan. I played the two-record album so many times I actually knew the lyrics as well as the Hail Mary and was able to sing them playing snooker at the corner and fishing in the French River.

So, I was prepared for the Rolling Thunder Revue at the Gardens, we had good seats in the reds, only $8.80, and the first whiff of the pine-tree fragrance of pot didn't faze me. "Pot!" I said, calmly but with a ring of authority.

The show went on and on. After listening to artists called Ramblin' Jack Eliot and Roger McGinn and Mick Ronson and Ronnee Blakely, none of whom I knew from a hole in the ground, I waited for the main event. The warm-up acts bored me. My right leg went to sleep. "You could hear better stuff at The Horseshoe," I said.

After listening to some little guy in a hat and jeans, one of us asked the couple in front who it was and a languorous young woman said, "Dylan." Oh, thank you. There hadn't been any introduction. He just suddenly appeared on the stage. When Frank Sinatra came out to his square walkway at the Gardens in May, we knew he was there.

Dylan later was joined by another singer and the lady next to me asked if it was Joan Baez. "Naw, it's a guy," I told her. It was Joan Baez.

On and on went the Rolling Thunder Revue. A nerve in my right knee twitched unmercifully. I asked the lady next to me if she'd mind if I straightened out my leg across her lap. It was midnight and still the guitars sent pulsating chords reverberating to the end greys, off the deserted press box, all around the heavy smoke-filled arena. Not once did he play Memphis Blues Again or Lay Lady Lay or Watching the River Flow or Don't Think Twice. At 1 a.m. I got up, walked out and patrolled the corridors, still listening to the crash of guitars and the wail of undistinguishable lyrics. People were leaving. They looked pretty hip, too, at least three years younger than I and still wearing ragged jeans and walking in that cool slouch of the sixties.

They were the ones in the thick of it when Dylan came on the scene. Now they were leaving early because it was a week night and they had to relieve their babysitters. It wasn't a great consolation, but it was some consolation. T'hell with it. The escargots were great.

The Globe and Mail. Wed., Dec. 3, 1975. Reprinted with permission from The Globe and Mail.

Thursday, December 4, 1975 --- Montreal Forum
Montreal, QC

Set List

	Song	From The Album	Released
1.	When I Paint My Masterpiece	Bob Dylan's Greatest Hits, Vol. 2	Nov. 17, 1971
2.	It Ain't Me, Babe	Another Side of Bob Dylan	Aug. 8, 1964
3.	The Lonesome Death of Hattie Carroll	The Times They Are A-Changin'	Feb. 10, 1964
4.	Tonight I'll Be Staying Here With You	Nashville Skyline	April 9, 1969
5.	A Hard Rain's A-Gonna Fall	The Freewheelin' Bob Dylan	May 27, 1963
6.	Romance in Durango (Bob Dylan/Jacques Levy)	Desire	Jan. 5, 1976
7.	Isis (Bob Dylan/Jacques Levy)	Desire	Jan. 5, 1976
8.	Blowin' in the Wind	The Freewheelin' Bob Dylan	May 27, 1963
9.	Dark as a Dungeon (Merle Travis)	–	–
10.	Mama, You Been on My Mind	The Bootleg Series Volumes 1-3	March 26, 1991
11.	Never Let Me Go (Joseph C. Scott)	–	–
12.	I Dreamed I Saw St. Augustine	John Wesley Harding	Dec. 27, 1967
13.	I Shall Be Released	Bob Dylan's Greatest Hits, Vol. 2	Nov. 17, 1971
14.	It's All Over Now, Baby Blue	Bringing It All Back Home	March 22, 1965
15.	Love Minus Zero/No Limit	Bringing It All Back Home	March 22, 1965
16.	Tangled Up in Blue	Blood on the Tracks	Jan. 20, 1975
17.	Oh, Sister (Bob Dylan/Jacques Levy)	Desire	Jan. 5, 1976
18.	Hurricane (Bob Dylan/Jacques Levy)	Desire	Jan. 5, 1976
19.	One More Cup of Coffee (Valley Below)	Desire	Jan. 5, 1976
20.	Sara	Desire	Jan. 5, 1976
21.	Just Like a Woman	Blonde on Blonde	May 16, 1966
22.	Knockin' on Heaven's Door	Pat Garrett & Billy The Kid	July 13, 1973
23.	This Land is Your Land (Woody Guthrie)	–	–

The Musicians

Bob Dylan (vocal, guitar & harmonica)

Guam — Bob Neuwirth (vocal & guitar), T-Bone J. Henry Burnett (guitar), Roger McGuinn (vocal & guitar), Steven Soles (guitar), Mick Ronson (guitar), David Mansfield (steel guitar, violin, mandolin & dobro), Rob Stoner (bass), Howie Wyeth (piano & drums), Luther Rix (drums & percussion), Ronee Blakley (vocal), Joan Baez (vocal & guitar), Scarlet Rivera (violin).

Notes

- 21st Bob Dylan concert in Canada; 9th Bob Dylan concert in Montreal.
- 1, Bob Neuwirth (shared vocal).
- 1-13, 17-23, Bob Dylan (vocal & guitar), Bob Neuwirth (guitar), T-Bone J. Henry Burnett (guitar), Roger McGuinn (guitar), Steven Soles (guitar), Mick Ronson (guitar), David Mansfield (steel guitar, violin, mandolin & dobro), Rob Stoner (bass), Howie Wyeth (piano & drums), Luther Rix (drums & percussion), Ronee Blakley (vocal).
- 2, 14-17, 20, Bob Dylan (harmonica).
- 5-7, 17-23, Scarlet Rivera (violin).
- 8-13, Joan Baez (vocal, guitar).
- 14-16, Bob Dylan solo (vocal, guitar & harmonica).
- 22, Roger McGuinn (shared vocal).
- 23, shared vocal by Bob Dylan and the entire ensemble for the evening.
- The songs performed by members of Guam, Joan Baez or other special guests are not included in the set list.

- Special guests included Joni Mitchell, Jack Scott and Allen Ginsberg.
- Many consider this show to be one of the best Bob Dylan has ever played in Canada. Nine of the twenty-three songs played later appeared as live tracks on official releases.

Official Releases

- Songs 5-7, 11, 19-20 released in the movie Renaldo and Clara, Jan. 25, 1978 (long version) and late 1978 (short version).
- Songs 6-7 released on Biograph, Nov. 7, 1985.
- Song 11 released on promotional maxi-EP 4 songs from "Renaldo and Clara," Jan. 1978.
- Songs 4-5, 14-15 released on The Bootleg Series, Vol. 5. Bob Dylan Live in 1975: The Rolling Thunder Revue, Nov. 26, 2002.
- Song 7 released both as a video and audio on the bonus DVD accompanying the first release of The Bootleg Series, Vol. 5. Bob Dylan Live in 1975: The Rolling Thunder Revue, Nov. 26, 2002.

Review

Dylan: son premier show

La Presse.

Il était près d'une heure ce matin, quand j'ai quitté le Forum qui hurlait encore à pleins poumons et ne tarissait point d'éloges sur le merveilleux spectacle auquel il venait d'assister, le "Rolling Thunder Review", dont la grande et locomotive vedette était Bob Dylan.

Un show de quatre heures très "country rock", très électrique et très "Nashville", ou figuraient Joan Baez, Joni Mitchell, Roger McGuinn (the Byrds), Ronee Blakley (la fille du film Nashville), Jack Scott et une bonne quinzaine des meilleurs musiciens rock et western américains. Une batterie, des percussions, beaucoup de cordes (de pianos, de guitares, de violons) et beaucoup de voix (d'hommes et de femmes). Un son étonnament bien balancé, solide, coloré. Une bonne grosse musique de cow-boys qui visiblement avaient un immense plaisir à jouer devant un aussi beau public, qui remplissait complètement le Forum, même l'arrière de la scène.

Il y eut, bien sûr, quelques temps morts. Et il est regrettable que le plus long d'entre eux soit venu sur la fin, quand Dylan qui s'était un moment éclipsé est remonté sur la scène pour nous faire (seul ou accompagné d'une violoniste et d'un bassiste) une série de chansons anciennes et nouvelles. Le public venait d'être renversé par l'extraordinaire Joan Baez qui possède beaucoup plus de présence physique et beaucoup plus de chaleur que Dylan. Elle nous parlait en français. Elle a chanté sans accompagnement, mais avec un "drive" incroyable, une grande chanson du vieux folklore américain, "Swing low, sweet charriot". Un tour de force. Peut-être le plus beau moment de la soirée.

Mais il y eut aussi ces moments terriblement émouvantes où Dylan reprenait ses plus grandes chansons, "It ain't me babe", "I shall be released", "It's all over now, baby blue", "A hard Rain", chansons qui se sont chargées de toutes sortes de significations depuis le temps. Nous avons grandi et passé avec elles et on les retrouve complètement transformées, épanouies, plus poignantes et plus belles que jamais dans ces nouveaux arrangements et dans cette musique pleine da folle et d'énergie.

Dylan, pour la première fois, nous donne un show. Il porte un chapeau dur à l'espagnol, une longue écharpe de sole, un blue jeans fripé. Et il est maquillé de rouge et de blanc. Avec du noir sur les yeux, comme la plupart des musiciens.

Un document

Jamais il ne sourit, rarement il parle. Mais il se garroche dans ses chansons comme jamais on ne l'a vu faire. Il pousse sa voix, il ouvre les bras, il bouge, il joue. Ça n'a pas grand chose à voir avec le dernier Forum qu'il a fait. Il donnait alors un récital très conventionnel et très austère en compagnie de the Band avec qui il effectuait péniblement (et avec l'air assez bête et des lunettes fumées un retour à la scène après cinq ou six ans de réclusions. Le "Rolling Thunder Review" est autre chose, heureusement. C'est une illumination, une vision, un événement.

Je ne sais pas quel esprit anime cette bande de fous. Mais tous à l'intérieur de cette revue semblent nous donner le meilleur d'eux-mêmes (sur scène). Joan Baez est belle comme un coeur, rayonnante, bouleversante. Beauté, vigueur, passion dans la voie et la guitare de Joni Mitchell, dans la voie et le piano de la fille de Nashville. Et il y avait aussi une fille vêtue comme un archange noir qui jouait du puissant violon et dont la foule s'est éprise immédiatement. La participation de Jack Scott et de Roger McGuinn était moins intéressante. Mais la musique filait toujours le parfait bonheur.

Il y avait des caméramen sur la scène. Et c'était parfois achalant, de même que les "cues" lumineux qu'ils recevaient à tout - bout de champs. Mais ça finissait par faire partie du show. Et l'on se disait que le film tiré de cette tournée devrait être férocement intéressant. Car il réunit les plus grandes figures d'un domaine musical immense dans lequel s'est exprimée toute une génération. La musique de Dylan n'est plus une création véritable. Mais ce "Rolling Thunder Review" est l'un des documents les plus complets et les plus passionnants que le rock américain ait soumis à notre atttention populaire.

La Presse. Fri., Dec. 5, 1975. Reprinted with permission of La Presse.

Additional Reviews

Dylan and friends bring intimacy to lofty Forum: Rolling Thunder warms crowd, by David Freeston. The Montreal Star. Fri., Dec., 5, 1975. p. C11.

Rolling Thunder spirits in peak form, by Juan Rodriguez. The Montreal Gazette. Sat., Dec. 6, 1975. p. 49.

1978

Introduction

The 1978 World Tour stopped in Canada for three concerts. Bob Dylan's first concerts in Canada since 1975.

These shows would mark Bob Dylan's 22nd, 23rd & 24th concert in Canada.

The Dates

Montreal, QC	Tues., Sept. 19, 1978
Toronto, ON	Thurs., Oct. 12, 1978
Vancouver, BC	Sun., Nov. 11, 1978

The shows would be Dylan's 10th concert in Montreal, 9th concert in Toronto and 3rd concert in Vancouver.

The Musicians

Bob Dylan (vocal, guitar & harmonica).

Billy Cross (lead guitar), Alan Pasqua (keyboards), Steven Soles (rhythm guitar & backup vocals), David Mansfield (violin & mandolin), Steve Douglas (horns), Jerry Scheff (bass), Bobbye Hall (percussion), Ian Wallace (drums), Helena Springs (backup vocals), Jo Ann Harris (backup vocals), Carolyn Dennis (backup vocals).

The Songs

Bob Dylan performed a total of 81 songs. Of those, 35 were different songs (32 were from albums, one was an unreleased song and 2 were cover and/or traditional songs).

Sixteen songs made their Canadian live debut.

My Back Pages	I Want You
I'm Ready	Señor (Tales of Yankee Power)
Is Your Love in Vain?	Masters of War
Shelter from the Storm	Baby, Stop Crying
Maggie's Farm	Changing of the Guards
Going, Going, Gone	Where Are You Tonight?
One of Us Must Know (Sooner or Later)	She's Love Crazy
Am I Your Stepchild?	We Better Talk This Over

Fours songs have been played only once in Canada.

Baby, Stop Crying	She's Love Crazy
Where Are You Tonight?	We Better Talk This Over

Bob Dylan performed songs from 12 different albums.

Album	Released	# of Songs Performed by Album
The Freewheelin' Bob Dylan	May, 27, 1963	3
The Times They Are A-Changin'	Feb., 10, 1964	1
Another Side of Bob Dylan	Aug. 8, 1964	5
Bringing It All Back Home	March 22, 1965	4
Highway 61 Revisited	Aug. 30, 1965	2
Blonde on Blonde	May 16, 1966	3
John Wesley Harding	Dec. 27, 1967	1
Bob Dylan's Greatest Hits, Vol. 2	Nov. 17, 1971	1
Planet Waves	Jan. 17, 1974	2
Blood on the Tracks	Jan. 20, 1975	3
Desire	Jan. 5, 1976	1
Street Legal	June 15, 1978	6

The Venues

It was Bob Dylan's 4th time playing at the Montreal Forum, 5th time playing at Maple Leaf Gardens in Toronto and debut concert at the Pacific National Exhibition Hall in Vancouver.

Tuesday, September 19, 1978 --- Montreal Forum
Montreal, QC

Set List

	Song	From The Album	Released
1.	My Back Pages	Another Side of Bob Dylan	Aug. 8, 1964
2.	I'm Ready (Willie Dixon)	–	–
3.	Is Your Love in Vain?	Street Legal	June 15, 1978
4.	Shelter from the Storm	Blood on the Tracks	Jan. 20, 1975
5.	It's All Over Now, Baby Blue	Bringing It All Back Home	March 22, 1965
6.	Tangled Up in Blue	Blood on the Tracks	Jan. 20, 1975
7.	Ballad of a Thin Man	Highway 61 Revisited	Aug. 30, 1965
8.	Maggie's Farm	Bringing It All Back Home	March 22, 1965
9.	I Don't Believe You (She Acts Like We Never Have Met)	Another Side of Bob Dylan	Aug. 8, 1964
10.	Like a Rolling Stone	Highway 61 Revisited	Aug. 30, 1965
11.	I Shall Be Released	Bob Dylan's Greatest Hits, Vol. 2	Nov. 17, 1971
12.	Going, Going, Gone	Planet Waves	Jan. 17, 1974
13.	One of Us Must Know (Sooner or Later)	Blonde on Blonde	May 16, 1966
14.	It Ain't Me, Babe	Another Side of Bob Dylan	Aug. 8, 1964
15.	Am I Your Stepchild?	Unreleased	–
16.	One More Cup of Coffee (Valley Below)	Desire	Jan. 5, 1976
17.	Blowin' in the Wind	The Freewheelin' Bob Dylan	May 27, 1963
18.	I Want You	Blonde on Blonde	May 16, 1966
19.	Señor (Tales of Yankee Power)	Street Legal	June 15, 1978
20.	Masters of War	The Freewheelin' Bob Dylan	May 27, 1963
21.	Just Like a Woman	Blonde on Blonde	May 16, 1966
22.	Baby, Stop Crying	Street Legal	June 15, 1978
23.	All Along the Watchtower	John Wesley Harding	Dec. 27, 1967
24.	All I Really Want to Do	Another Side of Bob Dylan	Aug. 8, 1964
25.	It's Alright, Ma (I'm Only Bleeding)	Bringing It All Back Home	March 22, 1965
26.	Forever Young	Planet Waves	Jan. 17, 1974
	Encore		
27.	Changing of the Guards	Street Legal	June 15, 1978

The Musicians

Bob Dylan (vocal, guitar & harmonica), Billy Cross (lead guitar), Alan Pasqua (keyboards), Steven Soles (rhythm guitar & backup vocals), David Mansfield (violin & mandolin), Steve Douglas (horns), Jerry Scheff (bass), Bobbye Hall (percussion), Ian Wallace (drums), Helena Springs (backup vocals), Jo Ann Harris (backup vocals), Carolyn Dennis (backup vocals).

Notes

- 22nd Bob Dylan concert in Canada; 10th Bob Dylan concert in Montreal.
- 1, instrumental without Bob Dylan.
- 5, 15, 21, Bob Dylan (harmonica).
- 14, Bob Dylan solo (vocal, guitar & harmonica).
- Canadian live debut of songs 1, 2, 3, 4, 8, 12, 13, 15, 18, 19, 20, 22 & 27.
- Song 22 has been performed only once in Canada.

Reviews

Grand chef Dylan cooks music banquet

By David Sherman, of The Gazette.

Bob Dylan's concert last night proved once and for all the Forum should be reserved for hockey, wrestling and roller derby.

Beside the high ticket prices and dismal acoustics, Dylan's visit brought a phalanx of gum chewing young men with muscles and short hair who were passed off as "Security."

Security did their best to add to the chaos of a full house by accosting people over and over for tickets, hassling people who stood still for more than a second and literally knocking people down and hustling them out of the arena.

Despite the over-zealous precautions, the Forum quickly descended to its usual sardine-can claustrophobia, with all aisles and stairwells jammed, seats were packed even behind the stage – as soon as the lights dimmed.

Was all things

But, with the darkness, came the 11 piece team from the *Street Legal* album. They warmed up to an instrumental and then came Dylan.

He was all things last night – the rock star, the blues balladeer, the folk hero and the dramatist. More animated then ever, Dylan strutted and danced, moved back and forth behind the mike, leaning into the vocals and even talking to the audience.

Dressed in black with a white shirt and grey scarf, alternating his stature between a stiff pose with his legs apart and his shoulders bent to the mike, and the more excitable prancing of a rock singer, Dylan has become the showman.

Changing the mood constantly, from the somber to hard-driving emotion, he moved the members of his band on and off the stage, keeping the show flowing and peaking with a mixture of old and new tunes.

Like a Grand Chef, never satisfied with the old recipes, Dylan is constantly toying with his arrangements, changing the tempo of the numbers, adding new phrasing and throwing in different lyrics.

The old tunes were inevitably powerful, the lush musical backdrop enhanced with the everpresent harmonies of his gospel vocal trio of Helena Springs, Carolyn Dennis and Jo Ann Harris.

He sang new treatments of *Maggie's Farm, Do You Mr. Jones, Shelter From the Storm,* and *Going, Going, Gone*, which alternated from a bluesy ballad to hard electric rock. There was a slower, more poignant *I Want You* with only sax and piano to back his voice and guitar, and he has added a new vocal arrangement to *Like a Rolling Stone*.

He was at his best for *Tangled up in Blue*. His voice throaty, almost hoarse, he strummed his guitar lightly in the true romantic Dylan style, as Steve Douglas blew a soft, lilting saxophone.

To some tunes, he remained faithful. *Just Like a Woman* was sang to a laid back band while for *It Ain't Me, Babe* he appeared with his harmonica clamped to his neck, accompanying himself on the acoustic guitar.

Once again, he was "the man with the stage fright," alone under half a dozen spotlights, singing from the soul about the inequities of romance.

The band was a rhythmic power house that played all night with smiling, good time enthusiasm. Unfortunately neither the hall nor the sound system could carry the load.

With 12 musicians playing with sometimes as many as four guitars going at once, the subtleties were totally lost.

Except for the lead guitar or piano and the drums and sax, the delicate combination of violin, congas and rhythm guitars were caught up in a maelstrom of high volume distortion.

Dylan's occasional harp blowing and wailing vocals often suffered an identical fate.

Only on the softer, more evocative ballads did the tenderness of the ensemble come out.

The emotional fire came from Dylan's smoother, less wrenching vocals and the guitar playing of Billy Cross. Bending notes and rifling through the high register, the silver-haired Cross blasted through lick after lick of tight, searing leads.

Also interesting was the conga work of Bobbye Hall, a female percussionist who has toured with Carol King and has numerous recording sessions to her credit. She keeps up a steady back beat, fitting in artful lines between the drumming of Ian Wallace.

In control

More the performer than ever, Dylan gave a little bit to every taste. Confident and totally in control, his lyrics sharp and his voice powerful with the experience of age, Dylan delivered a masterful performance.

Unusually talkative, he seemed to be having as good a time as the rest of the band. Playing with his voice, digging into the emotions of each song, pausing with theatrical perfection to heighten the drama between each phrase, he has traveled a long way from the silent, shy figure of mystery.

He ended off the formal concert with a soaring rendition of *Forever Young* – and then, for Montreal, he even delivered and encore – *Changing of the Guard* – with his band dressed in "home" and "away" Montreal Canadians hockey sweaters.

The Montreal Gazette. Wed., Sept. 20, 1978.

Dylan le troubadour n'existe plus

par Pierre Beaulieu.

La dernière visite de Bob Dylan à Montreal datait de décembre 1975, alors qu'en compagnie de Joan Baez, Joni Mitchell et quelques autres, il nous avait présenté le désormais célèbre «Rolling Thunder Review». Il nous avait présenté son «One man show» précédent en 1974. On se souviendra que The Band l'avait alors accompagné.

Les billets, pour ce nouveau spectacle, se sont donc vendus le temps de le dire. Même que certains «scalpers» ont réussi à écouler les leurs jusqu'à $30 l'unité. La salle était archipleine et les gens vendus d'avance. On remarquait, à part à peu près égale, des gens de 30 ans, la jeunesse des années 50, ceux de la génération de Dylan, et des jeunes, des tout jeunes gens, émerveillés par le mythe et la nouvelle musique de Dylan. Celle de «Street Legal» particulièrement.

Quand les lumières se sont éteintes, c'était déjà l'ovation.

Malgré tout, les réactions de la foule ont été plutôt froides (compte tenu qu'il s'agissait d'un show de Dylan), au cours de la première partie. Ses fans de longue date ont été sûrement les plus déçus. Il faut dire que le son était tout à fait horrible, autant pour la voix que pour la musique, forte et fort confuse. Il n'y eu qu'un seul moment vraiment exceptionnel au cours de cette première heure. Quand Dylan a chanté «Like a Rolling Stone», la foule s'est levée d'un trait.

Opinions partagées

A l'entracte, les opinions semblaient fort partagées. La plupart des gens rencontrés emblaient déçus. Accompagné par un immense «band» qui n'a vraiment rien à voir avec le précédent (il ne s'agit plus d'un groupe mais plutôt de musiciens accompagnateurs qui travaillaient auparavant chacun de leur côté. Le bassiste, entre autres, a travaillé huit ans avec Elvis Presley), Dylan semblait perdu, enfoui complètement sous une musique énorme qui prenait parfois des teintes de rythm and blues.

Tout le monde sait que Dylan a toujours refusé d'être prisonnier de ses propres succès, qu'il s'efforce de ne jamais les chanter comme il les a faits sur disque, pour ne pas voir tomber son public dans l'idolâtrie.

Il change donc sa voix, le rythme des chansons, son environnement musical. Mais là, vraiment, on ne le reconnaissait plus.

Son spectacle avait quelque chose d'anachronique. On avait vraiment l'impression que, pour pouvoir captiver les grandes salles, il avait décidé de les défoncer, de jouer le jeu des groupes rocks qui vous assomment de leurs dècibels.

C'est pourtant quand il se présentait seul (très rarement) avec sa guitare et son harmonica que les gens réagissaient davantage. Il nous semblait que sa seule voix, sa seule présence suffisaient à le faire passer.

La musique et le son

Heureusement, sa deuxième partie l'a racheté. Le son, tout d'abord, était meilleur. De beaucoup. L'evironnement musical, ressemblait davantage à celui qu'on connaît.

De plus, le rythme du spectacle était beaucoup plus rapide, les chansons, beaucoup plus impressionnantes et la voix, moins caricaturale. La foule a donc réagi beaucoup mieux. A la fin de son show, Dylan a eu droit à une longue ovation et quand ses musiciens se sont présentés sur la scène vêtu d'un chandail du Canadien (comme c'est devenu la mode), pour le rappel, ce fut le délire. Mais je me demande vraiment, si le seul fait d'avoir vu Dylan en personne n'aurait pas réussi a attirer une ovation semblable.

On va voir Dylan, le mythe. On ne va plus voir Dylan le troubadour contestataire, parce qu'il n'existe plus.

Le rêve

D'ailleurs, en ragardant une petite dépêche de l'AFP datant de 1966, dépêche que je vous lis à l'instant, je pensais à cette «sortie» par les cheveux qu'ont fait deux photographes qui ont eu le malheur de se présenter sur le parquet du Forum avec tout leur attirail (M. Dylan ne tolère que son photographe).

La dépêche dit ceci: «Bob Dylan fêtera ce soir ses 25 ans, au cours d'un spectacle à l'Olympia. L'idole des Beatniks s'est prêtée hier après-midi, dans les salons d'un hôtel du quartier des Champs-Elysées, au feu roulant des questions de la presse. Il lui arrive souvent de rêver, a-t-il dit, qu'il est poursuivi dans d'interminables escaliers par une meute de journalistes…»

La Presse. Wed., Sept. 20, 1978. Reprinted with permission of La Presse.

BOB DYLAN SE PREND POUR UN CHANTEUR POP

par Colette Perron.

Bob Dylan a été pendant des années le symbole d'une génération en crise; hurlant d'une voix dévastée les craintes et les aspirations d'une jeunesse alors beaucoup plus ardente qu'aujourd'hui, Dylan nous avait accoutumé à écouter ses paroles comme celle d'un prophète ou au moins d'un porte-parole. Mais cette génération a vieilli, Dylan aussi et les ardeurs, sinon éteintes, ont changé de direction…

Entouré de huit musiciens, de trois choristes, tous vêtus de noir et de blanc, propres, nets, (certains étaient même cravatés), Dylan offre un nouveau son, un son à la mode. Il n'a pas résisté à l'envie de faire comme tout le monde, beaucoup de bruit. Le guitariste joue des solos criants, plus électrisants que de vieux Black Sabbath. Le saxophoniste semble vouloir prêter à son instrument les mêmes sonorités que la voix du chanteur. Et cette voix, Dylan l'a brisé tout à fait, ne lui laissant même plus le charme d'un certain voile surprenant mais attirant. Bob Dyaln se prend pour un chanteur pop. Dans son nouveau spectacle, il interprète des tas de vieilles chansons, mais ne peut s'empêcher de les changer, de leur donner une allure plus moderne. On est déçus de voir pâlir ses chansons qui nous ont fait l'aimer… Des essais de blues, de rock, de R&B s'avèrent tout aussi décevants, et il arrive qu'on ne reconnaisse certaines mélodies qu'en plein milieu…

Le pouvoir d'attraction du chanteur est tout de même bizarre; sans aucune présence scénique (il n'attire pas plus d'attention physiquement que n'importe lequel de ses musiciens), il arrive pourtant à réunir 20,000 personnes parmi lesquelles beaucoup de jeunes, qui n'ont sans doute jamais porté d'attention aux textes, et qui par conséquent n'ont que peu de raisons, à prime abord, de s'intéresser à un artiste dont la carrière remonte presque à une quinzaine d'années. Après tout, les choses vont tellement vite ces temps-ci, que quand on a moins de 20 ans, on a peu de temps pour s'attacher à une «vieille» vedette. Il y en a trop… Toujours est-il que pendant que Bob Dylan présentait au public une très grosse production, presque «las-vegasienne» (la comparaison a d'ailleurs déjà été faite aux États-Unis), et dont le son ressemble parfois à un spectacle de Joe Cocker, c'est encore les moments privilégiés où Dylan abandonnait son cirque pour sa seule guitare qui étaient le plus appréciés. Les ovations réelles ont été gardées pour ces instants, alors que pour le reste du spectacle, le public du Forum est resté étonnamment calme.

Drôle de constater qu'alors qu'on se plaignait de voir notre Charlebois s'assagir, on pardonne mal à Bob Dylan d'avoir, lui, trop tenu à conserver un air de junesse qui ressemble un peu trop à une concession. Peut-être, au fond, a-t-il peur de mal vieillir…

Le Journal de Montréal. Wed., Sept. 20, 1978. Reprinted with permission of Le Journal de Montréal.

Bob Dylan: le poète maudit s'est radouci

par Nathalie Petrowski.

Ils sont venus avec leurs bébés et leurs souvenirs, chargés de nostalgie et de vieilles revoltes fanées, curieux de revoir une fois, peut-être la dernière, le messie. Ils ont entourés la scène complètement ont rempli tous les sièges, se sont empiles les uns sur les autrres pour mieux le voir mais tout au long de cette soirée privilégiée avec Bob Dylan, le prophéte des temps mordernes, ils sont restés calmes, presque endormis. Était-ce du respect ou de l'apathie, nul ne sait, sans doute un peu des deux.

Une chose est certaine, Bob Dylan n'est plus le même homme et il est encore difficile, impossible même à dire ce qu'il est devenu. La vérité c'est que depuis le temps, nous avons trop fait de chemin ensemble. Nous ne savons plus quelle attitude prendre devant Dylan, nous ne savons plus comment l'aborder, comment l'interpréter. Et Dylan selon sa bonne habitude ne nous aide toujours pas. Entouré cette fois-ci de 8 musiciens en tuxedos, de 3 choristes en robe du soir et arborant lui-même un pantalon lustré dans un style vestimentaire qui n'était pas sans rappeler celui des vedettes de Las Vegas, la maggie de Dylan n'a opéré qu'à moitié.

La premiére partie du spectacle, avec l'exception de trois chansons, a été complètement ratée à cause d'un son hasardeux, à cause surtout des nouvelles versions que Dylan fait de ses anciennes chansons. En fait, sa trouvaille musicale largement inspirée de rythm 'n blues dessert aussi bien sa voix stridente que sa musique souvent stérile. Refusant de rester figé dans une image et un son, Dylan a complètement remodelé ses chansons, a changé les accords, les arrangements, les a rendues méconnaissables et parfois insupportables. Mais c'est surtout dans le rock, que le chansonnier-poète devenu victime de son époque électrique, perd de son charme et de son impact. Le rock va mal à Dylan, lui donne aujourd'hui de villaines rides, brouille ses paroles et sa poésie, le fait paraître plus vieux que son âge et plus fatigué.

Malgré ceci, la deuxième partie du spectacle, plus rodée, plus décontractée, a largement compensé pour l'echec de la première. Dylan n'a plus l'âge de porter sur ses épaules toujours aussi frêles, le poids de deux heures de show. C'est pour cela aussi que la matière qu'il nous présente 15 ans plus tard n'est plus aussi rageuse, que la musique a perdu de sa force rauque et vive pour devenir plus nuancée, plus colorée avec des intrusions de la part du saxe, du violin, des airs de calypso et un rythme qui tient avant tout de la Jamaïque et du reggae. Il n'en reste pas moins qu'avec des chansons comme **Like a Rolling Stone, Just Like a Woman, I want you, Forever Young** qu'il chante avec autant d'ardente ferveur, on peut difficilement résister à Dylan; on peut difficilement ne pas partir la machine à vues et voir défiler les images d'une autre époque; on peut difficilement ne pas être profondément touché par ce mystérieux personnage, tantôt totalement présent, tantôt totallement absent, qui a resisté au temps et à l'usure qui est encore là, comme le témoin de ce que nous avons été et ne serons jamais plus.

Le Devoir. Wed., Sept. 20, 1978. Reprinted with permission of Le Devoir.

Thursday, October 12, 1978 --- Maple Leaf Gardens
Toronto, ON

Set List

	Song	From The Album	Released
1.	My Back Pages	Another Side of Bob Dylan	Aug. 8, 1964
2.	I'm Ready (Willie Dixon)	–	–
3.	Is Your Love in Vain?	Street Legal	June 15, 1978
4.	Shelter from the Storm	Blood on the Tracks	Jan. 20, 1975
5.	It's All Over Now, Baby Blue	Bringing It All Back Home	March 22, 1965
6.	Tangled Up in Blue	Blood on the Tracks	Jan. 20, 1975
7.	Ballad of a Thin Man	Highway 61 Revisited	Aug. 30, 1965
8.	Maggie's Farm	Bringing It All Back Home	March 22, 1965
9.	I Don't Believe You (She Acts Like We Never Have Met)	Another Side of Bob Dylan	Aug. 8, 1964
10.	Like a Rolling Stone	Highway 61 Revisited	Aug. 30, 1965
11.	I Shall Be Released	Bob Dylan's Greatest Hits, Vol. 2	Nov. 17, 1971
12.	Going, Going, Gone	Planet Waves	Jan. 17, 1974
13.	One of Us Must Know (Sooner or Later)	Blonde on Blonde	May 16, 1966
14.	It Ain't Me, Babe	Another Side of Bob Dylan	Aug. 8, 1964
15.	Am I Your Stepchild?	Unreleased	–
16.	One More Cup of Coffee (Valley Below)	Desire	Jan. 5, 1976
17.	Blowin' in the Wind	The Freewheelin' Bob Dylan	May 27, 1963
18.	Girl of the North Country	The Freewheelin' Bob Dylan	May 27, 1963
19.	Where Are You Tonight?	Street Legal	June 15, 1978
20.	Masters of War	The Freewheelin' Bob Dylan	May 27, 1963
21.	Just Like a Woman	Blonde on Blonde	May 16, 1966
22.	To Ramona	Another Side of Bob Dylan	Aug. 8, 1964
23.	All Along the Watchtower	John Wesley Harding	Dec. 27, 1967

24.	All I Really Want to Do	Another Side of Bob Dylan	Aug. 8, 1964
25.	It's Alright, Ma (I'm Only Bleeding)	Bringing It All Back Home	March 22, 1965
26.	Forever Young	Planet Waves	Jan. 17, 1974
	Encore		
27.	Changing of The Guards	Street Legal	June 15, 1978

The Musicians

Bob Dylan (vocal, guitar & harmonica), Billy Cross (lead guitar), Alan Pasqua (keyboards), Steven Soles (rhythm guitar & backup vocals), David Mansfield (violin & mandolin), Steve Douglas (horns), Jerry Scheff (bass), Bobbye Hall (percussion), Ian Wallace (drums), Helena Springs (backup vocals), Jo Ann Harris (backup vocals), Carolyn Dennis (backup vocals).

Notes

- 23rd Bob Dylan concert in Canada; 9th Bob Dylan concert in Toronto.
- 1, instrumental without Bob Dylan
- 5, 15, 21, Bob Dylan (harmonica).
- 14, Bob Dylan solo (vocal, guitar & harmonica).
- Canadian live debut of song 19.
- Song 19 has been performed only once in Canada.

Reviews

Dylan's showbiz slick shocks a lot of fans

He took enormous risks like a pro and it all worked

By Peter Goddard, Toronto Star.

The music swayed and snickered like a lounge drunk. But the singer moved with it like a pro. His hands played expertly with the mike cord, then he bent his knees to the beat. Turning his back to the band, he looked coyly over his shoulder, then facing the audience again, he spread his legs, put his head back and started belting it out. Solid.

Sinatra at the Copa? Tom Jones doing Vegas? No – just Bob Dylan doing Ballad Of A Thin Man at Maple Leaf Gardens last night, in a 2½-hour concert that was one of the most radical of his career.

It was the 37-year-old singer stripping away more masks, destroying more labels. It was Dylan "the song-and-dance man," as he once described himself, at once destroying old illusions while concocting new ones. It was Dylan playing himself as a show business and not a social figure. It was slick, full of jive, assured, and moving in many ways.

Some teenagers

And it caught many in the jam-packed crowd of nearly 19,000 completely by surprise. As they streamed through the gates before the show – some having picked up scalpers' tickets for up to $40 for a pair of $10 reds – it was possible to think that they looked like a Dylan crowd. While there were some teenagers, for the most part the crowd consisted of those in their 20s and 30s. As one woman remarked, "seeing Dylan every time he's through town, is a ritual, like phoning up old boyfriends when you go back to your home town."

But Dylan was to have his say in this ritual. By the time the show, with its encores, was finished, and he had completely re-vamped old songs like Blowin' In The Wind, Masters Of War and I Shall Be Released, some people had walked out.

"I couldn't stand it any longer, listening to what he was doing to all those songs," said 32-year-old Jack Robeson, throwing his jacket over his shoulders and practically running to the exit. "I grew up with those songs. They were mine, in a way, and I don't recognize them anymore."

Changed voice

Indeed! Just Like A Woman was completely altered for this tour, Dylan's first in two years. He changed the quality of his voice and the old edge he once brought to the bitter-sad words had been replaced by an almost tender crooning. The melody line itself had been re-vamped. In fact, as he sang his new – and I think improved – version you could hear, like a low undercurrent, the rest of the crowd softly singing the old version.

Dylan's fond of comparing his method of working with those of painters like Picasso or Cezanne who in the evolution of their techniques and thinking, frequently treated old themes in radical new ways. Last night's tormented rock version of Maggie's Farm, with its heavy back-beat and stark counterpoint, played by 22-year-old fiddler David Mansfield, was merely but another evolution of the song.

So radical were some of the alterations, from the chunky Bo Diddley treatment of One More Cup Of Coffee to the almost whispy melody-altered version of Blowin' In The Wind, the audience didn't catch on to what was happening until the title was sung.

"I just don't like the obvious," he once said. "Obvious things are a step backwards. Nobody should step backwards because nobody knows what's behind them. The only direction you can see is in front of you, not in back of you."

What he saw before last summer's European leg of this tour began was yet another criticism-prone way of portraying Dylan. So everyone is complaining that Dylan is selling out again? Okay – let's really go show business. So last night he introduced his three backing singers, Helena Springs, Carolyn Dennis, JoAnn Harris, as his cousin, his current girl friend and his fiance, respectively. Then, when he introduced the members of his eight-piece band, he pointed to the "phenomenal" woodwind player, Steven Douglas, and rhythm guitarist "Steve Soles, who doesn't speak English." That none of these throw-away lines was true didn't matter. This was showbiz.

Not that the band was above such blandishments. Billy Cross, the 32-year-old lead guitarist, uncorked some tremendous solos throughout the night and gave this otherwise conservative band whatever rock 'n' roll edge it had.

But, Dylan himself was working way beyond the already wide borders of rock 'n' roll. He was dealing with show business in the broadest sense. At one point he mentioned that Ronnie Hawkins was in the audience (in New York, it was Kinky Friedman) just as some comic might kibbitz from the stage of the MGM Grand about Charo being in the audience.

But it all worked. Not the way it worked in the past, certainly, but still in ways that were substantial and touching. Behind all the tossed-off chatter, Dylan was once again taking enormous risks. These weren't risks beyond what everyone else was doing and what everyone wanted him to do, as was the case when he "went electric" in the mid-'60s. These were risks taken at the very dead-centre of pop music today.

Once again he obliterated all expectations and re-defined for most of the crowd that cheered everything he did, what he was about. What's more, he established the idea that next time around he may do something just as radically different again.

The Toronto Star. Fri., Oct. 13, 1978. Reprinted with permission – Torstar Syndication Services.

DYLAN'S THEATRE GRIPS MLG

By Katherine Gilday.

He's said before that his songs are like pictures and last night at Maple Leaf Gardens Bob Dylan unveiled some of the moving images that constitute his private theatre of the mind. Flickering with the dance of the past and present in them, the songs penetrated the vast space with the power of his obsessively individual voice. And the audience, an older, mellower audience than the Arena is accustomed to, heard the changes and assented to them, without much apparent regret for the days of purity and simplicity long gone.

In the first half of the show, Dylan played performer – Harlequin mostly – a whimsical, ironical character who mimes the comedy of broken love and parodies his own pain. First the band played the introductory refrain that might be regarded as Dylan's theme, I was so much older then, I'm younger than that now. Then the troubadour himself emerged to begin with Is Your Love in Vain? from his new album – but in a campy sneering manner so we knew he wasn't *seriously* asking for a woman who could cook and sew. Then we got a thoroughly eccentric version if It's All Over Now, Baby Blue, where his angular phrasing and harshly passionate chords on the mouth organ made us consider the song completely anew.

All night, in fact, Dylan forced us to reconsider. Ballad of a Thin Man became an end-of-the-world cabaret number, with a torrid sax underlining the now-decadent "Something is happening here and you don't know what it is, do you, Mr. Jones?" It Ain't Me, Babe was delivered with a musical delicacy – Dylan on acoustic guitar without much accompaniment – and tenderness in the dismissal we hadn't heard before.

The arrangements of the old favorites became a revision of their meanings. All Along the Watchtower was done, believe it or not, in a whimsical style while All I Really Want to Do came across as a parody of Simon an Garfunkel's Feelin' Groovy.

By the second half of the show, Dylan the performer had more or less dissolved himself in Dylan the musician – or more aptly, perhaps, Dylan the stage-manager. Though the evening did not lack for sincerity of emotion throughout. Early on, he delivered a powerfully "confounded" rendition of Tangled Up in Blue and later on, a nuanced and nostalgic Girl From the North Country. Interestingly, however, the most emotionally charged song from the new album, Where Are You Tonight, was given a very direct, somewhat abstracted treatment.

The band of eight musicians and three back-up singers created a bewilderingly rich sound, filled with diverse textures and echoes. Dylan seems to be using the possibilities inherent in his accompaniment for multi-levelled speech to take the place of his old, convoluted imagery. The gospel sound the three women singers put out has widely different effects, from providing a potently ironic commentary on an emotion to a straight-out spiritual admonition and criticism of degraded times and degraded love. The last song I heard before I had to leave to make my deadline, was one of Dylan's best – It's Alright Ma. What he presented us with was an apocalyptic version, with a wicked violin weaving its way through and showing us, as the gospel singers exhorted us, "not much is really sacred." The energy of youthful indignation long ago transmuted into the energy of knowledge and loss but still making contact in the old vital way.

The Globe and Mail. Fri., Oct. 13, 1978. Reprinted with permission from The Globe and Mail.

Dylan sheds brooding image and captivates new generation

By Bruce Blackadar, Toronto Star.

He used to be a brooding, often bitter poet whose anguished howls riveted an earlier generation, but last night Bob Dylan turned into a friendly and smiling Mister Showbiz and conquered Toronto all over again.

The 37-year-old musician, whose silences during his concerts became a trademark right from the start of his career, has shifted gears and attracted new armies of teenagers under his banner.

"He's terrific," 16-year-old Darren Reid, a Grade 12 student at Lawrence Park Collegiate, said in the jammed corridor near a concession booth in Maple Leaf Gardens.

"Being a child of the 70s, well, you miss so much," he said. "All that rebellion from the 1960s.

"He just represents so much, and he's one of the last ones left, because so many have died off, you know?"

Ticket scalpers were more than usually ravenous for last night's concert, which attracted 19,000 people.

This reporter was "offered" two tickets for a whopping $160.

Pushy vendors sold Dylan T-shirts at $6 apiece and Dylan programs for $3, and two religious groups competed for attention.

The Toronto Star. Fri., Oct. 13, 1978. Reprinted with permission - Torstar Syndication Services.

Lyrics move to background

DYLAN WITH 11-PIECE BAND

By Wilder Penfield III.

"I had a head full of ideas that were driving me insane," sang Dylan. "And a mouthful of cotton candy," added the Firesign Theatre.

Bob Dylan, master of multi-layered lyric and the minimal accompaniment crammed our largest folk rink last night – but this time it was the musical arrangements that were multi-layered and the words seemed incidental.

While scalpers outside were asking (and getting) more than $50 for a good gold seat at what people obviously expected to be an event, the perverse star of the show was inside with his 11-piece band redefining the nature of that event.

Dylan could have come on in striped pyjamas or Edwardian dinner wear and affected fashion. He could have sung his own greatest hits or the hits of anyone else and the fans would have followed.

Instead he and the band were garbed here in subdued shades of white and vivid variations on black and they sampled songs from the entire Dylan songbook.

The concert started ambivalently as he loped through something borrowed, something new, something old and then something sort of blue with hurried indifference.

How does he make his voice DO that?? complained a friend, commenting on his use of a vibrato that would make a Bolshoi baritone blush and Muppet vocal filters. Indeed, he was singing as though the words would leave scars if he held them too long.

But quite luckily the spirited good feeling that had excited observers of early concerts on this tour had reasserted itself.

If you thought Bob Dylan would volunteer to lead a Bob Dylan tribute, you thought wrong. There are hundreds of out-of-work imitators who could do a much better job.

Dylan obviously finds staleness offensive – much as many of his self-appointed fans resent change and think he should be a combination of museum of memories and worker of minor variations of his now-acceptable folk-protest-styles.

The turnaround came with Maggie's Farm. He ain't gonna work there no more; the new version was jazz-rock, and the crowd loved it.

How did it feel? Like Rotary Connection or the Byrds or the Turtles. The words (which could be heard lots of the time) fulfilled syllabic requirements. The essence of the communication was in the grooves, and in the lyrics when they happened to fit the new patterns.

His Shelter made you long for the Storm, but how does it feel? Great! Standing ovation time. Thanks.

Him too. Once again Bob Dylan has been released. When it came time to introduce the intermission he damn near ran off at the tongue with cheerful chat. The pain that made the old words possible has been replaced by the freewheeling feeling of the new music making – an acquired taste that seems to take no more than one concert to acquire.

The Toronto Sun. Fri., Oct. 13, 1978. Reprinted with permission of The Sun Media Corp.

Sunday, November 11, 1978 --- Pacific National Exhibition Hall Vancouver, BC

Set List

	Song	**From The Album**	**Released**
1.	My Back Pages	Another Side of Bob Dylan	Aug. 8, 1964
2.	She's Love Crazy (Tampa Red)	–	–
3.	Mr. Tambourine Man	Bringing It All Back Home	March 22, 1965
4.	Shelter from the Storm	Blood on the Tracks	Jan. 20, 1975
5.	It's All Over Now, Baby Blue	Bringing It All Back Home	March 22, 1965
6.	Tangled Up in Blue	Blood on the Tracks	Jan. 20, 1975
7.	Ballad of a Thin Man	Highway 61 Revisited	Aug. 30, 1965
8.	Maggie's Farm	Bringing It All Back Home	March 22, 1965
9.	I Don't Believe You (She Acts Like We Never Have Met)	Another Side of Bob Dylan	Aug. 8, 1964
10.	Like a Rolling Stone	Highway 61 Revisited	Aug. 30, 1965
11.	I Shall Be Released	Bob Dylan's Greatest Hits, Vol. 2	Nov. 17, 1971

12.	Señor (Tales of Yankee Power)	Street Legal	June 15, 1978
13.	Rainy Day Women #12 & 35	Blonde on Blonde	May 16, 1966
14.	The Times They Are A-Changin'	The Times They Are A-Changin'	Feb. 10, 1964
15.	It Ain't Me, Babe	Another Side of Bob Dylan	Aug. 8, 1964
16.	Am I Your Stepchild?	Unreleased	–
17.	One More Cup of Coffee (Valley Below)	Desire	Jan. 5, 1976
18.	Blowin' in the Wind	The Freewheelin' Bob Dylan	May 27, 1963
19.	Girl of the North Country	The Freewheelin' Bob Dylan	May 27, 1963
20.	We Better Talk This Over	Street Legal	June 15, 1978
21.	Masters of War	The Freewheelin' Bob Dylan	May 27, 1963
22.	Just Like a Woman	Blonde on Blonde	May 16, 1966
23.	All Along the Watchtower	John Wesley Harding	Dec. 27, 1967
24.	All I Really Want to Do	Another Side of Bob Dylan	Aug. 8, 1964
25.	It's Alright, Ma (I'm Only Bleeding)	Bringing It All Back Home	March 22, 1965
26.	Forever Young	Planet Waves	Jan. 17, 1974
	Encore		
27.	Changing of The Guards	Street Legal	June 15, 1978

The Musicians

Bob Dylan (vocal, guitar & harmonica), Billy Cross (lead guitar), Alan Pasqua (keyboards), Steven Soles (rhythm guitar & backup vocals), David Mansfield (violin & mandolin), Steve Douglas (horns), Jerry Scheff (bass), Bobbye Hall (percussion), Ian Wallace (drums), Helena Springs (backup vocals), Jo Ann Harris (backup vocals), Carolyn Dennis (backup vocals).

Notes

- 24th Bob Dylan concert in Canada; 3rd Bob Dylan concert in Vancouver.
- 1, instrumental without Bob Dylan.
- 5, 22, Bob Dylan (harmonica).
- 13, Helena Springs, Jo Ann Harris, Carolyn Dennis (vocals) without Bob Dylan.
- 15, Bob Dylan solo (vocal, guitar & harmonica).
- Canadian live debut of songs 2 & 20.
- Songs 2 & 20 have been performed only once in Canada.

Review

May he stay forever

By Vaughn Palmer, *Express*ions.

Bob Dylan has rewritten the book again, and done so spectacularly. It seems we'll never catch up with him.

The enigmatic 37-year-old performer packed the Pacific Coliseum on Saturday night with almost 17,000 fans, the bulk of them undoubtedly attracted by his earlier incarnations: elemental folksinger, surging rocker, and mellow country singer.

He gave them none of it, though there were many old songs in the more than two-hour show – 17 of the 26 numbers dated from 1966 or earlier.

But in a move as risky as any he's ever attempted, Dylan has recast his best-known music on this, his biggest year of touring ever.

Heretofore noted for his sparse, unadorned music, Dylan has now crafted a "big" sound, with an eight-piece backup band and heresy of heresies, there are also three gospel-type female back-up singers.

The music flashes with gospel, R&B and soul, thanks largely to the rhythm section, the singers and the rich urban sax of Steve Douglas.

For his part Dylan has assembled his full repertoire of voices. He shouted, snarled, howled, racked, pleaded, confessed and even crooned. He also displayed the old Dylan wit, propelling the joyous nature of the show.

High points, and there were many, included an acoustic blues version of It Ain't Me Babe, a menacing All Along the Watchtower, an unsettling Senor, a Bo Diddley-style One More Cup of Coffee, a King Curtis-style Times They Are A Changin', and a vengeful, angry tour-de-force: Masters of War.

Perhaps the crowd would have preferred something familiar, a reminder of a Dylan they used to know. If so, he threw a final challenge, Forever Young, with the lines "May you have a strong foundation/when the winds of changes shift/and may you stay forever young."

In the end they loved it. A long, delirious ovation brought Dylan back for a retrospective tune from his latest album, Street Legal, an uncompromising uptown strut called Changing of the Guards:

"I have moved your mountains and marked your cards ... better prepare in your heart for a changing of the guards."

The Vancouver Express. Mon., Nov. 13, 1978.

1980

Introduction

The 1980 Gospel Tour came to Canada for eight concerts.

These shows would mark Bob Dylan's 25th, 26th, 27th, 28th, 29th, 30th, 31st & 32nd concert in Canada.

The Dates

Toronto, ON	Thurs., April 17, 1980
Toronto, ON	Fri., April 18, 1980
Toronto, ON	Sat., April 19, 1980
Toronto, ON	Sun., April 20, 1980
Montreal, QC	Tues., April 22, 1980
Montreal, QC	Wed., April 23, 1980
Montreal, QC	Thurs., April 25, 1980
Montreal, QC	Fri., April 25, 1980

The Tour stopped for four consecutive nights in both Toronto and Montreal.

The shows would be Dylan's 10th, 11th, 12th & 13th concert in Toronto and 11th, 12th, 13th & 14th concert in Montreal.

All four shows in Toronto were filmed and recorded for a possible concert film and/or live album, but never released.

The Musicians

Bob Dylan (vocal, guitar, harmonica & piano).

Fred Tackett (guitar), Spooner Oldham (keyboards), Tim Drummond (bass), Terry Young (piano), Jim Keltner (drums), Clydie King (backup vocals), Gwen Evans (backup vocals), Mary Elizabeth Bridges (backup vocals), Regina McCrary (backup vocals), Mona Lisa Young (backup vocals).

The Songs

Bob Dylan performed a total of 129 songs. Of those, 18 were different songs (15 were from albums and 3 were unreleased songs).

Eighteen songs made their Canadian live debut.

Gotta Serve Somebody	Solid Rock
I Believe in You	Saving Grace
When You Gonna Wake Up	Saved
Ain't Gonna Go to Hell for Anybody	What Can I Do For You?
Cover Down, Break Through	In the Garden
Precious Angel	Are You Ready?
Man Gave Names to All the Animals	Pressing On
Slow Train	Covenant Woman
Do Right to Me Baby (Do Unto Others)	I Will Love Him

Three songs made their worldwide live debut.

Ain't Gonna Go to Hell for Anybody	I Will Love Him
Cover Down, Break Through	–

Bob Dylan performed songs from 2 albums.

Album	**Released**	**# of Songs Performed by Album**
Slow Train Coming	Aug. 20, 1979	7
Saved	June 19, 1980	8

Opening Act

Mary Elizabeth Bridges, Gwen Evans, Clydie King, Regina McCrary & Mona Lisa Young with Terry Young on piano opened all eight shows.

The Venues

It was Bob Dylan's 4th, 5th, 6th & 7th time playing at Massey Hall in Toronto and debut concert, 2nd, 3rd & 4th time playing at Le Theatre Saint-Denis in Montreal.

Thursday, April 17, 1980 --- Massey Hall
Toronto, ON

Set List

	Song	On Stage
–	Let It Ride (McCoy/Dennis)	Mary Elizabeth Bridges, Gwen Evans, Clydie King, Regina McCrary & Mona Lisa Young with Terry Young on piano.
–	(You've Got To) Hold On (?)	Mary Elizabeth Bridges, Gwen Evans, Clydie King, Regina McCrary & Mona Lisa Young with Terry Young on piano.
–	Look Up and Live By Faith (Roberts Lawrence Curtis)	Mary Elizabeth Bridges, Gwen Evans, Clydie King, Regina McCrary & Mona Lisa Young with Terry Young on piano.
–	Show Me the Way Lord (?)	Mary Elizabeth Bridges, Gwen Evans, Clydie King, Regina McCrary & Mona Lisa Young with Terry Young on piano.
–	Freedom at the Wall (?)	Mary Elizabeth Bridges, Gwen Evans, Clydie King, Regina McCrary & Mona Lisa Young with Terry Young on piano.
–	This Train is Bound for Glory (This Train) (Big Bill Broonzy)	Mary Elizabeth Bridges, Gwen Evans, Clydie King, Regina McCrary & Mona Lisa Young with Terry Young on piano.

	Song	From The Album	Released
1.	Gotta Serve Somebody	Slow Train Coming	Aug. 20, 1979
2.	I Believe in You	Slow Train Coming	Aug. 20, 1979
3.	When You Gonna Wake Up	Slow Train Coming	Aug. 20, 1979
4.	Ain't Gonna Go to Hell for Anybody	Unreleased	–
5.	Cover Down, Break Through	Unreleased	–
6.	Precious Angel	Slow Train Coming	Aug. 20, 1979
7.	Man Gave Names to All the Animals	Slow Train Coming	Aug. 20, 1979
8.	Slow Train	Slow Train Coming	Aug. 20, 1979

	Song	On Stage
–	My Heart (Regina McCrary)	Regina McCrary with Terry Young on piano.
–	Stranger in the City (Healing) (?)	Mona Lisa Young with Terry Young on piano.

	Song	From The Album	Released
9.	Do Right to Me Baby (Do Unto Others)	Slow Train Coming	Aug. 20, 1979
10.	Solid Rock	Saved	June 19, 1980
11.	Saving Grace	Saved	June 19, 1980
12.	Saved (Bob Dylan/Tim Drummond)	Saved	June 19, 1980
13.	What Can I Do For You?	Saved	June 19, 1980
14.	In the Garden	Saved	June 19, 1980
	Encores		
15.	Are You Ready?	Saved	June 19, 1980
16.	Pressing On	Saved	June 19, 1980

The Musicians

Bob Dylan (vocal, guitar, harmonica & piano), Fred Tackett (guitar), Spooner Oldham (keyboards), Tim Drummond (bass), Terry Young (piano), Jim Keltner (drums), Clydie King (backup vocals), Gwen Evans (backup vocals), Mary Elizabeth Bridges (backup vocals), Regina McCrary (backup vocals), Mona Lisa Young (backup vocals).

Notes

- 25th Bob Dylan concert in Canada; 10th Bob Dylan concert in Toronto.
- 13, Bob Dylan (harmonica).
- 16, Bob Dylan (piano).
- Canadian live debut of songs 1, 2, 3, 4, 5, 6, 7, 8, 9, 10, 11, 12, 13, 14, 15 & 16.
- Worldwide live debut of songs 4 & 5.

Reviews

The times, they've changed

By Peter Goddard, Toronto Star.

"Hey Bobby," came the voice from the back row. "Do Lay Lady Lay."

"You should have been here 10 years ago," Bob Dylan said.

The times aren't a-changin' any more. They've changed. And with tambourines, slapping thighs, gospel girls hooting, fat and meaty chords rolling off the piano, and the spirit, yes the very spirit, in the air, Brother Bob's travelling salvation show, Bob Dylan presiding, found its way into Massey Hall last night for the first of four nights in town.

And there was more than just 15 years separating him – and us – from when he last played Massey Hall Nov. 14, 1965.

Charlie Reich's "true prophet of the new consciousness," the Napoleon in rags from the far away '60s, had become the affable, readily accessible, chatty figure in his late 30s, looking rather suburban in black pants, a dark shirt and leather jacket. Settled. Happy. This Dylan appeared comfortable and at ease with himself.

'Beautiful City'

So he took care of some business, first acknowledging Gordon Lightfoot's presence in the audience. "He's one of a Canada's national treasures," Dylan said. "It's been a long while, eh Gord?"

A little later, it was time for the city itself: "Always had a good time in Toronto – a beautiful city. It's trying to revive itself," he added.

All this acted as an enormous safety valve for a kind of speculative pressure that has been building up ever since the first rumors about his conversion to fundamentalist Christianity were circulated late in 1978. And with the arrival last August of the album Slow Train Coming – which formed the basis for last night's show – the wondering ended.

It didn't preach fire and brimstone exactly, but with song titles such as When He Returns and lines quoting Christ, there was no question about his leanings. The real question was, why Christianity? Was he searching for something after the messily public divorce from his wife, Sara, and the commercial failure of his 1978 movie, Renaldo And Clara?

It was also rumored that it was due to the influence of the new women in his life but his press agent, Paul Wasserman, squelched that suggestion earlier this week, by saying "Bob's over 21. He knows what he's doing. Besides, he has had a lot of women telling him a lot of things."

All in all, it was assumed that the reasons behind his spiritual re-birth just had to be dark, menacing. I mean, this is Bob Dylan, we're talking about, right?

Right.

Mini-tour

But this is no longer the Dylan Kris Kristofferson once called "a dozen different people." Now on a min-tour until May 10, he has never approached so close to those he wants to reach since he started out.

It's still theatre, of course, but now the play seems for real. And the moment last night's audience realized that, after he'd ignored repeated requests for old songs, after it was evident that gospel music and *the* Gospel were the subjects of the night, you could detect what amounted to a collective psychological sigh. The pressure was off. Enjoy.

"I know you're going to read in the newspapers that everyone walked out," he told the crowd during the two-hour show, referring to earlier newspaper reports. "Well, you tell everybody the truth."

Okay. There were only a few in last night's audience of what appeared to be veteran Dylan fans who walked out, and this was during the opening set by his backing singers, Mona Lisa Young, Regina Havis, Clydie King ("a legend in her own time," Dylan said), Gwen Edwards and Mary Bridges, along with piano player Terry Young.

This show was rich in swooping gospel harmonies and long, melismatic hollers. In a sense, it established a traditional framework for what was to follow. And everyone who'd left came back in.

Several years ago, the singer tried to explain his art work by saying that he's "learned as much from Cezanne as he had from Woody Guthrie. In 1965 he used one color combination, hard-rock applied directly on folk music's uneven surface. Last night merely showed his latest; gospel choral work added to a bottom-heavy pop band, led by bassist Tim Drummond and including keyboard player Spooner Oldham, guitarist Fred Tackett and drummer Jim Keltner.

Punchy Beat

The result was that the older material was nearly completely revamped at times. Man Gave Names was pretty, airy and magical; Gotta Serve Somebody had lost its sly piano vamp in favor of a punchy rock beat. The new music was, if anything, even more overtly religious than that on Slow Train. The last piece, I'm Pressing On (I guess this was the title), was as complex as anything he has done; a series of rising harmonic plateaus over which his voice, sounding more musically supple than ever, climbed.

Why, there was even a bit of preaching. Near the show's end, he mentioned he read about The Who's opening concert on tour Tuesday night and that Peter Townshend had apologized for being away so long. "He said, we'd never leave you alone again," Dylan said. "Just think about that for a moment."

People were smiling from this moment to the end.

Dylan's act a real revival

No ghost — Dylan threw everything but The Gnostic Gospels

By Paul McGrath.

Bob Dylan's fans have always had reason to fear the man. He's always been two or three years ahead of them, always told them what was going on in their heads before they were aware of it, and always preached his personal gospel to them in terrifying terms.

Now that he's switched over to the gospel of Jesus Christ, they fear him even more. At Massey Hall last night, where Dylan opened a four-night stint, they sat bewildered while he threw everything but the Gnostic Gospels at them in an attempt to provoke some participation.

Incredible gospel singing, rock and roll that out-raunched his pre-conversion days, uncommonly committed singing and superb playing from a state-of-the-art band – all of it elicited little more, until the very end, than polite applause, whistles and shouts for older, classic Dylan tunes which he now refuses to play. He's playing for and about Jesus now, and the fans don't know how to handle it. They came to be entertained.

And they were entertained, if they managed to get past the message. Even if rock and roll would appear to be hostile to any form of religion, organized or unorganized – it is, for those who need one, a religion unto itself – there is no conflict in Dylan's mind. Good rock can be put to a good end, and the new-found personal confidence was evident in the sometimes devastating power of his new songs.

The best tune of the evening was the only one whose title I missed, but those who were there will remember it because the first few bars were like sheet lightning in the hall, a wrenching shock to those who were there to see the ghost of a man they once knew. It was the hardest thing I've heard out of Dylan in years, and he was enthralled with the way it worked, allowing quick flashes of the old grin to move across his face as every member of his 11-person outfit worked double-time to prove to the crowd that this man is still very much alive.

Dylan was consistent; every single musical item of the evening addressed one or another aspect of the Christian experience. Abandonment and redemption, confusion and clarity, sin and salvation were all there – in that respect, he's no different from the late-night TV preachers, but the poet inside him made the statement of these themes far more palatable to non-Christians. Dylan's always been searching for some type of redemption, generally in the world itself, but because he's changed the direction of his search makes him no less gifted a craftsman.

His excellent band was packed with legends: Spooner Oldham, the Memphis session pianist whose work can be heard in the best recordings of Otis Redding, Aretha Franklin, Wilson Pickett and many others; Jim Keltner, traveling drummer best known for his work with Eric Clapton's Derek and The Dominoes; bassist Tim Drummond, also a well-known session player. The five women who started the show with half an hour of moving gospel music added an authority to his religious rock that would not have been there without them.

If Dylan is going to continue as a Christian performer, he'd better clear up the ambiguity in the traditional Christian lyrics with which those women opened the show. "Before I'll be a slave, I'll be buried in my grave," they sang, but later came this transparent snippet of Christian defeat: "I used to complain when my income was small, then I remembered who holds it all." The old Dylan would have raged at a line like that. You gotta serve somebody, sure Bob, just make sure it isn't the slave-drivers.

The Globe and Mail. Fri., April 18, 1980. Reprinted with permission from The Globe and Mail.

Dylan sings with conviction

By Jonathan Gross, Staff Writer.

"*Lay Lady Lay!*"

"*Highway 61! Like a Rolling Stone!*"

"Play something old Bob!"

When the frustrations of a vocal minority began to drift down from the upper reaches of Massey Hall about half way through last night's ride on Bob Dylan's Slow Train, you could sense, to a much lesser extent, what it was like back in 1965 at Forest Hills, N.Y. when his fans revolted at the sight of an electric guitar.

The new feature in his act is now Jesus Christ and Dylan was quick to put the disgruntled non-believers in their place.

"*Lay Lady Lay*? You should have been here 10 years ago.

"Why should I play something that I don't believe in.

"Besides, I don't have any friends to lose anyways."

That's right. Not only did Dylan break his code of silence but he prayed and sang with twice the conviction of his Vegas-slick Street Legal tour of a couple of years ago.

Although to some Dylan seems lost in space, his music is actually more accessible than ever.

His touring band, a group that is much more straight ahead than his studio outfit, filled the hall with a surprisingly punchy sound.

Five female back-up singers, clad in sequined shirts and tight jeans, added vocal excitement to rock and roll that had an almost New Wave edge to it.

For this is no accident. As a salesman for Christ, Dylan knows that he has to do a great job of packaging his product. He's not competing with the other headline hunters anymore; he's going for our heads.

And that's the biggest game of all.

Even his black leather jacket and tight pants came to be a way of appealing to the trendier sensibilities in his audience.

The new material continues in this direction, particularly *Ain't Going to Hell for Anybody* a rocker with an appeal so strong you have to like it even with sermonizing lyrics.

"I'd like to say hello to Gordon Lightfoot. He knows about not going to hell for anybody…yeh, Canada's most precious national treasure."

I'll be interested to see just how chatty Dylan is through the rest of his four-night stand, one of the longest running tent shows to hit this town.

The Toronto Sun. Fri., April 18, 1980. Reprinted with permission of The Sun Media Corp.

Friday, April 18, 1980 --- Massey Hall Toronto, ON

Set List

	Song	From The Album	Released
1.	Gotta Serve Somebody	Slow Train Coming	Aug. 20, 1979
2.	I Believe in You	Slow Train Coming	Aug. 20, 1979
3.	When You Gonna Wake Up	Slow Train Coming	Aug. 20, 1979
4.	Ain't Gonna Go to Hell for Anybody	Unreleased	–
5.	Cover Down, Break Through	Unreleased	–
6.	Precious Angel	Slow Train Coming	Aug. 20, 1979
7.	Man Gave Names to All the Animals	Slow Train Coming	Aug. 20, 1979
8.	Slow Train	Slow Train Coming	Aug. 20, 1979
9.	Do Right to Me Baby (Do Unto Others)	Slow Train Coming	Aug. 20, 1979
10.	Solid Rock	Saved	June 19, 1980
11.	Saving Grace	Saved	June 19, 1980
12.	What Can I Do For You?	Saved	June 19, 1980
13.	Saved (Bob Dylan/Tim Drummond)	Saved	June 19, 1980
14.	In the Garden	Saved	June 19, 1980
	Encores		
15.	Are You Ready?	Saved	June 19, 1980
16.	Pressing On	Saved	June 19, 1980

The Musicians

Bob Dylan (vocal, guitar, harmonica & piano), Fred Tackett (guitar), Spooner Oldham (keyboards), Tim Drummond (bass), Terry Young (piano), Jim Keltner (drums), Clydie King (backup vocals), Gwen Evans (backup vocals), Mary Elizabeth Bridges (backup vocals), Regina McCrary (backup vocals), Mona Lisa Young (backup vocals).

Notes

- 26th Bob Dylan concert in Canada; 11th Bob Dylan concert in Toronto.
- 12, Bob Dylan (harmonica).
- 16, Bob Dylan (piano).
- The songs by Mary Elizabeth Bridges, Gwen Evans, Clydie King, Regina McCrary & Mona Lisa Young with Terry Young on piano are not included in the set list.

Saturday, April 19, 1980 --- Massey Hall Toronto, ON

Set List

	Song	On Stage
–	Let It Ride (McCoy/Dennis)	Mary Elizabeth Bridges, Gwen Evans, Clydie King, Regina McCrary & Mona Lisa Young with Terry Young on piano.
–	(You've Got To) Hold On (?)	Mary Elizabeth Bridges, Gwen Evans, Clydie King, Regina McCrary & Mona Lisa Young with Terry Young on piano.
–	It's Gonna Rain (C. Johnson)	Mary Elizabeth Bridges, Gwen Evans, Clydie King, Regina McCrary & Mona Lisa Young with Terry Young on piano.
–	Show Me the Way Lord (?)	Mary Elizabeth Bridges, Gwen Evans, Clydie King, Regina

	Song	On Stage
		McCrary & Mona Lisa Young with Terry Young on piano.
–	Freedom (Over Me) (?)	Mary Elizabeth Bridges, Gwen Evans, Clydie King, Regina McCrary & Mona Lisa Young with Terry Young on piano.
–	Freedom at the Wall (?)	Mary Elizabeth Bridges, Gwen Evans, Clydie King, Regina McCrary & Mona Lisa Young with Terry Young on piano.
–	This Train is Bound for Glory (This Train) (Big Bill Broonzy)	Mary Elizabeth Bridges, Gwen Evans, Clydie King, Regina McCrary & Mona Lisa Young with Terry Young on piano.

	Song	From The Album	Released
1.	Gotta Serve Somebody	Slow Train Coming	Aug. 20, 1979
2.	Covenant Woman	Saved	June 19, 1980
3.	When You Gonna Wake Up	Slow Train Coming	Aug. 20, 1979
4.	Ain't Gonna Go to Hell for Anybody	Unreleased	–
5.	Cover Down, Break Through	Unreleased	–
6.	Man Gave Names to All the Animals	Slow Train Coming	Aug. 20, 1979
7.	Precious Angel	Slow Train Coming	Aug. 20, 1979
8.	Slow Train	Slow Train Coming	Aug. 20, 1979

	Song	On Stage
–	Calgary (?)	Clydie King with Terry Young on piano.
–	Put Your Hand in the Hand of the Man From Galilee (Gene MacLellan)	Regina McCrary with Terry Young on piano.

	Song	From The Album	Released
9.	Do Right to Me Baby (Do Unto Others)	Slow Train Coming	Aug. 20, 1979
10.	Solid Rock	Saved	June 19, 1980
11.	Saving Grace	Saved	June 19, 1980
12.	What Can I Do For You?	Saved	June 19, 1980
13.	Saved (Bob Dylan/Tim Drummond)	Saved	June 19, 1980
14.	In the Garden	Saved	June 19, 1980
	Encores		
15.	Are You Ready?	Saved	June 19, 1980
16.	I Will Love Him	Unreleased	

The Musicians

Bob Dylan (vocal, guitar, & harmonica), Fred Tackett (guitar), Spooner Oldham (keyboards), Tim Drummond (bass), Terry Young (piano), Jim Keltner (drums), Clydie King (backup vocals), Gwen Evans (backup vocals), Mary Elizabeth Bridges (backup vocals), Regina McCrary (backup vocals), Mona Lisa Young (backup vocals).

Notes

- 27th Bob Dylan concert in Canada; 12th Bob Dylan concert in Toronto.
- 12, Bob Dylan (harmonica).
- Canadian live debut of songs 2 & 16.
- Worldwide live debut of song 16.

Sunday, April 20, 1980 --- Massey Hall
Toronto, ON

Set List

	Song	On Stage
–	Let It Ride (McCoy/Dennis)	Mary Elizabeth Bridges, Gwen Evans, Clydie King, Regina McCrary & Mona Lisa Young with Terry Young on piano.
–	(You've Got To) Hold On (?)	Mary Elizabeth Bridges, Gwen Evans, Clydie King, Regina McCrary & Mona Lisa Young with Terry Young on piano.
–	It's Gonna Rain (C. Johnson)	Mary Elizabeth Bridges, Gwen Evans, Clydie King, Regina McCrary & Mona Lisa Young with Terry Young on piano.
–	Look Up and Live By Faith (Robert Lawrence Curtis)	Mary Elizabeth Bridges, Gwen Evans, Clydie King, Regina McCrary & Mona Lisa Young with Terry Young on piano.
–	Show Me the Way Lord (?)	Mary Elizabeth Bridges, Gwen Evans, Clydie King, Regina

	Song	On Stage
		McCrary & Mona Lisa Young with Terry Young on piano.
–	Freedom at the Wall (?)	Mary Elizabeth Bridges, Gwen Evans, Clydie King, Regina McCrary & Mona Lisa Young with Terry Young on piano.
–	This Train is Bound for Glory (This Train) (Big Bill Broonzy)	Mary Elizabeth Bridges, Gwen Evans, Clydie King, Regina McCrary & Mona Lisa Young with Terry Young on piano.

	Song	From The Album	Released
1.	Gotta Serve Somebody	Slow Train Coming	Aug. 20, 1979
2.	I Believe in You	Slow Train Coming	Aug. 20, 1979
3.	When You Gonna Wake Up	Slow Train Coming	Aug. 20, 1979
4.	Ain't Gonna Go to Hell for Anybody	Unreleased	–
5.	Cover Down, Break Through	Unreleased	–
6.	Man Gave Names to All the Animals	Slow Train Coming	Aug. 20, 1979
7.	Precious Angel	Slow Train Coming	Aug. 20, 1979
8.	Slow Train	Slow Train Coming	Aug. 20, 1979

	Song	On Stage
–	Stranger in the City (Healing) (?)	Mona Lisa Young with Terry Young on piano.
–	Walk Around Heaven All Day (Rev. James Cleveland & Cassietta George)	Mary Elizabeth Bridges with Terry Young on piano.

	Song	From The Album	Released
9.	Do Right to Me Baby (Do Unto Others)	Slow Train Coming	Aug. 20, 1979
10.	Solid Rock	Saved	June 19, 1980
11.	Saving Grace	Saved	June 19, 1980
12.	What Can I Do For You?	Saved	June 19, 1980
13.	Saved (Bob Dylan/Tim Drummond)	Saved	June 19, 1980
14.	In the Garden	Saved	June 19, 1980
	Encores		
15.	Are You Ready?	Saved	June 19, 1980
16.	Pressing On	Saved	June 19, 1980

The Musicians

Bob Dylan (vocal, guitar, harmonica & piano), Fred Tackett (guitar), Spooner Oldham (keyboards), Tim Drummond (bass), Terry Young (piano), Jim Keltner (drums), Clydie King (backup vocals), Gwen Evans (backup vocals), Mary Elizabeth Bridges (backup vocals), Regina McCrary (backup vocals), Mona Lisa Young (backup vocals).

Notes

- 28th Bob Dylan concert in Canada; 13th Bob Dylan concert in Toronto.
- 12, Bob Dylan (harmonica).
- 16, Bob Dylan (piano).
- Part of When You Gonna Wake Up (51 seconds) was released on the Interactive Music CD-ROM, Bob Dylan: Highway 61 Interactive in Feb. 1995.

Tuesday, April 22, 1980 --- Le Theatre Saint-Denis Montreal, QC

Set List

	Song	From The Album	Released
1.	Gotta Serve Somebody	Slow Train Coming	Aug. 20, 1979
2.	I Believe in You	Slow Train Coming	Aug. 20, 1979
3.	When You Gonna Wake Up	Slow Train Coming	Aug. 20, 1979
4.	Ain't Gonna Go to Hell for Anybody	Unreleased	–
5.	Cover Down, Break Through	Unreleased	–
6.	Precious Angel	Slow Train Coming	Aug. 20, 1979
7.	Man Gave Names to All the Animals	Slow Train Coming	Aug. 20, 1979
8.	Slow Train	Slow Train Coming	Aug. 20, 1979

Song	On Stage

–	Calgary (?)	Clydie King with Terry Young on piano.	
–	Lord Don't Move That Mountain (Mahalia Jackson)	Gwen Evans with Terry Young on piano.	
	Song	**From The Album**	**Released**
9.	Do Right to Me Baby (Do Unto Others)	Slow Train Coming	Aug. 20, 1979
10.	Solid Rock	Saved	June 19, 1980
11.	Saving Grace	Saved	June 19, 1980
12.	Saved (Bob Dylan/Tim Drummond)	Saved	June 19, 1980
13.	What Can I Do For You?	Saved	June 19, 1980
14.	In the Garden	Saved	June 19, 1980
	Encores		
15.	Are You Ready?	Saved	June 19, 1980
16.	Pressing On	Saved	June 19, 1980

The Musicians

Bob Dylan (vocal, guitar, harmonica & piano), Fred Tackett (guitar), Spooner Oldham (keyboards), Tim Drummond (bass), Terry Young (piano), Jim Keltner (drums), Clydie King (backup vocals), Gwen Evans (backup vocals), Mary Elizabeth Bridges (backup vocals), Regina McCrary (backup vocals), Mona Lisa Young (backup vocals).

Notes

- 29th Bob Dylan concert in Canada; 11th Bob Dylan concert in Montreal.
- 13, Bob Dylan (harmonica).
- 16, Bob Dylan (piano).
- The opening songs by Mary Elizabeth Bridges, Gwen Evans, Clydie King, Regina McCrary & Mona Lisa Young with Terry Young on piano are not included in the set list.

Review

Dylan lance son «trip» religieux

Le Journal de Montréal.

«La dernière fois que je suis venu à Montréal, je ne connaissais pas Jésus.Tel que vous me voyez, extérieurement, je ne suis pas différent. Mais au-dedans de moi, c'est comme si je renaissais!» Le message de Bob Dylan est très clair, net, à prendre ou à laisser. Hier soir au Théâtre St-Denis, il n'a peut-être pas converti grand-monde à son regain religieux; mais assurément, son message musical est passé.

Depuis tant d'années qu'il est là, on passe à peu près tout à Bob Dylan; ses phases de transition sont vues comme des évolutions admirables et quel que soit le rythme qu'il offre, celui-ci s'impose de lui-même. Sa nouvelle «lubie» (telle de moins qu'elle est vue par de nombreux sceptiques) risque toutefois de promettre plus qu'une simple folie passagère. Le «Slow Train Coming» qu'il propage est spacieux, confortable et sa destination a peu d'influence sur les passagers en puissance. On embarque, quitte à se retrouver dans un champ de coton du sud des Etats-Unis au temps de l'esclavage, quand les travailleurs harassés chantaient pour se donner du coeur à l'ouvrage. Bob Dylan fait goûter trip personnel en allant au plus profond du blues, du gospel, avec quelques incursions dans le reggae et dans le rock; la musique est belle, riche, puissante et beaucoup plus compréhensible du fait que le chanteur a choisi le St-Denis plutôt que le Forum, pour se «rapprocher du monde». S'il sourit beaucoup plus à sa vision intérieure qu'à son public, on le sent tout de même très proche.

Les musiciens sont calmes et concentrés, les cinq choristes sont déchaînées et pleines d'un entrain digne du missionnaire enthousiaste fraîchement arrivé en terre à conquérir. Ces jeunes femmes feront énormément pour créer l'atmosphère fervente de ce spectacle, pour donner une enveloppe soyeuse à la voix de Dylan (qui à ce niveau, n'a pas changé pour un sou…). Il est toujours aussi écorché vif, toujours aussi habile, surprenant dans sa façon d'arriver à la fin d'une mesure en même temps que tout le monde quand on le croit parti dans une croisade vocale!

Bob Dylan va-t-il relancer la mode des «Jesus Freaks»? Difficile à dire; mais tant qu'il continuera à offrir un tel véhicule musical à ses convictions, il pourra certes faire tous les sermons qu'il veut, on l'écoutera. Comme nous écouterions avec passion le «PTL Club» si les Rolling Stones en devenaient les vedettes...

Le Journal de Montréal. Wed., April 23, 1980. Reprinted with permission of Le Journal de Montréal.

Wednesday, April 23, 1980 --- Le Theatre Saint-Denis
Montreal, QC

Set List

	Song	On Stage
–	Let It Ride (McCoy/Dennis)	Mary Elizabeth Bridges, Gwen Evans, Clydie King, Regina McCrary & Mona Lisa Young with Terry Young on piano.
–	(You've Got To) Hold On (?)	Mary Elizabeth Bridges, Gwen Evans, Clydie King, Regina McCrary & Mona Lisa Young with Terry Young on piano.
–	It's Gonna Rain (C. Johnson)	Mary Elizabeth Bridges, Gwen Evans, Clydie King, Regina McCrary & Mona Lisa Young with Terry Young on piano.
–	Show Me the Way Lord (?)	Mary Elizabeth Bridges, Gwen Evans, Clydie King, Regina McCrary & Mona Lisa Young with Terry Young on piano.
–	Freedom at the Wall (?)	Mary Elizabeth Bridges, Gwen Evans, Clydie King, Regina McCrary & Mona Lisa Young with Terry Young on piano.
–	This Train is Bound for Glory (This Train) (Big Bill Broonzy)	Mary Elizabeth Bridges, Gwen Evans, Clydie King, Regina McCrary & Mona Lisa Young with Terry Young on piano.

	Song	From The Album	Released
1.	Gotta Serve Somebody	Slow Train Coming	Aug. 20, 1979
2.	I Believe in You	Slow Train Coming	Aug. 20, 1979
3.	When You Gonna Wake Up	Slow Train Coming	Aug. 20, 1979
4.	Ain't Gonna Go to Hell for Anybody	Unreleased	–
5.	Cover Down, Break Through	Unreleased	–
6.	Precious Angel	Slow Train Coming	Aug. 20, 1970
7.	Man Gave Names to All the Animals	Slow Train Coming	Aug. 20, 1979
8.	Slow Train	Slow Train Coming	Aug. 20, 1979

	Song	On Stage
–	Walk Around Heaven All Day (Rev. James Cleveland/Cassietta George)	Mary Elizabeth Bridges with Terry Young on piano.
–	Stranger in the City (Healing) (?)	Mona Lisa Young with Terry Young on piano.

	Song	From The Album	Released
9.	I Will Love Him	Unreleased	
10.	Do Right to Me Baby (Do Unto Others)	Slow Train Coming	Aug. 20, 1979
11.	Solid Rock	Saved	June 19, 1980
12.	Saving Grace	Saved	June 19, 1980
13.	Saved (Bob Dylan/Tim Drummond)	Saved	June 19, 1980
14.	What Can I Do For You?	Saved	June 19, 1980
15.	In the Garden	Saved	June 19, 1980
	Encores		
16.	Are You Ready?	Saved	June 19, 1980
17.	Pressing On	Saved	June 19, 1980

The Musicians

Bob Dylan (vocal, guitar, harmonica & piano), Fred Tackett (guitar), Spooner Oldham (keyboards), Tim Drummond (bass), Terry Young (piano), Jim Keltner (drums), Clydie King (backup vocals), Gwen Evans (backup vocals), Mary Elizabeth Bridges (backup vocals), Regina McCrary (backup vocals), Mona Lisa Young (backup vocals).

Notes

- 30th Bob Dylan concert in Canada; 12th Bob Dylan concert in Montreal.
- 14, Bob Dylan (harmonica).
- 17, Bob Dylan (piano).

Thursday, April 24, 1980 --- Le Theatre Saint-Denis Montreal, QC

Set List

	Song	On Stage
–	Let It Ride (McCoy/Dennis)	Mary Elizabeth Bridges, Gwen Evans, Clydie King, Regina McCrary & Mona Lisa Young with Terry Young on piano.
–	(You've Got To) Hold On (?)	Mary Elizabeth Bridges, Gwen Evans, Clydie King, Regina McCrary & Mona Lisa Young with Terry Young on piano.
–	It's Gonna Rain (C. Johnson)	Mary Elizabeth Bridges, Gwen Evans, Clydie King, Regina McCrary & Mona Lisa Young with Terry Young on piano.
–	Show Me the Way Lord (?)	Mary Elizabeth Bridges, Gwen Evans, Clydie King, Regina McCrary & Mona Lisa Young with Terry Young on piano.
–	Freedom at the Wall (?)	Mary Elizabeth Bridges, Gwen Evans, Clydie King, Regina McCrary & Mona Lisa Young with Terry Young on piano.
–	This Train is Bound for Glory (This Train) (Big Bill Broonzy)	Mary Elizabeth Bridges, Gwen Evans, Clydie King, Regina McCrary & Mona Lisa Young with Terry Young on piano.

	Song	From The Album	Released
1.	Gotta Serve Somebody	Slow Train Coming	Aug. 20, 1979
2.	Covenant Woman	Saved	June 19, 1980
3.	When You Gonna Wake Up	Slow Train Coming	Aug. 20, 1979
4.	Ain't Gonna Go to Hell for Anybody	Unreleased	–
5.	Cover Down, Break Through	Unreleased	–
6.	Precious Angel	Slow Train Coming	Aug. 20, 1970
7.	Man Gave Names to All the Animals	Slow Train Coming	Aug. 20, 1979
8.	Slow Train	Slow Train Coming	Aug. 20, 1979

	Song	On Stage
–	Calgary (?)	Clydie King with Terry Young on piano.
–	Ain't No Man Righteous (No Not One) (Bob Dylan)	Regina McCray Havis with Terry Young on piano.

	Song	From The Album	Released
9.	Do Right to Me Baby (Do Unto Others)	Slow Train Coming	Aug. 20, 1979
10.	Solid Rock	Saved	June 19, 1980
11.	Saving Grace	Saved	June 19, 1980
12.	Saved (Bob Dylan/Tim Drummond)	Saved	June 19, 1980
13.	What Can I Do For You?	Saved	June 19, 1980
14.	In the Garden	Saved	June 19, 1980
	Encores		
15.	Are You Ready?	Saved	June 19, 1980
16.	Pressing On	Saved	June 19, 1980

The Musicians

Bob Dylan (vocal, guitar, harmonica & piano), Fred Tackett (guitar), Spooner Oldham (keyboards), Tim Drummond (bass), Terry Young (piano), Jim Keltner (drums), Clydie King (backup vocals), Gwen Evans (backup vocals), Mary Elizabeth Bridges (backup vocals), Regina McCrary (backup vocals), Mona Lisa Young (backup vocals).

Notes

- 31st Bob Dylan concert in Canada; 13th Bob Dylan concert in Montreal.
- 13, Bob Dylan (harmonica).
- 16, Bob Dylan (piano).

Friday, April 25, 1980 --- Le Theatre Saint-Denis Montreal, QC

Set List

	Song	From The Album	Released
1.	Gotta Serve Somebody	Slow Train Coming	Aug. 20, 1979
2.	I Believe in You	Slow Train Coming	Aug. 20, 1979
3.	When You Gonna Wake Up	Slow Train Coming	Aug. 20, 1979
4.	Ain't Gonna Go to Hell for Anybody	Unreleased	–
5.	Cover Down, Break Through	Unreleased	–
6.	Precious Angel	Slow Train Coming	Aug. 20, 1970
7.	Man Gave Names to All the Animals	Slow Train Coming	Aug. 20, 1979
8.	Slow Train	Slow Train Coming	Aug. 20, 1979

	Song	On Stage
–	Walk Around Heaven All Day (Rev. James Cleveland & Cassietta George)	Mary Elizabeth Bridges with Terry Young on piano.
–	Lord Don't Move That Mountain (Mahalia Jackson)	Gwen Evans with Terry Young on piano.

	Song	From The Album	Released
9.	Do Right to Me Baby (Do Unto Others)	Slow Train Coming	Aug. 20, 1979
10.	Solid Rock	Saved	June 19, 1980
11.	Saving Grace	Saved	June 19, 1980
12.	Saved (Bob Dylan/Tim Drummond)	Saved	June 19, 1980
13.	What Can I Do For You?	Saved	June 19, 1980
14.	In the Garden	Saved	June 19, 1980
	Encores		
15.	Are You Ready?	Saved	June 19, 1980
16.	Pressing On	Saved	June 19, 1980

The Musicians

Bob Dylan (vocal, guitar, harmonica & piano), Fred Tackett (guitar), Spooner Oldham (keyboards), Tim Drummond (bass), Terry Young (piano), Jim Keltner (drums), Clydie King (backup vocals), Gwen Evans (backup vocals), Mary Elizabeth Bridges (backup vocals), Regina McCrary (backup vocals), Mona Lisa Young (backup vocals).

Notes

- 32nd Bob Dylan concert in Canada; 14th Bob Dylan concert in Montreal.
- 13, Bob Dylan (harmonica).
- 16, Bob Dylan (piano).
- The opening songs by Mary Elizabeth Bridges, Gwen Evans, Clydie King, Regina McCrary & Mona Lisa Young with Terry Young on piano are not included in the set list.

1981

Introduction

The 1981 Shot of Love Tour visited Canada for four concerts.

These shows would mark Bob Dylan's 33rd, 34th, 35th & 36th concert in Canada.

The Dates

Toronto, ON	Thurs., Oct. 29, 1981
Montreal, QC	Fri., Oct. 30, 1981
Kitchener, ON	Sat., Oct. 31, 1981
Ottawa, ON	Mon., Nov. 2, 1981

The shows would be Dylan's 14th concert in Toronto, 15th concert in Montreal, debut concert in Kitchener and 2nd concert in Ottawa.

The Musicians

Bob Dylan (vocal, guitar & harmonica).

Fred Tackett (guitar), Steve Ripley (guitar), Al Kooper (keyboards), Tim Drummond (bass), Jim Keltner (drums), Arthur Rosato (drums), Clydie King (backup vocals), Regina McCrary (backup vocals), Madelyn Quebec (backup vocals).

The Songs

Bob Dylan performed a total of 107 songs. Of those, 34 were different songs (31 were from albums, one was an unreleased song and 2 were cover and/or traditional songs).

Eight songs made their Canadian live debut.

I'll Be Your Baby Tonight	Dead Man, Dead Man
Gamblin' Man	Heart of Mine
Watered Down Love	It's All in the Game
Let It Be Me	Jesus Is the One

Two songs have been played only once in Canada.

It's All in the Game	Jesus Is the One

Bob Dylan performed songs from 14 different albums.

Album	Released	# of Songs Performed by Album
The Freewheelin' Bob Dylan	May, 27, 1963	5
The Times They Are A-Changin'	Feb., 10, 1964	1
Another Side of Bob Dylan	Aug. 8, 1964	1
Bringing It All Back Home	March 22, 1965	3
Highway 61 Revisited	Aug. 30, 1965	2
Blonde on Blonde	May 16, 1966	2
John Wesley Harding	Dec. 27, 1967	2
Self Portrait	June 8, 1970	1
Pat Garrett and Billy The Kid	July 13, 1973	1
Planet Waves	Jan. 17, 1974	1
Blood on the Tracks	Jan. 20, 1975	1
Slow Train Coming	Aug. 20, 1979	4
Saved	June 19, 1980	4
Shot of Love	Aug. 12, 1981	3

The Venues

It was Bob Dylan's 6th time playing at Maple Leaf Gardens in Toronto, 5th time playing at the Montreal Forum, debut concert at the Kitchener Memorial Auditorium and debut concert at the Ottawa Civic Centre.

Thursday, October 29, 1981 --- Maple Leaf Gardens
Toronto, ON

Set List

	Song	From The Album	Released
1.	Gotta Serve Somebody	Slow Train Coming	Aug. 20, 1979
2.	I Believe in You	Slow Train Coming	Aug. 20, 1979
3.	Like a Rolling Stone	Highway 61 Revisited	Aug. 30, 1965
4.	I Want You	Blonde on Blonde	May 16, 1966
5.	Man Gave Names to All the Animals	Slow Train Coming	Aug. 20, 1979
6.	Maggie's Farm	Bringing It All Back Home	March 22, 1965
7.	Girl of the North Country	The Freewheelin' Bob Dylan	May 27, 1963
8.	Ballad of a Thin Man	Highway 61 Revisited	Aug. 30, 1965
9.	Simple Twist of Fate	Blood on the Tracks	Jan. 20. 1975
10.	All Along the Watchtower	John Wesley Harding	Dec. 27, 1967
11.	I'll Be Your Baby Tonight	John Wesley Harding	Dec. 27, 1967
12.	Forever Young	Planet Waves	Jan. 17, 1974
13.	Gamblin' Man (trad.)	–	–
14.	The Times They Are A-Changin'	The Times They Are A-Changin'	Feb. 10, 1964
15.	A Hard Rain's A-Gonna Fall	The Freewheelin' Bob Dylan	May 27, 1963
16.	Watered Down Love	Shot of Love	Aug. 12, 1981
17.	Masters of War	The Freewheelin' Bob Dylan	May 27, 1963
18.	Mr. Tambourine Man	Bringing It All Back Home	March 22, 1965
19.	Solid Rock	Saved	June 19, 1980
20.	Let It Be Me (Pierre Delanoé/Gilbert Bécoud/Mann Curtis)	Self Portrait	June 8, 1970
21.	Dead Man, Dead Man	Shot of Love	Aug. 12, 1981
22.	When You Gonna Wake Up	Slow Train Coming	Aug. 20, 1979
23.	In the Garden	Saved	June 19, 1980
	Encores		
24.	Blowin' in the Wind	The Freewheelin' Bob Dylan	May 27, 1963
25.	It Ain't Me, Babe	Another Side of Bob Dylan	Aug. 8, 1964
26.	Knockin' on Heaven's Door	Pat Garrett & Billy The Kid	July 13, 1973

The Musicians

Bob Dylan (vocal, guitar & harmonica), Fred Tackett (guitar), Steve Ripley (guitar), Al Kooper (keyboards), Tim Drummond (bass), Jim Keltner (drums), Arthur Rosato (drums), Clydie King (backup vocals), Regina McCrary (backup vocals), Madelyn Quebec (backup vocals).

Notes

- 33rd Bob Dylan concert in Canada; 14th Bob Dylan concert in Toronto.
- 11, 20, Bob Dylan & Clydie King (shared vocals).
- 12, 14, 25-26, Bob Dylan (harmonica).
- 13, Clydie King, Regina McCrary, Madelyn Quebec (vocals).
- 25, Bob Dylan solo (vocal & guitar).
- Canadian live debut of songs 11, 13, 16, 20 & 21.

Reviews

God looks good on Dylan

By Bruce Blackadar, Toronto Star.

The notoriously mysterious thin man with the anguished and plaintive ballads has had more incarnations in his incredibly complicated career than a Dalai Lama on a hot streak.

But, let the good news be preached now that he is back – and he is back with a vengeance.

Yes, parishioners, the 40-year-old 'born again' Bob Dylan stormed joyously into Maple Leaf Gardens last night and conclusively demonstrated to a fervent audience of 17,000 – many of them high school kids, many of them people like Alderman John Sewell – that rumors of his immediate professional demise as a culture hero are being spread by people bearing false witness.

Better than ever

But the truth is that the man is now singing better than ever. He's a more improved entertainer; he's warmer, more communicative, and far less jumpy and arrogant and walled-in as a person than he used to be in the '60s, when his every word was dissected as if it were an entrail perused by an ancient priest who was searching for its cosmic meaning.

Bob Dylan has been lifted from a great burden, on the evidence of last night's performance, at any rate. Somehow, he was relaxed to the point where he doesn't seem to feel as if he is any longer an icon, a mythological figure fixed in stone.

Dylan used to be venerated, literally, and that is simply too much weight to be carried around by anyone for too long. And so it is very pleasant to see him now, free of the load, no longer in the superstar sweepstakes, no longer needed by too many of us who believed he once had the key to it all, that, yes, he had the various truths that would help us through the bumpy, messy times.

Asked too much

I think we all asked too much of the man before, and I think it damaged him badly. There were rumblings last night from some members of the audience that he wasn't giving them a replica of former concerts, that he re-arranged the music of their favorite songs, songs like Mr. Tambourine Man, and Like A Rolling Stone, and Simple Twist Of Fate, and Forever Young. These people reminded me of those who chose to boo the man when he 'went electric' in New York all those years ago, and was condemned roundly because he'd given up his folkie purity. Rigid is what you term people like that. And too nostalgic by half. And too unimaginative.

Dylan was hot last night; he had a very good band – three guitars, two keyboards, two drummers, and three fine women singers – and his voice, often accused of being too harsh, too nasal, and too angry, was in top form. He moves more on stage now, he's easy – heck, the man seems to be having some FUN – and that's something that Dylan rarely demonstrated in too many earlier concerts when he was idolized.

Dressed in black, wearing sunglasses, he looked sexy and vital, and no, he did not preach, he did not sermonize. Fact is, even when he was singing his Christian songs they were not heavy or pompous. They were musically sound on their own, and certainly not a discredit when compared to his earlier work.

He did an amazing version of It Ain't Me, Babe that brought the house down – and a tender, compassionate rendering of Forever Young that was heart-stopping.

Good show, Mr. Zimmerman. Christianity looks good on you. And how does it feel? Pretty fine. Really.

The Toronto Star. Fri., Oct. 30, 1981. Reprinted with permission - Torstar Syndication Services.

Times a-changin' back

By Wilder Penfield III.

The last time most of the 16,000 people at the Gardens last night had seen Bob Dylan in concert was at the same place three years ago. That was around the time of his celebrated re-birth in Christ, but he wasn't talking yet.

Maybe there were hints, though, in the lyrics he chose to present to us. He was asking us, "Are you willing to risk it all, or is your love in vain?" And telling us, "The only thing I knew how to do was to keep on keepin' on."

"It is his faithful followers," I wrote then, "who have established the religion and made him their high priest."

Nonetheless he wasn't "lookin' for you to feel like me, see like me, or be like me."

Since then there have been two albums of fundamentalist preachment, and a third – *Shot of Love* – that maintained a moral stance but tackled some secular concerns.

But, as he used to sing, "I couldn't believe that after all these years you didn't know me better than that."

Last night he was changing again. He started by telling those of us who knew the lyric implications of the chord changes that *You've Got to Serve Somebody*.

But he was gregarious: "It's nice to be here," he said, "it really is." And by the third song we were back into the classics – *Like a Rolling Stone, I Want You, Maggie's Farm, North Country Fair, Ballad of a Thin Man, A Hard Rain's a Going to Fall*. Old Bob was back.

Sure, he had re-worked the vocal lines so that the melodies were all but unrecognizable, and the arrangements had followed suit, but he often does that. To the lyrics of even the oldest song he seemed to be remaining faithful. And with some pruning of new material, a tape of last night's generous show would sound years older – especially *because* of the sound which had a muddiness we no longer associate with major league rock tours.

The lighting, coffee house dim mostly, took us even farther back – to the days when Bob Dylan imitators had jobs in every town.

But while this Dylan may be incorporating his past into his present now, he isn't stuck there. This Dylan is 40 years old, and has been singing professionally for a couple of decades. So there is art in his artlessness, and the band he can call on to come play with him is top drawer. Al Kooper on keyboards, Steve Ripley and Fred Tackett on guitars, Tim Drummond and Jim Keltner on bass and drums, Clydie King joining the back-up vocalists. (Too bad we couldn't hear their contributions more clearly).

But Dylan's re-birth has not been cancelled retroactively. It is just that in re-discovering his innocence, as Robert Fripp and other counter-culture heroes have done, he is evidently willing to take something from older, wiser artists such as his former self.

The Toronto Sun. Fri., Oct. 30, 1981. Reprinted with permission of The Sun Media Corp.

A surprising new Dylan incarnation

By Liam Lacey.

As the purple spotlights came up on Bob Dylan last night at Maple Leaf Gardens, he stood, lean and menacing, dressed from head to foot in black, with pointed dark shoes and a pair of shades covering his eyes, like a beat preacher of doom ready to whip the flesh of the profligates, fornicators and nay-sayers who had gathered to hear the word. Instead, Dylan wore another mask entirely, a new, and once again surprising, incarnation of the master of disguises, after it seemed he had just about blown his bolt of new manoeuvres.

He is, of course, still a born-again Christian, and the opening song was a straightforward, almost perfunctory, Gotta Serve Somebody, followed by another song, I Believe In You, that always sounds a bit like Dylan's compliment to God.

Then came the twist. While it has been widely reported that Dylan has been doing his old material again, nobody has mentioned exactly how he has been doing it. As he swung into what may be the greatest rock song ever written, Like a Rolling Stone, he altered the phrasing in ways that were a revelation. The song, which had always sounded like one long sneer, no longer has any sneer left, just the tremendous anguish of the chorus.

With the course of the evening established, the band began playing in earnest, alternating between the new hard-driving Christian songs, which the greatest ambiguity hunter in the world couldn't mistake a word of, and the older, richer songs, many transformed into strangely wistful laments by a voice that sounds more supple and more free from artifice than it has in years. Indeed, over-all, it was easily the best performance Dylan has offered here in the last five years. His band, (Fred Tackett and Steve Ripley on guitars, Tim Drummond on bass, Jim Keltner on drums and William Smith on keyboards) played with understated authority.

It was, nonetheless, a performance that seemed designed to perplex. Why, for example, does Dylan now find his older material acceptable when he so harshly repudiated it a couple of years ago when he converted? Why was a song like Mister Tambourine Man given a completely new melody, one that supplants the raggedly stoned surrealism of the first song with a song that feels much more directly about loss and emptiness? And, finally, why has Dylan addressed himself so passionately to reshaping his old social protest songs – songs such as Hard Rain's Gonna Fall, The Times They Are A Changin' and Masters of War?

The answer unfolded as the night progressed, and as Dylan took the audience through the strange autobiographical tour of his old material, showing in song after song the strong thematic and imagistic links between pre and post-Christian music.

Once in a while it was not so subtle, as, for example, when, for emphasis, he repeated the line in The Times They Are A Changin' that talks about "he who is first shall later be last." Of course he sang All Along the Watchtower, and here it was abundantly clear that Hard Rain is less an anti-nuke tune than it is a vision of the apocalypse.

To be fair, he occasionally threw in songs like I'll Be Your Baby Tonight that one would be hard-pressed to place in any good Christian context, and they seemed to be deliberate sops to the audience, in order to keep them listening to the important stuff. But the overall impression still holds: Dylan has progressed both as an artist and Christian since his first flush of rabid, vitriolic born-againism. The passion seems tempered with compassion, and songs about sex, revenge, rebellion and rage have found their place again in his repertoire. The path may be strait and narrow, but Dylan seems to have recognized that the soul is oceanic.

The Globe and Mail. Fri., Oct. 30, 1981. Reprinted with permission from The Globe and Mail.

A pleasant evening out with a 1960s demi-god

Nicely nostalgic Dylan, but is that all there is?

By Jason Mitchell, Special to The Record.

Toronto — Rolling Stone editor Jann Wenner has called him the greatest figure that rock has ever produced. He's been referred to as the spokesman for an entire generation, and few other musicians have had their every move scrutinized as closely as he.

He has a mystique that seems to draw people to him like a magnet. And yet, Thursday night onstage at Maple Leaf Gardens, Bob Dylan looked very fragile, very ordinary and very, very mortal.

Even clad all in black, with regulation shades, Dylan is not a very imposing character. In fact, when the lights go down a little, he disappears completely. This is certainly not the material of which demi-gods are made.

Dylan's performance is subdued, unsure and uneven, as if he is still smarting from the shellacking he took over his conversion to Christianity. At times, he sounds almost inspired, singing with a certain degree of feeling and playing with some fervor, yet, at other times, he seems almost listless, content to let his band roll through the song. He can't seem to make up his mind whether he wants to be there or not.

It's hard to understand how these songs could have even provoked an argument, let alone inspired people to action and changed lives. Was the door of the '60s that wide open that someone with an off-key nasal whine, a harmonica and a guitar, who was able to accurately reflect what everyone was thinking, could become a superstar?

To no one's surprise, most of Dylan's songs currently have a gospel feel to them, and it's not really unpleasant to listen to. In fact, backup singers Clydie King, Madelyn Quebec and Regina McCrary are at least as interesting to listen to as Dylan, and they certainly radiate more confidence.

I wonder, though, if Dylan realizes the extent of the irony of imbuing a free-spirit song like Blowing in the Wind with a religious tone. Or, for that matter, I wonder if he realizes just how ironic it is for both himself and the audience when he sings "You got to start swimming or you sink like a stone," in The Times They Are A-Changin.

Oh, the show wasn't all that bad. To answer the burning question, yes, he played a lot of the old stuff, though some of it was changed so drastically that it took half a verse to recognize. A Hard Rain's Gonna Fall sounded like a waltz and Like a Rolling Stone, Maggie's Farm, Hey Mr. Tambourine Man, All Along the Watchtower, The Times They Are A-Changin', Forever Young and Blowing in the Wind, are also re-arranged drastically. But what's important is that he did them, right?

For an evening's entertainment, which is undoubtedly all that the majority came for, Dylan provided what was necessary. The older members in the crowd probably had some pleasant memories stirred, and for a couple of hours, they could forget about their mortgage renewal, their increasing girth and the tuneup the car needs.

For the younger people, it was a chance to see a legend, the same thought process that takes people to Buffalo to see the Stones "before they retire." For everyone, it was a chance to tap a foot and relax, like one would listening to a singer and his guitar around a camp fire. Very cosy.

Perhaps it's silly to expect inspiration and leadership from a mere singer. But really, the question must be asked; What does Bob Dylan have to offer to those few of us who are neither nostalgia freaks or born-again Christians?

The answer, I fear, is not very much.

Friday, October 30, 1981 --- Montreal Forum
Montreal, QC

Set List

	Song	From The Album	Released
1.	Gotta Serve Somebody	Slow Train Coming	Aug. 20, 1979
2.	I Believe in You	Slow Train Coming	Aug. 20, 1979
3.	Like a Rolling Stone	Highway 61 Revisited	Aug. 30, 1965
4.	I Want You	Blonde on Blonde	May 16, 1966
5.	Man Gave Names to All the Animals	Slow Train Coming	Aug. 20, 1979
6.	Maggie's Farm	Bringing It All Back Home	March 22, 1965
7.	Girl of the North Country	The Freewheelin' Bob Dylan	May 27, 1963
8.	Ballad of a Thin Man	Highway 61 Revisited	Aug. 30, 1965
9.	Heart of Mine	Shot of Love	Aug. 12, 1981
10.	All Along the Watchtower	John Wesley Harding	Dec. 27, 1967
11.	I'll Be Your Baby Tonight	John Wesley Harding	Dec. 27, 1967
12.	Forever Young	Planet Waves	Jan. 17, 1974
13.	Gamblin' Man (trad.)	–	–
14.	The Times They Are A-Changin'	The Times They Are A-Changin'	Feb. 10, 1964
15.	A Hard Rain's A-Gonna Fall	The Freewheelin' Bob Dylan	May 27, 1963
16.	Watered Down Love	Shot of Love	Aug. 12, 1981
17.	Masters of War	The Freewheelin' Bob Dylan	May 27, 1963
18.	Mr. Tambourine Man	Bringing It All Back Home	March 22, 1965
19.	Solid Rock	Saved	June 19, 1980
20.	Let It Be Me (Pierre Delanoé/Gilbert Bécoud/Mann Curtis)	Self Portrait	June 8, 1970
21.	Just Like a Woman	Blonde on Blonde	May 16, 1966
22.	When You Gonna Wake Up	Slow Train Coming	Aug. 20, 1979
23.	In the Garden	Saved	June 19, 1980
	Encores		
24.	Blowin' in the Wind	The Freewheelin' Bob Dylan	May 27, 1963
25.	It's Alright, Ma (I'm Only Bleeding)	Bringing It All Back Home	March 22, 1965
26.	It Ain't Me, Babe	Another Side of Bob Dylan	Aug. 8, 1964
27.	Knockin' on Heaven's Door	Pat Garrett & Billy The Kid	July 13, 1973

The Musicians

Bob Dylan (vocal, guitar & harmonica), Fred Tackett (guitar), Steve Ripley (guitar), Al Kooper (keyboards), Tim Drummond (bass), Jim Keltner (drums), Arthur Rosato (drums), Clydie King (backup vocals), Regina McCrary (backup vocals), Madelyn Quebec (backup vocals).

Notes

- 34th Bob Dylan concert in Canada; 15th Bob Dylan concert in Montreal.
- 11, 20, Bob Dylan & Clydie King (shared vocals).
- 12, 14, 26-27, Bob Dylan (harmonica).

- 13, Clydie King, Regina McCrary, Madelyn Quebec (vocals).
- 25-26, Bob Dylan solo (vocal & guitar).
- Canadian live debut of song 9.

Reviews

Bob Dylan's old pop fire is rapidly fadin'

By John Griffin, Gazette Pop Music Critic.

Who could have ever predicted that Bob Dylan's own words would return to haunt him so horribly.

Yet there they were coming from the lips of the prophet himself, echoing with painful irony off the Forum rafters last night.

"Your old world is rapidly fadin" Dylan sang. "And the first ones now will later be last, for the times they are a changin."

That song was a classic of the protest era of the early and mid-1960s, an era Dylan virtually defined.

Back then, he was full of righteous rage directed at a political system that could rationalize the spectre of nuclear war, condone racial injustice and close its eyes to social inequalities.

Test of Time

Dylan's songs not only defined a generation, they passed the test of time as well.

Time hasn't been quite as kind to Dylan himself who picked up his paycheque courtesy of the 14,000 fans who paid $12.50 each to hear him at the Forum.

Gone is the anger of youth – the middle-aged Dylan has decided to play it safe.

For the first time in a controversial career that has been, for better or worse, conducted strictly on Dylan's own terms, the singer has decided to heed the advice of his critics to tone down the message.

Gone also are the more obvious allusions to his born-again Christianity and there is no sign of the bitter wit and seething rage that characterized his work between *Talking New York Blues* in 1961 and the amphetamine-fed paranoia of *Blonde On Blonde* in 1966.

There is no trace of the pastoral visions and utopian hope that nourished him in upstate New York in the early 1970s.

No more humor or sarcasm and no sign of that endlessly questing spirit that helped Dylan, and his fans, survive two decades.

A lifeless clone appears to have replaced the Dylan of old.

Clad in black, dark shades and with wild hair cool-personified, the clone looks just like the familiar Dylan of yesterday.

There the resemblance ends.

The Dylan that would once have given the finger to anyone disagreeing with his choice of material, has capitulated to an audience that wants to hear him grind out a pasteurized medley of his greatest hits.

Dylan has played his old material before, in tours with the Band and with the Rolling Thunder Revue of 1975, to name but two.

But that material was always totally rearranged to suit his mood of the moment, a situation that may have driven his sidemen crazy, but made for exciting, dangerous music.

No Longer.

Although Dylan and his nine-piece band did work over many of his better known songs last night, few sparkled with the flame of spontaneous creation.

The sound, for starters, was turgid.

For reasons best known to himself, Dylan has decided to tour with two drummers.

That hard-driving combination worked wonders for Rolling Thunder, when Dylan had the guitar firepower of a hard-rock monster like Mick Ronson to scream through the upper registers.

This time, Dylan has taken on the fine, but absolutely mannered stylings of Fred Tackett and Steve Ripley, two guitarists who would be better suited to the controlled rock of a band like Dire Straits.

When coupled with the booming, oft-distorted bass of Tim Drummond, the effect was about as exciting as watching a polluted river flow.

Still, Dylan has carried shows on the strength of his stage presence alone, and he could well have pulled this one off, had he so desired.

But few songs seemed to engage him last night.

Wistful memory

He treated his anthem – *Like A Rolling Stone* – as a kind of wistful musical memory and he sloughed off all the fear and loathing that lies at the heart of the terrifying anti-nuclear song *Hard Rain*.

The love song *I Want You* was given a spritely countrified beat that destroyed its original intent.

Only *Masters of War* captured the Dylan imagination and its relentless force was a high point of an otherwise exceedingly depressing evening.

The Times They Are A-Changin' indeed – even Bob Dylan has been affected.

The Montreal Gazette. Sat., Oct. 31, 1981.

Le retour de Dylan: un show plutôt terne

par Denis Lavoie.

Le producteur de spectacles Donald K. Donald avait bien pris soin, pour annoncer le spectacle de Bob Dylan au Forum, vendredi soir, de preciser que la grande idole américaine du folk rock nous revenait cette fois avec ses bons vieux «hits»: «Like a Rolling Stone» et «Girl from the North Country».

Cette fois, on s'attendait donc a retrouver le Dylan de sa meilleure epoque, celle des années '60, ce Dylan qui a marqué toute une génération par sa musique et l'intensité de ses chansons, qui en ont fait l'idole de la chanson engagée (contre la guerre et la pauvreté) et l'inspiration de toute une génération de rockers.

Mais Dylan est un original, un être bien à part et changeant, un artiste fort contesté et instable. Aussi, s'il a su conserver un très large et très fidele public, comme on a pu le constater vendredi soir, Dylan n'a plus autant de succes et ses derniers disques se vendent moins biens.

Sa fournée de l'an dernier en avait par ailleurs déçu plusieurs, car il avait décidé de ne chanter que sa nouvelle foi et de présenter un show «gospel», quoi. Juif américaine ne Bobby Zimmerman s'est en effet converti au christianisme il y a quelques années. On en a beaucoup parlé partout, et on en parle encore.

L'artiste a toute de même voulu contenter ses fans cette fois-ci en présentant ses plus populaires chansons, «I Want You, Just Like a woman», et, bien sûr, «Like a Rolling Stone» aux publics des 24 villes nord-américaines qu'il doit visiter du 17 octobre au 22 novembre (Milwaukee, Montréal, Toronto, Philadelphie, Boston, etc.).

Si Dylan nous offre ses meilleures chansons, son spectacle ne semble pas pour autant des meilleurs. C'est comme si le coeur n'y était pas. C'est froid. Le son n'est pas propulsé pour nous briser les tympans, comme c'est l'habitude lors des shows rock du forum, et l'artiste parle peu et manifeste peu d'entrain.

Le public, pour sa part, heureux de retrouver son idole, a surtout applaudi les titres les mieux connus et s'est soulevé au retour de la vedette qu'on réclamait à nouveau sur scène. Malheureusement, à la différence de ses fans, Dylan manquait d'enthousiasme pour faire son travail d'artiste.

Le spectacle a commence en retard (les billets ne se sont pas envoles rapidement et les revendeurs offraient de bonnes places pour $20, le prix officiel étant de $12.50) sans première partie et sans musique avant le show.

Sobre, la scène n'avait rien de spectaculaire. Dylan n'est d'ailleurs pas du genre démonstratif. L'intensité d'un spectacle de Bruce Springsteen ou du nouveau King Crimson (qu'on a pu voir sur la scène du Club Montréal il y a une semaine) est bien plus remarquable qu'un spectacle plutôt terne d'un Dylan absent ou divisé entre ce qu'il fut et ce qu'il est devenu.

Il n'en demeure pas moins que Dylan est Dylan et que sa musique et ses chansons, même presentées sans l'émotion qui leur a donne naissance, sont des perles qu'il fait toujours plaisir de réentendre.

La Presse. Mon., Nov., 2, 1981. Reprinted with permission of La Presse.

Une soirée nostalgique avec un Dylan immuable

par Nathalie Petrowski.

Lorsque les lumières blafardes du Forum se sont éteintes et que Bob Dylan tel un frêle fantôme surgi de la mémoire collective d'une certaine génération, est arrivé sur scène vendredi soir, je me suis dit qu'il ne se rendrait pas jusqu'au bout de la soirée ni jusqu'à la fin du spectacle. C'était sous-estimer la force intransigeante du personnage. Deux heures plus tard, je devais comprendre que cela fait maintenant 20 ans que Dylan menace de disparaître et 20 ans qu'il se débat pour rester au sommet de l'échelle. L'homme est aussi immuable que les chansons.

Ouvrant la soirée avec *Serve somebody*, le maître des masques, de mystères et des déguisements, vêtu de noir et portant ses anciennes lunettes fumées de poète de la bohème, a plongé immédiatement dans l'atmosphère fraternelle de cette réunion des élèves de la classe de 63. Pas de préambule, pas de première partie, Dylan du debut jusqu'à la fin. Interprétant quelques-uns de ses plus récents succès, il a consacré une grande partie de la soirée à ses classiques au cours d'un long voyage musical et biographique.

La nostalgie n'est plus ce qu'elle était. Après avoir déclaré qu'il ne chanterait plus jamais les chansons du passé, Dylan fait précisement le contraire. Tout le répértoire y passe depuis *Like a Rolling Stone, Mr. Tambourine Man, Forever young, Mister Jones, Blowin in the wind, All along the watchtower.* Combien d'autres encore. Les retouches rythmiques, le maquillage musical ont cependant rendu les chansons méconnaissables.

Rien de surprenant. Ceux qui l'on vu à maintes reprises affirment que Dylan n'interprète jamais une chanson de la même manière, qu'à chaque nouvelle tournée, il s'arrange pour modifier les mélodies et ne jamais s'enuyer avec des airs qu'il a chantés mille fois.

Mince silhouette squelettique qui se découpe sur la vaste scène tel un survivant sur les ruines du passé, Dylan chante mieux que jamais. Dans sa nouvelle ferveur chrétienne, sa nasalité exacerbée a retrouvé l'urgence cinglante des premiers temps. La musique hantée par la colère percutante de deux batteurs, par les éclats des guitares militantes et les voix célestes des choristes noires, ne perd pas son intérêt de la soirée.

Caché derrière ses lunettes, instable sur ses petities jambes trop maigres, il porte sa guitare blanche comme une armure contre les affres du temps et de la vieillesse. Malgré ses 40 ans, son énergie est vive et sa passion aussi intense qu'avant. Il parle pas ou peu entre les chansons. Le dos tourné à la foule amoureuse, il jette des regards obliques aux musiciens ou accorde ses nombreuses guitares. De temps à autre, il lance des réflexions teintées d'ironie comme «Vous devez tous être des Américains», ou encore, «J'espère que je chante dans la bonne clé!»

Vivement critiqué par les nombreux détracteurs qui n'acceptent pas son nouveau dogmatisme chrétien, Dylan a choisi cette fois de contourner le problème. Ses anciennes chansons sont maintenant autant de preuves à l'appui qui expliquent l'historique de sa récente conversion. Dylan a en fait toujours été préoccupé de façon inconsciente ou voilée par Dieu et les mystères de la vie. De la même façon, il a toujours cherché à provoquer, quitte à devenir l'artisan de sa propre persécution. Aujourd'hui il semble avoir atteint une sorte de réconciliation intérieure. Il n'a plus besoin d'aménager la scène à l'image d'un autel sacré et peut maintenant revenir dans les grandes arénas du rock contemporain. La musique et la religion sont complètement intégrées. Les temps ne changent pas autant qu'on le pense.

Arrivé au bout du chemin, Dylan est encore là, entouré de ses chansons comme d'immenses monuments érigés à ce que nous avons tous été en même temps que lui. Plus que jamais, on le sent prêt à communiquer avec la foule dont il s'est tant de fois sauvé. Il reste un point de repère dans le temps. Ceux qui aujourd'hui le renient après l'avoir adulé ont sans doute peur du temps qui passe trop vite peur de ce bref sentiment de fraternité qui peut encore se vivre un vendredi soir des années 80.

Saturday, October 31, 1981 --- Kitchener Memorial Auditorium Kitchener, ON

Set List

	Song	From The Album	Released
1.	Gotta Serve Somebody	Slow Train Coming	Aug. 20, 1979
2.	I Believe in You	Slow Train Coming	Aug. 20, 1979
3.	Like a Rolling Stone	Highway 61 Revisited	Aug. 30, 1965
4.	I Want You	Blonde on Blonde	May 16, 1966
5.	Man Gave Names to All the Animals	Slow Train Coming	Aug. 20, 1979
6.	Maggie's Farm	Bringing It All Back Home	March 22, 1965
7.	Girl of the North Country	The Freewheelin' Bob Dylan	May 27, 1963
8.	Ballad of a Thin Man	Highway 61 Revisited	Aug. 30, 1965
9.	Heart of Mine	Shot of Love	Aug. 12, 1981
10.	All Along the Watchtower	John Wesley Harding	Dec. 27, 1967
11.	It's All in the Game (Carl Sigman/Charles Gates Dawes)	–	–
12.	Forever Young	Planet Waves	Jan. 17, 1974
13.	Gamblin' Man (trad.)	–	–
14.	The Times They Are A-Changin'	The Times They Are A-Changin'	Feb. 10, 1964
15.	A Hard Rain's A-Gonna Fall	The Freewheelin' Bob Dylan	May 27, 1963
16.	Masters of War	The Freewheelin' Bob Dylan	May 27, 1963
17.	Watered Down Love	Shot of Love	Aug. 12, 1981
18.	Dead Man, Dead Man	Shot of Love	Aug. 12, 1981
19.	Just Like a Woman	Blonde on Blonde	May 16, 1966
20.	Solid Rock	Saved	June 19, 1980
21.	Mr. Tambourine Man	Bringing It All Back Home	March 22, 1965
22.	When You Gonna Wake Up	Slow Train Coming	Aug. 20, 1979
23.	In the Garden	Saved	June 19, 1980
	Encores		
24.	Blowin' in the Wind	The Freewheelin' Bob Dylan	May 27, 1963
25.	Don't Think Twice, It's All Right	The Freewheelin' Bob Dylan	May 27, 1963
26.	It's Alright, Ma (I'm Only Bleeding)	Bringing It All Back Home	March 22, 1965
27.	Are You Ready?	Saved	June 19, 1980
28.	Knockin' on Heaven's Door	Pat Garrett & Billy The Kid	July 13, 1973

The Musicians

Bob Dylan (vocal, guitar & harmonica), Fred Tackett (guitar), Steve Ripley (guitar), Al Kooper (keyboards), Tim Drummond (bass), Jim Keltner (drums), Arthur Rosato (drums), Clydie King (backup vocals), Regina McCrary (backup vocals), Madelyn Quebec (backup vocals).

Notes

- 35th Bob Dylan concert in Canada; Debut Bob Dylan concert in Kitchener.
- 11, Bob Dylan & Clydie King (shared vocals).
- 12, 14, 25, 28, Bob Dylan (harmonica).
- 13, Clydie King, Regina McCrary, Madelyn Quebec (vocals).
- 25-26, Bob Dylan solo (vocal & guitar).
- Canadian live debut of song 11.
- Song 11 has been performed only once in Canada.

Review

Listless Dylan in a sad show

Aud concert a lethargic flop with star stuck in neutral

By John Kiely, Record Staff Writer.

Bob Dylan's performance Saturday night at Kitchener Auditorium was plagued by sound problems that were gruesome by even the Aud's bargain-basement standards, but the failure of Saturday's concert cannot be placed conveniently on technical foulups.

Dylan, appearing listless, apathetic, bored and lazy, gave a performance that never got out of neutral except when it appeared to be a parody of itself. When the best song of the evening is a reprise of Jimmy Edwards' late '50s hit It's All In The Game, you pretty well know the game is over.

Dressed like Joey Ramone and playing to a house not quite full, Dylan fronted a large group for these lean times with two drummers, two guitars, bass, one and sometimes two keyboards and three backup singers providing vocal and rhythmic support.

For all the musicians on stage, the band, taking its cue from Dylan, was sloppy. If not exactly ragged, it never converged on anything approaching power or even interest.

The old songs, re-arranged to a non-lyrical monotony, were there, although when given the sappy approach of Blowin' in the Wind, it was easy to wish they weren't. Still, an entire concert of Dylan's new Christian material would be enough to drive one into the arms of any devil who happened along.

The man whose words were once studied in university poetry classes has now reached a level where profundity is found at the level of tracts. "For some people, it's Halloween every day," he said with a pregnant pause as if expecting an Amen from the audience. "They wear a mask every day."

Being preached to isn't so bad, but being bored to death is. If this new gospel music can't find an audience in the Gateway to the Ontario Bible Belt, where can it find an audience?

Only twice did Dylan find a glimmer of interest in his material. There was promise in a new arrangement of Mr. Jones and a wistfulness in Forever Young, but both were lost quickly when Dylan slipped into his preacher pose.

A reggae version of In The Beginning was dreadful and seemed likely to go on until the end. Dylan started the show with Sanctified, but whatever energy he had was used by the end of the song.

Dylan has never been excited about public performance, but this tour, unlike the 1974 Rolling Thunder when Dylan was still trying to re-capture the '60s, or his proselytizing 1979 tour, seems to have no point at all except contractual obligations.

Clydie King, Madelyn Quebec and Regina McCrary, Dylan's back-up singers, briefly brought some hand-clapping to the show with a soulful version of Gamblin' Man, but that was the only time the party mood which greeted the show was ever recaptured.

There were some devoted Dylan fans, either nostalgia freaks or fellow born-agains, who rushed to the stage after a totally listless final number, but they were in a minority. After an unforgiveably long time, Dylan returned for an encore of Blowin' in the Wind, but, by then, many had sought the exits. There seemed to be an equal number at the stage as there were leaving, but by far the majority simply sat and watched the stage.

It is hard to believe that a legend can be left irrelevant. Like an aging and crippled athlete, Dylan may not be washed up, but he will no longer dominate and win.

His days are over, and the man won't even let us say goodbye.

The Kitchener-Waterloo Record. Mon., Nov. 2, 1981. Reprinted with permission of The Kitchener-Waterloo Record.

Monday, November 2, 1981 --- Ottawa Civic Centre
Ottawa, ON

Set List

	Song	From The Album	Released
1.	Saved (Bob Dylan/Tim Drummond)	Saved	June 19, 1980
2.	I Believe in You	Slow Train Coming	Aug. 20, 1979
3.	Like a Rolling Stone	Highway 61 Revisited	Aug. 30, 1965
4.	I Want You	Blonde on Blonde	May 16, 1966
5.	Man Gave Names to All the Animals	Slow Train Coming	Aug. 20, 1979
6.	Maggie's Farm	Bringing It All Back Home	March 22, 1965
7.	Girl of the North Country	The Freewheelin' Bob Dylan	May 27, 1963
8.	Ballad of a Thin Man	Highway 61 Revisited	Aug. 30, 1965
9.	Heart of Mine	Shot of Love	Aug. 12, 1981
10.	All Along the Watchtower	John Wesley Harding	Dec. 27, 1967
11.	I'll Be Your Baby Tonight	John Wesley Harding	Dec. 27, 1967
12.	Forever Young	Planet Waves	Jan. 17, 1974
13.	Gamblin' Man (trad.)	–	–

14.	The Times They Are A-Changin'	The Times They Are A-Changin'	Feb. 10, 1964
15.	A Hard Rain's A-Gonna Fall	The Freewheelin' Bob Dylan	May 27, 1963
16.	Masters of War	The Freewheelin' Bob Dylan	May 27, 1963
17.	Watered Down Love	Shot of Love	Aug. 12, 1981
18.	Mr. Tambourine Man	Bringing It All Back Home	March 22, 1965
19.	Solid Rock	Saved	June 19, 1980
20.	Just Like a Woman	Blonde on Blonde	May 16, 1966
21.	When You Gonna Wake Up	Slow Train Coming	Aug. 20, 1979
22.	In the Garden	Saved	June 19, 1980
	Encores		
23.	Blowin' in the Wind	The Freewheelin' Bob Dylan	May 27, 1963
25.	It's Alright, Ma (I'm Only Bleeding)	Bringing It All Back Home	March 22, 1965
25.	Jesus Is the One	Unreleased	
26.	Knockin' on Heaven's Door	Pat Garrett & Billy The Kid	July 13, 1973

The Musicians

Bob Dylan (vocal, guitar & harmonica), Fred Tackett (guitar), Steve Ripley (guitar), Al Kooper (keyboards), Tim Drummond (bass), Jim Keltner (drums), Arthur Rosato (drums), Clydie King (backup vocals), Regina McCrary (backup vocals), Madelyn Quebec (backup vocals).

Notes

- 36th Bob Dylan concert in Canada; 2nd Bob Dylan concert in Ottawa.
- 11, Bob Dylan & Clydie King (shared vocals).
- 12, 14, 26, Bob Dylan (harmonica).
- 13, Clydie King, Regina McCrary, Madelyn Quebec (vocals).
- 24-25, Bob Dylan solo (vocal & guitar).
- Canadian live debut of song 25.
- Song 25 has been performed only once in Canada.

Reviews

Bob Dylan still doing it his way

By Bill Provick, Citizen Staff Writer.

Bob Dylan didn't get this far by standing still.

One of the most legendary figures in music since the early '60s – as much through social significance as record sales – Dylan has refused to repeat himself. Some words do stay the same but the times – and the tunes – continue to change.

So does Dylan.

Monday night at the Civic Centre, Dylan made his first appearance in Ottawa in 15 years. The show was a far cry from his 1966 performance but it had a number of things in common – it was different, it was Dylan and it was delightful.

For the 9,000 plus Dylan fans on hand, it was also fascinating, unsettling, entertaining, exhilarating and for assorted reasons, a somewhat rare experience.

Dylan's audience ranged in age from teens to mid 30s. In outlook, the crowd included young rockers, the newly religious and a few of the old '60s rebels.

Some would have preferred the Dylan of 15 years ago but Dylan, as always, was himself.

When he became a born-again Christian a few years back, many were upset when he discarded the old songs to concentrate on his own brand of gospel rock.

Dylan's back to doing the old songs, but on his terms and he blended them in well with his newer, more religious material.

Not everyone liked what they heard better than the originals but Dylan wasn't aiming for the easy applause for past glories. This was no mere 'greatest hits' package.

Dylan's a bit like the Rolling Stones in that he's been around so long and done so much, it's an event just to see him in the flesh. But Dylan doesn't play it as safe as the Stones. He doesn't stick to the old formats that become mere echoes of more exciting times.

He changes things – to the point where old favorites were not readily identifiable – but he gets you listening anew.

The applause may not always have been as exuberant as that awarded other legendary figures but it was better for being somewhat grudging. Dylan earned it rather than merely accepted it, and though I wouldn't always want to hear *I Want You* sound like it was being done by a country bar band, Dylan and his band made it at least an interesting experiment.

For many of the old songs, Dylan kept the framework and the lyrics, but gave the songs a facelift. *Like A Rolling Stone, Ballad of a Thin Man* and *All Along The Watchtower* retained some of their original power but took on new feeling – if not meaning – in the hands of Dylan the religious rocker rather than Dylan the rocking prophet.

Dylan's occasional pop vocals – *The Times They Are A Changin', Mr. Tambourine Man, Just Like a Woman* – were in sharp contrast to his more traditional hoarse growl but just when one might start to feel this bit of slickness might be undermining some old favorite tune, something in Dylan's voice, with the music swelling up behind, would create an eerie edge to the song – like it was a joke but it really wasn't.

It wasn't just that Dylan would take a classic like *Maggie's Farm* and turn it into a heavy metal number, it was that he and his band would carry it off so well.

Despite an uneven start, the concert was so good that even religious numbers like *Heart of Mine* went over quite well – especially with the dynamic assistance of Dylan's back-up singers Clydie King, Regina McCrary and Madelyn Quebec.

Dylan left the stage after an hour and 40 minutes but the crowd stood and applauded until he returned for a 20-minute encore.

After an energetic, gospel version of *Blowin' In The Wind*, Dylan returned to acoustic guitar and harmonica for a fairly straight solo version of *It's Alright Ma (I'm Only Bleeding)*. He rode the subsequent rhythmic handclapping all through a quick gospel tune and then closed out with *Knocking On Heaven' s Door*.

The Ottawa Citizen. Tues., Nov. 3, 1981. Reprinted with permission of The Ottawa Citizen.

La légende se perpétue

9,000 personnes venues entendre Bob Dylan

par Marthe Lemery.

Les gens ne vont pas voir un spectacle, bon ou mauvais, de Bob Dylan.

Ils vont voir Bob Dylan. Point.

Hier soir, ils étaient plus de 9,000 depuis les contestataires des années 60 maintenant bien installés dans la vie comme dans leur job de petits boss, jusqu'aux jeunes collégiens en bas de laine et chapeaux melons, qui avaient encore la couche aux fesses quand Dylan déversait son fiel existentiel dans Greenwich Village, et faisant peur aux honnêtes gens, en passent par les «décrochés» des années 70 qui se sont depuis raccrochés à l'agriculture biologique ou aux gurus du spiritisme. 9,000 à s'entasser pêle-mêle dans la vaste arène du Centre municipal, à se toucher mutuellement les coudes dans une atmosphère de grand-messe. 9,000 à être venus entendre le prophète, prêcher du haut de sa maigreur excessive le Peace and Love des années 80.

C'est la deuxième fois que Robert Zimmerman, depuis qu'il est Bob Dylan, rendait visite à ses fans d'Ottawa. Pour se faire pardonner d'avoir été à ce point infidèle, ou parce qu'il savait qu'il irait ainsi chercher son quota de «bravos», il n'a pas ménagé ses vieilles chansons dans son tour de chant, les Mr. Tambourine Man, Just Like a Woman, Like a Rolling Stone, Blowin in the Wind ou Ballad of a Thin Man qui, même éloignées de leurs rythmes initiaux, faisaient rouler des vagues d'applaudissements parmi les gradins.

Non, un spectacle de Dylan n'est ni bon ni mauvais. Il est la représentation vibrante d'une légende qui, à l'ocassion, daigne venir nourrir son public et alimenter son mythe. Par moments, il semble se désintéresser complétement de cette grande scène tendue de noir, se foutre éperdument des milliers de visages tendus vers lui pour y boire jusqu'aux moindres goutes de paroles, torturées, déformées par l'accent nasillard. Tandis qu'à d'autres tantôts, son intensité, sa gravité, sa concentration sont tels qu'ils illuminent sa voix, transfigurent sa frêle personne jusqu'à la rendre électrisante.

Paradoxalement, c'est lorsqu'il interprète ses plus récentes chansons, celles que lui ont inspirées sa conversion au christianisme, que la légende Dylan trouve une justification, dans des chansons oú le souci de provoquer tant par la voix que par une musique étriquée disparaît alors au profit d'une musique plus inventive, d'une voix assagie. Appuyé par trois excellentes choristes, Regina McCrary, Madelyn Quebec et Clydie King, Dylan déplace alors ce gospel nouveau genre avec puissance et conviction, même s'il est évident que le public, lui, n'embarque pas toujours dans cette croisade qui devrait mener droit au ciel.

Qu'on lui reproche aujourd'hui de trop lire la Bible et de ne plus tapper sur la tête du pouvoir n'a, dans le fond, que peu de pertinence. C'est l'angoisse qui vit tapie quelque part en lui et qui ronge son corps jusqu'à le rendre émouvant dans sa fragilité. C'est ce courage qui le force à tout remettre en question, constamment, qui lui assurera toujours plusieurs longueurs d'avance sur une humanité bien trop occupée à idolâtrer ses veaux d'or pour chercher elle-même les bonnes réponses.

LeDroit. Tues., Nov. 3, 1981. Reprinted with permission of LeDroit.

1986

Introduction

The 1986 True Confessions Tour in which Bob Dylan's backing band was Tom Petty & the Heartbreakers played only one concert in Canada. It was the first Canadian concert for Dylan since 1981.

The single date would mark Bob Dylan's 37th concert in Canada.

The Date

The show was Dylan's 4th concert in Vancouver.

Vancouver, BC	Fri., Aug 1, 1986

The Musicians

Bob Dylan (vocal, guitar & harmonica).

Tom Petty & the Heartbreakers — Tom Petty (guitar, bass, & shared vocals), Mike Campbell (guitar), Benmont Tench (keyboards), Howie Epstein (bass & electric slide guitar), Stan Lynch (drums).

The Queens of Rhythm — Carolyn Dennis (backup vocals), Queen Esther Marrow (backup vocals), Madelyn Quebec (backup vocals), Louise Bethune (backup vocals).

The Songs

Bob Dylan performed a total of 25 songs (19 were from albums, one was an unreleased song and 5 were cover and/or traditional songs).

Fourteen songs made their Canadian live debut.

Bye Bye Johnny	Band of the Hand (It's Hell Time Man!)
Clean-Cut Kid	When the Night Comes Falling from the Sky
Emotionally Yours	Lonesome Town
Shot of Love	Seeing the Real You at Last
That Lucky Old Sun	Across the Borderline
One Too Many Mornings	I and I
I Forgot More Than You'll Ever Know	Shake a Hand

Eleven songs have been played only once in Canada.

Bye Bye Johnny	Band of the Hand (It's Hell Time Man!)
Clean-Cut Kid	When the Night Comes Falling from the Sky
Emotionally Yours	Lonesome Town
Shot of Love	Across the Borderline
That Lucky Old Sun	Shake a Hand
I Forgot More Than You'll Ever Know	–

Bob Dylan performed songs from 13 different albums.

Album	Released	# of Songs Performed by Album
The Freewheelin' Bob Dylan	May, 27, 1963	3
The Times They Are A-Changin'	Feb., 10, 1964	1
Another Side of Bob Dylan	Aug. 8, 1964	1
Highway 61 Revisited	Aug. 30, 1965	2
Blonde on Blonde	May 16, 1966	1
John Wesley Harding	Dec. 27, 1967	1
Self Portrait	June 8, 1970	1
Pat Garrett and Billy The Kid	July 13, 1973	1
Slow Train Coming	Aug. 20, 1979	1
Saved	June 19, 1980	1
Shot of Love	Aug. 12, 1981	1
Infidels	Oct. 27, 1983	1
Empire Burlesque	May, 30, 1985	4

The Venue

It was Bob Dylan's debut concert at BC Place in Vancouver.

Friday, August 1, 1986 --- BC Place Vancouver, BC

Set List

	Song	From The Album	Released
1.	Bye Bye Johnny (Chuck Berry)	–	–
2.	All Along the Watchtower	John Wesley Harding	Dec. 27, 1967
3.	Clean-Cut Kid	Empire Burlesque	May 30, 1985
4.	Emotionally Yours	Empire Burlesque	May 30, 1985
5.	Shot of Love	Shot of Love	Aug. 12, 1981
6.	That Lucky Old Sun (Haven Gillespie/Beasley Smith)	–	–
7.	Masters of War	The Freewheelin' Bob Dylan	May 27, 1963
8.	To Ramona	Another Side of Bob Dylan	Aug. 8, 1964
9.	One Too Many Mornings	The Times They Are A-Changin'	Feb. 10, 1964
10.	A Hard Rain's A-Gonna Fall	The Freewheelin' Bob Dylan	May 27, 1963
11.	I Forgot More Than You'll Ever Know (Cecil A. Null)	Self Portrait	June 8, 1970
12.	Band of the Hand (It's Hell Time Man!)	Unreleased	–
13.	When the Night Comes Falling from the Sky	Empire Burlesque	May 30, 1985
14.	Lonesome Town (Baker Knight)	–	–
15.	Ballad of a Thin Man	Highway 61 Revisited	Aug. 30, 1965
16.	Rainy Day Women #12 & 35	Blonde on Blonde	May 16, 1966
17.	Gotta Serve Somebody	Slow Train Coming	Aug. 20, 1979
18.	Seeing the Real You at Last	Empire Burlesque	May 30, 1985
19.	Across the Borderline (Ry Cooder/John Hiatt & Jim Dickinson)	–	–
20.	I and I	Infidels	Oct. 27, 1983
21.	Like a Rolling Stone	Highway 61 Revisited	Aug. 30, 1965
22.	In the Garden	Saved	June 19, 1980
	Encores		
23.	Blowin' in the Wind	The Freewheelin' Bob Dylan	May 27, 1963
24.	Shake a Hand (Joe Morris)	–	–
25.	Knockin' on Heaven's Door	Pat Garrett & Billy The Kid	July 13, 1973

The Musicians

Bob Dylan (vocal, guitar & harmonica).

Tom Petty and the Heartbreakers — Tom Petty (guitar, bass & shared vocals), Mike Campbell (guitar), Benmont Tench (keyboards), Howie Epstein (bass & electric slide guitar), Stan Lynch (drums).

The Queens of Rhythm — Carolyn Dennis (backup vocals), Queen Esther Marrow (backup vocals), Madelyn Quebec (backup vocals), Louise Bethune (backup vocals).

Notes

- 37th Bob Dylan concert in Canada; 4th Bob Dylan concert in Vancouver.
- 8-9, 25, Bob Dylan (harmonica).
- 8-10, Bob Dylan solo (vocal & guitar).
- 11, 23, 25, Bob Dylan and Tom Petty (shared vocals).
- 16, Howie Epstein (electric slide guitar), Tom Petty (bass).
- Canadian live debut of songs 1, 3, 4, 5, 6, 9, 11, 12, 13, 14, 18, 19, 20 & 24.
- Songs 1, 3, 4, 5, 6, 11, 12, 13, 14, 19 & 24 have been performed only once in Canada.
- Tom Petty and the Heartbreakers performed four of their own songs after song 7 (Straight Into Darkness, Think About Me, The Waiting & Breakdown). After song 15 they played another four songs (Even the Losers, Spike, Tonight Might Be My Night & Refugee).

Reviews

Dylan lives up to billing with a marathon show

By John Mackie.

HE'S STILL GOT that big bushy neo-Afro, still sings like he has a clothes-pin on his nose and, yes, still appears to have *it*. Bob Dylan's highly-touted appearance with Tom Petty and the Heartbreakers lived up to all its advance billing Friday night with a marathon (33 songs spaced out over nearly three hours) show filled with some of Dylan's most invigorating work in years.

The concert opened with Petty leading the band through a rollicking version of Chuck Berry's Bye Bye Johnny, then Dylan took over for a gospel-tinged reading of All Along the Watchtower. From then on, he alternated between radical reworkings of old standards (Knockin' on Heaven's Door, Ballad of a Thin Man) to charged-up renditions of his latter-day stuff, a lot of it in the religious vein. Dylan also did a three-song solo set and the Heartbreakers took over the stage for two mini-sets (four songs each) themselves, but almost all the evening's highlight's came when they appeared together.

Dylan and the Heartbreakers are a fine match. With guitarist Mike Campbell and keyboardist Benmont Tench leading the way, the Heartbreakers gave Dylan superb support, keeping the songs simple, with a kick. It may or may not have been their doing but one of the real pluses of the concert was that Dylan's arrangements were infinitely more direct than the last time he played Vancouver in 1978. With Petty and company he may have strayed from the original versions of his classics but at least you could still figure out what songs he was playing this time.

Killers? Well, at the end of his three-song solo set he did away with the lilting melody of A Hard Rain's A-Gonna Fall and delivered it with classic Bob Dylan punctuation and phrasing (as in "ah saw a *hah* way of *di* monds with *no* body on it").

Then there was the loping mid-tempo treatment of Like a Rolling Stone, with keyboardist Tench chipping in some gorgeous piano and the gliding encore of Blowin' in the Wind, with Tench again providing the instrumental beauty, this time on organ. Simply amazing, the stuff of which legends are made. There are gonna be some great bootlegs coming out of this tour, let me tell ya.

It definitely was an event as much as a concert. Security kept hurling water over the crowd crushed in front of the stage to help them cool out while farther away a giant party was in progress, a party with lots of beer, doobers and hooting. It was one of the oddest assortment of fans at a rock gig ever, ranging from studious, reserved Dylan worshippers (mainly in the seats) to some real party animals punching the air down on the floor. It's hard to say the split between Petty and Dylan fans but, when the Heartbreakers finished up Refugee, it got the biggest cheer of the night – until Dylan followed it with Rainy Day Women #12 & 35, which got a whole mess of people screaming along the "everybody must get stoned!" chorus.

All that said, it was rather ridiculous to see Bob Dylan in a venue like B.C. Place Stadium. For most of the 25,000 fans, he was a little speck only visible through binoculars, and for some reason most of the house lights were kept on throughout the concert, ruining the ambience. Plus this was Bob Dylan, not the Rolling Stones or Prince; you don't come to Dylan's concerts to just see and listen to him, you come to try to *understand* him, to figure out what the hell he's saying and how's he's saying it. The sound may have been okay in most spots – on the side, it most definitely wasn't – but there just isn't any intimacy and, without intimacy, it just isn't Bob Dylan.

The Vancouver Sun. Sat., Aug. 2, 1986.

Dylan lost in Place

By Tom Harrison, Music Critic.

The tour is called True Confessions but there is little to hear of Bob Dylan and Tom Petty within the expanse of B.C. Place.

This is especially true of Dylan, who is distant anyway and whose teaming with Petty's Heartbreakers on this Friday night produces three hours of random impressions.

Bye Bye Johnny is an appropriate Chuck Berry song to begin this made-in-Hollywood tour; All Along The Watchtower establishes the Dylan image from a block away, even with the muffled sound that sends unhappy fans to the floor for their only chance to be immersed in the supple, wiry music Dylan and Petty are making.

That Lucky Old Sun is Bob's first surprise; a mostly solo rendition of The Waiting is Petty's means of keeping pace; the avalanche of images of A Hard Rain's Gonna Fall is reduced to a snow drift under the dome; I Forgot More Than You'll Ever Know is a glimpse of the potential of the Dylan-Petty match;

When The Night Comes Falling From The Sky is the first number in which everything clicks.

Ballad Of A Thin Man wields its power, but is upstaged by Refugee, the reaction to which suggesting that Petty may be a twerp compared to Dylan, but he is carrying the show.

The grace of Just Across That Borderline doesn't count for much in a football stadium and may be why Petty's straight-up rock is more effective.

Sadly, apart from the triumph of Like A Rolling Stone, nothing has happened to clarify the reason for this tour and illuminate it.

In the song Brownsville Girl from his new Knocked Out Loaded LP, Dylan sings, "if there's an original thought out there, I could use it right now."

True Confessions doesn't admit even that much.

The Vancouver Province. Sun., Aug. 3, 1986.

1988

Introduction

The Never-Ending Tour began in 1988. There were eight concerts in Canada.

These shows would mark Bob Dylan's 38th, 39th, 40th, 41st, 42nd, 43rd, 44th and 45th concert in Canada.

The Dates

Montreal, QC	Fri., July 8, 1988
Ottawa, ON	Sat., July 9, 1988
Hamilton, ON	Mon., July 11, 1988
Vancouver, BC	Sun., Aug. 21, 1988
Calgary, AB	Tues., Aug. 23, 1988
Edmonton, AB	Wed., Aug. 24, 1988
Winnipeg, MB	Fri., Aug. 26, 1988
Toronto, ON	Mon., Aug. 29, 1988

The shows would be Dylan's 16th concert in Montreal, 3rd concert in Ottawa, debut concert in Hamilton, 5th concert in Vancouver, debut concert in Calgary, debut concert in Edmonton, debut concert in Winnipeg and 15th concert in Toronto.

The Musicians

Bob Dylan (vocal & guitar).

G. E. Smith (guitar, electric slide guitar & backup vocals), Kenny Aaronson (bass), Christopher Parker (drums).

The Songs

Bob Dylan performed a total of 123 songs. Of those, 43 were different songs (38 were from albums and 5 were cover and/or traditional songs).

Fifteen songs made their Canadian live debut.

Subterranean Homesick Blues	Absolutely Sweet Marie
Stuck Inside of Mobile with the Memphis Blues Again	Silvio
Hallelujah	I'll Remember You
Highway 61 Revisited	Barbara Allen
Lakes of Pontchartrain	Eileen Aroon
Boots of Spanish Leather	You're a Big Girl Now
Driftin' Too Far from Shore	She's About a Mover
Joey	–

Five songs have been played only once in Canada.

Hallelujah	Eileen Aroon
Lakes of Pontchartrain	She's About a Mover
Joey	–

One song made its worldwide live debut.

She's About a Mover	–

Bob Dylan performed songs from 17 different albums.

Album	Released	# of Songs Performed by Album
The Freewheelin' Bob Dylan	May, 27, 1963	4
The Times They Are A-Changin'	Feb., 10, 1964	4
Another Side of Bob Dylan	Aug. 8, 1964	2
Bringing It All Back Home	March 22, 1965	6
Highway 61 Revisited	Aug. 30, 1965	4
Blonde on Blonde	May 16, 1966	3
John Wesley Harding	Dec. 27, 1967	2
Bob Dylan's Greatest Hits, Vol. 2	Nov. 17, 1971	1
Pat Garrett and Billy The Kid	July 13, 1973	1
Blood on the Tracks	Jan. 20, 1975	4
Desire	Jan. 5, 1976	1
Slow Train Coming	Aug. 20, 1979	1
Saved	June 19, 1980	1
Empire Burlesque	May, 30, 1985	1

Knocked Out Loaded	July 14, 1986	1
Down in the Groove	May 19, 1988	1
The Bootleg Series Volumes 1-3	Match 26, 1991	1

Opening Acts

The Alarm was the opening act in Montreal, Ottawa, and Hamilton. Tracy Chapman was the opening act in Vancouver, Calgary, and Edmonton. Timbuk 3 was the opening act in Winnipeg and Toronto.

Special Guests

Tracy Chapman joined Dylan on stage to sing Knockin on Heaven's Door at all three shows that she opened. Doug Sahm of the Sir Douglas Quintet joined Dylan on stage for one song in Edmonton. They played Sahm's classic She's About Mover.

The Venues

It was Bob Dylan's 6th time playing at the Montreal Forum, 2nd time playing at the Ottawa Civic Centre, debut concert at Copps Coliseum in Hamilton, debut concert at the Pacific Coliseum in Vancouver, debut concert at the Saddledome in Calgary, debut concert at the Northlands Coliseum in Edmonton, debut concert at the Winnipeg Arena and debut concert at the CNE Grandstand in Toronto.

Friday, July 8, 1988 --- Montreal Forum
Montreal, QC

Set List

	Song	From The Album	Released
1.	Subterranean Homesick Blues	Bringing It All Back Home	March 22, 1965
2.	I Shall Be Released	Bob Dylan's Greatest Hits, Vol. 2	Nov. 17, 1971
3.	Stuck Inside of Mobile with the Memphis Blues Again	Blonde on Blonde	May 16, 1966
4.	Hallelujah (Leonard Cohen)	–	–
5.	Ballad of a Thin Man	Highway 61 Revisited	Aug. 30, 1965
6.	Highway 61 Revisited	Highway 61 Revisited	Aug. 30, 1965
7.	Lakes of Pontchartrain (trad.)	–	–
8.	A Hard Rain's A-Gonna Fall	The Freewheelin' Bob Dylan	May 27, 1963
9.	Boots of Spanish Leather	The Times They Are A-Changin'	Feb. 10, 1964
10.	Tangled Up in Blue	Blood on the Tracks	Jan. 20, 1975
11.	In the Garden	Saved	June 19, 1980
12.	Like a Rolling Stone	Highway 61 Revisited	Aug. 30, 1965
	Encores		
13.	It Ain't Me, Babe	Another Side of Bob Dylan	Aug. 8, 1964
14.	All Along the Watchtower	John Wesley Harding	Dec. 27, 1967

The Musicians

Bob Dylan (vocal & guitar), G. E. Smith (guitar, electric slide guitar & backup vocals), Kenny Aaronson (bass), Christopher Parker (drums).

Notes

- 38th Bob Dylan concert in Canada; 16th Bob Dylan concert in Montreal.
- 1, G. E. Smith (backup vocals).
- 6, G. E. Smith (electric slide guitar).
- 7-9, 13, Bob Dylan (vocal & guitar), G. E. Smith (guitar).
- Canadian live debut of songs 1, 3, 4, 6, 7 & 9.
- Songs 4 & 7 have been performed only once in Canada.
- The Alarm was the opening act.

Reviews

BOB DYLAN, C'EST PRESQUE ENCORE CE BON VIEUX DYLAN

25 and plus tard

par Martin Smith.

Il y a exactement vingt-cinq ans, aujourd'hui, un jeune artiste, nommé Robert Allen Zimmerman, voyait son premier disque embarquer dans les palmarès américaines.

Le titre était *The freewheelin' Bob Dylan*... une légende était née!

Hier soir, ce même Bob Dylan a joué au Forum devant environ 7,000 personnes. En 1974, il y avait 20,000 personnes pour le voir et l'entendre dans la même enceinte.

The times, they are a'changin?

Dieu

Au début des années 80, Dylan a rencontré Dieu et est devenu un *born again*. Ses deux derniers disques, *Knocked out loaded* et le récent *Down in the groove*, témoignent éloquemment de la place prépondérante que le Christ a prise dans la vie de Dylan.

La foule ne savait donc pas trop à quoi s'attendre de cette légende vivante: un show à la gloire de Dieu ou un retour dans le passé avec une interprétation de ses plus grands hits?

Au grand soulagement de tous, Dylan, accompagné de trois musiciens, a attaqué d'emblée avec *Subterranean homesick blues* et a enchaîné avec *I shall be released*.

Si la communication avec le public est totalement absente et si l'équipement est réduit au minimum, il n'en reste pas moins qu'il est impossible de ne pas se laisser emporter quand les premières notes de *Memphis Blues again* résonnent.

Contrecoeur

Dylan, à 47 ans, resemble à un de ces dinosaures qui sort de sa tanière une fois de temps en temps pour humer l'air environnant, pour examiner où en est rendue cette société qu'il condamnait déjà à vingt ans et qu'il refuse de suivre dans ses développements superficiels.

Il monté sur scène à contrecoeur, dirait-on, mais s'il est d'un froid glacial, il peut encore se laisser emporter par le véhicule artistique qu'il a choisi pour exprimer ses convictions, ses colères, ses peines, ses amours et ses déceptions.

Lorsqu'il a interprété *Highway 61* et, surtout, l'admirable *A hard rain's gonna fall*, accompagné uniquement par le guitariste G.E. Smith, la magie était totale.

Si son attitude a changé avec les ans, s'il trouve de plus en plus difficile de continuer à exister dans une industrie où la jeunesse et l'image sont deux conditions *sine qua non* de la popularité, Bob Dylan peut encore faire la barbe à n'importe quel jeunot avec un *Like a rolling stone* aussi transcendant que celui qu'il a interprété hier.

Bob Dylan a perdu des plumes mais il n'a pas à se présenter sur une scène avec un attirail de lasers et de gadgets technologiques pour faire vibrer une foule.

Les 7,000 croyants qui étaient présents, hier soir, le lui ont fait comprendre en lui accordant plusieurs ovations monstres.

Le Journal de Montréal. Sat., July 9, 1988. Reprinted with permission of Le Journal de Montréal.

Bob Dylan, comme un rendez-vous manqué

par Mario Roy.

Il faudra un jour écrire un livre sur cette sorte d'instinct suicidaire qui habite Dylan, sur sa tendance perverse à faire les mauvais choix, sur la manie masochiste qu'il cultive de réduire en pièces ce qu'il a, depuis un quart de siècle, si habilement bâti.

Bob Dylan était au Forum, vendredi soir, devant une foule qui n'atteignait pas les 7000 spectateurs.

Il est monté sur scène après The Alarm. Il n'y a pas grand chose à dire de ce groupe, sinon que leur musique et leur comportement sur scène font d'eux un énorme cliché ambulant; leur ultime originalité aura été de terminer leur prévisible prestation par Bound For Glory, une toune – et en même temps le titre d'un livre que Dylan, semble-t-il, a lu et relu – de Woody Guthrie, considéré comme le père spirituel de cette légende vivante qu'est devenu l'auteur de The Times They Are A-Changing.

Exit The Alarm.

Les techniciens vident la scène de l'instrumentation superflue, ne laissant sur les planches que deux ou trois Fender beiges (les vieux amplis à tubes utilisés dans les années 60...). Pas de piano, pas de claviers. Les projecteurs s'allument: on se trouve en face de trois accompagnateurs – guitare, basse, batterie – et d'un Dylan un peu bouffi, sévère, tête basse, grattant sa Strato avec morosité, muet comme une carpe entre les pièces qu'il donne en enfilade; à aucun moment, même lorsque cela serait impérieux, il ne touchera à l'harmonica, dont il est pourtant un virtuose.

Mauvais choix. Pourquoi un band aussi minimal, alors que peu de chansons de Dylan, et encore moins celles de ces dix dernières années, s'accomodent d'une telle frugalité? Au théâtre Saint-Denis, à l'été 1980, n'avait-il pas conscrit cinq musiciens et trois choristes pour donner les tounes de sa période charismatique – de Street-Legal à Saved, – atteignant alors une stupéfiante perfection musicale?

Il ne faut pas juger par continuelles références au passé, dira-t-on? Alors, pourquoi Dylan a-t-il choisi d'ouvrir son show par des tounes comme Subterranean Homesick Blues, qui date de 1965, par Memphis Blues Again (1966) et par Highway 61 Revisited (1965 également)?

Et, pendant qu'on est dans ce genre de considérations, n'y a-t-il pas quelque chose d'indécent à passer à la moulinette une pièce comme Ballad Of A Thin Man? A banaliser ce monsieur Jones passé à l'histoire comme le plus grand archétype dylanesque? A en détruire les arrangements si habilement construits par Bloomfield et Kooper pour en donner une version scénique que toute la bonne volonté du guitariste G.E. Smith n'aura pas réussi à rendre potable?

Il y a parfois chez Dylan, dirait-on, une inclination morbide à gâcher les bons moments.

Car il y en a eu. Par exemple, lorsque lui et Smith se sont accrochés au cou des guitares sèches pour interpréter A Hard Rain's A-Gonna Fall, cette fresque cauchemardesque peinte en 1963 après la crise des missiles cubains. Il y a eu de l'électricité dans l'air à ce moment-là, au Forum. Alors pourquoi Dylan a-t-il pris sur lui de chambarder le refrain – brisant le rythme, rendant le phrasé méconnaissable – au moment où le public s'apprêtait à l'entonner avec lui?

N'insistons pas sur sa version de Like A Rolling Stone. Par une quelconque magie, cette chanson semble résister à tous les mauvais traitements, même à ceux que lui inflige son auteur. Parce que c'est un chef d'oeuvre, «peut-être la plus grande chanson de l'histoire du rock», disait John Cougar il y a un mois. Dylan l'avait massacrée au Forum en 1981; il a recommencé la boucherie, vendredi. Malgré cela, malgré le tempo trop rapide, malgré les excès d'une guitare et d'une batterie pognées pour remplacer à elles seules tout un vrai band, malgré l'incapacité de Dylan à recréer sur scène la subtilité vocale dont il fait preuve en studio, Like A Rolling Stone a été émouvant. Très émouvant. Le public (des gens de tous les âges, mais surtout de celui qui permet d'avoir écouté Freewheelin' le jour même de sa sortie chez les disquaires...), déjà ébloui par l'aura qui enveloppe toujours Dylan, a été littéralement subjugué dès que l'homme s'est mis à cracher:

Once upon a time You dressed so fine...

En dehors de cela, Dylan a peu touché à ses tounes bondieusiennes; encore moins à celles de son dernier microsillon, Down In The Groove.

Il a accordé un rappel, All Along The Watchtower, qui était un des bons moments du microsillon John Wesley Harding et un meilleur moment encore du répertoire de Jimi Hendrix. Puis, Dylan est sorti de scène et, malgré l'ovation pressante de la foule, n'est jamais revenu.

Un employé du Forum a ramené l'éclairage dans les gradins. Et on est resté quelques-uns plantés là, déçus, blessés comme on peut l'être par un rendez-vous manqué avec quelqu'un que l'on adule.

La Presse. Sun., July 10, 1988. Reprinted with permission of La Presse.

Additional Review

A mere 6,000 for a living legend, by Mark LePage. The Montreal Gazette. Sat., July 9, 1988. p. D1.

Saturday, July 9, 1988 --- Ottawa Civic Centre Ottawa, ON

Set List

	Song	From The Album	Released
1.	Subterranean Homesick Blues	Bringing It All Back Home	March 22, 1965
2.	It's All Over Now, Baby Blue	Bringing It All Back Home	March 22, 1965
3.	Masters of War	The Freewheelin' Bob Dylan	May 27, 1963
4.	Just Like Tom Thumb's Blues	Highway 61 Revisited	Aug. 30, 1965
5.	Driftin' Too Far from Shore	Knocked Out Loaded	July 14, 1986
6.	Stuck Inside of Mobile with the Memphis Blues Again	Blonde on Blonde	May 16, 1966
7.	A Hard Rain's A-Gonna Fall	The Freewheelin' Bob Dylan	May 27, 1963
8.	Mama, You Been on My Mind	The Bootleg Series Volumes 1-3	March 26, 1991
9.	It's Alright, Ma (I'm Only Bleeding)	Bringing It All Back Home	March 22, 1965
10.	I Shall Be Released	Bob Dylan's Greatest Hits, Vol. 2	Nov. 17, 1971
11.	Joey (Bob Dylan/Jacques Levy)	Desire	Jan. 5, 1976
12.	Like a Rolling Stone	Highway 61 Revisited	Aug. 30, 1965
	Encores		
13.	The Times They Are A-Changin'	The Times They Are A-Changin'	Feb. 10, 1964
14.	Maggie's Farm	Bringing It All Back Home	March 22, 1965

The Musicians

Bob Dylan (vocal & guitar), G. E. Smith (guitar & backup vocals), Kenny Aaronson (bass), Christopher Parker (drums).

Notes

- 39th Bob Dylan concert in Canada; 3rd Bob Dylan concert in Ottawa.
- 1, 5, 11, G. E. Smith (backup vocals).
- 7-9, 13, Bob Dylan (vocal & guitar), G. E. Smith (guitar).
- Canadian live debut of songs 5 & 11.
- Song 11 has been performed only once in Canada.
- The Alarm was the opening act.

Reviews

Dylan sizzles at Centre

Strong musicianship delivers old favorites in fine form

By Chris Cobb, Citizen Staff Writer.

A rock concert in the melting heat of the Ottawa Civic Centre was probably not the wisest choice of activity for Saturday night.

The air conditioning made heroic, if creakingly ineffective attempts to keep the temperature below 50 degrees, but a look at the flood of sweat pouring from Bob Dylan's face made the discomfort of the passive participants seem relatively insignificant.

Dylan was hot in more ways than one. This was a concert of such polish and remarkable musicianship that one had to be impressed almost from beginning to end.

Impressed particularly by Dylan and the brilliant transformations he has put his older material through. This was not a night for new songs – not even his current hit *Silvio* – but an unabashed greatest hits concert. Dylan seems to have found a balance between the desires of his audience and his own inherent need to become a rock and roll singer.

The setting and lighting was sparse, the three-man band was brilliant, keeping tight rein on Dylan's musical meanderings and heightening the emotional impact of his songs.

The likes of *It's Alright Ma (I'm Only Bleeding)* and *Mama You've Been on My Mind* played acoustically was bettered only by the brilliant *Hard Rain*, arguably Dylan's finest piece of writing. Even on a sweltering night, Dylan singing *Hard Rain* in (close to) its original form sent shivers down the spine.

But while every fan loves the acoustic material, it has become expected that he plays predominately rock and roll. Of all the Dylan incarnations in the past 10 to 15 years, this current trio travelling with him is providing the most punkish backup – sophisticated, polished punk, certainly, but basic. No keyboards and back-up singers: just guitar, bass and drums.

The concert was relatively short with Dylan ending the pre-encore period with *Like a Rolling Stone*. There were maybe a dozen or so songs in all and perhaps if the Glebe Inferno had been a little more comfortable, we may have heard more.

Dylan, who has not always met with roaring success during his periods of musical experiment, came through this one in fine style. It was often clever, always dynamic and certainly modern – the latter point probably being Dylan's main concern.

A hot show for sure.

The Ottawa Citizen. Mon., Jul 11, 1988. Reprinted with permission of The Ottawa Citizen.

Dylan: un spectacle on ne peut plus sobre

par Carole Grenier, collaboration spéciale.

Étrange ce Bob Dylan. Son spectacle presénté au Centre municipal d'Ottawa samedi soir contraste avec ce que l'on est en droit d'attendre d'un personnage dont la réputation est depuis si longtemps solidement établie.

Un spectacle on ne peut plus sobre, au point qu'il aurait pu faire très intime n'eut été des 6 500 personnes qui y assistaient. Principalement, à cause de la simplicité la plus complète qui régnait à tous les niveaux. Une scène pratiquement dénudée, des éclairages très modestes, et un orchestre composé de seulement trois musiciens: guitariste, bassiste et batteur. Un retour au rock élémentaire si l'on peut dire anisi.

D'accord, Bob Dylan est un chanteur à textes originalement. Les mots doivent donc prendre la plus grande importance en spectacle. Mais considérant la grandeur du Centre municipal, il est impossible de capter tout le langage du chanteur; on en perd presque la moitié.

D'autre part, il ne fait aucune intervention entre ses chansons. Pas un mot de tout le spectacle. À croire qu'il ne s'adresse à son public qu'à travers ses chansons. Cela paraît un peu surprenant de la part d'une vedette, qui plus est, d'un auteur qui a tant de choses à dire dans ses textes.

Un autre fait bizarre réside dans la répertoire des chansons du spectacle. Il a pris son envol avec *Subterranean Homesick Blues*, qui remonte à 1965, et a poursuit dans la même veine jusqu'à la fin. Aucune chanson de son dernier album, *Down in the Groove*. Pourquoi ce voyage dans le passé? Après tout, la rareté de ses visites à Ottawa aurait permis un renouveau.

Un des bons côtés reste sans doute son exécution de *A Hard Rain's A-Gonna Fall* et de quelques autres avec pour unique accompagnement sa guitare sèche, secondée par son guitariste G.E. Smith. La foule est quand même restée sage. Des gens de presque tous les âges s'étaient déplacés pour ce spectacle.

Un spectacle qui a eu une ovation complète avant même la première note de musique. Le phénomène ne s'est pas répété cependant. Incluant les rappels, on a eu pas plus de 90 minutes de spectacle. Quand les lumières se sont allumées, j'avais l'impression d'être restée sur ma faim. Il semble que plusieurs auraient enduré la chaleur écrasante quelques minutes de plus pour jouir un peu plus de leur idole.

LeDroit. Mon., July 11, 1988. Reprinted with permission of LeDroit.

Monday, July 11, 1988 --- Copps Coliseum
Hamilton, ON

Set List

	Song	From The Album	Released
1.	Subterranean Homesick Blues	Bringing It All Back Home	March 22, 1965
2.	Absolutely Sweet Marie	Blonde on Blonde	May 16, 1966
3.	Stuck Inside of Mobile with the Memphis Blues Again	Blonde on Blonde	May 16, 1966
4.	Ballad of a Thin Man	Highway 61 Revisited	Aug. 30, 1965
5.	Simple Twist of Fate	Blood on the Tracks	Jan. 20, 1975
6.	All Along the Watchtower	John Wesley Harding	Dec. 27, 1967
7.	It Ain't Me, Babe	Another Side of Bob Dylan	Aug. 8, 1964
8.	To Ramona	Another Side of Bob Dylan	Aug. 8, 1964
9.	Mr. Tambourine Man	Bringing It All Back Home	March 22, 1965
10.	I Shall Be Released	Bob Dylan's Greatest Hits, Vol. 2	Nov. 17, 1971
11.	Silvio (Bob Dylan/Robert Hunter)	Down in the Groove	May 19, 1988
12.	Like a Rolling Stone	Highway 61 Revisited	Aug. 30, 1965
	Encores		
13.	A Hard Rain's A-Gonna Fall	The Freewheelin' Bob Dylan	May 27, 1963
14.	Gotta Serve Somebody	Slow Train Coming	Aug. 20, 1979
15.	Maggie's Farm	Bringing It All Back Home	March 22, 1965

The Musicians

Bob Dylan (vocal & guitar), G. E. Smith (guitar & backup vocals), Kenny Aaronson (bass), Christopher Parker (drums).

Notes

- 40th Bob Dylan concert in Canada; Debut Bob Dylan concert in Hamilton.
- 1, 11, G. E. Smith (backup vocals).
- 7-9, 13, Bob Dylan (vocal & guitar), G. E. Smith (guitar).
- Canadian live debut of songs 2 & 11.
- The opening act was The Alarm.

Review

Minstrel of the '60s plays honest music

Alternately fiery, stirring and bluesy, Dylan provides 1¼ hours of coffeehouse classics

By Nick Krewen, The Spectator.

THE TIMES, they are a-changin'.

Used to be a time when Bob Dylan – who had been labelled a poetic prophet on more occasions than he probably cares to remember – performed 90-minute shows of mostly new and obscure material, travelled with a bloated backing band, whined the night away as his trademark nasal wail mimicked his bleating harmonica (and vice-versa) and ignored the audience.

Reclusive by nature (to the point where he's now suffering from Ann Wilson syndrome and refuses to allow photographs by any media), Dylan still ignores the audience, and his show has been trimmed to 60 minutes (although he did insert a 15-minute encore at Copps Coliseum last night).

But Bob seems to be shucking the ornaments for a straightforward, no frills approach to his music these days. Maybe he's reminiscing about his days as a balladeer, the happy-go-lucky wandering minstrel who sojourned to Woody Guthrie's hospital bedside – the freewheelin' Bob Dylan.

Whatever the reason, the estimated 11,000 fans last night were treated to a generous selection of coffeehouse classics upon which Dylan built his reputation. And there were moments during his show – Robert Zimmerman's first appearance in Hamilton since he filmed Hearts of Fire in late '86 – where he actually seemed to be enjoying himself.

At the very least, the music played by Dylan and his accompanying trio of former Hall And Oates and current Saturday Night Live guitarist G.E. Smith, Billy Idol bassist Kenny Aaronson and drummer Chris Parker was compassionate and honest.

G.E.'s initials might as well stand for General Electric, since he carried the entire show with high-voltage licks and energetic crunch chords while Dylan had his electric guitar volume control turned down. His fiery solos during Subterranean Homesick Blues and All Along The Watchtower were fine works of art.

Smith also became a foil for Dylan when both men abandoned the rhythm section for a spell and strummed acoustics guitars, surprising the audience with stirring renditions of It Ain't Me Babe and Mr. Tambourine Man.

Aaronson on bass also did a fine job of filling in the holes, often adding countermelodies during I Shall Be Released and Silvio –

the only reference to Dylan's latest album, Down In The Groove.

After a messy version of Stuck Inside Of Mobile With The Memphis Blues Again, Dylan and company performed their best number of the night – a bluesy, reflective Simple Twist Of Fate, with Dylan going to great lengths to turn out a consistent, if unspectacular, vocal performance.

But the beauty of the music is that you never know how it's going to be performed. Like A Rolling Stone had an understated melody, while Gotta Serve Somebody was served up as a tasty two-step with motoring bass line. Almost all the songs were stretched into jams, with more false endings tagged on than in a mystery novel.

Welsh rockers The Alarm were a strong balance to the card, providing a tensely rousing opening set that undoubtedly won some new converts from the Dylan camp.

Concentrating on material from their last two albums, Strength and Eye Of The Hurricane, vocalist Mike Peters sang Blaze Of Glory with the crowd, later throwing himself into a heap of bodies during Rescue Me because "I want everyone who believes in live music to stand up!"

The request brought the crowd to their feet, and The Alarm were promptly summoned back for an encore at the conclusion of their set – Woody Guthrie's Bound For Glory.

Once again, Dylan and The Alarm – two international travellers from different sunsets – share the same traditions. Musically, anyway, the global village is becoming smaller.

The Hamilton Spectator. Tues., July 12, 1988. Reprinted with permission of The Hamilton Spectator.

Sunday, August 21, 1988 --- Pacific Coliseum Vancouver, BC

Set List

	Song	From The Album	Released
1.	Subterranean Homesick Blues	Bringing It All Back Home	March 22, 1965
2.	I'll Remember You	Empire Burlesque	May 30, 1985
3.	Masters of War	The Freewheelin' Bob Dylan	May 27, 1963
4.	Stuck Inside of Mobile with the Memphis Blues Again	Blonde on Blonde	May 16, 1966
5.	It's All Over Now, Baby Blue	Bringing It All Back Home	March 22, 1965
6.	Highway 61 Revisited	Highway 61 Revisited	Aug. 30, 1965
7.	Boots of Spanish Leather	The Times They Are A-Changin'	Feb. 10, 1964
8.	The Lonesome Death of Hattie Carroll	The Times They Are A-Changin'	Feb. 10, 1964
9.	One Too Many Mornings	The Times They Are A-Changin'	Feb. 10, 1964
10.	Barbara Allen (trad.)	–	–
11.	Silvio (Bob Dylan/Robert Hunter)	Down in the Groove	May 19, 1988
12.	In the Garden	Saved	June 19, 1980
13.	Like a Rolling Stone	Highway 61 Revisited	Aug. 30, 1965
	Encores		
14.	The Times They Are A-Changin'	The Times They Are A-Changin'	Feb. 10, 1964
15.	All Along the Watchtower	John Wesley Harding	Dec. 27, 1967
16.	Knockin' on Heaven's Door	Pat Garrett & Billy The Kid	July 13, 1973

The Musicians

Bob Dylan (vocal & guitar), G. E. Smith (guitar, electric slide guitar & backup vocals), Kenny Aaronson (bass), Christopher Parker (drums).

Notes

- 41st Bob Dylan concert in Canada; 5th Bob Dylan concert in Vancouver.
- 1, 11, G. E. Smith (backup vocals).
- 6, G. E. Smith (electric slide guitar).
- 7-10, 14, Bob Dylan (vocal & guitar), G. E. Smith (guitar).
- Canadian live debut of songs 2 & 10.
- Tracy Chapman was the opening act and shared vocals on song 16.

Reviews

Dylan dynamite in Coliseum Concert

By John Mackie.

A BOB DYLAN concert can be many things to many people. Enlightening, to the hardcore fans who study his lyrics and collect bootleg records and tapes filled with his seemingly endless supply of new songs and/or new arrangements of old standards. Confusing, to the casual fan baffled by his unpredictability and playing around with those same old standards.

But rarely had there been a Dylan concert so downright entertaining as Sunday night's show at the Coliseum. Dylan has gone back to basics, stripping his songs down to their rock, folk and country roots, and he has recruited just the band to make the songs come to life.

Led by stellar guitarist G. E. Smith, the band played Dylan's music with a controlled fury, injecting a passionate energy into the music that made Dylan's 1986 concert at B.C. Place with Tom Petty's Heartbreakers seem tame by comparison.

Not that Dylan went out of his way to be entertaining. He didn't say boo to the audience (not one word in Sunday's show), never bothered to announce any of the songs, and, of course, twisted familiar melodies around so much they were almost unrecognizable.

But he did bring out the acoustic guitar for five songs, hauling The Times They Are A Changin' and The Lonesome Death Of Hattie Carroll out of mothballs and performing them relatively straight.

And if you concentrated, you could make out the lyrics to Stuck Inside of Mobile With The Memphis Blues Again, Highway 61, It's All Over Now, Baby Blue, Like A Rolling Stone and All Along The Watchtower, all in shiny new arrangements.

Dylan looked thin and fit in a black cowboy jacket, black pants and black cowboy boots. His big, frizzy mop of hair is still his most distinctive feature, and he still sings in a nasal wheeze, with the world's most unique sense of timing.

He's still a pretty somber guy onstage, but did manage a few smiles when guitarist Smith played a particularly exceptional solo, and when opening act Tracy Chapman came up to duet on Knockin' On Heaven's Door.

Chapman played an all too brief nine song, 40 minute set (Dylan's was 15 songs, 80 minutes). Appearing solo, she had the 9,000 in attendance enthralled with her stark, emotional protest songs.

Chapman is a refreshingly direct songwriter, someone who's not afraid to ask the age old question of why babies starve "when there's enough food to feed the world," who throws her lot in with the poor and the oppressed, and promises she won't abandon them for the trappings of fame.

On stage, she comes across as extremely shy (neither she nor Dylan would allow photographers), but songs like Talkin' 'Bout a Revolution, Fast Car, Mountains of Things and Across The Lines are all strong, moving statements on the problems of modern America.

She's an important artist, and an original one as well – Tracy Chapman's going to be prodding the collective consciousness for a long time to come.

The Vancouver Sun. Mon., Aug. 22, 1988.

Fans fill Bob's garage

By Tom Harrison, Music Critic.

Being at the coliseum Sunday night was more like being in Bob Dylan's garage.

He had a small band there, and a new friend named Tracy Chapman, and he was going over some old tunes. Just having a bash, you know, and evoking those old days when the world puzzled over the identity of the sad-eyed lady of the lowlands and Napoleon in rags.

Nobody really worries about them anymore. But a few people still puzzle over Bob Dylan and what he's thinking.

There were 8,000 curious and committed at the PNE and although they cheered and hollered for him when he sang The Times They Are A-Changing', Bob proved that he hasn't changed much. He still isn't giving people what they really want.

It was a short concert – 85 minutes. The lights were low, the need for spectacle superfluous.

Tracy came, sang her songs of stark, forthright, realistic beauty; Tracy left.

Then Dylan arrived with drummer Christopher Parker, bassist Kerry Aaronson and guitarist G.E. Smith and wailed the Subterranean Homesick Blues.

Immediately it was apparent that this was going to be a magnetic rock and roll show even if the distance between Dylan and the audience was measured in years of mystery, confusion and suspicion.

This was a high powered garage-band. It exuded cool and played with a feeling that was unforced yet sinewy and muscular.

The set list itself, which included Like A Rolling Stone, It's All Over Now Baby Blue and Memphis Blues Again, was less adventurous, but the songs lived again in this new guitar-powered context.

Despite this, the atmosphere for most of the show was too respectful. It wasn't until a hard-rocking Silvio that the crowd rushed the stage, and suddenly there was a rock and roll concert going on.

Among the night's surprises were an acoustic segment by Dylan and Smith highlighted by the ancient folk song, Barb'ra Allen, and The Lonesome Death of Hattle Carroll; and Tracy Chapman returning for the last encore number, Knockin' on Heaven's Door.

Chapman smiled and Dylan smiled, both for the first time, and this was enough. Between the two – the icon and the fast-rising acolyte – they'd spoken perhaps 10 words. Instead, their collaboration spoke for them.

The Vancouver Province. Tues., Aug. 23, 1988.

Tuesday, August 23, 1988 --- Olympic Saddledome Calgary, AB

Set List

	Song	From The Album	Released
1.	Subterranean Homesick Blues	Bringing It All Back Home	March 22, 1965
2.	Just Like a Woman	Blonde on Blonde	May 16, 1966
3.	Driftin' Too Far from Shore	Knocked Out Loaded	July 14, 1986
4.	Simple Twist of Fate	Blood on the Tracks	Jan. 20, 1975
5.	I'll Be Your Baby Tonight	John Wesley Harding	Dec. 27, 1967
6.	Highway 61 Revisited	Highway 61 Revisited	Aug. 30, 1965
7.	Don't Think Twice, It's All Right	The Freewheelin' Bob Dylan	May 27, 1963
8.	Girl of the North Country	The Freewheelin' Bob Dylan	May 27, 1963
9.	It's Alright, Ma (I'm Only Bleeding)	Bringing It All Back Home	March 22, 1965
10.	Eileen Aroon (trad., arr. Clancy Brothers/Tommy Makem)	–	–
11.	It Ain't Me, Babe	Another Side of Bob Dylan	Aug. 8, 1964
12.	I Shall Be Released	Bob Dylan's Greatest Hits, Vol. 2	Nov. 17, 1971
13.	Silvio (Bob Dylan/Robert Hunter)	Down in the Groove	May 19, 1988
14.	Like a Rolling Stone	Highway 61 Revisited	Aug. 30, 1965
	Encores		
15.	Mr. Tambourine Man	Bringing It All Back Home	March 22, 1965
16.	Maggie's Farm	Bringing It All Back Home	March 22, 1965
17.	Knockin' on Heaven's Door	Pat Garrett & Billy The Kid	July 13, 1973

The Musicians

Bob Dylan (vocal & guitar), G. E. Smith (guitar, electric slide guitar & backup vocals), Kenny Aaronson (bass), Christopher Parker (drums).

Notes

- 42nd Bob Dylan concert in Canada; Debut Bob Dylan concert in Calgary.
- 1, 3, 13, G. E. Smith (backup vocals).
- 6, G. E. Smith (electric slide guitar).
- 7-11, 15, Bob Dylan (vocal & guitar), G. E. Smith (guitar).
- Canadian live debut of song 10.
- Song 10 has been performed only once in Canada.
- Tracy Chapman was the opening act and shared vocals on song 17.

Reviews

Rich legend left in tatters

By James Muretich, Herald Staff Writer.

Bob Dylan has always gone his way, paying no mind to what critics or the public thought of him.

However, after Tuesday night's performance at the Saddledome, his Calgary fans would have every right to also pay no attention to anything Dylan does on stage from here on in.

To say that Dylan's first ever Calgary appearance was a letdown would be a major understatement.

His show ranged from haphazard and sloppy to insensitive and boorish. Dylan and his three-piece backing band raced through his songs with nary a care as to their intellectual or emotional intent.

As a result, tunes such as Subterranean Homesick Blues and Simple Twist Of Fate were given the bum's rush while the ballad I'll Be Your Baby Tonight was reduced from a love song to a sexless rock shuffle devoid of any longing whatsoever.

And while not possessed of an operatic voice, Dylan can have an expressive, emotional singing style when he wants. However, he certainly showed no signs of wanting any such thing.

He spat the words out, almost with disdain. The result was a legacy of evocative, inventive imagery left in tatters. Rather than prick the subconscious with his lyrics, as so very many of his classic tunes have done, Dylan's songs in concert merely shot the words out with all the delicacy of a machine-gun.

On top of that, his band seldom seemed to gel with any authority, save for a strong version of I Shall Be Released. Led by the showboat antics of Saturday Night Live's G. E. Smith on guitar, the group tried to rock but seldom found the groove.

Needless to say, the majority of the approximately 12,000 paying customers on hand still cheered. After all, this was THE Bob Dylan on stage making his belated Calgary debut.

It was if they poured decades of reverential devotion into the hollow but hallowed figure on stage, creating in their mind's eye the image of Dylan that they most cherished, whether that as folkie, gospel troubadour, social critic or romantic poet.

Dylan may knock publicly his status of musical legend, but he should really be glad people view him that way. If they didn't, he would've been booed off the stage Tuesday night for a pitiful performance. Instead, he was applauded.

Meanwhile, opening act Tracy Chapman seems to have gone to the Dylan school of charm and concert etiquette as well.

In keeping with her powerful debut disc, the popular singer/songwriter proved to have a riveting voice and muscular material to match, full of social import and soul.

Unfortunately, Chapman didn't say boo between tunes during her solo set, stifling much of the impact of her impassioned vocals and lyrics.

The end result was a strange evening where the music of an old master and a promising young artist was strangely remote in concert. Not even a respectable wrap-up with Knockin' On Heaven's Door (where Chapman joined Dylan on stage) could put a lasting glow on the evening.

Oh well, it was only rock 'n' roll, right Bob? It's not meant to be taken seriously. Certainly, you didn't take it that way.

Attendance: about 12,000.

The Calgary Herald. Wed., Aug. 24, 1988.

DYLAN!

Bob's fire still burns

By David Veitch, Calgary Sun.

To answer Bob Dylan's immortal question, it felt wonderful.

A near-capacity crowd at the Olympic Saddledome last night caught Dylan bringing his music all back home as he eschewed show-biz glitz for rock 'n' roll grind and folkie simplicity.

Fronting a ragged four-piece band, well-versed in roadhouse blues 'n' boogie, Dylan turned many of his familiar standards into lean and mean rave-ups.

The music – performed with only two guitars, bass and drums – was pure, raw and unembellished.

But this chaotic, bar-band approach seemed to inspire Dylan, who was singing and playing with sheer force.

It's difficult to believe that 10 years ago, Dylan's road show was dangerously close to imitating a Las Vegas revue.

Though Dylan built the show around pre-*John Wesley Harding* material, he stripped his songs down to their most basic components and rebuilt them.

One couldn't even recognize *Subterranean Homesick Blues*, *Just Like A Woman* or *Like A Rolling Stone* until Dylan sang their first few lines.

After a fiery version of *Highway 61 Revisited*, the rhythm section exited, leaving Dylan and his guitarist to play a lengthy acoustic set of pre-electric material, including *Girl From The North Country, Don't Think Twice, It's All Right, It Ain't Me Babe and It's Alright Ma (I'm Only Bleeding)*.

These songs were older than some members of the very eclectic audience but Dylan's interpretations were as urgent as ever, as if he wrote these songs days ago, not decades ago.

This acoustic set recalled Dylan's stellar 1965 tour of Britain, preserved in Don Pennebaker's acclaimed film documentary, *Don't Look Back*.

The rhythm section returned to close the show with *I Shall Be Released, Silvio*, and *Like A Rolling Stone*.

For an encore, Dylan treated fans to acoustic versions of *Mr. Tambourine Man* and *Knockin' On Heaven's Door*, the latter being a duet with opening act, Tracy Chapman (whose solo acoustic set received a thunderous ovation).

Many stars of the '60s have embarrassed themselves in the '80s.

But Dylan's latest road show lives up to the legend. His songs have proven to be timeless and, though he's showing every minute of his 47 years, a fire still burns within his soul.

It was a true pleasure to be stuck in the Saddledome with the Dylan blues again.

The Calgary Sun. Wed., Aug. 24, 1988.

Wednesday, August 24, 1988 --- Northlands Coliseum
Edmonton, AB

Set List

	Song	From The Album	Released
1.	Subterranean Homesick Blues	Bringing It All Back Home	March 22, 1965
2.	Just Like a Woman	Blonde on Blonde	May 16, 1966
3.	All Along the Watchtower	John Wesley Harding	Dec. 27, 1967
4.	You're a Big Girl Now	Blood on the Tracks	Jan. 20, 1975
5.	Shelter from the Storm	Blood on the Tracks	Jan. 20, 1975
6.	Highway 61 Revisited	Highway 61 Revisited	Aug. 30, 1965
7.	To Ramona	Another Side of Bob Dylan	Aug. 8, 1964
8.	Girl of the North Country	The Freewheelin' Bob Dylan	May 27, 1963
9.	Mr. Tambourine Man	Bringing It All Back Home	March 22, 1965
10.	Silvio (Bob Dylan/Robert Hunter)	Down in the Groove	May 19, 1988
11.	In the Garden	Saved	June 19, 1980
12.	Like a Rolling Stone	Highway 61 Revisited	Aug. 30, 1965
	Encores		
13.	It Ain't Me, Babe	Another Side of Bob Dylan	Aug. 8, 1964
14.	Maggie's Farm	Bringing It All Back Home	March 22, 1965
15.	Knockin' on Heaven's Door	Pat Garrett & Billy The Kid	July 13, 1973
16.	She's About a Mover (Doug Sahm)	–	–

The Musicians

Bob Dylan (vocal & guitar), G. E. Smith (guitar, electric slide guitar & backup vocals), Kenny Aaronson (bass), Christopher Parker (drums).

Notes

- 43rd Bob Dylan concert in Canada; Debut Bob Dylan concert in Edmonton.
- 1, 10, G. E. Smith (backup vocals).
- 6, G. E. Smith (electric slide guitar).
- 7-9, 13, Bob Dylan (vocal & guitar), G. E. Smith (guitar).
- 16, Doug Sahm (lead vocal).
- Canadian live debut of songs 4 & 16.
- Song 16 has been performed only once in Canada.
- Worldwide live debut of song 16.
- Tracy Chapman was the opening act and shared vocals on song 15.

Reviews

Aggressive Dylan makes his oldies memorable

By Helen Metella, Journal Staff Writer.

Objections to seeing Bob Dylan live in 1988 were plentiful in the weeks preceding Wednesday night's far-from-sold-out show.

But virtually all those anxieties were exactly what made his aggressive concert of predominantly oldies memorable.

Instead, unexpected bugaboos such as a short program (one hour with a 15-minute encore), muddy sound and a total lack of material from such sterling LPs as Blood On The Tracks, Desire, Empire Burlesque, Infidels and Slow Train Coming contributed to the disappointing side of the ledger for 10,000 fans.

But the unpredictable, moody risk-taker – who phrases with dangerous abandon – re-arranged familiar material with challenging fury and has to convince us of his contemporary relevance again and again, made it an event not to be missed.

Dylan's unique independence surfaced immediately as the 47-year-old troubadour with a cockeyed crop of curls and nondescript black clothes roared into heavily amplified versions of Just Like A Woman and All Along The Watchtower.

Guitarist G.E. Smith, an alumnus of The Saturday Night Live Band, matched his leader's ferocity with solos that had the tingle of electrified barbed wire.

A country-and-western two-step tempo for Shelter From The Storm emphasized Dylan's long-held theory that audiences should be jarred by the depth of his material.

As for his dubious relevance, it was a revelation to find new resonance in the lines, "I'm not sleepy and there ain't no place I'm going to," and "You don't have to be a weatherman to know which way the wind blows," in these years of high unemployment and deceitful political candidates.

As for the moody anti-show-biz moroseness noted on his last two tours with the Grateful Dead and Tom Petty, his lack of between-song chatter meant more songs back to back, including blistering renditions of Highway 61, Like A Rolling Stone, Maggie's Farm and It Ain't Me, Babe.

While the occasional acoustic guitar sections were agreeably organic (as Mr. Tambourine Man's many mistakes and run-on hootenany ending attested), the most compelling of the slow songs was Knockin' On Heaven's Door, in which Tracy Chapman joined him for a spiritual and symbolic exchange of values.

Nonetheless, considering the breadth of his 26 years worth of material and his many different waves of popularity, Dylan was true to his legendary status as a succinct philosophizer, provocative band leader and a gripping rock and roller.

Opening act Tracy Chapman, a 24-year-old black from Boston via Cleveland, commanded the stage with her abrasive, wounded vocals and her frank observations on hypocrisy. (This despite the fact that she insists on communicating solely through her songs.)

She reminded us all of the power of a strong composition simply sung without the smokescreens of complicated arrangements and blipping, popping synthesizers and percussion machines.

Rarely if ever have I experienced the shivers that accompanied the spontaneous, applause for the chorus, "I had a feelin' I could be someone," on her hit single Fast Car. It makes you want to pick up a guitar and learn it immediately and there are few chart-toppers that have done that in years.

When all around we are crying at the unstoppable juggernaut of power and greed that steals from the defenceless in our population, it's extraordinarily heartening to know that there remains a channel where someone can say out loud "Why are the missiles called peacekeepers, when they're aimed to kill."

The Edmonton Journal. Thurs., Aug. 25, 1988. Reprinted with the permission of The Edmonton Journal.

Bob Dylan

By Neal Watson, Staff Writer.

Looking more like a man with his mind on his work than a bonafide living legend, Bob Dylan and his crack three-piece band wasted no time going to work cranking out one very famous tune after another last night at the Coliseum.

It was a tough, gutsy, and at times, even sentimental show by a musician not noted for his sentiment.

Making his first appearance in Edmonton before a surprisingly small crowd of just under 10,000, the 47-year-old singer was in a typical 'Dylan mood.' That meant no photography – press or otherwise. He said nothing to the audience and he studiously avoided the usual rituals of a rock concert.

But he did seem to be enjoying himself and he even smiled a few times.

Dylan's never been afraid to tamper with the original conception of his songs and he toughened up the arrangements on many of the songs giving the show a real rock 'n' roll feel.

He was aided and ably abetted in this pursuit by his three-piece band – G.E. Smith on guitar, Chris Parker on drums and Ken Aaronson on bass. In particular, Smith was the musical mainstay of the night, providing scorching lead guitar at every turn.

The result was rough, energized and deliberately raggedy versions of songs like *Just Like a Woman*, *Shelter From The Storm*, *Like a Rolling Stone*, *Highway 61* and *Maggie's Farm* among others. Smith also joined Dylan on stage for acoustic versions of *Mr. Tambourine Man* and *North Country Fair*.

Opening act Tracy Chapman joined Dylan for an encore version of *Knockin' On Heaven's Door*.

At first glance, it was fitting that Chapman, an artist in the tradition of the socially conscious singer/songwriters, open for Dylan.

Chapman is one of the biggest music stories of 1988 and a No. 1 album in both Canada and the U.S. have taken her almost overnight from obscurity to playing arena shows.

A painfully shy performer, Chapman is not ready for a venue this size. Her songs are stark and unadorned, but tender and often wrenching statements on issues like racial hatred and family violence.

There is power to the words in *Talkin' Bout a Revolution*, *Across The Lines* and *Behind The Wall* and emotion to her plaintive presentation of her songs.

But last night the intimate and often haunting quality of these songs was lost in the Coliseum. Appearing alone and usually standing in almost complete darkness between songs, Chapman said nothing to an audience that would have loved to have heard from her.

Perhaps she was silenced by some in the crowd who yelped and hooted between every pause in her songs – particularly *Behind The Wall*, which is a emotional song about domestic violence. Chapman, who did receive a standing ovation, will learn to deal with the larger sizes and the inattentive in the audience. And this is a performer whose voice will only get stronger as she gains confidence.

The Edmonton Sun. Thurs., Aug. 25, 1988. Reprinted with permission of The Sun Media Corp.

Friday, August 26, 1988 --- Winnipeg Arena
Winnipeg, MB

Set List

	Song	From The Album	Released
1.	Subterranean Homesick Blues	Bringing It All Back Home	March 22, 1965
2.	I'll Remember You	Empire Burlesque	May 30, 1985
3.	Highway 61 Revisited	Highway 61 Revisited	Aug. 30, 1965
4.	You're a Big Girl Now	Blood on the Tracks	Jan. 20, 1975
5.	Driftin' Too Far from Shore	Knocked Out Loaded	July 14, 1986
6.	Ballad of a Thin Man	Highway 61 Revisited	Aug. 30, 1965
7.	She Belongs to Me	Bringing It All Back Home	March 22, 1965
8.	Mr. Tambourine Man	Bringing It All Back Home	March 22, 1965
9.	To Ramona	Another Side of Bob Dylan	Aug. 8, 1964
10.	Girl of the North Country	The Freewheelin' Bob Dylan	May 27, 1963
11.	I Shall Be Released	Bob Dylan's Greatest Hits, Vol. 2	Nov. 17, 1971
12.	Silvio (Bob Dylan/Robert Hunter)	Down in the Groove	May 19, 1988
13.	Like a Rolling Stone	Highway 61 Revisited	Aug. 30, 1965
	Encores		
14.	The Times They Are A-Changin'	The Times They Are A-Changin'	Feb. 10, 1964
15.	Maggie's Farm	Bringing It All Back Home	March 22, 1965

The Musicians

Dylan (vocal & guitar), G. E. Smith (guitar, electric slide guitar & backup vocals), Kenny Aaronson (bass), Christopher Parker (drums).

Notes

- 44th Bob Dylan concert in Canada; Debut Bob Dylan concert in Winnipeg.
- 1, 5, 12, G. E. Smith (backup vocals).
- 3, G. E. Smith (electric slide guitar).
- 7-10, 14, Bob Dylan (vocal & guitar), G. E. Smith (guitar).
- The opening act was Timbuk 3.

Reviews

Dylan wows crowd eager to be pleased

By Stephen Ostick.

There was a moment towards the end of music legend Bob Dylan's concert last night that pretty well summed up the spirit of the whole show.

The Man and his three-piece back-up band were winding up Like A Rolling Stone when suddenly he broke a string on his electric guitar.

It was a bass string, too, and band leader G. E. Smith's guitar was already out of tune so their instruments quickly deteriorated to sounding like two sick cats.

All the big-shots nowadays have roadies that would've jumped from the wings with a replacement or, at the worst, the song would've been cut short.

Couldn't care less

Bob Dylan didn't even seem to notice. Head slightly bowed, he kept building the song to a climax, strumming the chords and singing with that nasal, lamenting voice until he was good and ready to end it.

The crowd couldn't have cared less. Dylan could have stood and sung his way through the phone book and been a smash.

This was, pure and simple, a night for fans to bask in their hero's first appearance here.

And judging by the emotional response, it's a good bet most of the 9,500 in attendance were longtime devotees.

As it was, the 47-year-old worked his way through a song catalogue dating back about 26 years, perhaps explaining the absence of the usual roars of recognition when superstars break into one of their hits.

More than half of the 13 tunes in his 65-minute set went unrecognized. Only the first notes to Mr. Tambourine Man and Like A Rolling Stone were greeted enthusiastically.

The choice of repertoire was obviously deliberate, what with Dylan's penchant for constantly changing his show. He wasn't out to prove anything or to win new converts to his cause. It seemed as though he just wanted to get up there and play.

And he chose well in picking Smith and company to back him up. Smith, drummer Christopher Parker and bassist Kenny Aaronson were as raw and ragged as Dylan's voice.

There rough edges would have overpowered the tenderness of Lay Lady Lay, for instance (had he played it), but Dylan wasn't after that quality last night.

Even the second half hour, which was an all-acoustic affair between just Dylan and Smith, attacked more than it caressed. Smith took more of a back seat, allowing Dylan the space to play chord pattern leads. These extended breaks evoked wild applause.

The feeling presented there, however, and indeed inherent in the entire set, was not one of sweet melody but rather one of power.

Cast a spell

The man on stage and his music have been arguably the most potent musical influence on this generation. Knowing that seemed to cast a spell over the crowd, which, not having seen Dylan before, saw magic in his performance where perhaps there wasn't any. Genius is, after all, a tough billing to live up to every day.

Openers Timbuk 3 announced this was the largest crowd they'd ever played for. That's too bad, because their delightful satire was a treat. Pat MacDonald and wife Barbara K's sarcastic wit was delivered cleverly and with good humor.

Dylan

Still fickle, still angry – and his fans wouldn't have it any other way

By John Kendle, For The Sun.

In a pop world dominated by commercialism, consumerism and mass marketing strategies, Bob Dylan is one of the few artists who can remain oblivious to everything but himself.

This was made painstakingly plain to 10,000 Winnipeggers Friday night at the Winnipeg Arena.

The 47-year-old rock icon, didn't give a concert in the acknowledged sense of the term; instead he provided a demonstration of his mastery over the intangible, intoxicating power of popular music.

Speaking nary a word to the audience, Dylan let his music do the talking through his 81 minute set, and the angry buzz of his tunes spoke volumes on his behalf.

Dylan, in 1988, is still angry; still exploring his soul, and still looking to come to terms with a world which held so much promise and fear for him when he first rose to prominence in the early '60s.

The fact he's accorded almost Herculean status by his fans certainly allows wide leeway. Playing here for the first time, his every move was greeted with wild, rapturous applause, despite the fact he played only 81 minutes, much of which was devoted to rearranged versions of lesser known songs spanning his 26 year career.

Following less than satisfactory, often sprawling excursions with Tom Petty and The Grateful Dead over the past two summers, Dylan has assembled a compact touring unit this time out, and the players – G.E. Smith on guitar, bassist Kenny Aaronson and drummer Christopher Parker – provided a rock-solid bluesy backdrop to the piercing nasal whine and jagged rhythm playing of their boss.

Indeed, the group brought new life to songs like Highway 61 Revisited, which was given a new, vitriolic treatment. Like A Rolling Stone was completely revised, Dylan choosing to retain only the chorus and bridge while reworking the rest of the song.

He even changed the inflection and phrasing of his lyrics, shedding new light on their meanings. Mr. Jones would have wilted in his seat if he heard the venomous way in which Dylan spat out his name.

Mr. Tambourine Man, played during a five song acoustic break featuring Dylan, Smith and some expressive guitar noodling, was faithful to the original, and elicited the thrôatiest response of the evening. Silvio, a number from his latest L.P., Down In The Groove, was a sensuous blues workout, and I Shall Be Released turned into an eerie cue to the crowd to get off their feet and rush closer to the stage.

Dylan closed with an acoustic version of The Times They Are A Changin' and a throbbing rendition of Maggie's Farm. He could have gone on forever – he's certainly got the material to choose from, and the audience was clamoring for more – but chose instead to stride quickly offstage directly into his waiting tour bus.

Openers Timbuk 3, playing before a crowd they admitted was the largest they'd ever seen from a stage, did a fine job of warming things up. Pat MacDonald and Barbara K.'s wry wit and textured guitar playing, particularly during Assholes On Parade, struck the right chord with a crowd sympathetic to their cynical world view. The duo drew a hearty cheer by introducing Welcome To The Human Race as a song about rich people who lose all their money.

Monday, August 29, 1988 --- CNE Grandstand
Toronto, ON

Set List

	Song	From The Album	Released
1.	Subterranean Homesick Blues	Bringing It All Back Home	March 22, 1965
2.	Absolutely Sweet Marie	Blonde on Blonde	May 16, 1966
3.	Masters of War	The Freewheelin' Bob Dylan	May 27, 1963
4.	Simple Twist of Fate	Blood on the Tracks	Jan. 20, 1975
5.	Shelter from the Storm	Blood on the Tracks	Jan. 20, 1975
6.	Highway 61 Revisited	Highway 61 Revisited	Aug. 30, 1965
7.	Girl of the North Country	The Freewheelin' Bob Dylan	May 27, 1963
8.	Don't Think Twice, It's All Right	The Freewheelin' Bob Dylan	May 27, 1963
9.	One Too Many Mornings	The Times They Are A-Changin'	Feb. 10, 1964
10.	Barbara Allen (trad.)	–	–
11.	I Shall Be Released	Bob Dylan's Greatest Hits, Vol. 2	Nov. 17, 1971
12.	Silvio (Bob Dylan/Robert Hunter)	Down in the Groove	May 19, 1988
13.	Like a Rolling Stone	Highway 61 Revisited	Aug. 30, 1965
	Encores		
14.	It Ain't Me, Babe	Another Side of Bob Dylan	Aug. 8, 1964
15.	All Along the Watchtower	John Wesley Harding	Dec. 27, 1967
16.	Knockin' on Heaven's Door	Pat Garrett & Billy The Kid	July 13, 1973

The Musicians

Bob Dylan (vocal & guitar), G. E. Smith (guitar, electric slide guitar & backup vocals), Kenny Aaronson (bass), Christopher Parker (drums).

Notes

- 45th Bob Dylan concert in Canada; 15th Bob Dylan concert in Toronto.
- 1, 12, G. E. Smith (backup vocals).
- 6, G. E. Smith (electric slide guitar).
- 7-10, 14, Bob Dylan (vocal & guitar), G. E. Smith (guitar).
- Timbuk 3 was the opening act.

Reviews

Dylan shocks audience out of confusion

By Greg Quill, Toronto Star.

You can never second guess Bob Dylan.

That, and his inability after all these years to start and finish a song with a modicum of style, are about the only things of which Dylan fans and students can be reasonably sure.

Last night at the CNE Grandstand, the man whose songs in the mid-1960s actually changed the way the world still thinks about fundamental issues like war and racism, politics, personal freedom, love, our responsibilities to each other and perhaps our very destiny, started out by throwing away some of his best work.

Fronting a dull three-piece band that might have been picked up at some roadhouse in northern Minnesota, and dressed in a natty dark suit, white shirt and tie, Dylan made nonsense of "Subterranean Homesick Blues", "Sweet Marie", "Masters Of War', and "A Simple Twist Of Fate" by racing through them at breakneck speed, pinning them to basic rock 'n' roll tempos and bellowing out their lyrics apparently without respect for the 10,000 or so people who'd turned out to see him.

It was awful. These were some of Dylan's finest recorded pieces, bled of every trace of emotional power, of drama, even of logic. Unimaginative solos by an unnamed guitarist, clearly insensitive to the pieces on which he laid his grubby hands, merely filled the space between verses with absurd bar-room cliches. Each song rolled out of a jumble of chords and ended with big, silly flourishes that obliterated whatever faint original flavor still lingered.

"Any true Dylan fan would forgive him for this," a man nearby said in a thick northern English accent. "We've been through everything with him."

Still, he seemed not to recognize "Shelter From The Storm", rendered in a hoarse, syncopated shout over a rapid, hokey two-four, until the end of the first verse.

He was not alone. The audience of Dylan fans from the 1960s, folk music fans from an earlier generation and the young and curious, drawn perhaps by the songwriter's weighty reputation (although he hasn't had a hit record in more than a decade), was confused and static mid-way through the show.

Then something happened. The band gelled suddenly for a rip-snorting, spiritually faithful version of "Highway 61", one of Dylan's most vicious and rousing songs, and disappeared. Alone on stage, with an acoustic guitar slung around his neck, Dylan strummed his way into one of his earliest pieces, the love ballad "North Country Blues", as resonant as ever with rich, inventive chords, and with rhythms puncuated not by metered time, but as they were in the singer's best days, by emotional pulses.

The spell continued, through "Don't Think Twice", whose verses were joined by half the audience, through the little known "One Too Many Mornings", with Dylan still weaving those wonderful, timeless chords, and on to a heartstopping revision of the traditional "Barbara Allen", which seemed to pour from Dylan's heart like the blood of the doomed lovers in the song.

By then, Dylan seemed to have retraced his very first steps back to his folk roots and discovered a well of emotional power there. He need only to return to the anthems "I Shall Be Released" and "Like A Rolling Stone", given a passionate boost by his band, to complete the coup.

Made redundant by pop music's ever-shifting fashions, Dylan last night simply reminded us, after some idiosyncratic self-parody, that his best work will live forever.

Bob Dylan: OUT OF SIGHT

By Bob Thompson.

Bob Dylan offered his vocal nasal passages as only he could at the Grandstand last night.

He was also generous in recounting his legendary folk-rock songwriting past with a mixture of pensive and passionate song productions.

Although, he proved to be decidedly stingy about a picture recollection of the Grandstand event by banning newspaper photographers.

So picture this.

Dylan, replete with puffy hair and dark suit, straddled the microphone as he took us down his moan-drone singing highway of thought-talk rock.

Which was more than most of 13,000 Dylan fans could ever hope to receive.

But there was more.

There was the electric guitar of G.E. Smith.

He single-handedly turned the Dylan homage into a stylishly down-to-earth example of guitar playing – acoustically intricate or rock 'n' roll bold.

But Dylan didn't go gentle into the night either.

He moved from guitar clanging four-man band renditions of *Shelter From The Storm* and *Masters Of War* to a few uptempo strummers, including *Don't Think Twice It's Alright.*

I Shall Be Released provided one of the better moments of the night, and allowed Smith some high-flying guitar jags.

And a Beatles type rockin' *Like A Rolling Stone* prompted the fans in the outback to push forward to the stage front.

How did it feel?

Like we were being revisited.

Opening was Timbuck 3, a two-member husband-and-wife band from Austin featuring folk harmonies, electric guitars and an always reliable beat box.

Pat MacDonald and Barbara K. also tended to deliver their selectively cynical lyrics with a sly wink.

Sometimes they were successful – for example *The Future's So Bright (I Gotta Wear Shades).*

Sometimes their high-minded busker posing was a little to much to handle.

Once the prolific songwriter, Bob Dylan plays the interpreter

By Chris Dafoe, The Globe and Mail.

"Pass the shovel Martha, it's time to bury Bob Dylan."

Yes, kids it's that time again. Time to say once again that Bob Dylan is washed up and has nothing left to say and is worthless and meaningless and has burned out and, well, who does he think he is anyway?

Dylan, who played his first Toronto show in six years last night at the CNE Grandstand, has been the subject of this sort of talk before. When he went electric in 1965. When he went born-again Christian in 1979. Whenever.

The cause for the latest talk is Dylan's most recent album, Down In The Groove, most of which he didn't write and most of which he ignored last night in favour of material from the full range of his 27-year career.

And in spite of his favoring old ground over of new, Dylan showed (once again) that it would be premature to start tossing the dirt on Bob's head.

Playing on an almost bare stage, Dylan, backed by guitarist G.E. Smith – formerly of Hall and Oates' band – bassist Kenny Aaronson and drummer Christopher Parker, revived songs like Subterranean Homesick Blues and Absolutely Sweet Marie with a lean, uncompromising approach that was both unforgivingly tough and undeniably elegant.

In part it was Dylan taking his music back to its roots – or to parallel roots. There was country (Highway 61 Revisited, indeed!), there was raw rock and roll (Silvio, his most recent hit, penned with Robert Hunter of the Grateful Dead) and there were some cool blues, with Smith adding slide guitar accents to Dylan's solid but unspectacular rhythm guitar work. And there was folk, not just songs like Don't Think Twice It's All Right and Shelter from the Storm and A Thousand Miles Behind, but real chestnuts like North Country Fair and Barbara Allen, a song perhaps best known these days from the bowdlerized version sung each Christmas during the annual airing of the Alistair Sim version of Dicken's A Christmas Carol.

Along with the impeccable version of Like a Rolling Stone that closed the set, Dylan's performance and his song selection was a sign that the covers of songs such as Shenendoah and Let's Stay Together that dominated Down in The Groove were not evidence that Dylan has run out of steam. While he has admitted to a shortage of material of late, Monday's show suggested that Dylan – the mercurial man of many disguises – now intends to present himself as an interpreter of songs. It's an odd role for one of the most prolific songwriters of the last thirty years, but Dylan – adenoidal drawl and all – has made a stirring go of it. Of course, the songs he's interpreting are for the most part his own, but his versions of them, solid readings full of pleasant surprises and stylish touches from the band – and devoid of sentimentality or nostalgia – suggest that Dylan is capable of pulling on even this unlikely mask.

"Martha, he's not dead yet. Better forget about the shovel."

1989

Introduction

The Never-Ending Tour continued in 1989 with three concerts in Canada.

These shows would mark Bob Dylan's 46th, 47th & 48th concert in Canada.

The Dates

Toronto, ON	Sat., July 29, 1989
Ottawa, ON	Sun., July 30, 1989
Joliette, QC	Mon., July 31, 1989

The shows would be Dylan's 16th concert in Toronto, 4th concert in Ottawa and debut concert in Joliette.

The Musicians

Bob Dylan (vocal, guitar & harmonica).

G. E. Smith (guitar, electric slide guitar & backup vocals), Tony Garnier (bass), Christopher Parker (drums).

The Songs

Bob Dylan performed a total of 47 songs. Of those, 36 were different songs (31 were from albums and 5 were cover and/or traditional songs).

Seven songs made their Canadian live debut.

Trouble	Pretty Peggy-O
Early Mornin' Rain	One Irish Rover
Tears of Rage	Don't Pity Me
Hey La La (Hey La La)	–

Three songs have been played only once in Canada.

Trouble	Don't Pity Me
Hey La La (Hey La La)	–

Bob Dylan performed songs from 16 different albums.

Album	Released	# of Songs Performed by Album
Bob Dylan	March 19, 1962	1
The Freewheelin' Bob Dylan	May, 27, 1963	4
The Times They Are A-Changin'	Feb., 10, 1964	3
Another Side of Bob Dylan	Aug. 8, 1964	1
Bringing It All Back Home	March 22, 1965	4
Highway 61 Revisited	Aug. 30, 1965	4
Blonde on Blonde	May 16, 1966	4
John Wesley Harding	Dec. 27, 1967	1
Self Portrait	June 8, 1970	1
Bob Dylan's Greatest Hits, Vol. 2	Nov. 17, 1971	1
Blood on the Tracks	Jan. 20, 1975	2
The Basement Tapes	July 1, 1975	1
Saved	June 19, 1980	1
Shot of Love	Aug. 12, 1981	1
Empire Burlesque	May, 30, 1985	1
Down in the Groove	May 19, 1988	1

Opening Act

Steve Earle and the Dukes opened all three shows.

The Venues

It was Bob Dylan's debut concert at Kingswood Music Theatre in Toronto, 3rd time playing at the Ottawa Civic Centre and debut concert at the Lanaudière Outdoor Amphitheatre in Joliette.

Saturday, July 29, 1989 --- Kingswood Music Theatre
Toronto, ON

Set List

	Song	From The Album	Released
1.	Trouble	Shot of Love	Aug. 12, 1981
2.	Early Mornin' Rain (Gordon Lightfoot)	Self Portrait	June 8, 1970
3.	Tears of Rage (Bob Dylan/Richard Manual)	The Basement Tapes	July 1, 1975
4.	I Don't Believe You (She Acts Like We Never Have Met)	Another Side of Bob Dylan	Aug. 8, 1964
5.	Just Like a Woman	Blonde on Blonde	May 16, 1966
6.	Simple Twist of Fate	Blood on the Tracks	Jan. 20, 1975
7.	It's Alright, Ma (I'm Only Bleeding)	Bringing It All Back Home	March 22, 1965
8.	Don't Think Twice, It's All Right	The Freewheelin' Bob Dylan	May 27, 1963
9.	Gates of Eden	Bringing It All Back Home	March 22, 1965
10.	Hey La La (Hey La La) (McBride)	–	–
11.	In the Garden	Saved	June 19, 1980
12.	Silvio (Bob Dylan/Robert Hunter)	Down in the Groove	May 19, 1988
13.	Like a Rolling Stone	Highway 61 Revisited	Aug. 30, 1965
	Encores		
14.	The Times They Are A-Changin'	The Times They Are A-Changin'	Feb. 10, 1964
15.	All Along the Watchtower	John Wesley Harding	Dec. 27, 1967

The Musicians

Bob Dylan (vocal, guitar & harmonica), G. E. Smith (guitar & backup vocals), Tony Garnier (bass), Christopher Parker (drums).

Notes

- 46th Bob Dylan concert in Canada; 16th Bob Dylan concert in Toronto.
- 2, 4-6, 8, 14, Bob Dylan (harmonica).
- 7-9, 14, Bob Dylan (vocal & guitar), G. E. Smith (guitar).
- 10, 12, G. E. Smith (backup vocals).
- Canadian live debut of songs 1, 2, 3 & 10.
- Songs 1 & 10 have been performed only once in Canada.
- The opening act was Steve Earle and the Dukes.

Reviews

Dylan gives his fans the silent treatment

By Mitch Potter, Toronto Star.

Trust Bob Dylan to be conspicuous in his silence.

Scant days before the entertainment industry's planned canonization of the Woodstock generation, Dylan has virtually nothing to say on that or any other subject.

Not in so many words, at least. Pop music's most overanalyzed poet gave a capacity crowd of 14,000 the silent treatment Friday during an 80-minute set at Kingswood Theatre. No hello, no goodbye, not so much as a how do you do.

Not a peep.

Depending on which decade you tuned in to Dylan's prolific body of work, the show was alternately confounding, bemusing, infuriating or delightful. Most of the old folkies and middle-aged yuppies got it: most of the neo-Deadheads and fresh-faced teens didn't.

In an era when video spells it out for one and all, this had the makings of a refreshingly enigmatic, spartan affair: just three subdued backing musicians playing beneath a smattering of lights that left the stage in a constant state of silhouette.

But in purely musical terms, it was less than satisfying. Mixing a repertoire that bounced from the obvious ("Like A Rolling Stone", "Just Like A Woman", "The Times They Are A-Changin' ", "All Along The Watchtower") to the unknown (much of it, presumably, culled from his forthcoming album), Dylan occasionally sparked and sputtered but never really caught fire.

Repeatedly, the Minnesota native rearranged his own standards with a casualness verging on contempt – skewed, uncoordinated chording and half-hearted guitar leads, matched by trill, two-note toots on harmonica. For the most part, he spat out his lyrics like nails, making no attempt to turn his ravaged pipes on those famous melodies: in fact, during "Watchtower" he defined the melody by singing everything but.

That alone was probably a good thing. After all, feel-good nostalgia is the last thing we'd want from Mr. Zimmerman.

But occasionally, as in "Silvio" (a southern roots workout from last year's *Down In The Groove* album), Dylan was awakened from his aloof trance and coaxed into a more spirited effort by the bristling efficiency of bassist Tony Garnier, drummer Christopher Parker, and, worthy of particular mention, guitarist

G.E. Smith (the pony-tailed veteran of the Saturday Night Live band).

Still driven by equal parts country and rock, songwriter Steve Earle and his Dukes band proved the ideal complement to Friday's show, delivering an edited, more articulate version of their springtime sets at the Concert Hall.

From "Snake Oil" and "Copperhead Road" to "Nothing But A Child", Earle's newest pennings successfully convey an unlikely blend of raging "white trash" rebel sensibilities and astute social conscience. Earle's music is rooted with an undeniably southern signpost: his words are as far from redneck as it gets.

The Toronto Star. Mon., July 31, 1989. Reprinted with permission - Torstar Syndication Services.

Sharing Dylan's vision

Toronto Sun.

Bob Dylan was back with his trademark nasal honk at the Kingswood last night.

Indeed, it was a rather familiar evening.

In fact, it was very similar to last summer's Dylan show at the CNE Grandstand.

He played a selective profile of music from his past and present.

And he was helped along by his three-piece band, but especially guitarist G.E. Smith.

Dylan was also camera shy again. No concert photographs.

Which was a shame.

He was resplendent in a black ensemble with white trim. His hair was medium length and extra fuzzy.

Anyway, 13,500 fans shared his vision and his songs. And they were respectful.

This was Dylan, after all.

And so what if his voice cracked occasionally. So what if some of the versions of his famous folk-rock songs didn't quite hold together. His living-legend image did.

His *Early Morning Rain* was also a nice tribute to Gordon Lightfoot, who was in the crowd.

And don't forget crisp renditions of *Like A Rolling Stone*, *The Times They Are a-Changin'* and *All Along The Watchtower*.

Who could?

Dylan did them like nobody else could.

Besides that, two things became clear after Steve Earle and his band opened the evening's entertainment.

Toronto audiences can't seem to get enough of Earle. And just as many fans came to see him as they did Dylan.

Certainly, the reaction to Earle's driving roadhouse country-rock suggested it. The fact that most of the crowd arrived early enough to catch his set confirmed it.

Earle, of course, responded with a quick, but earnest, profile of his outlaw sounds epitomized by the rousing *Copperhead Road*.

The Toronto Sun. Sun., July 30, 1989. Reprinted with permission of The Sun Media Corp.

Sunday, July 30, 1989 --- Ottawa Civic Centre
Ottawa, ON

Set List

	Song	From The Album	Released
1.	Most Likely You Go Your Way and I'll Go Mine	Blonde on Blonde	May 16, 1966
2.	Pretty Peggy-O (trad. arr. Bob Dylan)	Bob Dylan	March 19, 1962
3.	Masters of War	The Freewheelin' Bob Dylan	May 27, 1963
4.	I Want You	Blonde on Blonde	May 16, 1966
5.	Ballad of a Thin Man	Highway 61 Revisited	Aug. 30, 1965
6.	Highway 61 Revisited	Highway 61 Revisited	Aug. 30, 1965
7.	It Takes a Lot to Laugh, It Takes a Train to Cry	Highway 61 Revisited	Aug. 30, 1965
8.	It's All Over Now, Baby Blue	Bringing It All Back Home	March 22, 1965
9.	Girl of the North Country	The Freewheelin' Bob Dylan	May 27, 1963
10.	The Lonesome Death of Hattie Carroll	The Times They Are A-Changin'	Feb. 10, 1964
11.	One Irish Rover (Van Morrison)	–	–
12.	Silvio (Bob Dylan/Robert Hunter)	Down in the Groove	May 19, 1988
13.	I Shall Be Released	Bob Dylan's Greatest Hits, Vol. 2	Nov. 17, 1971
14.	Like a Rolling Stone	Highway 61 Revisited	Aug. 30, 1965

	Encores		
15.	Barbara Allen (trad.)	–	–
16.	Blowin' in the Wind	The Freewheelin' Bob Dylan	May 27, 1963
17.	All Along the Watchtower	John Wesley Harding	Dec. 27, 1967

The Musicians

Bob Dylan (vocal, guitar & harmonica), G. E. Smith (guitar, electric slide guitar & backup vocals), Tony Garnier (bass), Christopher Parker (drums).

Notes

- 47th Bob Dylan concert in Canada; 4th Bob Dylan concert in Ottawa.
- 1, 4, 7-10, 15-16, Bob Dylan (harmonica).
- 6, G. E. Smith (electric slide guitar).
- 8-10, 15-16, Bob Dylan (vocal & guitar), G. E. Smith (guitar).
- 12, G. E. Smith (backup vocals).
- Canadian live debut of songs 2 & 11.
- The opening act was Steve Earle and the Dukes.

Reviews

BARE BONES BOB

By Rick Overall.

The anticipation was high – legends tend to do that to a crowd.

However, walking into the Civic Centre last night, this reporter was already a little miffed, no media personnel were allowed to photograph either Bob Dylan or opening act Steve Earle – fancy that!

Legends sometimes act in a strange fashion but hey, this was Bob Dylan. I figured we owed it to him to respect the edict.

It was basically a bare bones show which the 4,000 in attendance saw last night – Dylan switched off between his three-piece back-up band and a more acoustic scenario featuring himself and an additional acoustic backup. It was this format which seemed to illicit a stronger response from the crowd.

If there was a fault with the electric side it was that Dylan and company tended to wander off into jam-land a bit too often.

The performance featured a pot-pourri of songs from the extensive lyric history of Dylan – in almost every case, arrangements had been changed and tempos bumped into overdrive.

This re-working was most noticeable on tunes like *I Want You* and *I Shall Be Released*.

What one walked away from after last night's show really depended on what you walked into it expecting.

If it was wall to wall hits, then you'd have been disappointed – if it was an evening with one of contemporary music's great figures than you probably were pleased.

Dylan's performance was void of any onstage amenities – no bells and whistles, thank you very much.

He's an artist who doesn't need to perform and there are those who subscribe to the theory that he shouldn't – what we saw last night was an indication that he can still cut the mustard musically, even if it does come off a little lackluster in spots.

In keeping with his status as opening act – Steve Earle's stage appearance and overall projection had been scaled down.

But despite the downsizing there was no lack of on-stage enthusiasm as Earle and the Dukes romped through a shortened version of the killer show we saw at the NAC in February – favorites like *Guitar Town*, *I Ain't Ever Satisfied* and *Copperhead Road* served to get the evening off to a splendid start.

His encore version of the Stone's classic *Dead Flowers* sounded as if he owned the publishing rights himself.

The Ottawa Sun. Mon., July 31, 1989. Reprinted with permission of The Sun Media Corp.

Dylan pushes darkly into the future

By Susan Beyer, Citizen Correspondent.

While some may have been hoping for a sweet trip back to the sixties, Bob Dylan delivered a dark push into the '90s Sunday night at the Civic Centre.

Backed by a three-piece band led by G.E. Smith, as he was last year, Dylan opened with a disjointed rendition of *When You Go Your Way And I Go Mine*.

The strange chaotic playing drowned out the vocal as the sound board got adjusted. The harmonica was pitiful. Dylan's random rhythm guitar strumming seemed in competition with Smith's lead as they stood in a darkly-lit, high-tech tableau.

Even those willing to follow Dylan anywhere may have found their paths diverging here.

He followed with one of the many old tunes he played, *Pretty Peggy-O*, standing all in shadow, dressed in western-cut trousers, a dark striped shirt and vest, wearing Cuban heel boots, the harmonica slung round his neck.

Not even the next song, a driving, furious version of *Masters of War* was the sound mix clean.

The band whipped things up into a fierce storm while the audience fought to hear the words. What is the point of hearing Bob Dylan if you can't hear the words?

By the fourth song things seemed to have been adjusted and we could hear the lyrics, as Dylan spat out the words "I wan choo."

In this most strange of lust songs, he dropped the winsome tone of the 1965 version and delivered a scathing sort of denunciation.

Still seeming rather tentative at the mouth harp, which he kept adjusting in a fidgety manner, there was an improvised feel to the number which may not have been intentional.

Ballad Of A Thin Man, which has always had a bleak feel to it, was next.

The stage version was a brilliant reworking of the original. Smith on guitar gives Dylan's songs an edge like a razor: super sharp and deadly.

Gone are any vestiges of a honky tonk feel to the material Dylan played from *Highway 61 Revisited*.

Smith played aggressively and Dylan continued to release the lyrics from his mouth with re-invented melodies and a tonal flatness.

There was no singing from Bob Dylan. Recitations, speeded up to fit the new charging arrangements, yes.

Poetry written in the '60s transformed into a warp-speed, undifferentiated rap.

At the start of each new song, Dylan seemed reluctant to sing, approaching and then withdrawing from the mike, leading to extended intros.

The drummer and the bass player left the stage leaving Smith and Dylan on acoustic guitars. Dylan sang *It's All Over Now Baby Blue*, throwing a weird, near-hysterical spin on some of the lines.

The show progressed with more acoustic numbers and more band members.

Dylan came back to encore with the oldest of oldies *Barbara Allen*, then a strong *Blowin' in the Wind*.

Just when the crowd thought it was over and were ready to file out, out of the darkness came the shattering opening chords to *All Along the Watchtower*, sending a dark apocalyptic feel to the entire evening.

This was extremely powerful stuff, reminding us of just who we had been listening to for the past 90 minutes.

Steve Earle, in a 45-minute opening set, returned to his enthusiastic Ottawa fans, this time more open, more enjoyable than his last performance here.

Playing a condensed set of his best material Earle impressed with the fine songs he has written, all of them with good hooks. Especially fine was his *Fearless Heart*.

Without the dark trappings of his *Copperhead Road* persona, Earle pulled off a good set, enjoyed by a crowd which included families with "tiny-boppers" in tow, teenagers, youths and parents.

On y va parce que c'est Dylan…

La légende du folk n'attire que 5,000 personnes

par Marc André Joanisse, LeDroit.

On ne se déplace pas pour voir un spectacle bon ou mauvais de Bob Dylan.

On y va parce que c'est Dylan. Point à la ligne.

Hier soir, quelque 5,000 personnes tout au plus, ont été témoin du troisième spectacle à Ottawa de Robert Zimmerman.

Des *Flower People* devenus yuppies et qui fêtent cette année le 20e anniversaire de leur Woodstock aux jeunes collégiens en bermudas qui avaient encore la couche aux fesses quand Dylan crachait son fiel dans Greenwich Village, chacun avait sa raison de se retrouver dans un Centre municipal surchauffé dû à l'absence d'air climatisé et souligner le retour de la légende du folk.

Peu communicatif – il n'a pas dit un traître mot de la soirée – Dyan donnait carrément l'impression de se foutre éperdument de ces inconditionnels qui le dévisageaint et l'écoutaient comme s'il était un guru.

L'écouter représentait pratiquement une mission impossible. Pendant la majeure partie de son show, Dylan s'est retrouvé au beau milieu d'une guerre de décibels où les solos de guitare se sont succédés à un rythme effréné. Les nouvelles pièces interprétées hier en ont laissé plusieurs sur leur appétit. Dylan forcant sa voix à plus d'une reprise, torturant et déformant ainsi les textes de son dernier cru qu'on avait peine à saisir.

Le même problème a surgi lorsqu'il s'est lancé dans une version saccadée de *Like A Rolling Stone*. Il a fallu se tourner les pouces une bonne minute avant de saisir les notes de base de ce classique des années 60. Il était également méconnaissable dans l'interprétation de *I Want You*.

Le seul moment où Dylan a donné l'impression d'être vraiment en possession de ses moyens fut lorsqu'il a livré des versions «acoustiques» de quelques-unes de ses meilleures pièces.

Brilamment accompagné par son guitariste, G.E. Smith, l'artiste a livré une émouvante version de *It's All Over Now Baby Blue* et *Blowin'g In The Wind* qu'il a offerte en rappel.

L'espace de quelques minutes, le poète-chanteur de Greenwich Village qui a déplacé tant d'air à une certaine époque venait de descendre sur la patinoire des 67's d'Ottawa.

Il est malheureusement aussitôt remonté pour redescendre dans la peau d'un gars qui donne l'impression de vouloir briser les liens avec le passé.

Mais Dylan c'est Dylan.

On ne peut pas le trouver bon ni mauvais.

Et dans deux ans, peut-être trois, il sera de retour.

Et encore une fois, il sera fidèle à sa réputation…mi-bon, mi-mauvais.

LeDroit. Mon., July 31, 1989. Reprinted with permission of LeDroit.

Monday, July 31, 1989 --- Lanaudière Outdoor Amphitheatre Joliette, QC

Set List

	Song	From The Album	Released
1.	Most Likely You Go Your Way and I'll Go Mine	Blonde on Blonde	May 16, 1966
2.	Don't Pity Me (?)	–	–
3.	Ballad of Hollis Brown	The Times They Are A-Changin'	Feb. 10, 1964
4.	Shelter from the Storm	Blood on the Tracks	Jan. 20, 1975
5.	I Want You	Blonde on Blonde	May 16, 1966
6.	Ballad of a Thin Man	Highway 61 Revisited	Aug. 30, 1965
7.	Don't Think Twice, It's All Right	The Freewheelin' Bob Dylan	May 27, 1963
8.	One Too Many Mornings	Blonde on Blonde	May 16, 1966
9.	Mr. Tambourine Man	Bringing It All Back Home	March 22, 1965
10.	Seeing the Real You at Last	Empire Burlesque	May 30, 1985
11.	One Irish Rover (Van Morrison)	–	–
12.	Silvio (Bob Dylan/Robert Hunter)	Down in the Groove	May 19, 1988
13.	Like a Rolling Stone	Highway 61 Revisited	Aug. 30, 1965
	Encores		
14.	It Ain't Me, Babe	Another Side of Bob Dylan	Aug. 8, 1964
15.	All Along the Watchtower	John Wesley Harding	Dec. 27, 1967

The Musicians

Bob Dylan (vocal, guitar & harmonica), G. E. Smith (guitar & backup vocals), Tony Garnier (bass), Christopher Parker (drums).

Notes

- 48th Bob Dylan concert in Canada; Debut Bob Dylan concert in Joliette.
- 4, 5, 7-9, 14, Bob Dylan (harmonica).
- 4-6, Bob Dylan (acoustic guitar).
- 7-9, 14, Bob Dylan (vocal & guitar), G. E. Smith (guitar).
- 12, G. E. Smith (backup vocals).
- Canadian live debut of song 2.
- Song 2 has been performed only once in Canada.
- Only live performance of song 2 anywhere in the world, to date.
- The opening act was Steve Earle and the Dukes.

Review

Un guitariste avant tout

BOB DYLAN

par Jean Sébastien.

DYLAN folkloriste, Dylan hippie, Dylan militant, Dylan chrétien, Dylan maître de cérémonie – l'Américain qui a dominé la musique populaire des années 60 a tenu tous ces rôles.

Aujourd'hui il veut nous dire qu'il est aussi, et avant tout, Dylan guitariste.

Nous le dire… Est-ce le bon mot? Pas vraiment puisque Bob Dylan ne s'est pas adressé à la foule une seule fois au cours du spectacle qu'il a donné lundi soir dans le cadre du festival de Lanaudière. Ni bonjour à l'entrée, ni merci au rappel. Seulement ses chansons et sa guitare.

La « rumeur » voulait que Dylan tourne maintenant le dos au public. Vrai et faux à la fois. C'est plutôt à la la relation traditionnelle entre le public et l'artiste que Dylan tourne le dos.

Les éclairages sobres traçaient un jeu d'ombres contrastées sur son visage dont on devinait les traits plus qu'on ne les voyait, mais jetaient ses mains, son jeu de guitare, en pleine lumière. Ses musiciens, comme l'éclairage, cherchaient à mettre en valeur le travail de Dylan. Comme la plomberie bien faite d'une maison, les rythmes forts du bassiste Kenny Aaronson et le jeu des cymbales de Chris Parker laissaient couler la guitare.

Vers la mi-spectacle, le guitariste G. E. Smith est resté seul sur scène avec Dylan, tous deux à la guitare acoustique, l'un tenant le contrepoint de jeu de l'autre. Les trois pièces qu'ils ont interprétées ont créé une tension qui a trouvé sa catharsis dans le classique *Mr Tambourine Man*.

Ici le choix des chansons disait à lui seul tout ce que Dylan avait à dire. Sur la première pièce de ce triplé, Dylan à mots couverts nous laissait voir son âme de *hobo*, difficile d'approche : « *We never did too much talking anyway.* » Et l'homme silencieux qu'il a chanté sur la pièce suivante complétait le portrait.

Dylan a immédiatement relancé le spectacle avec des pièces plus dures, de la musique qui s'écoute debout, terminant le spectacle avec *Where the Dean Men Go*, puis *Like a Rolling Stone*. Le service de sécurité, habitué aux « bonnes moeurs » des concerts de musique classique, avait fort à faire pour que le public resta assis. Quand la salle était debout sur les bancs, c'est du feu qu'a dû s'inquiéter la sécurité alors qu'un spectateur allumait quelques feux de Bengale sur la butte gazonnée de l'amphithéâtre.

Dylan, maître de la situation, a quitté discrètement la scène, puis est revenu avec son guitariste interpréter en rappel *It Ain't Me, Babe*; puis avec le groupe complet, il a entonné *All Along the Watchtower*.

Steve Earle a, lui aussi, entamé sa jeune carrière en bousculant la tradition. Avec *Back to the Wall*, on a compris pourquoi il a pris Nashville à rebrousse-poil. Et le solo de guitare fou sur la chanson très country *Good Ol Boy (Gettin' Tough)* vous hérissait tous les poils du corps.

Earle bien sûr n'a pas la stature de Dylan. Il ne peut se permettre de garder le silence devant son public. Il nous a donc entretenu du son rapport à la tradition.

Le chanson *Copperhead Road* avec laquelle il a fermé son spectacle en est un bon exemple. Le Texas de Earle n'est plus celui des cowboys mais celui des motards.

Et si Earle dit ressembler à George Bush, dans leurs rôles semblables d'orateur public, il s'en est différencié en présentant l'Amérique démunie. Pourfendant ceux qui se cache la pauvreté, il a chanté l'autre Amérique en trafiquant le country-blues.

Additional Review

Bob Dylan catches fire: Steve Earle raw, raucous at idyllic Laurentian site. No byline. The Montreal Gazette. Tues., Aug. 1, 1989. p. C6.

1990

Introduction

The Never-Ending Tour stormed through Canada in 1990 with sixteen concerts. The most concerts in Canada for any given year.

These shows would mark Bob Dylan's 49th, 50th, 51st, 52nd, 53rd, 54th, 55th, 56th, 57th, 58th, 59th, 60th, 61st, 62nd, 63rd & 64th concert in Canada.

The Dates

Montreal, QC	Tues., May 29, 1990
Kingston, ON	Wed., May 30, 1990
Ottawa, ON	Fri., June 1, 1990
Ottawa, ON	Sat., June 2, 1990
London, ON	Mon., June 4, 1990
Toronto, ON	Tues., June 5, 1990
Toronto, ON	Wed., June 6, 1990
Toronto, ON	Thurs., June 7, 1990
Winnipeg, MB	Sun., June 17, 1990
Winnipeg, MB	Mon., June 18, 1990
Edmonton, AB	Sun., Aug. 12, 1990
Edmonton, AB	Mon., Aug. 13, 1990
Calgary, AB	Wed., Aug. 15, 1990
Calgary, AB	Thurs., Aug. 16, 1990
Victoria, BC	Sun., Aug. 19, 1990
Vancouver, BC	Mon., Aug. 20, 1990

Ottawa, Winnipeg, Edmonton and Calgary each hosted two-night stands. Toronto fans were treated to a three-night run.

The shows would be Dylan's 17th concert in Montreal, debut concert in Kingston, 5th & 6th concert in Ottawa, debut concert in London, 17th, 18th & 19th concert in Toronto, 2nd & 3rd concert in Winnipeg, 2nd & 3rd concert in Edmonton, 2nd & 3rd concert in Calgary, debut concert in Victoria and 6th concert in Vancouver.

The Musicians

Bob Dylan (vocal, guitar & harmonica).

G. E. Smith (guitar, acoustic slide guitar, electric slide guitar & backup vocals), Tony Garnier (bass), Christopher Parker (drums).

The Songs

Bob Dylan performed a total of 295 songs. Of those, 60 were different songs (54 were from albums and 6 were cover and/or traditional songs).

Seventeen songs made their Canadian live debut.

Everything is Broken	What Was It You Wanted?
What Good Am I?	One More Night
No More One More Time	Queen Jane Approximately
Where Teardrops Fall	Political World
Disease of Conceit	Nowhere Man
Tight Connection to My Heart (Has Anybody Seen My Love)	The Water is Wide
Tomorrow is a Long Time	Man of Constant Sorrow
John Brown	Shooting Star
I've Been All Around This World	–

Six songs have been played only once in Canada.

Where Teardrops Fall	One More Night
Disease of Conceit	Nowhere Man
Tight Connection to My Heart (Has Anybody Seen My Love)	The Water is Wide

Two songs made their worldwide live debut.

No More One More Time	Nowhere Man

Bob Dylan performed songs from 18 different albums.

Album	Released	# of Songs Performed by Album
Bob Dylan	March 19, 1962	1
The Freewheelin' Bob Dylan	May, 27, 1963	4

The Times They Are A-Changin'	Feb., 10, 1964	5
Another Side of Bob Dylan	Aug. 8, 1964	2
Bringing It All Back Home	March 22, 1965	8
Highway 61 Revisited	Aug. 30, 1965	6
Blonde on Blonde	May 16, 1966	5
Bob Dylan's Greatest Hits	March 27, 1967	1
John Wesley Harding	Dec. 27, 1967	1
Nashville Skyline	April 9, 1969	2
Bob Dylan's Greatest Hits, Vol. 2	Nov. 17, 1971	2
Blood on the Tracks	Jan. 20, 1975	3
The Basement Tapes	July 1, 1975	1
Slow Train Coming	Aug. 20, 1979	2
Saved	June 19, 1980	1
Empire Burlesque	May, 30, 1985	2
Oh Mercy	Sept. 12, 1989	7
MTV Unplugged	June 30, 1995	1

Opening Act

Sue Medley opened all sixteen shows.

Special Guests

Ronnie Hawkins joined Dylan on stage at the June 7th show in Toronto for One More Night. Steve Bruton auditioned live with the band in both Victoria and Vancouver.

The Venues

It was Bob Dylan's debut concert at the Centre Sportif de l'Université de Montréal, debut concert at the Kingston Memorial Centre, debut concert & 2nd time playing at the National Arts Centre Opera in Ottawa, debut concert at Alumni Hall in London, debut concert, 2nd & 3rd time playing at the O'Keefe Centre for the Performing Arts in Toronto, debut concert & 2nd time playing at the Centennial Centre Concert Hall in Winnipeg, debut concert & 2nd time playing at the Jubilee Auditorium in Edmonton, debut concert & 2nd time playing at the Jubilee Auditorium in Calgary, debut concert at Memorial Arena in Victoria and 2nd time playing at the Pacific Coliseum in Vancouver.

Tuesday, May 29, 1990 --- Centre Sportif de l'Université de Montréal Montréal, QC

Set List

	Song	From The Album	Released
1.	Absolutely Sweet Marie	Blonde on Blonde	May 16, 1966
2.	Lay, Lady, Lay	Nashville Skyline	April 9, 1969
3.	Maggie's Farm	Bringing It All Back Home	March 22, 1965
4.	You're a Big Girl Now	Blood on the Tracks	Jan. 20, 1975
5.	Highway 61 Revisited	Highway 61 Revisited	Aug. 30, 1965
6.	The Times They Are A-Changin'	The Times They Are A-Changin'	Feb. 10, 1964
7.	Desolation Row	Highway 61 Revisited	Aug. 30, 1965
8.	The Lonesome Death of Hattie Carroll	The Times They Are A-Changin'	Feb. 10, 1964
9.	Girl of the North Country	The Freewheelin' Bob Dylan	May 27, 1963
10.	To Ramona	Another Side of Bob Dylan	Aug. 8, 1964
11.	Everything is Broken	Oh Mercy	Sept. 12, 1989
12.	All Along the Watchtower	John Wesley Harding	Dec. 27, 1967
13.	What Good Am I?	Oh Mercy	Sept. 12, 1989
14.	No More One More Time (Troy Seals/Dave Kirby)	–	–
15.	Simple Twist of Fate	Blood on the Tracks	Jan. 20, 1975
16.	I Shall Be Released	Bob Dylan's Greatest Hits, Vol. 2	Nov. 17, 1971
17.	Like a Rolling Stone	Highway 61 Revisited	Aug. 30, 1965
	Encores		
18.	Mr. Tambourine Man	Bringing It All Back Home	March 22, 1965
19.	Stuck Inside of Mobile with the Memphis Blues Again	Blonde on Blonde	May 16, 1966

The Musicians

Bob Dylan (vocal, guitar & harmonica), G. E. Smith (guitar & electric slide guitar), Tony Garnier (bass), Christopher Parker (drums).

Notes

- 49th Bob Dylan concert in Canada; 17th Bob Dylan concert in Montreal.
- 4, 6, 8, 10, 13, 15, 18, Bob Dylan (harmonica).
- 6-10, 18, acoustic with the band.
- 5, G. E. Smith (electric slide guitar).
- Canadian live debut of songs 11, 13 & 14.
- Worldwide live debut of song 14.
- The opening act was Sue Medley.

Review

Bob Dylan: un show correct, mais sans plus

par Alain Brunet.

Bob Dylan est certainement l'un des personnages les plus célèbres de la musique populaire. Archevêque du protest song dans les années soixante, fondateur du folk-rock, il représente un grand mythe américain.

Mais en ce qui a trait à la bête de scène et au musicien hors pair, on repassera.

Au Centre Sportif de l'Université de Montréal, plus de deux mille fans de toutes les générations étaient venus visionner le mythe hier soir. Et les "vieux" comme moi pouvaient en apprendre de leurs cadets. Prenez la jeune femme ma gauche; en début de vingtaine, elle savait tout du répertoire dylanesque! Évidemment, les nostalgiques plus âgés étaient aussi de la partie. Bob achève la quarantaine, il atteint au moins trois décennies de tympans.

Malgré les failles majeures qui truffent le concert de Dylan, il est tout de même excitant de voir cet être ébouriffé gratouiller ses guitares électrique et acoustique, l'entendre baragouiner ses grands succès de sa voix ultra-nasillarde, le voir déployer ses gestes anguleux et maladroits.

Il est cependant moins agréable d'observer l'artiste pomper l'huile en certains moments, manquer de magnétisme... pour reprendre vie par la suite. Et comment une célébrité qui a trente ans de métier derrière la cravate peut-elle réussir à fausser totalement avec son harmonica en jouant un de ses mythiques succès? Ah ces anti-stars...

On sait que récemment, notre personnage s'était refait une santé musicale avec Oh Mercy, le plus brillant de ses microsillons depuis plusieurs années. Sur scène, Robert Zimmerman n'a malheureusement joué que deux titres de cette extraordinaire galette: Everything Is Broken et What Good Am I?.

Dommage, d'autant plus que le trio qui accompagne Dylan ne reproduit vraiment pas l'esprit de ce mémorable enregistrement produit par Daniel Lanois. Le guitariste J.E. Smith (un régulier de l'émission Saturday Night Live) et ses collègues sont de respectables professionnels, mais livrent un produit qui semble parfois inachevé. Lorsqu'on donne dans le rock, certains moments peuvent s'avérer inspirés; lorsque'on prend une pause folk, il faut aimer le style Dylan pour demeurer magnétisé. Quoi qu'il en soit, l'auditoire semblera conquis, surtout en fin de concert.

Fidèle à ses habitudes (c'est ce qu'on dit), Dylan a truffé son spectacle de vieux tubes, pour la plupart inscrits au panthéon du folk-rock américain: Lay Lady Lay, Highway 61 Revisited, The Times They Are A-Changing, We Shall Be Released, All Along The Watch Tower, Twist Of Faith... Était-ce possible d'éviter Like A Rolling Stone, Mister Tambourine Man ou Stuck Inside Of Mobile With The Memphis Blues Again? Probablement pas. On ne va pas à l'Université de Montréal pour rien. Une heure et demie de Dylan 101, version intensive. La pauvre Sue Medley, en première partie, n'a pu faire lever l'auditoire, vu la mauvaise qualité sonore - qui, soit dit en passant, affligeait Dylan aussi, mais à un moindre degré.

As appeared in La Presse. Wed., May 30, 1990. Reprinted with permission of Alain Brunet.

Additional Review

Dylan beats odds with classic performance, by Mark LePage. The Montreal Gazette. Wed., May 30, 1990. p. E9.

Wednesday, May 30, 1990 --- Kingston Memorial Centre
Kingston, ON

Set List

	Song	From The Album	Released
1.	Most Likely You Go Your Way and I'll Go Mine	Blonde on Blonde	May 16, 1966
2.	Ballad of a Thin Man	Highway 61 Revisited	Aug. 30, 1965
3.	Stuck Inside of Mobile with the Memphis Blues Again	Blonde on Blonde	May 16, 1966
4.	Just Like a Woman	Blonde on Blonde	May 16, 1966
5.	Masters of War	The Freewheelin' Bob Dylan	May 27, 1963
6.	Gotta Serve Somebody	Slow Train Coming	Aug. 20, 1979

7.	Love Minus Zero/No Limit	Bringing It All Back Home	March 22, 1965
8.	It's Alright, Ma (I'm Only Bleeding)	Bringing It All Back Home	March 22, 1965
9.	She Belongs to Me	Bringing It All Back Home	March 22, 1965
10.	Ballad of Hollis Brown	The Times They Are A-Changin'	Feb. 10, 1964
11.	One Too Many Mornings	The Times They Are A-Changin'	Feb. 10, 1964
12.	Mr. Tambourine Man	Bringing It All Back Home	March 22, 1965
13.	Where Teardrops Fall	Oh Mercy	Sept. 12, 1989
14.	Everything is Broken	Oh Mercy	Sept. 12, 1989
15.	I Shall Be Released	Bob Dylan's Greatest Hits, Vol. 2	Nov. 17, 1971
16.	All Along the Watchtower	John Wesley Harding	Dec. 27, 1967
17.	What Good Am I?	Oh Mercy	Sept. 12, 1989
18.	Like a Rolling Stone	Highway 61 Revisited	Aug. 30, 1965
	Encores		
19.	Blowin' in the Wind	The Freewheelin' Bob Dylan	May 27, 1963
20.	Highway 61 Revisited	Highway 61 Revisited	Aug. 30, 1965

The Musicians

Bob Dylan (vocal, guitar & harmonica), G. E. Smith (guitar & electric slide guitar), Tony Garnier (bass), Christopher Parker (drums).

Notes

- 50th Bob Dylan concert in Canada; Debut Bob Dylan concert in Kingston.
- 2, 7, 9, 11-13, 16-17, 19, Bob Dylan (harmonica).
- 7-12, 19, acoustic with the band.
- 20, G. E. Smith (electric slide guitar).
- Canadian live debut of song 13.
- Song 13 has been performed only once in Canada.
- The opening act was Sue Medley.

Review

Dylan tries hard but disappoints crowd

Dylan wasn't a success but he did try hard, pumping out 22 songs in an energetic 100-minute set

By Greg Burliuk, Whig-Standard Staff Writer.

Is Bob Dylan a control freak or a truly shy guy? Is he a tease or a true artist? Does he remember the tunes to his old songs? Is he too cheap to afford a decent sound system? Is he singing with passion or just croaking off-key?

As always with Bob Dylan, the questions outnumber the answers. The 2,869 in attendance in the Kingston Memorial Centre last night were vociferous in their appreciation of him but what were they going to do, boo a legend? Besides, there was such a nice friendly feeling in the air as people renewed old acquaintances at perhaps the first concert they'd attended in many years.

They included a babe in arms, a little girl in gold lame shoes and a guy with pink sneakers who could have passed for my double in a dark room. (Sounds like a Dylan song, eh?) And after all, this is the man whose canon includes some of the greatest songs in popular music.

Still, the concert has to rank as a disappointment. I'd be surprised if many of 2,869 would go see Bob Dylan again. It's not that the diminutive singer didn't try hard: he pumped out 22 songs in a 100-minute set which, if nothing else, was energetic.

But there were problems from the beginning. Opening act Sue Medley started promptly on time at 7:30 p.m. with a third of the audience not yet in their seats. There were sound problems with her set until she played a couple of quieter songs.

Louisiana guitar player Sonny Landreth and his excellent fills, for example, were largely inaudible but for a couple of songs.

Ms. Medley is a much better artist than she was allowed to show, although the songs Blue Skies and Dangerous Times were at least not damaged.

After a short intermission, the audience was told not to smoke, not to take pictures or sound recordings and to sit down because Mr. Dylan was about to come on. When he did, it was on a stage which had a six-foot barrier between the apron and the audience. And it was with a three-piece band led by Saturday Night Live guitarist G.E. Smith.

While this was a group who could rock, they weren't particularly adept at illuminating Mr. Dylan's music and that's crucial because his singing has never particularly done so on its own. This minimalist accompaniment meant that more ambitious songs, especially several created in the last 10 years, could not be attempted.

It may seem facetious to wonder whether Mr. Dylan remembers the tunes to his older stuff but I wasn't too sure when he sang Blowin' In The Wind in an encore to no melody you could recognize.

But surely one could recognize the songs from his lyrics, those unforgettable words imprinted on so many of our minds. That's true but the sound system was so muddy, if you didn't recognize the song you had no idea what he was saying. And let's not blame the Memorial Centre acoustics again, please.

That's a canard since performers as disparate as Willie Nelson and Alice Cooper have had no problems being heard in recent months. Not that Mr. Dylan helped any. He raced through Like A Rolling Stone as if he was apologetic that it was six minutes long.

I don't know if that's why I couldn't recognize some of the songs or it was just obscure material but at least Mr. Dylan did play some of his older hits. He seemed particularly interested in his mid-Sixties repertoire and especially the albums Bring It All Back Home, The Times They Are A Changin' and Highway 61 Revisited.

From them he chose songs like One Too Many Mornings, Love Minus Zero/No Limit, Mr. Tambourine Man, Like A Rolling Stone, Ballad Of A Thin Man and Highway 61 Revisited.

Other golden oldies included Just Like A Woman, I Shall Be Released, and a version of All Along The Watchtower which was vigorous but simplistic beside Jimi Hendrix's superb cover of it.

Mr. Dylan was even disappointing when performing songs from his latest album Oh Mercy. He performed three: Where Teardrops Fall, Everything Is Broken and What Good Am I?, and each came up well short of the stark drama contained on record.

For me, at least, something good came out of this exercise. In preparing for this concert, I went back to many of the albums Bob Dylan has made in the last 10 years and some of them are truly underrated classics. Albums like Saved, Infidels, and Empire Burlesque are brilliant pieces of work and now that he's proven he can still rock I'd love to hear Mr. Dylan come back with a full band and perform music from them.

Friday, June 1, 1990 --- National Arts Centre Opera
Ottawa, ON

Set List

	Song	From The Album	Released
1.	Most Likely You Go Your Way and I'll Go Mine	Blonde on Blonde	May 16, 1966
2.	Ballad of a Thin Man	Highway 61 Revisited	Aug. 30, 1965
3.	Stuck Inside of Mobile with the Memphis Blues Again	Blonde on Blonde	May 16, 1966
4.	Just Like a Woman	Blonde on Blonde	May 16, 1966
5.	Masters of War	The Freewheelin' Bob Dylan	May 27, 1963
6.	Gotta Serve Somebody	Slow Train Coming	Aug. 20, 1979
7.	Love Minus Zero/No Limit	Bringing It All Back Home	March 22, 1965
8.	It's Alright, Ma (I'm Only Bleeding)	Bringing It All Back Home	March 22, 1965
9.	She Belongs to Me	Bringing It All Back Home	March 22, 1965
10.	It Takes a Lot to Laugh, It Takes a Train to Cry	Highway 61 Revisited	Aug. 30, 1965
11.	Disease of Conceit	Oh Mercy	Sept. 12, 1989
12.	Everything is Broken	Oh Mercy	Sept. 12, 1989
13.	In the Garden	Saved	June 19, 1980
14.	Like a Rolling Stone	Highway 61 Revisited	Aug. 30, 1965
	Encores		
15.	Mr. Tambourine Man	Bringing It All Back Home	March 22, 1965
16.	Highway 61 Revisited	Highway 61 Revisited	Aug. 30, 1965

The Musicians

Bob Dylan (vocal, guitar & harmonica), G. E. Smith (guitar & electric slide guitar), Tony Garnier (bass), Christopher Parker (drums).

Notes

- 51st Bob Dylan concert in Canada; 5th Bob Dylan concert in Ottawa.
- 2, 4, 7, 9, 14, 15, Bob Dylan (harmonica).
- 7-9, 15, acoustic with the band.
- 16, G. E. Smith (electric slide guitar).
- Canadian live debut of 11.
- Song 11 has been performed only once in Canada.
- The opening act was Sue Medley.

Reviews

Who's that man mumbling those great lyrics?

By Chris Cobb, Citizen Staff Writer.

Frustrating though it obviously is for some people, Bob Dylan doesn't bother communicating with his audience – except, of course, through his songs, which he would likely say is quite enough.

In the inhibiting surroundings of The National Arts Centre Opera on Friday, however, Dylan could have gone a little farther in pandering to his audience.

"Say a few words," someone shouted, somewhat pathetically.

"Happy birthday," shouted someone else.

"Happy birthday to you too," he replied. That was it. That was all he said, all night.

Dylan traditionally chooses to perform this way. No idle banter. No banter at all, in fact. Just one song after another, sung in frail voice, the old songs altered a little to accommodate the aging vocal chords.

The concert Friday featured many of his great songs – well, he's written so many of them.

You Go Your Way, I'll Go Mine gave the concert a shaky opening. He went on to sing *Masters of War*, *Just Like a Woman*, *Serve Somebody*. And, as always, he split his show into electric and acoustic sets helped out by a three-piece band led by G.E. Smith of *Saturday Night Live* fame. The music was good, solid, technically excellent but at times lacked any real spirit.

Many of the lyrics were inaudible and the singing often monotonous.

It is sad to hear a song like *Masters of War* rendered without enthusiasm, the brilliant words obscured by a wall of electric sound.

And sad it was too to see people leaving the hall midway through the show. A noticeable number did.

The band could have benefited from a few backup singers. Dylan has often travelled with singers and besides adding vocal strength to the performance, they have given him something to play off. His band, which often looked bored, didn't give him that.

Dylan, of course, is a wonderful writer and a true icon. But as his mass popularity dwindles and he finds himself playing to smaller halls a long way from stadiums and arenas, he would do well to think about reaching out to his audience a little more.

The Ottawa Citizen. Sat., June 2, 1990. Reprinted with permission of The Ottawa Citizen.

DYLAN FALLS FLAT!

By Rick Overall.

The bigger they are, the harder they fall.

It's an old adage but never truer than when applied to Bob Dylan's appearance at the NAC this weekend.

There's no denying the incredible contribution Dylan's heaped on contemporary music over the past 20 years but the man we saw in concert on Friday was a shadow of the legend he'd sculpted with his own hands.

It was like watching Muhammed Ali try to make a comeback – we all respect the legend but the reality was pretty darn embarrassing to watch.

Backed by a functional three-piece band, Dylan wallowed through the wash of distortion which rendered his vocals almost unintelligible – save for the most familiar of songs.

Throughout the show he swaggered around the stage, seemingly oblivious to what was going on – like some punch-drunk boxer long past his prime.

It was an evening where Dylan and company methodically plodded on through a selection of classics and only when they switched to acoustic guitars did it feel comfortable.

A lot of the material offered up during the Friday show was drawn from early LPs.

From *It's All Right Ma, I'm Only Bleeding* to *Masters of War* to the monster hit *Like A Rolling Stone*, there was certainly a lot of Dylan to choose from.

But the special subtlety and trademark lyrical ferocity, so important, were missing.

The saddest aspect of the whole exercise was the fact that this music, which "meant" so much to those in attendance, was treated in such an offhand manner.

Why even External Affairs Minister Joe Clark – who was in attendance – deserves better treatment than what bashful Bob dealt out.

Despite the misfortune of Dylan's performance, the evening was still a memorable one.

The memories all flowed from the considerable talent dealt out by Canadian up and comer Sue Medley.

Her opening set completely addressed the promise of her self-titled debut LP – she's simply dynamite.

Joined by a captivating band, Medley got every second's worth of her 40-minute set.

From the hard edge of tracks like *That's Life*, *Dangerous Times*, *Love Thing* and *57 Chevy*, she moved effortlessly through the gentler sounds of *Blue Skies* and *Blue Train*.

Medley's strength lies in a delicious marriage of pure vocal beauty and a hint of raunch – for someone who's just moved into the "bigs," she's surprisingly strong on stage.

Without a doubt, Sue Medley is on her way and it's to her credit she was there to toss a musical liferaft to a show that would have drowned without her.

The Ottawa Sun. Sun., June 3, 1990. Reprinted with permission of The Sun Media Corp.

Quelle belle soirée inoubliable

Bob Dylan au CNA

par Mariloup Malboeuf, LeDroit.

OTTAWA Il est venu et, tel un dieu, a été salué et applaudi par ses disciples, avant même d'ouvrir la bouche.

Bob Dylan est apparu de noir vêtu, au Centre national des arts, hier, pour la première des deux représentations qu'il offre à Ottawa.

Son auditoire, dont l'âge variait entre 18 et 55 ans, l'attendait.

Personne n'a été déçu.

De «You Go Your Way, I'll Go Mine», à « t's All Right, Ma», Bob Dylan a été égal à luimême, et fidèle à ses enregistrements.

Trois musiciens l'accompagnaient, dont le fantastique G.E. Smith à la guitare.

Deuxième visite

Applaudissements, encouragements et accompagnements de voix ont salué sa presentation sur scène, à sa deuxième visite en un peu plus d'un an.

Dans «Just Like a Woman», Dylan s'est emparé de son harmonica, et le public a pu l'écouter en solo. Les fausses notes ont fusé... Mais Dylan, c'est Dylan!

Avares de paroles, généreux en chansons

Avare de paroles, il a lancé un «Happy Birthday to You» après la 11e toune, et Dieu sait à qui il s'adressait!, le gourou du folk américain a laissé couler ses paroles et sa musique sur la foule, subjuguée.

Contrairement à d'autres occasions où sa prestation méritait d'être oubliée, Bob Dylan a offert ce que l'on attendait de lui. On souhaitait voir du Dylan pur et simple, sans flafla, et se fût le cas.

Le décor sobre de la scène a aidé à créer un environnement intime, où les messieurs et dames habillés de jeans ou portant la cravate se sont retrouvés.

«Oh Mercy»

Il a chanté quelques tounes de son plus récent album, «Oh, Mercy», produit par le Hullois Daniel Lanois.

Ce soir, il sera de retour au CNA, pour une dernière représentation. Après quoi, il poursuivra sa tournée canadienne. C'est à voir!

Une belle entrée

Auteure-compositeur, Sue Medley a relevé le défi de jour en première partie du spectacle de Bob Dylan. Un mélange de pop, de rock et de folk, une voix forte et chaude, et le tour était joué!

Même si sa performance ne mérite guère un cinq étoiles, Sue Medley a sû se faire apprécier de la foule. Des chansons d'amour, des chansons d'espoir ont été chantées par l'artiste acompagnée, au départ, de cinq musiciens.

Des paroles parfois difficiles à entendre. Mais on se surprenait quelquefois à branler le pied, à suivre le rythme...

Une bien belle soirée!

LeDroit. Sat., June 2, 1990. Reprinted with permission of LeDroit.

Saturday, June 2, 1990 --- National Arts Centre Opera
Ottawa, ON

Set List

	Song	From The Album	Released
1.	Subterranean Homesick Blues	Bringing It All Back Home	March 22, 1965
2.	Ballad of a Thin Man	Highway 61 Revisited	Aug. 30, 1965
3.	Stuck Inside of Mobile with the Memphis Blues Again	Blonde on Blonde	May 16, 1966
4.	Tight Connection to My Heart (Has Anybody Seen My Love)	Empire Burlesque	May 30, 1985
5.	Masters of War	The Freewheelin' Bob Dylan	May 27, 1963
6.	Gotta Serve Somebody	Slow Train Coming	Aug. 20, 1979
7.	It Ain't Me, Babe	Another Side of Bob Dylan	Aug. 8, 1964
8.	Desolation Row	Highway 61 Revisited	Aug. 30, 1965
9.	The Lonesome Death of Hattie Carroll	The Times They Are A-Changin'	Feb. 10, 1964

10.	It's Alright, Ma (I'm Only Bleeding)	Bringing It All Back Home	March 22, 1965
11.	Boots of Spanish Leather	The Times They Are A-Changin'	Feb. 10, 1964
12.	Everything is Broken	Oh Mercy	Sept. 12, 1989
13.	All Along the Watchtower	John Wesley Harding	Dec. 27, 1967
14.	What Good Am I?	Oh Mercy	Sept. 12, 1989
15.	Leopard-Skin Pill-Box Hat	Blonde on Blonde	May 16, 1966
16.	Simple Twist of Fate	Blood on the Tracks	Jan. 20, 1975
17.	Like a Rolling Stone	Highway 61 Revisited	Aug. 30, 1965
	Encores		
18.	The Times They Are A-Changin'	The Times They Are A-Changin'	Feb. 10, 1964
19	Highway 61 Revisited	Highway 61 Revisited	Aug. 30, 1965

The Musicians

Bob Dylan (vocal, guitar & harmonica), G. E. Smith (guitar & electric slide guitar), Tony Garnier (bass), Christopher Parker (drums).

Notes

- 52nd Bob Dylan concert in Canada; 6th Bob Dylan concert in Ottawa.
- 2, 7, 9-11, 13-15, 18, Bob Dylan (harmonica).
- 7-11, 18, acoustic with the band.
- 19, G. E. Smith (electric slide guitar).
- Canadian live debut of song 4.
- Song 4 has been performed only once in Canada.
- The opening act was Sue Medley.

Review

Bob Dylan recovers stolen guitar

By Greg Barr, Citizen Music Writer.

Bob Dylan didn't fare too well at the NAC on the weekend. But at least he got his guitar back.

Dylan's 30-year-old Stratocaster guitar was taken from the National Arts Centre late Friday. An employee found a smashed fire-exit door at about 12:30 a.m. Saturday. A preliminary police report suggested that a suspect hid in the backstage area and then broke through the door.

Early on during Saturday's show at the NAC Opera, Dylan made a personal plea to the audience, saying no questions would be asked, as long as the vintage guitar returned to him.

"The band wasn't going to do anything about it, they just wanted the damn thing and that was all," concert promoter Dennis Ruffo said Monday.

What Dylan didn't know at the point was that Ruffo had been approached by an unidentified person, who told Ruffo that he was upset that the guitar had been stolen. If no questions would be asked, he would take them to the place where the guitar was taken.

Later on during Saturday's show, lead guitarist G.E. Smith walked off stage briefly while still playing, when he was called over by one of Dylan's crew. After the song was over, Smith passed the news to Dylan that the guitar had been found.

Smith, by the way, was not a happy camper after Friday's show, which was by all accounts a disaster. Smith could only cover up for Dylan's errors to a certain point, and had a few words with old Bob after the set.

That little chat, plus a scathing review in Saturday's *Citizen*, which Dylan commented on during Saturday's show, seemed to click. Although the first five songs stunk, I thought he turned it around Saturday with *Serve Somebody*.

Despite the fact that Smith, Dylan and the bassist had to huddle like football players at the end of every song to ensure that Dylan would stop when he was supposed to, old Bob seemed to actually get into the swing of things.

Lost in the shuffle was the very satisfying performance by Vancouver's Sue Medley. Her vocals and Sonny Landreth's slidework in *Blue Skies* were the highlight.

The Ottawa Citizen. Tues., June 5, 1990. Reprinted with permission of The Ottawa Citizen.

Monday, June 4, 1990 --- University of Western Ontario, Alumni Hall London, ON

Set List

	Song	From The Album	Released
1.	Subterranean Homesick Blues	Bringing It All Back Home	March 22, 1965
2.	I'll Remember You	Empire Burlesque	May 30, 1985

3.	Stuck Inside of Mobile with the Memphis Blues Again	Blonde on Blonde	May 16, 1966
4.	Tears of Rage (Bob Dylan/Richard Manual)	The Basement Tapes	July 1, 1975
5.	Masters of War	The Freewheelin' Bob Dylan	May 27, 1963
6.	Gotta Serve Somebody	Slow Train Coming	Aug. 20, 1979
7.	Ballad of Hollis Brown	The Times They Are A-Changin'	Feb. 10, 1964
8.	Gates of Eden	Bringing It All Back Home	March 22, 1965
9.	Don't Think Twice, It's All Right	The Freewheelin' Bob Dylan	May 27, 1963
10.	One Too Many Mornings	The Times They Are A-Changin'	Feb. 10, 1964
11.	Mr. Tambourine Man	Bringing It All Back Home	March 22, 1965
12.	Everything is Broken	Oh Mercy	Sept. 12, 1989
13.	Simple Twist of Fate	Blood on the Tracks	Jan. 20, 1975
14.	All Along the Watchtower	John Wesley Harding	Dec. 27, 1967
15.	I Shall Be Released	Bob Dylan's Greatest Hits, Vol. 2	Nov. 17, 1971
16.	Like a Rolling Stone	Highway 61 Revisited	Aug. 30, 1965
	Encores		
17.	Girl of the North Country	The Freewheelin' Bob Dylan	May 27, 1963
18.	Highway 61 Revisited	Highway 61 Revisited	Aug. 30, 1965

The Musicians

Bob Dylan (vocal, guitar & harmonica), G. E. Smith (guitar, electric slide guitar & backup vocals), Tony Garnier (bass), Christopher Parker (drums).

Notes

- 53rd Bob Dylan concert in Canada; Debut Bob Dylan concert in London.
- 1, G. E. Smith (backup vocals).
- 2, 4, 9-11, 13, 17, Bob Dylan (harmonica).
- 7-11, 17, acoustic with the band.
- 18, G. E. Smith (electric slide guitar).
- The opening act was Sue Medley.

Review

The old Dylan shines through

Backed by sideman G. E. Smith, the rock legend mined a bottomless bag of crowd-pleasing favorites.

By Allan Casey, The London Free Press.

As the athletes like to say after close, hard-fought sporting matches, it coulda gone either way.

It was like that for Bob Dylan's more-than-sold-out show at Alumni Hall Monday night. Dylan ended up turning in a performance which proved that, of all the old rock stars on the circuit, he's still the one to watch. But he had to overcome a precariously slow start, a feat he managed with a little help from the audience.

Dylan and his Saturday Night Live pal G. E. Smith, backed by the rhythm section of Tony Garnier and Kenny Aaronson, opened with Subterranean Homesick Blues. Dylan and Smith have been playing together three summers now, and their double-barrelled guitar sound can be a little overbearing. The subtleties of I Remember You from the Empire Burlesque album got lost in all this hard-edged guitar.

When the identical treatment was given to Stuck Inside Of Mobile, the pair looked more than slightly guilty of painting by numbers. Dylan was, after all, wearing the same studded jacket he had on at his 1988 CNE show.

But Dylan kept rooting in his bottomless bag of songs to find the right fit for the music and he came up with a clear winner in Master's Of War, delivered as a brooding, pressure-cooker guitar onslaught.

ACOUSTIC SET: The pleasant surprises kept coming when Dylan and Smith launched into a five-song acoustic set. This regular feature of Dylan's recent shows just doesn't work from arena stages, but in the relative intimacy of Alumni Hall, unusual song selections like droning Ballad Of Hollis Brown and One Too Many Mornings, both from the The Times They Are A-Changin', truly let a bit of the old Dylan shine through.

DID NOT DISTURB: Smith, television's best-known freelance guitarist, takes his share of the criticism for being just a little too uptown to play with the likes of Dylan. But on the acoustic numbers, you get a sense of his reverence for the boss' music. Though he can play rings around him, but he's careful not to disturb Dylan's wonderfully erratic phrasing.

By the time Dylan got back to the more familiar territory of All Along The Watchtower and I Shall Be Released and was working toward the close of the show, the crowd had come completely onside. All it took was a few bars of Like A Rolling Stone, and everyone got up – a few lit up.

Dylan, who had earlier complained of a recent bout of illness ("Even Madonna got sick last week, so it can happen to anybody"), seemed to prefer a sea of waving arms to people sitting in rows, and he grinned at the people crammed in the front while pounding out a few extra bars of the tune.

Sue Medley and a crack six-piece band led by Sonny Landreth on slide guitar opened with a terrific set of bluesy country-rock from her debut album. This is a Canadian with a voice big enough to fill three Alumni Halls, but she couldn't overcome someone's crummy organizing.

A thorough frisking of the audience meant that her set was half done before she had anyone to hear her.

See her when she's back in town.

The London Free Press. Tues., June 5, 1990. Reprinted with permission of The London Free Press.

Tuesday, June 5, 1990 --- O'Keefe Centre for the Performing Arts Toronto, ON

Set List

	Song	From The Album	Released
1.	Subterranean Homesick Blues	Bringing It All Back Home	March 22, 1965
2.	I'll Remember You	Empire Burlesque	May 30, 1985
3.	Stuck Inside of Mobile with the Memphis Blues Again	Blonde on Blonde	May 16, 1966
4.	Tears of Rage (Bob Dylan/Richard Manual)	The Basement Tapes	July 1, 1975
5.	Masters of War	The Freewheelin' Bob Dylan	May 27, 1963
6.	Gotta Serve Somebody	Slow Train Coming	Aug. 20, 1979
7.	Tomorrow is a Long Time	Bob Dylan's Greatest Hits, Vol. 2	Nov. 17, 1971
8.	Desolation Row	Highway 61 Revisited	Aug. 30, 1965
9.	The Lonesome Death of Hattie Carroll	The Times They Are A-Changin'	Feb. 10, 1964
10.	John Brown	MTV Unplugged	June 30, 1995
11.	One Too Many Mornings	The Times They Are A-Changin'	Feb. 10, 1964
12.	Everything is Broken	Oh Mercy	Sept. 12, 1989
13.	Simple Twist of Fate	Blood on the Tracks	Jan. 20, 1975
14.	All Along the Watchtower	John Wesley Harding	Dec. 27, 1967
15.	I Shall Be Released	Bob Dylan's Greatest Hits, Vol. 2	Nov. 17, 1971
16.	Like a Rolling Stone	Highway 61 Revisited	Aug. 30, 1965
	Encores		
17.	Barbara Allen (trad.)	_	_
18.	The Times They Are A-Changin'	The Times They Are A-Changin'	Feb. 10, 1964
19.	Highway 61 Revisited	Highway 61 Revisited	Aug. 30, 1965

The Musicians

Bob Dylan (vocal, guitar & harmonica), G. E. Smith (guitar, acoustic slide guitar, electric slide guitar & backup vocals), Tony Garnier (bass), Christopher Parker (drums).

Notes

- 54th Bob Dylan concert in Canada; 17th Bob Dylan concert in Toronto.
- 1, G. E. Smith (backup vocals).
- 2, 4, 7, 9, 11, 18, Bob Dylan (harmonica).
- 7-11, 18, acoustic with the band.
- 10, G. E. Smith (acoustic slide guitar).
- 17, Bob Dylan (guitar & vocal), G. E. Smith (guitar).
- 18-19, G. E. Smith (electric slide guitar).
- Canadian live debut of songs 7 & 10.
- The opening act was Sue Medley.

Reviews

The times, they are a-changin'

Dylan SPEAKS! Smiles, even

By Mitch Potter, Toronto Star.

Okay, it has been quite a year. Walls toppled. Iron curtains parted. But fans of one Bob Dylan were served what is for them an even greater shock last night at O'Keefe Centre.

Dylan smiled, laughed and . . . wait for it . . . actually spoke to his audience during the first of three nights at the plummy Front St. venue.

Was this the same Zimmy who barked and caterwauled a disaffected concert last summer at Kingswood Theatre? Or, indeed, the same Old Papa Folk whose infrequent live shows over the past decade have amounted to little more than aimless wheezing?

It would seem so. The dishevelled mat of hair and scratchy beard matched the phlegmatic honk to a T.

Whatever his reasons, Dylan brought surprisingly fresh spirit to a near-capacity crowd that spanned three generations (some tickets remain for tonight and tomorrow's performances).

Dividing the 90-minute set into three parts, Dylan and his supporting cast of G.E. Smith (guitar), Tony Garnier (bass) and Christopher Parker (drums) bookended an acoustic middle section with electric passages in presenting a three-decade survey of the Minnesotan songwriter's work.

With the stage backlit, Dylan hacked through "Stuck Inside Of Mobile With The Memphis Blues Again", the vintage "Masters Of War" and his late-1970s neo-Christian opus, "Gotta Serve Somebody", before trading his electric for a six-string acoustic.

Then, turning to earlier work, Dylan loosened up with "Seems Like A Long Time", a marathon arrangement of "Desolation Row", "The Lonesome Death Of Hattie Carroll" and the early '70s "One Too Many Mornings", before pointing out with a mischievous grin that several seats in the front row remained empty.

"C'mon down here an' fill them."

The ensuing rush for the stage, which converted the orderly O'Keefe into a mass of standing patrons, only served to bolster Dylan's mood, as he returned to electrics for "Simple Twist Of Fate", from 1975's Blood On The Tracks.

Guitarist Smith, the pony-tailed leader of the Saturday Night Live group, played his usual role as damage control for much of the concert, lending gentle heft to the mix when Dylan was keeping proper time, but assertively leading the rhythm back to place during those occasional moments when Dylan wanders off into some melody nobody else happens to be hearing.

Still, the closing segment, "All Along The Watchtower", "I Shall Be Released", "Like A Rolling Stone" and an encore of "The Times They Are A-Changin' ", did much to convince that Zimmy was alert to what was happening. Later, Dylan dusted off a rustic version of the traditional "Barbara Allen", allowing that "It's not as good as Gordon Lightfoot's version, but we'll try it anyway."

Vancouver's Sue Medley, whose warm, easy vibrato has elements of country, southern rock, folk and pop, didn't bother to introduce her group during last night's opening set, but it would have made sense.

The talents of slide guitarist Sonny Landreth, fretless bassist Blair DePape and the rest of her inestimable crew pretty much squeezed Medley herself to the bottom of the mix during the solo artist's warmly-received eight-song performance. A promising set nonetheless, Medley is almost certain to return in the near future for a proper headline show.

Dylan thaws

The chill is (almost) gone

By Bob Thompson.

Bob Dylan was being almost intimate at the sold-out O'Keefe Centre last night at the first of three nights.

Well, let's say he was being nearly personable.

Actually, Dylan was back-slapping chummy compared to the glum silence that highlighted two previous concert visits here.

Mind you, Dylan was negative about cameras, which meant concert photographs were, again, out of the question – and that included opening act Sue Medley.

But, despite that, he did joke with the crowd between songs on a few occasions. Once he even mumbled something about appreciating the fact that he was in Toronto.

Really up close and personal stuff was saved for the assorted re-invented Dylan tunes, which used the fine talents of his three-piece band. As usual, guitarist G.E. Smith was flashy, while drummer Christopher Parker and bassist Tony Garnier were solid.

All four rocked some Dylan folk material, and acoustically re-worked some ol' favorites.

Some of his newer songs seemed old, too. But that's more because of the familiarity that arrives with Dylan's nasal nuances than trite retreading of a good thing.

In the end, Dylan showed last night that he didn't need to live on legend alone, although it helped.

Opening act, Sue Medley and her group served up an earnest mix of boogie rock and rural pop with an aim to please.

Medley's vivacious voice sure did.

A bonus came with guest guitarist Sonny Landreth, who added some southern-fried slides to Robbie Steininger's more conventional string stings.

Well done.

Electric Dylan builds to a rockin' climax

By Alan Niester, Special to The Globe and Mail.

At the Newport Folk Festival in 1965, Bob Dylan wrapped himself in controversy by playing his folk music on an electric guitar. At Toronto's O'Keefe Centre Tuesday night, Dylan showed just how far that transition has progressed as he led a tight, aggressive four-piece band through what must have been the most electric and electrifying performance he has ever given here.

The tone was set in the first number, a barely recognizable version of the classic Subterranean Homesick Blues. While Dylan ripped off the lyrics in almost indecipherable hunks, guitarist G. E. Smith (he of the blond ponytail and Saturday Night Live house band) laid down a raw and chunky instrumental frenzy. Dylan himself, hunched over his guitar, seemed more intent on playing fills than singing, and the song came across as a rousing rock and roll opener.

The next five numbers were performed in the same energetic manner, with the band (which also included bassist Tony Garnier and drummer Christopher Parker) sounding more like roadhouse rockers than folk-rocking traditionalists.

The songs in this part of the show represented the breadth of Dylan's career, including Stuck Inside Of Mobile With The Memphis Blues Again, Masters of War and the Christian rocker, Gotta Serve Somebody.

At this point, Dylan switched to acoustic guitar, Garnier to standup acoustic bass, and the performance slipped into cruise. After such an energetic first half-hour, this middle segment seemed to drag.

The highlight came just before Dylan's blurred version of One Too Many Mornings, when he mumbled something about there being two or three empty seats up near the stage, and invited fans to come down and fill them. This resulted in a lemming-like rush by about 1,000 cheap-seat faithful, all of whom got to watch the final section of the concert from relatively close to the stage, much to the distress of the expensive-seat faithful, who were forced to stand for the rest of the evening.

But they probably would have been standing anyway, because the last third of the concert was overdrive time. Dylan built to his climax slowly, beginning with a heartfelt version of Simple Twist of Fate, his most emotional rendering of the evening. At this point, Smith began a few mystery chords, which were ultimately transformed into All Along The Watchtower. It wasn't exactly Hendrix, but it certainly tried to be. Then, I Shall Be Released, and finally, a furious version of Like A Rolling Stone.

Dylan played about unmercifully with our memories and his vocal phrasing, stressing spots that have probably never been stressed before. But with the band now seriously into overdrive, and Dylan spitting and ranting like the Dylan of old, this last number was easily worth the price of admission.

Wednesday, June 6, 1990 --- O'Keefe Centre for the Performing Arts Toronto, ON

Set List

	Song	**From The Album**	**Released**
1.	Absolutely Sweet Marie	Blonde on Blonde	May 16, 1966
2.	Early Mornin' Rain (Gordon Lightfoot)	Self Portrait	June 8, 1970
3.	Ballad of a Thin Man	Highway 61 Revisited	Aug. 30, 1965
4.	Stuck Inside of Mobile with the Memphis Blues Again	Blonde on Blonde	May 16, 1966
5.	You're a Big Girl Now	Blood on the Tracks	Jan. 20, 1975
6.	Masters of War	The Freewheelin' Bob Dylan	May 27, 1963
7.	Gotta Serve Somebody	Slow Train Coming	Aug. 20, 1979
8.	Love Minus Zero/No Limit	Bringing It All Back Home	March 22, 1965
9.	It's Alright, Ma (I'm Only Bleeding)	Bringing It All Back Home	March 22, 1965
10.	I've Been All Around This World (trad.)	–	–
11.	Gates of Eden	Bringing It All Back Home	March 22, 1965
12.	Boots of Spanish Leather	The Times They Are A-Changin'	Feb. 10, 1964
13.	Everything is Broken	Oh Mercy	Sept. 12, 1989
14.	What Was It You Wanted?	Oh Mercy	Sept. 12, 1989
15.	One More Night	Nashville Skyline	April 9, 1969
16.	All Along the Watchtower	John Wesley Harding	Dec. 27, 1967
17.	What Good Am I?	Oh Mercy	Sept. 12, 1989
18.	In the Garden	Saved	June 19, 1980
19.	Like a Rolling Stone	Highway 61 Revisited	Aug. 30, 1965
	Encores		
20.	It Ain't Me, Babe	Another Side of Bob Dylan	Aug. 8, 1964
21.	Highway 61 Revisited	Highway 61 Revisited	Aug. 30, 1965

The Musicians

Bob Dylan (vocal, guitar & harmonica), G. E. Smith (guitar & electric slide guitar), Tony Garnier (bass), Christopher Parker (drums).

Notes

- 55th Bob Dylan concert in Canada; 18th Bob Dylan concert in Toronto.
- 2-3, 7-8, 12, 20, Bob Dylan (harmonica).
- 8-12, 20, acoustic with the band.
- 15, Ronnie Hawkins (vocal), Bob Dylan (backup vocals).
- 21, G. E. Smith (electric slide guitar).
- Canadian live debut of songs 10, 14 & 15.
- Song 15 has been performed only once in Canada.
- The opening act was Sue Medley.

Thursday, June 7, 1990 --- O'Keefe Centre for the Performing Arts Toronto, ON

Set List

	Song	From The Album	Released
1.	Most Likely You Go Your Way and I'll Go Mine	Blonde on Blonde	May 16, 1966
2.	I'll Remember You	Empire Burlesque	May 30, 1985
3.	Stuck Inside of Mobile with the Memphis Blues Again	Blonde on Blonde	May 16, 1966
4.	I Believe in You	Slow Train Coming	Aug. 20, 1979
5.	Masters of War	The Freewheelin' Bob Dylan	May 27, 1963
6.	Gotta Serve Somebody	Slow Train Coming	Aug. 20, 1979
7.	It's Alright, Ma (I'm Only Bleeding)	Bringing It All Back Home	March 22, 1965
8.	Love Minus Zero/No Limit	Bringing It All Back Home	March 22, 1965
9.	Ballad of Hollis Brown	The Times They Are A-Changin'	Feb. 10, 1964
10.	Gates of Eden	Bringing It All Back Home	March 22, 1965
11.	Desolation Row	Highway 61 Revisited	Aug. 30, 1965
12.	What Was It You Wanted?	Oh Mercy	Sept. 12, 1989
13.	What Good Am I?	Oh Mercy	Sept. 12, 1989
14.	All Along the Watchtower	John Wesley Harding	Dec. 27, 1967
15.	I Shall Be Released	Bob Dylan's Greatest Hits, Vol. 2	Nov. 17, 1971
16.	Like a Rolling Stone	Highway 61 Revisited	Aug. 30, 1965
	Encores		
17.	I've Been All Around This World (trad.)	–	–
18.	Maggie's Farm	Bringing It All Back Home	March 22, 1965

The Musicians

Bob Dylan (vocal, guitar & harmonica), G. E. Smith (guitar), Tony Garnier (bass), Christopher Parker (drums).

Notes

- 56th Bob Dylan concert in Canada; 19th Bob Dylan concert in Toronto.
- 2, 4, 8, 17, Bob Dylan (harmonica).
- 7-11, 17, acoustic with the band.
- The opening act was Sue Medley.

Sunday, June 17, 1990 --- Centennial Centre Concert Hall Winnipeg, MB

Set List

	Song	From The Album	Released
1.	Most Likely You Go Your Way and I'll Go Mine	Blonde on Blonde	May 16, 1966
2.	Lay, Lady, Lay	Nashville Skyline	April 9, 1969
3.	Stuck Inside of Mobile with the Memphis Blues Again	Blonde on Blonde	May 16, 1966

4.	Tears of Rage (Bob Dylan/Richard Manual)	The Basement Tapes	July 1, 1975
5.	Masters of War	The Freewheelin' Bob Dylan	May 27, 1963
6.	Gotta Serve Somebody	Slow Train Coming	Aug. 20, 1979
7.	It's Alright, Ma (I'm Only Bleeding)	Bringing It All Back Home	March 22, 1965
8.	Gates of Eden	Bringing It All Back Home	March 22, 1965
9.	Don't Think Twice, It's All Right	The Freewheelin' Bob Dylan	May 27, 1963
10.	Desolation Row	Highway 61 Revisited	Aug. 30, 1965
11.	Boots of Spanish Leather	The Times They Are A-Changin'	Feb. 10, 1964
12.	Mr. Tambourine Man	Bringing It All Back Home	March 22, 1965
13.	Everything is Broken	Oh Mercy	Sept. 12, 1989
14.	No More One More Time (Troy Seals/Dave Kirby)	–	–
15.	All Along the Watchtower	John Wesley Harding	Dec. 27, 1967
16.	I Shall Be Released	Bob Dylan's Greatest Hits, Vol. 2	Nov. 17, 1971
17.	Like a Rolling Stone	Highway 61 Revisited	Aug. 30, 1965
	Encores		
18.	Blowin' in the Wind	The Freewheelin' Bob Dylan	May 27, 1963
19.	Highway 61 Revisited	Highway 61 Revisited	Aug. 30, 1965

The Musicians

Bob Dylan (vocal, guitar & harmonica), G. E. Smith (guitar & electric slide guitar), Tony Garnier (bass), Christopher Parker (drums).

Notes

- 57th Bob Dylan concert in Canada; 2nd Bob Dylan concert in Winnipeg.
- 2, 4, 9, 11-12, 18, Bob Dylan (harmonica).
- 7-12, 18, acoustic with the band.
- 19, G. E. Smith (electric slide guitar).
- The opening act was Sue Medley.

Reviews

Dylan's interest shows in manner musicianship

By Stephen Ostick.

OK, so music legend Bob Dylan wouldn't let photographers take his picture last night at Centennial Concert Hall. Big Deal.

Because that's the only part of the show that might've reminded Winnipeggers of his last visit to town.

That uninterested Dylan walked through a brief 60-minute Winnipeg Arena concert without a word in 1988. It seemed he was up there only because some clever person had somehow tricked him into it.

But this Dylan gave the impression there was nowhere else he'd rather be. During a 90-minute set, encores still to come, he spoke to the crowd, included old hits along with new material, and sent the audience home with memories to pass on to the grandkids.

Like seeing Dylan end the show with an electrifying version of the 25-year-old Like A Rolling Stone, his first major hit, from 1965. "You've been an incredible crowd tonight," he told the sell-out crowd before launching into the classic.

Carried by guitarist G.E. Smith (the ultra-cool player who leads TV's Saturday Night Live band), bassist Tony Garnier and drummer Christopher Parker, the tune built to an excitement level to rival the climax of any rock show.

Which explains mostly why this night was such a smash to the sell-out crowd of mid-20s-and-uppers: make no mistake about it – this was the Bob Dylan show.

It had a pacing – a 30-minute acoustic mini-set produced subtleties and tenderness in that love-it-or-hate-it nasal whine but also allowed opportunities for good old coffee-house jamming, chances that didn't elude Dylan and co.

Even the folk hit Don't Think Twice, It's Alright faded to just Dylan, his guitar and harp while Smith manufactured a rather neat facsimile of a mandolin.

It also had the hits, played with urgency and affection – and he wasted no time getting to them. The sensuous Lay Lady Lay was second on the bill, followed by an appropriately ragged Stuck Inside of Mobile with the Memphis Blues Again.

In Smith, Dylan has found perhaps his best playing partner since his days with the Band in the mid-'60s. Smith's rough but authoritative playing is the perfect foil to Dylan's writing and singing, which share those same qualities.

Vancouver's Sue Medley opened the show and did her best to duplicate a set of tunes from her terrific debut LP. Blessed with singing and songwriting skills, Medley has produced some of the most distinctive songs of the year, in an alluring honky-tonk rock style.

But only great slide player Sonny Landreth, whose feather-light touch has been borrowed from John Hiatt's Goners, played with the sensitivity and dynamics so apparent – and necessary – on the record.

Only Landreth and Medley seemed to listen to, or care at all about, what anybody else onstage was playing.

Both acts play again tonight.

Dylan served up one hot concert

By John Kendle, Sun Staff Writer.

It could have been the warmth of the day, the warmth of the crowd, or maybe the warm sound of the room.

Whatever the reason, Bob Dylan turned in a scorcher of a set last night before a capacity crowd at the Centennial Concert Hall.

Often maligned (privately, mind you) by devout fans who nevertheless think he should be more forthcoming in concert, Dylan was anything but shy last night.

Musically he was in a playful, ebullient mood, pulling plenty of old nuggets from his sleeve, and personally, well, he looked a far cry from the near-catatonic soul who played the Arena two years ago.

He even addressed Winnipeg by name (something he didn't do in '88), saying that "any place Neil Young grew up has got to be incredible."

But it was really the show that was incredible last night.

Squeezing an acoustic passage in between two solid 40-minute electric forays, Dylan delivered a solid 110 minutes of tunes.

And it was impressive right off the bat as he, guitarist G.E. Smith, bassist Tony Garnier and drummer Christopher Parker launched a three-song punch including Most Likely You Go Your Way, Lay Lady Lay and the country-blues of Stuck Inside Of Mobile With The Memphis Blues Again.

From there the rollicking quartet roared into an electric re-working of Masters Of War and a radically re-interpreted Gotta Serve Somebody.

Indeed, musical recidivism was the main order of business last night. Dylan's a musician who enjoys rearranging and rephrasing his songs – often in mid-show – and it was a credit to his supporting players (especially bandleader Smith) that they managed to keep up.

Mr. Tambourine Man was obviously pulled out of the hat and brushed off in mid-stream, but it sounded all the better for the spontaneity, as did It's Alright Ma I'm Only Bleeding.

Rehearsed tunes, like an acoustic Desolation Row and electric versions of All Along The Watchtower and I Shall Be Released, also sounded fresher for the new treatments, and the uptempo version of Like A Rolling Stone that came just before the encores was simply a treat.

Of course, just hearing that familiar nasal whine and seeing that shuffling, black-clad figure was a treat in and of itself.

Further surprises came after regulation time, as Dylan offered up Blowin' In the Wind and the bluesy shuffle of Highway 61.

Opener Sue Medley certainly had the best voice of the night, and her crack band (including Winnipeg bassist Blair DePape and ex-goner Sony Landreth on slide guitar) added extra magic to spry little tunes like Dangerous Times and That's Life.

But at eight songs, her set was too brief to be the dynamic outing it will be when she attains headlining status in her own right.

Both acts do it all again tonight. Showtime at the Concert Hall is 8 p.m.

Monday, June 18, 1990 --- Centennial Centre Concert Hall Winnipeg, MB

Set List

	Song	From The Album	Released
1.	Absolutely Sweet Marie	Blonde on Blonde	May 16, 1966
2.	Ballad of a Thin Man	Highway 61 Revisited	Aug. 30, 1965
3.	Stuck Inside of Mobile with the Memphis Blues Again	Blonde on Blonde	May 16, 1966
4.	Queen Jane Approximately	Highway 61 Revisited	Aug. 30, 1965
5.	Masters of War	The Freewheelin' Bob Dylan	May 27, 1963
6.	Gotta Serve Somebody	Slow Train Coming	Aug. 20, 1979
7.	It's Alright, Ma (I'm Only Bleeding)	Bringing It All Back Home	March 22, 1965
8.	It's All Over Now, Baby Blue	Bringing It All Back Home	March 22, 1965
9.	Boots of Spanish Leather	The Times They Are A-Changin'	Feb. 10, 1964
10.	John Brown	MTV Unplugged	June 30, 1995
11.	Gates of Eden	Bringing It All Back Home	March 22, 1965
12.	Everything is Broken	Oh Mercy	Sept. 12, 1989
13.	Political World	Oh Mercy	Sept. 12, 1989
14.	All Along the Watchtower	John Wesley Harding	Dec. 27, 1967
15.	I Shall Be Released	Bob Dylan's Greatest Hits, Vol. 2	Nov. 17, 1971
16.	Like a Rolling Stone	Highway 61 Revisited	Aug. 30, 1965
	Encores		
17.	Blowin' in the Wind	The Freewheelin' Bob Dylan	May 27, 1963
18.	Highway 61 Revisited	Highway 61 Revisited	Aug. 30, 1965

The Musicians

Bob Dylan (vocal, guitar & harmonica), G. E. Smith (guitar, acoustic slide guitar & electric slide guitar), Tony Garnier (bass), Christopher Parker (drums).

Notes

- 58th Bob Dylan concert in Canada; 3rd Bob Dylan concert in Winnipeg.
- 2, 4, 8-9, Bob Dylan (harmonica).
- 7-11, 17, acoustic with the band.
- 10, G. E. Smith (acoustic slide guitar).
- 18, G. E. Smith (electric slide guitar).
- Canadian live debut of songs 4 & 13.
- The opening act was Sue Medley.

Sunday, August 12, 1990 --- Jubilee Auditorium
Edmonton, AB

Set List

	Song	From The Album	Released
1.	Maggie's Farm	Bringing It All Back Home	March 22, 1965
2.	Shelter from the Storm	Blood on the Tracks	Jan. 20, 1975
3.	Stuck Inside of Mobile with the Memphis Blues Again	Blonde on Blonde	May 16, 1966
4.	Nowhere Man (John Lennon/Paul McCartney)	–	–
5.	Masters of War	The Freewheelin' Bob Dylan	May 27, 1963
6.	Gotta Serve Somebody	Slow Train Coming	Aug. 20, 1979
7.	Ballad of Hollis Brown	The Times They Are A-Changin'	Feb. 10, 1964
8.	The Water is Wide (trad.)	–	–
9.	Gates of Eden	Bringing It All Back Home	March 22, 1965
10.	Don't Think Twice, It's All Right	The Freewheelin' Bob Dylan	May 27, 1963
11.	Everything is Broken	Oh Mercy	Sept. 12, 1989
12.	Political World	Oh Mercy	Sept. 12, 1989
13.	It Takes a Lot to Laugh, It Takes a Train to Cry	Highway 61 Revisited	Aug. 30, 1965
14.	In the Garden	Saved	June 19, 1980
15.	Like a Rolling Stone	Highway 61 Revisited	Aug. 30, 1965
	Encores		
16.	Blowin' in the Wind	The Freewheelin' Bob Dylan	May 27, 1963
17.	All Along the Watchtower	John Wesley Harding	Dec. 27, 1967

The Musicians

Bob Dylan (vocal, guitar & harmonica), G. E. Smith (guitar), Tony Garnier (bass), Christopher Parker (drums).

Notes

- 59th Bob Dylan concert in Canada; 2nd Bob Dylan concert in Edmonton.
- 2, 8, 10, 15-16, Bob Dylan (harmonica).
- 7-10, 16, acoustic with the band.
- Canadian live debut of songs 4 & 8.
- Songs 4 & 8 have been performed only once in Canada.
- Worldwide live debut of song 4.
- The opening act was Sue Medley.

Reviews

Dylan no one to rest on well-deserved laurels

By Helen Metella, Journal Staff Writer.

How many songs can a man tear down, before he stops being in demand?

Every one, apparently, if you're Bob Dylan.

The wholesale reconstruction of melodies and rhythms that the 49 year-old king of troubadours undertakes in virtually every concert appearance would be sheer suicide for any other performer.

But Sunday night, nearly 3,000 people gave Dylan a standing ovation before he sang a single word in the first of his two Edmonton performances, and revered every slurred, acoustically mangled syllable that followed.

And difficult as it is to explain to someone who didn't consider the evening, "bigger than what's going on in the Middle East," (as one Dylan aficionado only half-jokingly quipped in the lobby), this homage is neither madness nor obsession.

Dylan is popular music's greatest iconoclast, one who's always instinctively known that good songs are social statements that breathe and grow, reflecting their subject; that arbitrary rules must be wrenched wildly if we're to crawl forward at all.

So although it was an oftimes baffling and challenging experience to identify which song it was Dylan was presenting in fearfully amplified, mumbled manner, his brash impudence was exactly what his fans had come to hear.

Moreover, when a writer has imbedded in a culture, scores of songs as succinctly and strongly put as *Everything Is Broken*, (from last year's album *Oh, Mercy*) or *You Gotta Serve Somebody*, (from 1979's *Slow Train Coming*), he's on safe turf when he takes liberties. The souls of those songs certainly weren't fundamentally altered by Dylan's eccentric enunciation any more than they were hurt by the scorching lead guitar reeled off by G. E. Smith, the fleet-fingered alumnus of the last Dylan tour and *The Saturday Night Live Band*.

Opening with clanging, crashing renditions of *Maggie's Farm, Shelter From The Storm, Stuck Inside Of Mobile* and – eccentrically – Lennon and McCartney's *Nowhere Man*, Dylan, Smith and the brittle rhythm section of Tony Garnier and Christopher Parker formed a mighty band of minimalists.

Lit by harsh white spotlights which created deep, enigmatic shadows, the secretive visual image they selected to present loud, blunt and angry rock 'n' roll underlined the double-edge to songs such as *Political World*.

Although only marginally more talkative than when he last appeared here in 1988, Dylan grinned about as often as he grimaced and stuck his tongue out in self-effacing dismay during a particularly clumsy harmonica solo in *Don't Think Twice, It's Alright*.

As usual, the audience was left to puzzle over such things as the origin of an obscure old folk song, introduced to honor, "the big folk festival going on this weekend," and several other intriguing, but unfamiliar tunes played during a quieter, but no less muttered, acoustic segment.

Still, the rumpled but rigorous performer, who played three completely different shows during the Toronto stop on this tour, seemed inclined to please rather than irritate the audience with his set list. With 28 years worth of fine material to choose from he finished the night with an acoustic rendition of *Blowing in the Wind* and a searing *All Along The Watchtower*.

Sue Medley warmed the room in 45 feisty minutes as she presented the radiant country-rock of her dynamic debut album. With John Hiatt's slide guitar player Sonny Landreth, stellar gut-string classical guitar by Robbie Steninger Medley, the singing keyboards of Richard Sera and the sturdy rhythm section of Vince Ditrich and Blair DePape, this band can't help but cook.

The Edmonton Journal. Mon., Aug. 13, 1990. Reprinted with permission of The Edmonton Journal.

Dylan dazzles

By Peter North.

Bob Dylan fans sought out their own shelter from today's storm of musical mediocrity and packed the Jubilee Auditorium last night.

The man whose audience is getting both younger and older as the years roll by didn't disappoint in his second visit here in as many years.

Backed again by a stripped-down trio of guitar, bass and drums, the master tunesmith worked through material that runs from the very beginning of his career.

The foursome, looking comfortable yet serious when necessary, ripped through versions of classic songs.

Moments into the first tune, *Maggie's Farm*, it was apparent this was the ideal condition in which to catch him.

Words lost in hockey rink concerts came alive, although Dylan doesn't have the greatest gift for enunciation.

Shooting directly into *Shelter From the Storm*, Dylan and company gathered up a strong, driving rhythm at about three times the pace the song was recorded at.

Maybe it was the lengthy roaring and chanting that preceded the house lights' dimming that gave Dylan room to relax, but this time around he even talked to the crowd.

"This is one of my favorite songs by John Lennon. It's a special occasion today," he said before lighting into the Beatles' *Nowhere Man*.

His execution of the song shied away from the original's built-in sarcasm, instead almost showing pity for the ones the song was pointed at.

He also made a comment regarding the success of our folk festival.

Rainy Day Women featured some intricate playing by *Saturday Night Live* bandleader G.E. Smith, who tossed out pinpoint fills and solos from the word go. The guitarist's strength as a commanding rhythm player above Chris Parker's perfect time-keeping came to light when Dylan blew out his trademark, shrill harp solos.

A knockout version of *Serve Somebody* had the tempo slowed a touch and the conviction of the word seemed to drop out of his mouth like lead weights dropping on to a hardwood floor.

Dylan and band complete their two night stand with opening act Sue Medley tonight.

The Edmonton Sun. Mon., Aug. 13, 1990. Reprinted with permission of The Sun Media Corp.

Monday, August, 13, 1990 --- Jubilee Auditorium
Edmonton, AB

Set List

	Song	From The Album	Released
1.	Maggie's Farm	Bringing It All Back Home	March 22, 1965
2.	Shelter from the Storm	Blood on the Tracks	Jan. 20, 1975
3.	No More One More Time (Troy Seals/Dave Kirby)	–	–
4.	Stuck Inside of Mobile with the Memphis Blues Again	Blonde on Blonde	May 16, 1966
5.	Masters of War	The Freewheelin' Bob Dylan	May 27, 1963
6.	Gotta Serve Somebody	Slow Train Coming	Aug. 20, 1979
7.	It's Alright, Ma (I'm Only Bleeding)	Bringing It All Back Home	March 22, 1965
8.	It's All Over Now, Baby Blue	Bringing It All Back Home	March 22, 1965
9.	Gates of Eden	Bringing It All Back Home	March 22, 1965
10.	Mr. Tambourine Man	Bringing It All Back Home	March 22, 1965
11.	Everything is Broken	Oh Mercy	Sept. 12, 1989
12.	Queen Jane Approximately	Highway 61 Revisited	Aug. 30, 1965
13.	Political World	Oh Mercy	Sept. 12, 1989
14.	All Along the Watchtower	John Wesley Harding	Dec. 27, 1967
15.	I Shall Be Released	Bob Dylan's Greatest Hits, Vol. 2	Nov. 17, 1971
16.	Like a Rolling Stone	Highway 61 Revisited	Aug. 30, 1965
	Encores		
17.	Blowin' in the Wind	The Freewheelin' Bob Dylan	May 27, 1963
18.	Highway 61 Revisited	Highway 61 Revisited	Aug. 30, 1965

The Musicians

Bob Dylan (vocal, guitar & harmonica), G. E. Smith (guitar & electric slide guitar), Tony Garnier (bass), Christopher Parker (drums).

Notes

- 60th Bob Dylan concert in Canada; 3rd Bob Dylan concert in Edmonton.
- 2, 8, 10, 12, 17, Bob Dylan (harmonica).
- 7–10, 17, acoustic with the band.
- 18, G. E. Smith (electric slide guitar)
- The opening act was Sue Medley.

Wednesday, August 15, 1990 --- Jubilee Auditorium
Calgary, AB

Set List

	Song	From The Album	Released
1.	Maggie's Farm	Bringing It All Back Home	March 22, 1965
2.	Simple Twist of Fate	Blood on the Tracks	Jan. 20, 1975
3.	Early Mornin' Rain (Gordon Lightfoot)	Self Portrait	June 8, 1970
4.	Stuck Inside of Mobile with the Memphis Blues Again	Blonde on Blonde	May 16, 1966
5.	Masters of War	The Freewheelin' Bob Dylan	May 27, 1963
6.	Gotta Serve Somebody	Slow Train Coming	Aug. 20, 1979
7.	It's Alright, Ma (I'm Only Bleeding)	Bringing It All Back Home	March 22, 1965
8.	Girl of the North Country	The Freewheelin' Bob Dylan	May 27, 1963
9.	Desolation Row	Highway 61 Revisited	Aug. 30, 1965
10.	Don't Think Twice, It's All Right	The Freewheelin' Bob Dylan	May 27, 1963
11.	Everything is Broken	Oh Mercy	Sept. 12, 1989
12.	Tears of Rage (Bob Dylan/Richard Manual)	The Basement Tapes	July 1, 1975
13.	Political World	Oh Mercy	Sept. 12, 1989
14.	It Takes a Lot to Laugh, It Takes a Train to Cry	Highway 61 Revisited	Aug. 30, 1965
15.	I Shall Be Released	Bob Dylan's Greatest Hits, Vol. 2	Nov. 17, 1971
16.	Like a Rolling Stone	Highway 61 Revisited	Aug. 30, 1965
	Encores		
17.	Blowin' in the Wind	The Freewheelin' Bob Dylan	May 27, 1963
18.	All Along the Watchtower	John Wesley Harding	Dec. 27, 1967

The Musicians

Bob Dylan (vocal, guitar & harmonica), G. E. Smith (guitar), Tony Garnier (bass), Christopher Parker (drums).

Notes

- 61st Bob Dylan concert in Canada; 2nd Bob Dylan concert in Calgary.
- 2-6, 8, 10, 17, Bob Dylan (harmonica).
- 7-10, 17, acoustic with the band.
- The opening act was Sue Medley.

Reviews

Dylan fans get treat of rich, heartfelt music

By Alison Mayes, Herald Writer.

Maybe the reason why Bob Dylan's shoulders are so hunched is that he has to carry the weight of all our expectations.

Two summers ago, some fans viewed his Saddledome concert as a triumph, while others condemned it as an empty exercise. Bearing that in mind, some listeners at Wednesday's intimate Jubilee show may have found the legendary folk poet too taciturn or been frustrated by the way he twists and reinvents his material.

But it's hard to imagine anyone going away truly disappointed after an evening so rich in convincingly heartfelt music.

Kicking things off with the nasal baying of Maggie's Farm, then a hard-to-decipher Simple Twist Of Fate, the neatly dressed, slight framed troubadour at first seemed twitchy and somewhat ill at ease.

Backed by drums, bass, and usually one but occasionally two guitars, he was so sparingly lit that his face almost never emerged from shadow during the 90-minute show.

His third number was a quirky, countrified version of Gordon Lightfoot's Early Morning Rain. He seemed to loosen up with a playful Stuck Inside Of Mobile (With The Memphis Blues Again), on which he made odd hand gestures, bounced his bony knees, and rocked against his mike stand while blowing the harp.

Finally, when he and the band (all playing electric instruments for this opening section) kicked into a superbly rhythmic Serve Somebody, the show clicked: it became a masterful showcase of mostly classic material, served up by a Dylan who was truly communicating.

An acoustic segment saw Dylan and ponytailed Saturday Night Live guitarist G. E. Smith strumming with obvious camaraderie while bassist Tony Garnier played upright bass. Returning to the electric sound, Dylan did a couple of tunes from last year's Oh Mercy, including the swampy Everything Is Broken.

Shortly after that, the tight security surrounding the show (no one was allowed to take photos) became suddenly apparent when two young men who rushed enthusiastically up to the stage were pounced upon by burly guards and hustled out.

The final song was a howling version of Like A Rolling Stone, even more visceral than the original. Dylan went off to a thunderous ovation, returned on acoustic and told the crowd as he led into the final encore, "Somebody once told me if I kept playing this song I'd be a star."

The song was Blowin' In The Wind, and if anyone was put off by its altered melody and speeded-up tempo, they probably should have known better than to experience Dylan in person.

Attendance: 2,000.

The Calgary Herald. Thurs., Aug. 16, 1990.

Dylan delivers dynamite package

By John Bachusky, Calgary Sun.

For more than 25 years, Bob Dylan has never surrendered.

His moods and artistic detours are legendary.

In the late '70s, Dylan's conversion to a born-again Christian brought moans from critics and fans who lamented the passion – his old resonance – that articulated an entire generation's outrage.

But Dylan, who's influenced everyone from the **Beatles** to **Tom Petty** to **Tracy Chapman**, has never retreated from what matters most – his soul.

Last night he proved once again there is another side of Bob Dylan – one who absolutely refuses to fade away.

He shook the neck of rock 'n' roll pretenders last night at the Jubilee and was positively electric.

Dylan's songs – grand symbols of protest in the '60s – remain as vital as ever.

Unlike **The Who** and **The Rolling Stones**, Dylan refuses to lay back and play his standard oldies the way we'd expect to hear them.

He ripped open his show with ferocious versions of *Maggie's Farm*, *Simple Twist of Fate*, *Early Mornin' Rain* and *Gotta Serve Somebody*.

It was a relentless attack and for the most part, the audience wasn't expecting it.

Even during the acoustic sets, Dylan and his superb band hardly slowed a beat.

He pounded furiously through *Desolation Row* and *Girl From the North Country*, grinding and wrenching the spirits that have tormented him to find the perfect note.

He wasn't trying to match the sound of his records.

Even *Political World* from his latest album, *Oh Mercy*, was rocked up to maintain the flow.

Dylan kept the show easy.

There was no chit-chat to the audience and the lighting was simplistic.

It was the music that mattered.

He ended the show with *Blowin' in the Wind* and it took on a different feeling – another dimension to this man who is one of rock's greatest treasures.

The Calgary Sun. Thurs., Aug. 16, 1990. Reprinted with permission of The Calgary Sun.

Thursday, August 16, 1990 --- Jubilee Auditorium Calgary, AB

Set List

	Song	From The Album	Released
1.	Maggie's Farm	Bringing It All Back Home	March 22, 1965
2.	Lay, Lady, Lay	Nashville Skyline	April 9, 1969
3.	Ballad of a Thin Man	Highway 61 Revisited	Aug. 30, 1965
4.	Stuck Inside of Mobile with the Memphis Blues Again	Blonde on Blonde	May 16, 1966
5.	Masters of War	The Freewheelin' Bob Dylan	May 27, 1963
6.	Gotta Serve Somebody	Slow Train Coming	Aug. 20, 1979
7.	Don't Think Twice, It's All Right	The Freewheelin' Bob Dylan	May 27, 1963
8.	Gates of Eden	Bringing It All Back Home	March 22, 1965
9.	Mr. Tambourine Man	Bringing It All Back Home	March 22, 1965
10.	One Too Many Mornings	The Times They Are A-Changin'	Feb. 10, 1964
11.	Everything is Broken	Oh Mercy	Sept. 12, 1989
12.	I Believe in You	Slow Train Coming	Aug. 20, 1979
13.	All Along the Watchtower	John Wesley Harding	Dec. 27, 1967
14.	What Good Am I?	Oh Mercy	Sept. 12, 1989
15.	I Shall Be Released	Bob Dylan's Greatest Hits, Vol. 2	Nov. 17, 1971
16.	Like a Rolling Stone	Highway 61 Revisited	Aug. 30, 1965
	Encores		
17.	Blowin' in the Wind	The Freewheelin' Bob Dylan	May 27, 1963
18.	Highway 61 Revisited	Highway 61 Revisited	Aug. 30, 1965

The Musicians

Bob Dylan (vocal, guitar & harmonica), G. E. Smith (guitar & electric slide guitar), Tony Garnier (bass), Christopher Parker (drums).

Notes

- 62nd Bob Dylan concert in Canada; 3rd Bob Dylan concert in Calgary.
- 1-3, 7, 9-10, 14, 17, Bob Dylan (harmonica).
- 7-10, 17, acoustic with the band.
- 18, G. E. Smith (electric slide guitar).
- The opening act was Sue Medley.

Sunday, August 19, 1990 --- Memorial Arena Victoria, BC

Set List

	Song	From The Album	Released
1.	Maggie's Farm	Bringing It All Back Home	March 22, 1965
2.	Shelter from the Storm	Blood on the Tracks	Jan. 20, 1975
3.	Positively 4th Street	Bob Dylan's Greatest Hits	March 27, 1967
4.	Stuck Inside of Mobile with the Memphis Blues Again	Blonde on Blonde	May 16, 1966

5.	Masters of War	The Freewheelin' Bob Dylan	May 27, 1963
6.	Gotta Serve Somebody	Slow Train Coming	Aug. 20, 1979
7.	Man of Constant Sorrow (arr. by Bob Dylan)	Bob Dylan	March 19, 1962
8.	Don't Think Twice, It's All Right	The Freewheelin' Bob Dylan	May 27, 1963
9.	Gates of Eden	Bringing It All Back Home	March 22, 1965
10.	Mr. Tambourine Man	Bringing It All Back Home	March 22, 1965
11.	Boots of Spanish Leather	The Times They Are A-Changin'	Feb. 10, 1964
12.	Everything is Broken	Oh Mercy	Sept. 12, 1989
13.	I Believe in You	Slow Train Coming	Aug. 20, 1979
14.	All Along the Watchtower	John Wesley Harding	Dec. 27, 1967
15.	I Shall Be Released	Bob Dylan's Greatest Hits, Vol. 2	Nov. 17, 1971
16.	Like a Rolling Stone	Highway 61 Revisited	Aug. 30, 1965
	Encores		
17.	Blowin' in the Wind	The Freewheelin' Bob Dylan	May 27, 1963
18.	Highway 61 Revisited	Highway 61 Revisited	Aug. 30, 1965

The Musicians

Bob Dylan (vocal, guitar & harmonica), G. E. Smith (guitar & electric slide guitar), Tony Garnier (bass), Christopher Parker (drums) and Steve Bruton (guitar).

Notes

- 63rd Bob Dylan concert in Canada; Debut Bob Dylan concert in Victoria.
- 2, 7-13, 16-17, Bob Dylan (harmonica).
- 7-11, 17, acoustic with the band.
- 18, G. E. Smith (electric slide guitar).
- Canadian live debut of song 7.
- Live audition for Steve Bruton on guitar.
- The opening act was Sue Medley.

Review

Laughing Dylan still has the power to move

By Adrian Chamberlain, Times-Colonist Staff Review.

The Beatles, the Rolling Stones and Bob Dylan were the mega-stars of the '60s. But it's Dylan who has best retained the air of mystery and legend that once enveloped all three.

Bob the Legend made his first ever Victoria appearance Sunday night. He had the same week's growth of beard, black biker jeans and boots, strapped-on harmonica and acoustic guitar he's been sporting since the early '60s.

Dylan's older now, of course – a year shy of 50. And his voice, once a keen nasal whine, has evolved into a guttural rasp.

But that didn't stop some of the sold-out crowd at the Memorial Arena from rushing the stage (or at least the barricade) half-way through his set to boogie with Bob.

The interesting question is: Were they merely worshipping at the altar of The Legend, or were they responding to a stunning musical performance?

The answer, not surprisingly, is a little of both.

Dylan's at the stage where he can do little wrong in performance. Gruff wheedling singing? That's just Bob's style. Odd, tuneless harmonica solos? That's Bob's trademark. A somewhat detached stage presence? Well, the man is an enigma, after all.

And yet Dylan still has the power to move. *Boots of Spanish Leather*, played during a selection of acoustic numbers, had the timeless, mystical quality found in his best work. So did *Gates of Eden*.

But it was the big hits that got the crowd on its feet. During the rocking *All Along the Watchtower*, the usually unsmiling Dylan actually laughed out loud in response to the audience's cheers.

And it was a searing workout, with guitarist and bandleader G.E. Smith (best known as the musical director on *Saturday Night Live*) taking a Hendrix-inspired solo.

The obligatory *Like a Rolling Stone* was transformed from a scathing accusation to a victorious anthem. Dylan, sweat dripping from his face, grinned and drawled without reserve (*Now you don't seem so proooooooooouuuuud*). He also took a couple of harmonica solos, including an extended improvisation at the end.

Almost as fascinating as seeing Dylan was watching Smith lead the band. Dylan is notorious for changing what he does on stage from night to night. Accordingly, Smith kept an eagle eye on the singer, looking for cues (or perhaps clues) and doing an amazing job of keeping this terrific band together.

The four-piece back-up band also did a fine job of not overshadowing Dylan, while at the same time acting as a powerful musical force.

A seemingly relaxed Dylan and company played a good sampling from his career, including *Maggie's Farm, Positively 4th Street, Masters of War, Stuck Inside of Mobile With the Memphis Blues Again* (for which he assumed a wide-legged Keith Richards stance), *You've Got to Serve Somebody, Don't Think Twice, It's All Right, Hey Mr. Tambourine Man, I Believe in You, I Shall be Released* (dedicated to the late Pearl Bailey) and encores *Blowin' in the Wind* and *Highway 61 Revisited*.

His voice sounded a little fractured at first, but warmed up to a tuneful croak after about 15 minutes. Typical of his live shows, the lyrics were difficult to make out. And the arena's hockey-rink acoustics didn't help out those sitting far from the stage.

A serious rocking *Highway 61 Revisited* ended the approximately 75-minute performance. Dylan ignored a broken guitar string. Smith produced some sizzling slide guitar lines, and the band surged ahead like an unrelenting freight train.

Singer Sue Medley, who hails from Courtenay, and her band opened the show with a distinctive set of Southern-style rock, ranging from ballads such as *Blue Skies* to harder hitting tunes like her single, *That's Life*.

Medley sounds something like Bonnie Raitt, although her style is less bluesy and her voice less husky. A strong singer and a powerful presence. It seems good things lie ahead for this musician.

The Victoria Times Colonist. Tues., Aug. 21, 1990.

Monday, August 20, 1990 --- Pacific Coliseum Vancouver, BC

Set List

	Song	From The Album	Released
1.	Maggie's Farm	Bringing It All Back Home	March 22, 1965
2.	Shelter from the Storm	Blood on the Tracks	Jan. 20, 1975
3.	Ballad of a Thin Man	Highway 61 Revisited	Aug. 30, 1965
4.	Stuck Inside of Mobile with the Memphis Blues Again	Blonde on Blonde	May 16, 1966
5.	Masters of War	The Freewheelin' Bob Dylan	May 27, 1963
6.	Gotta Serve Somebody	Slow Train Coming	Aug. 20, 1979
7.	Man of Constant Sorrow (arr. by Bob Dylan)	Bob Dylan	March 19, 1962
8.	Don't Think Twice, It's All Right	The Freewheelin' Bob Dylan	May 27, 1963
9.	It's Alright, Ma (I'm Only Bleeding)	Bringing It All Back Home	March 22, 1965
10.	Girl of the North Country	The Freewheelin' Bob Dylan	May 27, 1963
11.	It's All Over Now, Baby Blue	Bringing It All Back Home	March 22, 1965
12.	Everything is Broken	Oh Mercy	Sept. 12, 1989
13.	I Believe in You	Slow Train Coming	Aug. 20, 1979
14.	All Along the Watchtower	John Wesley Harding	Dec. 27, 1967
15.	Shooting Star	Oh Mercy	Sept. 12, 1989
16.	I Shall Be Released	Bob Dylan's Greatest Hits, Vol. 2	Nov. 17, 1971
17.	Like a Rolling Stone	Highway 61 Revisited	Aug. 30, 1965
	Encores		
18.	Blowin' in the Wind	The Freewheelin' Bob Dylan	May 27, 1963
19.	Highway 61 Revisited	Highway 61 Revisited	Aug. 30, 1965

The Musicians

Bob Dylan (vocal, guitar & harmonica), G. E. Smith (guitar & electric slide guitar), Tony Garnier (bass), Christopher Parker (drums).

Notes

- 64th Bob Dylan concert in Canada; 6th Bob Dylan concert in Vancouver.
- 2-3, 8, 10-11, 13, 15, 17-18, Bob Dylan (harmonica).
- 7-11, 18, acoustic with the band.
- 19, G. E. Smith (electric slide guitar).
- Live audition for Steve Bruton on guitar.
- Canadian live debut of song 15.
- The opening act was Sue Medley.

Reviews

Dylan still stalks watchtower

Icon of '60s shows great songs always can win audience

By John Mackie.

SATURDAY NIGHT, Cher drew 10,000 people to the Pacific Coliseum. Monday, Bob Dylan drew 6,500.

Seems trash is always more popular than art – even among '60s icons. But don't be surprised if old Bob makes a strong comeback, commercially speaking, in the near future. His last album (Oh Mercy) was his best in eons, and there's quite a buzz about his next one, due in September.

To top it off, the 49-year-old tunesmith seems to have gotten new life as a concert performer. Notoriously inconsistent in his past stage appearances, the Dylan onstage at the Coliseum Monday was at the top of his form, revitalizing old classics and whipping through new contenders in a sparkling 19-song, 85-minute set.

Backed by a crack four member band (including G.E. Smith, guitarist/bandleader for the Saturday Night Live band), Dylan offered his version of the greatest hits shows that are all the rage these days. With one big difference – when Bob Dylan does his hits, he reworks them so radically you can barely recognize them.

He opened with a jaunty country-swamp-rock number that sort of sounded-familiar, but the combination of not-so-great sound and his clothespin-on-the-nose vocal whine made the lyrics virtually indecipherable. After much frowning (and conferring with neighbours), it was ascertained that the tune in question was Maggie's Farm.

God only knows what the second song was, but the tell-tale "there's something happening here and you don't know what it is, do you, Mr. Jones?" made the third number, a bluesy Ballad of a Thin Man, (relatively) easy to peg. With each successive number, you seemed to be able to clue in a little more to his distinctive phrasing and cadence, until eventually you could pretty well understand every tune.

You never got to sit back and relax to a reasonable facsimile of a sentimental favourite, though, Dylan always keeps you on the edge of your seat, trying to figure out what he's going to do next.

That said, he did trot out a glorious collection of ye olde "timeless classics," including Stuck Inside of Mobile With The Memphis Blues Again, Don't Think Twice, It's Alright, It's Alright Ma (I'm Only Bleeding), Girl From The North Country, It's All Over Now, Baby Blue, I Shall Be Released, Blowin' In The Wind and Highway 61 Revisited. The real crowd-pleasers, though, were Like a Rolling Stone and All Along The Watchtower (which prompted a mass rush towards the stage).

Dylan also seemed in far better spirits than on past occasions, striking up dramatic poses with his guitar and even talking to the crowd. It helped to demystify his larger than life legend, and set the tone for a real fine concert.

Opener Sue Medley proved she's got the goods to make it on the big stage, filling the Coliseum with her powerful voice and canny mix of rock, country and blues. With ace slide guitarist Sonny Landreth (from John Hiatt's Goners) back on board, Medley and her band ripped it up through tunes like That's Life and Dangerous Times, tunes that show Medley to be a real comer in the heartland rock field.

The Vancouver Sun. Tues., Aug 21, 1990.

Pop legend renders familiar unfamiliar in night of nonchalance

By Tom Harrison, The Province.

It was precisely when Bob went to play a harmonica solo during Don't Think Twice (It's Alright) that you could figure out why some people were going to love last night's concert at the Coliseum and others were going to hate it.

Like Moses before him, Bob Dylan has that power to part seas – whether it's a sea of 6,000 people at the PNE or a sea of opinion. Last night, he did it again, simply by walking up to the microphone and drawing on his harp, only to discover it was in the wrong key.

Ambling off to put the right one in his holder, Dylan let his four musicians casually ride through the changes on their guitars, returning in time for barely a few notes on the correct harp.

The display was so random, as was most everything His Bobness did last night, and it was that kind of nonchalance which dominated the evening.

Anyone who went to the Coliseum, actually expecting to witness some variation on or version of 28 years of a different Bob Dylan that was fixed in time or trapped in the grooves of a record, was bound to be disappointed.

Odd to say it, but Bob Dylan is like Cher, who put on a completely different show Saturday at the PNE, yet one which worked on a similar principal of attraction. Here are two pop icons who, at this point in their careers, are the centres of a social event. Their presence makes everything else secondary.

Bob Dylan's presence differs in that he keeps heading off-centre, throwing familiar songs at the audience in completely unfamiliar arrangements, rendering some of them (Maggie's Farm, Shelter from the Storm, Blowin' in the Wind) virtually unrecognizable; or throwing in forgotten gems (You've Gotta Serve Somebody, I Believe In You) with unforgettably powerful results.

Working within a loose ensemble format led by guitarist G.E. Smith has given Dylan an extraordinary maneouvrability, which the band demonstrated in the lengthy acoustic portion of the set.

Songs such as It's All Over Now, Baby Blue or Girl of the North Country simply meandered until they found the right emotional tenor, whereas the electric segments showed a band that burrowed into the guts of All Along the Watchtower or Ballad of a Thin Man or Like a Rolling Stone, kept the bones and the sinews, and dug their way back out again.

It was natural, it was right, and they could do it at will – randomly.

Sue Medley, who has been Dylan's opening act on this tour, came back to Vancouver to celebrate her birthday on the weekend and to receive a gold disc for the 50,000 sales of her first album.

The Coliseum is a daunting place to celebrate a hometown triumph, however, and Sue more or less kept the set businesslike.

With a five-piece band that is mindful of the subtleties of Blue Skies or Queen of the Underground or able to shift gears on the rockers That's Life and Love Thing, and with a voice big enough to take on a hockey rink, Medley indicated that she hadn't even begun to tap her potential or even tap into her audience. When that happens, she'll also be able to take a few chances, and then watch out.

The Vancouver Province. Tues., Aug. 21, 1990.

1991

Introduction

The fourth year of the Never-Ending Tour saw Dylan play only one concert in Canada.

The only Canadian date would mark Bob Dylan's 65th concert in Canada.

The Date

Toronto, ON	Fri., July 26, 1991

The show was Dylan's 20th concert in Toronto.

The Musicians

Bob Dylan (vocal, guitar & harmonica).

John Jackson (guitar), Tony Garnier (bass), Ian Wallace (drums).

The Songs

Bob Dylan performed 18 songs (16 were from albums and 2 were cover and/or traditional songs).

Six songs made their Canadian live debut.

New Morning	Trail of the Buffalo
Wiggle Wiggle	Visions of Johanna
Lenny Bruce	Folsom Prison Blues

Three songs have been played only once in Canada.

Lenny Bruce	Folsom Prison Blues
Trail of the Buffalo	–

Bob Dylan performed songs from 12 different albums.

Album	Released	# of Songs Performed by Album
Another Side of Bob Dylan	Aug. 8, 1964	1
Bringing It All Back Home	March 22, 1965	1
Highway 61 Revisited	Aug. 30, 1965	2
Blonde on Blonde	May 16, 1966	1
John Wesley Harding	Dec. 27, 1967	2
New Morning	Oct. 21, 1970	1
Blood on the Tracks	Jan. 20, 1975	2
Slow Train Coming	Aug. 20, 1979	1
Shot of Love	Aug. 12, 1981	1
Empire Burlesque	May, 30, 1985	1
Oh Mercy	Sept. 12, 1989	2
Under the Red Sky	Sept. 11, 1990	1

Opening Act

Paul James opened the show.

The Venue

It was Bob Dylan's 2nd time playing at the Kingswood Music Theatre in Toronto.

Friday, July 26, 1991 --- Kingswood Music Theatre Toronto, ON

Set List

	Song	From The Album	Released
1.	New Morning	New Morning	Oct. 21, 1970
2.	I'll Remember You	Empire Burlesque	May 30, 1985
3.	All Along the Watchtower	John Wesley Harding	Dec. 27, 1967
4.	Shelter from the Storm	Blood on the Tracks	Jan. 20, 1975
5.	Gotta Serve Somebody	Slow Train Coming	Aug. 20, 1979
6.	Wiggle Wiggle	Under the Red Sky	Sept. 11, 1990
7.	Lenny Bruce	Shot of Love	Aug. 12, 1981
8.	I'll Be Your Baby Tonight	John Wesley Harding	Dec. 27, 1967
9.	Trail of the Buffalo (trad. arr. Woody Guthrie)	–	–
10.	Visions of Johanna	Blonde on Blonde	May 16, 1966
11.	Mr. Tambourine Man	Bringing It All Back Home	March 22, 1965
12.	It Ain't Me, Babe	Another Side of Bob Dylan	Aug. 8, 1964
13.	Folsom Prison Blues (Johnny Cash)	–	–
14.	Everything is Broken	Oh Mercy	Sept. 12, 1989
15.	Simple Twist of Fate	Blood on the Tracks	Jan. 20, 1975
16.	Highway 61 Revisited	Highway 61 Revisited	Aug. 30, 1965
	Encores		
17.	What Good Am I?	Oh Mercy	Sept. 12, 1989
18.	Ballad of a Thin Man	Highway 61 Revisited	Aug. 30, 1965

The Musicians

Bob Dylan (vocal, guitar & harmonica), John Jackson (guitar), Tony Garnier (bass), Ian Wallace (drums).

Notes

- 65th Bob Dylan concert in Canada; 20th Bob Dylan concert in Toronto.
- 1-2, 4, 7, 11-12, 16-18, Bob Dylan (harmonica).
- 9, Bob Dylan (vocal & guitar), John Jackson (guitar).
- 10-12, acoustic with the band.
- Canadian live debut of songs 1, 6, 7, 9, 10 & 13.
- Songs 7, 9 & 13 have been performed only once in Canada.
- The opening act was Paul James.

Reviews

Dylan rambles for a mere 6,500

By Peter Howell, Toronto Star.

Anyone searching for cosmic significance from Bob Dylan last night could have pondered his choice of encore tunes: "What Good Am I?" followed by "Ballad Of A Thin Man."

After a 90-minute show at Kingswood Theatre in Canada's Wonderland, in which he lurched and rambled over material from his earliest days to his most recent album, he seemed to be saying in the first song, "What do you think of this, everybody? Do you still like Bob Dylan?"

And with "Thin Man," his attack on the journalists who used to try so hard to figure him out ("Something is happening here, and you don't know what it is, do you, Mr. Jones?") the message seemed to be, "What are you going to write about this crazy show?"

That was about as deep as it got last night, in a wildly uneven performance viewed by a mere 6,500 souls. That was less than half the 14,000 who jammed the same place this past Monday to see another old-timer, the "Space Cowboy" Steve Miller, rock the house with a much more solid show.

The ever-enigmatic Dylan, dressed all in black, Johnny Cash-style, opened with an extended harmonica intro that made him seem as though he were simply the harp player for his excellent three-piece band: John Jackson on guitar, Tony Garnier on bass and Ian Wallace on drums.

Then it was on to "New Morning," the title track from his 1970 album, and in which he slurred the words so badly, it was almost unrecognizable.

It was the same with "All Along The Watchtower," which if you didn't recognize the distinctive guitar riffs supplied by Jackson, you likely wouldn't have figured out what Bobby was singing up there.

In better days, Dylan used to spit out the words to songs like that, sending a chill up your backbone.

Was he bored with singing songs he's sung a thousand times? It seemed that way at times, although he also seemed to be in a pretty good mood, for Dylan.

He didn't say much to the crowd – not even the obligatory, "How ya doin' Toronto?" – but he did observe that there were some empty seats up front available for fast-moving fans.

On most of his other songs, Dylan changed his arrangements around drastically.

It really cooked mid-show on "Visions Of Johanna" from Blonde On Blonde, in which the suddenly energized Mr. D. finally found his voice and cranked his harmonica up full-blast.

But a lounge lizard version of "Simple Twist Of Fate," from his 1975 album Blood On The Tracks seemed a sad way to treat one of his most moving ballads.

There were curiousity items, such as a deliberate in-your-face playing of "Wiggle Wiggle," his dumb ecology song on his most recent album, Under The Red Sky, which was singled out by critics as one of his worst-ever songs when it was released last fall.

And then soon he was on the tour bus and driving out of Wonderland before the house lights even came on.

In contrast, Toronto blues singer Paul James provided a solo acoustic set earlier on that showed him in great form, and delighted to be entertaining a crowd that had come to see his long-time friend and mentor, Dylan.

He looks and sounds so much like the early Dylan, but without Dylan's anger. It was the best reminder we got all night of a musical legend.

The Toronto Star. Sat., July 27, 1991. Reprinted with permission - Torstar Syndication Services.

Myth-ster Bob Dylan

By John Sakamoto, On Music.

There are two schools of thought about what Bob Dylan is up to on his so-called Never-Ending tour, now in its second decade and still going strong.

One grandiose theory holds that he takes great glee in mangling his best-known songs because he wants to play with our expectations and thereby subvert his own myth so he can be viewed as just another human.

Either that, or he's bored.

Last night, in front of 6,500 believers at Kingswood, he provided enough ammo to keep both sides yelling at each other for years.

Strolling onstage at a couple of minutes before 9, he played a two-minute harmonica solo before launching into New Morning. The only thing was, his three-piece band seemed to be playing Series of Dreams, a recent number from his Bootleg retrospective.

It was either a genuine mix-up or Dylan's way of signalling, "Let the games begin."

As any life-long fan will tell you, half the fun of going to a Dylan show is trying to guess what the hell he's playing.

So, the classic ballad, Shelter From The Storm, was sung at the same jaunty tempo as, say, Tie A Yellow Ribbon 'Round The Ole Oak Tree, while You Gotta Serve Somebody was so incomprehensible, the chorus sounded like a long, polysyllabic whine.

The crowd loved it.

On the non-musical side, Dylan, 50, actually spoke between songs. Early on he cracked, "There's some empty seats down in front." Later he introduced the inane Wiggle Wiggle with, "This is another religious song." (At least that's what it sounded like.)

Later still, he cracked. "These are my serious songs now," before reeling off Lenny Bruce and a virtually unrecognizable I'll Be Your Baby Tonight, which came out sounding like "Hunh ee yurr bee tight." (Then again, so did All Along The Watchtower.)

While all of this myth-bashing/plain old boredom was pretty funny, Dylan threw us off by abruptly switching gears half an hour in. Strapping on a black acoustic guitar, he played it almost straight, running through everything from Visions Of Johanna to Mr. Tambourine Man to It Ain't Me Babe.

Although the band this time around didn't feature any big names – no G.E. Smith or any of Tom Petty's Heartbreakers – it displayed an endless capacity to go with the flow no matter which way it went. Drummer Ian Wallace, guitarist John Jackson, and basist Tony Garnier fielded everything that came their way, and were especially impressive on the two-song encore, a sombre What Good Am I? and a raucous Ballad Of A Thin Man.

In the end, Dylan probably didn't settle any arguments about what he's up to. Instead, he did something more unexpected – he delivered a weird, fascinating, unpredictable, and riveting night of rock 'n' roll.

Captured Live

By Wilfred Langmaid, For The Daily Gleaner.

While he has continued to release a huge number of albums through the years, and always supports these albums with tours, Bob Dylan's concerts have often been big disappointments to people who come out to see a living legend perform his craft. Performances that are, at best, detached and, at worst, scornful of his audience have been marked by rapid-fire run-throughs of beautiful classics which lose their individual charm. Couple that with deteriorating vocals and an often showboating group of side men, and the picture is not promising.

However, Dylan silenced the skeptics with a fervent, sometimes beautiful, and occasionally sizzling 100-minute performance at Kingswood, the amphitheatre at Canada's Wonderland. Spurred by his young new band of drummer Ian Wallace, guitarist John Jackson, and bassist Tony Garnier, he clearly got into performing for a packed house. From the time that he began the concert by giving New Morning a full instrumental run through before beginning the vocals, things rocked.

What often made Dylan concerts of the 80s particularly boring was the fact every song sounded the same; performances were bereft of imagination or virtuosity. (Check out the 1984 album Real Live, for instance.) On this night, though, there were wonderful surprises, largely attributed to the fact that his band had an insatiable urge to rock with conviction on tracks both fast and slow. Shelter From The Storm worked surprisingly well as a frenetic rocker, while the ballad I'll Remember You got new life as a slow rocker. I'll Be Your Baby Tonight gets a mid-tempo rock feel catalyzed by Garnier's walking bass, while Dylan enjoys similar success with a rock-ized It Aint Me Babe. Even Mr. Tambourine Man got a loose jamming feel which even threatened to kick into Tangled up In Blue; as an example of the relaxed nature of this band, Dylan reconsidered a harp break, deferring to lead guitarist Jackson before he kicked in on harmonica 30 seconds or so later. The neatest metamorphosis happened to All Along The Watchtower; by no means Bobby mindlessly running through a classic, as he and his band gave this an ingenious new cadence.

For the Dylan fan, the treats never ended: a version of Gotta Serve Somebody which was the slinky, down-to-dirty rock that this band did best; an encore-closing Ballad Of A Thin Man which itself featured a little cadence shift; a version of the newer track Everything Is Broken which was dominated, interestingly enough, by bass licks from Green Onions by Garnier; and even a fun cover of Johnny Cash's Folsom Prison Blues. As for the ballads, they were highlighted by Visions Of Johanna, where Bob started on solo acoustic, and was gradually joined by Jackson on acoustic guitar and Garnier on stand-up bass before drummer Wallace entered on the second stanza; Simple Twist Of Fate and What Good Am I were also beautifully-performed ballads.

The best concerts are often pleasant surprises. Bob Dylan's 1991 summer tour is a good example.

As appeared in The Fredericton Daily Gleaner. Sat., Aug. 3, 1991. Reprinted with permission of Wilfred Langmaid

1992

Introduction

The Never-Ending Tour continued on in 1992 with seven concerts in Canada.

These shows would mark Bob Dylan's 66th, 67th, 68th, 69th, 70th, 71st & 72nd concert in Canada.

The Dates

Toronto, ON	Mon., Aug. 17, 1992
Toronto, ON	Tues., Aug. 18, 1992
Hamilton, ON	Fri., Aug. 21, 1992
Ottawa, ON	Sat., Aug. 22, 1992
Sudbury, ON	Mon. Aug. 24, 1992
Sault Ste. Marie, ON	Tues., Aug. 25, 1992
Thunder Bay, ON	Thurs., Aug 27, 1992

The shows would be Dylan's 21st and 22nd concert in Toronto, 2nd concert in Hamilton, 7th concert in Ottawa, debut concert in Sudbury, debut concert in Sault Ste. Marie and debut concert in Thunder Bay.

The Musicians

Bob Dylan (vocal, guitar & harmonica).

Bucky Baxter (mandolin, pedal steel guitar & electric slide guitar), John Jackson (guitar), Tony Garnier (bass), Ian Wallace (drums), Charlie Quintana (drums & percussion).

The Songs

Bob Dylan performed a total of 125 songs. Of those, 50 were different songs (47 were from albums and 3 were cover and/or traditional songs).

Ten songs made their Canadian live debut.

Watching the River Flow	Cat's in the Well
Little Moses	Don't Let Your Deal Go Down
Female Rambling Sailor	Unbelievable
Idiot Wind	To Be Alone with You
2 x 2	Man in the Long Black Coat

Two songs have been played only once in Canada.

Female Rambling Sailor	2 x 2

One song made its worldwide live debut.

Unbelievable	–

Bob Dylan performed songs from 21 different albums.

Album	Released	# of Songs Performed by Album
Bob Dylan	March 19, 1962	1
The Freewheelin' Bob Dylan	May, 27, 1963	2
The Times They Are A-Changin'	Feb., 10, 1964	4
Another Side of Bob Dylan	Aug. 8, 1964	3
Bringing It All Back Home	March 22, 1965	5
Highway 61 Revisited	Aug. 30, 1965	5
Blonde on Blonde	May 16, 1966	3
Bob Dylan's Greatest Hits	March 27, 1967	1
John Wesley Harding	Dec. 27, 1967	3
Nashville Skyline	April 9, 1969	1
New Morning	Oct. 21, 1970	1
Bob Dylan's Greatest Hits, Vol. 2	Nov. 17, 1971	1
Blood on the Tracks	Jan. 20, 1975	3
The Basement Tapes	July 1, 1975	1
Shot of Love	Aug. 12, 1981	1
Infidels	Oct. 27, 1983	1
Empire Burlesque	May, 30, 1985	1
Down in the Groove	May 19, 1988	1
Oh Mercy	Sept. 12, 1989	4
Under the Red Sky	Sept. 11, 1990	4
MTV Unplugged	June 30, 1995	1

Opening Acts

Moxy Fruvous opened the shows in Toronto. Junkhouse opened the show in Hamilton. In Ottawa, Michelle Shocked opened the show, The Neville Brothers were next and Joe Cocker followed. Sue Medley opened the shows in Sudbury & Sault Ste. Marie.

The Venues

It was Bob Dylan's 8th & 9th time playing at Massey Hall in Toronto, debut concert at Hamilton Place, debut concert at Lansdowne Stadium in Ottawa, debut concert at the Sudbury Arena, debut concert at Memorial Gardens in Sault Ste. Marie and debut concert at the Fort William Gardens in Thunder Bay.

Monday, August 17, 1992 --- Massey Hall Toronto, ON

Set List

	Song	From The Album	Released
1.	Wiggle Wiggle	Under the Red Sky	Sept. 11, 1990
2.	Heart of Mine	Shot of Love	Aug. 12, 1981
3.	All Along the Watchtower	John Wesley Harding	Dec. 27, 1967
4.	Positively 4th Street	Bob Dylan's Greatest Hits	March 27, 1967
5.	Tangled Up in Blue	Blood on the Tracks	Jan. 20, 1975
6.	She Belongs to Me	Bringing It All Back Home	March 22, 1965
7.	Watching the River Flow	Bob Dylan's Greatest Hits, Vol. 2	Nov. 17, 1971
8.	Little Moses (Bert A. Williams/Earle C. Jones)	–	–
9.	Female Rambling Sailor (trad.)	–	–
10.	Boots of Spanish Leather	The Times They Are A-Changin'	Feb. 10, 1964
11.	It's Alright, Ma (I'm Only Bleeding)	Bringing It All Back Home	March 22, 1965
12.	I Dreamed I Saw St. Augustine	John Wesley Harding	Dec. 27, 1967
13.	It Takes a Lot to Laugh, It Takes a Train to Cry	Highway 61 Revisited	Aug. 30, 1965
14.	Like a Rolling Stone	Highway 61 Revisited	Aug. 30, 1965
15.	Idiot Wind	Blood on the Tracks	Jan. 20, 1975
	Encores		
16.	What Good Am I?	Oh Mercy	Sept. 12, 1989
17.	Highway 61 Revisited	Highway 61 Revisited	Aug. 30, 1965

The Musicians

Bob Dylan (vocal, guitar & harmonica), Bucky Baxter (mandolin, pedal steel guitar & electric slide guitar), John Jackson (guitar), Tony Garnier (bass), Ian Wallace (drums), Charlie Quintana (drums & percussion).

Notes

- 66th Bob Dylan concert in Canada; 21st Bob Dylan concert in Toronto.
- 5, 8, 10, 13, 16, Bob Dylan (harmonica).
- 8-9, 18, Bob Dylan solo (acoustic guitar & vocal).
- 10-11, acoustic with the band.
- Canadian live debut of songs 7, 8, 9 & 15.
- Song 9 has been performed only once in Canada.
- The opening act was Moxy Fruvous.

Reviews

Befuddled Bob still manages to muddle through

By Peter Howell.

People were actually enjoying themselves at the Bob Dylan show in Massey Hall last night.

I saw it with my own eyes. A fabulous blonde got up and started dancing right in front of Zimmy during "Like A Rolling Stone", and the next thing you knew, the joint was jumpin' like it was pay day in a Sudbury bar.

The uncharacteristically mellow Massey security people even allowed dancing up front, and the spotlights were turned to illuminate the crowd.

Dylan even seemed to enjoy it. He cracked his first smile of the evening during "Idiot Wind", and started pointing at the dancers and hamming it up on his guitar.

He was a regular Napoleon in rags up there, and it was all so jolly it almost made me forget the feeling I'd had for most of the show – that I was sitting up with the ghost of an old friend.

Was this hunched-over figure slurring his barely audible words the same guy whose every phrase used to inspire intense reflection?

The pop bard whose poetry more than made up for his vocal shortcomings?

Was this the same travelling minstrel whose Rolling Thunder Revue I once travelled seven hours in a cramped bus to see, savoring every minute of the trip?

It sure was hard to tell, especially as Dylan's mind appeared to be miles away from Massey.

In the middle of "All Along The Watchtower" he stopped to adjust his mike stand and his harmonica, and then started rubbing his hair – something he did a lot during the evening.

At one point during another song, he lost his harmonica altogether, and just continued to play without his usual harp flourishes.

There was his regular trick of rearranging all of his old material, but his changes were so drastic this time, even old fans had to play "Name That Tune" well into each song.

He and his five-piece band starting playing what sounded like "Rainy Day Women No. 12 & 35" (his "everybody must get stoned" song that a few brazen tokers were already heeding) but the tune suddenly turned into a fractured version of "It Takes A Lot To Laugh, It Takes A Train To Cry".

"Positively 4th Street" was stripped of its urban angst to become a country rock number, with pedal steel provided by new Dylan player Bucky Baxter.

But one thing hasn't changed – Dylan still has a sense of humor.

He chose local up-and-comers Moxy Fruvous as opening act, possibly the cheekiest group ever to warm up a Dylan audience.

The fast-rising Fruvous, friends of working people everywhere, at first seemed a strange choice as opening act.

But the warm acoustics of Massey were perfect for the quartet's mainly a cappella material, and even the zany, Dr. Seuss-inspired rap song "Green Eggs And Ham" went down well with an audience that included "a lot of leftover '60s people," to use the words of band member Jean Ghomeshi.

The fans came to revere a living legend; they heard Moxy Fruvous twist a Dylan song title to make "Sad-Eyed Lisa Of The Lowlands" out of the "unspeakable Queen Lisa" in the Fruvous hit "King Of Spain".

They also saw Bob Dylan in the most befuddled state he's ever been in on a Toronto stage.

Yet still they thundered applause at him and at Moxy Fruvous, and they probably will again for tonight's second show, for which about 100 tickets remain unsold.

But was that the real Bob Dylan up there?

The Toronto Star. Tues., Aug. 18, 1992. Reprinted with permission - Torstar Syndication Services.

The crimes they are a-changing

By John Sakamoto, Music.

By now, it no longer matters if Bob Dylan is good or bad.

As a near-capacity crowd proved last night at the first of two nights at Massey Hall, all Dylan has to be these days is perverse enough to be entertaining.

Now, you can still make a good argument that Dylan knows exactly what he's doing, that he deliberately goes out of his way to make his songs unrecognizable so he can reinvent them every night, or that he's rebelling against the tired convention of playing his songs the same way each time out.

But there comes a point when even the most ardent fan has to face up to the possibility that Dylan's performances no longer deserve that kind of theoretical speculation.

Maybe, just maybe, Dylan puts on these kinds of wildly careless, unintelligible concerts because it's simply all he's capable of doing.

Even those fans who continue to show up just to revel in Dylan's unqualified weirdness, must have noticed the horrendous sound that all but buried guitarist John Jackson's fluid playing.

Or the fact that Dylan couldn't even be bothered to tune his guitar before launching into a woeful It Takes A Lot To Laugh, It Takes A Train To Cry.

Or the fact that the five-piece band featured, for no apparent reason, two drummers when most of the songs could've gotten along quite nicely without one. It was akin to carrying a pair of bassists, and telling them just to play two strings each.

All this added up to was a bizarre game of "name that tune."

You could look around during almost any song and see people whispering in each other's ears, trying to figure out what the hell Dylan was playing.

So, after a merciless trashing of All Along The Watchtower, he reeled off virtually unrecognizable versions of Positively 4th Street, Tangled Up In Blue (Mangled Up In Blue would've been more like it), She Belongs To Me, and Boots Of Spanish Leather – or at least a song that contained the words "Boots of Spanish Leather" somewhere among its lines.

It was easy to laugh at all this, at least for a while.

But, for those of us who still think of these songs as something special, something like, I don't know, art, it got progressively more difficult to take pleasure in hearing them destroyed.

Convincing yourself that that was what Dylan had in mind all along is little comfort.

SUN RATING: 2 OUT OF 5

The Toronto Sun. Tues., Aug. 18, 1992. Reprinted with permission of The Sun Media Corp.

Dylan has lost a lot but fans still love him

A former great who is a mere shell of former self plays to sell-out Toronto crowd

By Alan Niester. Special to The Globe and Mail.

Imagine a sketch on *Saturday Night Live* in which Dana Carvey portrays Bob Dylan in the year 2022. He would don a grey wig, totter out to the front of the stage with requisite guitar and harmonica, and mumble versions of *Like A Rolling Stone* and *Rainy Day Women #12 and 35* in a nasal drone that would border on the indecipherable. North American audiences would howl.

But Dana Carvey won't be performing this particular skit, because it's already been done. It's undoubtedly been done on every night of Dylan's current tour, and last night the unintentional comedy was played out again before a full house at Toronto's Massey Hall.

Dylan arguably is or was the most influential musician of his generation, and there was a time when a local appearance really, really mattered. But watching the venerable balladeer, who looks and sounds so much older than his 51 years, it quickly became obvious that his importance waned years ago. Today, Dylan is a relic, an anachronism, a total irrelevant. He has not mattered in any real musical, social or political sense in over two decades, and the only reason anyone would have for going to see him and cheer him would be for purposes of nostalgia, respect or history. Certainly no one would come for the music. He has become little more than a humourless version of Flo and Eddie, churning out a succession of old songs to audiences desperate to turn back the clock. What's sad about it all is that, unlike Flo and Eddie singing their old Turtles hits, Dylan still takes it all so very, very seriously.

Dylan's voice and vocal style, at this point, can only be described as wretched. His tone is so incredibly nasal that lyrical interpretation is hopeless. His phrasing, always difficult, now borders on the absurd, and, no, his mumbling problem has not gotten any better since his last local appearance.

But presumably he is aware of his worsening vocal talents. He has managed to take the strain off his voice by turning many of his older numbers into extended instrumental workouts. He has surrounded himself with a passable six-piece band (highlighted by guitarist John Jackson) that turns every song into a Grateful Dead-like experience. Old standards such as *All Along The Watchtower* and *Watching The River Flow* were turned into looping, Jerry Garcia-styled vocal/instrumentals. Dylan would mumble a few lines, sit back and strum along with the band on his acoustic guitar, then interject himself back into the song at the finish.

But for all that, the audience still ate it up. In fact, during the inevitable version of *Like A Rolling Stone*, many rushed to the foot of the stage to bask in the master's aura, swaying along like reeds in a very light breeze.

Dylan performs again at Massey Hall tonight. There are, as they say on the radio, still good seats available (which is a story in itself). No doubt they will be snapped up by much the same type of people who slow down to inspect a car wreck.

As appeared in The Globe and Mail. Tues., Aug. 18, 1992. Reprinted with permission of Alan Niester.

Tuesday, August 18, 1992 --- Massey Hall
Toronto, ON

Set List

	Song	From The Album	Released
1.	2 x 2	Under the Red Sky	Sept. 11, 1990
2.	All Along the Watchtower	John Wesley Harding	Dec. 27, 1967
3.	Tears of Rage (Bob Dylan & Richard Manual)	The Basement Tapes	July 1, 1975
4.	Maggie's Farm	Bringing It All Back Home	March 22, 1965
5.	Just Like Tom Thumb's Blues	Highway 61 Revisited	Aug. 30, 1965
6.	I Don't Believe You (She Acts Like We Never Have Met)	Another Side of Bob Dylan	Aug. 8, 1964
7.	Wiggle Wiggle	Under the Red Sky	Sept. 11, 1990
8.	Little Moses (Bert A. Williams &Earle C. Jones)	–	–
9.	To Ramona	Another Side of Bob Dylan	Aug. 8, 1964
10.	Gates of Eden	Bringing It All Back Home	March 22, 1965
11.	Don't Think Twice, It's All Right	The Freewheelin' Bob Dylan	May 27, 1963
12.	Cat's in the Well	Under the Red Sky	Sept. 11, 1990
13.	Idiot Wind	Blood on the Tracks	Jan. 20, 1975
14.	Stuck Inside of Mobile with the Memphis Blues Again	Blonde on Blonde	May 16, 1966
15.	Highway 61 Revisited	Highway 61 Revisited	Aug. 30, 1965
	Encores		
16.	Ballad of a Thin Man	Highway 61 Revisited	Aug. 30, 1965
17.	Everything is Broken	Oh Mercy	Sept. 12, 1989
18.	It Ain't Me, Babe	Another Side of Bob Dylan	Aug. 8, 1964

The Musicians

Bob Dylan (vocal, guitar & harmonica), Bucky Baxter (mandolin, pedal steel guitar & electric slide guitar), John Jackson (guitar), Tony Garnier (bass), Ian Wallace (drums), Charlie Quintana (drums & percussion).

Notes

- 67th Bob Dylan concert in Canada; 22rd Bob Dylan concert in Toronto.
- 5-6, 8-10, 13-14, 18, Bob Dylan (harmonica).
- 8-9, 18, Bob Dylan solo (acoustic guitar & vocal).
- 10, Bob Dylan (acoustic guitar & vocal), Tony Garnier (bass).
- 11, Bob Dylan (acoustic guitar & vocal), John Jackson (guitar), Tony Garnier (bass).
- Canadian live debut of songs 1 & 12.
- Song 1 has been performed only once in Canada.
- The opening act was Moxy Fruvous.

Friday, August 21, 1992 --- Hamilton Place
Hamilton, ON

Set List

	Song	From The Album	Released
1.	Don't Let Your Deal Go Down (trad.)		
2.	Pretty Peggy-O (arr. by Bob Dylan)	Bob Dylan	March 19, 1962
3.	All Along the Watchtower	John Wesley Harding	Dec. 27, 1967
4.	Tangled Up in Blue	Blood on the Tracks	Jan. 20, 1975
5.	I'll Be Your Baby Tonight	John Wesley Harding	Dec. 27, 1967
6.	Simple Twist of Fate	Blood on the Tracks	Jan. 20, 1975
7.	Everything is Broken	Oh Mercy	Sept. 12, 1989
8.	Little Moses (Bert A. Williams/Earle C. Jones)	–	–
9.	Boots of Spanish Leather	The Times They Are A-Changin'	Feb. 10, 1964
10	The Lonesome Death of Hattie Carroll	The Times They Are A-Changin'	Feb. 10, 1964
11.	Mr. Tambourine Man	Bringing It All Back Home	March 22, 1965
12.	Cat's in the Well	Under the Red Sky	Sept. 11, 1990
13.	The Times They Are A-Changin'	The Times They Are A-Changin'	Feb. 10, 1964
14.	Idiot Wind	Blood on the Tracks	Jan. 20, 1975
15.	Maggie's Farm	Bringing It All Back Home	March 22, 1965
	Encores		
16.	What Good Am I?	Oh Mercy	Sept. 12, 1989
17.	Highway 61 Revisited	Highway 61 Revisited	Aug. 30, 1965
18.	It Ain't Me, Babe	Another Side of Bob Dylan	Aug. 8, 1964

The Musicians

Bob Dylan (vocal, guitar & harmonica), Bucky Baxter (mandolin, pedal steel guitar & electric slide guitar), John Jackson (guitar), Tony Garnier (bass), Ian Wallace (drums), Charlie Quintana (drums & percussion).

Notes

- 68th Bob Dylan concert in Canada; 2nd Bob Dylan concert in Hamilton.
- 4-6, 9-11, 14, 16, 18, Bob Dylan (harmonica).
- 4, 14, Bucky Baxter (mandolin).
- 8-9, 18, Bob Dylan solo (acoustic guitar & vocal).
- 10, Bob Dylan (acoustic guitar & vocal) & Tony Garnier (bass).
- 11, Bob Dylan (acoustic guitar & vocal), Tony Garnier (bass) & Ian Wallace (drums).
- Canadian live debut of song 1.
- The opening act was Junkhouse.

Review

Dylan gets repeated standing ovations

By Nick Krewen, The Spectator.

EXCELLENT!

Bob Dylan and company cooked up a mean gumbo last night at Hamilton Place in what could be considered one of the legendary songwriter's more consistent performances.

For two hours, Dylan entertained the near-capacity crowd of hippies, baby boomers and naturalists with choice selections from his 30-year career, causing such a wave of excitement that several people in the crowd repeatedly gave him a standing ovation after each number.

What's more, he and his proficient entourage – which included guitarist John Jackson, bassist Tony Garnier, pedal steel guitarist/mandolinist Bucky Baxter and the drumming pair of Ian Wallace and Charlie Quintana – thoroughly deserved it.

Those familiar with Dylan's shaky performance past are well aware that the pendulum can swing as easily left as to the right and how easily a moment of magical brilliance can be replaced by awkward hackneyedness.

Not last night, however. The 51-year-old singer's approach with his compatriots could pretty much be compared with a whirlpool, in that it was a casual affair that had everybody contribute their stroke of the brush to complete the aural painting.

As usual, Dylan led – everyone followed – and eventually the musical locomotive would pull out of the station, chug along for awhile while everybody explored the scenery and slow to a gradual stop once Bob the Conductor had decided the destination had been reached.

At times, the chemistry would be extremely fragile, as Jackson and Garnier would listen hard to determine where Dylan was going. After the first few numbers, they were in tune with the master of reinvention and their improvisation was nothing short of brilliant.

And the performance also revealed another side of Dylan we haven't seen so much recently: the guitarist. While everyone was barrelling ahead with whatever momentum certain songs called for, Bob was picking some very sweet melodic solos on his acoustic. It was an unexpected, delightful surprise.

But then, Dylan is full of them. Sporting a black polka-dot shirt, black slacks and cowboy boots, the songsmith (who, as usual, didn't allow any photographers into the building) continually pulled rabbits out of his hat throughout the concert. Usually he'd spring an unfamiliar riff done in a foreign style, warm up the band and then begin singing the last tune you'd expect to accompany the vamp.

Thus, Maggie's Farm was performed over a soul-stirred fun-kee treadmill that came perilously close to disco, while Mr. Tambourine Man was thrown out as a country two-step shuffle.

Not everything about the man has changed, of course. At times he still sounded like a graduate of the Buckwheat School of Broadcasting, running together his words and editing his lines, with that nasal whine that was born to shear sheep.

But there were moments – like the tender, bluesy rendition of Simple Twist Of Fate and the solo renditions of Little Moses and Boots Of Spanish Leather – where Bob was definitely singing sensitively and passionately.

Other gold nuggets from the treasure-filled Dylan catalogue: The Lonesome Death Of Hattie Carroll, All Along The Watchtower, Tangled Up In Blue, Idiot Wind, Everything Is Broken and I'll Be Your Baby Tonight, and an amazing rendition of The Times They Are A-Changin'.

The openers, local band Junkhouse, did Hamilton proud.

Led by singer Tom Wilson, the team of guitarist Dan Achen, drummer Ray Ferruga and bassist Russ Wilson left no doubt in anyone's mind that these guys are ready for the big leagues.

Handling themselves with charismatic confidence, Junkhouse combined David Lynchian guitar riffs, driving rhythms and intense musicality into a potent sonic aphrodisiac and seduced the crowd into whistling, applauding appreciation.

No wonder the majors are battling to sign Junkhouse. They deserve it.

Saturday, August 22, 1992 --- Landsdowne Stadium
Ottawa, ON

Set List

	Song	From The Album	Released
1.	Rainy Day Women #12 & 35	Blonde on Blonde	May 16, 1966
2.	Pretty Peggy-O (arr. by Bob Dylan)	Bob Dylan	March 19, 1962
3.	All Along the Watchtower	John Wesley Harding	Dec. 27, 1967
4.	Stuck Inside of Mobile with the Memphis Blues Again	Blonde on Blonde	May 16, 1966
5.	Watching the River Flow	Bob Dylan's Greatest Hits, Vol. 2	Nov. 17, 1971
6.	Simple Twist of Fate	Blood on the Tracks	Jan. 20, 1975
7.	Just Like a Woman	Blonde on Blonde	May 16, 1966
8.	Little Moses (Bert A. Williams/Earle C. Jones)	–	–

9	Boots of Spanish Leather	The Times They Are A-Changin'	Feb. 10, 1964
10.	Gates of Eden	Bringing It All Back Home	March 22, 1965
11.	Don't Think Twice, It's All Right	The Freewheelin' Bob Dylan	May 27, 1963
12.	Unbelievable	Under the Red Sky	Sept. 11, 1990
13.	I and I	Infidels	Oct. 27, 1983
14.	The Times They Are A-Changin'	The Times They Are A-Changin'	Feb. 10, 1964
15.	Maggie's Farm	Bringing It All Back Home	March 22, 1965
	Encores		
16.	What Good Am I?	Oh Mercy	Sept. 12, 1989
17.	To Be Alone with You	Nashville Skyline	April 9, 1969
18.	Girl of the North Country	The Freewheelin' Bob Dylan	May 27, 1963

The Musicians

Bob Dylan (vocal, guitar & harmonica), Bucky Baxter (mandolin, pedal steel guitar & electric slide guitar), John Jackson (guitar), Tony Garnier (bass), Ian Wallace (drums), Charlie Quintana (drums & percussion).

Notes

- 69th Bob Dylan concert in Canada; 7th Bob Dylan concert in Ottawa.
- 1, 4-7, 9, 11, 15-16, 18, Bob Dylan (harmonica).
- 8-9, 18, Bob Dylan solo (acoustic guitar & vocal).
- 10, Bob Dylan (acoustic guitar & vocal), Tony Garnier (bass).
- 11, Bob Dylan (acoustic guitar & vocal), Tony Garnier (bass), Ian Wallace (drums).
- 14, acoustic with the band.
- 14, Bucky Baxter (mandolin).
- Canadian live debut of songs 12 & 17.
- Worldwide live debut of song 12.
- The opening act was Michelle Shocked, followed by The Neville Brothers, followed by Joe Cocker.

Reviews

Dylan's meteoric magic lights up star-studded night at Super Ex

By Lynn Saxberg, Citizen Staff Writer.

The Dylan doubters were wrong. To those of you who said Bob Dylan is washed-up, burnt out and can't sing, you were mistaken.

The legendary singer-songwriter was in fine form Saturday night at the Super Ex Grandstand. In fact, he rocked.

It wouldn't have spoiled the day if Dylan had an off night. Each band gave fantastic performances. It would have been satisfying to go home having seen Joe Cocker, The Neville Brothers and Michelle Shocked.

But, thankfully, the magic didn't end. Dylan came out blasting *Everybody Must Get Stoned* with all the power and intensity of the old days.

The powerstart continued with mindblowing versions of *All Along The Watchtower* and *Stuck Inside of Mobile With the Memphis Blues Again* coming soon after.

Dylan had a crack band backing him, including two drummers, two guitarists and a bassist who played electric and acoustic bass. He also took the stage alone for a hypnotizing acoustic session, maintaining the energy of the music the whole time.

His voice was confident, surprisingly clear and he focused intently on his microphone stand, moving only occasionally. Highlights of the set, which was approaching the two hour mark at deadline, were *The Times They Are A-Changing*, *All Along The Watchtower* and an electric *Maggie's Farm.*

It was one of the best days of music for Ottawa in a long time. The between-set changes were quick and the bands almost precisely on schedule.

One of the most stirring moments of the evening came during Joe Cocker's renowned rendition of *With A Little Help From My Friends.*

Cocker had been pacing himself during his hour-long set, concentrating on his specialty, ballads, no doubt to ensure his voice lasted to the end. It doesn't seem any easier for him to sing; he still grimaces like he's pushing himself to the limit.

His voice and the show peaked during *With A Little Help*, as Cocker and his backup singers belted their hearts out.

Hard to follow; but he had one more ace up his sleeve, a spectacular version of *You Are So Beautiful.*

During their performance as the second act, the Neville Brothers guided the crowd into the sizzling atmosphere of a New Orleans nightclub.

Brothers Aaron, Charles, Cyril and Art Neville served up a tasty set of spicy R&B, with African, Caribbean, funk, and rap thrown in for extra flavor.

It was a mélange guaranteed to get feet moving. The band members' incredible vocals and punchy rhythm section didn't let for an hour, mixing old favorites like *Aaron* Neville's poignant version of *Tell It Like It Is* to newer gems such as *One More Day*, which the band dedicated to the children of the planet Earth, and *Saxafunk*, both tracks from the *Family Groove* disc. The highlight of the set was the New Orleans Mardi Gras standard, *Iko Iko*, which the band dedicated to the Grateful Dead's Jerry Garcia, who is recovering from exhaustion.

The Super Ex concert series got off to a fine start Saturday evening with a great set by Texas-born singer-songwriter Michelle Shocked. Unlike so many opening acts where artists with plenty of potential are plagued with below-grade sound and a distracted audience, Shocked's siren like voice was impossible to ignore.

With her songs, she took the crowd on a rambling journey through the backstreets and backwoods of America.

Backed by a three-piece band on fiddle, guitar and banjo and bass, Shocked blends the music of the country — bluegrass, country and folk — with lyrics that tell stories of urban life.

She performed a half-hour set (too short, really), about half of which consisted of songs from her latest album, *Arkansas Traveler*, a collection of songs recorded with the help of various artists, including Hothouse Flowers, Doc Watson, and the Band's Garth Hudson and Levon Helm. The challenge was to replicate those performances without the artists, and she managed extremely well.

The Ottawa Citizen. Sun., Aug. 23, 1992. Reprinted with permission of The Ottawa Citizen.

STELLAR START

SuperEx show a winning mix

By Rick Overall, On Music.

Let just call it a rocker's buffet – a little taste of something special for every appetite.

Yesterday's SuperEx Grandstand's opening concert offered up a wide range of styles, making it pretty well impossible for anyone to walk away unimpressed.

A least from a seniority aspect, Dylan was the headliner – and the word from the road indicated he was in better form than the debacle he passed off as a concert at the NAC.

Well Dylan wasn't only in better form – he was GREAT.

The voice is a little shakier, but with a gutsy band behind him, Dylan just sat back and cranked out the classics.

Rainy Day Women, *All Along The Watchtower*, *Pretty Peggy-O* and *Memphis Blues Again* – get the idea?

This was Bob Dylan the way he needs to be seen – offering up an astounding repertoire that's brought him into the hearts of millions.

The mood and atmosphere he created during the show was a treasure – transporting us back to an age when things were simpler and Dylan was a hero.

He obviously still is.

The afternoon rolled into action with a visit from Michelle Shocked – long a favorite with the alternative crowd, she was riding a new wave of success generated by her latest disc *Arkansas Traveller*.

Pulling about 60% of her material from that disc, Shocked delivered the goods with stirring versions of *Jump Jim Crow*, *Over The Water Fall* (a traditional tune with Shocked adding her own lyrics), *Weaving Way* and her exquisite finish *Secret Of A Long Life*.

I've never seen Shocked in concert before but this short 40-minute set made me an instant fan. Her strong voice and excellent combination of a bare bones traditional feel mixed well with the street soul of the'90s.

Now, Joe Cocker's been through the wringer on a personal level – but more recently succeeded in absolving himself of those nasty dependencies which nearly cost him his career.

And this new, improved version of the man who invented air guitar hit the spot with a dyno combination of all his mega-hits and a little taste of *Night Calls*, his latest.

With A Little Help From My Friends, *Feelin' Alright* and *Hitchcock Railroad* represented the past while *Up Where We Belong*, *You Can Leave Your Hat On* and *Shelter Me* gave us a peek at the middle of his career.

And finally he dropped in his remake of Gary Wright's *Love Is Alive* for good measure.

The Neville Brothers are no strangers to Ottawa – in the leaner years they were a staple on the club circuit, playing to packed houses at places like Barrymore's.

Led by the amazing vocals of Aaron, the boys rollicked through a superb set. Their portion of the show was simply brilliant – like the rollicking version of *Devil Moon* which highlighted their ability to cross-pollinate styles as mixed as straight-ahead rock, reggae, rap and funk.

Aaron Neville gave us a great tune with the Main Ingredient hit *Everybody Plays The Fool* and a stellar version of *Tell It Like It Is*.

Brother Cyril's no slouch either, grinding out a gutsy version of *Let My People Go*.

All in all, not a bad start to SuperEx – with nearly 10,000 happy fans in attendance, things got off to a super start.

The Ottawa Sun. Sun., Aug. 23, 1992. Reprinted with permission of The Sun Media Corp.

Un Dylan exceptionnel à la SuperEx

Joe Cocker, Michelle Shocked et les frères Neville au même programme

par Marc André Joanisse, LeDroit.

Bob Dylan a parlé... Il a dit bonsoir au monde.

On s'en fiche qu'il n'aspire pas aux grands concours oratoires.

Que voulez-vous, le pape de Greenwich Village est peu bavard, mais quand il se donne la peine d'offrir un «vrai» spectacle, il n'a pas son pareil.

Samedi, il a été exceptionnel, à la mesure de son talent, pour ce premier soir de spectacle à la SuperEx.

Rien de moins que l'apothéose pour la grande majorité des 10 000 personnes. Une belle foule qui s'est dandinée une partie de la soirée. Tranquille et respectueuse. Non, il n'y a pas eu d'émeute, samedi, au parc Lansdowne.

Bob Dylan se devait de tirer les marrons du feu, car les artistes qui l'ont précédé, Michelle Shocked, les frères Neville et Joe Cocker, avaient déjà dressé la table.

Beaucoup plus rock n' roll que par les années passées avec ses cinq musiciens dont deux batteurs, Dylan ne s'est pas contenté de cracher des mucosités comme il en avait l'habitude de le faire.

Il a joué de la guitare et de l'harmonica comme lui seul sait le faire et il a chanté (un sacrilège pour les gens qui ne peuvent le blairer) avec un énergie qu'on croyait endormie à tout jamais. L'homme y a mis du coeur et de la passion et aurait esquissé un sourire à quelques reprises, foi d'un fan assis dans la deuxième rangée.

On le répète, l'exécution était serrée et parfaite, principalement chez *Rainy Day Woman*, pièce qui a tout déclenché, *All Along The Watchtower*, *Maggie's Farm* et *Watching the Ri-ver Flow*.

Une prestation tantôt électrique, tantôt acoustique, puisque l'ami Bob a flairé le courant.

Il a retrouvé ses allures de barde et le parc Lansdowne s'est vite transformé en café, probablement le plus gros de la planète.

Plus de 10 000 personnes, dont plusieurs hippies qui n'ont jamais décroché et des «conscrits», ces nouveaux ténors du *Peace and Love*, l'ont accompagné dans des versions en solo de ses plus grands crédos. Pas les plus connus, les plus « punchés ».

Quelle joie de réentendre *Gates of Eden*, *Don't Think Twice*, *Outlaw Blues* et en quatuor acoustique, *The Time's They Are a Changin*: de grands moments d'une grande quiétude.

Volontairement, avec lui le contraire étonnerait, Dylan a choisi de laisser de côté ses chansons les plus commerciales. Non, il n'a pas chanté *Blowing In The Wind* et *Like A Rolling Stone*, au grand dam d'un jeune spectateur, Benoît, qui assistait au premier concert rock de son existence.

Michelle Shocked

Ce jeune amant de la musique a bien résumé la soirée de samedi: Couci-couça, Michelle Shocked, emballé par les frères Neville – il a fait la coversation avec Cyril après son spectacle – et littéralement submergé par Joe Cocker.

Du haut de ses 15 ans, on comprend son indifférence à Michelle Shocked. Il n'est pas donné à quiconque d'apprécier le Bluegrass, nouveau dada de la chanteuse. Il a quand même saisi la portée de sa chanson *Graffiti Limbo* et sa sortie à l'endroit de la justice américaine.

Graffiti Limbo, c'est l'histoire de Michael Stewart, un jeune Noir arrêté puis étranglé à mort par des policiers de Los Angeles alors qu'il écrivait des graffitis sur des murs. «C'était bien avant les incidents de South Central L.A.» a crié la chanteuse du Texas. La justice américaine est aveugle.

Les quartre frères Neville

Si Michelle Shocked a laissé Benoît sur son appétit, il a été séduit par les frères Neville. Et on le comprend. Quatre musiciens de New Orleans qui défendent la même musique et la même cause, l'égalité sur terre, depuis 25 ans.

On se serait cru au Mardi gras, tellement l'atmosphère était carnavalesque avec les *Iko Iko*, chanson dédiée à Jerry Garcia des Grateful Dead et *One More Day*, aux enfants de la planète.

Il n'y a pas de trou dans une prestation des Neville, aussi courte soit-elle. Le rythme est soutenu, les chanteurs sont sympathiques et on est en présence d'un phénomène, Aaron Neville, une voix angélique dans un corps d'haltérophile. On a eu des frissons quand il a interprété, *Tell It Like It Is* et *Everybody Plays The Fool*.

Mais le clou de la soirée, avant l'entrée en scène de sieur Dylan, aura été Joe Cocker, une force de la nature.

Cocker capable de grandes choses

Le simple fait qu'il puisse encore chanter tire du miracle. Après 25 ans à s'époumoner, Joe Cocker est toujours capable de grandes choses.

Et de grandes interprétations. Cocker était manifestement dans une forme impeccable. Et c'est avec ses merveilleuses ballades «bluesées» qu'il nous a fait mordre à l'appât.

Tout simplement divines ses interprétations de *With A Little Help From My Friend*, *Up Where We Belong* et *You Are so Beautiful*.

Les spectacles de SuperEx se sont poursuivis, hier, avec Lynyrd Skynyrd et le groupe canadien April Wine.

On reprend, ce soir, avec les B-52's et Violent Femmes, euh... et demain avec les Beach Boys et Southside Johnny.

Mercredi, ce sera la fête à Bryan Adams. Prenez note, déjà 20 000 billets se sont envoles a-t-on appris samedi.

LeDroit. Mon., Aug. 24, 1992. Reprinted with permission of LeDroit.

Monday, August 24, 1992 --- Sudbury Arena
Sudbury, ON

Set List

	Song	From The Album	Released
1.	New Morning	New Morning	Oct. 21, 1970
2.	Pretty Peggy-O (arr. by Bob Dylan)	Bob Dylan	March 19, 1962
3.	All Along the Watchtower	John Wesley Harding	Dec. 27, 1967
4.	Just Like a Woman	Blonde on Blonde	May 16, 1966
5.	Tangled Up in Blue	Blood on the Tracks	Jan. 20, 1975
6.	I Don't Believe You (She Acts Like We Never Have Met)	Another Side of Bob Dylan	Aug. 8, 1964
7.	Simple Twist of Fate	Blood on the Tracks	Jan. 20, 1975
8.	Little Moses (Bert A. Williams/Earle C. Jones)	–	–
9.	Boots of Spanish Leather	The Times They Are A-Changin'	Feb. 10, 1964
10.	John Brown	MTV Unplugged	June 30, 1995
11.	Don't Think Twice, It's All Right	The Freewheelin' Bob Dylan	May 27, 1963
12.	Unbelievable	Under the Red Sky	Sept. 11, 1990
13.	Man in the Long Black Coat	Oh Mercy	Sept. 12, 1989
14.	The Times They Are A-Changin'	The Times They Are A-Changin'	Feb. 10, 1964
15.	Maggie's Farm	Bringing It All Back Home	March 22, 1965
	Encores		
16.	What Good Am I?	Oh Mercy	Sept. 12, 1989
17.	To Be Alone with You	Nashville Skyline	April 9, 1969
18.	It Ain't Me, Babe	Another Side of Bob Dylan	Aug. 8, 1964

The Musicians

Bob Dylan (vocal, guitar & harmonica), Bucky Baxter (mandolin, pedal steel guitar & electric slide guitar), John Jackson (guitar), Tony Garnier (bass), Ian Wallace (drums), Charlie Quintana (drums & percussion).

Notes

- 70th Bob Dylan concert in Canada; Debut Bob Dylan concert in Sudbury.
- 3, 5, 7, 11, 15-16, 18, Bob Dylan (harmonica).
- 5, 14, Bucky Baxter (mandolin).
- 8-9, 18, Bob Dylan solo (acoustic guitar & vocal).
- 10, Bob Dylan (acoustic guitar & vocal), Tony Garnier (bass).
- 11, Bob Dylan (acoustic guitar & vocal), Tony Garnier (bass), Ian Wallace (drums).
- 14, acoustic with the band.
- Canadian live debut of song 13.
- The opening act was Sue Medley.

Review

Bob Dylan impressive

By Daisy Debolt, Star Correspondent.

A lot of us were reluctant to see Bob Dylan.

We heard the rumors, read the press, saw him mumble on David Letterman.

None of us wanted our legend to be less than great.

And any songwriter worth his or her salt was weaned on Dylan.

On Monday, Aug. 24 at Sudbury Arena, the first song was definitely mumbled, unrecognizable.

But then he played Peggio, and then the hits just kept on coming. Next was All Along the Watchtower, guitars screaming as the "winds begin to howl" and Bob's irreverent harmonica and his two drummers doing a breakneck crescendo that left me breathless.

Then came Just Like a Woman with some energetic guitar solos from Bob, Blame it on a Simple Twist of Fate, and then just Dylan and the stand-up bass, singing sweet, singing the old spiritual Little Moses, Boots of Spanish Leather and Don't Think Twice, It's Alright.

This solo section was quite magic.

He and the band tore into Long Black Coat, the Times They Are A-Changin' and the most incredible version of Maggie's Farm I've ever heard, burnin' rock and roll, full-steam ahead.

His program finished (apparently he doesn't stick to a set list), he left the stage to a deafening roar and a standing ovation. He returned with the band to play What Good Am I and To Be Alone With You. He did one more encore, solo, It Ain't Me Babe.

No, we weren't let down.

This was a concert by the prime innovator of contemporary music, the man who put poetry to music.

The man who liberated us from the Chad Mitchell Trio and the rest of the folk drivel from the early 1960s. His unique voice and astounding phrasing made every song new.

Dylan got out of the spotlight and go back to drums and his amp and improvise with the guitar player and the bass player. It had a loose and playful feeling, bordering on jazz.

Bob Dylan might be one of the greatest singers and writers of our age. If only arenas had good acoustics, then maybe we could hear all the words.

After the concert, I spoke with Rob Boman from Toronto – a disc jockey at CKLN-Ryerson Community Radio who also teaches a course in popular music at York University and who pioneered the first course in rock 'n' roll in Canada.

He saw four concerts of this tour, and felt this concert was one of the best.

We talked of Dylan's phrasing.

"The timbre of his voice may not be a sound that some people find pleasing to their ear, but as an actual vocalist, in terms of what he does, with his phrasing, he's to me one of the greatest, most gifted vocalists I've ever heard in my life in any genre," said Boman.

We both agreed that he sang his pants off.

Dylan has been touring nonstop since 1988. At this point in time, he doesn't seem to really care about making gestures to his audience.

Instead, he is a musician's musician who goes out and plays. With his reputation, he can continue to tour and draw an audience and play whenever and however often he wants.

The opening act, Sue Medley, got a warm reception from a crowd that was waiting for Dylan.

After the bass and drums stopped rolling back from the end of the arena and the sound settled down, we were treated to her ballads.

Her voice soared in Somebody's Callin' Somebody's Goin' Down, the band cut back and started to space away from the heavy rock, right down to a drum and guitar solo that was burnin'.

The band was hot and gave her voice a lot of space. Five songs were not enough.

Five-star verdict: * * * *

An evening of magic: songs from every phase of his career and we wanted more. Thanks Bob.

Attendance: 2,300.

The Sudbury Star. Wed., Aug. 26, 1992. Reprinted with permission of The Sudbury Star.

Tuesday, August 25, 1992 --- Memorial Gardens Sault Ste. Marie, ON

Set List

	Song	From The Album	Released
1.	Don't Let Your Deal Go Down (trad.)	–	–
2.	Pretty Peggy-O (arr. by Bob Dylan)	Bob Dylan	March 19, 1962
3.	All Along the Watchtower	John Wesley Harding	Dec. 27, 1967
4.	Just Like a Woman	Blonde on Blonde	May 16, 1966
5.	She Belongs to Me	Bringing It All Back Home	March 22, 1965
6.	Simple Twist of Fate	Blood on the Tracks	Jan. 20, 1975
7.	Silvio (Bob Dylan/Robert Hunter)	Down in the Groove	May 19, 1988
8.	Little Moses (Bert A. Williams/Earle C. Jones)	–	–
9.	Boots of Spanish Leather	The Times They Are A-Changin'	Feb. 10, 1964
10.	Ballad of Hollis Brown	The Times They Are A-Changin'	Feb. 10, 1964
11.	Don't Think Twice, It's All Right	The Freewheelin' Bob Dylan	May 27, 1963
12.	Unbelievable	Under the Red Sky	Sept. 11, 1990
13.	The Times They Are A-Changin'	The Times They Are A-Changin'	Feb. 10, 1964
14.	Man in the Long Black Coat	Oh Mercy	Sept. 12, 1989
15.	Maggie's Farm	Bringing It All Back Home	March 22, 1965
	Encores		
16.	Shooting Star	Oh Mercy	Sept. 12, 1989
17.	Highway 61 Revisited	Highway 61 Revisited	Aug. 30, 1965
18.	It Ain't Me, Babe	Another Side of Bob Dylan	Aug. 8, 1964

The Musicians

Bob Dylan (vocal, guitar & harmonica), Bucky Baxter (mandolin, pedal steel guitar & electric slide guitar), John Jackson (guitar), Tony Garnier (bass), Ian Wallace (drums), Charlie Quintana (drums & percussion).

Notes

- 71st Bob Dylan concert in Canada; Debut Bob Dylan concert in Sault Ste. Marie.
- 3-4, 6-7, 11, 18, Bob Dylan (harmonica).
- 8-9, 18, Bob Dylan solo (acoustic guitar & vocal).
- 10, Bob Dylan (acoustic guitar & vocal), Tony Garnier (bass).
- 11, Bob Dylan (acoustic guitar & vocal), Tony Garnier (bass), Ian Wallace (drums).
- 13, acoustic with the band.
- 13, Bucky Baxter (mandolin).
- The opening act was Sue Medley.

Review

Bob Dylan shows that he can still thrill a crowd

By Angela Wierzbicki, The Sault Star.

Where were you on Tuesday night?

Maybe you had tickets for the cancelled Trooper concert at the Eastgate.

Or perhaps you went to the movies – after all, it was cheap night.

But no matter where you were, you weren't anywhere unless you were at the Bob Dylan concert.

No glitz, no glam.

Just Bob Dylan.

Live – with his harmonica, his guitar, a phenomenal back-up band.

And about 1,500 die-hard fans at the Memorial Gardens.

Mr. Dylan, at age 51, put on an amazing two-hour show that would put most new acts to shame.

He was here to perform, and perform he did. Playing songs representative of his 30-year plus career, Mr. Dylan delivered intensity and energy to the enthusiastic, albeit small, crowd in the Sault.

Opening to a standing ovation precisely at 9 p.m., Mr. Dylan didn't stop pumping out the tunes until 2 hours later.

With a plain black backdrop and a stage simply lighted in shades of purple, blue and red, Mr. Dylan's music was the focus of this show.

Offering no chatter between songs, he got straight to the point of the performance with classic folk tunes and newer heavier rock songs. He was just doing his job, but what a job it was.

Despite the lack of conversation and supporting props, Mr. Dylan was able to produce an effect that not many singers can equal.

He pleased young and old alike.

The younger crowd came in hopes of catching a glimpse of a music legend, who was in the prime of his career before many of these admirers were born.

The older crowd came to relive memories of the time when they were young and free. And maybe, just maybe, they wanted to recreate that spirit of demonstration and protest for peace that Bob Dylan was all about in the 1960s. Even though the Gardens was only at about half capacity, Mr. Dylan's music filled the arena, making it seem fuller than it was.

The evening was punctuated with traditional favorites like Just Like a Woman, Rainy Day Women and Memphis Blues Again, all played with the heart and soul of a legend and his obviously experienced supporting band.

Although Mr. Dylan neglected to introduce his fellow stage mates, the swing of this band was an important part of the overall atmosphere of the show.

In fact, the band was so good that one might have wondered if Mr. Dylan was actually playing his guitar, until he began a solo acoustic set.

After a heavy jam that left audience members breathless, the band members abandoned the stage to let Mr. Dylan shine on his own.

With nothing but his guitar, harmonica and trademark voice, Mr. Dylan rambled from song to song in a style all of his own.

By the end of his five-song acoustic set, Mr. Dylan had successfully worked his band back into full force, adding one instrument at a time to reach a tumultuous climax at the end of It's All Right.

After an electric version of Unbelievable, Mr. Dylan barked out his thanks to the crowd and muttered a few unintelligible syllables before moving right into The Times They Are A-Changing.

The session ended with another fabulous jam, concluding with a funked-out version of Maggie's Farm.

But a wild crowd brought the song writing master back to the stage for a three-song encore consisting of Shooting Star, Highway 61 and an acoustic solo of It Ain't Me Babe.

It's a pity that more people from the Sault and area couldn't shell out the $26.75 required to see this veteran musician. Mr. Dylan taught a valuable lesson in folk-rock education as his fingers flew over the guitar fretboard.

Many young radio listeners don't know that Mr. Dylan is the man behind songs like The Mighty Quinn, Knocking on Heaven's Door, and Steel Bars, a recent top 40 hit that Mr. Dylan wrote with the song's performer, Michael Bolton.

Sue Medley, who opened the show in place of Michelle Shocked, was also a powerful performer.

Ms. Medley played a bluesy brand of rock that most of the audience appreciated. Her voice was strong, deep and filled with emotion as she sang original songs like Dangerous Times, Maybe the Next Time and That's Life.

This Vancouver native seemed to be best friends with her guitar and gave the audience an honest effort and a good, clean sound.

Thursday, August 27, 1992 --- Fort William Gardens
Thunder Bay, ON

Set List

	Song	From The Album	Released
1.	Everything is Broken	Oh Mercy	Sept. 12, 1989
2.	Man in the Long Black Coat	Oh Mercy	Sept. 12, 1989
3.	All Along the Watchtower	John Wesley Harding	Dec. 27, 1967
4.	Seeing the Real You at Last	Empire Burlesque	May 30, 1985
5.	Simple Twist of Fate	Blood on the Tracks	Jan. 20, 1975
6.	Like a Rolling Stone	Highway 61 Revisited	Aug. 30, 1965
7.	I'll Be Your Baby Tonight	John Wesley Harding	Dec. 27, 1967
8.	Little Moses (Bert A. Williams/Earle C. Jones)	–	–
9.	Boots of Spanish Leather	The Times They Are A-Changin'	Feb. 10, 1964
10.	John Brown	MTV Unplugged	June 30, 1995
11.	Don't Think Twice, It's All Right	The Freewheelin' Bob Dylan	May 27, 1963
12.	Unbelievable	Under the Red Sky	Sept. 11, 1990
13.	The Times They Are A-Changin'	The Times They Are A-Changin'	Feb. 10, 1964
14.	I and I	Infidels	Oct. 27, 1983
15.	Maggie's Farm	Bringing It All Back Home	March 22, 1965
	Encores		
16.	What Good Am I?	Oh Mercy	Sept. 12, 1989
17.	Silvio (Bob Dylan/Robert Hunter)	Down in the Groove	May 19, 1988
18.	It Ain't Me, Babe	Another Side of Bob Dylan	Aug. 8, 1964

The Musicians

Bob Dylan (vocal, guitar & harmonica), Bucky Baxter (mandolion, pedal steel guitar & electric slide guitar), John Jackson (guitar), Tony Garnier (bass), Ian Wallace (drums), Charlie Quintana (drums & percussion).

Notes

- 72nd Bob Dylan concert in Canada; Debut Bob Dylan concert in Thunder Bay.
- 2-6, 9, 11, 15-16, 18, Bob Dylan (harmonica).
- 8-9, 18, Bob Dylan solo (acoustic guitar & vocal).
- 10, Bob Dylan (acoustic guitar & vocal), Tony Garnier (bass).
- 11, Bob Dylan (acoustic guitar & vocal), Tony Garnier (bass), Ian Wallace (drums).
- 13, Bucky Baxter (electric mandolin).
- 14 acoustic with the band.

Review

A legend visits

In our view: Many missed Dylan in fine form … in the Auditorium

By Ian Pattison, The Chronicle-Journal.

NO THANKS to the hundreds of people who didn't take seats at Fort William Gardens; no thanks to the thousands of people opposed to the Community Auditorium; no thanks to rumors he was a strung-out has-been, Bob Dylan was alive and well in Thunder Bay this week.

The poet laureate of popular music took his audience on a smooth, solid ride through his entire career. Dylan was probably near as fine a form as he's been for his many years. And the music was honest, authentic and well-played as the day it came from the mind of the world's finest modern lyricist.

But why were there empty seats in the Gardens? It defies belief that probably the largest living force in popular music came to Thunder Bay, Ontario, and didn't sell out in one afternoon. What did these people do with the $30 that could have bought them a date with greatness? Buy a case of beer and rent a movie? This was Bob *Dylan* for Pete's sake! What more do people want?

The people who did witness a living legend will have wished it was in their downsized music showcase instead of the dingy Gardens. The sound crew did a remarkable job with Dylan's awkward voice considering the acoustics they had to work with. What might it have sounded like in the Auditorium? But the city's ABC faction (Anything But Culture) cowed the politicians into halfing the seating capacity, effectively forcing all 'expensive' acts back into the Gardens. But all the fixtures and systems that surround the seats have to be there anyway. A 3,000-seat auditorium, it is said, would have added no more than 10 per cent to the current ticket price structure. So, for $33, Bob Dylan could have been seen in the acoustically-superb Auditorium by the crowd that paid $30 to see him in the hockey din bin on Myles Street.

But see him they did, and in fine form. Knowing about Dylan is knowing that the legend includes surprises. This night's was a band with two drummers for a wide percussive backdrop to lead guitar, pedal steel and bass, with Dylan plucking and strumming his own, big flattop through it all. His trademark wailing harmonica brought applause with nearly every use.

This was the working Dylan, intent on making good and having fun. And it was an audience, from teens to folks in their 50s, with a love and appreciation and knowledge of Dylan's decades of masterful music. He sensed this quickly and it seemed to urge him to more and better playing as the night went on. It may also have convinced him to present more of the standard songs of his thick portfolio than he might otherwise have played. Repeating 'the great songs' can get to be a bore over the years, unless an audience is special to the artist.

Dylan, whether rocking with the boys in the band or standing alone in splendid, acoustic isolation – black garb, white light, great songs... mesmerizing – got a kick out of playing in Thunder Bay. It's too bad more people didn't share the joy of a great performer at his best.

The Thunder Bay Chronicle-Journal. Sat., Aug. 29, 1992. Reprinted with permission of The Thunder Bay Chronicle-Journal.

1993

Introduction

The sixth year of the Never–Ending Tour stopped in Canada for two shows in 1993.

These shows would mark Bob Dylan's 73rd & 74th concert in Canada.

The Dates

Vancouver, BC	Sun., Aug. 22, 1993
Toronto, ON	Thurs., Sept. 2, 1993

The shows would be Dylan's 7th concert in Vancouver and 23rd concert in Toronto.

The Musicians

Bob Dylan (vocal, guitar & harmonica).

Bucky Baxter (mandolin, pedal steel guitar, lap steel guitar, concertina & electric slide guitar), John Jackson (guitar), Tony Garnier (bass), Winston Watson (drums & percussion).

The Songs

Bob Dylan performed 25 songs. Of those, 19 were different songs (18 were from albums and one was a cover song).

Three songs made their Canadian live debut.

You're Gonna Quit Me	God Knows
Under the Red Sky	–

One song made its worldwide live debut.

You're Gonna Quit Me	–

Bob Dylan performed songs from 13 different albums.

Album	Released	# of Songs Performed by Album
The Freewheeelin' Bob Dylan	May 27, 1963	2
The Times They Are A-Changin'	Feb., 10, 1964	2
Another Side of Bob Dylan	Aug. 8, 1964	1
Bringing It All Back Home	March 22, 1965	1
Highway 61 Revisited	Aug. 30, 1965	1
Blonde on Blonde	May 16, 1966	3
John Wesley Harding	Dec. 27, 1967	1
Bob Dylan's Greatest Hits, Vol. 2	Nov. 17, 1971	1
Blood on the Tracks	Jan. 20, 1975	1
Infidels	Oct. 27, 1983	1
Oh Mercy	Sept. 12, 1989	1
Under the Red Sky	Sept. 11, 1990	2
Good As I Been to You	Nov. 3, 1992	1

Opening Acts

The Wailing Souls were the opening act followed by Santana.

The Venues

It was Bob Dylan's 3rd time playing at the Pacific Coliseum in Vancouver and 2nd time playing at the CNE Grandstand in Toronto.

Sunday, August 22, 1993 --- Pacific Coliseum
Vancouver, BC

Set List

	Song	From The Album	Released
1.	You're Gonna Quit Me (arr. by Bob Dylan)	Good As I Been to You	Nov. 3, 1992
2.	Stuck Inside of Mobile with the Memphis Blues Again	Blonde on Blonde	May 16, 1966
3.	All Along the Watchtower	John Wesley Harding	Dec. 27, 1967
4.	Just Like a Woman	Blonde on Blonde	May 16, 1966
5.	Tangled Up in Blue	Blood on the Tracks	Jan. 20, 1975
6.	Under the Red Sky	Under the Red Sky	Sept. 11, 1990
7.	Little Moses (Bert A. Williams/Earle C. Jones)	–	–
8.	Boots of Spanish Leather	The Times They Are A-Changin'	Feb. 10, 1964
9.	Don't Think Twice, It's All Right	The Freewheelin' Bob Dylan	May 27, 1963
10.	God Knows	Under the Red Sky	Sept. 11, 1990
11.	Highway 61 Revisited	Highway 61 Revisited	Aug. 30, 1965
	Encores		
12.	What Good Am I?	Oh Mercy	Sept. 12, 1989
13.	Girl of the North Country	The Freewheelin' Bob Dylan	May 27, 1963

The Musicians

Bob Dylan (vocal, guitar & harmonica), Bucky Baxter (mandolin, pedal steel guitar, lap steel guitar, concertina & electric slide guitar), John Jackson (guitar), Tony Garnier (bass), Winston Watson (drums & percussion).

Notes

- 73rd Bob Dylan concert in Canada; 7th Bob Dylan concert in Vancouver.
- 1, 4-5, 8-10, 12-13, Bob Dylan (harmonica).
- 1, 7-9, 13, acoustic with the band.
- 7, Bucky Baxter (concertina).
- Canadian live debut of songs 1, 6 & 10.
- Worldwide live debut of song 1.
- The opening act was Wailing Souls, followed by Santana.

Review

The times they are a changin' and so, alas, is Dylan's voice, by John Armstrong. The Vancouver Sun. Tues., Aug. 24, 1993. p. C5.

Thursday, September 2, 1993 --- CNE Grandstand Toronto, ON

Set List

	Song	From The Album	Released
1.	You're Gonna Quit Me (arr. by Bob Dylan)	Good As I Been to You	Nov. 3, 1992
2.	Stuck Inside of Mobile with the Memphis Blues Again	Blonde on Blonde	May 16, 1966
3.	All Along the Watchtower	John Wesley Harding	Dec. 27, 1967
4.	I Don't Believe You (She Acts Like We Never Have Met)	Another Side of Bob Dylan	Aug. 8, 1964
5.	Tangled Up in Blue	Blood on the Tracks	Jan. 20, 1975
6.	Watching the River Flow	Bob Dylan's Greatest Hits, Vol. 2	Nov. 17, 1971
7.	Little Moses (Bert A. Williams/Earle C. Jones)	–	–
8.	Girl of the North Country	The Freewheelin' Bob Dylan	May 27, 1963
9.	The Lonesome Death of Hattie Carroll	The Times They Are A-Changin'	Feb. 10, 1964
10.	I and I	Infidels	Oct. 27, 1983
11.	Maggie's Farm	Bringing It All Back Home	March 22, 1965
	Encore		
12..	Rainy Day Women #12 & 35	Blonde on Blonde	May 16, 1966

The Musicians

Bob Dylan (vocal, guitar & harmonica), Bucky Baxter (mandolin, pedal steel guitar, lap steel guitar, concertina & electric slide guitar), John Jackson (guitar), Tony Garnier (bass), Winston Watson (drums & percussion).

Notes

- 74th Bob Dylan concert in Canada; 23rd Bob Dylan concert in Toronto.
- 1, 4-5, 8-9, Bob Dylan (harmonica).
- 1, 7-9, acoustic with the band.
- 7, Bucky Baxter (concertina).
- The opening act was Wailing Souls, followed by Santana.

Reviews

Santana soared, Dylan squawked

This memorable pairing at the CNE's closing Grandstand concert showed guitarist Carlos Santana in fine form and the legendary Bob Dylan reinvented as a Texas roadhouse rocker

By Alan Niester, Special to The Globe and Mail.

There are lots of ways a performing artist can connect with the audience – a revealing anecdote, a foray into the aisles, a call-and-response type number. But veteran guitarist Carlos Santana undoubtedly hit upon the Ultimate Bond while performing at Exhibition Stadium Thursday night. In the middle of a deluge, Santana reached down and distributed plastic raincoats to a few of the drowning located in the front row.

Thursday night's pairing of Santana with enigmatic rock legend Bob Dylan marked the end of this year's Canadian National Exhibition Grandstand concert series, and the torrential rain that began around the dinner hour undoubtedly played a large part in limiting the audience to an announced 7,500. But those willing to brave the elements were certainly well rewarded. This was one of the most memorable events of the summer concert season.

Santana's opening set offered few surprises. In some ways, this could have been a performance given a year or so after his breakthrough at the Woodstock Festival. But that was fine. Santana's unique style, a blend of jazz, rock and traditional Mexican, never grows tiresome, and he is creative enough to constantly add new shadings even to older numbers like *Black Magic Woman* and *Oye Como Va*.

In fact, the only moments in the set that at all dragged were when Santana allowed members of his eight-piece backing band (which included long-time vocalist Alex Ligertwood and Carlos' brother Jorge on guitar) to stretch out.

Make Someone Happy started out as an odd but appealing combination of Afro-Cuban rhythms and Philly Soul vocals, but eventually deteriorated into a *Living Colour*-type funk workout. And the boring drum solo that punctuated Santana's well-deserved encore kicked the momentum out of what had been otherwise an enjoyable set.

It must have taken a certain amount of nerve for Dylan to follow Santana's satisfying opening, especially since his performances over the past few years have become increasingly unappealing, often marred by incoherent vocals and unrecognizable versions of his own tunes.

But Thursday night, Dylan chose to reinvent himself once again, this time as a Texas roadhouse rocker. His choice of material was surprisingly mainstream (*All Along the Watchtower, Watchin' the River Flow*), but the renditions of the songs were not. Dylan's *modus operandi* this time out was to squawk his way through the lyrics, then sit back as his four-piece backing band (John Jackson on guitars, Tony Garnier on bass, Winston Watson on drums and Bucky Baxter on assorted stringed things) rambled along like some sort of countrified version of the Grateful Dead. That the band only got through about a dozen or so numbers in the entire 90-minute-plus set is indication enough of how much time each number was given room to grove.

This set was evenly divided between acoustic (*Girl From the North Country, Hattie Caroll*) and electric (*Tangled Up in Blue, Rainy Day Women #12 & 35*) numbers, but one number that wasn't performed was *A Hard Rain's A-Gonna Fall*. The rain had eased to an insignificant drizzle during Dylan's set, thereby allowing Dylan's long-suffering audience to better revel in his newly re-discovered sense of the freewheelin'.

As appeared in The Globe and Mail. Sat., Sept. 4, 1993. Reprinted with permission of Alan Niester.

Killer Bob and Super Santana

By Peter Howell, Toronto Star.

All together now: It's a hard rain's a-gonna fall . . .

Hey, nobody ever said that being a Bob Dylan fan was easy. With the buckets o' rain that were lashing down last night at CNE Grandstand, you had to be a true believer, and the 7,500 present obviously were.

And they were amply rewarded, with the best show Dylan has played here in years, and with an equally fine opening set by co-headliner Santana.

Guitarist Carlos Santana and his eight bandmates (including brother Jorge on rhythm guitar) opened in the face of a monsoon. But they played like the rain didn't matter.

After leading with "Spirits Dancing In The Flesh", Santana was joined by several members of the third act on the bill, Wailing Souls, for a fine reggae jam that made all those cliches about hot music warming up a cold and damp crowd suddenly seem very true.

Carlos still acts as if Woodstock was yesterday, dressing in tie-dye and laying on hippie love platitudes about how we were "completely surrounded by angels" – although those angels looked more like umbrellas.

Yet give the man and his band full credit for making us concentrate on his music instead of the rising damp.

The expected oldies like "Black Magic Woman" and "Oye Como Va" were played with plenty of heart, and new song "Make Somebody Happy" was an extended exercise that started out as a Philly soul number and turned into a funk freakout between the bass player and one of three drummers.

It was only when the same drummer noodled away the encore with a too-long drum solo that the weather seemed to be getting the upper hand again. But after a half-hour break, it was Dylan's turn to try to make us forget the rain, and did he ever.

After an acoustic country opening, Bob and his superb four backing players charged into rock 'n' roll, for brilliant versions of "Stuck Inside Of Mobile With The Memphis Blues Again", "All Along The Watchtower" and "Watching The River Flow".

The stage was in semi-darkness throughout – there were no spotlights for anti-legend Dylan. But none were needed. Sparks flew in the axe interplay between Dylan and lead guitarist John Jackson, while Bucky Baxter added textures with lap steel and mandolin, and the rhythm section of bassist Tony Garnier and drummer Winston Watson made it rock.

Here's the most amazing thing about it: Dylan stuck close to the "traditional" arrangements on many numbers, something he rarely does any more, and he actually enunciated his words. Finally, after years of messing with our minds, he didn't make us play Name That Tune, and since he appeared to be following a set list, the band didn't have to guess either.

The great songs rolled out, both the lesser-known and the familiar: "I Don't Believe You (She Acts Like We Never Have Have Never Met)", "Girl From The North Country", "The Lonesome Death Of Hattie Carroll", a butt-kicking "Maggie's Farm" and many more.

If you stayed home last night because of the rain or to watch the MTV Awards, too bad. You missed Killer Bob and Super Santana, a great end to a great CNE concert series.

The Toronto Star. Fri., Sept. 3, 1993. Reprinted with permission - Torstar Syndication Services.

Bob Dylan still hasn't a-changed

By Ira Band, Toronto Sun.

There are probably no more than two reasons for attending a Bob Dylan concert in the '90s.

One is the opportunity – however illusory – to see a legend at work. This rationale might have explained the significant number of teenagers in the audience of 7,500 last night at the Grandstand.

The other reason is a morbid curiosity to see the ongoing unravelling of a once great artist.

Last night's performance offered only a little of both. Musically, Dylan and his four-man band generated a clean, and, at times, polished sound.

Contrary to reports that he tortures his songs beyond recognition, Dylan and his musicians offered relatively faithful performances of *Watching The River Flow*, *Stuck Inside Of Mobile With Those Memphis Blues Again* and *Maggie's Farm*.

On the other hand, *Tangled Up In Blue* – from his last classic album, 1975's *Blood On The Tracks* – was badly distorted, as was *Girl From the North Country*. Talk about blood on the tracks.

If a certain measure of restraint and respect was shown on many of the songs, Dylan's vocal delivery was – depending on your mood – either hilarious or tragically sad.

Once revered as a master of evocative personal, political and folkloric imagery, Dylan's lyrics – mangled in his wheezing whine and phlegm-soaked bray – were virtually unintelligible.

Dylan dropped a few hints of former greatness, but not many, in a concert where disappointments outnumbered rewards.

Still in fine form after 25 years was Carlos Santana, who preceded Dylan with a more spirited and energetic show than the one he rendered on his SkyDome visit last November.

Although no one in the seven-man band is an original member, collectively they performed exuberant and faithful renditions of the early Santana tunes, *Black Magic Woman* and *Oye Como Va*. They also formed a smoothly precise and cohesive unit on the newer songs, *Spirits Dancing In The Flesh* and *Angel*, adding spicy rhythms and melodies around Santana's mellifluous, free-flowing and passionate guitar exercises.

SUN RATING: 3 OUT OF 5

1996

Introduction

The Never–Ending Tour stopped in Canada for four shows in 1996. The first Canadian dates since 1993.

These shows would mark Bob Dylan's 75th, 76th, 77th & 78th concert in Canada.

The Dates

Montreal, QC	Fri., April 26, 1996
Toronto, ON	Sat., April 27, 1996
Toronto, ON	Sun., April 28, 1996
London, ON	Sun., May 12, 1996

The shows would be Dylan's 18th concert in Montreal, 24th & 25th concert in Toronto and 2nd concert in London.

The Musicians

Bob Dylan (vocal, guitar & harmonica).

Bucky Baxter (dobro, mandolin, pedal steel guitar, electric slide guitar & backup vocals), John Jackson (guitar & backup vocals), Tony Garnier (bass), Winston Watson (drums & percussion).

The Songs

Bob Dylan performed 59 songs. Of those, 37 were different songs (35 were from albums and two were cover songs).

Nine songs made their Canadian live debut.

Drifter's Escape	This Wheel's on Fire
If You See Her, Say Hello	Crash on the Levee (Down in the Flood)
Obviously Five Believers	Friend of the Devil
Alabama Getaway	Seven Days
If Not for You	–

Three songs have been played only once in Canada.

Obviously Five Believers	Seven Days
Friend of the Devil	–

Bob Dylan performed songs from 16 different albums.

Album	Released	# of Songs Performed by Album
The Freewheeelin' Bob Dylan	May 27, 1963	3
Another Side of Bob Dylan	Aug. 8, 1964	3
Bringing It All Back Home	March 22, 1965	2
Highway 61 Revisited	Aug. 30, 1965	3
Blonde on Blonde	May 16, 1966	5
Bob Dylan's Greatest Hits	March 27, 1967	1
John Wesley Harding	Dec. 27, 1967	2
Nashville Skyline	April 9, 1969	1
New Morning	Oct. 21, 1970	1
Bob Dylan's Greatest Hits, Vol. 2	Nov. 17, 1971	2
Blood on the Tracks	Jan. 20, 1975	3
The Basement Tapes	July 1, 1975	1
Empire Burlesque	May, 30, 1985	2
Down in the Groove	May 19, 1988	1
Oh Mercy	Sept. 12, 1989	3
The Bootleg Series Volumes 1-3	Match 26, 1991	2

Opening Act

Aimee Mann opened the shows in Montreal and Toronto.

Special Guest

Paul James joined Dylan on stage at the second show in Toronto for Rainy Day Women #12 & 35. He also came on stage in London for Alabama Getaway and Rainy Day Women #12 & 35.

The Venues

It was Bob Dylan's debut concert at Verdun Auditorium in Montreal, debut concert and 2nd time playing at the Concert Hall in Toronto and 2nd time playing at Alumni Hall in London.

Friday, April 26, 1996 --- Verdun Auditorium Montreal, QC

Set List

	Song	From The Album	Released
1.	Drifter's Escape	John Wesley Harding	Dec. 27, 1967
2.	If You See Her, Say Hello	Blood on the Tracks	Jan. 20, 1975
3.	All Along the Watchtower	John Wesley Harding	Dec. 27, 1967
4.	Just Like Tom Thumb's Blues	Highway 61 Revisited	Aug. 30, 1965
5.	Most Likely You Go Your Way and I'll Go Mine	Blonde on Blonde	May 16, 1966
6.	Silvio (Bob Dylan/Robert Hunter)	Down in the Groove	May 19, 1988
7.	Tangled Up in Blue	Blood on the Tracks	Jan. 20, 1975
8.	Masters of War	The Freewheelin' Bob Dylan	May 27, 1963
9.	Don't Think Twice, It's All Right	The Freewheelin' Bob Dylan	May 27, 1963
10.	Maggie's Farm	Bringing It All Back Home	March 22, 1965
11.	I'll Remember You	Empire Burlesque	May 30, 1985
12.	Obviously Five Believers	Blonde on Blonde	May 16, 1966
	Encores		
13.	Alabama Getaway (Robert Hunter/Jerry Garcia)	–	–
14.	Girl of the North Country	The Freewheelin' Bob Dylan	May 27, 1963
15.	Rainy Day Women #12 & 35	Blonde on Blonde	May 16, 1966

The Musicians

Bob Dylan (vocal, guitar & harmonica), Bucky Baxter (dobro, mandolin, pedal steel guitar, electric slide guitar & backup vocals), John Jackson (guitar & backup vocals), Tony Garnier (bass), Winston Watson (drums & percussion).

Notes

- 75th Bob Dylan concert in Canada; 18th Bob Dylan concert in Montreal.
- 1, 6, 13, John Jackson, Bucky Baxter (backup vocals).
- 1-2, 7, 15, Bob Dylan (harmonica).
- 7-9, 14, acoustic with the band.
- Canadian live debut of songs 1, 2, 12 & 13.
- Song 12 has been performed only once in Canada.
- The opening act was Aimee Mann.

Reviews

Le mythe vivant ne s'est pas tourné les pouces

par Alain Brunet.

Robert Zimmerman n'était pas venu à l'Auditorium de Verdun pour y retirer un cachet faramineux après avoir livré machinalement quelques joyaux de son répertoire mythique.

C'était à craindre, pourtant; lors de l'escale montréalaise précédente (au Centre sportif de l'Université de Montréal, en 1990), Bob Dylan baillait aux corneilles, malgré les sparages effectués par son orchestre – dirigé alors par E.G. Smith. Plusieurs de ses admirateurs s'étaient plutôt emmerdés, se promettant de ne s'en tenir qu'aux enregistrements de l'artiste. Pourquoi, au fait, assister à un concert de Dylan? Pourquoi Dylan se produisait-il sur scène? Ses droits d'auteur ne suffisaient-ils pas amplement à garnir sa cagnotte?

Hier soir, le mythe vivant ne s'est pas tourné les pouces. Il est apparu sur scène affublé d'un veston de... crooner! Refusant de s'immobiliser derrière sa guitare, il a démarré avec un aplomb que l'on ne lui soupçonnait plus. Les éclairages conféraient à ses habits une teinte bleu poudre digne des plus beaux minets de Las Vegas.

N'ayez crainte, Bob Dylan n'avait pas retourné sa veste, ne s'était pas vraiment converti au showbusiness à grand déploiement. Les spots informatisés étaient généreux, voire considérables, mais aussi échevelés que leur cible. Joyeux bordel de lumière, en somme!

Ainsi donc, l'auteur-compositeur-interprète allait nous asséner une ponction stupéfiante de folk rock, fort d'un groupe ayant parfaitement saisi la rugosité potentielle de son art chansonnier – Winston Watson à la batterie, Bucky Baxter au pedal steel, John Jackson à la guitare et Tony Garnier, ex-Lounge Lizard, à la basse.

Le dinosaure de la chanson américaine a ainsi mâchonné avec inspiration plusieurs de ses rimes cruciales. La machine a d'abord tourné rondement sur le mode électrique, enfilant des titres tels *Positively 4th Street*, *All Along The Watch Tower*, *Tom Thumb Blues*, *You Go Your Way I Go Mine*. Le quinquagénaire assurait même à la guitare solo, sa Stratocaster brillait de tous ses feux. Les notes ont été joliment écorchées, les accords ont brûlé sur les planches, ça trépignait partout dans l'aréna - jeunes fans de chanson amerloque et vieux hippies avaient bondé l'amphithéâtre.

Vers le milieu de la prestation, Tony Garnier a troqué sa basse électrique pour l'acoustique, ses collègues ont fait de même, et nous avons assisté à la plus belle séquence de la soirée. *Tangled Up In Blue*, *Masters Of War* et *Don't Think Twice* rappelaient la facture originelle de l'art dylanesque.

L'hydro-électricité québécoise servira de nouveau lorsque l'artiste entamera *Maggie's Farm*, *When I Paint A Masterpiece* et autres classiques aussi savoureux les uns que les autres. On finira bien par s'apaiser au rappel, lorsque Dylan servira *North Country*, une autre de ses incontournables.

En sortant ainsi de sa tanière, le vieux loup nous aura offert un récital inspiré, confondant les sceptiques - dont j'étais. On se sera ainsi rappelé que Bob Dylan demeure le maître incontesté du premier jet, tant dans sa façon de coucher la rime que dans sa dégaine sur scène. Un jour, Leonard Cohen m'a raconté avoir rencontré son collègue Zimmerman. Ils ont causé de la confection de leur dernière chanson : «J'avais mis des mois à fignoler la mienne. Lui avait mis... 25 minutes! Et je ne peux déterminer laquelle est la meilleure», avait confié l'artiste montréalais, hilare.

L'as du premier jet, je vous dis.

La Presse. Sat., April 27, 1996. Reprinted with permission of La Presse.

BOB DYLAN A COMBLÉ SES FANS

A l'Auditorium de Verdun

par Paul-Henri Goulet.

Fidèle au mythe qui a toujours entouré le chef de file du *folk-rock*, Bob Dylan s'est fait attendre jusqu'à 21 heures 05, hier soir, à l'Auditorium de Verdun. Là où quelque 5 000 admirateurs – des adolescents et de jeunes adultes pour la plupart – s'impatientaient depuis déjà 20 heures.

Non, le *pape* des troubadours n'a pas vraiment joué au retardataire par exprès, puisqu'il y avait une première partie au programme. Mais entre vous et moi, croyez-vous qu'ils étaient nombreux, hier, à s'être déplacés jusqu'à l'Auditorium de Verdun pour venir voir et entendre l'ex *Til Tuesday*, Aimée Mann.

Bref, celui que nous attendions tous s'est pointé sur scène, avec seulement un micro en mains, pour partir le bal – sous de généreux applaudisements – avec un puissant rock issu d'une couvée moins connu de son oeuvre, on ne peut plus prolifique.

Accompagné de son nouveau groupe, (formé du batteur Winston Waston, du percussionniste Bucky Baxter, du bassiste Tony Garnier et du guitariste John Jackson), Dylan poursuit de plus belle, cette fois, guitare électrique en bandoulière, avec l'un de ses plus beaux «classiques» *All Along the Watchtower*.

Et ça continue, presque sans relâche, avec *Maggie's Farm* puis *Tangled up in blue*, sur des arrangements beaucoup plus rock. Cette dernière, qui marie admirablement le *blues* et le *folk*, est de tous les airs à succès qu'il a repris hier, celle qui nous a le mieux ramené le poète-chanteur des beaux jours.

Trois p'tits tours et puis s'en va!

Comblés les spectateurs? Cela ne fait aucun doute, d'autant plus que cette très courte tournée (qui a débutée le 16 avril dernier au Massachusetts pour se terminer le 18 mai prochain en Pennsylvanie) ne comporte que deux villes canadiennes (Montréal et Toronto).

Voir et entendre celui qui, plus que tout autre, a vraiment su porter le lourd fardeau (qui généralement tue les *légendes vivantes*), vaut effectivement le déplacement. Et qu'importe si le phénomène, à l'aube de ses 56 ans, n'a plus la voix ni l'inspiration aussi puissantes.

Ce qui importe c'est qu'il soit encore là, reprenant pour la millième fois son *Don't Think Twice, It's All Right* ainsi que son immortelle *Like a Rolling Stone*.

Car il ne faudrait jamais perdre de vue que celui que nous avons applaudi jusqu'à tard dans la soirée, hier, à l'Auditorium de Verdun, est celui-là même qui a vraiment réussi l'*opération du Saint-Esprit*, exécutant presque à lui seul la fusion entre la musique traditionnelle (*folk, country, blues*) et le rock 'n' roll. Et ce avec des textes qui n'appartenaient, auparavant, qu'à la littérature.

Chapeau, et merci!

Le Journal de Montréal. Sat., April 27, 1996. Reprinted with permission of Le Journal de Montréal.

Dylan à Verdun: le musicien a supplanté la légende

par Sylvain Cormier.

Difficile de se trouver devant Bob Dylan sans idées préconçues. Quand les projecteurs ont finalement concentré leurs faisceaux sur le costard argenté et la tête frisée qui le surmontait, ce n'est pas le juif américain de 54 ans, ses rides, ses ongles trop longs, ses rictus plus ou moins involontaires, que les quelque 5000 disciples rassemblés vendredi soir à l'Auditorium de Verdun ont vu et acclamé: c'est la légende vivante. Deux heures, une quinzaine de chansons et trois rappels plus tard, c'était l'homme.

Avant d'entamer *Drifter's Escape*, la première chanson, tout ce qu'a été Dylan pour tous ces gens, toutes les chansons qui ont tant compté, tous les faits marquants de cette vie mille fois écrite remontaient à la surface: en vrac se mêlaient l'héritier de Woody Guthrie, les cafés de Greenwich Village, *Blowin' In The Wind*, Joan Baez, le hipster qui a fait fumer de la mari aux Beatles, *Mr Tambourine Man*, le pied de nez aux puristes folk à Newport, *Like A Rolling Stone*, *Blonde On Blonde*, l'accident de moto, le virage country, les *Basement Tapes* avec le futur Band à Woodstock, *Lay Lady Lay*, l'île de Wight, le concert pour le Bangladesh, *Knockin' On Heaven's Doors*, *Blood On The Tracks*, le *Rolling Thunder Review*, l'entrée en religion, le fiasco de *Live-Aid*, les Traveling Wilburys, la tournée sans fin, le Bobfest du 30e anniversaire. Beaucoup de visages pour une seule tête de pipe.

L'autre idée toute faite, au moins aussi pesante dans l'esprit des gens que le parcours, c'est que que Dylan vieillit mal. Que sa voix, de nasillarde qu'elle était, est devenue si irritante que les chiens aboient en l'entendant. Qu'il fait exprès de saper sa légende en rendant méconnaissable ses classiques. Qu'assister à l'un de ses spectacles risque d'entacher le souvenir que l'on a gardé de ses grandes années. De fait, plusieurs d'entre nous pénétrions dans l'amphi verdunois avec méfiance et hantise. Réputé insonorisable, l'édifice n'annonçait rien de bon. Le déménagement de site, en raison de la fermeture du Métropolis, et l'amalgame conséquent en une seule foule des deux salles combles originellement prévues, annulait tout potentiel d'intimité: ce spectacle-là n'allait certainement pas ressembler à l'excellent *Unplugged*, enregistré dans les studios Sony à New York l'an dernier. N'empêche, Dylan étant Dylan, on était tous là. Prêts au pire.

Le meilleur

Surprise, on a eu le meilleur. On a eu un show qui brassait, des versions jouées avec compétence et abandon (avec des ralentis dans les finales!), des séquences acoustiques pur folk, un bel équilibre d'immortelles et d'obscures, presque deux heures de vraie musique. On a eu Dylan tel qu'il est aujourd'hui: un gars coriace qui essaie de justifier que la vie continue, mythe ou pas, et qui trouve le salut, soir après soir, en jouant de la guitare et de l'harmonica avec un petit groupe de bons musiciens. Dylan n'est pas un grand instrumentiste, tant s'en faut, mais on avait vendredi un guitariste *lead* qui s'assume, cherchant la bonne *lick*, la trouvant souvent (ses impros dans *All Along The Watchtower* et *Sylvio* étaient particulièrement heureuses). S'il ne souriait pas (quand même!), on le sentait intense, dédié à l'instant présent, multipliant les échanges avec John Jackson, l'autre guitariste, comme le ferait n'importe quel musicien dans un bon groupe de folk-rock alternatif.

Tout faisait plaisir: la sono était acceptable, le timbre de voix bien moins râpeux qu'on le redoutait, et l'on comprenait enfin que la propension de Dylan à changer les mélodies n'est pas qu'une manie de vieux saligaud. Il les simplifie pour que les chansons vivent, comme Springsteen en janvier à la PdA quand il dénudait *Born In The USA*. Rendues en *talking blues*, les électriques *Most Likely You Go Your Way And I'll Go Mine*, *Maggie's Farm*, *If You See Her, Say Hello*, tout comme les acoustiques *Tangled Up In Blue* et *Girl From The North Country*, gagnaient en efficacité ce qu'elles perdaient en joliesse. À preuve, lorsqu'une interprétation plus fidèle s'imposait, notamment pour les essentielles *Masters Of War* et *Don't Think Twice, It's All Right* (avec mandoline et *lap steel*, un rêve!), Dylan respectait sans problème les mélodies de base.

Mais surtout, Dylan était vendredi le rockeur qu'il rêve d'être depuis les années cinquante, quand Little Richard était son idole. Et un rockeur fait danser les foules: telles qu'envoyées, les versions de Sylvio, de *Rainy Day Women #12 & 35*, n'avaient pas d'autre fonction. Et la foule, moitié babacools, moitié jeunots, se trémoussait en conséquence. On s'était rendu à Verdun comme on va à l'église: on est ressorti en sueur, avec une seule certitude: Dylan est vivant.

Le Devoir. Mon., Apr. 29, 1996. Reprinted with permission of Le Devoir.

Additional Review

Dylan still blurs the line between art and instinct: Rocks in Verdun show before 5,000 believers, by Mark LePage. The Montreal Gazette. Sat., April 27, 1996. p. D3.

Saturday, April 27, 1996 --- The Concert Hall
Toronto, ON

Set List

	Song	From The Album	Released
1.	Drifter's Escape	John Wesley Harding	Dec. 27, 1967
2.	If Not for You	New Morning	Oct. 21, 1970
3.	All Along the Watchtower	John Wesley Harding	Dec. 27, 1967
4.	Positively 4th Street	Bob Dylan's Greatest Hits	March 27, 1967
5.	Watching the River Flow	Bob Dylan's Greatest Hits, Vol. 2	Nov. 17, 1971
6.	Silvio (Bob Dylan/Robert Hunter)	Down in the Groove	May 19, 1988
7.	Tangled Up in Blue	Blood on the Tracks	Jan. 20, 1975
8.	Masters of War	The Freewheelin' Bob Dylan	May 27, 1963
9.	Mama, You Been on My Mind	The Bootleg Series Volumes 1-3	March 26, 1991
10.	Seeing the Real You at Last	Empire Burlesque	May 30, 1985
11.	This Wheel's on Fire (Bob Dylan/Rick Danko)	The Basement Tapes	July 1, 1975
12.	Maggie's Farm	Bringing It All Back Home	March 22, 1965

	Encores		
13.	Alabama Getaway (Robert Hunter/Jerry Garcia)	–	–
14.	My Back Pages	Another Side of Bob Dylan	Aug. 8, 1964

The Musicians

Bob Dylan (vocal, guitar & harmonica), Bucky Baxter (dobro, mandolin, pedal steel guitar, electric slide guitar & backup vocals), John Jackson (guitar & backup vocals), Tony Garnier (bass), Winston Watson (drums & percussion).

Notes

- 76th Bob Dylan concert in Canada; 24th Bob Dylan concert in Toronto.
- 1-2, 7, 11, 14, Bob Dylan (harmonica).
- 1, 6, 11-13, John Jackson, Bucky Baxter (backup vocals).
- 7-9, 14, acoustic with the band.
- Canadian live debut of songs 2 & 11.
- The opening act was Aimee Mann.

Reviews

Dylan doesn't disappoint faithful

By Peter Howell, Rock Critic.

It's been said of the Bible that as a work of a literature, it's more revered than read.

An analogy could be drawn with Bob Dylan and his career in the 1990s. Remembered fondly for his heights of greatness in the '60s and '70s – Dylan freaks now call him "Uncle Bob" – he's been championed by the faithful, even as his songwriting pen dried up, his voice became a feeble croak and his audience shrank.

He's playing the club-sized Concert Hall on Yonge St. this weekend (200 extra tickets are on sale today at 10 a.m. through Ticketmaster) not so much because it's intimate, but because he can no longer fill Maple Leaf Gardens. The mostly standing-room venue is more suited for newer acts like Aimee Mann, who was politely received last night by an audience of mainly over-30 Dylan fans.

And yet the obviously faithful believers who made the trek were more than amply rewarded. Just a few weeks shy of his 55th birthday, Dylan showed he can once again spark his old fire.

He and his band gave a performance that is arguably Dylan's best in this town in 20 years. A major reason was that for the first time in memory, he actually enunciated his words, and thought about them.

In previous shows, Dylan has mumbled his famous lyrics – when he wasn't forgetting them altogether – and often seemed in a hurry to leave.

It looked like more of the same when he arrived on stage lounge lizard style, mic in hand, sans guitar, to sing the John Wesley Harding rarity "Drifter's Escape," followed by "If Not For You." But Dylan was delivering the songs, not just tossing them off, and the excellent drumming by Winston Watson helped them make their mark.

Then the familiar riff of "All Along The Watchtower" sounded, and the band was off and running, with Dylan grabbing his Fender to spar with lead guitarist John Jackson. That led to "Positively Fourth Street," not as biting as the original, but still good, and a double-time "Watching The River Flow," with the multi-talented Bucky Baxter supplying fine dobro picking.

So far so wonderful, and then came one of the evening's highlights, "Silvio," a song Dylan co-wrote with Grateful Dead lyricist Robert Hunter. A hat-tip to the recently departed Dead guitarist Jerry Garcia, whom Dylan has called his "big brother," the song is packed with meaning: "Stake my future on a hell of a past/Looks like tomorrow is coming on fast/Ain't complaining 'bout what I got/Seen better times, but who has not?"

With Jackson singing back-up, and jamming on guitar with Dylan, Grateful Dead style, this otherwise minor song in the Dylan canon became a revelation. It even looked like Bob was smiling up there, just a bit.

The show down-shifted to acoustic as this point, Watson leaving the stage, bassist Tony Garnier switching to stand-up bass, Baxter to mandolin, but the intensity kept building.

Dylan's reborn vocal skills made "Tangled Up In Blue" as good as new, the crowd singing along for the first time, and "Masters Of War" was restored as the prophet's warning – remember how he slurred it and wasted it at the Grammys in '91? There was similar acoustic redemption for "Mama, You Been On My Mind," a song he used to do in a duet with Joan Baez.

The return to electric guitar included the rarely heard "This Wheel's On Fire" and the frequently heard "Maggie's Farm," but on that song, Dylan didn't sound like Maggie was forcing him to plow the back 40. The rebel in him has returned.

So has his sentimental heart. The encore included another nod to Jerry Garcia, the rocking "Alabama Getaway," followed by "My Back Pages," with those memorable lines, "I was so much older then/I'm younger than that now."

These lines have possibly never had greater meaning. He sounds so much younger now than he has for years. Dylan is back, and the best thing about it is he's back again tonight.

I'm already there.

No blood on these tracks as real Dylan shows up

By Paul Cantin, Ottawa Sun.

TORONTO -- So there was Bob Dylan onstage, leading his band through a charged-up, Stonsey rendition of Seeing The Real You At Last, and the wry smile that spread across his face seemed like his acknowledgement of what an ironic moment this was.

After watching Dylan slide by for a half-dozen years with listless performances occasionally enlightened by glimpses of true inspiration, Saturday's opening concert of a two-night stand at Toronto's intimate Concert Hall was truly a chance to see the real Bob, at last.

Dylan's lacklustre attitude has, on past tours, made it so easy to dismiss the greatest living songwriter as a tired old has-been. But egged on by a fired-up audience of 1,800 and inspired by the ornate venue (formerly a Masonic Temple) and crisp acoustics, Dylan served notice he is still capable of spinning your head around with the unexpected.

Take his entrance. When the lights came up, there was His Bobness, decked out not in his trademark black but in a shocking, shiny pink jacket (with white belt), and without his guitar. As his backing quartet cranked out a snarling blues arrangement of the rarely performed Drifter's Escape, a guitar-less Dylan barked the lyrics into his mike Sinatra-style.

The surprises continued like that all night, with Dylan constantly delighting the attentive listener, reaching way back into his songbook for obscurities like Mama, You Been On My Mind and This Wheel's On Fire (from his Bootleg Tapes and Basement Tapes respectively), or rearranging familiar material in fresh, most often superior fashion.

During the encores, Dylan and company even raced through The Dead's Alabama Getaway.

An unrecognizable rockabilly shuffle turned into a spirited Watching The River Flow. And Tangled Up In Blue, the ever-evolving masterful epic from Blood On The Tracks, was transformed into a gorgeous bluegrass ballad, arranged for two guitars, acoustic bass and mandolin.

Full marks must go to his backing troupe, which has weathered hundreds of shows on Dylan's so-called Never Ending Tour (which has continued, with the occasional interlude and lineup change, since the late 1980s) and has now coalesced into a peerless team. They locked into a mesmerizing groove on Maggie's Farm, and all the players seemed so overcome with the pure joy of performing, they could have gone all night.

Guitarist J.J. Jackson seemed to bring out the best in his boss, even leaving room for Dylan to take his own occasional ragged solos. Steel guitarist Bucky Baxter is capable of coaxing a bizarre array of sounds from his instrument – atmospheric sustained chords, Hammond B3 organ-like fills and more straightforward countrified grace notes during a tender If Not For You.

Dylan's voice was ragged but right, with no sign of the wasted wheeze that has spoiled so many recent tours. His delivery was intense and he never seemed less than absolutely in the moment, investing each song with conviction and heart.

I'm at a loss to pick a highlight. Was it the extra muscle the one-time fundamentalist put into Positively Fourth Street's line, "You have no faith to lose AND YOU KNOW IT"? Or the way he prowled the stage like some doomsday prophet reciting This Wheel's On Fire? Or the tasty exchange of solos on All Along The Watchtower? Or the heart-melting country-waltz treatment of My Back Pages, served up as an exquisite final encore?

He is a notoriously erratic performer who picks his own moments of inspiration and could quite easily retreat back into his shell of indifference and enigma. That's the risk you take with Dylan, but on this night, the gamble was richly rewarded.

Former 'Til Tuesday leader Aimee Mann provided a tentative opening set that drew heavily from her fine recent release I'm With Stupid. The glammy Sugarcoated (which recounts the bust-up of the British group Suede), the buoyant Fifty Years After The Fair and outstanding Choice In The Matter found favor with the crowd.

JAM! RATING: 5 out of 5

The Ottawa Sun. Mon., April 29, 1996. Reprinted with permission of The Sun Media Corp.

The mighty Dylan

Bob's better than ever

By Jane Stevenson, Music.

Reports of Bob Dylan's musical death have been greatly exaggerated.

At least if the legendary folk singer-songwriter's stellar performance before a standing-room-only crowd at the Concert Hall on Saturday night is any indication.

Gone was the dazed-and-confused Dylan of recent years who mumbled his way through televised performances, looking disinterested, even pained at times.

In his place was a slick and attentive folk-country-and-blues artist still at the top of his game at age 54. And in all senses.

Not only did Dylan look great – slim and sleek-looking in head-to-toe black with the exception of a startingly hot pink satin shirt and thin white belt – "but boy could he play guitar," to quote another gracefully aging music-maker.

Particularly when he got caught up in duelling with lead guitarist John Jackson on such songs as All Along The Watchtower, Positively 4th Street, Watching The River Flow and Silvio.

When he really got into it, Dylan struck an almost Presley-like pose, feet spread part, shoulders shaking, and fingers flying.

It's an image not easily forgotten.

The rest of Dylan's tight, four-piece band was also outstanding – with a big nod to drummer Winston Watson, divided from the rest of the band by a plexiglass sound barrier as per Dylan's request.

The accompanying laser light show brought a cool intimacy to the proceedings, especially for a three song acoustic set - Tangled Up In Blue (which prompted the first singalong of the night), Masters Of War and Mama, You Been On My Mind. For these songs, Watson was excused from the stage and bassist Tony Garnier converted to the standup variety.

The night became electric again with rousing versions of This Wheel's On Fire and Maggie's Farm. In between, Dylan spoke for the first time to introduce his band.

His nasal, Porky Pig-like voice has never been Dylan's strong suit, but for better or worse, it's his calling card and a large part of his charm.

After an hour and a half on stage, Dylan came back for two encores, Alabama Getaway and My Back Pages. The latter song includes the somewhat prophetic line: "I was so much older then, I'm younger than that now."

It certainly appeared that way on Saturday night, with another performance scheduled last night.

Poor Aimee Mann didn't really stand a chance as backup act.

The older, Dylan-obsessed crowd (who started clapping for their hero even before he walked on stage for the first song, Drifter's Escape, with harmonica in hand) talked through her 45 minute set despite some pretty decent songs from her latest album, I'm With Stupid.

But hey, she's touring with the new and revitalized Bob Dylan. Things could be a lot worse.

SUN RATING: 5 OUT OF 5

Dylan delivers loud (still comically nasal) and clear

Resplendent in purple, the singer and his excellent quartet gave good roadhouse rock

By Alan Niester, Special to The Globe and Mail.

Bob Dylan awoke, as he always did, with the morning sun. After his morning ablutions and a strong cup of java, he rounded up the terriers for a brisk walk to the Quickie Mart. The morning of Aug. 10, 1995, was beginning just like any other day in this, his semi-retirement.

Bidding a jaunty 'top o' the morning' to the friendly shopkeeper, Dylan picked up a copy of his favourite morning newspaper, The Woodstock Daily Gleaner. The moment his eyes hit the headline, Dylan's life began to change once again.

For he learned of the death the day before of his old friend Jerry Garcia of The Grateful Dead. A sad event, to be sure, and Dylan spent the next few days, like so many of his contemporaries, in mourning. But as time passed, Dylan began to realize that a little bit of good comes from everything, that Garcia's death might mean new career opportunities for himself. After all, there were millions of Deadheads out there who would still need to be entertained. Perhaps he, once the voice of his generation, could fill the void...

Okay, so maybe it didn't happen quite like that, but watching and listening to what can only be described as "The New Bob Dylan" Saturday night certainly gets the imagination moving. For unlike past performances here, which have ranged from passable at best to downright mystifying at worse, this was a Dylan that could be seen, heard and enjoyed.

Several years ago at O'Keefe Centre, Dylan played on a stage so underlit he could barely be seen. The new Dylan arrived like some kind of Space Cowboy, resplendent in a loud purple satin shirt, black T-shirt, silver belt and black pants with a thin stripe down the side. Sure he was a fashion victim, but he was trying. His voice, while still comically nasal, was strong and discernible. For once, the listener could actually hear what was being sung.

But what set this concert apart from recent Dylan performances was his band, a skilled quartet that, while short on name power, was long on jam potential. And this was what this concert was mostly all about, Dylan leading his players (John Jackson on guitar, Tony Garnier on bass, Winston Watson on drums and Bucky Baxter on guitar, dobro and mandolin) through remarkably skilled and supple versions of some of his best-known numbers. This was Dylan doing roadhouse rock, and the fact that he and his band did only 14 songs in a nearly two-hour set (with absolutely no between-song patter) shows just how Dead-like this performance was.

Starting slowly with the lesser-known *Drifter's Escape* from *John Wesley Harding*, the evening didn't really get off the ground until Dylan strapped on the old Fender to lead his band through a remarkably trippy version of *All Along the Watchtower*. With Dylan trading lead lines with guitarist Jackson, this was a perfect bar-band workout, a number that cried out for a pitcher of draft and a sawdusted dance floor.

Positively Fourth Street, which followed, was a country waltz, with Baxter's steel guitar adding a graceful sheen, and the subsequent *Watching the River Flow* was done as a pure country rag, more like Commander Cody's *Hot Rod Lincoln* than classic Dylan.

The middle of the set was all-acoustic, with Watson taking a smoke break while the remaining quartet did some wonderful picking and grinning. Numbers like *Tangled Up in Blue* and *Masters of War* seemed to be a direct grab for the younger audience (of which there were a surprising number on hand), the types who have made stars out of such rootsy, back-to-the-basics outfits as Blues Traveller and The Dave Matthews Band. *Mama, You Been On My Mind*, which followed, came out virtually bluegrass.

Dylan and band returned to the electric mode for the home stretch. *This Wheel's on Fire* had an organic *Music from Big Pink* feel, while the set-ending *Maggie's Farm* featured more magic guitar interplay, coming across like something from Eric Clapton's *461 Ocean Blvd.*

Two encores later (a trippy *Alabama Getaway*, which finally and firmly re-established the Jerry Garcia connection, and a poignant and sing-alongable *My Back Pages*) and Dylan was gone, leaving the sold-out throng loudly screaming for more.

No, it certainly wasn't the Bob Dylan of the mid-sixties. Those days are gone forever. But based on Dylan's performance here Saturday, it seems he has found a new place he is comfortable with, a way to deliver the old songs not merely as exercises in nostalgia, but a living, breathing, works-still-in-progress. And for that, he should be applauded yet again.

As appeared in The Globe and Mail. Mon., April 29, 1996. Reprinted with permission of Alan Niester.

Sunday, April 28, 1996 --- The Concert Hall
Toronto, ON

Set List

	Song	From The Album	Released
1.	Crash on the Levee (Down in the Flood)	Bob Dylan's Greatest Hits, Vol. 2	Nov. 17, 1971
2.	Tonight I'll Be Staying Here With You	Nashville Skyline	April 9, 1969
3.	All Along the Watchtower	John Wesley Harding	Dec. 27, 1967
4.	I Don't Believe You (She Acts Like We Never Have Met)	Another Side of Bob Dylan	Aug. 8, 1964
5.	It Takes a Lot to Laugh, It Takes a Train to Cry	Highway 61 Revisited	Aug. 30, 1965
6.	Silvio (Bob Dylan/Robert Hunter)	Down in the Groove	May 19, 1988
7.	Mr. Tambourine Man	Bringing It All Back Home	March 22, 1965
8.	Desolation Row	Highway 61 Revisited	Aug. 30, 1965
9.	Friend of the Devil (Jerry Garcia/Robert Hunter/John Dawson)	–	–
10.	Stuck Inside of Mobile with the Memphis Blues Again	Blonde on Blonde	May 16, 1966
11.	What Good Am I?	Oh Mercy	Sept. 12, 1989
12.	Seven Days	The Bootleg Series Volumes 1-3	March 26, 1991
	Encores		
13.	Alabama Getaway (Robert Hunter/Jerry Garcia)	–	–
14.	Girl of the North Country	The Freewheelin' Bob Dylan	May 27, 1963
15.	Rainy Day Women #12 & 35	Blonde on Blonde	May 16, 1966

The Musicians

Bob Dylan (vocal, guitar & harmonica), Bucky Baxter (dobro, mandolin, pedal steel guitar, electric slide guitar & backup vocals), John Jackson (guitar & backup vocals), Tony Garnier (bass), Winston Watson (drums & percussion).

Notes

- 77th Bob Dylan concert in Canada; 25th Bob Dylan concert in Toronto.
- 1, 12, 14, Bob Dylan (harmonica).
- 6, 9, 13, John Jackson, Bucky Baxter (backup vocals).
- 7-9, 14, acoustic with the band.
- 15, Paul James (electric guitar).
- Canadian live debut of songs 1, 9 & 12.
- Songs 9 & 12 have been performed only once in Canada.
- The opening act was Aimee Mann.

Sunday, May 12, 1996 --- University of Western Ontario, Alumni Hall
London, ON

Set List

	Song	From The Album	Released
1.	Leopard-Skin Pill-Box Hat	Blonde on Blonde	May 16, 1966
2.	Man in the Long Black Coat	Oh Mercy	Sept. 12, 1989
3.	All Along the Watchtower	John Wesley Harding	Dec. 27, 1967
4.	Simple Twist of Fate	Blood on the Tracks	Jan. 20, 1975
5.	It Takes a Lot to Laugh, It Takes a Train to Cry	Highway 61 Revisited	Aug. 30, 1965
6.	Silvio (Bob Dylan/Robert Hunter)	Down in the Groove	May 19, 1988

7.	Mr. Tambourine Man	Bringing It All Back Home	March 22, 1965
8.	Desolation Row	Highway 61 Revisited	Aug. 30, 1965
9.	To Ramona	Another Side of Bob Dylan	Aug. 8, 1964
10.	Everything is Broken	Oh Mercy	Sept. 12, 1989
11.	This Wheel's on Fire (Bob Dylan/Rick Danko)	The Basement Tapes	July 1, 1975
12.	Maggie's Farm	Bringing It All Back Home	March 22, 1965
	Encores		
13.	Alabama Getaway (Robert Hunter/Jerry Garcia)	–	–
14.	Girl of the North Country	The Freewheelin' Bob Dylan	May 27, 1963
15.	Rainy Day Women #12 & 35	Blonde on Blonde	May 16, 1966

The Musicians

Bob Dylan (vocal, guitar & harmonica), Bucky Baxter (dobro, mandolin, pedal steel guitar, electric slide guitar & backip vocals), John Jackson (guitar & backup vocals), Tony Garnier (bass), Winston Watson (drums & percussion).

Notes

- 78th Bob Dylan concert in Canada; 2nd Bob Dylan concert in London.
- 1, 7, 11, 14, Bob Dylan (harmonica).
- 6, 11-13, John Jackson, Bucky Baxter (backup vocals).
- 7-9, 14, acoustic with the band.
- 13, 15, Paul James (electric guitar).

Reviews

Dylan brings some to feet, keeps others in their seats

The music rocked loud and skillfully but the voice and the poetry were gone

By Joe Matyas, Free Press Arts & Entertainment Reporter.

The Bob Dylan who played at Alumni Hall Sunday night was past his prime, but his concert wasn't a callous box-office grab by a fading star.

Dylan cut it, not totally and not on every count, but the audience dynamics showed he satisfied at least half and maybe more of the crowd of 2,600.

About 75 minutes into a non-stop show that lasted about 100 minutes, dozens of fans stormed to the front of the hall and hundreds more stood in their seats, moving and grooving, swinging and swaying to a driving rock beat driven by no compromise bass and drum rhythms.

HIGH LEVEL: As a rock concert, as an electric blues concert, the Dylan show was performed at a high level of musicianship and volume, including on the long instrumental breaks which featured clean and crisp delivery from a heart-pounding tower of power – 32 amps arranged in two banks of 16 on each side of the stage.

Dylan's rock crowd loved it and committed themselves to the concert and its atmosphere.

Fans who admire Dylan more for his street poetry and his ability to sell his songs with a quirky rasp and hypnotic pacing were left sadly wanting.

Dylan's voice, never much of an instrument, was once a performance tool, but it's spent now.

It was virtually impossible to recognize any of his tunes by his singing, which bore little or no resemblance to recorded versions. Such changes could be accepted if they were new arrangements, but Dylan simply couldn't hold his songs together vocally. He sounded lousy and his delivery was a jumble of mumble.

For Dylan's oldest fans, it was an act of faith to attend Sunday's concert.

Rumors of his demise as a live performer have been circulating for months and up to three decades of memories were at risk of being tarnished if they were true.

WASHED UP: The grapevine said Dylan was washed up, that he looked wasted and sounded worse.

But those who followed Dylan's music for more than three decades were willing to give their cultural idol the benefit of the doubt.

Dylan, after all, is the guy who ticked off his folk fans by going electric at the Newport Folk Festival in 1965, who shook his rock fans by going country in 1968 and stunned everyone with his born-again Slow Train Coming album in 1979.

Like a visual artist, Dylan has had "periods" and at the dawning of each has lost fans and won new ones. He's recorded 28 albums and sold 35 million copies since 1962 and you don't write a guy like that off any more than you would Wayne Gretzky on a hockey rink.

Dylan's oldest fans, the ones who've stuck with him through thick and thin, had to buy tickets, had to take the chance that he could deliver some of his old magic. Some of them sat dismayed and left disappointed.

The London Free Press. Mon., May 13, 1996. Reprinted with permission of The London Free Press.

1997

Introduction

The Never-Ending Tour rolled on in 1997 with eight concerts in Canada.

These shows would mark Bob Dylan's 79th, 80th, 81st, 82nd, 83rd, 84th, 85th & 86th concert in Canada.

The Dates

St. John's, NL	Mon., March 31, 1997
St. John's, NL	Tues., April 1, 1997
Moncton, NB	Sat., April 5, 1997
Halifax, NS	Sun., April 6, 1997
Fredericton, NB	Mon., April 7, 1997
Saint John, NB	Tues., April 8, 1997
Montreal, QC	Tues., Aug. 5, 1997
Toronto, ON	Thurs., Aug. 7, 1997

The shows would be Dylan's debut concert and 2nd concert in St. John's, debut concert in Moncton, debut concert in Halifax, debut concert in Fredericton, debut concert in Saint John, 19th concert in Montreal and 26th concert in Toronto.

The Musicians

Bob Dylan (vocal, guitar & harmonica).

Bucky Baxter (dobro, mandolin, pedal steel guitar, electric slide guitar & backup vocals), Larry Campbell (guitar, bouzouki & backup vocals), Tony Garnier (bass), David Kemper (drums & percussion).

The Songs

Bob Dylan performed a total of 118 songs. Of those, 54 were different songs (52 were from albums and 2 were cover and/or traditional songs).

Six songs made their Canadian live debut.

Oh Baby It Ain't No Lie	You Ain't Goin' Nowhere
Born in Time	Cocaine Blues
Tough Mama	Blind Willie McTell

One song has been played only once in Canada.

Born in Time	–

One song made its worldwide live debut.

Blind Willie McTell	–

Bob Dylan performed songs from 21 different albums.

Album	Released	# of Songs Performed by Album
The Freewheelin' Bob Dylan	May, 27, 1963	3
The Times They Are A-Changin'	Feb., 10, 1964	2
Another Side of Bob Dylan	Aug. 8, 1964	3
Bringing It All Back Home	March 22, 1965	4
Highway 61 Revisited	Aug. 30, 1965	6
Blonde on Blonde	May 16, 1966	7
Bob Dylan's Greatest Hits	March 27, 1967	1
John Wesley Harding	Dec. 27, 1967	2
Nashville Skyline	April 9, 1969	2
New Morning	Oct. 21, 1970	1
Bob Dylan's Greatest Hits, Vol. 2	Nov. 17, 1971	3
Planet Waves	Jan. 17, 1974	2
Blood on the Tracks	Jan. 20, 1975	4
The Basement Tapes	July 1, 1975	1
Street Legal	June 15, 1978	1
Infidels	Oct. 27, 1983	1
Empire Burlesque	May, 30, 1985	1
Down in the Groove	May 19, 1988	1
Oh Mercy	Sept. 12, 1989	3
Under the Red Sky	Sept. 11, 1990	3
The Bootleg Series Volumes 1-3	Match 26, 1991	1

Opening Acts

BR5-49 and Ani DiFranco opened the shows in Montreal and Toronto.

The Venues

It was Bob Dylan's debut concert and 2nd time playing at St. John's Memorial Stadium, debut concert at the Moncton Coliseum, debut concert at the Metro Centre in Halifax, debut concert at the Aitken Centre in Fredericton, debut concert at Harbour Station in Saint John, debut concert at du Maurier Stadium in Montreal and debut concert at the Molson Amphitheatre in Toronto.

Monday, March 31, 1997 --- St. John's Memorial Stadium
St. John's, NL

Set List

	Song	From The Album	Released
1.	Crash on the Levee (Down in the Flood)	Bob Dylan's Greatest Hits, Vol. 2	Nov. 17, 1971
2.	Lay, Lady, Lay	Nashville Skyline	April 9, 1969
3.	All Along the Watchtower	John Wesley Harding	Dec. 27, 1967
4.	Just Like a Woman	Blonde on Blonde	May 16, 1966
5.	I'll Be Your Baby Tonight	John Wesley Harding	Dec. 27, 1967
6.	Silvio (Bob Dylan/Robert Hunter)	Down in the Groove	May 19, 1988
7.	Oh Baby It Ain't No Lie (Elizabeth Cotton)	–	–
8.	Mr. Tambourine Man	Bringing It All Back Home	March 22, 1965
9.	Masters of War	The Freewheelin' Bob Dylan	May 27, 1963
10.	Seeing the Real You at Last	Empire Burlesque	May 30, 1985
11.	Shooting Star	Oh Mercy	Sept. 12, 1989
12.	Highway 61 Revisited	Highway 61 Revisited	Aug. 30, 1965
	Encores		
13.	Like a Rolling Stone	Highway 61 Revisited	Aug. 30, 1965
14.	Girl of the North Country	The Freewheelin' Bob Dylan	May 27, 1963
15.	Rainy Day Women #12 & 35	Blonde on Blonde	May 16, 1966

The Musicians

Bob Dylan (vocal, guitar & harmonica), Bucky Baxter (dobro, mandolin, pedal steel guitar, electric slide guitar & backup vocals), Larry Campbell (guitar & backup vocals), Tony Garnier (bass), David Kemper (drums & percussion).

Notes

- 79th Bob Dylan concert in Canada; Debut Bob Dylan concert in St. John's.
- 4, 8, 14, Bob Dylan (harmonica).
- 6, Larry Campbell & Bucky Baxter (backup vocals).
- 7-9, 14, acoustic with the band.
- Canadian live debut of song 7.

Reviews

Dylan plays doorman for Tely

By Gary Hebbard, The Evening Telegram.

When Evening Telegram photographer Jonathan Hayward set out to get a picture of Bob Dylan, little did he know he'd need the intervention of the rock legend himself to get it.

Hayward arrived at Memorial Stadium draped in his usual assortment of camera gear Monday night only to find that, despite signed agreements with Dylan's music label – Sony Music Canada – there was no press pass waiting for him and no chance of making it past security.

"They said, 'Wait, we'll try and get hold of someone,' " Hayward said of the two women at the box office. "The two ladies tried to help me out."

But to no avail. They said they'd been told by Dylan's people that the agreement was off and there would be no access for him, nor would they contact concert promoter David Carver to come out and speak to him.

"They said, 'there's nothing we can do' and Dylan's people won't come out and talk to you because they're too busy."

At this point, Hayward decided his best bet might be to hang out at gate four, located near the dressing room, in hopes of grabbing a quick shot of the big man should he arrive.

But a beefy security guard warned him to get away from the door or he "might pop off," Hayward said.

"All of a sudden the door opens up and Dylan comes out to have a smoke. I see this guy in this gold metallic suit and my first reaction was to pick up my camera and start shooting," said Hayward.

But instead, he struck up a conversation.

"I said look I've had permission from Sony Music Canada in Toronto… but now that I'm here I'm being told I'm not allowed to photograph and there's no explanation. I need to get a picture," Hayward said.

"So Dylan says, 'I'll let you in for two songs,' " said the now impressed photographer.

And with that, the security guard took Hayward to a spot on stage.

The singer, meanwhile, stayed outside by himself, having a quiet smoke before the show.

The St. John's Telegram. Tues., April 1, 1997. Reprinted with permission of The St. John's Telegram.

Review

By Hans Rollman.

Just came from the Dylan concert in St. John's, Newfoundland. Terrific show, four encores. There was originally only one concert planned, tomorrow, but today's was put on after the quick sellout of Tuesday's tickets. The program was mixed with some predictable favourites like Lay Lady Lay, Mr. Tambourine Man, Masters of War… His voice was better than I had expected. The times, they are a-changin', but Bob still rocked the audience, which consisted of a mix of nostalgic Baby Boomers, like myself, but also quite a few young people.

Posted to bobchronicles.com. Mon., March 31, 1997. Reprinted with permsission of Hans Rollmann.

Tuesday, April 1, 1997 --- St. John's Memorial Stadium St. John's, NL

Set List

	Song	From The Album	Released
1.	Crash on the Levee (Down in the Flood)	Bob Dylan's Greatest Hits, Vol. 2	Nov. 17, 1971
2.	Señor (Tales of Yankee Power)	Street Legal	June 15, 1978
3.	All Along the Watchtower	John Wesley Harding	Dec. 27, 1967
4.	Simple Twist of Fate	Blood on the Tracks	Jan. 20, 1975
5.	Just Like Tom Thumb's Blues	Highway 61 Revisited	Aug. 30, 1965
6.	Silvio (Bob Dylan/Robert Hunter)	Down in the Groove	May 19, 1988
7.	Oh Baby It Ain't No Lie (Elizabeth Cotton)	–	–
8.	Tangled Up in Blue	Blood on the Tracks	Jan. 20, 1975
9.	Don't Think Twice, It's All Right	The Freewheelin' Bob Dylan	May 27, 1963
10.	God Knows	Under the Red Sky	Sept. 11, 1990
11.	Ballad of a Thin Man	Highway 61 Revisited	Aug. 30, 1965
12.	Everything is Broken	Oh Mercy	Sept. 12, 1989
	Encores		
13.	Like a Rolling Stone	Highway 61 Revisited	Aug. 30, 1965
14.	Forever Young	Planet Waves	Jan. 17, 1974
15.	Rainy Day Women #12 & 35	Blonde on Blonde	May 16, 1966

The Musicians

Bob Dylan (vocal, guitar & harmonica), Bucky Baxter (dobro, mandolin, pedal steel guitar, electric slide guitar & backup vocals), Larry Campbell (guitar & backup vocals), Tony Garnier (bass), David Kemper (drums & percussion).

Notes

- 80th Bob Dylan concert in Canada; 2nd Bob Dylan concert in St. John's.
- 6, Larry Campbell & Bucky Baxter (backup vocals).
- 7-9, 14, acoustic with the band.
- 8, 14, Bob Dylan (harmonica).

Saturday, April 5, 1997 --- Moncton Coliseum
Moncton, NB

Set List

	Song	From The Album	Released
1.	Crash on the Levee (Down in the Flood)	Bob Dylan's Greatest Hits, Vol. 2	Nov. 17, 1971
2.	I Want You	Blonde on Blonde	May 16, 1966
3.	All Along the Watchtower	John Wesley Harding	Dec. 27, 1967
4.	Positively 4th Street	Bob Dylan's Greatest Hits	March 27, 1967
5.	Watching the River Flow	Bob Dylan's Greatest Hits, Vol. 2	Nov. 17, 1971
6.	Silvio (Bob Dylan/Robert Hunter)	Down in the Groove	May 19, 1988
7.	Oh Baby It Ain't No Lie (Elizabeth Cotton)	–	–
8.	Desolation Row	Highway 61 Revisited	Aug. 30, 1965
9.	Don't Think Twice, It's All Right	The Freewheelin' Bob Dylan	May 27, 1963
10.	God Knows	Under the Red Sky	Sept. 11, 1990
11.	She Belongs to Me	Bringing It All Back Home	March 22, 1965
12.	Highway 61 Revisited	Highway 61 Revisited	Aug. 30, 1965
	Encores		
13.	Like a Rolling Stone	Highway 61 Revisited	Aug. 30, 1965
14.	It Ain't Me, Babe	Another Side of Bob Dylan	Aug. 8, 1964
15.	Rainy Day Women #12 & 35	Blonde on Blonde	May 16, 1966

The Musicians

Bob Dylan (vocal, guitar & harmonica), Bucky Baxter (dobro, mandolin, pedal steel guitar, electric slide guitar & backup vocals), Larry Campbell (guitar & backup vocals), Tony Garnier (bass), David Kemper (drums & percussion).

Notes

- 81st Bob Dylan concert in Canada; Debut Bob Dylan concert in Moncton.
- 2, 5, 9, Bob Dylan (harmonica).
- 6, 15, Larry Campbell & Bucky Baxter (backup vocals).
- 7-9, 14, acoustic with the band.
- The date of this show was changed from April 4th to April 5th due to a storm. The trucks carrying Bob's equipment were held up at the ferry terminal in Port aux Basques, Newfoundland.

Reviews

A blast from the past

Timeless troubadour Bob Dylan delivers fast paced, hard driving two-hour show that leaves 7,000 fans in Moncton satisfied

By Mike Tenszen, In Moncton for The Telegraph Journal.

HE IS 55, looks it, moves like it, and sounds as pained as ever, but the old coffee house folkie, rockabilly, poet, balladeer and American song-writing genius held teens and pensioners alike in his thrall here Saturday with a passionate, hard-rocking roll call of Bob Dylan's beloved best.

The haystack-haired Mr. Dylan, in silky black suit with silver trim and black cowboy bow tie, screeched, barked and belted the ballads that has made the Minnesotan high school dropout a wealthy man over the last 36 years.

The audience of about 7,000 at Moncton Coliseum heard what they came to hear from their vocally challenged, stooped superstar – *All Along the Watchtower, I Want You, Desolation Row, Don't Think Twice, Highway 61 Revisited, Like A Rolling Stone* and *It Ain't Me Babe.*

Old gold, with a few fresh ones, from his countless, million-seller albums, vinyl LPs, tapes, CDs. Columbia label.

University and high school kids – not born when Bob Zimmerman left Hibbing, Minn., for The City – danced, hooted and hollered in the aisles and crowded the stage, while misty eyed senior citizens swayed in their seats and mouthed the timeless troubadour's angry, lovely and literate poems.

Two young women were moved to mount the stage and plant kisses on the grandfatherly folk rocker and he beamed, seemed genuinely pleased, and then the band's rugged roadies gently scooped up the overheated fans and planted them back into the front row teenage throng. Several people held up "Welcome to Moncton, Bob Dylan" signs from the front rows, but the city's most famous visitor, who may have seen the greetings through the cigarette and marijuana smoke, remained stone faced. The rolling stone.

It was a hard-driving, fast paced, two hour show that kicked off at 8:25 p.m., 25 minutes after the scheduled starting time, with no warm-up band, and only seconds between songs.

"Ladies and gentlemen, please welcome Columbia recording artist Bob Dylan," was the only loudspeaker introduction. The lights came up in red on the American legend and several generations of Bobby Zimmerman fans were already on their feet, where they remained for much of the night.

The secretive showman granted no interviews, and the signs on the Coliseum doors ordered "No Cameras, and No Recording Devices," and they meant it. He mouthed only a few words of appreciation into the microphone, and the somber and scowling Mr. Dylan did not smile until about 30 minutes into the show when it was happily obvious that the lights, sound system, sidemen, fired-up audience, and the artist's own nasal twang and road-weary larynx were working well. Or as well as Dylanites, who worship their voice-vexed hero nonetheless, could have expected. Mr. Dylan – first time in Moncton on his first trip to eastern Canada – took charge with his first song, *I Want You*, boosted by those plaintive licks on his harmonica. And every time he positioned that trademark harmonica on his tired old folkie face, the audience screamed and cheered. And they even cheered when the old New York coffee house strummer – who broke in, unplugged, in Greenwich Village in 1961 – picked through some pleasing, not quite Hendrixian, electric guitar solos to the smiles and understanding nods from his more musically accomplished sidemen, a pick-up band who were introduced by name by Mr. Dylan, and the star's mandatory "How about this band right here!"

But it was not the musicianship, nor the voice, but the middle-aged man and his biting, esoteric, and wondrous words that the audience craved and invested $30 a seat to receive.

It was a sound investment, according to the faithful.

"He looked great; he sounded great," said Shirley Kaye, in her 40s, from Joggins, N.S. "It was a great show and, you know, he smiled right at me," added Ms. Kaye, who had a front row seat.

Jim Wood, from Hopewell Cape, heard his favourites, *Watchtower* and *Highway 61*. "You know, it was the young people here who got this (concert) going," Mr. Wood said.

"I just like his message, I like his style," said Dave Colbourne, 25 of Miramichi.

Mike Kelly, a 40ish miner down from Bathurst, has all Dylan's recordings and claims "it's the words; there's a meaning to every one of his songs. He never could sing. Who cares?"

After 90 minutes, the lights went down and Dylan left the stage, but then the lighters and matches and rock concert sparkles came out and no one was leaving. Shouts of "more," and "Bob" and "Dylan," and the black and silver suit swaggered out of the darkness and set the place ablaze with *Like a Rolling Stone*, 10 minutes of tears and cheers and joy. Lights down again, but Dylan was not leaving the building, until his final, show-stopping encore closer *It Ain't Me Babe*. All lights up and he's gone.

Dan Koch, 22, of Miramichi, who loves "folk-type music," was hoping to hear the classics *Mr. Tambourine Man* and *Blowin' In The Wind*. So were we all, but perhaps down easters have had enough wind lately.

But, quite obviously – from the adulation shown here Saturday – they've not had enough of the old, rock solid folk rocker. And, on this jingle jangle morning, with more concerts planned for New Brunswick, they'll be afollowing him.

The New Brunswick Telegraph-Journal. Mon., April 7, 1997. Reprinted with permission of The New Brunswick Telegraph-Journal.

Dylan delivers musical feast

Music legend shows he still has 'the right stuff' after more than 30 years

By Alan Cochrane, Times-Transcript Staff.

Better late than never.

Music legend Bob Dylan rolled on stage in Moncton Saturday night, playing a solid two-hour set to a capacity crowd at the Coliseum.

At 55, he may have been the oldest person at the concert, but he thrilled the more than 6,000 fans with a cool 15 song mix of thumping blues rock, chicken pickin' country and rejigged folk. Dressed in a black suit with shiny silver trim and backed by a five-piece band, the music legend played such crowd favorites as Down in the Flood, Sweet Marie, All Along the Watchtower, Fourth Street and Silvio. The crowd reacted with cheers, claps and puffs of white smoke.

But the loudest response from the fans came when Bob bobbed on his harmonica, sending young and old alike into hysterical screaming fits. In fact the crowd was so enthusiastic, Dylan could have stood there and blown just a single note into his harp and the fans still would have roared with delight.

For the first half of the show, Dylan stuck with an electric Fender Stratocaster guitar, and then switched to an acoustic for O Babe It Ain't No Lie and Desolation Row. He then moved back to an electric guitar for the second half, which ended with Highway 61. The crowd cheered Dylan back for three encores, for which he played his best-known hit, Like a Rolling Stone.

As the concert wore on, the crowd in the Coliseum edged closer and closer to the stage, with several people breaking through the barrier of security men to touch, hug or kiss Dylan. One female fan scrambled onto the stage during Rolling Stone, stood next to him and showed him a slip of paper. He nodded at the note, she kissed him on the cheek and escaped back into the crowd. Crowd reaction among the 20-somethings was the most fervent, as the wrinkled and greying guru of rock teased and fiddled with their 'I Want to Be a Hippie' mentality. Clearly, it was gramps showing the grandchildren how to have a good time.

The crowd at the Coliseum was one of the largest in recent memory. Manager Ralph Hayden considered the show a sellout, with approximately 6,000 people in the building. The crowd ranged through the ages, from fresh-faced school kids to spike-haired punk rockers to mellowed hippies. Many well-known local musicians were also in the crowd, seeking both inspiration and knowledge from this pioneer of modern music. The show was actually delayed by half an hour as a long lineup of fans stretched outside the building, waiting for what would likely be a once in a lifetime opportunity.

But it almost didn't happen.

Dylan had played in Newfoundland March 31 and April 1. While he arrived in Halifax safely last week, the trucks and roadies transporting his lights and sound equipment were marooned on the ferry between Newfoundland and Sydney. The situation caused postponement of the Halifax show to Sunday night and the Moncton show from Friday to Saturday. He was scheduled to perform at the Fredericton Aitken Centre tonight at 7:30 p.m. and at Harbour Station in Saint John Tuesday at 8 p.m.

As the gear was stuck on the ferry, promoter David Carver scrambled to rent light and sound equipment from other sources and have it trucked to Moncton. While it was a bare-bones affair with just enough lights and sound to get by, it was more then adequate for the Coliseum.

"It was incredible," said Shelly Pullen of Moncton, who was in the front row. "I would have been disappointed if it was cancelled, but after seeing him now, I REALLY would have been disappointed."

Her friend, Hammond Joshi, also of Moncton, said several people cancelled rooms at the hotel he manages because they thought it wasn't going to happen.

But Dylan delivered. In two hours, he barely spoke a word to the crowd, other than to do the obligatory introduction of the band members. He spoke about a favorite song of beat generation poet Allen Ginsberg, who died earlier in the day. And as he sang, it was the same nasal rambling voice fans have come to love over the years.

They all joined together as Dylan closed the show with the '60s anthem Rainy Day Women. The crowd responded by jumping to their feet, swinging their bodies and clapping their hands as Dylan dragged the 30-year-old song on for more than five minutes as the main lights lit up the building.

He ended, put his guitar down and walked away, pointing at the cheering crowd. And then he was gone.

The Maritime dates open a world tour that will keep Dylan going until July. From here, he will travel through New Jersey, Pennsylvania, West Virginia and Tennessee. He will play dates in Ireland, Scotland and England in July.

Sunday, April 6, 1997 --- Metro Centre
Halifax, NS

Set List

	Song	From The Album	Released
1.	Crash on the Levee (Down in the Flood)	Bob Dylan's Greatest Hits, Vol. 2	Nov. 17, 1971
2.	Man in the Long Black Coat	Oh Mercy	Sept. 12, 1989
3.	All Along the Watchtower	John Wesley Harding	Dec. 27, 1967
4.	Just Like a Woman	Blonde on Blonde	May 16, 1966
5.	It Takes a Lot to Laugh, It Takes a Train to Cry	Highway 61 Revisited	Aug. 30, 1965
6.	Silvio (Bob Dylan/Robert Hunter)	Down in the Groove	May 19, 1988
7.	Oh Baby It Ain't No Lie (Elizabeth Cotton)	–	–
8.	Mr. Tambourine Man	Bringing It All Back Home	March 22, 1965
9.	Tangled Up in Blue	Blood on the Tracks	Jan. 20, 1975
10.	Maggie's Farm	Bringing It All Back Home	March 22, 1965
11.	You're a Big Girl Now	Blood on the Tracks	
12.	Everything is Broken	Oh Mercy	Sept. 12, 1989
	Encores		
13.	Like a Rolling Stone	Highway 61 Revisited	Aug. 30, 1965
14.	My Back Pages	Another Side of Bob Dylan	Aug. 8, 1964
15.	Rainy Day Women #12 & 35	Blonde on Blonde	May 16, 1966

The Musicians

Bob Dylan (vocal, guitar & harmonica), Bucky Baxter (dobro, mandolin, pedal steel guitar, electric slide guitar & backup vocals), Larry Campbell (guitar& backup vocals), Tony Garnier (bass), David Kemper (drums & percussion).

Notes

- 82nd Bob Dylan concert in Canada; Debut Bob Dylan concert in Halifax.
- 4, 8, 11, 14, Bob Dylan (harmonica).
- 6, Larry Campbell & Bucky Baxter (backup vocals).
- 7-9, 14, acoustic with the band.
- The date of this show was changed from April 3rd to April 6th due to a storm. The trucks carrying Bob's equipment were held up at the ferry terminal in Port aux Basques, Newfoundland.

Reviews

Storm can't hold Dylan back

By Sandy MacDonald, The Daily News.

Was fate testing the resolve of 10,000 Bob Dylan fans this week? Could a little pack ice, a howling North Atlantic gale and a couple of stranded semis hobble the hometown concert that die-hard Dylanites have waited for since, well, since forever?

Undaunted by the three-day wait, a packed house turned out last night and no one was disappointed as the enigmatic singer romped and rocked through a non-stop two-hour concert that covered much of his 35-year career.

Dylan has always been tagged as a sporadic performer – sometimes riveting, other times disinterested. But last night he seemed genuinely engaged, offering extended versions of tunes and even grabbing several guitar solos.

In the midst of an ocean-hopping tour that wrapped up in Japan and is now heading south into the U.S., Dylan and his four backup musicians keep an edge to the shows by shifting setlists nightly. In fact, the band often sounded barroom-raggedy and the tunes were the better for it. With the addition of guitarist Larry Campbell last week (replacing J.J. Jackson), there was some obvious Band-aid playing outfront – Dylan, Campbell and pedal steel player Bucky Baxter covering little miscues as the rhythm section held the tunes together with brick and mortar. That edge kept everyone sharp and energized many of the tunes.

For all the hullabaloo about missing equipment, there was precious little sound gear blocking the stage. With flying stacks of PA speakers high out of the viewplane, the stage was uncluttered. And the band – drums, bass, guitar and pedal steel/mandolin – were all cosily wrapped round Dylan, giving the feel of a bar band tucked in the corner of a smoky little dance hall.

Unmistakable

Overhead, the scores of light cans were used to beautiful effect, as washes of warm greens and deep blues flooded the stage. There was no need for eye-bugging light tricks or swinging ladders and jack-up drum risers. Everyone came to see the charismatic Dylan – and he delivered in spades.

He looked the world like a slightly dishevelled riverboat gambler, clean-shaven in a light grey frock coat, black stovepipe pants and white wing-tipped cowboy boots. Even from the back of the hall, he was unmistakable with that famous tangled mop of greying curls.

What has kept Dylan relevant and musically interesting into the late '90s is his constant innovation, even with his old classics. Several tunes were dressed up in new clothes last night – more aggressive rhythms and shifted phrasing freshened the songs, while retaining their nostalgic magnetism.

Fifteen minutes late, the house lights of the Metro Centre blackened, and out strolled the band with little fanfare. A one-two count from the drummer, and the crunchy band launched into Crash on the Levee. From the first notes, Dylan's singing was aggressive and very animated. After some tweaking of the sound system through the first couple of tunes, everything fell into place – lots of presence for the vocals, big warm bass and snapping drums.

The band hit a ferocious romp on the old warhorse All Along the Watchtower, a tune that's been covered for 20 years by every garage band that figured out the A minor chord. And like every garage-band version, the band obliged with guitar solos that went nowhere for too long – perfect.

A half-hour into the show, the band traded the electric instruments for acoustic guitars, stand-up bass and dobro. Dylan wandered over to his guitar amp, grabbed a shiny harp and sauntered back to the mike. As a rumble of applause spread through the crowd, he hee-hawed an extended intro for Just Like a Woman. There are few sounds in popular music like Dylan's harmonica playing. Raw and piercing, it's an acquired taste, like fresh-from-the-still moonshine. But if you just let it slide down without fighting, it eventually does the trick.

Through the rest of the show, Dylan plucked tunes from all over his discography. Silvio, from his Down In The Groove album, had the band in full steam, as rhythms tumbled in front of the big drumbeats and churning guitars.

The musical highlight came on a marvellous acoustic version of Mr. Tamborine Man, retooled from a straight-ahead radio hit to a slow loping groove. Dylan turned the phrasing around and the melody upside down. Hey, it's his tune; he can sing it anyway he wants.

Ragged glory

As the show rolled past the 100-minute mark, Dylan offered up Tangled Up In Blue and a rocking version of Maggie's Farm. The set closer, Everything is Broken, had the hall on its feet as Dylan indulged in a playful guitar windout.

Three encore tunes, including a rasping take on Like a Rolling Stone and show closer Rainy Day Women #12 & 35, cemented a performance that was well worth the wait. With his rootsy band and the greatest collection of rock songs ever written, Dylan was in all his ragged glory last night. Even the Canadian winter can't keep him down.

The Halifax Daily News. Mon., April 7, 1997. Reprinted with permission of The Halifax Daily News.

Bob Dylan

By Shirley Newhook, The Hectic Pace.

One fan who attended the Bob Dylan concert in Halifax claimed "Carver really earned his money."

Promoter David Carver had the coup of the year when he managed to bring the legendary rock star to St. John's and he also arranged the Atlantic tour.

The tour fell on hard times when two semi-trailers of concert equipment got stuck in the ice between Newfoundland and Cape Breton and the crew got stuck in a Stephenville snowstorm.

Carver's popularity had fallen in Halifax because of a cancellation… but he managed to juggle all the mainland dates and keep everyone happy.

The appearance scheduled for Thursday night in the Halifax Metro Centre finally went off on Sunday night. Normally a quiet night in the city, "downtown bars loved it… everyone went in for a drink before and after the concert; just a mixture of everyone from 22 to 50 plus."

Ten thousand fans demanded three encores. With spectacular cowboy boots and dressed as a riverboat gambler BD roused the audience to a frenzy with Blonde on Blonde selections and probably increased record sales in the city. "Fantastic"… "fabulous"… and "the sound was spectacular… not what you expect in a stadium."

The young promoter, who started out selling tickets to theme parties at university, has come of age!

The St. John's Telegram. Fri., April 11, 1997. Reprinted with the permission of The St. John's Telegram.

Dylan wows with full-throttle delivery

By Stephen Pedersen, Staff Reporter.

It was worth the wait. After 35 years and four jittery days, the more than 8,000 Bob Dylan fans who jammed into the Metro Centre Sunday night achieved closure as Dylan stepped out onto a Halifax stage for the first time in his life.

It was, in typical Dylan style, a full-throttle delivery of some of his best work, without frills, sucking up to the fans, or showbiz shtick.

Lights there were, and pristine sound, and maybe a little smoke and incense at the start of the show, but no circus tricks or side-show hoopla. Just Dylan, three guitars and drums, and a voice whose once youthful in-your-face edginess has mellowed into a melodious growl, though it is as full as ever of moaning vowels and bruised consonants.

Dylan addressed only seven words directly to the audience, and they came in the form of a rhetorical question. "How about a hand for this band?" he asked halfway through the show, and introduced them with his usual flawled enunciation – that is, no one could make out a single word.

For Dylan fans, it didn't matter a bit. They know all his songs by heart anyway.

For others, you could only catch a line here and there, and that was usually a title like "Jase laik a wooman" (translated from the original Dylanese).

When he brought out the harmonica, everybody went nuts. There's no sound that better typifies the Sixties as a time of youthful unrest, rebellion and thrilling causes like civil rights and anti-war demonstrations than Dylan's harmonica playing.

It's the sound of protest and compassion.

There was variety in his show: songs with lyrics that he not so much sang as chanted with a high, raspy croak in a voice like old, cracked, water-burned leather.

After 35 years, it's remarkable how well many of those powerful songs Dylan wrote, beginning in 1961, have worn. Tambourine Man, the song with which the Byrds invented folk-rock in 1965, can still bring a tear to your eye. Like A Rolling Stone can still bring a crowd of thousands to their feet.

The audience was a real cross-section – teenagers, twenty-somethings, aging folkies, fiftyish rock 'n' rollers – proof that Dylan is a culture hero with a powerful and universal attraction even though he currently occupies a musical backwater well off the mainstream.

It was ever thus. Dylan, of all the great legends of the Sixties, always maintained an aloofness. But today, on the stage, he is kinder. He smiles more. He's jowly, and his guitar has to be pressed into his middle-aged belly.

But he looks dignified up there. And he gives an honest show. And people drive miles to see him.

Reg Oderkirk and his wife Heather first heard Dylan in 1965. Reg owns all his albums, knows all his songs.

They came up from Truro on Friday, spent the night in a hotel, went home annoyed and came back Sunday.

"He's a hundred per cent better than in Ontario seven years ago." Reg says. He had been mad about the postponement, but not last night.

"I had fun," he said. "All is forgiven."

John Drew and John Cross, scallop draggermen from Lunenburg, set out to drive to Halifax to see Dylan three times over the weekend.

Sunday night was the last chance. On Monday, the T. K. Pierce sailed with them on board.

"I'm still shocked he's here," Drew said.

"You're never going to see him and hear him again," added Cross. "Bob Dylan's a legend."

"He's opened everybody's mind to freedom," said Drew, explaining why Dylan is such a hero to him.

They are both middle-aged, which might lead you to think Dylan's influence is limited to those who knew him 30 years ago.

But down on the main floor of the Metro Centre, two very young women with headbands in their hair, wearing tunics straight out of Haight-Ashbury, throw their arms across each other's shoulders, and gaze up at Dylan with radiant expressions, their faces glowing in the soft light of the candles each of them holds.

Want to bet that 35 years from now they'll be talking about the night they heard Dylan sing?

The Halifax Chronicle-Herald. Tues., April 8, 1997. Republished with permission from The Halifax Herald Limited.

Monday, April 7, 1997 --- Aitken Centre --- UNB
Fredericton, NB

Set List

	Song	From The Album	Released
1.	Crash on the Levee (Down in the Flood)	Bob Dylan's Greatest Hits, Vol. 2	Nov. 17, 1971
2.	Tonight I'll Be Staying Here With You	Nashville Skyline	April 9, 1969
3.	All Along the Watchtower	John Wesley Harding	Dec. 27, 1967
4.	Under the Red Sky	Under the Red Sky	Sept. 11, 1990
5.	Most Likely You Go Your Way and I'll Go Mine	Blonde on Blonde	May 16, 1966
6.	Silvio (Bob Dylan/Robert Hunter)	Down in the Groove	May 19, 1988
7.	Oh Baby It Ain't No Lie (Elizabeth Cotton)	–	–
8.	Masters of War	The Freewheelin' Bob Dylan	May 27, 1963
9.	It's All Over Now, Baby Blue	Bringing It All Back Home	March 22, 1965
10.	Seeing the Real You at Last	Empire Burlesque	May 30, 1985
11.	I and I	Infidels	Oct. 27, 1983
12.	Highway 61 Revisited	Highway 61 Revisited	Aug. 30, 1965
	Encores		
13.	Like a Rolling Stone	Highway 61 Revisited	Aug. 30, 1965
14.	The Times They Are A-Changin'	The Times They Are A-Changin'	Feb. 10, 1964
15.	Rainy Day Women #12 & 35	Blonde on Blonde	May 16, 1966

The Musicians

Bob Dylan (vocal, guitar & harmonica), Bucky Baxter (dobro, mandolin, pedal steel guitar, electric slide guitar & backup vocals), Larry Campbell (guitar & backup vocals), Tony Garnier (bass), David Kemper (drums & percussion).

Notes

- 83rd Bob Dylan concert in Canada; Debut Bob Dylan concert in Fredericton.
- 7-9, 14, acoustic with the band.
- 14, Bob Dylan (harmonica).
- All Along the Watchtower is played in concert worldwide for the 1,000th time!

Reviews

Dylan Dazzles Devoted Audience

By Wilfred Langmaid, for The Daily Gleaner.

Though the show was delayed by inclement weather and tucked away as the smallest-venue stop in a five-show run, one could suggest that the biggest name in Aitken Centre concert history appeared last night.

Bob Dylan treated three generations of fans in a nearly-full Aitken Centre to an energetic 15-song show that bridged 35 years of songwriting and recording. In the process, he showed that he can still profoundly move a wide range of people with his exquisite craft.

There have certainly been more spectacular visual sights at the AUC over the past few decades. There have undoubtedly been more skilful musicians honing more tightly-rehearsed chops. There have unquestionably been more textbook-perfect vocalists.

The joy was that none of this was an issue. Dylan's singing style, if anything, has evolved to fit his vocal limitations. His band of sidemen – relative Dylan band vets Tony Garnier on bass and Bucky Baxter on pedal steel, mandolin, and acoustic guitar, long-time Jerry Garcia band drummer David Kemper, and relatively young guitarists Larry Campbell (ex-sideman for singers ranging from k.d. lang to Cyndi Lauper) – was basically a garage band, albeit a consummately competent one. If anything, Dylan was the lead guitarist at least as often as was Campbell, be it on electric or acoustic-cored numbers.

And it worked like a charm. Dylan ran through some old nuggets that have been part of every show this tour, to wit *Down In The Flood* and *All Along The Watchtower*. He also delivered other well known classics like *Highway 61 Revisited*, *Masters of War*, *Tonight I'll Be Staying Here With You*, *It's All Over Now, Baby Blue*, and *Someday You'll Go Your Way (And I'll Go Mine)*.

Fans of every age are, unquestionably, more than familiar with Dylan's exceptional canon of material from the 1960s when he redefined rock and added new standards of literacy to contemporary music. Last night's show also had new discoveries for many listeners in nuggets from the 1980s. That songs like *Sylvio*, *I and I*, *Seeing The Real You At Last*, and *Under The Red Sky* were just as impassioned and just as vital is a testimony to the ongoing power of Dylan's songwriting.

For Bob Dylan is, first and foremost, a songwriter – a lyrical prophet of the last decades of this millennium. As he closed his show with three encores – the ode of common alienation *Like A Rolling Stone*, the anthem of defiant hope *The Times They Are A Changin'*, and the tongue-in-cheek tale of nonconformity *Rainy Day Woman #12 & 35*, he was speaking for the age-spanning crowd who counted it a thrill to actually see him live in Fredericton.

"Come writers and critics who prophesize with your pen, and keep your eyes wide the chance won't come again, Dylan sang in the next-to-last song *The Times They Are A Changin'*. Far more than a bank commercial, this song is an admonition to Dylan the songwriter himself, and to those who are privileged to listen. If his unforgettable stop in the capital moves a listener or two to act with wisdom and charity in these changing times, Dylan is continuing to entertain – to inspire – to move his legion of fans. In his mid-50s and at the end of a tour with plenty of weather and scheduling headaches, it may have been our last chance "in creation where one's nature neither honors or forgives" to hear one of rock's principal sages first-hand. It was a privilege.

As appeared in The Fredericton Daily Gleaner. Tues., April 8, 1997. Reprinted with permission of Wilfred Langmaid.

Dylan's Fans Cross The Age Barrier

By Lisa Gregoire, The Daily Gleaner.

There he was in the eighth row in a beige patterned sweater and thinning grey hair.

To his left and right, three teenaged children – all tie-dyes and ponytails and braces – bounce and whisper and glance back and forth between the stage and the crowd.

They spot a friend, perhaps a crush. They lean into Dad's ear. Words are exchanged. And they're off like a breeze, disappearing into the throng of young shoulders now thick before the stage.

He's alone.

The house lights thankfully dim. He settles back into the fold-out chair on the floor of the Aitken Centre and taps his hand to the beat, the odd yawn passing his lips.

No doubt, 25 years ago he would have been on his feet.

Bob Dylan and his band of classic minstrels hit the stage shortly after 8 p.m. last night in Fredericton to a patchwork of young hippie teens, nose-pierced university students, a few ball-hats louder than most and a herd of nostalgic baby boomers.

And for an hour and a half, that quilt of lawyers, teachers and young Dead-heads swayed, whooped and punched the air. Shouts of approval rang out from the rafters as various contingents recognized songs from long-past, leisurely youth.

Plastic Canadian beer and American soft drink cups litter the floor as decades of American and Canadian pop culture once again merge. Yuppie birders with their sleeves rolled up forego winged sightings and squint through tiny binoculars to catch a glimpse of the fading vagabond.

What did they see?

"Well, he didn't really get into it and smile until the end," says Carol Cunningham, a ninth-row fan, as she dusts off her purse and slings it over her shoulder. The final riffs of a rollicking third encore, *Everybody Must Get Stoned*, echo into memory and the crowd quietly dissolves into a post-show traffic jam.

"I was king of hoping there'd be more of that. He was just starting to get into it."

When asked if she and her husband are big Dylan fans, she replies, "Oh well, he's a legend."

Her husband Jack juts his chin over her shoulder, smiling. "Long time," he says, "See this?" and he strokes back the few remaining hairs on his smooth head, laughing, "Long time fan."

Perhaps it was the omnipresent and over-zealous venue security or maybe the bar closing down at 9:15 that kept the crowd for the most part seated and subdued. Maybe it was the dusk lighting – never quite dark enough to offer the kind of anonymity most concerts afford.

Maybe it was the man himself on stage, practising solos and slow cascading song endings in preparation for bigger gigs yet to come in Dylan '97.

Or maybe it was just the reverence and admiration felt by a small Canadian crowd, lulled into awe by an American legend on a pared-down stage in a city he'd never been to and probably won't visit again.

Clad in a silver-grey suit and string tie, the balladeer strikes a question-mark pose for most of the show, bleating out a suitcase full of musical repertoire. Images of American Civil War and the Klu Klux Klan trade places on the back screen and popcorn teenagers bounce through electric and acoustic tunes alike.

But the awakening finally comes. Gently, like a slow train a-comin' – so to speak – the momentum begins building toward the end of the show. More people get up on their feet and the cheering increases.

Dylan strums the last few bars of the set, waves to the crowd and exits stage left with the band.

The house erupts into earsplitting whistles. People in the stands bang their wooden chairs to add to the din.

Bob hits the stage with *Like a Rollin' Stone* in what would be the first of three encores. The security slackens and people rush to the aisles to get a closer look at their childhood and new-found hero. More playful now, the fuzzy-headed man of prose smiles and gestures to the crowd before him.

This was what Carol Cunningham had been waiting for.

The man in row eight with the beige sweater stands up. A woman joins him, they lock arms and start to dance. He shakes his head, claps and smiles in disbelief.

It seems Bob Dylan and his faithful entourage still have a little juice left.

The Fredericton Daily Gleaner. Tues., April 8, 1997. Reprinted with permission of The Fredericton Daily Gleaner.

Tuesday, April 8, 1997 --- Harbour Station
Saint John, NB

Set List

	Song	From The Album	Released
1.	Crash on the Levee (Down in the Flood)	Bob Dylan's Greatest Hits, Vol. 2	Nov. 17, 1971
2.	If Not for You	New Morning	Oct. 21, 1970
3.	All Along the Watchtower	John Wesley Harding	Dec. 27, 1967
4.	Simple Twist of Fate	Blood on the Tracks	Jan. 20, 1975
5.	I Don't Believe You (She Acts Like We Never Have Met)	Another Side of Bob Dylan	Aug. 8, 1964
6.	Silvio (Bob Dylan/Robert Hunter)	Down in the Groove	May 19, 1988
7.	Oh Baby It Ain't No Lie (Elizabeth Cotton)	–	–
8.	Tangled Up in Blue	Blood on the Tracks	Jan. 20, 1975
9.	Girl of the North Country	The Freewheelin' Bob Dylan	May 27, 1963
10.	Stuck Inside of Mobile with the Memphis Blues Again	Blonde on Blonde	May 16, 1966
11.	Born in Time	Under the Red Sky	Sept. 11, 1990
12.	Maggie's Farm	Bringing It All Back Home	March 22, 1965
	Encores		
13.	Like a Rolling Stone	Highway 61 Revisited	Aug. 30, 1965
14.	Don't Think Twice, It's All Right	The Freewheelin' Bob Dylan	May 27, 1963
15.	Rainy Day Women #12 & 35	Blonde on Blonde	May 16, 1966

The Musicians

Bob Dylan (vocal, guitar & harmonica), Bucky Baxter (dobro, mandolin, pedal steel guitar, electric slide guitar & backup vocals), Larry Campbell (guitar & backup vocals), Tony Garnier (bass), David Kemper (drums & percussion).

Notes

- 84th Bob Dylan concert in Canada; Debut Bob Dylan concert in Saint John.
- 2, 11, Bob Dylan (harmonica).
- 7-9, 14, acoustic with the band.
- Canadian live debut of song 11.
- Song 11 has been performed only once in Canada.

Review

Sixties icon justifies his status to new fans

By Derek Shelly, Telegraph Journal Staff Writer.

I'm not old enough to worship Bob Dylan for what he's supposed to represent. Certainly, I can't see the man the way my father does. He's a brilliant songwriter whose best years were, for the most part, behind him by the time I became old enough to appreciate his work. His music – and, indeed, much of his message – would seem to belong to my parent's generation.

But still he tours, still he records, and still we flock to see him in concert. That he has left a great body of songwriting work in his wake is uncontestable. Whether he himself is great, as the 1990s fade into the next millennium, is up for grabs.

To make a long story short: yes, when he performs before me live, he's got something to prove.

And my father would not have been disappointed in his performance last night at Harbour Station. Okay, Bob, you win.

The teen-age girls who shrieked and danced to *All Along the Watchtower* – perhaps more familiar with U2's version of the song than the original, and likely more familiar with Jimi Hendrix's – seemed stumped by *Tangled Up in Blue* last night. But Dylan's original fans were likely just as baffled when their coffee-house hero embraced electricity back when the earth was young. Both songs churned with intensity last night, *Watchtower* a steamy, half choked cry of frustration and *Tangled Up in Blue* a leisurely journey across distance and years to the place that love calls home.

A Simple Twist of Fate was loosely elegant, with spare, looping guitar lines underlining Dylan's lyric; *Silvio* was nothing more than a rock song, as it should be.

Dylan did not sway from the pattern he's already established on this Atlantic tour: about a dozen songs followed by a three-song encore. Two hours. No break, except for the brief – almost cynical – period allowed at concert's end, during which Dylan and his band left the stage just long enough to be sure they were duly appreciated by the Saint John crowd.

Dylan himself was the most animated figure on stage, surprisingly into his music and the mood of the show, given his reputation for sullen recalcitrance – almost every chord change saw him bend low, shuffle and shake. He spoke but once to introduce his backing band.

Not surprisingly his lyrics were near to unintelligible. Who cares? Anyone who cares enough to know them already does, and thankfully, the band was tight enough and Dylan's singing good enough that anyone who didn't still get their money's worth in entertainment.

What at one time I considered the stupidest concert review I'd ever read took Bruce Springsteen to task for not playing enough of his classics. Since Springsteen had just released two albums in the previous year, and was touring to promote them, the criticism to me seemed a little harsh. The review came to mind when Dylan announced this concert tour. With no new material to promote, a greatest hits concert was the only possible option. I was less than excited about the prospect.

I've since changed my mind. When an artist's body of work is so worthy of respect, it's worth bringing to new generations of fans. Certainly there must be greatest-hits shows. If only more were like this; songs older than I am played either with the passion inspired by new love, or with the affection only decades of companionship can bring. Yes, Dylan is of my father's generation. He's also of mine, and those girls who delighted in his music last night, some of them for perhaps the first time.

A man for all seasons, then. Long may he reign.

Tuesday, August 5, 1997 --- du Maurier Stadium Montreal, QC

Set List

	Song	From The Album	Released
1.	Absolutely Sweet Marie	Blonde on Blonde	May 16, 1966
2.	Lay, Lady, Lay	Nashville Skyline	April 9, 1969
3.	Tough Mama	Planet Waves	Jan. 17, 1974
4.	You Ain't Goin' Nowhere	Bob Dylan's Greatest Hits, Vol. 2	Nov. 17, 1971
5.	Silvio (Bob Dylan/Robert Hunter)	Down in the Groove	May 19, 1988
6.	Mr. Tambourine Man	Bringing It All Back Home	March 22, 1965
7.	Tangled Up in Blue	Blood on the Tracks	Jan. 20, 1975
8.	Cocaine Blues (trad.)	–	–
9.	Watching the River Flow	Bob Dylan's Greatest Hits, Vol. 2	Nov. 17, 1971
10.	Blind Willie McTell	The Bootleg Series Volumes 1-3	March 26, 1991
11.	Highway 61 Revisited	Highway 61 Revisited	Aug. 30, 1965
	Encores		
12.	Like a Rolling Stone	Highway 61 Revisited	Aug. 30, 1965
13.	It Ain't Me, Babe	Another Side of Bob Dylan	Aug. 8, 1964
14.	Rainy Day Women #12 & 35	Blonde on Blonde	May 16, 1966

The Musicians

Bob Dylan (vocal, guitar & harmonica), Bucky Baxter (dobro, mandolin, pedal steel guitar, electric slide guitar & backup vocals), Larry Campbell (guitar, bouzouki & backup vocals), Tony Garnier (bass), David Kemper (drums & percussion).

Notes

- 85th Bob Dylan concert in Canada; 19th Bob Dylan concert in Montreal.
- 4-5, 8, 14, Larry Campbell & Bucky Baxter (backup vocals).
- 6-8, 13, acoustic with the band.
- 6, 13, Bob Dylan (harmonica).
- 10, Larry Campbell (bouzouki).
- Canadian live debut of songs 3, 4, 8 & 10.
- Worldwide live debut of song 10.
- The opening act was BR5-49, followed by Ani DiFranco.

Reviews

Dylan égal à lui-même: tantôt brillant, tantôt nul

par Richard Labbé.

Le stade du Maurier présentait hier soir le premier spectacle rock de sa jeune histoire. L'homme désigné pour l'occasion ? Le chanteur américain Robert Zimmerman, mieux connu sous le nom de Bob Dylan. Encore une fois, Dylan a été égal à lui-même : parfois brillant, parfois carrément nul.

Un petit mot sur la version rock de ce stade du Maurier, tout d'abord. Une possibilité de 7500 spectateurs, une très bonne sono, des sièges confortables, bref, tout va très bien madame la marquise.

Et il régnait là-bas une ambiance propre au baseball avec l'odeur des hot-dogs et du maïs soufflé, et ces vendeuses de bière qui déambulaient dans les allées. Vivement un autre spectacle au stade du Maurier!

Dylan, maintenant. Fidèle à sa réputation, le bon vieux Bob est arrivé sur la scène en titubant légèrement, guitare Les Paul à la main. Quelques accords grattés péniblement, et voilà *Absolutely Sweet Mary* qui donne le signal de départ. Première constatation : Dylan est bien entouré. Quatre solides musiciens, dont un joueur de «lap steel» pas piqué des vers. Dylan a beau se gourer, multiplier les notes étouffées, son band reste solide et implacable, prêt à colmater les failles.

Lay Lady Lay, de l'album *Nashville Skyline*, vient ensuite.

Excellente version. Le vieux Bob entonne le premier couplet de sa voix nasillarde si caractéristique, et les 4000 spectateurs se lèvent d'un trait. Jusqu'ici, ça va. Le band assure, Dylan lance parfois quelques bons riffs de guitare, et il n'oublie pas ses textes.

Entre les chansons, l'homme se fait toujours aussi énigmatique. Il marmonne trois ou quatre mots, tourne le dos, et enchaîne avec la pièce suivante. Remarquez, c'est peut-être mieux comme ça. On le sait, l'ami Bob n'est pas fort côté «social». S'il n'y a pas de photo sur cette page, ce n'est pas un ha- sard. On ne photographie pas Monsieur Dylan. «Cela n'est pas nouveau», me confiait une porte-parole des productions Fogel-Sabourin hier soir. «Il n'aime pas les entrevues et il n'aime pas les photos. Il a toujours été comme ça.» Bon...

Après quatre ou cinq chansons, Dylan se retire pour réapparaître ensuite avec une six-cordes acoustique. Les fans de la première heure se lèvent, les nombreux jeunes hippies, eux, ne se peuvent plus. Dylan pose les lèvres sur le micro. Il regarde son guitariste, et chante: «Hey mister tambourine man, play a song for me...»

Là, c'est le côté exécrable de Bob Dylan qui nous saute au visage. Le voilà qui retombe dans ses mauvaises habitudes et qui massacre une de ses plus belles chansons. À ma droite, un confrère se tient la tête à deux mains, incapable d'assister à un tel carnage musical. Impossible de chanter le refrain ; Dylan ne respecte pas le phrasé original, accélère le débit sans crier gare. Et comme si ce n'était pas assez, il sort son harmonica vers la fin, histoire de jouer quelques notes tonitruantes.

Surprise, Dylan revient ensuite avec une très bonne version de *Tangled Up In Blue*. La magie est de retour... Au rappel, toutefois, Dylan se permet de passer au tordeur son *Like A Rolling Stone*, pourtant une des plus grandes pièces de toute l'histoire du rock. Le refrain que chante l'ami Bob est méconnaissable. Mais le public est debout quand même...

Hier soir, Bob Dylan aura donc été égal à lui-même. Pour le meilleur et pour le pire.

As appeared in La Presse. Wed., Aug. 6, 1997. Reprinted with permission of Richard Labbé.

La résurrection de Bob Dylan

par Patrick Gauthier.

Il y a quelques mois, on le croyait en train de creuser sa tombe, agonisant sur un lit d'hôptial, pensant bientôt aller rejoindre le King au paradis. Hier soir, au Stade du Maurier, Bob Dylan a pourtant paru en grande forme à quelque 4 000 de ses admirateurs.

De Bob Dylan, on est en droit de s'attendre au meilleur comme au pire. Hier soir, il était manifestement en forme, presque en voix, poussant même souvent l'audace jusqu'à tenter de chanter.

Un Bob Dylan plus a rock 'a' billy que rock, plus bluegrass que folk. Un Bob Dylan revisitant ses racines, comme il le faisait en 69 avec l'album *Nashville Skyline*.

Un Bob Dylan livrant *Lay Lady Lay*, *Mr. Tambourine Man* ainsi que *Like a Rolling Stone* et *It Ain't Me* au rappel et, finalement, *Rainy Day Woman*, mais aussi une très longue et très swinguante version de *Desolation Row*.

Le patriarche avait d'ailleurs décidé de miser sur l'aspect musical de son œuvre étirant souvent ses finales, ne livrant finalement qu'une dizaine de pièces pendant l'heure qu'a duré son spectacle (avant les rappels).

Pour ce premier concert présenté au Stade de Maurier, on ne pouvait espérer passer meilleure soirée. Surtout après l'excellente performance d'Ani DiFranco qui livrait une espèce de *funk-folk-rap* en première partie.

Parlant du Stade du Maurier, il faut absolument souligner, outre la praticabilité du site, l'excellence de l'acoustique.

Car hier, le son était digne des meilleurs salles de concerts.

Le Journal de Montréal. Wed., Aug. 6, 1997. Reprinted with permission of Le Journal de Montréal.

Le coeur bien accroché

Bob Dylan au Stade du Maurier

par Sylvain Cormier.

Dylan était là. Ce qui était en soi une raison de se réjouir, après les alarmantes nouvelles de fin mai. Le pire, constations-nous hier au baptême rock du tout neuf Stade du Maurier, n'était finalement pas au plus mal, et ce n'est pas une infection de rien du tout à l'enveloppe cardiaque qui aura raison de Saint-Bob, lequel a tout simplement repris là où il avait laissé sa tournée sans fin. Ce n'était jamais que le troisième show de son retour à l'ordinaire, mais Dylan n'a à aucun moment joué au convalescent.

Le Dylan d'hier était au moins aussi solide sur ses pieds que l'an dernier, à son surprenant passage à l'Auditoriun de Verdun. Prenez là-dessus ma parole: aucune photo n'était permise.

Présenté sans emphase en «Columbia Recording Artist», Dylan s'est remis à la tâche sans tarder, lançant une version absolument pas doucereuse d'*Absolutely Sweet Marie*, suivie de quelques «*thank you*» presque trop affables après cinq petites minutes de spectacle. Contre toute attente, la romantique ballade *Lay Lady Lay* enchaînait, une superbe version qui révélait un Dylan au timbre raffermi (séquelle de l'hospitalisation, comme en 1968 après l'accident de moto?). Entre les Sylvio et autres poncifs des récents shows de Dylan s'immiscaient des titres inespérés, comme si le goût de les jouer lui était revenu avec la signature de son nouveau bail sous le soleil: le country-folk *You Ain't Goin' Nowhere*, livré à la Byrds (avec les refrains en harmonie à trois voix), et surtout l'ode aux troubadours *Mr. Tambourine Man*, classique parmi les classiques, magnifiquement rendu par Dylan à l'acoustique et à l'harmonica, entouré de contrebasse et de mandoline. Moment de totale communion pour cette foule d'âge varié (dont un bon nombre d'ados) qui en laissait présager d'autres. Sur les talons de l'homme-orchestre, *Tangled Up In Blue*, titre majeur de l'album *Blood On The Tracks* (1974), était encore plus resserré qu'à Verdun. Tombée oblige, je suis parti alors que Dylan entamait un blues à la Jimmie Rodgers. Pour Robert Allen Zimmerman, la vie continuait là où elle a le plus de sens: sur scène.

Plus tôt en soirée, Ani DiFranco a obtenu son propre petit triomphe auprès des disciples de sa Sainteté. Il faut dire qu'elle plantait ses bottes plate-forme en plein dans les plates-bandes du folk tel que propagé par Dylan. Plus dur et plus alternatif, son folk à elle n'était pas moins familier pour cette foule (assez réduite, la foule, soit dit en passant: seuls 4000 sièges sur 7500 étaient occupés). Avoir aimé Dylan, c'était se reconnaître en cette jeune artiste irréductible qui a su percer le marché américain à la seule force du poignet, créant et menant avec succès sa propre compagnie de disques (Righteous Babe Records). Ravie d'un accueil aussi chaleureux (à l'opposé du show de la veille, précisait-elle), DiFranco poussait avec d'autant plus d'ardeur ses refrains moitié chantés, moitié déblatérés, confinant parfois au *spoken-word*, cette poésie sur fond de congas, typique de l'âge d'or des *coffeshouses* de Greenwich Village. Tel Dylan à son époque la plus vitale, DiFranco représentait pour les années 90 l'artiste intraitable. Hier, Bob et elle menaient le même combat.

En ouverture, directement du Robert's Western World, fameux bar de Nashville, nous parvenait le plus vivifiant groupe de hillbilly boogie en activité, les BR5-49 (c'est le numéro de téléphone de l'endroit). Les voir chez nous, c'était se sentir étrangement ailleurs. Les nouveaux groupes de Nashville ne se rendent jamais jusque dans nos contrées. On a bien nos propres Crazy Rhythm Daddies dans le genre, mais c'est un secret pour initiés. L'auditoire, qui pénétrait peu à peu l'enceinte durant leur séquence, a vite manifesté son approbation: on ne pouvait trouver mieux pour entrer en matière que ces frétillants boogies (*Little Ramona, Hometown Boogie*), ces balançants shuffles (*Heartaches By The Numbers*) et ces irrépressibles swings texans (*Honky Tonk Song, I Ain't Never*). On n'aurait pu souhaiter affiche plus conséquente. La musique américaine, c'est ça. De Mel Tillis à Ani DiFranco, en passant par Dylan l'increvable.

Le Devoir. Thurs., Aug. 7, 1997. Reprinted with permission of Le Devoir.

Additional Review

Dylan croaks: Voice is still all it's cracked up to be, by Mark LePage. The Montreal Gazette. Wed., Aug. 6, 1997. p. F6.

Thursday, August 7, 1997 --- Molson Amphitheatre Toronto, ON

Set List

	Song	From The Album	Released
1.	Absolutely Sweet Marie	Blonde on Blonde	May 16, 1966
2.	If You See Her, Say Hello	Blood on the Tracks	Jan. 20, 1975
3.	Tough Mama	Planet Waves	Jan. 17, 1974
4.	I'll Be Your Baby Tonight	John Wesley Harding	Dec. 27, 1967
5.	Silvio (Bob Dylan/Robert Hunter)	Down in the Groove	May 19, 1988
6.	Don't Think Twice, It's All Right	The Freewheelin' Bob Dylan	May 27, 1963
7.	One Too Many Mornings	The Times They Are A-Changin'	Feb. 10, 1964
8.	Cocaine Blues (trad.)	–	–

9.	Watching the River Flow	Bob Dylan's Greatest Hits, Vol. 2	Nov. 17, 1971
10.	This Wheel's on Fire (Bob Dylan/Rick Danko)	The Basement Tapes	July 1, 1975
11.	Leopard-Skin Pill-Box Hat	Blonde on Blonde	May 16, 1966
	Encores		
12.	Like a Rolling Stone	Highway 61 Revisited	Aug. 30, 1965
13.	Forever Young	Planet Waves	Jan. 17, 1974
14.	Rainy Day Women #12 & 35	Blonde on Blonde	May 16, 1966

The Musicians

Bob Dylan (vocal, guitar & harmonica), Bucky Baxter (dobro, mandolin, pedal steel guitar, electric slide guitar & backup vocals), Larry Campbell (guitar & backup vocals), Tony Garnier (bass), David Kemper (drums & percussion).

Notes

- 86th Bob Dylan concert in Canada; 26th Bob Dylan concert in Toronto.
- 5, 8, 10, 13-14, Larry Campbell & Bucky Baxter (backup vocals).
- 6-8, 13, acoustic with the band.
- 13, Bob Dylan (harmonica).
- The opening act was BR5-49, followed by Ani DiFranco.

Reviews

Dylan's back in business

Brush with death hasn't softened legend's gritty vocal delivery

By Betsy Powell, Pop Music Critic.

Fans feared Bob Dylan was knockin' on heaven's door only eight weeks ago after the 56-year-old singing-songwriting legend cancelled his summer European tour after being hospitalized with a serious chest infection.

But lingering concerns about the popular music icon's health were put at ease last night as he strolled on to the Molson Amphitheatre stage before a crowd of 9,000, signalling that he's carrying on business as usual. Dressed in a dark gentleman's cowboy suit, with silver rhinestones stitched along the sides of his pants, the graying Dylan appeared strong and fit, though he wouldn't allow photographers to snap his picture. His poker face even cracked a smile or two as he led his four-piece band through a set of oldies while keeping hits to a minimum. Nor was there a harmonica in sight.

Dylan's bout with the potentially fatal histoplasmosis – he resumed touring earlier this week – didn't soften his gritty vocal delivery, which at times seemed even more ragged than usual. The repertoire consisted of songs culled from albums he released in the '60s and '70s with no hint of what lies ahead on a CD coming out this fall that he co-produced with Canadian Daniel Lanois.

Dylan opened with "Absolutely Sweet Marie," a steady rocker from 1966's Blonde On Blonde and followed with an uptempo "If You See Her Say Hello" from Blood On The Tracks (1975). He introduced the relatively obscure "Tough Mama," a track from his days with The Band and one he hasn't played since 1974, before tipping his hat to the Grateful Dead with "Silvio," a song from 1987's Down In The Groove and the most recent song played last night.

The curtains at the back of the dry-ice filled stage parted during "Don't Think Twice, It's Alright," initiating a series of sepia slide projections.

The show picked up steam with the the bluesy "Cocaine," a 35-year-old tune (not by J.J. Cale) that some fans believe has surfaced now as a nod to Dylan's brush with death. "This ol' cocaine is makin' me sick/Cocaine/all around my brain."

After quickening the tempo of "Watching The River Flow" to nearly twice its pace on record, the band launched into a standout version of "Leopard-Skin Pill-box Hat," a song that prompted a young woman to jump on stage wearing a pill-box style hat. Dylan glanced at her several times as she danced on her own until the song ended. He saved his biggest hit, "Like A Rolling Stone," for the encore. As is customary, Dylan spoke few words during the 65-minute show, though he introduced his band and asked the crowd for a show of appreciation for openers BR5-59 and young singer-songwriter Ani DiFranco.

It was a nice gesture but unnecessary since both acts, particularly DiFranco, were enthusiastically received after solid and entertaining sets.

The Toronto Star. Fri., Aug. 8, 1997. Reprinted with permission - Torstar Syndication Services.

Resurrected Dylan shows he can outjam the Dead

Reviewed by Alan Niester.

With so many rock 'n' roll icons in rock 'n' roll heaven, it's downright delightful to have one who, metaphorically at least, dodged the bullet.

A mere couple of months ago, Spokesman of His Generation Bob Dylan was hospitalized with a condition known as histoplasmosis pericarditis, a potentially fatal infection of the sac that surrounds the heart. But last night at the Molson Amphitheatre, he was right back on stage where he belonged, leading his four-piece band through a rollicking set that suggested that infected hearts were no more serious than ingrown toenails.

Physically, the condition seems not to have taken much of a toll. Dylan looked hale and hearty (or at least as hale and hearty as he ever gets), and while he didn't bounce around the stage much, he never was a Peter Townsend type anyway.

The condition seems, however, to have taken a significant toll on his voice. His range has shrunk to about two notes (that's notes, not octaves): he spews forth lyrics in an almost indecipherable mumble, and his voice occasionally exhibits a frog-like croak when it's supposed to be reaching past the two-note limit. Although, come to think of it, that was pretty much the way it was before the infection, too.

At any rate, to compensate for his deficiencies, Dylan arrived last night ready to outjam the Grateful Dead. Backed by a band that included a steel guitarist and a lead guitarist to compliment his own instrumental work, Dylan and company eschewed lyricism for meaty rock 'n' roll jams, rolling and complex rhythmic arrangements with the guitars and the steel intertwining like the threads in a fine tapestry.

The first half-dozen numbers were pure Grateful Dead-style jams, highlighted by a sashaying version of *I'll Be Your Baby Tonight* that started out as a country waltz, but built to a J.-Geils-styled roadhouse rocker.

After this, the lights went down, and when they came up again, the quintet had morphed into an Appalachian string band, with upright bass replacing electric, and mandolin replacing electric steel. This segment featured some of Dylan's better known numbers, including a croaking *Don't Think Twice, It's Alright*, and a bluesy version of J. J. Cale's classic *Cocaine*.

Then it was back to electricland for a few more numbers, including a dirge-like *This Wheel's on Fire*, and a low-speed version of *Like a Rolling Stone*, done in the encore, that was sung almost as a dirge.

If Dylan showed any effects of his recent illness, it was in the length of the performance. For a headliner, this was a pretty truncated show, stretching not much more that an hour. Perhaps the effects of the illness have indeed weakened him to some degree.

Or perhaps it was simply that Dylan was the third act of the night, and it was felt that the audience had already got its money's worth. Opening for Dylan were Buffalo-based guerilla feminist folkie Ani DiFranco, and Nashville retro outfit BR5-49.

DiFranco is poised for superstar status, and a goodly portion of the estimated 10,000 on hand last night were undoubtedly there to see her. But DiFranco works best in an intimate setting when the audience is totally her own. Usually, she interacts with her audience from the stage, reflecting, storytelling, cajoling and bantering. Last night, she simply got on with it, perhaps intimidated by performing before an audience of, relatively speaking, greybeards.

She did tell one story about being brought to Ontario Place by her parents when she was younger. But other than that, she was pure business, and came across less like the next big thing, and more like one-half of the Indigo Girls.

As for BR5-49, the traditional-minded country quintet was limited to an early-evening half-hour set that was performed mostly in front of rows of empty seats. It was hardly an inspiring performance, but the combination of Commander-Cody-styled goofiness and precise Nashville traditionalism suggested that they too would have benefited from more intimate surroundings and a more knowledgeable and hence appreciative audience.

As appeared in The Globe and Mail. Fri., Aug. 8, 1997. Reprinted with permission of Alan Niester.

Dylan Still on Fire

By Kieran Grant, Toronto Sun.

To say that Bob Dylan's reputation precedes him would be a great understatement.

He is, after all, an icon, widely considered to be the best songwriter in the history of rock and folk.

Balancing the scales, however, is another reputation that has dogged him for over a decade: He's lost it.

Dylan's show at the Molson Amphitheatre last night blew the latter theory out of the water.

The singer's act was as intact as you could expect from someone who's spent the last ten years on a so-called "Neverending tour."

Not to mention the fact that Dylan, 56, was in hospital just two months ago with a potentially fatal chest infection.

Suited up like a Civil War-era dandy and quite alive, Dylan and his four-man band treated a crowd of 9,000 to a 95-minute set of straight-up country rockers.

And while the sounds were conventional, Dylan wasn't resting on his laurels as a hitmaker.

With the exception of two inescapable encore numbers, Like A Rolling Stone and a bluesy rave-up of Rainy Day Women #12 & 35 – both show highlights – he laid off the best-known classics.

He deviated from his prepared set list and scrapped a run-through of Tangled Up In Blue during a slippery acoustic passage in favor of This Wheel's On Fire.

Still, the many Dylanologists in attendence were obviously impressed with his venturing back to 1966's Blonde On Blonde album for his opening tune Absolutely Sweet Marie.

Other favorites included I'll Be Your Baby Tonight, from 1968's John Wesley Harding, Don't Think Twice, One Too Many Mornings, and even 1988's Silvio.

Dylan's stature as a performer does let him get away with a few, shall we say, idiosyncrasies that wouldn't work for a lesser artist: He frequently took wrong turns on the guitar. His inventive take on the English language left some of his best lyrics in need of a Dylanese translator.

Fortunately, his band – which included longtime bassist Tony Garnier and steel guitarist Bucky Baxter – followed him attentively and never let him slide.

Dylan even took to duelling with lead guitarist Larry Campbell. He became quite animated and laughed when a young girl in a pillbox hat emerged from the crowd and danced along to Pillbox.

Dylan doesn't take performing for granted. As he slumped offstage, his appreciative audience decided he deserves the same respect.

Opener Ani DiFranco proved you didn't have to be a legend to win two encores last night.

After a set by old-school country godsends BR5-49, DiFranco went over like gangbusters with a remarkable set.

A one-woman rhythm section on acoustic guitar, the Buffalo-reared singer's sound became a triple-threat with her Torontonian band, drummer Andy Stochansky and former Bourbon Tabernacle Choir bassist Jason Mercer.

Things have come a long way in the 27 years since those beards at Newport booed Dylan for going electric.

SUN RATING: 3 OUT OF 5

The Toronto Sun. Fri., Aug. 8, 1997. Reprinted with permission of The Sun Media Corp.

1998

Introduction

The Never-Ending Tour stopped for nine concerts in Canada in 1998. The third most concerts in any given year.

These shows would mark Bob Dylan's 87th, 88th, 89th, 90th, 91st, 92nd, 93rd, 94th & 95th concert in Canada.

The Dates

Vancouver, BC	Wed., May 13, 1998
Vancouver, BC	Wed., May 14, 1998
Calgary, AB	Thurs., Oct. 15, 1998
Edmonton, AB	Fri., Oct. 16, 1998
Saskatoon, SK	Sun., Oct. 18, 1998
Regina, SK	Tues., Oct. 20, 1998
Winnipeg, MB	Wed., Oct. 21, 1998
Toronto, ON	Thurs., Oct. 29, 1998
Ottawa, ON	Fri., Oct. 30, 1998

The shows would be Dylan's 8th & 9th concert in Vancouver, 4th concert in Calgary, 4th concert in Edmonton, debut concert in Saskatoon, debut concert in Regina, 4th concert in Winnipeg, 27th concert in Toronto and 8th concert in Ottawa.

The Musicians

Bob Dylan (vocal, guitar & harmonica).

Bucky Baxter (dobro, mandolin, pedal steel guitar, electric slide guitar & backup vocals), Larry Campbell (guitar & backup vocals), Tony Garnier (bass), David Kemper (drums & percussion).

The Songs

Bob Dylan performed a total of 146 songs. Of those, 47 were different songs (43 were from albums and 4 were cover and/or traditional songs).

Ten songs made their Canadian live debut.

Not Fade Away	I'm Not Supposed to Care
Cold Irons Bound	Til I Fell In Love With You
Make You Feel My Love	Love Sick
Stone Walls and Steel Bars	Can't Wait
Million Miles	Every Grain of Sand

Two songs have been played only once in Canada.

Not Fade Away	Stone Walls and Steel Bars

Bob Dylan performed songs from 19 different albums.

Album	Released	# of Songs Performed by Album
The Freewheelin' Bob Dylan	May, 27, 1963	4
The Times They Are A-Changin'	Feb., 10, 1964	3
Another Side of Bob Dylan	Aug. 8, 1964	2
Bringing It All Back Home	March 22, 1965	3
Highway 61 Revisited	Aug. 30, 1965	4
Blonde on Blonde	May 16, 1966	6
Bob Dylan's Greatest Hits	March 27, 1967	1
John Wesley Harding	Dec. 27, 1967	1
Nashville Skyline	April 9, 1969	1
Bob Dylan's Greatest Hits, Vol. 2	Nov. 17, 1971	2
Planet Waves	Jan. 17, 1974	1
Blood on the Tracks	Jan. 20, 1975	3
Street Legal	June 15, 1978	1
Slow Train Coming	Aug. 20, 1979	1
Shot of Love	Aug. 12, 1981	1
Empire Burlesque	May, 30, 1985	1
Down in the Groove	May 19, 1988	1
The Bootleg Series Volumes 1-3	Match 26, 1991	1
Time Out of Mind	Sept. 30, 1997	6

Opening Acts

Ron Sexsmith opened the show at the Rage in Vancouver. The second show in Vancouver was a historic triple bill with Bob Dylan, Van Morrison and Joni Mitchell. Jann Arden opened the shows in Calgary, Edmonton, Saskatoon, Regina and Winnipeg. Dave Alvin and the Guilty Men opened the shows in Toronto and Ottawa and Joni Mitchell followed.

The Venues

It was Bob Dylan's debut concert at the Rage in Vancouver, debut concert at GM Place in Vancouver, 2nd time playing at the Saddledome in Calgary, 2nd time playing at the Coliseum in Edmonton, debut concert at Saskatchewan Place in Saskatoon, debut concert at the Agridome in Regina, 2nd time playing at the Winnipeg Arena, 7th time playing at Maple Leaf Gardens in Toronto and debut concert at the Corel Centre in Ottawa.

Wednesday, May 13, 1998 --- The Rage
Vancouver, BC

Set List

	Song	From The Album	Released
1.	Not Fade Away (Norman Petty/Charles Hardin)	–	–
2.	Tonight I'll Be Staying Here With You	Nashville Skyline	April 9, 1969
3.	Cold Irons Bound	Time Out of Mind	Sept. 30, 1997
4.	Make You Feel My Love	Time Out of Mind	Sept. 30, 1997
5.	Silvio (Bob Dylan/Robert Hunter)	Down in the Groove	May 19, 1988
6.	Stone Walls and Steel Bars (Ray Pennington/Ray Marcum)	–	–
7.	It's All Over Now, Baby Blue	Bringing It All Back Home	March 22, 1965
8.	Tangled Up in Blue	Blood on the Tracks	Jan. 20, 1975
9.	Million Miles	Time Out of Mind	Sept. 30, 1997
10.	I'm Not Supposed to Care (Gordon Lightfoot)	–	–
11.	Highway 61 Revisited	Highway 61 Revisited	Aug. 30, 1965
	Encores		
12.	Til I Fell In Love With You	Time Out of Mind	Sept. 30, 1997
13.	It Ain't Me, Babe	Another Side of Bob Dylan	Aug. 8, 1964
14.	Love Sick	Time Out of Mind	Sept. 30, 1997
15.	Rainy Day Women #12 & 35	Blonde on Blonde	May 16, 1966

The Musicians

Bob Dylan (vocal & guitar), Bucky Baxter (dobro, mandolin, pedal steel guitar, electric slide guitar & backup vocals), Larry Campbell (guitar & backup vocals), Tony Garnier (bass), David Kemper (drums & percussion).

Notes

- 87th Bob Dylan concert in Canada; 8th Bob Dylan concert in Vancouver.
- 6-8, 13, acoustic with the band.
- Canadian live debut of songs 1, 3, 4, 6, 9, 10, 12 & 14.
- Songs 1 & 6 have been performed only once in Canada.
- The opening act was Ron Sexsmith.

Reviews

1,000 lucky fans get an early taste of Dylan live

By Kerry Gold, Sun Pop Music Critic.

Bob Dylan's show at the Rage Wednesday night was a sizzling start to a series of back-to-back concerts featuring three of the '60s most influential icons, including Joni Mitchell and Van Morrison.

It's been about a month since Dylan last performed, and his club show at the Rage served as a rehearsal for an extremely lucky audience of about 1,000 fans of all ages. Diehard fans in the crowd came from as far away as Toronto and California to see the legend. One man in the audience even played harmonica to the old Dylan songs. On the balcony, Van Morrison was spotted, but he only stayed for three tunes.

Dressed nattily in silvery suit, white shoes and tie, Dylan seemed initially reserved, but perked up by the time he got to a rousing version of an old standby, Silvio.

Dylan opened with the blues classic, Not Fade Away, and mixed it up with fast and slow tunes, including a spot-on version of Tangled Up In Blue, It's All Over Now, Baby Blue, It Ain't Me Babe, Steel Bars, Million Miles, Gordon Lightfoot's

I'm Not Supposed to Care, I'll Be Your Baby Tonight, Love Sick, the gorgeously serene To Make You Feel My Love and a blessedly raunchy Highway 61 Revisited.

He played both electric and acoustic guitar, and his encore included a wonderful surprise, Rainy Day Women #12 and 35.

As expected, his four-piece back-up band was top-notch. Not expected was Dylan's obvious delight and his eloquent delivery. Not a word was mumbled. He often smiled, bobbed his head to the music, and shuffled across the stage between band mates.

Near the evening's end, he accepted a big bouquet of red roses from a fan in the audience – a fitting tribute to a class act.

Thursday night's show, for a crowd of 15,000 at GM Place, is the inaugural concert for Dylan, Mitchell and Morrison as a triple bill. It marks the start of a seven-city West Coast tour that continues in the U.S. The tour sold out almost immediately, partly because it is history-making, and partly because these three artists are enjoying renewed interest in their music.

In comparison, Lilith Fair, which is also playing at the Gorge venue, hasn't yet sold out.

Morrison added a second show at the Queen Elizabeth Theatre tonight, which took five hours to sell out. If anyone thought the influence of these '60s icons had waned, they stand corrected.

Mitchell's performance is of particular interest, since she hasn't toured in 15 years. She last played in Vancouver in September 1979 at the Pacific Coliseum.

Morrison was last here in July 1986 at the Expo Theatre.

The Vancouver Sun. Fri., May 15, 1998.
Material reprinted with the express permission of: "Pacific Newspaper Group Inc.", a CanWest Partnership.

His Bobness delivers the goods

Reviewed by Chris Dafoe.

MAKE of this what you will. On Wednesday morning, a Vancouver newspaper carried letters from heartbroken girls and angry parents, upset that ticket brokers were asking as much as $350 for tickets to see the Spice Girls play GM Place in August. On Wednesday evening, a scalper outside The Rage would sell you a ticket for Bob Dylan's show at the 1,000-seat club for $70, less than $20 over cost.

Well, as the man once said, money doesn't talk, it swears.

Whatever you make of that bit of rock economics, it's probably impossible to put a price on the performance Dylan gave on Wednesday as a warmup for last night's show at GM Place with Joni Mitchell and Van Morrison. Backed by a four-piece band – a basic rock trio joined by a steel guitar and mandolin player – Dylan played a 90-minute set that moved between electrifying rock 'n' roll abandon, delicate, graceful country-tinged introspection and deep, haunting blues grooves. Dylan, decked out in the same silver country gentleman suit he wore at the recent Grammy Awards, seemed as delighted by the proceedings as the two – or was it three? – generations of fans who packed the club. There was a glint in his eye and the hint of a grin on his craggy old mug as he traded guitar solos with band leader Larry Campbell and there was a sense of connection that came as a real surprise to anyone who hadn't seen Dylan since his distant, indifferent and sometimes downright perverse shows of the late 1980s and early 1990s.

It was apparent from the moment that he opened the show with Buddy Holly's *Not Fade Away* that it was going to be a rollicking evening. The song is a little rockabilly number about love, written by a kid barely out of his teens, but when it's sung by a man who nearly bought the farm a bit more than a year ago, it's hard not to hear it as rock 'n' roll's version of John Donne's and Dylan Thomas's defiant letters to death: a promise that the beat and the word will live on.

The rest of the show made that promise seem credible indeed. After winding down the energy with a couple of folk and blues-tinged numbers, including a lovely and generous version of *To Make You Feel My Love*, Dylan cranked it up again with an electrifying version of *Silvio*, a song he wrote with Grateful Dean lyricist Robert Hunter for 1988's *Down in the Groove*. As the song turned into a jam, the band pushed the energy level higher and higher, weaving guitar and steel guitar lines into the groove as Dylan wailed out the chorus.

And so it continued, a delicate acoustic treatment of *It's All Over Now, Baby Blue* giving way to a smoking version of *Tangled Up in Blue*; the blues of *Million Miles* setting up the wild ride of *Highway 61 Revisited*; old hits such as *It Ain't Me Babe* giving way to the new, but hauntingly timeless numbers such as *Love Sick*. Fans threw flowers or, in the case of one middle-aged woman, crowd-surfed to the front of the stage to deliver a bouquet to His Bobness. By the time Dylan wrapped up the evening with *Rainy Day Women #12 and #35*, the whole room was part of the show. As balding grey-beards passed joints to skinny young *nouveau*-hippies, 1,000 people sang in unison, "Everybody must get stoned."

The Globe and Mail. Fri., May 15, 1998. Reprinted with permission from The Globe and Mail.

Additional Review

Emotions high at Dylan club show, by Denise Sheppard. Jam! Music. Posted on Thurs., May 14, 1998.

Thursday, May 14, 1998 --- GM Place Vancouver, BC

Set List

	Song	From The Album	Released
1.	Absolutely Sweet Marie	Blonde on Blonde	May 16, 1966
2.	Señor (Tales of Yankee Power)	Street Legal	June 15, 1978
3.	Cold Irons Bound	Time Out of Mind	Sept. 30, 1997
4.	You're a Big Girl Now	Blood on the Tracks	Jan. 20, 1975
5.	Silvio (Bob Dylan/Robert Hunter)	Down in the Groove	May 19, 1988
6.	Cocaine Blues (trad.)	–	–
7.	Mr. Tambourine Man	Bringing It All Back Home	March 22, 1965
8.	Tangled Up in Blue	Blood on the Tracks	Jan. 20, 1975
9.	Stuck Inside of Mobile with the Memphis Blues Again	Blonde on Blonde	May 16, 1966
10.	I Shall Be Released	Bob Dylan's Greatest Hits, Vol. 2	Nov. 17, 1971
11.	Highway 61 Revisited	Highway 61 Revisited	Aug. 30, 1965
	Encores		
12.	Forever Young	Planet Waves	Jan. 17, 1974
13.	Love Sick	Time Out of Mind	Sept. 30, 1997
14.	Rainy Day Women #12 & 35	Blonde on Blonde	May 16, 1966

The Musicians

Bob Dylan (vocal & guitar), Bucky Baxter (dobro, mandolin, pedal steel guitar, electric slide guitar & backup vocals), Larry Campbell (guitar & backup vocals), Tony Garnier (bass), David Kemper (drums & percussion).

Notes

- 88th Bob Dylan concert in Canada; 9th Bob Dylan concert in Vancouver.
- 6-8, 12, acoustic with the band
- The triple bill also featured Van Morrison and Joni Mitchell.

Reviews

Historic night like revisiting the past

By Tom Harrison, The Province.

They are storytellers who seem to draw from the same well of inspiration and yet they tell their stories to different rhythms.

Bob Dylan, Joni Mitchell and Van Morrison's historic triple bill last night at GM Place ostensibly placed three of the most influential songwriters of the past 35 years on the same stage, as if underlining their similarities and characterizing them as one sole expression of the culture that made them and they helped to shape.

Instead, the four-hour evening exposed their differences – or at least how they drew from that well of inspiration exactly what they wanted and used it to develop and modify what has since become wells of inspiration to those who've come along since.

Morrison, who began the evening (and who will perform two shows on his own this evening at the QET), hears his muse in the jazz and soul with which he began. With his eight-piece band putting down a fluid rolling rhythm over which the horns effortlessly floated, the dapper looking Irish soulman mined a rich seam that evoked Ben E. King and gave everything away when he climaxed his set with James Brown's stunningly elegant blues ballad, It's a Man's World.

"It's payback time," he announced and, indeed, this four minute tribute showed that the muse is getting back as good as it gives.

Joni Mitchell, by contrast, uses rhythm like an underlay, something that pushes along her narratives, which themselves move along like psychological travelogues.

With a rhythm section that included ex-husband Larry Klein on bass, plus multi-instrumentalist Greg Liesz playing off Mitchell's own liquid guitar tone to create a musical horizon befitting her Saskatchewan upbringing, she told stories that found their own accents and highlights in Mitchell's eye for detail.

She dropped in a new song, the Crazy Cries of Love, transposing W.B. Yeats' the Second Coming as Slouching to Bethlehem and choosing some of her more esoteric songs.

The overall effect was to create her own musical environment entirely her own, rather than to take her place as second in line in providing a cosy evening that hollowly revisited the past.

She did, however, reward the sell out crowd for visiting this world with Big Yellow Taxi.

Who would have expected Silvio, a minor song in Bob Dylan's bulging bag of album toss-offs, to be a highlight of what was a highly charged and focused set of primal rural blues and country that started at the Rage the night before?

Compared to the uptown rhythm and blues of Van Morrison and the blue sky ambience of Joni Mitchell, the swampy gumbo of

Dylan cut raw and deep, the effect ragged but ineffably right on older songs such as Wednesday's highlight, Tangled Up In Blue and the troubled reflections of the newer Cold Irons Bound, Lovesick or Stone Walls and Steel Bars.

In the comparatively intimate setting of the Rage, Dylan was the most invigorated and animated he's been on a Vancouver stage in years.

With a set list that changes from night to night but a band that seems to read him as well as anyone can, the Bob Dylan Vancouver witnessed this week showed that there are years of vital music in him yet.

The Vancouver Province. Fri., May 15, 1998.

Dylan dominates sizzling concert

By Mike Devlin, Times Colonist.

Ironically, Dylan showed all the desire and fight of a battling heavyweight champion on this historical night – the first time since The Band's 1976 farewell show, The Last Waltz, that Joni Mitchell, Van Morrison and Bob Dylan have shared the same stage together.

Die-hard fans of each performer were certainly vocal about their artist of choice throughout the evening, but Dylan was clearly the unanimous winner when it was all said and done.

Van Morrison began the night's festivities at Vancouver's GM Place, taking the stage to a well-received ovation from the crowd. Van The Man proceeded to run through a set of his classics, which ranged from a tight, up-tempo version of Domino to a swinging version of Jackie Wilson Said. His seven-piece band was in fine form, countering Van's stage presence with similar moves of flashy showmanship that brought back memories of vintage James Brown.

Morrison and his crew not only emulated the Godfather of Soul, they payed homage to him by covering his classic ballad, It's a Man's World, all the while awash in an ocean of blue stage lights.

Wearing his trademark black fedora and a sharp tailored suit, Van ruled his backing band with an iron fist – calling for and receiving cues on perfect time with flamboyant hand gestures. Morrison, proving why he is one of the world's most respected musicians, tore the roof off with a 75-minute set of classy Irish soul.

After a short change of equipment, Joni Mitchell glided onto the stage and proceeded to lull the crowd into a dreamlike state. With a coastal horizon backdrop and backup players who seemed to have their feet cemented to the ground, Mitchell and her spare songs tended to get lost in the afterglow of Morrison's performance.

She opened her set with a subdued version of Night Ride Home, setting the tone for her seemingly endless set. Though she did play a triple-shot of songs from her moody 1976 album, Hejira – Coyote, Amelia and the album's title song – it was obvious the crowd was anticipating more accessible songs such as This Flight Tonight and Blue. Unfortunately, they had to wait until her encore to hear anything widely recognizable, a somewhat rushed but nonetheless heartfelt version of Big Yellow Taxi.

Clearly moved by the adoring ovation and a lone red rose tossed at her feet, Mitchell finally broke down with emotion upon completing the first show of her first tour since 1982. Needless to say, it was a set for die-hard fans only.

Mitchell likely suffered from the immense pressure of opening in the shadow of the evening's headliner, Bob Dylan. Though it was billed as an equal-opportunity event, with each performer receiving a 75-minute slot, Dylan was clearly the reason 18,000 fans paid $90 per seat.

The boisterous crowd erupted at the first glimpse of their icon, who strolled out in a makeshift tuxedo with awkward looking white shoes. For the first time in years, Dylan looked to be enjoying himself – both with his expert new band as well as with his devoted fans. Often a smile crossed his lips during this up-tempo performance, just as it did the night before during his surprise gig at the small Vancouver club, The Rage.

Dylan ditched his trademark acoustic guitar for much of the evening, forsaking his folk roots for his electric sound; the plan worked, and Dylan turned in what has to be one of his finest performances in years.

Despite the up-tempo electric feel of the evening, likely brought on by his crackerjack band of young musicians, Dylan did manage to quiet things down with a melancholic acoustic set of tunes that was highlighted by a mandolin-heavy version of Mr. Tambourine Man. After the brief set of acoustic magic, it was back to the rockers: Tangled Up in Blue, Highway 61 Revisited and I Shall Be Released.

Dylan finally left the stage, but not before an encore that included Forever Young, his new single Love Sick and an absolutely rambunctious version of Rainy Day Women #12 & 35.

When the lights came up, they revealed a crowd that was united by one common bond – Bob Dylan, the legend.

The Victoria Times Colonist. Sat., May 16, 1998.

The triple bill of the decade

General Motors Place, Vancouver - May 14, 1998

By Mike Ross, For Jam! Music.

VANCOUVER – Which is more culturally relevant?: The Seinfeld finale or a Bob Dylan concert?

For the 15,000 baby boomers who filled Vancouver's General Motors Place last night, the answer was as obvious as the hair on Kramer's head. Throw in Van Morrison and Joni Mitchell and it was no contest. It was the triple bill of the decade, the first stop of a seven-city tour winding its way down the West coast.

It could've been a case of loving them for who they are rather then what they did, but this trio of rock legends – together for the first time since The Last Waltz more than two decades ago – elivered a stellar show that lasted nearly four hours. Each three 75-minute sets could've stood as a complete concert in its own right – Van the Man with his blue-eyed soul, Joni with her provocative songs you need an English degree to fully appreciate, and Bob rocking out the hits till midnight, warts and all. All three were brilliant.

Jerry who?

Dylan was an especially pleasant surprise last night. He displayed real passion, from the opening country rocker "Absolutely Sweet Marie" to the last encore, the famous "Rainy Day Women #12 & #35", which brought the crowd to its feet shouting "everybody must get stoned"! Given the amount of fragrant blue smoke in the arena, the sentiment went over well.

It was a remarkable transformation.

Dylan had been in an apathetic fog for years, not seeming to care that he'd written some of the most vital songs in pop history – and then he mysteriously bounced back. Maybe it was his near-death experience last year from a heart ailment. Maybe it was the gig playing for the Pope. Or maybe it was winning three Grammy awards. Who knows? Dylan is not one to explain himself.

As he said while introducing "Tangled Up In Blue", "There's a story behind this song, but I'm not going to tell it."
With a solid country-rock-flavored band behind him, the highlights were many: The loose groove of "Cold Irons Bound", a boogie-woogie blast of "Silvio", the swampy back-porch feel of "Cocaine Blues", a strange, folky take on "Mr. Tambourine Man", and many more. The crowd ate it up.

Dylan may be a terrible singer who can't play a guitar solo to save his life, but he proved last night that he's still a powerful performer, a true original and utterly free of pretension. He is, in a word, untouchable.

Making an exceedingly rare live appearance, Joni Mitchell lost some of the crowd with her pensive, self-indulgent set, but for those willing to pay attention, she was mesmerizing. With her beautiful, smoky voice in fine form, Mitchell showcased many of the songs from her upcoming album, Taming the Tiger, along with some obscure material from her past.

She played only one hit, "Big Yellow Taxi", which she performed solo and introduced as if she were doing everybody a huge favor. "I'll just give this one to you", she said. Impersonating Dylan during the third verse was a nice touch.

As for Van Morrison, the man has to be the best white soul shouter in the business. With a tasty set of '50s-style soul that spanned "Astral Weeks" to his latest album, "The Healing Game", he made the Blues Brothers (which he happened to dress like) look lame. He had help, of course, from a killer eight-piece band that grooved like nobody's business.

Overall, it was an exhaustingly glorious trio of shows that will surely go down in history as the best package tour of the '90s. Condolences to those who decided to watch Seinfeld instead.

JAM! RATING: 5 out of 5

Unpredictable icons can still rock when they want to

Three of the most potent musical forces from the 1960s and '70s prove to the delight of baby boomers that they haven't lost their touch.

By Chris Dafoe, Western Arts Correspondent, Vancouver.

WHEN it was first announced that Bob Dylan, Joni Mitchell and Van Morrison would be playing a series of dates together, the response was predictable. This was to be a baby boomer's wet dream, a trifecta in the nostalgia sweepstakes.

Just as predictably, it didn't turn out that way when the trio took the stage Thursday at GM Place to launch the tour. While Dylan, Mitchell and Morrison may be icons of the 1960s – or in Mitchell's case, the early 1970s – they have all continued to grow and change. They've also all made albums recently that stand up with the best of their back catalogue. On top of that, they're three of the most contrary-minded and unpredictable artists in popular music.

That contrariness was very apparent in Mitchell's set, which took the middle slot on Thursday's triple bill. Dressed in a blue jacket and yellow skirt and looking as willowy as a teenager, Mitchell opened her set with the cool flow of *Night Ride Home*, the title track from her 1991 album. From there on, however, Mitchell seemed to take her lead from the title of D. A. Pennebaker's famous film about Dylan, *Don't Look Back.*

Rather than revisit such hits as *Carey, Help Me* or *Free Man in Paris*, Mitchell went full-on fusion, plucking out silvery, liquid chords on an electric guitar as her drummer played jazzy fills and bass player (ex-husband Larry Klein) laid down elliptical lines. While she tossed in a couple of tracks from her last album, 1994's *Turbulent Indigo*, including *Sex Kills* and *The Magdalene Laundries*, and offered an intriguing adaptation of W. B. Yeats's *The Second Coming*, most of the songs seemed to be drawn from an as-yet-unreleased album.

There were a few standouts among the new tunes, including *Happiness is the Best Facelift*, a wry response to Mitchell's mother's objections to shacking up with fellow Canadian songwriter Don Freed. For the most part, however, they seemed shapeless and vague. The sellout crowd remained polite, rising to their feet to applaud after every song, but one had the feeling that they did so not out of appreciation of the song that preceded, but in hopes that, if they clapped loud enough, the one that followed would be something they recognized. Mitchell finally delivered on her second encore, knocking off a solo version of *Big Yellow Taxi*, and she was rewarded with hoots and cheers.

The sheer perversity of Mitchell's set was almost worth the price of admission (well, maybe not the top ticket price was nearly $90), but Dylan and Morrison showed that you can visit your back pages without shame, artistic compromise or accusations of pandering.

Dylan reprised some of the more popular selections from his Wednesday-night club date: rocking out with *Silvio* and a stomping version of *Highway 61 Revisited*, digging into the deep blues of *Cold Steel Bound* and *Love Sick*, and doing a delicate and intricate country dance with *Tangled Up in Blue*. But on Thursday, he delved even further into the past, offering up *Mr. Tambourine Man*, *I Shall Be Released* and a moving version of *Forever Young* before turning on the house lights and leading the crowd in a giddy version of *Rainy Day Women #12 and 35*.

Dylan's four-piece band, lead by guitarist Larry Campbell, may not be most stellar outfit to work with him, but it does seem to bring out the best in him. Dressed in a black suit with white shoes – white shoes! – he struck knock-kneed rock 'n' roll poses as he traded off solos with Campbell.

Morrison, who opened the evening, kicked off his set with a track from last year's magnificent *The Healing Game* and followed up with the best performance of the evening. With a homburg perched on his head and his eyes hidden behind shades, he looked like an enforcer for the Irish mafia, but he sang like a force of nature as he rolled out the hits – *Domino*, *Jackie Wilson Says*, *Tupelo Honey*, *Crazy Love* – and invoked classic R&B songs – *Flip, Flop and Fly*, *Shake, Rattle and Roll* – as if they were the names of saints.

While the songs may have been from the past, Morrison's performance was always in the moment, always unpredictable. His nine-piece band, which included keyboardist Georgie Fame and backup singer Brian Kennedy, matched him at every step. He closed with a cover of James Brown's *It's a Man's Man's Man's World*, roaring through it once, then turning the song over to Kennedy, who threw a gender curve ball by singing it again in a sweet falsetto, before Morrison returned to close it out with the insistent refrain, "It's too late to stop now!"

That phrase may be a Morrison trademark, but on Thursday it felt like it applied to all three acts. They will, no doubt, be amply rewarded for this two-week jaunt down the coast, but unlike some acts of similar vintage, they sound like they play because they have to, because it is what they do.

The Globe and Mail. Sat., May 16, 1998. Reprinted with permission from The Globe and Mail.

BOB DYLAN, JONI MITCHELL, VAN MORRISON

Concert Review

By Tony Montague.

When three artists whose music and poetry has altered the shape of popular culture over the past several decades appear together on the same bill, clapped-out epithets like legendary and historic insinuate their way back to mind. But legends are not truthful, history can distort (and, more to the point, so can the acoustics at BC Place). On the last occasions when I'd heard Bob Dylan, Joni Mitchell, and Van Morrison they had all sounded great – would they prove disappointing playing a hockey arena in cocooned middle-age? Having been lured back 8,000 miles that very day for the gig, it was with some apprehension that I joined the throng eddying in and around the stadium.

First up was Van Morrison, starting bang-on time and sending thousands of 40 and 50-somethings scurrying for their places and their specs, like a disturbed ant-nest in reverse. From his initial number "Burning Ground" it was clear that Morrison has lost nothing of his vocal power and unique mastery of phrasing. The diminutive figure with the black fedora and dark glasses was also in complete control of his eight-piece band – which included a punchy brass-section of trumpet and saxophone – as he pumped his right arm up and down to keep measure and orchestrate the changes. Morrison meant business, but mixed it with serious pleasure. Backed-up on vocals by the impressive and youthful Brian Kennedy, he sang for well over an hour with scarcely a moment's pause.

Van the Man ranged over his repertoire of old and new songs, really rousing the crowd with kick-ass versions of "Domino" and "Jackie Wilson Said". By the time he launched the band into the more sultry grooves of "Tupelo Honey", Morrison's voice was soaring and swooping with delight, and he segued with seamless ease into "Crazy Love". The arrangements were very tight, yet left room for some tantalizingly brief, superb solos by saxophonist Pee Wee Ellis. (Next evening, in the first of two concerts at the Queen Elizabeth Theatre, every band-member got the chance to solo on an extended version of "Moondance"). Morrison finished with a funky tribute to James Brown "It's a Man's World". As an encore he sang "Cypress Avenue", parodying himself playfully as his "t-t-t-t-tongue" got completely "t-t-t-tied" up once again, and ending ironically with his familiar cry "It's too late to stop now!"

Joni Mitchell was also in fine voice for her first Vancouver concert in almost 20 years. Accompanied by an excellent trio of musicians (with former spouse Larry Klein on bass) she was determined to show that she is still very much a current artist – playing electric guitar only, and presenting material that was almost exclusively recent and relatively unfamiliar. Mitchell even courageously performed one unrecorded new song "The Crazy Price of Love" and an evocatively jazzy setting of W.B. Yeats' dark poem "The Second Coming", which she entitled "Slouching Towards Bethlehem". But it was difficult to engage properly with her finely-wrought, intimate lyrics and her melodic and chordal subtleties in the cavernous setting, and there was a steady stream away to the concession stands. Many fans were clearly disappointed that Mitchell failed to deliver her hits of yesteryear, and when for her last number she conceded by singing "Big Yellow Taxi" solo the stadium erupted in belatedly happy recognition.

Bob Dylan didn't make that mistake. From the opening chords of "Absolutely Sweet Marie" it was apparent he was intent on revisiting and revitalizing his back pages. Though he remained deadpan throughout the 90 minute set Dylan – dressed in white boots and black suit and still sporting an unruly shock of hair – was obviously enjoying himself as he shimmied and shuffled niftily across the stage, belying his years. Indeed the energy between Dylan and his four-piece band, which featured both lead and pedal-steel guitars, was palpable and often thrilling. A brooding "Señor, Señor " preceded a rocking "Cold Irons Bound" from his latest album Time out of Mind, "You're a Big Girl Now", and the more obscure "Sylvio" – before Dylan swopped electric for acoustic axe to perform a bouncy version of the traditional and subversive "Cocaine".

Though his voice sounded somewhat raw and limited in range at times, there was still great feeling behind Dylan's delivery of "Mr Tambourine Man" (reduced to three verses) and a magnificent "Tangled up in Blue". Then it was back to full-tilt electric swamp-boogie for "Stuck inside of Mobile with the Memphis Blues Again" and "Highway 61 Revisited". Dylan bowed out with a poignant rendition of "Forever Young" only to return for two encores – the sombre new "Lovesick" and, by contrast, a joyful and rollicking version of "Rainy Day Women # 12 & 35 that had the entire stadium howling out the lines "everybody must get stoned". It was the climax of the longest day I can recall and I'd received an emphatic answer to my earlier question – or, more precisely, I'd been given an order. We'll all be high for weeks.

As appeared in The Georgia Straight. Thurs., May 21, 1998. Reprinted with permission of Tony Montague.

Additional Review

Growing old with Joni, Van and Bob, by John MacLachlan Gray. The Vancouver Sun. Sat., May 23, 1998. p. I5.

Thursday, October 15, 1998 --- Canadian Airlines Saddledome Calgary, AB

Set List

	Song	From The Album	Released
1.	Leopard-Skin Pill-Box Hat	Blonde on Blonde	May 16, 1966
2.	I'll Remember You	Empire Burlesque	May 30, 1985
3.	Cold Irons Bound	Time Out of Mind	Sept. 30, 1997
4.	Just Like a Woman	Blonde on Blonde	May 16, 1966
5.	Can't Wait	Time Out of Mind	Sept. 30, 1997
6.	Silvio (Bob Dylan/Robert Hunter)	Down in the Groove	May 19, 1988
7.	Mr. Tambourine Man	Bringing It All Back Home	March 22, 1965
8	Masters of War	The Freewheelin' Bob Dylan	May 27, 1963
9.	One Too Many Mornings	The Times They Are A-Changin'	Feb. 10, 1964
10.	Tangled Up in Blue	Blood on the Tracks	Jan. 20, 1975
11.	Make You Feel My Love	Time Out of Mind	Sept. 30, 1997
12.	Til I Fell In Love With You	Time Out of Mind	Sept. 30, 1997
	Encores		
13.	Love Sick	Time Out of Mind	Sept. 30, 1997
14.	Rainy Day Women #12 & 35	Blonde on Blonde	May 16, 1966
15.	Blowin' in the Wind	The Freewheelin' Bob Dylan	May 27, 1963
16.	Highway 61 Revisited	Highway 61 Revisited	Aug. 30, 1965
17.	Forever Young	Planet Waves	Jan. 17, 1974

The Musicians

Bob Dylan (vocal, guitar & harmonica), Bucky Baxter (dobro, mandolin, pedal steel guitar, electric slide guitar & backup vocals), Larry Campbell (guitar & backup vocals), Tony Garnier (bass), David Kemper (drums & percussion).

Notes

- 89th Bob Dylan concert in Canada; 4th Bob Dylan concert in Calgary.
- 4, Bob Dylan (harmonica).
- 7-9, 14-15, acoustic with the band.
- Canadian live debut of song 5.
- The opening act was Jann Arden.

Reviews

Dylan show all any man can give

By James Muretich, Calgary Herald.

How many roads must Bob Dylan walk down before his fans realize he's just a man?

A talented man, a man whose music has given poetic voice to so many of life's puzzles and passions, but nonetheless a man despite his seemingly eternal status as spokesman for this or legend of that.

Here was a man performing at the Saddledome Thursday night, a man whose songs have echoed throughout the world from the early '60s to today, and yet there was a smallish crowd of about 6,500 on hand for his musical voice and vision.

And you couldn't help but get the feeling from the decidedly baby-boomer audience, that they wanted Bob the legend more than the flesh and blood Dylan in front of them, that somehow he just couldn't live up to their expectations, couldn't blow them all away in the wind.

Which is why Dylan was greeted with generous applause when he played the harmonica during his Sixties' classic Just Like a Woman, while his newer songs were enjoyed but not with the same enthusiasm as the soundtrack he's provided for people's lives.

Still, none of that mattered to Dylan. He's always gone his own way and, no matter how his personal times have forever been a-changin', he's remained true to himself.

The Dylan at the 'Dome Thursday was not the slurrin', guess what song-he's-playin' Bob who last graced Calgary nearly a decade ago, but rather a Dylan backed by a four piece band that kept things rock simple yet expressive (like it's use of mandolin during Mr. Tambourine Man).

Attired in simple black slacks, jacket, tie and a white shirt, the smell of incense wafting through the arena, he reworked his repertoire as always (such as his souped-up version of Leopard Skin Pill-Box Hat) but kept far more to the original style of the songs (be it epic tracks like Masters of War and Tangled Up in Blue or lesser-known, equally deserving, songs from last year's gem Time Out of Mind).

With a blues and folk-rock backbone to his show, alternately electric and acoustic, it was the sound of Dylan returning to his roots, playing spirited versions of his songs and proving that he remains a man who can still touch one to the core with his amazing honesty, imagery and moving music.

He cannot walk on water, he cannot provide the concert of your life (though Thursday night's was damn close), but Bob Dylan can – and does – write and perform songs that fans will take to their grave, and beyond.

Meanwhile, the ubiquitous opening act of Calgary's Jann Arden began the evening with her usual balance of emotionally articulate songs, expertly played by her always tight 'n' tasty band, and between-song humour — such as her promise not to play Calgary again for five years since she's becoming too much of a regular at these shows, having also opened for Eric Clapton recently at the 'Dome.

(There is no concert photo from Thursday's show accompanying this review since Dylan would not allow photographers into the Saddledome).

Attendance: about 6,500.

The Calgary Herald. Fri., Oct. 16, 1998.
Material reprinted with the express permission of: "Calgary Herald Group Inc.", a CanWest Partnership.

Not A Legend For Nothing

Dylan rolls out the old magic

By David Veitch, Calgary Sun.

Unless I'm mistaken, I'd say ol' Bob Dylan had himself a good time last night at the Saddledome.

And that's really saying something.

After all, Dylan invested little joy in his last two Calgary concerts in 1988 and 1990.

And his last studio album, the bleak and bitter Time Out of Mind, sounded like the work of a man who's fixin' to die.

Yet I could detect a reasonably wide grin cross his face as he watched 7,000 fans dance during Tangled Up In Blue.

He even briefly attempted a Chuck Berry-style duckwalk while soloing during a shuffling version of Highway 61 Revisited.

The 30-plus-minute encore ultimately confirmed my suspicions.

Dylan's excellent four-piece band seemed ready to retire for the night on several occasions, but Dylan would round them up, probably say something like, 'Let's do one more song, boys,' and they'd rip into another tune. And another. And another after that.

As you can tell, it was a great show.

The concert got off to a playful start with Leopard-Skin Pill-box Hat, one of many Blonde on Blonde beauties on the night's set list.

Best of all, the song sounded like you remember it.

This time around, Dylan did not deconstruct his most beloved songs, as he was prone to do during the 1980s and early '90s.

And, throughout the show, he sang forcefully and he enunciated clearly – at least by Dylan's standards – rather than wheezing and mumbling the words.

A lot of the credit also rests with his versatile band.

If you closed your eyes during the beautiful instrumental intro to Just Like a Woman, you could imagine it was Mike Bloomfield or Robbie Robertson unreeling that tasteful guitar solo and Al Kooper or Richard Manuel supplying those warm organ textures.

It was the sound of classic Dylan.

There was some phenomenal guitar and mandolin interplay during a scintillating, bluesy take on one of Dylan's old protest songs, Masters of War, while Spanish-style guitar gave a fresh feel to another old protest song, Blowin' in the Wind,

Yet the band could also re-create that rickety, rattling, swamp-blues vibe of Cold Irons Bound, one of many Time out of Mind songs Dylan would play. The ballad Make You Feel My Love, recently turned into a hit by Garth Brooks, also made the cut, as did the bluesy, embittered Lovesick.

The set list was a master stroke, offering up old and new, familiar and obscure.

Near the end of the show, the house lights came up and Dylan and his band launched into Rainy Day Women #12 & 35. Much of the audience leapt to their feet, danced in a crazy, woozy way and shouted "everybody must get stoned," in unison. And in genuine glee.

If Dylan was indeed having fun onstage, then that sense of enjoyment was definitely contagious.

Jann Arden may stand no more than 5-ft.-4 – on her tippy toes – but she is in no way dwarfed in the presence of giants. The local singer-songwriter earned a standing ovation opening for Eric Clapton last month, and her opening set last night was just as seductive and alluring.

"I try to play the Saddledome every month," she quipped dryly after her opening number, Could I Be Your Girl.

What followed was classic Jann: Songs about friendship and family, romantic longing and personal independence, gussied up in shimmering arrangements and delivered with a supple, heart-rending voice.

Friday, October 16, 1998 --- Edmonton Coliseum
Edmonton, AB

Set List

	Song	From The Album	Released
1.	Gotta Serve Somebody	Slow Train Coming	Aug. 20, 1979
2.	I'll Remember You	Empire Burlesque	May 30, 1985
3.	Cold Irons Bound	Time Out of Mind	Sept. 30, 1997
4.	Just Like a Woman	Blonde on Blonde	May 16, 1966
5.	Can't Wait	Time Out of Mind	Sept. 30, 1997
6.	Silvio (Bob Dylan/Robert Hunter)	Down in the Groove	May 19, 1988
7.	It Ain't Me, Babe	Another Side of Bob Dylan	Aug. 8, 1964
8.	Masters of War	The Freewheelin' Bob Dylan	May 27, 1963
9.	Mama, You Been on My Mind	The Bootleg Series Volumes 1-3	March 26, 1991
10.	Tangled Up in Blue	Blood on the Tracks	Jan. 20, 1975
11.	Make You Feel My Love	Time Out of Mind	Sept. 30, 1997
12.	Til I Fell In Love With You	Time Out of Mind	Sept. 30, 1997
	Encores		
13.	Love Sick	Time Out of Mind	Sept. 30, 1997
14.	Rainy Day Women #12 & 35	Blonde on Blonde	May 16, 1966
15.	Blowin' in the Wind	The Freewheelin' Bob Dylan	May 27, 1963
16.	Highway 61 Revisited	Highway 61 Revisited	Aug. 30, 1965
17.	Forever Young	Planet Waves	Jan. 17, 1974

The Musicians

Bob Dylan (vocal, guitar & harmonica), Bucky Baxter (dobro, mandolin, pedal steel guitar, electric slide guitar & backup vocals), Larry Campbell (guitar & backup vocals), Tony Garnier (bass), David Kemper (drums & percussion).

Notes

- 90th Bob Dylan concert in Canada; 4th Bob Dylan concert in Edmonton.
- 7-10, 15, 17, acoustic with the band.
- 9, Bob Dylan (harmonica).
- The opening act was Jann Arden.

Reviews

Wow, Bob, Wow!

Music Legend Turns It Up For Skyreach Centre Crowd

By Mike Ross, Edmonton Sun.

It was a case of substance over style.

He was sloppy, his nasal bray can be compared to that of a donkey, he plays guitar solos like he never learned how to play guitar and he hardly says anything – but Bob Dylan was still the greatest concert of the decade.

At least that was what 7,500 fans in Skyreach Centre obviously thought last night – and they weren't too far off the mark. Dylan gave a revitalized, raw-boned performance of timeless songs that transcend style or context. Destined to be remembered long after we're dead, his music was rendered with a focus on interpretation, emotion and originality rather than mere entertainment. You wanted flash and hit after hit after hit? Try Reba McEntire.

To many, it scarcely mattered how "good" Dylan was. Local songwriter Mike McDonald – who's such a rabid fan that he once drove all the way to Minnesota to hear Dylan play – said he holds the Poet in such high esteem it was an honour even being in the same room with him. Besides, given all the flack Dylan's taken from his fans over everything from going rock to finding God, he's entitled to put on a weak show now and then. So consider last night's solid concert a bonus.

Backed by a four-piece band that blurred the line between rock and country, Dylan opened with You've Got To Serve Somebody. (His black-suited "cosmic country gentleman" look went well with the vibe.) Couched in a messy wall of electric guitars, I Remember You, Cold Irons Bound and the classic Just Like a Woman followed. The crowd was hooked. They cheered Dylan's every move – a precious few notes on a harmonica, powerful and distinctive vocals, his rudimentary but spirited three-note solos. Obviously into it, Dylan even pulled a little Chuck Berry move every now and then. The crowd went wild.

Ironically (considering the famous folk-rock schism that occurred the '60s), the concert really became magical when the acoustic guitars and upright bass were brought out. Dylan mangled It Ain't Me, Babe into a country two-step, traded some surprisingly technical licks with his guitarist and ended the "unplugged" portion of the evening with a fiery rendition of Tangled Up in Blue – once again so twisted it was hard to even tell what it was. "Name that tune before he gets to the chorus" seemed to be a popular game.

But like I said, style wasn't really a factor. Dylan made his entrance to a basic introduction, did his thing with a complete lack of pretension or contrivance and politely thanked the crowd for coming. That was it. Ending with a loud and dirty blues number, Dylan grabbed a thrown bouquet of flowers from the throng that had rushed the front of the stage and left them screaming for the encore.

Sure, he could attract larger crowds if he spent a bit more on production, took some guitar lessons, maybe did a few TV talk shows to pump up the hype. Of course, that would ruin the magic of a true original. The faithful attending their hero last night would surely take great pains to prevent that.

Opening act Jann Arden has taken some grief over playing this market too much lately. But what's she going to do – say no to Dylan? While the promised "Soy Bomb" gag didn't materialize, Arden and band gave yet another wonderful show, rich in beautiful melancholy and deadpan humour. I for one could stand to hear her perform every two months, no problem.

Tangled up in Dylan's magic

It was Heaven's Door for fans

By Peter North.

Master songwriter Bob Dylan was true to his opening words last night as he and his sensational four-piece band lit into the snarly and very direct Gotta Serve Somebody from his 20-year-old Slow Train Comin' album.

He commenced to serve up a wired house of hard-core fans a great show – and one that will long be remembered in this city.

Gone are the memories of visits he made here in the late '80s and early '90s.

If he was born again when he cut Slow Train he must be "born again once more" judging by the way he stoked a roaring fire under many of his classic tunes and a handful of new ones including a couple from the Grammy-winning Time Out of Mind.

The man may not be a great singer but he sure has a great voice and it's one – when he's into it as he was last night -- that delivers his thoughts, emotions, and short stories with clarity and power.

Kicking off the show in an electric format, Dylan and his crew added character to each tune on an instrumental level that probably hasn't been achieved in a live setting since his days with The Band.

Off the top Dylan sang I Remember You and Just Like A Woman with no shortage of intensity as his ace sidemen continually dug into the heart of the songs.

The sound was never slick, but the grooves were always in the pocket. That allowed Dylan and guitarist Larry Campbell to peel off some reasonably lengthy solos while weaving some harmony lines onto each other's leads.

The first electric portion was highlighted by a rollicking take of Silvio from 1988's Down In The Groove.

The song, which he wrote with Grateful Dead lyricist Robert Hunter, was built on another unshakable rhythm pattern that the quintet tore into like a prize fighter hammers away on a staggering opponent.

Each song found Dylan's enunciation becoming a tad clearer, and it wasn't bad to begin with.

Drummer David Kemper, who was a member of Jerry Garcia's Almost Acoustic Band, picked up a pair of brushes, Bucky Baxter moved from steel to mandolin and the electric guitars were traded for acoustics.

All of a sudden the timbre of the evening changed dramatically.

Shelter From The Storm and It Ain't Me Babe were served up as country shuffles.

Shortly afterward, Dylan's rant at the world's hate-mongers came in the form of a very effective and instrumentally brittle Masters of War.

Not a word was lost in the mix as he sang it like he had just written it a couple of hours prior to the show.

Between tunes we may not have gotten much more than "Thank you very much ladies and gentlemen."

During the action though, the man let go of a grin here and there, lightly shuffled his feet across the stage in time to the tunes, and kicked up a leg now and then as he burrowed into a guitar solo holding his axe like he was pitching hay.

The audience threw thunderous applause back at him as his distinctive harmonica sound announced the opening chords of Tangled Up In Blue from his classic Blood On The Tracks album.

Then it was back to an electric format. The overall sound was akin to The Dead meets electric Lightnin' Hopkins meets Jimmy Rodgers in a Delta juke joint.

These guys were on the same page at all times, throwing dashes of instrumental colour onto melodies engrained in our minds.

His encore started with the aching Love Sick from his latest album but it was the intro to Rainy Day Women 12 and 35 that had the hall vibrating and, as this scribe had to leave, it was pretty clear that Bob Dylan is very much alive and well and inspired.

As appeared in The Edmonton Journal. Sat., Oct. 17, 1998. Reprinted with permission of Peter North.

Sunday, October 18, 1998 --- Saskatchewan Place Saskatoon, SK

Set List

	Song	From The Album	Released
1.	Gotta Serve Somebody	Slow Train Coming	Aug. 20, 1979
2.	I'll Remember You	Empire Burlesque	May 30, 1985
3.	Cold Irons Bound	Time Out of Mind	Sept. 30, 1997
4.	Just Like a Woman	Blonde on Blonde	May 16, 1966
5.	It Takes a Lot to Laugh, It Takes a Train to Cry	Highway 61 Revisited	Aug. 30, 1965
6.	Silvio (Bob Dylan/Robert Hunter)	Down in the Groove	May 19, 1988
7.	The Times They Are A-Changin'	The Times They Are A-Changin'	Feb. 10, 1964
8.	Masters of War	The Freewheelin' Bob Dylan	May 27, 1963
9.	Don't Think Twice, It's All Right	The Freewheelin' Bob Dylan	May 27, 1963
10.	Tangled Up in Blue	Blood on the Tracks	Jan. 20, 1975
11.	Ballad of a Thin Man	Highway 61 Revisited	Aug. 30, 1965
12.	Highway 61 Revisited	Highway 61 Revisited	Aug. 30, 1965
	Encores		
13.	Love Sick	Time Out of Mind	Sept. 30, 1997
14.	Rainy Day Women #12 & 35	Blonde on Blonde	May 16, 1966
15.	Blowin' in the Wind	The Freewheelin' Bob Dylan	May 27, 1963
16.	Til I Fell In Love With You	Time Out of Mind	Sept. 30, 1997
17.	Forever Young	Planet Waves	Jan. 17, 1974

The Musicians

Bob Dylan (vocal, guitar & harmonica), Bucky Baxter (dobro, mandolin, pedal steel guitar, electric slide guitar & backup vocals), Larry Campbell (guitar & backup vocals), Tony Garnier (bass), David Kemper (drums & percussion).

Notes

- 91st Bob Dylan concert in Canada; Debut Bob Dylan concert in Saskatoon.
- 4, 7, Bob Dylan (harmonica).
- 7-10, 15, 17, acoustic with the band.
- The opening act was Jann Arden.

Review

Times may be a'changin' but Dylan's music stands

By Cam Fuller, of The StarPhoenix.

It was history that did the talking Sunday night at SaskPlace as a totally cool, almost aloof Bob Dylan rocked, strummed and proved, for those who needed reminding, that there's no one like him.

The stage was free of clutter, the four-person back-up band nattily attired and the man himself black-clad and pointy of shoe.

He didn't talk. He almost never moved. His expression almost never changed. But the key word is almost.

By not doing much, Dylan made every eyebrow raise, every knee bend seem to have some significance.

It was the definitive old bull at work, and it was great to see.

Dylan's raspy nasal shout took a bow in I'll Remember You, the second of about 17 songs in the fast-moving, 90-minute set. It started loud and heavily electric.

Dylan demolished and rebuilt Just Like a Woman, omitting the melody in the reconstruction, unfortunately. You couldn't tell what it was until the song title popped up in the lyrics.

Sadly, the anything-goes sound on stage was contradicted by the thought police in the audience, doing Dylan's bidding and eradicating people with purloined cameras. (Some women even had their purses checked at the door to keep the world safe from photography.)

Gosh, you'd think one harmless guy was smoking contraband the way he was rousted for possession of an Instamatic.

The wonderful, great big guitar groove of Silvio made it seem impossible that Dylan ever held an acoustic guitar.

Then, almost ironic in the timing, he and the band switched to a full-bore acoustic segment starting with The Times They Are A-Changin.' (More irony popped up with the lyric "come mothers and fathers throughout the land, don't criticize what you don't understand." An erstwhile cry of rebellion changes to a kind of admonishment when you're the one who has kids.)

Tangled up in Blue was another great strummer, outdone only by a fine, mandolin-flavoured, almost bluegrassy version of Don't Think Twice.

Not quite country, not quite blues, not quite rock, Dylan is a master of brushing by influences and picking the best parts of them up without owing any one genre too big a debt.

Jann Arden had a great warm-up set, impressing as she always does with her seductive voice and warm sense of humour.

"Because of my pathetic personal life, I'm a very wealthy woman," she joked before singing one of those cheque-writers, Insensitive.

Could I Be Your Girl?, Holy Moses, The Sound Of, Saved, Ode to A Friend and Living Under June were all perfectly played by Arden and her five-piece.

Having an actual star as the opener, and having her do a legitimate multi-song set was a real bonus.

The Saskatoon StarPhoenix. Mon., Oct. 19, 1998.

Tuesday, October 20, 1998 --- The Agridome
Regina, SK

Set List

	Song	From The Album	Released
1.	Gotta Serve Somebody	Slow Train Coming	Aug. 20, 1979
2.	I'll Remember You	Empire Burlesque	May 30, 1985
3.	Cold Irons Bound	Time Out of Mind	Sept. 30, 1997
4.	Just Like a Woman	Blonde on Blonde	May 16, 1966
5.	Can't Wait	Time Out of Mind	Sept. 30, 1997
6.	Silvio (Bob Dylan/Robert Hunter)	Down in the Groove	May 19, 1988
7.	Mr. Tambourine Man	Bringing It All Back Home	March 22, 1965
8.	Masters of War	The Freewheelin' Bob Dylan	May 27, 1963
9.	Tangled Up in Blue	Blood on the Tracks	Jan. 20, 1975
10.	My Back Pages	Another Side of Bob Dylan	Aug. 8, 1964
11.	She Belongs to Me	Bringing It All Back Home	March 22, 1965
12.	Til I Fell In Love With You	Time Out of Mind	Sept. 30, 1997
	Encores		
13.	Love Sick	Time Out of Mind	Sept. 30, 1997
14.	Rainy Day Women #12 & 35	Blonde on Blonde	May 16, 1966
15.	Blowin' in the Wind	The Freewheelin' Bob Dylan	May 27, 1963
16.	Highway 61 Revisited	Highway 61 Revisited	Aug. 30, 1965
17.	Forever Young	Planet Waves	Jan. 17, 1974

The Musicians

Bob Dylan (vocal, guitar & harmonica), Bucky Baxter (dobro, mandolin, pedal steel guitar, electric slide guitar & backup vocals), Larry Campbell (guitar & backup vocals), Tony Garnier (bass), David Kemper (drums & percussion).

Notes

- 92nd Bob Dylan concert in Canada; Debut Bob Dylan concert in Regina.
- 4, 10, Bob Dylan (harmonica).
- 7-10, 15, 17, acoustic with the band.
- The opening act was Jann Arden.

Review

Dylan show one for the ages

By Nick Miliokas, L-P Entertainment Writer.

Years from now, people who were nowhere near the Agridome last night will be telling friends and family they were there the night Bob Dylan played Regina.

Who could blame them?

This was one for the ages, undoubtedly the biggest concert event ever held in this city, and it will be talked about for a long time to come, by more than just the (estimated) 5,000 or so spectators who cared to take advantage of what truly was a once-in-a-lifetime opportunity.

It was an opportunity to see and hear a pop music icon, a singer-songwriter who does in fact deserve to be called a legend, having influenced not only fellow musicians but the course of music history itself.

A crowd spanning several generations had gathered in anticipation, and they rose to their feet in unison, with chants of "Bobby! Bobby! Bobby!"

He walked briskly onto the stage, ushered in by strobelights, and welcomed by a public-address announcer who delivered a deadpan and decidedly understated greeting, introducing a man of myth as simply "Columbia recording artist Bob Dylan."

The mood was electrifying, and Dylan and his four-piece band – Larry Campbell, Tony Garnier, Bucky Baxter, and David Kemper – were electrified.

They moved back and forth, smoothly and effortlessly, from electric to acoustic, and whether they were plugged-in or unplugged, their delivery was polished, their sound vibrant with energy.

It would have been impossible, of course, for Dylan to satisfy every last one of his fans in terms of honouring requests for favourite songs, but he did play a surprising number of classics, from a lively and electric "Gotta Serve Somebody" which opened the show to a laid-back and acoustic "Forever Young" which closed it, 17 songs later.

In between, Dylan presented a succession of tunes with evocative lyrics and powerful instrumentation as if to remind his listeners that he is a fine player as well as an inspired writer.

Dylan was dynamite from start to finish, hitting high points with "Just Like A Woman," "Mr. Tambourine Man," and "Blowin' In The Wind."

He played soulful acoustic guitar and screaming electric guitar, and when he picked up that harmonica, it was Dylan at his purest.

He seemed to be enjoying himself, and it was contagious. Dylan certainly hasn't lost anything over the years. He has retained his stage prescence, his charisma, and his ability to control the emotions of his audience.

Whether he was playing selections from his latest album, *Time Out Of Mind*, or instantly recognizable hits from years gone by, Dylan was at his spine-tingling best, putting on a show that was sincere, emotional, nostalgic.

The stage for Dylan was set by Canadian superstar Jann Arden, who played a short set of eight songs, the majority of them from her current release *Happy*?.

Arden's performance also included her characteristic between-songs banter.

She has a lively sense of humour, and on this night gave several indications that she was thrilled to be sharing a stage with a hall-of-famer.

Chastising late-comers, with a tongue-in-cheek put-down, Arden said: "I'll be an opening act for Dylan, but that's it!"

Later on, she took her leave with the words: "You guys are in for probably the night of your lives."

Arden wasn't kidding.

It was one for the age.

I hope you kept your stub.

The Regina Leader-Post. Wed., Oct. 21, 1998.

Wednesday, October 21, 1998 --- Winnipeg Arena
Winnipeg, MB

Set List

	Song	From The Album	Released
1.	Gotta Serve Somebody	Slow Train Coming	Aug. 20, 1979
2.	I'll Remember You	Empire Burlesque	May 30, 1985
3.	Cold Irons Bound	Time Out of Mind	Sept. 30, 1997
4.	Just Like a Woman	Blonde on Blonde	May 16, 1966
5.	It Takes a Lot to Laugh, It Takes a Train to Cry	Highway 61 Revisited	Aug. 30, 1965
6.	Silvio (Bob Dylan/Robert Hunter)	Down in the Groove	May 19, 1988
7.	It Ain't Me, Babe	Another Side of Bob Dylan	Aug. 8, 1964
8.	Masters of War	The Freewheelin' Bob Dylan	May 27, 1963
9.	Tangled Up in Blue	Blood on the Tracks	Jan. 20, 1975
10.	The Lonesome Death of Hattie Carroll	The Times They Are A-Changin'	Feb. 10, 1964
11.	Make You Feel My Love	Time Out of Mind	Sept. 30, 1997
12.	Til I Fell In Love With You	Time Out of Mind	Sept. 30, 1997
	Encores		
13.	Love Sick	Time Out of Mind	Sept. 30, 1997
14.	Rainy Day Women #12 & 35	Blonde on Blonde	May 16, 1966
15.	Blowin' in the Wind	The Freewheelin' Bob Dylan	May 27, 1963
16.	Highway 61 Revisited	Highway 61 Revisited	Aug. 30, 1965
17.	Forever Young	Planet Waves	Jan. 17, 1974

The Musicians

Bob Dylan (vocal, guitar & harmonica), Bucky Baxter (dobro, mandolin, pedal steel guitar, electric slide guitar & backup vocals), Larry Campbell (guitar & backup vocals), Tony Garnier (bass), David Kemper (drums & percussion).

Notes

- 93rd Bob Dylan concert in Canada; 4th Bob Dylan concert in Winnipeg.
- 4, 9, Bob Dylan (harmonica).
- 7-10, 15, 17, acoustic with the band.
- The opening act was Jann Arden.

Review

Bob Dylan

Folk-Rock legend delivers a spare, but satisfying set for 4,600 fans at Winnipeg Arena

By Bartley Kives, Music Reporter.

SIX HUNDRED and sixty two thousand, five hundred and a wee bit more.

That's how many Winnipeggers failed to take advantage of the opportunity to see one of music's greatest living legends in his best form in decades, assuming everyone attended last night's Bob Dylan concert at Winnipeg Arena lives within the city limits.

Dylan, the 57-year-old folk-rock icon who's inarguably the most important active pop musician on the planet, delivered a spare, utilitarian but ultimately satisfying set to only 4,600 fans.

Grizzly-looking

It started off as a big, noisy rock show. After the customary understated introduction – "Ladies and Gentlemen, please welcome Columbia recording artist Bob Dylan" – the grizzly looking, fuzzy-haired singer/guitarist and His Sensational Four-Piece Band kicked into Gotta Serve Somebody.

Dressed in a grey, vintage-looking two-piece suit, a puffy black bow tie and pointy black shoes, Dylan struck a bent-knee stance during the crescendo of the scathing Carter-Reagan transition-era number.

The backing band (bass, drums, guitar and a steel guitarist/mandolinist) confined themselves to the centre of a spare, simply lit stage that seemed larger than usual, thanks to the absence of silly props and other rock 'n' roll gadgetry. The only adornment: a tray of plastic-wrapped cigars sitting on a guitar amplifier directly behind Dylan.

For the first six songs, Dylan brought up the volume steadily. I'll Remember You gave way to the stomping Cold Irons Bound, from 1997's Grammy-winning Time Out Of Mind CD, before he launched into his first harmonica solo, a 90-second run at the beginning of Just Like A Woman.

By the time Silvio rolled around, the band was truly rocking, the guitars clashing in a wonderful cacophony that would make Crazy Horse proud.

Then, on cue, it was time for a string of acoustic numbers, beginning with the mandolin-guitar interplay of It Ain't Me Babe and the driving rhythm of Masters Of War.

For a notoriously unintelligible singer in a notoriously muddy-sounding building, Dylan's delivery was clear enough to elicit cheers before he even reached his choruses. Trust me, that's a good sign at any arena concert.

ABOUT THIS time, a few hundred fans on the floor decided to rush to the front of the stage, adding a bit more intimacy to the show. Security let them be – after all, we are talking about Bob Dylan fans here, not moshpit enthusiasts.

With the acoustic quotient satisfied, it was time for more electric guitars, just to crank up the volume before the inevitable encore. To any fan who's been following Dylan's tour across Western Canada, the suspense was minimal – the break in every previous show also took place following song No. 12.

After enthusiastic applause from the undersized crowd, Dylan returned amid the mid-tempo strains of Time Out Of Mind's Love Sick.

The stage-front crowd actually started dancing during Rainy Day Women #12 & 35, and the entire floor was up on its feet. Then came the opening strains of a countrified version of Blowin' In The Wind, which the crowd initially did not recognize, thanks to an odd guitar rearrangement.

After a second encore, Dylan unleashed the bluesy, extended-jam pyrotechnics of Highway 61 Revisited. But in a relatively anticlimax, the show closed with the slightly sappy Forever Young.

Still, the Bard of Hibbing presented a reasonably diverse sample of material from throughout his career, and that appeared to satisfy most fans. Sure, many would have loved to hear other Dylan classics, namely Like A Rolling Stone or Mr. Tambourine Man.

But for a late '90s performance from a Yoda sound-alike who changed the face of pop music more than 30 years ago, this just slightly idiosyncratic song selection was more than adequate.

* * * * out of five.

Attendance: 4,600.

Thursday, October 29, 1998 --- Maple Leaf Gardens Toronto, ON

Set List

	Song	From The Album	Released
1.	Gotta Serve Somebody	Slow Train Coming	Aug. 20, 1979
2.	Million Miles	Time Out of Mind	Sept. 30, 1997
3.	Just Like Tom Thumb's Blues	Highway 61 Revisited	Aug. 30, 1965
4.	I'm Not Supposed to Care (Gordon Lightfoot)	–	–
5.	Cold Irons Bound	Time Out of Mind	Sept. 30, 1997
6.	Tomorrow is a Long Time	Bob Dylan's Greatest Hits, Vol. 2	Nov. 17, 1971
7.	Masters of War	The Freewheelin' Bob Dylan	May 27, 1963
8.	My Back Pages	Another Side of Bob Dylan	Aug. 8, 1964
9.	Tangled Up in Blue	Blood on the Tracks	Jan. 20, 1975
10.	Every Grain of Sand	Shot of Love	Aug. 12, 1981
11.	Highway 61 Revisited	Highway 61 Revisited	Aug. 30, 1965
	Encores		
12.	Love Sick	Time Out of Mind	Sept. 30, 1997
13.	Rainy Day Women #12 & 35	Blonde on Blonde	May 16, 1966
14.	Blowin' in the Wind	The Freewheelin' Bob Dylan	May 27, 1963
15.	Til I Fell In Love With You	Time Out of Mind	Sept. 30, 1997
16.	It Ain't Me, Babe	Another Side of Bob Dylan	Aug. 8, 1964

The Musicians

Bob Dylan (vocal, guitar & harmonica), Bucky Baxter (dobro, mandolin, pedal steel guitar, electric slide guitar & backup vocals), Larry Campbell (guitar & backup vocals), Tony Garnier (bass), David Kemper (drums & percussion).

Notes

- 94th Bob Dylan concert in Canada; 27th Bob Dylan concert in Toronto.
- 6, 9, 13, 16, Bob Dylan (harmonica).
- 6-9, 14, 16, acoustic with the band.
- Canadian live debut of song 10.
- The opening act was Dave Alvin and the Guilty Men, followed by Joni Mitchell.

Reviews

A very fine show from Joni 'n' Bob

By Peter Howell, Entertainment Reporter.

Joni Mitchell and Bob Dylan are rock's two giant refuseniks, staunch believers that creativity must come before marketing, or even popular demand.

For most of their decades-long careers they've thumbed their noses at sentiment, preferring to deconstruct their biggest songs rather than simply play them. In Mitchell's case, she had almost giving up touring altogether.

So what a surprise last night, in their show at a three-quarters-full Maple Leaf Gardens, to see this fun couple "stoking the starmaker machinery behind the popular song," as Mitchell sang.

The line is from "Free Man In Paris," which she performed with her four-member band, as well as "Just Like This Train," another tune off her best-selling album, *Court & Spark.*

She opened her set with "Big Yellow Taxi," stepping up to the plate *sans* band, shimmying and smiling in flowing cloth of red and gold. She plucked her electric guitar with the same casual hand toss as Keith Richards, and sang a verse just like "Bobby," but informal didn't mean indifference.

Mitchell was eager to please, and delighted to be back on stage. She borrowed the giggle from "Big Yellow Taxi" and put it into "Hejira," the latter a song once judged difficult for her pop fans: familiarity has aged it like fine wine.

Same with the jazzy "Don Juan's Reckless Daughter," and well-chosen covers in Marvin Gaye's "Trouble Man" and "Comes Love" by Billie Holiday. When she encored with a dramatically rearranged "Woodstock" the circle game was complete.

Dylan, as always, had his own way of pleasing his mostly Boomer audience. The latest version of his Never-Ending Tour band started the proceedings with electric rock, and such well-loved tunes as "Gotta Serve Somebody," "Just Like Tom Thumb's Blues" and Gordon Lightfoot's "I'm Not Supposed To Care," which Dylan dedicated to the Bard of Rosedale. For once, you didn't need to be a lip reader to name that tune.

And Zimmy and his mates gave us an acoustic section worthy of the name, with impeccable musicianship that helped mask the legend's rusty pipes. Guitars, pedal steel and double bass united behind "Tomorrow Is A Long Time," "My Back Pages" and a toe-tapping "Tangled Up In Blue."

A very fine show from Bob and Joni, who are leaving the '90s in far better shape than they entered them. How many of us can say that about ourselves?

Times a-change, but these veterans can still deliver

By Finbarr O'Reilly, National Post.

A broad spectrum of rock history curved its arc over a half-full Maple Leaf Gardens last night as cultural icons Bob Dylan and Joni Mitchell drew upon a combined six decades of professional experience to deliver a solid and, at times, moving performance.

Mitchell set the tone for her portion of the show early by strolling casually onto the stage and getting nostalgia out of the way quickly with her first number, Big Yellow Taxi. She sang it solo with only her electric guitar for company, and immediately cast an intimate feel into what could otherwise have been a hollow musical environment. Mitchell also jazzed the song up with a funky extro filled with the warbling guitar washes that flowed throughout her performance.

Rolling up the sleeves of her blood red, crushed velvet outfit, the 54-year-old Mitchell was joined on stage for her third song by her band, which then eased its way into the smooth, almost sultry groove of Night Ride.

There was little chatter between numbers, but Mitchell did stray forth at one point to graciously accept a bouquet of flowers from a front-row fan. She then settled back into a comfortable musical realm that was filled with a smoky jazz flavour only heightened by the seductive drone of a gently played cornet.

Dylan picked up where Mitchell left off, adding foot-stomping rock, guitar-plucking blues, and the twang of country to the evening's musical march down memory lane. Dressed all in white, Dylan growled his unintelligible but legendary lyrics over the high-octane grind of his backing band, barely visible through a hazy glow of machine-made smoke. The 8,000-strong crowd swelled by a few thousand for Dylan's appearance and, through a set of better and lesser-known numbers, he reminded people why he's not just the father of his heartthrob son, Jakob.

Predictably, the crowd consisted mostly of baby boomers. But there were enough fresh faces to acknowledge that here were two artists who influenced the generation of musicians, who in turn influenced the current crop of imitators.

Together, Mitchell and Dylan proved that, unlike the Rolling Stones, they still have a sound worth paying good money for. And if you can forget for a moment they are aging icons, it's easy to allow yourself to enjoy music that's timeless, even if those who are playing it aren't.

Legends

Dylan, Mitchell play on their own terms

Disappointing crowd of 8,000 turns out for performances of mostly newer material

Reviewed by Alan Niester.

Pop music has traditionally fed on its past. Who can forget, for example, those great Golden-Oldie bills that used to roll into the old Ontario Place Forum – The Grassroots, The Outsiders, Herman's Hermits, and Gerry and the Pacemakers, all playing nothing but Top Ten for 25 minutes apiece?

Yeah, well, last night's pairing of Bob Dylan and Joni Mitchell – played out before a disappointing crowd of 8,000 – decidedly wasn't one of those shows, even though both artists are legitimate contemporaries of the previously mentioned bands.

These are two artists who – though their fans might prefer otherwise – have consciously decided not to wallow in nostalgia. Instead, they continue to perform on their own terms, not the terms of customers paying the freight.

While Dylan at least superficially delves into his storied past (although many of the songs are so reworked as to be, at times, virtually unrecognizable), the enigmatic Ms. Mitchell almost seems to sneer at hers. Last night's appearance centred almost exclusively on either newer material or lesser-known older album cuts. With only a couple of exceptions (*Big Yellow Taxi* and *Woodstock*, which opened and closed her performance), Mitchell's set list contained numbers known only to her most dedicated fans.

Backed by a quartet – which contained, as usual, "my dear ex-husband Larry Klein" on fretless bass – Mitchell was at times sombre (*Harry's* House), at times upbeat (*Black Crow*) and at times angry and aggressive (*Sex Kills*). But she was rarely playful or accommodating. In fact, the two numbers which did strike a familiar chord were played solo, oddly enough, with *Woodstock* as a virtual lament.

Predictably, many in the audience grew restless and annoyed (calls to "play something" and for "Boooobbbbb" occasionally rained down), but Mitchell carried on regardless. It was, overall, a somewhat self-indulgent set met with what can only be described as a mixed reaction.

The last few times Dylan played Toronto, he came across as something like Donald Duck fronting The Grateful Dead, his pinched vocals being laid overtop long and satisfying rock grooves.

Last night, he came across as more approachable, earthier and more humanistic. With the band performing a large portion of the set acoustically, this time he came across more like Donald Duck fronting The Nitty Gritty Dirt Band.

Like Mitchell's, his set list was totally unpredictable and he dredged up numbers that few would have expected to hear on this night. He opened with *Serve Somebody*, a song that seemed to suggest that this would be an evening of decipherable lyrics. But as soon as he launched into *Million Miles*, from last years stunning comeback album *Time Out Of Mind*, he was pretty much back into garbled slurs.

But for Dylan fans, this was a night of considerable treats, as numbers like *Younger Than Yesterday* and *Masters Of War* were dredged up from the archives. Particularly enjoyable was his revisiting of *Tangled Up In Blue* from 1975's *Blood On The Tracks* album, a number that had the audience up and on their collective feet.

The long evening was opened by roots rocker Dave Alvin, who parlayed a Johnny Cash singing voice, some Woody Guthrie numbers (notably *Promised Land* and *Dough-Re-Mi*) and Little Richard-styled retro-rock into a short set that – had more people been around early in the evening to see it – could very nearly have stolen the headliner's thunder.

As appeared in The Globe and Mail. Fri., Oct. 30, 1998. Reprinted with permission of Alan Niester.

Lookin' to live up to their legends

By Jane Stevenson, The Toronto Sun.

The meeting of two music legends – Joni Mitchell and Bob Dylan – on one stage comes along so rarely you'd think there'd be high expectations.

But judging from the weak attendance of last night's Maple Leaf Gardens show – only 10,000 tickets were sold leaving another 6,000 seats empty – you gotta wonder just how high.

For the more curious, younger types in the audience, whose numbers were impressive, maybe it was a chance to finally see what they've been told about these two '60s and '70s folk icons for all these years.

For the older die-hard Dylan and Mitchell fans, it must have been – come on, admit it – a bit of a nostalgia trip.

The truth of how the show played out last night falls somewhere in between.

There should have been less Joni and more Bob.

Mitchell, who released yet another album of laid-back jazz-and-folk fusion, Taming The Tiger, less than a month ago, wasted no time in getting to the hits as she began her hour-and-twenty-minute set with Big Yellow Taxi while strumming an electric guitar on stage alone.

Looking dazzling – those taut cheekbones can still be seen from a mile away despite her turning 55 on Nov. 7 – in a flowing pantsuit of gold-embosssd red velvet and gold sandals, Mitchell was also relaxed as she addressed some in the audience by their nicknames.

"Is Killer out there?" she asked, before dedicating her new song, Face Lift, to this person. (Possibly her Toronto-based daughter Kilauren Gibb who she gave up for adoption in 1965 but reunited with last year?)

However, despite Mitchell's solid stage presence – one front row guy in a white top hat and tails even presented her with flowers – and accomplished four piece band, led by her ex-husband-producer Larry Klein on bass, most of the older material appeared to fall on restless ears.

There was polite applause but even when Mitchell returned for a one-song encore with Woodstock, it seemed overwhelmingly obvious the crowd was ready for Dylan.

It was only when she put down her guitar to sing a jazzy version of her hit, Free Man, and a Billie Holiday cover, Comes Love, that she really hit her stride.

Dylan, meanwhile, had no problem in the crowd connection department as flashing lights indicated he and his four-piece band (all dressed in snazzy suits and hats) were about to take the stage.

The excitement was palpable as the audience, suddenly rowdier and seemingly drunker, lept to their feet when Dylan opened his hour-and-five minute show with Serve Somebody.

That was followed by Million Miles, from his most recent album, 1997's triple Grammy-winner Time Out Of Mind, which has seen him enter a new phase of his career, playing way more shows than Mitchell, who hasn't toured in 16 years, and get only better as a performer.

Dylan, 57, and Mitchell test drove the idea of a road trip together in May when they played a select number of West Coast dates with Van Morrison – deemed "the holy trinity" of singer-songwriters by some – also along for the ride. But the hype for those shows was considerably bigger out there, with the show at GM Place in Vancouver (the only Canadian stop on that tour) selling out in 24 hours.

(As one music colleague whispered to me last night: "There's more ex-hippies out there.")

A sweeping generalization maybe, but if you want either Dylan or particularly Mitchell to keep performing live, you've got to support them.

Dylan's standout numbers, by the way, were Masters Of War, Forever Young, Tangled Up In Blue and Highway 61, all of which brought about standing ovations.

SUN RATING: 4 out of 5

The Toronto Sun. Fri., Oct. 30, 1998. Reprinted with permission of The Sun Media Corp.

Review

By Jerry Tenenbaum.

I see him every time he comes to Toronto.

The last time he was this brilliant, in my opinion, was in Jan. 74 (That's not to say he hasn't been good on many other occasions).

Tonight was something special.

Dylan was really into it. He was having a good time and it showed. Some interesting selections reappeared.

Gotta Serve Somebody - punchy
Million Miles - smooth
Just Like Tom Thumb's Blues - true blues
I'm Not Supposed To Care - an unusual treat beautifully executed
Cold Irons Bound - it doesn't get better than this
Tomorrow Is A Long Time - heartfelt sensitive
Masters of War - venomous
My Back Pages - disarming and personal
Tangled Up In Blue - freight train powered/superb
Every Grain Of Sand - spiritually uplifting
Highway 61 Revisited - footstomping rock & roll at its best
Love Sick - soul baring
Rainy Day Women # 12 & 35 - too much fun to miss
Blowin' In The Wind - a singalong with some lighters/flashback
Til' I Fell In Love With You - more soul baring
It Ain't Me, Babe - finishes a theme with dignity

Dylan was at the top of his game. Singing excellent. Dancing. Enjoyed the guitar and played well. The mouth harp was stirring on both occasions.

I think he said hello to Hurricane Carter. (sometimes its hard to tell what he says.)

Thanks ev'rybody.

Posted to Bob Links. Reprinted with permission of Jerry Tenenbaum.

Friday, October 30, 1998 --- Corel Centre Ottawa, ON

Set List

	Song	From The Album	Released
1.	Gotta Serve Somebody	Slow Train Coming	Aug. 20, 1979
2.	I Want You	Blonde on Blonde	May 16, 1966
3.	All Along the Watchtower	John Wesley Harding	Dec. 27, 1967
4.	Simple Twist of Fate	Blood on the Tracks	Jan. 20, 1975
5.	Cold Irons Bound	Time Out of Mind	Sept. 30, 1997
6.	Girl of the North Country	The Freewheelin' Bob Dylan	May 27, 1963

7.	The Lonesome Death of Hattie Carroll	The Times They Are A-Changin'	Feb. 10, 1964
8.	Masters of War	The Freewheelin' Bob Dylan	May 27, 1963
9.	Tangled Up in Blue	Blood on the Tracks	Jan. 20, 1975
10.	Positively 4th Street	Bob Dylan's Greatest Hits	March 27, 1967
11.	Highway 61 Revisited	Highway 61 Revisited	Aug. 30, 1965
	Encores		
12.	Love Sick	Time Out of Mind	Sept. 30, 1997
13.	Rainy Day Women #12 & 35	Blonde on Blonde	May 16, 1966
14.	Blowin' in the Wind	The Freewheelin' Bob Dylan	May 27, 1963
15.	Til I Fell In Love With You	Time Out of Mind	Sept. 30, 1997
16.	Forever Young	Planet Waves	Jan. 17, 1974

The Musicians

Bob Dylan (vocal, guitar & harmonica), Bucky Baxter (dobro, mandolin, pedal steel guitar, electric slide guitar & backup vocals), Larry Campbell (guitar & backup vocals), Tony Garnier (bass), David Kemper (drums & percussion).

Notes

- 95th Bob Dylan concert in Canada 8th Bob Dylan concert in Ottawa.
- 1, 13-14, 16, Larry Campbell & Bucky Baxter (backup vocals).
- 6-9, 14, 16, acoustic with the band.
- 7, Bob Dylan (harmonica).
- The opening act was Dave Alvin and the Guilty Men, followed by Joni Mitchell.

Reviews

Dylan rocks, Joni balks

Bob played his oldies like a pro, while Mitchell disappointed

By Chris Cobb.

You never know with Bob Dylan.

The voice of the Sixties generation gained his reputation as a soft spoken coffee-house troubadour/poetic genius. Then he moved through a long and troubled period when his performances (and himself) were often a sad, pathetic shadow of what they had once been.

Now, for heaven's sake, he wants to be Eric Clapton or some other guitar hero.

Dylan at the Corel Centre was … well, dynamic. On several occasions he seemed poised to launch into a Chuck Berry-patented duck walk across the front of the stage.

Dynamic Dylan's voice was clear and his words satisfyingly enunciated. But the biggest surprise? He's playing the lead guitar like a seasoned rock legend, not an old three-chord folkie.

While a disappointing Joni Mitchell played little from her back catalogue during an 80-minute set, Dylan played little else. Clearly, he accepts that people want to hear his older material. Still, these weren't stale versions sung by note but freshly crafted songs with musical overhauls.

He opened with an ear-splitting *Gotta Serve Somebody*, continued with *I Want You*, *All Along the Watchtower* and on through *Girl from the North Country*, *The Lonesome Death of Hattie Carroll*, *Masters of War*, *Blowin' in the Wind*. All the hits, all the time.

A few times the music became a blurred cacophony but mostly it was well-balanced, and rarely was Dylan's voice lost in noise.

The concert culminated with stunning versions of *Highway 61* and *Forever Young*. Confusion during the last 20 minutes of the show suggested that Dylan was having more fun than usual. Twice the band bowed and waved to the crowd and twice Dylan appeared to change his mind about leaving.

In contrast, Joni Mitchell had many in the two-thirds full arena twiddling their thumbs. People were shouting for a taste of her early work but she responded with some condescending comment about not having her piano with her – "this is a guitar concert" she said.

Mitchell has often criticized the music industry, journalists and even her own fans for not understanding her musical desire to explore. That is baloney. Far better to thread the new music through the old. Give the people what they want and a taste of what you want to give them.

Her old friend and hero Bob Dylan could have told her that.

Long Live These Legends

Folk Icons Continue To Work Without Dwelling On Past

By Rick Overall, Ottawa Sun.

IT SEEMED fitting that with Halloween only a night away the ghosts of the '60s arrived to haunt the Corel Centre last night. The question for the 6,000 in attendance was whether or not any zombies were going to climb on that stage as well.

Despite the fact that both Bob Dylan and Joni Mitchell have travelled many musical miles since they first appeared over three decades ago, the pair are living, breathing icons who continue the minstrel tradition they made such a mark with all those years ago.

Anyone who's been at a Dylan concert in Ottawa over the past few years knows full well that buying a ticket for his shows was a crapshoot at best.

In the past Dylan has been at best marginally understandable and at his worst he blathered through an evening at the NAC that was one of the most embarrassing and uncomfortable events I've ever witnessed.

But whatever has happened to big Bob in the interim has to be viewed as a major step forward, because the man we saw last night emoted the kind of acoustic wanderlust and razor sharp lyrical bite that set him apart from the crowd and vaulted him to icon status.

From the crack of the bat, the band kicked into a grinding groove on Gotta Serve Somebody, and it became obvious the skeletons in Dylan's closet tonight were all solid gold. And as the incense machine filled the arena with the palpable sensory amenities to recreate the mood of a time long gone, Dylan did his part in the usual unkempt but exhilerating jagged line that is folk/rock – and he did it better than we've seen in years.

The great feel we picked up from the opening continued as Bob and the band rolled out an urban-country feel and laced up classics like I Want You with a new vigour – an electric feel that actually reminded you why this man turned some fans into worshippers. In fact, the way they attacked All Along The Watchtower with full-bore guitar fury was almost scary, the song had the urgency it was meant to have.

The evening was divided into moody fragments, wavering from the aforementioned wall of electric angst to gentle acoustic segments that brought the sensitivity factor to the forefront – with a more intimate feel up front as he poured out the grit on Masters Of War, or the jumpy new approach to Tangled Up In Blue – a feeling that gave the song a lot more oomph.

Although Dylan's set certainly didn't feel nostalgic, it was. But the hard-nosed approach the whole unit gave to benchmarks like Highway 61 Revisited was the divergence.

It was old Dylan that sounded new just because of the freshness and energy that the tunes were given.

For those of us who believed so strongly in Dylan's musical magnetism in its infancy, it was an absolute shot in the arm to see that at 57, the man seems close to being reborn as a performer. He's once again able to inject his music with the required dosage of whatever magic he summons up from inside to grab us by the collective scruff of the neck and get that special charge that only a few performers can.

Welcome back Bob, we missed this side of you.

Like Dylan, Joni Mitchell has covered a lot of territory since her fresh-faced Both Sides Now and Chelsea Morning signalled the arrival of Canada's first folk superstar.

Rather than allowing the evening to be straightforward nostalgia, Mitchell brought to the table a nice little evolutionary package.

The tone of her attack was instantaneous as she brought the screams of approval into play by launching into her classic Big Yellow Taxi. However, as was to be the case all night, Mitchell gave the tune a slap on the butt with jazzy and even hip-hoppish tinges creeping into the delivery.

She moved freely into a second solo version of a song that's stood by her like an old friend Just Like This Train – but again, taking a more soulful approach to the vocals

It was at this point that Mitchell brought out her stellar backup unit, and the whole focus moved into the king of slow, lusty bottom-driven jazzy groove that gave you the feeling you were in some smoky beatnik bar on the Left Bank.

And so it would be for the better part of the evening, with the romance of Night Ride Home, her newly recorded Crazy Cries of Love and the bouncy Court and Spark winner Free Man In Paris and the drama of Harry's House, and Magdalene Laundries.

It was a refreshing sight to see an artist like Mitchell continue to work without dwelling too much on the past.

She's become one of the most well-rounded of all the women who began as straight folk artists. The gentleness is still there, but when she approaches the tender feel of Amelia and Face Lift, the songs moved from a straight acoustic reading to something with a tad more soul – delivery is everything with Mitchell, and last night she was comfortable and it showed.

In fact, Mitchell seemed to be really enjoying herself, romping through the likes of Don Juan's Reckless Daughter with all the energy of a funky flower child. Especially when she comes out with the straight-ahead soul we hear on her version of Marvin Gaye's Trouble Man and evocative Closer Comes Love. Her straight-ahead cat attack on Woodstock was a marvel.

This was Mitchell at her jazzy best.

The evening was opened by a solid set from Dave Alvin and the Guilty Men, who divided their short time up with a cross-section of rockin' blues-based countrified folk.

It was one of those hurried little opening sets that showed these guys had something really intriguing to offer, with a sound that gave us a taste of what Dire Straits might have sounded like if they'd been from Austin, Tex. and Junior Brown was playing lead instead of Mark Knopfler.

Very cool.

Un vieux punk et une gente dame se sont croisés au centre Corel

Visite (con) sacrée

par Michel Defoy.

L'un est allé s'entretenir avec saint Pierre l'année dernière. L'autre revient de presque aussi loin. Pourtant, hier soir, Bob Dylan et Joni Mitchell ont remué le centre Corel avec la vigueur de leurs 20 ans. Enfin, c'est tout comme. Compte rendu d'une soirée évaluée à l'échelle (réduite) de Richter.

Le parterre était plus ou moins fourni. Les gradins supérieurs mal remplis. N'empêche, dans les fauteuils comblés, on s'est délecté du passage combiné de deux icônes ressuscitées.

Joni Mitchell d'abord. Tout de velours rouge vêtue, madame est montée sur scène d'un pas décidé pour aussitôt se lancer dans une version solo de *Big Yellow Taxi*. Ses acolytes sont ensuite venus la retrouver au début d'un segment jazzé pour initiés.

Il fallait être intime avec le grand oeuvre de la dame pour s'y retrouver dans un répertoire assez hermétique. A-t-on même entendu un seul refrain extrait de l'album *Taming the Tiger*, encore tout frais? Un ou deux, tout au plus (dont le très feutré *Face Lift*).

Manque

Cela dit, la livraison était quasi impeccable. La sono plutôt bien calibrée. Manquait simplement quelques titres plus familiers pour plaire aux becs fins.

À son tour, Bob Dylan s'est installé confortablement entre deux chaises. Beaucoup plus tard que prévu, en fait. C'est que Joni Mitchell avait pris son temps.

Un peu plus et on signait notre texte sans même avoir entraperçu «His Bobness». Trente minutes avant l'heure de tombée, le vieux punk s'est enfin montré le nez. L'éternelle tignasse ébouriffée. Le geste moins leste, mais encore précis. La diction plus claire qu'anticipée.

On se demandait bien avec quoi il allait lancer les hostilités. Avec *You Gotta Serve Somebody*, solide morceau de l'époque médiane, poussé à fond la caisse par un orchestre inspiré.

La suite est de la même eau: une version libre de *I Want You* fait mouche. *All Along the Watchtower*, rendue pesamment, déplace beaucoup d'air.

Accompagné de musiciens certifiés, Dylan se sent à l'aise. Il s'aventure dans l'exécution de quelques petits pas de danse. Ne va pas jusqu'à converser avec la foule, mais se fend quand même de deux ou trois *Thank You*! sincères. Et ça repart de plus belle avec l'imparable *Cold Irons Bound*, morceau phare du dernier album, *Time Out of Mind*

Qu'un type comme Dylan brûle encore sur scène d'une telle énergie après avoir flirté avec l'au-delà n'est pas sans étonner. C'est comme s'il avait trouvé dans cette épreuve l'énergie d'une autre vie.

L'énergie d'une vie ancienne documentée sur l'enregistrement *live* au Royal Albert Hall, qui rappelle la jeunesse agitée du barde. Trente ans plus tard, notre homme est toujours aussi vert.

LeDroit. Sat., Oct. 31, 1998. Reprinted with permission of LeDroit.

1999

Introduction

The Never-Ending Tour kept rolling along but only stopped for one concert in Canada in 1999.

The only Canadian date would mark Bob Dylan's 96th concert in Canada.

The Date

Vancouver, BC	Fri., June 11, 1999

This show was Dylan's 10th concert in Vancouver.

The Musicians

Bob Dylan (vocal, guitar & harmonica).

Charlie Sexton (guitar), Larry Campbell (guitar, mandolin, fiddle, pedal steel guitar & electric slide guitar), Tony Garnier (bass), David Kemper (drums & percussion).

The Songs

Bob Dylan performed 17 songs (13 were from albums and 4 were cover and/or traditional songs).

Six songs made their Canadian live debut.

Hallelujah, I'm Ready to Go	The Sound of Silence
Tryin' To Get To Heaven	I Walk the Line
Not Dark Yet	Blue Moon of Kentucky

Five songs have been played only once in Canada.

Hallelujah, I'm Ready to Go	I Walk the Line
Tryin' To Get To Heaven	Blue Moon of Kentucky
The Sound of Silence	–

One song made its worldwide live debut.

Hallelujah, I'm Ready to Go	–

Bob Dylan performed songs from 9 different albums.

Album	Released	# of Songs Performed by Album
The Freewheeelin' Bob Dylan	May 27, 1963	1
Another Side of Bob Dylan	Aug. 8, 1964	1
Bringing It All Back Home	March 22, 1965	2
Highway 61 Revisited	Aug. 30, 1965	2
Blonde on Blonde	May 16, 1966	1
John Wesley Harding	Dec. 27, 1967	1
Pat Garrett & Billy The Kid	July 13, 1973	1
Blood on the Tracks	Jan. 20, 1975	1
Time Out of Mind	Sept. 30, 1997	3

Opening Act

Bob Dylan opened the show and Paul Simon headlined. They would switch back and forth throughout the Tour.

Special Guest

Paul Simon joined Dylan on stage for four songs.

The Venue

It was Bob Dylan's 2nd time playing at GM Place in Vancouver.

Friday, June 11, 1999 --- GM Place
Vancouver, BC

Set List

	Song	From The Album	Released
1.	Hallelujah, I'm Ready to Go (trad.)	_	_
2.	Mr. Tambourine Man	Bringing It All Back Home	March 22, 1965
3.	Masters of War	The Freewheelin' Bob Dylan	May 27, 1963
4.	It's All Over Now, Baby Blue	Bringing It All Back Home	March 22, 1965
5.	Tangled Up in Blue	Blood on the Tracks	Jan. 20, 1975
6.	All Along the Watchtower	John Wesley Harding	Dec. 27, 1967
7.	Tryin' To Get To Heaven	Time Out of Mind	Sept. 30, 1997
8.	Stuck Inside of Mobile with the Memphis Blues Again	Blonde on Blonde	May 16, 1966
9.	Not Dark Yet	Time Out of Mind	Sept. 30, 1997
10.	Highway 61 Revisited	Highway 61 Revisited	Aug. 30, 1965
	Encores		
11.	Love Sick	Time Out of Mind	Sept. 30, 1997
12.	Like a Rolling Stone	Highway 61 Revisited	Aug. 30, 1965
13.	It Ain't Me, Babe	Another Side of Bob Dylan	Aug. 8, 1964
14.	The Sound of Silence (Paul Simon)	_	_
15.	I Walk the Line (Johnny Cash)	_	_
16.	Blue Moon of Kentucky (Bill Monroe)	_	_
17.	Knockin' on Heaven's Door	Pat Garrett & Billy The Kid	July 13, 1973

The Musicians

Bob Dylan (vocal, guitar & harmonica), Charlie Sexton (guitar), Larry Campbell (guitar, mandolin, fiddle, pedal steel guitar & electric slide guitar), Tony Garnier (bass), David Kemper (drums & percussion).

Notes

- 96th Bob Dylan concert in Canada; 10th Bob Dylan concert in Vancouver.
- 1–5, 13-16, acoustic with the band.
- 2, 5, 13-14, Bob Dylan (harmonica).
- 14-17, Paul Simon (vocal & acoustic guitar)
- 15, Larry Campbell (fiddle).
- Canadian live debut of songs 1, 7, 9, 14, 15 & 16.
- Songs 1, 7, 14, 15 & 16 have been performed only once in Canada.
- Worldwide live debut of song 1.
- Bob Dylan was the opening act and Paul Simon headlined.

Reviews

Legends on common ground

By Kerry Gold, Sun Pop Music Critic.

The jarring sight of disparate legends Bob Dylan and Paul Simon singing the pop-folk anthem Sounds of Silence was enough of a weird scenario to make Friday's concert worth the expense for the crowd of nearly 10,000 at GM Place.

Anyone who read advance stories that mentioned the duet would have been wondering how, exactly, the two 57-year-old superstars of the same musical era and two completely different stylistic worlds might pull it off. As improbable as it sounds, it came off, partly because Dylan let Simon lead the way vocally and partly because the two found a happy neutral ground in roots territory. It's not so strange after all, to hear Dylan speak-singing words like, "and the people bowed and prayed to the neon god they made." Simon played electric guitar, Dylan squeezed in a little harmonica solo, and the two spun a little magic in the midst of an evening that got off to a solid but tepid start.

Simon, dressed as if he just happened to be dropping in after a ball game, upped the energy level significantly when he strolled onto the stage after Dylan's hour and a half set. The man may be tiny, but he's got a big personality conveyed by sheer presence alone. Simon joined Dylan on Knockin' on Heaven's Door and Johnny Cash's I Walk the Line and Blue Moon of Kentucky.

Easy-going Simon playing guitar alongside docile Dylan created a sense of something strange and eventful underway, especially when they closed the short duet set with a warm and affectionate exchange. It's a sight in itself to see the normally staid Dylan beam broadly and deliver a playful slap in Simon's direction.

Dylan opened the show wordlessly a little after 8 p.m., launching into I'm Ready to Go before most of the floor seats had even filled. Joined by a four-piece band he chewed out selections new and old, including a speedy version of Mr. Tambourine Man, It's All Over Now Baby Blue and Like a Rolling Stone, which got the most timid dancers among the crowd on their feet. Dylan gets big points for giving fans a different flavour from last year's concert with Joni Mitchell and Van Morrison. This show was less rock, more country, and he suitably re-worked most of the phrasing on old songs. The compliment goes out in equal measure to Paul Simon, whose enormous, percussion heavy band took the drama out of Bridge Over Troubled Water and opted for a simplified, earthier version. Simon continued to please with a variety pack of his best songs, including Mrs. Robinson, Graceland, Slip, Slidin' Away, Diamonds on the Soles, Call Me Al, Late in the Evening and Still Crazy.

The Vancouver Sun. Sat., June 12, 1999.

Bob 'n' Paul: Folk triumph

Touring traditionalist, 'Big Idea' artist share stage

By Tom Harrison, Music Critic.

The pairing of Bob Dylan and Paul Simon would seem to be a perfect match based on urban folk lore: Two giants of the modern song, graduates of the '60s folk boom, together on the same stage.

Well, Bob 'n' Paul did sing Sounds of Silence on the stage of GM Place, and if Simon's Sounds of Silence owes its status to a little thing called folk-rock that Bob Dylan inadvertently invented, Friday's concert before "10,000 people maybe more" (to quote Sounds of Silence's lyric) showed that this also is where the two depart.

Backed by an intuitively brilliant four-piece band that unexpectedly included (but benefitted from the presence of) Charlie Sexton, Dylan opened the show with an acoustic first half that embraced gospel and country and the by-now routine recasting of old songs in new settings which made singing along to Mr. Tambourine Man a little like one-on-one basketball as you tried to figure out which way the singer was going to bob or weave.

Above the electric versions of Highway 61 Revisited or the still-monumental Like a Rolling Stone, was Masters of War.

In juxtaposition with last week's events in Kosovo, the song had extra poignance. Dylan continues to sing it at key times, as if to remind us that we need to hear it every so often until the message lands home.

Similarly, Dylan enlivens and informs his music with relevance just by continuing to tour, in effect keeping himself and his songs in the public consciousness – in the folk tradition.

By contrast, Paul Simon retreated to his artist's garret years ago and now only comes out when he has a Big Idea, or it suits him.

Appearing with up to 11 musicians, Simon's 75 minutes were an example of his dedication to precise musical organization and of an intellectual at play. Songs such as Mrs. Robinson, Me and Julio, Boy in the Bubble or The Trailways Bus vividly connected the dots between the different phases of his career as well as linked the many cultures these phases have explored to one celebratory pulse. But if Dylan's triumph was partly due to a loose and natural artlessness, Simon's was based on a colder esthetic that contorts indigenous, natural music into highly stylized conceptual art.

The Vancouver Province. Sun., June 13, 1999.

Chairman Bob's fountain of youth

By Chris Dafoe, Western Arts Correspondent, Vancouver.

Who would have guessed, if asked in the late 1960s, that Bob Dylan would end up spending his 50s as a tireless road warrior, playing dozens and dozens of dates around the world every year? Who would have guessed that popular music's most mysterious character would be the one to lure his reclusive contemporaries out of exile to face their fans? And who would have guessed he'd be so good at it?

Over the past two years, Dylan has emerged as the emcee of a touring operation that might be called Chairman Bob Brings Boomers Their Youth. Last year, he lured Joni Mitchell and Van Morrison out to play a triple bill. This year, he called up Paul Simon.

On Friday at GM Place in Vancouver, the only Canadian date the duo are scheduled to play, Dylan even let Simon headline and put on his best Ed Sullivan impersonation to introduce him to the crowd.

"I'd like you to welcome a young man who's written some fine hit songs," drawled Dylan, 58, in welcoming Simon, 57, to the stage in the middle of a show that stretched over four hours. Out came Simon, casually dressed in a T-shirt and baseball cap. The pair played a duet for *Sounds of Silence*, their voices coming together carefully and a little warily, like two men trying to get around each other on a slippery log, and then cut loose with covers of *I Walk the Line* and *Blue Moon of Kentucky* before ending with *Knockin' On Heaven's Door*.

Simon returned, backed by an 11-piece band that included three percussionists and a horn section. While he sounded a little rusty at times and the band wasn't as dazzling as some Simon has worked with in the past, it was hard to argue with the repertoire. After opening with a Middle Eastern take on *Bridge Over Troubled Waters*, Simon and company played it straight, delivering the hits pretty much the way you remembered them. *Mrs. Robinson* bounced along agreeably, *Me and Julio* set the crowd moving and dancing in the aisles, and tunes like *Diamonds on the Soles of Her Shoes* and *Call Me Al* kept them there. The energy lagged a little when Simon trotted out tunes *Rhythm of the Saints* and *The Capeman*, but it picked up again as he reached back for old favourites such as *The Boxer* and *Still Crazy After All These Years*.

If Simon offered faithful renditions of old favourites, Dylan had no patience for such niceties, figuring that his songs are sturdy enough to get kicked around a little.

On Friday, he opened with an acoustic set that included an extended reading of *Mr. Tambourine Man*, a menacing *Masters of War* and the warm embrace of *Tangled Up In Blue*, a song that has become a cornerstone of his live show. Then he plugged in and blew the roof off with roaring, primal versions of songs such as *All Along the Watchtower* and *Highway 61 Revisited*.

There were some quiet, tender moments as well, reminders that Dylan can cover more emotional range with that unpretty croak than most divas can with their five-octave instruments. What lingered, however, was the raw power of songs such as *Like a Rolling Stone*, the band pushing the groove until it broke like a wave as Dylan delivered the wailing taunt, "How does it feeeeeeeeel?" It feels pretty good, thanks.

The Globe and Mail. Mon., June 14, 1999. Reprinted with permission from The Globe and Mail.

BOB DYLAN & PAUL SIMON

GM Place, Vancouver, Canada

By Tony Montague.

Three songs into his set, Bob Dylan launched into a snarling rendition of *Masters Of War*, one of his most powerful protest-songs from the early '60s. Its selection was presumably significant, just days after the "death planes" had been pulled back from their assault missions in the Balkans. No comment was forthcoming from the laconic Dylan but, following a rather limp-sounding *Mr Tambourine Man*, there was a fire in his delivery that brought the audience, which included a sizeable contingent young enough to be Dylan's grandkids, to its feet in anticipation. They were not to be disappointed. After a rousing, bouncy *Tangled Up In Blue*, Dylan and the four musicians supporting him traded acoustic for electric instruments, and kicked straight in to a searing *All Along The Watchtower* – a nod of acknowledgement towards Hendrix's celebrated version. Dylan may be no virtuoso on the axe but he proved that he's no slouch either, trading nifty licks with his excellent lead-guitarist Larry Campbell on *Stuck Inside Of Mobile With The Memphis Blues Again*.

The famously unpredictable voice held up well as he trawled through a repertoire of his classics from the '60s, along with a smattering from the 1997 Grammy Award-winning *Time Out Of Mind*. While the songs themselves may have been familiar, their melodies had all been reconfigured – in accordance with Dylan's custom when on tour. Some parts of the altered versions sounded flat and awkwardly nuanced, as with *It's All Over Now Baby Blue*, but *Highway 61*, the set's closer, was given a new charge of vitality. Dylan's deadpan face, usually animated only by movements of his eyebrows, broke into a smile as he bobbed and swayed along. For an encore we got a hard-rocking *Like A Rolling Stone* that brought out all the song's magnificent structural dynamics, before switching back to acoustic for *It Ain't Me Babe* – with extended harmonica-break, played one-handed waving free.

Accompanied by the musicians of Dylan's band, the two '60s icons then ran through Simon's *Sounds Of Silence* and Johnny Cash's *I Walk The Line* – which segued seamlessly into an upbeat *Blue Moon Of Kentucky*. Fortunately that's as close to Nashville as we got. The first half ended with them swapping leads and sharing the chorus on Dylan's *Knockin' On Heaven's Door*. With such contrasting vocal styles, the harmonies could have benefitted from a little fine-tuning.

There was also a sharp distinction in musical approach. Whereas Dylan these days favours performing with small combos of rock musicians, Simon has – since *Graceland* at least – chosen to work with large bands for his forays into arty pop and world music. On his first concert tour in eight years he was joined by a bevy of 10 excellent musicians – including three full-kit drummers, two keyboardists and a three-man horn section of trumpet, trombone, and sax. Their collective sound was accordingly big, but not brash – and though the arrangements were highly polished, space was still provided for individual players to stretch out.

Simon had the good sense to stay away from his most recently-recorded songs, from his Broadway musical flopperoo *The Capeman*, and to concentrate instead on familiar, fan-pleasing material. He started out with *Bridge Over Troubled Water* – spacier and less schmaltzy than the original – then turned to songs from the *Graceland* and *Rhythm Of The Saints* albums. The biggest cheer of the evening went out for the opening chords on squeezebox of *Boy In The Bubble*, played with a thumping back-beat and a great percussive rumble at the end.

The 90-minute set was cleverly paced. Sing-along numbers like Simon's early classic *Mrs Robinson* and the peppy *Me And Julio Down By The Schoolyard* were balanced by more meditative pieces such as *Further To Fly*, with muted trumpet. And after a gentle *Slip Sliding Away* which highlighted the supple elegance of his voice, Simon got everybody up and dancing, to finish with *Diamonds On The Soles Of Her Shoes* and *You Can Call Me Al*. It represented a triumphant comeback for a musician who only a year earlier had said he would never tour again.

He returned to the stage for the wistful *Still Crazy After All These Years*, and the response was so raucous that he pulled out one last chestnut. "I haven't played this song in a long time," he confided before striking up the chords to *The Boxer* – played without snapping synthesizer on the chorus. Nostalgia ain't what it used to be – mercifully.

As appeared in fRoots. Oct. 1999. Reprinted with permission of Tony Montague.

2000

Introduction

The Never-Ending Tour continued into the new millennium with one concert in Canada in 2000.

The only Canadian date would mark Bob Dylan's 97th concert in Canada.

The Date

Toronto, ON	Tues., July 18, 2000

This show was Dylan's 28th concert in Toronto.

The Musicians

Bob Dylan (vocal, guitar & harmonica).

Charlie Sexton (guitar), Larry Campbell (guitar, mandolin, pedal steel guitar & electric slide guitar), Tony Garnier (bass), David Kemper (drums & percussion).

The Songs

Bob Dylan performed 17 songs (15 were from albums and 2 were cover and/or traditional songs).

Five songs made their Canadian live debut.

Duncan and Brady	Country Pie
Song to Woody	Things Have Changed
This World Can't Stand Long	–

Three songs have been played only once in Canada.

Duncan and Brady	Country Pie
Song to Woody	–

Bob Dylan performed songs from 10 different albums.

Album	Released	# of Songs Performed by Album
Bob Dylan	March 19, 1962	1
The Freewheelin' Bob Dylan	May 27, 1963	2
Bringing It All Back Home	March 22, 1965	2
Highway 61 Revisited	Aug. 30, 1965	3
Blonde on Blonde	May 16, 1966	1
John Wesley Harding	Dec. 27, 1967	1
Nashville Skyline	April 9, 1969	2
Blood on the Tracks	Jan. 20, 1975	1
Slow Train Coming	Aug. 20, 1979	1
The Essential Bob Dylan	Oct. 31, 2000	1

Opening Act

Bob Dylan opened the show and Phil Lesh and Friends headlined. They would switch back and forth throughout the Tour.

The Venue

It was Bob Dylan's 2nd time playing at the Molson Amphitheatre in Toronto.

Tuesday, July 18, 2000 --- Molson Amphitheatre
Toronto, ON

Set List

	Song	From The Album	Released
1.	Duncan and Brady (trad.)	–	–
2.	Song to Woody	Bob Dylan	March 19, 1962
3.	Desolation Row	Highway 61 Revisited	Aug. 30, 1965
4.	Love Minus Zero/No Limit	Bringing It All Back Home	March 22, 1965
5.	Tangled Up in Blue	Blood on the Tracks	Jan. 20, 1975
6.	This World Can't Stand Long (Jim Anglin)	–	–
7.	Country Pie	Nashville Skyline	April 9, 1969
8.	Lay, Lady, Lay	Nashville Skyline	April 9, 1969
9.	Gotta Serve Somebody	Slow Train Coming	Aug. 20, 1979
10.	She Belongs to Me	Bringing It All Back Home	March 22, 1965
11.	Drifter's Escape	John Wesley Harding	Dec. 27, 1967
12.	Leopard-Skin Pill-Box Hat	Blonde on Blonde	May 16, 1966
	Encores		
13.	Things Have Changed	The Essential Bob Dylan	Oct. 31, 2000
14.	Like a Rolling Stone	Highway 61 Revisited	Aug. 30, 1965
15.	Don't Think Twice, It's All Right	The Freewheelin' Bob Dylan	May 27, 1963
16.	Highway 61 Revisited	Highway 61 Revisited	Aug. 30, 1965
17.	Blowin' in the Wind	The Freewheelin' Bob Dylan	May 27, 1963

The Musicians

Bob Dylan (vocal, guitar & harmonica), Charlie Sexton (guitar), Larry Campbell (guitar, mandolin, pedal steel guitar & electric slide guitar), Tony Garnier (bass), David Kemper (drums & percussion).

Notes

- 97th Bob Dylan concert in Canada; 28th Bob Dylan concert in Toronto.
- 1-6, 15, 17, acoustic with the band.
- 2, 6, Larry Campbell (mandolin).
- 5, 11, 15, Bob Dylan (harmonica).
- Canadian live debut of songs 1, 2, 6, 7 & 13.
- Songs 1, 2 & 7 have been performed only once in Canada.
- Bob Dylan was the opening act and Phil Lesh and Friends headlined.

Reviews

Adored folkie Dylan comes full circle

Folk first, rock later a crowd-pleasing recipe

By Vit Wagner, Pop Music Critic.

Thirty-five years after the fact, it is hard to fathom the outcry that attended Bob Dylan's decision to plug in and rock out.

Had the adored, young folkie given in to his disciples' pleas to resist amplification, some of the finest music of the past 3 1/2 decades would never have found its natural voice.

Not only that, but last night's crowd at the Molson Amphitheatre would never have been in the position to enjoy a superbly paced and varied set in which Dylan, 59, and his bandmates glided effortlessly through folk, country, blues and rock, fusing styles and switching between electric and acoustic instruments as they went.

Initially, it was shaping up to resemble one of Dylan's bifurcated, post-Newport gigs. Folk first, rock later.

The first half-dozen songs received the acoustic treatment – or as acoustic as a stadium-style show gets these days – with Dylan reaching back to his debut album for the Guthrie tribute "Song To Woody," before breaking into the countrified jam of "Desolation Row" and then quickening the pulse beat yet again for a rousing rendition of "Tangled Up In Blue."

Seven numbers in, when Bob and company strapped on the electric guitars, a ripple ran through the 10,000-plus in attendance. The response probably had as much to do with a curtain dropping down behind the band at that point, as it did with a promised shift in instrumental approach.

The band ripped into "Country Pie," a song that came as close as any to reflecting the country-rock tenor of the evening. "Lay Lady Lay," with its bed of pedal steel guitar, was next, followed by a cut-loose assault on "Gotta Serve Somebody." By the end of the set, Dylan and his four accompanists, led by guitarist Charlie Sexton, were turning "Leopard-Skin Pill Box Hat" into a full-bore, rock 'n' roll revival that rose to a blistering harmonica finish.

During a five-song encore that began with Dylan's latest recorded tune, "Things Have Changed," the band switched gear a couple of times, gloriously rocking through "Like A Rolling Stone" and "Highway 61 Revisited" and strumming to "Don't Think Twice, It's All Right" and show-closer "Blowin' In The Wind." The latter seemed to complete the circle, except that the familiar folk standard had been given an up-beat, Nashville spin.

Dylan, despite banning photographers from the gig, was a gracious, if business-like maestro, displaying none of the indifference for which he is sometimes known. Contentment is not a word often used to describe Dylan, but on this night he seemed unshakably – and happily – in a groove.

When it came time to give way to former Grateful Dead bassist Phil Lesh, who has been alternating shows as headliner, Dylan conversed briefly with a stagehand before taking his final bows. You could have sworn he was trying to negotiate for more time.

The Toronto Star. Wed., July 19, 2000. Reprinted with permission - Torstar Syndication Services.

Dylan was Dylan, Lesh was a bit Dead

By Nate Hendley.

A heavy 1960s vibe hung over the Molson Amphitheatre last night as Bob Dylan shared a double-bill with former Grateful Dead bassist Phil Lesh. Dylan played first, at the relatively early hour of 7 p.m., and a carnival atmosphere reigned from the start.

Tie-dye T-shirts, pot smoke and dancing hippie girls were seen everywhere as the grey confines of the amphitheatre took on the air of a Woodstock-era rock festival.

Oddly, the only person present who didn't seemed imbued with the party spirit was Dylan himself. Dressed in black and scowling for most of the show, Dylan plunked himself down at centre-stage and barely moved from this spot all night.

Many of those in attendance were clearly there to see Lesh. Multi-coloured Grateful Dead T-shirts outnumbered Dylan T-shirts, by 100 to one.

Still, the crowed adored Dylan.

The audience, who filled maybe three-quarters of the amphitheatre, cheered throughout the set and gave him a standing ovation even before he set foot on stage.

Backed by a solid four-piece band, Dylan alternated between acoustic and electric numbers and avoided playing it easy. Almost as a rebuke to his hootenanny/folk roots, Dylan played his opening numbers in country and western fashion, with plenty of pedal steel guitar and mandolin.

A few songs into the set, he played *Tangled Up In Blue* and segued neatly into rock 'n' roll. Band members traded acoustic guitars for electric and began to rock out, tearing through *Lay Lady Lay* and *You Gotta Serve Somebody* – the latter tune being Dylan's peculiar paean to born-again Christianity.

Considering that Dylan was once booed off-stage for playing an electric guitar, the audience responded warmly to these abrupt musical changes. The incident happened back in 1965 at the Newport Folk Festival, when Dylan had been enshrined as a folk god, the musical equal of the Beatles and Rolling Stones.

Folk music is no longer quite as popular as it once was, but Dylan endures. His songs can still be heard in everything from bank commercials to recent film releases. (Dylan's Web site, proudly notes the inclusion of new Dylan tunes in a bomb of a film called the *Wonder Boys*). It's probably to safe to assume that bar bands and pub singers will still be warbling their way through the Bob Dylan song-book a 100 years from now.

The same cannot be said about the Grateful Dead. Never any good at writing memorable songs, the Dead achieved cult-like popularity on the strength of their long, spaced out rock jams.

Now that the Dead have broken up, Lesh is eager to continue this dreary musical tradition. His set was notable for long, indulgent jams played with the same sense of stoned listlessness that marked the Dead as one of the worst products of the 1960s.

As appeared in The National Post. Wed., July 19, 2000. Reprinted with permission of Nate Hendley.

Dylan, Dead bassist freshen classic tunes

By Robert Everett-Green, The Globe and Mail.

The attraction of opposites has seldom seemed more strange than last night at the Molson Amphitheatre. There on the same stage, though not at once, were Bob Dylan, unflagging veteran of the sixties folk revival, and Phil Lesh, bassist with the legendary jam band, the Grateful Dead.

Dylan's career has taken many turns, but he always made songs that could, in theory, be sung at any campfire. Lesh and the Dead have produced many songs, but the core of their art has always been expansive improvisation and artful segues.

Hence the confusion crossing the faces of some Dylan fans who stayed after their man's rugged yet tidy 90-minute opening set.

Lesh and his five-piece ensemble committed many clever turns of phrase, and some truly eloquent transitions, but tidy this band was not.

In truth, the chasm between the two veterans is not so wide. Both feed deeply on the vernacular roots of American music, from folk to blues to several distillations of country. And both rebel against the tyranny of the same old thing, though in different ways, Lesh improvises his way out of corners, while Dylan files the corners off and reworks songs.

Dylan's set included some striking deviations from those false canonical specimens; the studio recordings. *Highway 61*

Revisited roared out in a rock-hard electric version. The vocal line of *Like a Rolling Stone* was so far from the original as to stand almost as a variation on an unstated theme. Throughout the set, it was clear that Dylan's grizzled vocal technique, with its baroque dabs and arabesques, has evolved into a way of keeping him from falling into his own shadow.

It didn't always work. *Lay, Lady, Lay,* one of his tenderest ballads, sounded almost sinister as Dylan replaced its lyric yearning with a leer.

But such missteps couldn't derail a show that demonstrated such masterly control of pacing and idiom. The whole range of the Dylan sound was there, from the almost humble style of the acoustic opening tunes, to the distinctive country blend that first emerged in the late sixties, to the kind of hard urban blues that turned *Drifter's Escape* into a truly arena-sized composition.

I heard only the first 40-minute medley by Phil Lesh & Friends, and it was an awesome, intricate, and whimsical event. Medley seems an insufficient word – it was an archipelago of songs, linked by an endlessly changing ocean current.

Some Dead standards – *Shakedown Street, Broke Down Palace* – loomed up unexpectedly, yet inevitably from the subtle harmonic and rhythmic modulations wrought by the band. At its best, the music seemed unled and unbidden. It just happened, like a dream that you know is going to have a happy ending, and a happy middle as well.

The Globe and Mail. Wed., July 19, 2000. Reprinted with permission from The Globe and Mail.

Cool night with Bob

Bob Dylan keeps his distance throughout Molson Amphitheatre concert

By Jane Stevenson, Music.

Anyone who's witnessed Bob Dylan's extraordinary musical comeback of the last few years probably expected a lot from his concert last night at the Molson Amphitheatre.

Like I did, for example, having seen him turn in some truly thrilling shows on the heels of his Grammy Award-winning 1997 release,Time Out Of Mind .

But until the five-song-encore of his hour-and-45-minute performance, the 59-year-old legendary folkie seemed stuck in neutral, despite some solid musicianship by him and his excellent four-piece band, including Charlie "Cheekbones" Sexton on guitar. (Sexton was a budding star in his own right at one time.)

Inexplicably opening last night for Phil Lesh & Friends (Dylan and the former Grateful Dead bassist have been rotating headlining spots) Dylan was a man of few words.

He only muttered, and I do mean muttered, the occasional "Thank-you," and indecipherably introduced his band towards the end.

Even when he left the stage, Dylan stood stone-faced alongside his band members as the crowd (which included local folkies Gordon Lightfoot and Hayden) jumped to their feet while applauding and cheering in appreciation.

It's almost as if he's decided being detached is the way to go.

Oh, well.

At least, Dylan – who along with Lesh didn't allow any cameras to take their pictures last night – scored major points during the latter half of the evening as he performed some seldom played hits Lay Lady Lay and You Gotta Serve Somebody.

The guitar interplay between Dylan and multi-instrumentalist Larry Campbell was also impressive, particularly during Desolation Row, Tangled Up In Blue and Leopard-Skin Pillbox Hat, with Campbell particularly smoking on that last one.

Then came the encore.

Dylan, who occasionally brought out his harmonica, kicked things off with his newest song, Things Have Changed, from the excellent Wonderboys soundtrack. He then moved into classics from his nearly 40-year-old catalogue – Like A Rolling Stone, Don't Think Twice, It's Allright, Highway 61 Revisited and Blowin' In The Wind.

If only the whole evening, which saw the pale-faced singer-songwriter in a retro suit perform in front of a ruffled ivory curtain, had gone as well.

As for the jam-oriented Lesh, his status amongst Deadheads lead to an abundance of tie-dyed shirts, Birkenstocks and crystal necklaces amongst the peace-sign-flashing, dance-happy crowd last.

One obvious Dead fan even hugged an usher who tried to move him out of the aisle where he was engaged in some serious interpretive dance moves.

SUN RATING: 4 out of 5

The Toronto Sun. Wed., July 19, 2000. Reprinted with permission of The Sun Media Corp.

Review

By Jerry Tenenbaum.

Madonna and Cher... Gotta Serve Somebody: Song and Dance Man... Slight Return

Toronto was no exception. It is the professionalism that made the biggest impression. The band is extremely tight. Arguably, this is the best backup band that Dylan has had in recent years. The bonus is that they can sing and harmonize and give the songs something extra... something special.

Six minutes past seven and out they came... no fanfare... just the usual, "Ladies and Gentleman; Would you please welcome..." and into "Duncan and Brady". What struck me immediately was the confidence. Bob Dylan was supremely confident and it showed. It wasn't like most times I have seen him where it took 3 or 4 songs to get things ironed out to get going. The show was excellent from the getgo."Song To Woody" was sweet and "Desolation Row" was alive... the characters were all there in technicolor. "Love Minus Zero/No Limit" was reborn. How many times can a song be reborn? I never get tired of "Tangled". "Tangled" is alive and got the people jumpin'. They were standing up from the start but with "Tangled" they were dancing on the spot. It was sweet and joyous. "This World Can't Stand Too Long" is a beautiful countrified gem and the band did it justice. "Country Pie" was hard and raucous and bore little resemblance in its electrification to the song from Nashville Skyline. "Lay Lady Lay" was a wonderful rendition of a great song. The audience appreciated it and it showed.

Then came "Gotta Serve Somebody". I couldn't make out all the lyrics but Madonna and Cher made the fourth or fifth verse. I think that a few other new lyrics appeared... or have these been used before: I just don't know. (I'm sure if Madonna and Cher have been heard before, someone out there will correct me.) "She Belongs To Me" returned to the beautiful acoustic presentation heard throughout this entire concert. Then it was as if Jimi Hendrix was raised from the dead. "Drifter's Escape" was hard and the guitar work was astounding. This was a real counterpoint to the country acoustic feel of most of the rest of the show. I always admired Bob's blues, and "Leopard-Skin" didn't disappoint.

Then the 30 second pose. The disappearing act. And the 5 song encore. The only song after 1979 was "Things Have Changed". (Where did "Time Out of Mind" go and why? I really like that album. Oh well, you can't have everything all the time.) "Things" was good and quite enjoyable. "Like A Rolling Stone" for the umpteenth time... I still love it and it was very alive and well tonight. "Highway 61" rocked and "Blowin' in the Wind" was beautiful and harmonious and a lovely way to finish a lovely evening. (Yes I went home afterwards.)

Throughout, Bob was bending at the knees, doing little dance steps and in general having a good time. But this was a tight, well presented set in an evolution of "The Song and Dance Man" as the ultimate performer. No one plays sweet acoustics like this band does and not many can rock in the way I heard tonight. And..oh yes..congratulations to the sound people and the system and the Amphitheatre for a job and presentation well done.

Posted to Bob Links. Reprinted with permission of Jerry Tenenbaum.

2001

Introduction

The Never-Ending Tour would stop only once in Canada in 2001.

The only Canadian date would mark Bob Dylan's 98th concert in Canada.

The Date

Toronto, ON	Thurs., Nov. 8, 2001

The show was Dylan's 29th concert in Toronto.

The Musicians

Bob Dylan (vocal, guitar & harmonica).

Charlie Sexton (guitar & backup vocals), Larry Campbell (guitar, mandolin, pedal steel guitar, banjo, bouzouki, steel guitar, electric slide guitar & backup vocals), Tony Garnier (bass), David Kemper (drums & percussion).

The Songs

Bob Dylan performed 22 songs (20 were from albums and 2 were cover and/or traditional songs).

Seven songs made their Canadian live debut.

Humming Bird	Sugar Baby
Cry A While	The Wicked Messenger
High Water (for Charlie Patton)	Honest With Me
Summer Days	–

Two songs have been played only once in Canada.

Humming Bird	Sugar Baby

Bob Dylan performed songs from 11 different albums.

Album	Released	# of Songs Performed by Album
The Freewheelin' Bob Dylan	May 27, 1963	2
The Times They Are A-Changin'	Feb., 10, 1964	1
Bringing It All Back Home	March 22, 1965	1
Highway 61 Revisited	Aug. 30, 1965	3
Blonde on Blonde	May 16, 1966	2
John Wesley Harding	Dec. 27, 1967	2
Planet Waves	Jan. 17, 1974	1
Blood on the Tracks	Jan. 20, 1975	1
MTV Unplugged	June 30, 1995	1
The Essential Bob Dylan	Oct. 31, 2000	1
Love and Theft	Sept. 11, 2001	5

Special Guest

Paul James joined Dylan on stage for Highway 61 Revisited and Like a Rolling Stone.

The Venue

It was Bob Dylan's debut concert at the Air Canada Centre in Toronto.

Thursday, November 8, 2001 --- Air Canada Centre
Toronto, ON

Set List

	Song	From The Album	Released
1.	Humming Bird (Johnnie Wright/Jim Anglin/Jack Anglin)	–	–
2.	The Times They Are A-Changin'	The Times They Are A-Changin'	Feb. 10, 1964
3.	Desolation Row	Highway 61 Revisited	Aug. 30, 1965
4.	This World Can't Stand Long (Jim Anglin)	–	–
5.	Cry A While	Love and Theft	Sept. 11, 2001
6.	Just Like a Woman	Blonde on Blonde	May 16, 1966
7.	High Water (for Charlie Patton)	Love and Theft	Sept. 11, 2001
8.	Maggie's Farm	Bringing It All Back Home	March 22, 1965
9.	A Hard Rain's A-Gonna Fall	The Freewheelin' Bob Dylan	May 27, 1963
10.	John Brown	MTV Unplugged	June 30, 1995
11.	Tangled Up in Blue	Blood on the Tracks	Jan. 20, 1975
12.	Summer Days	Love and Theft	Sept. 11, 2001
13.	Sugar Baby	Love and Theft	Sept. 11, 2001
14.	The Wicked Messenger	John Wesley Harding	Dec. 27, 1967
15.	Rainy Day Women #12 & 35	Blonde on Blonde	May 16, 1966
	1st Encores		
16.	Things Have Changed	The Essential Bob Dylan	Oct. 31, 2000
17.	Highway 61 Revisited	Highway 61 Revisited	Aug. 30, 1965
18.	Like a Rolling Stone	Highway 61 Revisited	Aug. 30, 1965
19.	Forever Young	Planet Waves	Jan. 17, 1974
20.	Honest With Me	Love and Theft	Sept. 11, 2001
21.	Blowin' in the Wind	The Freewheelin' Bob Dylan	May 27, 1963
	2nd Encore		
22.	All Along the Watchtower	John Wesley Harding	Dec. 27, 1967

The Musicians

Bob Dylan (vocal, guitar & harmonica), Charlie Sexton (guitar & backup vocals), Larry Campbell (guitar, mandolin, pedal steel guitar, banjo, bouzouki, steel guitar, electric slide guitar & backup vocals), Tony Garnier (bass), David Kemper (drums & percussion).

Notes

- 98th Bob Dylan concert in Canada; 29th Bob Dylan concert in Toronto.
- 1-4, 9-11, 19, 21, acoustic with the band.
- 1, 4, 19, 21, Larry Campbell & Charlie Sexton (backup vocals).
- 2, 6, 11, 14, Bob Dylan (harmonica).
- 4, Larry Campbell (mandolin).
- 6, Larry Campbell (pedal steel guitar).
- 7, Larry Campbell (banjo).
- 9-10, Larry Campbell (bouzouki).
- 12-13. Tony Garnier (standup bass).
- 15, Larry Campbell (steel guitar).
- 17-18, Paul James (electric guitar).
- Canadian live debut of songs 1, 5, 7, 12, 13, 14 & 20.
- Songs 1 & 13 have been performed only once in Canada.

Reviews

Dylan delights again

By Vit Wagner, Music Critic.

It never pays to read too much into anything that Bob Dylan does, but the 60-year-old troubadour's bang-on set at the Air Canada Centre last night certainly had its share of post-Sept. 11 resonance.

Not that Dylan offered any particular acknowledgement of the event or its aftermath. As usual, Dylan let his music speak for him, his only direct address to the audience being the customary band introduction.

But the large, appreciative, multi-generational crowd was willing to draw its own conclusions from the early inclusion of such numbers as "This World Can't Stand Long" and "A Hard Rain's A-Gonna Fall," followed later by the anti-war ballad "John Brown," as well as the inclusion, in the extended encore, of "Blowin' In The Wind."

If we didn't already know it, the old sage in the white suit and guitar had come to warn us that war is hell and danger lurks. Or maybe he planned to play those songs anyway. Who can say for sure?

What is more certain is that Dylan's rededication to live performance has not waned in the slightest since his equally bracing visit to Molson Amphitheatre in the summer of 2000.

Much of the credit goes to his crack team of accompanists: guitarist Charlie Sexton, multi-instrumentalist Larry Campbell, bassist Tony Garnier and drummer David Kemper. It's no insult to say that these guys would have put on a fine show, even in the absence of their celebrated leader. Missing a certain charismatic dimension, to be sure, but fine none the less.

Dylan and his cohorts gathered momentum as the 2½-hour show progressed, switching effortlessly between acoustic offerings such as "Desolation Row" and plugged-in rips through "Maggie's Farm." Any doubts that this was going to be a night to remember were permanently laid to rest with a rhythmically irresistible mid-set assault on "Tangled Up In Blue" that brought the house to its feet.

The only hint of disappointment was the omission of "Mississippi," the masterpiece from the new *Love And Theft* disc. Dylan did not ignore the album, however, delivering fine renditions of the cautionary "High Water," the old-time rock 'n' roll flavoured "Summer Days," the mellow "Sugar Baby," the bluesy "Cry A While."

After wrapping up with "Rainy Day Women #12 & 35," the band returned for a six-song encore that began with the Oscar-winning "Things Have Changed" and also included such crowd pleasers as "Highway 61 Revisited" and "Like A Rolling Stone." Then they returned one final time for a thundering gallop through "All Along The Watchtower."

Brilliant.

The Toronto Star. Fri., Nov. 9, 2001. Reprinted with permission - Torstar Syndication Services.

Folk-rock Buddha

Dylan as relevant now as he's ever been

By Jane Stevenson, Toronto Sun.

Given Bob Dylan's songbook and the turbulent times we currently find ourselves in, it would have been easy for him to kick off his Air Canada Centre show last night with a protest song.

But then the 60-year-old music legend is anything but predictable.

Instead, Dylan – joined by a four-piece band on a stripped-down stage – launched his two-and-a-half-hour concert with the innocent, rollicking country song, Hummingbird, a tune more reflective of his two-month-old latest album, Love And Theft.

Still, he didn't waste any time getting to his classics and pretty much stuck with them for the rest of the night.

The follow-up songs were The Times They Are A-Changin', as relevant now as it was when Dylan wrote it back in the early '60s, and Desolation Row.

Dressed in a country gentleman's beige suit, with matching beige and black cowboy boots, Dylan stayed on acoustic guitar for the first four numbers, occasionally whipping out his harmonica, much to the crowd's delight.

His electric guitar made its debut for the new bluesy song, Cry A While, but he delivered another standout acoustic set later with A Hard Rain's A-Gonna Fall, Searchin' For A Soldier's Grave and, especially, Tangled Up In Blue.

And whatever Dylan lacked in terms of elocution – words were often undecipherable – the folk-rock Buddha more than made up for in his guitar playing and, frankly, just by being Bob.

His tight-sounding band, meanwhile, all dressed in matching burgundy suits with black shirts, looked ready to play the Grand Ole Opry instead of a hockey arena. Adding to the Nashville feel was talented multi-instrumentalist Larry Campbell playing everything from mandolin to pedal steel to banjo, along with a retro-looking black-and-white-diamond patterned stage floor, and a curtained backdrop.

Still, Dylan in the year 2001 obviously isn't the draw he once was, given the crowd of 10,000 who turned out to see one of the best songwriters of the 20th Century. That number was said to be about 2,000 shy of a sell-out but there sure were a lot of empty seats in the upper sections of the ACC.

Doesn't everyone know that Dylan's at his musically strongest in years with both Love And Theft and its darker, Grammy-winning predecessor 1997's Time Out Of Mind?

All of his newer material, High Water, Summer Days and Sugar Baby, in particular, dovetailed nicely with older gems Just Like A Woman, Maggie's Farm, Everybody Must Get Stoned, Like A Rolling Stone and Blowin' In The Wind.

And when he returned for his first encore, it was his 2001 Oscar-winning-song, Things Have Changed, from the film Wonder Boys, that he played first.

His last number – during a second encore – was, most appropriately, a blistering rendition of All Along The Watchtower.

SUN RATING: 4 1/2 out of 5

The Toronto Sun. Fri., Nov. 9, 2001. Reprinted with permission of The Sun Media Corp.

Aged to perfection

Reviewed by Alan Niester, Special to The Globe and Mail.

Forty-odd years ago, when Bob Dylan and his contemporaries were young men and women, they sat (figuratively speaking – literally, maybe, a few times) at the feet of the men who were then the masters of the arts that the new generation was pursuing: folk giants like Woody Guthrie and Pete Seeger, bluesmen like John Lee Hooker, country singers like Hank Williams, and others.

Now that Dylan has reached 60, he has inherited the crown of the artists he once studied. He is one of the old masters, and the young people sit at his feet, absorbing the wisdom of age.

But as Bob Dylan showed to a reverent and appreciative crowd of about 10,000 at the Air Canada Centre on Thursday night, old age and wisdom do not necessarily come at the expense of dynamism. Bob Dylan has undergone an artistic rebirth, and the evidence is clearly visible when he performs on-stage: Dylan is as captivating at 60 as he was at 20, and a lot more so than when he was 40.

Dylan's rebirth seems to have begun in 1997, with the release of the critically acclaimed *Time Out of Mind*, an album that found him waking up and confronting his own mortality. That re-awakening seems to have stirred long-lost interests and passions that resulted in the recent release of *Love and Theft*, an album that trolls America's musical past, and which finds Dylan dabbling in bluegrass, blues, R & B, swing, jump blues and other almost-forgotten genres.

Mix all this together with what amounts to one of the most storied back catalogues in popular music, and the unfolding war in Afghanistan, and the possibilities on this night were endless. Dylan seemed less a chef than the owner of a buffet restaurant, laying out bits and pieces of his musical past, but providing them with a relevance, and performing them with a spirit that seems indomitable.

Though it can be difficult to ascertain, it would seem that Toronto was treated to a relatively upbeat Dylan on Thursday night. He appeared in a natty white suit, matched with flashy print shirt and grounded by Pat Boone-style white bucks. And he drew more from his back catalogue for this performance than he has on other stops on this tour. Unexpected numbers like *Desolation Row* and *Just Like a Woman* were only two of the treasures dropped into the set.

He began in Grand Ole Opry mode, with he and his four-piece band (led by Charlie Sexton and Larry Campbell on guitar) chugging acoustically through a handful of numbers that included *Hummingbird*, *Desolation Row* and *The Times They Are A-Changin'*. It is typical of the mature Dylan to reconstruct his lyric and melody so drastically that certain songs become almost unrecognizable. Such was the case with the last of those, which ended up being sung in what sounded like a drunken drawl, almost a self-parody. But it did feature an extended harmonica solo on the outro that managed to connect the number to its early '60s origins.

It was not until five songs in (the bluesy *Cry a While* from *Love and Theft*) that the band swapped its acoustic instruments for electric, but even then it took a while to get into the kind of jam mode that has typified Dylan performances over the past decade or so. *Just Like a Woman*, the first real highlight of the evening, had a *Lay Lady Lay* mood. *High Water* (again from *Love and Theft*) had a Poco-ish feel, this time spurred by Campbell's banjo. And while *Maggie's Farm* was fueled by a driving Sexton lead, sombre takes on *A Hard Rain's A-Gonna Fall* (which these days has taken on new relevance) and the traditional *Searchin' for a Soldier's Grave* brought things back down to troubled earth.

But from that point on, things began to soar. *Tangled up in Blue* was a rambling, electric jam, one of those numbers obviously influenced by Dylan's dalliances with the Grateful Dead. And by the time he closed out the main body of his set, the whole room seemed to be in ecstasy (in it, not on it).

There have been moments in years past when Dylan's live performances were, frankly, of questionable worth. One went to see a legend; whatever magical musical moments presented themselves were a bonus. Those days, it seems, are gone. Bob Dylan has resurrected himself as a live performer, a road warrior. While he may sing on occasion about *Masters of War*, he is using his seemingly never-ending road tours to remind us that he is, above all else, a master of song.

As appeared in The Globe and Mail. Sat., Nov. 10, 2001. Reprinted with permission of Alan Niester.

A Minimalist Review

By Jerry Tenenbaum.

Dylan and Band were ideal.

Hummingbird - pure joy
Times - spoken word
Desoluaton Row - heartfelt
This World - wonderful harmony
Cry A While - hard blues/glorious
Just Like A Woman - sweetness/wonderful harp
High Water- ethereal
Maggie's Farm - like a welcome coffee break
Hard Rain - ominous
John Brown - melancholy
Tangled - a joyous triumph
Summer Days - more joy
Sugar Baby - cynical pain
Wicked Messenger - can this band ever rock!
Rainy Day Women - Dancing in the aisles
Things Have Changed - what a tight band!
Highway 61 - Paul James looked so happy
Rolling Stone - it never gets old
Forever Young - It was getting late and he was tucking us all in
Blowin' - fervent wishing
Watchtower - Is there a better band behind Bob.

All in all, another glorious affair. I want you to image a man in an electric wheelchair spinning behind the soundsquare on the floor with others with sound legs spinning madly about him. That's what was happening from half way through to the end. I don't recall seeing this kind of response in any of the shows I have ever been to. And the ages were 7 to 75. The average age around me was maybe 25 to 30.

This is a true renaissance by a renaissance man. See it if you can. It's worth it!

Posted to Bob Links. Reprinted with permission of Jerry Tenenbaum.

Toronto 2001

By Shawn Pulver.

It is always nice to see Bob when he returns to my hometown. Although I think the ACC isn't the best venue to see a Dylan show, the acoustics were very good from where I was in front of the stage. The show started with a strong version of Hummingbird, which my brother thought sounded like it could fit on the O Brother, Where Art Thou Soundtrack. Times was nice, although he flubbed a few words in the second verse. This World also featured a nice vocal, and a few short but sweet mandolin solos supplied by Larry. Cry A While was a real treat, despite sounding like It Takes A Lot to Laugh at the intro. Just Like a Woman was standard, although it featured what seemed to be a four minute harp solo at the end. Very nice! Maggie's Farm was a dramatic new arrangement, with a very cool drum refrain on the solo. Unfortunately, Bob was not happy, and gave Charlie what I would describe as the ultimate "death stare." At the end, Charlie put his hand around Bob, and I thought I could read his lips as he said "sorry." I guess it isn't always easy working for Bob. The acoustic set was the highlight of the show. It was my 30th show, and I've always wanted to hear Hard Rain. I always seemed to miss it by a show or two. Fortunately, Bob nailed all the words, and even had a nice sing along with the crowd. John Brown was dramatic, with Larry playing a cool intro with his Bazouki. Tangled got a nice crowd reaction, although I have to admit it was the first time that I ever ran to use the washroom in the middle of a show (hey, I only missed two verses). As usual, Sugar Baby was sublime. (In case anyone was wondering, that was me yelling "We love you Paul James, see you in London Ontario," before the song started). Wicked Messenger, Summer Days and RDW ended the main set in a rocking fashion. In terms of the encores, they were, as expected, well done, but short of any real surprises. I was happy when Paul James was finally brought on after watching most of the show from the side of the stage. I think I have the unusual distinction of seeing every show that Paul James has ever played with Bob. I saw him in '96 at the Concert Hall, in Buffalo in '99 and now in Toronto at the ACC. Anyways, it brought a smile to Bob's face, and I liked his slide work on Hwy61. Watchtower ended the show on a very high note, and I just can't get over how good that ending is. All in all, a great night and a great show (even though I almost told off the usher about six times for telling me that I was two inches past the aisle. We are, after all, at a Dylan show, not at a performance of Bizet's Carmen. Anyways, thanks for reading.

Posted to the Dylan Pool. Fri., Nov. 9, 2001. Reprinted with permission of Shawn Pulver.

2002

Introduction

The Never-Ending Tour rolled on with eleven concerts in Canada in 2002. The second most concerts in Canada for any given year.

These shows would mark Bob Dylan's 99th, 100th, 101st, 102nd, 103rd, 104th, 105th, 106th, 107th, 108th & 109th concert in Canada.

The Dates

Halifax, NS	Tues., Aug. 6, 2002
Moncton, NB	Thurs., Aug. 8, 2002
Saint John, NB	Fri., Aug. 9, 2002
Quebec City, QC	Sat., Aug. 10, 2002
Montreal, QC	Mon., Aug. 12, 2002
Ottawa, ON	Tues., Aug. 13, 2002
Toronto, ON	Fri., Aug. 16, 2002
Winnipeg, MB	Sat., Aug. 24, 2002
Saskatoon, SK	Mon., Aug. 26, 2002
Edmonton, AB	Tues., Aug. 27, 2002
Calgary, AB	Wed., Aug. 28, 2002

The shows would be Dylan's 2nd concert in Halifax, 2nd concert in Moncton, 2nd concert in Saint John, 2nd in Quebec City, 20th concert in Montreal, 9th concert in Ottawa, 30th concert in Toronto, 5th concert in Winnipeg, 2nd concert in Saskatoon, 5th concert in Edmonton and 5th concert in Calgary.

The Musicians

Bob Dylan (vocal, guitar & harmonica).

Charlie Sexton (guitar, dobro & backup vocals), Larry Campbell (guitar, mandolin, peddle steel guitar, fiddle, cittern, steel guitar, electric slide guitar & backup vocals), Tony Garnier (bass), George Recile (drums & percussion).

The Songs

Bob Dylan performed a total of 200 songs. Of those, 65 were different songs (61 were from albums and 4 were cover and/or traditional songs).

Eleven songs made their Canadian live debut.

I Am the Man, Thomas	Somebody Touched Me
Moonlight	Floater (Too Much To Ask)
Lonesome Day Blues	A Voice From On High
Never Gonna Be the Same Again	The Man in Me
Tweedle Dee & Tweedle Dum	Standing in the Doorway
If Dogs Run Free	–

Four songs have been played only once in Canada.

Never Gonna Be the Same Again	A Voice From On High
If Dogs Run Free	The Man in Me

Bob Dylan performed songs from 23 different albums.

Album	Released	# of Songs Performed by Album
The Freewheelin' Bob Dylan	May, 27, 1963	4
The Times They Are A-Changin'	Feb., 10, 1964	2
Another Side of Bob Dylan	Aug. 8, 1964	3
Bringing It All Back Home	March 22, 1965	5
Highway 61 Revisited	Aug. 30, 1965	4
Blonde on Blonde	May 16, 1966	7
John Wesley Harding	Dec. 27, 1967	3
Nashville Skyline	April 9, 1969	1
New Morning	Oct. 21, 1970	2
Bob Dylan's Greatest Hits, Vol. 2	Nov. 17, 1971	4
Pat Garrett and Billy The Kid	July 13, 1973	1
Planet Waves	Jan. 17, 1974	1
Blood on the Tracks	Jan. 20, 1975	2
Street Legal	June 15, 1978	1
Saved	June 19, 1980	1
Shot of Love	Aug. 12, 1981	1
Empire Burlesque	May, 30, 1985	1

Oh Mercy	Sept. 12, 1989	1
Under the Red Sky	Sept. 11, 1990	1
The Bootleg Series Volumes 1-3	Match 26, 1991	2
Time Out of Mind	Sept. 30, 1997	5
The Essential Bob Dylan	Oct. 31, 2000	1
Love and Theft	Sept. 11, 2001	8

The Venues

It was Bob Dylan's 2nd time playing at the Metro Centre in Halifax, 2nd time playing at the Moncton Coliseum, 2nd time playing at Harbour Station in Saint John, debut concert at l' Agora du Vieux-Port in Quebec City, debut concert at the Molson Centre in Montreal, 2nd time playing at the Corel Centre in Ottawa, 3rd time playing at the Molson Amphitheatre in Toronto, 3rd time playing at the Winnipeg Arena, 2nd time playing at Saskatchewan Place in Saskatoon, 3rd time playing at the Skyreach Centre in Edmonton and the 3rd time playing at the Saddledome in Calgary.

Tuesday, August 6, 2002 --- Metro Centre Halifax, NS

Set List

	Song	From The Album	Released
1.	I Am the Man, Thomas (Ralph Stanley/Larry Sparks)	–	–
2.	Señor (Tales of Yankee Power)	Street Legal	June 15, 1978
3.	Don't Think Twice, It's All Right	The Freewheelin' Bob Dylan	May 27, 1963
4.	Tangled Up in Blue	Blood on the Tracks	Jan. 20, 1975
5.	Subterranean Homesick Blues	Bringing It All Back Home	March 22, 1965
6.	Moonlight	Love and Theft	Sept. 11, 2001
7.	Blind Willie McTell	The Bootleg Series Volumes 1-3	March 26, 1991
8.	Lonesome Day Blues	Love and Theft	Sept. 11, 2001
9.	Mama, You Been on My Mind	The Bootleg Series Volumes 1-3	March 26, 1991
10.	Masters of War	The Freewheelin' Bob Dylan	May 27, 1963
11.	Forever Young	Planet Waves	Jan. 17, 1974
12.	Summer Days	Love and Theft	Sept. 11, 2001
13.	Make You Feel My Love	Time Out of Mind	Sept. 30, 1997
14.	Drifter's Escape	John Wesley Harding	Dec. 27, 1967
15.	Rainy Day Women #12 & 35	Blonde on Blonde	May 16, 1966
	Encores		
16.	Like a Rolling Stone	Highway 61 Revisited	Aug. 30, 1965
17.	Honest With Me	Love and Theft	Sept. 11, 2001
18.	Blowin' in the Wind	The Freewheelin' Bob Dylan	May 27, 1963
19.	All Along the Watchtower	John Wesley Harding	Dec. 27, 1967

The Musicians

Bob Dylan (vocal, guitar & harmonica), Charlie Sexton (guitar, dobro & backup vocals), Larry Campbell (guitar, fiddle, cittern, steel guitar, electric slide guitar & backup vocals), Tony Garnier (bass), George Recile (drums & percussion).

Notes

- 99th Bob Dylan concert in Canada; 2nd Bob Dylan concert in Halifax.
- 1-4, 9-11, 18, acoustic with the band.
- 1, 11, 18, Larry Campbell & Charlie Sexton (backup vocals).
- 2, Larry Campbell (fiddle).
- 3, 14, 18, Bob Dylan (harmonica).
- 5, 8, 17, Larry Campbell (electric slide guitar).
- 6, 12, Tony Garnier (standup bass).
- 7, Larry Campbell (cittern).
- 10, Charlie Sexton (dobro).
- 15, Larry Campbell (steel guitar).
- Canadian live debut of songs 1, 6 & 8.

Reviews

Dylan, band pack a punch

Familiar songs delivered like you've never heard them before

By Bruce Erskine, Staff Reporter.

Things may have changed during Bob Dylan's 40-year career, but the pop culture legend proved in Halifax on Tuesday that he still cares.

Dylan, 61, just off a triumphant return to the Newport Folk Festival, where he was booed off the stage 37 years ago for going electric – and virtually creating folk rock on the spot – rocked a mixed crowd of young and old at the Halifax Metro Centre with a selection of classics and new tunes from his latest CD, Love and Theft.

Dressed in a black cowboy hat, black western suit with red trim and matching cowboy boots, the taciturn Dylan was backed by a crack four-piece band that included Texas guitar slinger Charlie Sexton – heard most recently on Lucinda Williams' critically acclaimed work – string wizard Larry Campbell on guitar, mandolin and steel, Tony Garnier on bass and George Ricelli on drums.

"If there's a better band playing now, I've never heard them," Dylan said after introducing the group just before launching into Like a Rolling Stone.

It was his only direct communication to the crowd all evening.

The two-hour show, which had much of the capacity crowd on its feet even before the band hit the stage, proved that Dylan's music still has power, and he still has the power to deliver it forcefully.

Swaying on his toes and bending at the knees like a latter-day Hank Williams, Dylan played with conviction, even as he toyed with the familiar rhythms of classics like Don't Think Twice and Tangled Up in Blue.

He also unearthed a rollicking Subterranean Homesick Blues, a wistful Moonlight, from Love and Theft, and from the same CD, Summer Days, a hot jump blues straight out of the late '40s that featured blistering guitar work by Sexton and Campbell.

Other highlights included Rainy Day Women 12 and 35 – "Everybody must get stoned" – Forever Young and Senor.

Dylan ended the concert after an hour and a half of non-stop music with a rousing version of his best-known classic, Like a Rolling Stone, that had the crowd begging – and hollering, whistling and stomping – for more.

He obliged with an encore that included Honest with Me, from Love and Theft, followed by one of his earliest and most notable protest songs, Blowin' in the Wind, and finally, All Aong the Watchtower, delivered with a sound and fury that rivalled Jimi Hendrix's famous cover.

All in all, proof that – if you have the goods – you can still rock after 60, which might be something many of the follically challenged middle-aged men in the audience wanted to affirm.

Endnote – the straightforward staging was notable for a small silver statuette on a back riser that looked from a distance a lot like an Oscar – an inscrutable totem or a reminder of Dylan's own 2000 Oscar for the tune Things Have Changed from the film Wonder Boys?

The Halifax Chronicle-Herald. Thurs., Aug. 8, 2002. Republished with permission from The Halifax Herald Limited.

Basic blues

Concert Review

By Sandy MacDonald, The Daily News.

Bob Dylan boiled it all down to the blues. Last night, the musical icon filtered 40 years of his music through the gritty shuffles and limber swing of his streamlined four-piece band, to the delight of the full house at the Metro Centre in Halifax. The concert kicked off the Canadian leg of his summer tour.

Dressed in a black Nudie-style western suit trimmed in red, a big black stetson and two-toned cowboy boots, Dylan sauntered to centre-stage as the house lights dropped.

Then his band launched into the country stomp of I Am The Man, Thomas with three acoustic guitars in front of Tony Garnier's doghouse bass and George Ricelli's tasty drumming.

That famous voice started off pretty creaky. But like a road-weary car that needs an early morning idle, the voice warmed up and held its own fronting the hard-driving band. And the band gave the boss some warm-up room, with a nice acoustic half-set, including Senor, a striding version of Don't Think Twice, It's All Right and Tangled Up In Blue.

Raucous blues revue

With Dylan starting to purr, the band plugged in and the show shifted into a raucous blues revue. Subterranean Homesick Blues got a Chicago blues overhaul, with guitarists Larry Campbell and Charlie Sexton pushing the tune, and Dylan himself grabbing most of the solos. Even with the two powerhouse guitar pickers on either side, Dylan seemed in a mood to play his Fender Stratocaster, grabbing his fair share of lead breaks.

(He certainly wasn't in the mood to chat – the eloquent songwriter never uttered a word until the end of the near-two-hour set. "If there's a better band working out there, I've never heard one," he garbled while introducing the musicians.)

With the rootsy tone well established, Dylan slipped in the swinging Moonlight from last year's Grammy-winning Love and Theft album, with Sexton comping fat jazz chords. The lanky, good-looking Texan too frequently got elbowed out of the action, as Campbell and Dylan jumped over the lead breaks.

The band pushed the intensity through a roaring version of Blind Willie McTell before backing off the gas and slinging on the acoustic guitars again.

Dylan was all business

Though it's hard to penetrate that inscrutable old face, Dylan seemed to be having a good time, even favouring the crowd with a couple of subtle hip shakes and a halfways twist. Beyond that, it was all business.

The lighting was gorgeous, including a change that lit up four onstage table lamps to give a relaxed "sitting in Bob's rec room" feel to the stage. With the intimate mood set, Dylan revisited two classics – Masters Of War and Forever Young.

He tumbled the familiar phrasing and even changed some melody notes.

Dylan shows less reverence for his canon of tunes than some of his die-hard fans. These songs aren't dusty archival relics, but vehicles in motion that frequently need a new coat of paint and the occasional engine overhaul to keep them purring.

Last night, everything got redrawn in shades of blue. Even the set closer, Rainy Day Women #12 and 35, got invigorated with a charged-up Jimmy Reed shuffle.

After a quick towel-off, the band returned for a four-song encore, including Like A Rolling Stone, Blowin' In the Wind and capping the night with All Along The Watchtower.

The Halifax Daily News. Wed., Aug. 7, 2002. Reprinted with permission of The Halifax Daily News.

Thursday, August 8, 2002 --- Moncton Coliseum
Moncton, NB

Set List

	Song	From The Album	Released
1.	I Am the Man, Thomas (Ralph Stanley/Larry Sparks)	–	–
2.	Just Like Tom Thumb's Blues	Highway 61 Revisited	Aug. 30, 1965
3.	Don't Think Twice, It's All Right	The Freewheelin' Bob Dylan	May 27, 1963
4.	Masters of War	The Freewheelin' Bob Dylan	May 27, 1963
5.	Cry A While	Love and Theft	Sept. 11, 2001
6.	Moonlight	Love and Theft	Sept. 11, 2001
7.	I Don't Believe You (She Acts Like We Never Have Met)	Another Side of Bob Dylan	Aug. 8, 1964
8.	High Water (for Charlie Patton)	Love and Theft	Sept. 11, 2001
9.	Tomorrow is a Long Time	Bob Dylan's Greatest Hits, Vol. 2	Nov. 17, 1971
10.	It's Alright, Ma (I'm Only Bleeding)	Bringing It All Back Home	March 22, 1965
11.	My Back Pages	Another Side of Bob Dylan	Aug. 8, 1964
12.	Summer Days	Love and Theft	Sept. 11, 2001
13.	Never Gonna Be the Same Again	Empire Burlesque	May 30, 1985
14.	The Wicked Messenger	John Wesley Harding	Dec. 27, 1967
15.	Rainy Day Women #12 & 35	Blonde on Blonde	May 16, 1966
	Encores		
16.	Like a Rolling Stone	Highway 61 Revisited	Aug. 30, 1965
17.	Honest With Me	Love and Theft	Sept. 11, 2001
18.	Blowin' in the Wind	The Freewheelin' Bob Dylan	May 27, 1963
19.	All Along the Watchtower	John Wesley Harding	Dec. 27, 1967

The Musicians

Bob Dylan (vocal, guitar & harmonica), Charlie Sexton (guitar, dobro & backup vocals), Larry Campbell (guitar, cittern, fiddle, pedal steel guitar, steel guitar, electric slide guitar & backup vocals), Tony Garnier (bass), George Recile (drums & percussion).

Notes

- 100th Bob Dylan concert in Canada; 2nd Bob Dylan concert in Moncton.
- 1-4, 9-11, 18, acoustic with the band.
- 1, 18, Larry Campbell & Charlie Sexton (backup vocals).
- 2, 13, Larry Campbell (pedal steel guitar).
- 4, 9, 11, 14, Bob Dylan (harmonica).
- 4, 10, Charlie Sexton (dobro).
- 5, 17, Larry Campbell (electric slide guitar).
- 6, 12, Tony Garnier (standup bass).
- 10, Larry Campbell (cittern).
- 11, Larry Campbell (fiddle).
- 15, Larry Campbell (steel guitar).
- Canadian debut of song 13.
- Song 13 has been performed only once in Canada.

Reviews

Whatever planet they're from must have some rockin' concerts

Getting to see Bob Dylan perform in Moncton had to rank up there with thrills of a lifetime, at least so far.

By Alix MacLean, The Guardian.

I have this extraterrestrial theory. Most people might disagree with me, but frankly, I don't care.

To me, there are four people that had a huge part in shaping music as we know it today. I mean, there are more than four people, but I'm talking about the four major guys: John Lennon, Bob Dylan, Paul McCartney, and Jimi Hendrix. These guys just came along in the 1960s and possessed more talent than anyone had seen in a long time.

So my theory is, these four guys are aliens that were sent to earth to reform popular music. Think about it. Without Lennon, Dylan, McCartney Hendrix, we would still be listening to doo-wop music. (Basically every song would have about as much substance as a Britney Spears song – what a scary prospect).

So anyway, here I am in a van on my way to see one of those alleged aliens LIVE IN CONCERT!! Bob Dylan, the man who gave pop music a brain, is playing Moncton. I am so excited, I can't even function properly. This is Bob Dylan we're talking about, not some '80s hair-band reunion or the Backstreet Boys. Bob freakin, Dylan. And wait for the best part of it all.

My super amazing uncle, John gave my brother and I tickets to the show. I have no idea how I'm going to thank him, but this is about one of the coolest gifts I've ever gotten. It will have to involve something extravagant, like giving him my soul or first born child.

I think it's fairly obvious that my brother and I are a good choice to give Dylan tickets to, seeing as I think he's so talented that he can't even be human, and was sent from outer space.

We get to the Moncton Coliseum about seven o'clock. The show is supposed to start at 7:30. My uncle, my brother, my uncle's friend, and I all place bets on what song Dylan will sing first, and what song he will do for an encore. (I picked Subterranean Homesick Blues for an encore, but he didn't play it. He made up for it by playing two of my other favourites.)

So as we head inside, I check out the numbers on the ticket. It says we're in section 34, and because it's a high number, I assume that it's near the back. Honestly, that fact doesn't bother me. To see Dylan, I would hang from the ceiling holding on with only my teeth. Now for the second best part. Not only is section 34 nowhere near the back, it's the very first section in front of the stage. I am in row M, section 34, which means that in a very few moments, I will be less than 50 feet from one of my heroes.

We grab our seats, and the aging hippie in front of us turns around. She warns us politely that she will be on her feet for most of the show, and she gives us her reasoning for it: "You can sit down after the concert, you can sit down all day and all night, and every day of your life, but for Dylan, you stay on your feet."

That pretty much said it all. I wasn't sure what to think when she said that, but when the concert started, I knew exactly what she meant. I couldn't believe it. I still can't. Here I was, seeing one of my all-time heroes in the flesh.

When he walked out on stage I thought I was going to go into cardiac arrest. He played 19 songs, the majority of which I wasn't familiar with because they were new. But I didn't care at all.

The ones he played that I really knew were Masters of War, Rainy Day Women #12 and 35, and then for his encore he played my two favourite Dylan songs, Like a Rolling Stone and All Along the Watchtower. His band was amazing, and he rocked Moncton so hard it will never be the same again.

Neither will I. (Thank you so much, Uncle John!)

The Charlottetown Guardian. Sat., Aug. 17, 2002. Reprinted with permission of Alix MacLean and The Charlottetown Guardian.

2002-08-08 Moncton, NB

By Kyle Valanne.

Great concert!! Bob and the band really looked like they were enjoying themselves. The L&T songs sound great; Bob pulled out 5 if my count is right tonight. Blistering guitar work during Wicked Messenger, Summer Days, Honest With Me, and Rainy Day Women; Charlie and Bob seemed to interact a great deal on stage. Bob was shuffling, and dipping, and moving around the stage. He seemed to be into it from the first song!! Saw the Oscar. There was a beware of dog sign on one of the stacks on stage. Bob was wearing black suit with red trim on pocket and collar, and a black cowboy hat. His voice sounds great and I cannot wait until tomorrow!!

Posted to the Dylan Pool. Thurs., Aug. 8, 2002. Reprinted with permission of Kyle Valanne.

Friday, August 9, 2002 --- Harbour Station
Saint John, NB

Set List

	Song	From The Album	Released
1.	I Am the Man, Thomas (Ralph Stanley/Larry Sparks)	–	–
2.	Man in the Long Black Coat	Oh Mercy	Sept. 12, 1989
3.	Tangled Up in Blue	Blood on the Tracks	Jan. 20, 1975
4.	Mr. Tambourine Man	Bringing It All Back Home	March 22, 1965
5.	Tweedle Dee & Tweedle Dum	Love and Theft	Sept. 11, 2001
6.	Lay, Lady, Lay	Nashville Skyline	April 9, 1969
7.	Highway 61 Revisited	Highway 61 Revisited	Aug. 30, 1965
8.	Moonlight	Love and Theft	Sept. 11, 2001
9.	Masters of War	The Freewheelin' Bob Dylan	May 27, 1963
10.	Visions of Johanna	Blonde on Blonde	May 16, 1966
11.	If Dogs Run Free	New Morning	Oct. 21, 1970
12.	Summer Days	Love and Theft	Sept. 11, 2001
13.	Every Grain of Sand	Shot of Love	Aug. 12, 1981
14.	Cold Irons Bound	Time Out of Mind	Sept. 30, 1997
15.	Leopard-Skin Pill-Box Hat	Blonde on Blonde	May 16, 1966
	Encores		
16.	Honest With Me	Love and Theft	Sept. 11, 2001
17.	Blowin' in the Wind	The Freewheelin' Bob Dylan	May 27, 1963
18.	All Along the Watchtower	John Wesley Harding	Dec. 27, 1967

The Musicians

Bob Dylan (vocal, guitar & harmonica), Charlie Sexton (guitar, dobro & backup vocals), Larry Campbell (guitar, cittern, pedal steel guitar, electric slide guitar & backup vocals), Tony Garnier (bass), George Recile (drums & percussion).

Notes

- 101st Bob Dylan concert in Canada; 2nd Bob Dylan concert in Saint John.
- 1-4, 9-11, 17, acoustic with the band.
- 1, 17, Larry Campbell & Charlie Sexton (backup vocals).
- 2, Larry Campbell (cittern).
- 3, 13, 17, Bob Dylan (harmonica).
- 6, Larry Campbell (pedal steel guitar).
- 8, 12, Tony Garnier (standup bass).
- 9, Charlie Sexton (dobro).
- 16, Larry Campbell (electric slide guitar).
- Canadian live debut of songs 5 & 11.
- Song 11 has been performed only once in Canada.

Reviews

On the watchtower with Bob Dylan

By Chisholm Pothier, Politics.

I'm late and Bob Dylan's in the middle of Tangled Up in Blue.

Tangled Up in Blue, the song for my first serious girlfriend. Learned it on guitar so I could play it for her. She dumped me anyway. We didn't love each other. But we both loved that song.

Dylan is in Saint John, singing the soundtrack of the last four decades. My personal soundtrack.

The poet laureate of rock 'n roll, of folk, folk rock, country rock, sometimes of gospel.

He's old now, in his 60s, a skinny little guy who moves like a singer in a honky tonk, doing little country steps as his guitar players wail. He's Hank Williams if he lived to old age, if his body didn't give out in the backseat of a car in a cold and lonely parking lot one New Year's Eve.

Neil Young was wrong. It's better to rust than to burn out. Rusting makes you wise. When Dylan says something, he's got 60 years of living to back it up, 60 years of trying to get ready for the next life.

He's so cool. He's live in Harbour Station. I'm in the same room as Bob Dylan. It's transcendent. Transplendent, even.

He's singing Mr. Tambourine Man. I almost didn't recognize it until the chorus. Now I'm thinking about the first time I took a trip upon a magic swirling ship.

I was probably listening to Dylan. Maybe Jimi Hendrix singing All Along the Watchtower.

"Then take me disappearin' through the smoke rings of my mind, Down the foggy ruins of time, far past the frozen leaves, the haunted frightened trees, out to the windy beach, far from the twisted reach of crazy sorrow."

Imagine hearing that in the early 1960s in a pop song.

Dylan sings All Along the Watchtower later. He does it more like Hendrix than Dylan.

Now it's Lay, Lady Lay, the song people don't recognize as Dylan because he had quit smoking before recording Nashville Skyline and his voice was thick and rich. They'd recognize it as Dylan now. The quitting didn't take and the voice has almost become a caricature of itself.

Who cares. Dylan's a good singer. He gets his point across. And it's the words that matter, anyhow.

"I long to see you in the morning light, I long to reach for you in the night."

As a kid, I had never heard anything so chastely erotic. It still excites me. What else would you need to say? How could the object of your affection resist?

This is supposed to be a column about politics. Bob Dylan's about music.

But Dylan's music is politics. Brave, unpopular politics sometimes.

The United States is looking for an excuse, any excuse to use bombs on Iraq. Is it a justified war or is it a playground for the military/industrial complex, an opportunity to fill out new multi-million dollar orders and test new hardware? Dylan stands on stage in Saint John and sings about the masters of war who have built the big bombs.

"Let me ask you a question, is your money that good? Will it buy you forgiveness? Do you think that it should? ... And I hope that you die, and your death will come soon ... I'll watch while your lowered down to your deathbed. And I'll stand o'er your grave, 'til I'm sure that you're dead."

You don't hear that on CNN.

Why is he dragging that old nugget out of the archives now? Dylan's still relevant.

He's still good too, as he smashes through Tweedle Dee and Tweedle Dum, a rocker from his newest album.

"Every song's the same," complains the Celine Dion fan standing behind me, as Dylan sings a glorious version of Blowin' In the Wind, the harmonies swinging low, coming for to carry us home. The songs aren't the same. You just have to listen harder.

"How many times must the cannon balls fly, before they're forever banned?"

It seems like a naive sentiment now. It seemed like a good question when I was a kid.

Sex, drugs, politics, rock 'n roll. With Dylan as Pied Piper, Dylan like Virgil guiding Dante through heaven and hell. The soundtrack of a life, the soundtrack of a generation, a few generations even, as the grandparents and teenagers in Friday's crowd would attest.

"Thanks Bob," Neil Young said drily on Dylan's 30th anniversary as a performer. "Thanks for having Bob Fest."

Bob Fest today is a never-ending tour of the world with hockey rinks filling in for roadhouses. He gets off the beaten path, coming here twice in five years. About 6,000 people were screaming their thanks for Bob Fest and for Bob Friday night.

Joe Strummer of the Clash said playing in front of Dylan was like playing in front of God.

Last Friday, I saw God.

He was wearing a cowboy hat.

The Fredericton Daily Gleaner. Fri., Aug. 16, 2002. Reprinted with permission of The Fredericton Daily Gleaner.

Saturday, August 10, 2002 --- l'Agora du Vieux-Port Quebec City, QC

Set List

	Song	From The Album	Released
1.	I Am the Man, Thomas (Ralph Stanley/Larry Sparks)	–	–
2.	Man in the Long Black Coat	Oh Mercy	Sept. 12, 1989
3.	Tangled Up in Blue	Blood on the Tracks	Jan. 20, 1975
4.	Love Minus Zero/No Limit	Bringing It All Back Home	March 22, 1965
5.	Tweedle Dee & Tweedle Dum	Love and Theft	Sept. 11, 2001
6.	Just Like a Woman	Blonde on Blonde	May 16, 1966
7.	Stuck Inside of Mobile with the Memphis Blues Again	Blonde on Blonde	May 16, 1966
8.	Moonlight	Love and Theft	Sept. 11, 2001
9.	Masters of War	The Freewheelin' Bob Dylan	May 27, 1963
10.	Mama, You Been on My Mind	The Bootleg Series Volumes 1-3	March 26, 1991
11.	It's All Over Now, Baby Blue	Bringing It All Back Home	March 22, 1965
12.	Summer Days	Love and Theft	Sept. 11, 2001
13.	Lay, Lady, Lay	Nashville Skyline	April 9, 1969
14.	Drifter's Escape	John Wesley Harding	Dec. 27, 1967
15.	Rainy Day Women #12 & 35	Blonde on Blonde	May 16, 1966

	Encores		
16.	Honest With Me	Love and Theft	Sept. 11, 2001
17.	Blowin' in the Wind	The Freewheelin' Bob Dylan	May 27, 1963
18.	All Along the Watchtower	John Wesley Harding	Dec. 27, 1967

The Musicians

Bob Dylan (vocal, guitar & harmonica), Charlie Sexton (guitar, dobro & backup vocals), Larry Campbell (guitar, cittern, pedal steel guitar, electric slide guitar & backup vocals), Tony Garnier (bass), George Recile (drums & percussion).

Notes

- 102nd Bob Dylan concert in Canada; 2nd Bob Dylan concert in Quebec City.
- 1-4, 9-11, 17, acoustic with the band.
- 1, 17, Larry Campbell & Charlie Sexton (backup vocals).
- 2, Larry Campbell (cittern).
- 4, 6, 11, 13, Larry Campbell (pedal steel guitar).
- 4, 6, 14, 17, Bob Dylan (harmonica).
- 8, 12, Tony Garnier (standup bass).
- 9, Charlie Sexton (dobro).
- 16, Larry Campbell (electric slide guitar).

Reviews

Bob Dylan… 27 ans plus tard

par Kathleen Lavoie.

Si Bob Dylan n'existait pas, il faudrait l'inventer. Parce que Dylan redonne espoir en l'avenir.

Je m'explique. En pénétrant dans l'Agora, hier, je savais que je n'assisterais pas à un spectacle conventionnel. C'est connu: depuis toujours, le père du folk-rock fait mentir les faiseurs d'images avec son attitude rebelle et ses prestations anticonformistes...

Ces dernières, loin de proposer des costumes flamboyants et des mises en scène spectaculaires, brillent plutôt par leur sobriété.

Certains s'en plaindront? Pas moi. C'est fou comme une prestation dénuée de toute intervention superflue, d'artifices visuels ou de pas chorégraphiés laisse toute la place... à la musique.

Avec Dylan, il y a longtemps que ses fans ont accepté ce trait caractéristique de leur idole. Pour les autres, habitués aux démonstrations plus exubérantes, il y aura toujours de l'éducation à faire, diront les premiers.

N'empêche. Assister à un spectacle de Bob Dylan demeure une expérience à vivre. Les oreilles bien ouvertes, à part ça. Parce qu'à 61 ans, le grand Bob est toujours aussi délinquant, toujours aussi frondeur, toujours aussi désespérément audacieux. Qui, après tout, prendrait le risque de monter sur scène sans adresser un seul mot à la foule (à part, bien sûr, pour présenter ses musiciens...)? Qui prendrait le risque d'offrir des versions presque méconnaissables de ses succès les plus aimés? Qui se mettrait constamment au défi en réinventant chaque soir le spectacle de la veille?

À cette question, il n'y a qu'une réponse: Bob Dylan. Il ne suffit de passer que quelques instants dans l'univers passionnant des dylanomanes pour comprendre ce qui a pu les mener au culte. Cette idée d'un créateur qui se réinvente constamment, qui défie les prévisions et qui ose sans se préoccuper de la critique ne saurait être plus emballante pour un mélomane. Moi la première.

Devrait-on alors s'émouvoir que Dylan ait laissé de côté des «hits» comme *Like a Rolling Stone*, *The Times They Are A-Changin'* ou *Mr Tambourine Man*? Pas du tout. Parce que leur absence a permis d'apprécier bon nombre de pièces du dernier album, *Love and Theft*, soit les *Tweedle Dee & Tweedle Dum*, *Summer Days*, *Moonlight* et, en rappel, *Honest with Me*. Des pièces, comme toujours, refaçonnées en des blues légers, des rock énergiques, des ballades folk vibrantes, sous les doigts agiles de Dylan lui-même, de Tony Garnier (basse), de Larry Campbell, (guitare), de George Ricelli (batterie) et de l'incroyable Charlie Sexton (guitare).

Devrait-on mettre en question les versions surprenantes de classiques tels que *Blowin' in The Wind*, *Masters of War*, *Just Like a Woman* (plutôt fidèle à l'enregistrement, hier), *Tangled Up in Blue*, *Lay, Lady, Lay* et la très percutante *All Along the Watchtower*? Si c'est pour les renouveler, certainement pas.

Devrait-on encore une fois ramener sur le tapis la question de la voix de Dylan? Allez donc savoir! Certains apprécient ses failles comme d'autres les décrient. Je ferais plutôt partie des premiers. Dans cette voix éraillée qui casse constamment, il y a plus de vécu, d'intensité, de conviction et de passion que dans bien des grandes voix lisses.

Chose certaine, les 5200 spectateurs présents dans l'enceinte de l'Agora, hier, n'ont pas trouvé à s'en plaindre. Il faut dire que tous les éléments – naturels surtout – étaient réunis pour faire de ces retrouvailles avec un Dylan en pleine possession de ses moyens, un moment mémorable.

Voilà pourquoi Dylan donne espoir en l'avenir. Parce qu'il fait la preuve par quatre qu'il est possible dans le monde de la musique d'aujourd'hui d'être authentique, de faire passer la musique en avant, de lutter contre les diktats de l'image.

N'eût été de l'organisation catastrophique de l'Agora, le spectacle de plus de deux heures, avec ses trois rappels, aurait pu être l'un des plus agréables que l'on ait connus à la belle étoile depuis belle lurette. Comment se fait-il alors qu'on ait attendu à la toute dernière minute pour ouvrir les accès à la salle? Comment se fait-il qu'il y en ait si peu alors que se présentait une foule aussi considérable?

Ces interrogations, il faudra les adresser aux organisateurs. Parce que dans les estrades se trouvaient de nombreux mécontents, hier. Il n'y a rien de trop intéressant dans le fait de manquer trois pièces parce qu'on est pris dans un entonnoir à la porte...

On veut bien retourner à l'Agora, mais encore faudrait-il qu'on nous y accueille toutes portes ouvertes... À bon entendeur!

Le Soleil. Sun., Aug. 11, 2002. Reprinted with permission of Le Soleil.

Une présence hypnotique et des chansons méconnaissables

par Pierre O. Nadeau.

Sacré Dylan! Il a complètement hypnotisé ses fans de Québec, hier, au cours d'une véritable soirée magique, sous le ciel complice de l'Agora du Vieux-port de Québec, où il a fait le bonheur de ses fans, même en leur offrant de nouvelles versions presque méconnaissables de ses succès!

Il aurait été difficile d'imaginer des retrouvailles plus chaleureuses, après 27 ans d'absence. Il fallait voir la foule suspendue à la démarche pourtant très statique du légendaire personnage, qui est apparu fidèle à son image énigmatique.

Attendu depuis une éternité, il était enfin là, le frêle petit homme, venu nous livrer quelques pages de son catalogue géant devant 5200 admirateurs conquis d'avance.

Nonchalant

Coiffé de son chapeau de cow-boy, il était là, debout, presque effacé, son éternelle allure nonchalante en bandoulière.

Pas un mot de départ, pas un mot plus tard. Bob Dylan nous a parlé strictement par ses chansons, de plus anciennes aux plus nouvelles, avec l'appui de quatre efficaces musiciens, guidés par le solide guitariste Charlie Sexton.

Même si ça ne bougeait pas beaucoup en scène, il s'en dégageait une belle magie, à la faveur de la complicité d'un quatuor qui s'en donnait joyeusement sur les rythmes funk, country et rock, toujours chauffés à l'électricité!

On a eu droit à un imposant *show* de guitares rehaussé à l'occasion de quelques souffles d'harmonica, qui provoquaient les frissons à tout coup. Aucun moment en solo.

Aucun son acoustique. Dylan s'est livré en gang!

Le spectacle, dont le contenu varie d'un soir à l'autre, accordait une grande place à son dernier album, *Love and Theft*, tout en favorisant le plus merveilleux voyage dans le temps, à commencer par les airs de *Tangled Up in Blue* et de *Just Like a Woman*.

Lay, Lady, Lay a ensuite fait résonner cette voix écorchée, rauque et plus nazillarde que jamais.

Des *tounes* transformées

La foule a pu apprécier l'esprit créateur de l'artiste qui se réinvente continuellement en remodelant ses classiques, comme l'incontournable *Blowin'in the Wind*, dont les nouvelles couleurs en ont sûrement dérouté plusieurs.

Bob Dylan, c'est l'homme des paradoxes. La froideur qu'il dégage en scène se transforme en chaleur à travers ce magnétisme envoûtant, qui lui est particulier.

Après deux heures de *show*, sans entracte, Bob Dylan s'est éclipsé, de nouveau sans mot dire, sur les notes du classique *All Along the Watchtower*, en nous laissant sur notre appétit de *Like a Rolling Stone*.

Ce sera sans doute pour la prochaine fois...

Le Journal de Québec. Sun., Aug. 11, 2002. Reprinted with permission of Le Journal de Québec.

Monday, August 12, 2002 --- Molson Centre
Montreal, QC

Set List

	Song	From The Album	Released
1.	I Am the Man, Thomas (Ralph Stanley/Larry Sparks)	–	–
2.	Just Like Tom Thumb's Blues	Highway 61 Revisited	Aug. 30, 1965
3.	It's Alright, Ma (I'm Only Bleeding)	Bringing It All Back Home	March 22, 1965
4.	It's All Over Now, Baby Blue	Bringing It All Back Home	March 22, 1965
5.	Tweedle Dee & Tweedle Dum	Love and Theft	Sept. 11, 2001
6.	Moonlight	Love and Theft	Sept. 11, 2001
7.	Subterranean Homesick Blues	Bringing It All Back Home	
8.	High Water (for Charlie Patton)	Love and Theft	Sept. 11, 2001
9.	One Too Many Mornings	The Times They Are A-Changin'	Feb. 10, 1964
10.	A Hard Rain's A-Gonna Fall	The Freewheelin' Bob Dylan	May 27, 1963
11.	Don't Think Twice, It's All Right	The Freewheelin' Bob Dylan	May 27, 1963
12.	Summer Days	Love and Theft	Sept. 11, 2001
13.	Make You Feel My Love	Time Out of Mind	Sept. 30, 1997
14.	The Wicked Messenger	John Wesley Harding	Dec. 27, 1967

15.	Rainy Day Women #12 & 35	Blonde on Blonde	May 16, 1966
	Encores		
16.	Honest With Me	Love and Theft	Sept. 11, 2001
17.	Blowin' in the Wind	The Freewheelin' Bob Dylan	May 27, 1963
18.	All Along the Watchtower	John Wesley Harding	Dec. 27, 1967

The Musicians

Bob Dylan (vocal, guitar & harmonica), Charlie Sexton (guitar, dobro & backup vocals), Larry Campbell (guitar, cittern, pedal steel guitar, steel guitar, electric slide guitar & backup vocals), Tony Garnier (bass), George Recile (drums & percussion).

Notes

- 103rd Bob Dylan concert in Canada; 20th Bob Dylan concert in Montreal.
- 1-4, 9-11, 17, acoustic with the band.
- 1, 17, Larry Campbell & Charlie Sexton (backup vocals).
- 2, 4, 9, Larry Campbell (pedal steel guitar).
- 3, Charlie Sexton (dobro).
- 3, 10, Larry Campbell (cittern).
- 4, 13-14, 17, Bob Dylan (harmonica).
- 6, 12, Tony Garnier (standup bass).
- 7, 16, Larry Campbell (electric slide guitar).
- 15, Larry Campbell (steel guitar).

Reviews

Dylan delivers before 8,000

By T'cha Dunlevy, Gazette New Music Critic.

Bob Dylan makes concessions for no one. Luckily, he's a heck of a talented guy. And so, 40 years into a colourful and textured career, he pulled off a rare feat before 8,000 fans at the Molson Centre last night.

He managed to play the part of incredibly influential pop (rock? blues? folk?) artist aging gracefully. And with attitude.

That's not as easy it sounds. Look around. Pick any of his 1960s (or '70s) rock peers, put them on a stage and try not to either cringe, make excuses for the decline in their impact or at least lose yourself in a bubble of denial.

Bob Dylan strode out on stage in a black cowboy hat and black suit – with a red stripe down his pants legs – and made four decades of music mean something.

He didn't do it with witty between-song banter – there wasn't an off-the-cuff word exchanged with the crowd. He didn't do it with a flood of golden oldies; he chose a select few classics and interspersed them tastefully, and playfully.

He did it by getting down to business; the business of music, that is.

Accompanied by a tight, adaptable four-piece band, Dylan showed as much respect for his often poetic, prescient lyrics as for the heart and soul of the largely blues-based jams that many of the songs turned into.

And there was mischief.

That his voice is not what it once was is an ill-kept secret. But Dylan seemed to run with the idea, contorting his vocals into a variation of garbled, nasal mumbles and evocatively weathered and accomplished attempts at capturing beauty.

The patient, enthusiastic crowd was with him throughout. And as the night went on, a unity built. Cheers erupted as much for recognizable songs as for inspired jamming.

A breakthrough came about halfway in, as he dropped into a gentle, acoustic version of Don't Think Twice, It's Alright, from his 1963 album The Freewheelin' Bob Dylan. His gravelly voice countered with a darkish twist.

And the nostalgia came as it should, with meaning and a sense of real-life, time-worn struggle. As the song wound down, the band turned it into a heavy, near-riotous blues, without overdoing it.

A couple of songs later, he was into the silly, festive classic Rainy Day Women #12 & 35, better known by its chorus, "Everybody must get stoned." Throwing his lyrics about with gruff irreverence, Dylan was having fun with it, as were his musicians.

That, apparently, is what it's still all about. Cool.

The Montreal Gazette. Tues., Aug. 13, 2002.

Bob Dylan: 40 ans en deux heures

par Philippe Renaud.

LES ROLLING STONES mijotent leur tournée soulignant l'anniversaire de 40 ans passés sur les scènes. Pour l'heure, c'est Bob Dylan professionnellement quadragénaire qui brille sous les projecteurs de son aura de monstre du rock et du folk. Sous un Stetson aussi noir que son complet, le cow-boy de la pop a dégainé 18 chansons en deux heures devant un parterre de 8000 fans- eux de la première heure comme les plus jeunes. Quatre décennies de chansons, davantage dans l'histoire de la musique américaine: l'admirateur de Woody Guthrie a décliné son concert en des tons country, folk, blues et rock, appuyé par un groupe de vrais pros.

Monsieur Zimmerman n'a pas mis de temps à démarrer son concert au Centre Molson hier. "Good evening, ladies & gentlemen, please welcome Columbia recording artist... Bob Dylan!": à 19 h 50, sans autre fla fla qu'une bande-son de fanfare, il attaquait *I Am the Man, Thomas* façon bluegrass, sage mais impeccable. Dès la deuxième chanson (*Just Like Tom Thumb's Blues*), l'auditoire se mettait à son aise, allumait son petit joint pour se replonger dans l'atmosphère de guitares électriques et acoustiques qui se pointait.

Fallait aussi se faire à la voix du grand Dylan. Ce n'est plus une surprise pour personne, elle est carrément incompréhensible. Un mélange de mots mâchouillés et de bruits gutturaux. Heureusement que la qualité du groupe venait compenser pour cette voix nasillarde. Nous pouvions ainsi compter sur l'ancien-jeune-prodige-guitariste Charlie Sexton en tête, Larry Campbell aux guitares *slide*, électrique et mandoline et Tony Garner à la basse- ces mêmes trois musiciens dont on peut savourer le jeu sur *Love and Theft*.

De ce plus récent album, cinq chansons ont passé la rampe jusqu'à la scène: l'excellente *Tweedle Dee & Tweedle Dum* – qui a annoncé un virage plus électrique, après 30 minutes de folk à lent décollage – la jazzée *Moonlight*, le blues-rock de *High Water*, *Summer Days* et *Honest With Me* (en rappel). Un bon équilibre entre les chansons récentes et les classiques que tous espéraient, et un concert très différent de celui présenté à Québec samedi soir dernier.

Encore fallait-il les reconnaître, ces classiques! Surtout que Bob Dylan n'a rien fait pour nous aider; non seulement ses paroles étaient difficiles à décoder, mais ces vieilles chansons étaient bonifiées de nouveaux arrangements, voire de nouvelles mélodies.

Tentons notre coup. *It's Allright Ma (I'm Only Bleeding)* arriva troisième dans l'ordre et fut étirée en un long jam applaudi, à tout rompre, par les fans qui l'avaient replacée. Doublé de succès avec une version de *It's All Over Now, Baby Blue*, joliment remaniée country, avec harmonica et slide guitar. Un country rock punché a poussé dans le dos de *Subterranian Homesick Blues* puis, trois chansons plus tard, *A Hard Rain's A-Gonna Fall* poursuivait un passage acoustique qui s'est conclu par la coulante et soyeuse *Don't Think Twice, It's All Right*.

Le public, excité au début du concert, a suivi le courant country-folk imposé par Dylan. L'écoute attentive était de mise, au moins pour la première heure du concert. Nous baignions dans ce retour aux sources de l'Americana, captivés par ce qui semblait un long coucher de soleil sur les plaines. Couché, mais pas éteint: à 61 ans, Bob Dylan n'a visiblement pas tout dit, ne serait-ce que pour redire la musique qui l'a nourri dans sa jeunesse et pour croasser la fine poésie qu'il nous pond encore à son âge de rock star honorable.

Comme un vieux pro, après nous avoir gavé de cordes acoustiques et d'ambiances qui tanguent, il nous a asséné *Rainy Day Woman #12 & 35 ("Everybody must get stoned!")* rugueusement électrifiée-encore une tournée de pétards dans le Centre Molson! Après l'entracte qui a suivie, une nouvelle chanson, puis une version méconnaissable de *Blowin' in the Wind* (nouveaux arrangements, nouvelle mélodie) et, enfin, une lecture blues-rock, probablement inspirée de Hendrix, de *All Along the Watchtower*. Magnifique et éloquent coup de poing sonore au final.

Il égrène péniblement ses solos de guitare et cause bruyamment plus qu'il ne chante. Mais tant qu'il sera vivant, nous irons revoir Bob Dylan pour y passer une aussi belle soirée que celle d'hier.

As appeared in La Presse. Tues., Aug. 13, 2002. Reprinted with permission of Philippe Renaud.

Du mythe au musicien, le fossé se creuse

Bob Dylan au Centre Molson

par Sylvain Cormier.

Qu'attendait-on hier de Bob Dylan, sinon qu'il soit lui-même, c'est-à-dire intraitable? Si l'on espérait de ce passage au Centre Molson le sing-along nostalgique des chansons tant aimées en quelque 40 ans de route n'amassant pas mousse, on ne pouvait que sortir frustré. Je l'étais, même si je savais qu'il nous saboterait exprès l'accès aux mélodies, et par là le plaisir trop sucré du souvenir. C'est ainsi. Dylan refuse que ses chansons existent autrement qu'au présent, quitte à en réinventer chaque soir les airs. Mais imaginais-je qu'il pouvait s'en éloigner à ce point? Qu'il parviendrait à nous rendre si étrangères les *It's Alright, Ma (I'm Only Bleeding), It's All Over Now, Baby Blue, A Hard Rain's A-Gonna Fall* et autres *Don't Think Twice, It's All Right*

Pour un peu, à le voir ainsi attifé en Zorro de carnaval, on aurait cru qu'il nous traçait un grand Z ironique avec sa Fender Stratocaster, nous signifiant la pure vanité de notre désir de retrouvailles. Heureusement qu'il y avait Dylan le musicien, et les musiciens de Dylan, pour que cette entreprise de déconstruction du mythe ait sa contrepartie. Et quelle formidable contrepartie! Dylan a-t-il été mieux accompagné depuis The Band? Doutons-en: avec l'as texan Charlie Sexton aux guitares, avec ces gars que mille millions de spectacles avec Dylan ont soudés jusqu'à la totale flexibilité, avec Bon lui-même devenu véritable guitariste soliste à force de se payer des solos, ce groupe est si performant, si solide dans toutes les formes des musiques de racines, que le meilleur du spectacle en dépend.

De fait, on ne retrouvait la saveur originale des chansons que dans les solos d'accords à la mexicaine que se partageaient Sexton et Dylan: à ces moments, quand Dylan ne chantait plus et jouait avec l'intensité d'un possédé (avec la patte elvissienne en mouvement constant!), la musique ressuscitait les mélodies et les 8 000 spectateurs renouaient avec leur héritage. C'était d'autant plus flagrant que Dylan offrait un idéal point de comparaison, rendant les nouveautés de l'album *Love & Theft* très exactement comme sur le disque: la craquante *Tweedle Dee & Tweedle Dum*, la joliment swing *Moonlight*, le fumantrockabilly *Summer Days*, la non moins ronflante *Honest With Me* étaient non seulement reconnaissables, mais d'élocution presque soignée, alors que les grandes anciennes était mâchouillées comme de vieilles chiques.

Que restait-il de *Stuck Inside Of Mobile With The Memphis Blues Again*, épique rock du milieu des années 60? Le riff. De l'hymne *Blowin' In The Wind*? Le refrain. De *Rainy Day Women #12 & #35*, de *Subterranean Homesick Blues*? Les mots d'ordres, tout juste intelligibles: "*Everybody must get stoned*"; "*Don't follow leaders / Watch the parking meters*". Plus moyen, en effet, de suivre Dylan. Libéré de ses mots, il va où le mène soir après soir son *band*, ne servant plus que la musique. La foule, elle, n'a plus qu'à jouir du moment. Et merde à l'oeuvre.

Le Devoir. Tues., Aug. 13, 2002. Reprinted with permission of Le Devoir.

DYLAN

Le temps passe et le vieux Bob se surpasse

par Philippe Rezzonico.

Le premier hymne, *Blowin' in the Wind*, ouvrait son deuxième 33-tours, *The Freewheelin'Bob Dylan*, en 1963. Tant de gens l'ont connu par cette chanson folk épique. D'autres l'ont découvert avec l'incontournable *Like a Rolling Stone*, livrée sur *Highway 61 Revisited*, alors qu'il était passé en mode électrique.

Il y a même des jeunes qui l'ont découvert tout récemment, par l'entremise de *Hurricane* qui a joué dans un film fort bien défendu par Denzel Washington.

Peu importe.

Avec la guitare sèche ou le manche électrique, Bob Dylan peut être encore fort convaincant, comme il l'a démontré, hier, dans l'amphithéâtre du Centre Molson dont les 8 000 sièges étaient occupés.

Ouverture

Habillé en noir et chapeau sur la tête – on vous le précise parce que les photographes n'étaient pas admis –, le troubadour a ouvert son set de deux heures avec *I Am the Man, Thomas*. En effet.

Sans appui visuel – un écran géant n'aurait pas été superflu – et au sein d'une scène dénudée, hormis de larges rideaux, *His Bobness* a alterné entre classiques et récents crus, entre monuments et chansons méconnues.

Dans la foule ou se trouvaient une quantité impressionnante de jeunes de moins de 30 ans, on célébrait en buvant gaiement et en fumant sans restriction. Durant le splendide pont de *It's All Over Now, Baby Blue*, le type assis à côté de nous a offert son joint à toute la rangée de journalistes.

Qualité de son

Le son était d'une qualité insensée. Même à distance, on pouvait discerner à la perfection les solos de *slide* de Larry Campbell. Dylan, parfois inaudible sur scène, était presque probant sur le plan vocal... du moins, selon ses standards.

S'il a tendance à marmonner principalement ses chansons plus connues (*A Hard Rain's A-Gonna Fall, Don't Think Twice, It's All Right*), il pétait le feu sur *Summer Days* qui semblait tirée d'une session de Sun Records; *High Water*, lourde à souhait; ainsi que lors des livraisons hautement électriques et meurtrières de *Rainy Day Women # 12 and # 35* et *All Along the Watchtower*.

En forme

Ce type à la jambe gauche si leste a vraiment 40 ans de carrière derrière lui? Avec la forme affichée, hier, Bob, tu peux revenir nous voir quand tu veux.

Le Journal de Montréal. Tues., Aug. 13, 2002. Reprinted with permission of Le Journal de Montréal.

2002-08-12 Montréal, QC

By David Hanley.

And here's another view of the Montreal show.

Before concert stuff:

I had to work, so I missed out on the Peel Pub get together, but I got to Moe's at 5:30-ish and met a few poolers: Sweet Melinda, Boiled Guts Of Birds, Tuff Mama, a couple of others. A highlight was Boiled Guts explaining that he had put aside several albums that he won't listen to until Bob dies, making sure that he'll always have new Bob music to listen to. Among the titles: John Wesley Harding, Baement Tapes, Empire Burlesque, etc. So he's a little eccentric. Aren't we all? A bit later, Toomraider staggered over from the other gathering and other than immediately knocking over a glass and dousing a guy, you'd never have known he'd been drinking for 5 hours or so (just kidding man!). I then moved on to the Molson Centre and at last met the fabled Dearest Puppy. He was in a very mellow mood, probably from the afternoon of beer and lollipops. As he'd promised/threatened, he gave me a big kiss as a greeting. Most of you will have to wait until his picture is posted to realize just how terrifying this was (the horror, the horror). Actually, Puppy was very friendly and, along with Tuff Mama, we loitered with intent near the rail. Puppy was moved along (nice guy, but he'll never be inconspicuous), but we were left alone and when the show started Tuff Mama and I were able to grab spots right on the rail. Nice view.

Concert stuff:

Bob came on dressed in black with the fashion victim red piping on his trousers and jacket pockets and the show started. Bob's voice was strong and the band was very tight. There seemed to be a good rapport going on between Bob and the band and within the band itself. Larry was grinning through much of the show, particularly when Charlie would pull a mock guitar hero move. There was frequent eye contact between them and they seemed to be really into the music and enjoying themselves. They can play a little too.

I Am The Man, Thomas: Snappy, upbeat opener with the harmonies nicely done.

Just Like Tom Thumb's Blues: Very tasty acoustic guitar on this one with a great vocal. The song's pretty good too. This was a highlight for me.

It's Alright Ma: Bob growled through a pretty good version of this.

It's All Over Now, Baby Blue: The arrangement was nice, which is about all I can think to say about it.

Tweedle Dee & Tweedle Dum: The electric set began with my least favourite L&T song, but the band really rocked this one and there was some nice guitar work from Charlie. For some reason, the crowd hadn't gotten into the show until this point, but this seemed to wake them up.

Moonlight: Smooth.

SHB: Another highlight. It was energetic and bouncy, and Bob seemed to enjoy doing it. I guess he messed up some of the words, but since they're somewhat nonsensical to begin with, it didn't bother me much. It was fun.

High Water: One of the best L&T songs. I prefer the arrangement on the album, but Bob was commanding on this song. The words come with the authority of a sage. Yet another highlight. (I haven't seen Bob that often, so I might be easier to please than others – I thought there were quite a few high spots, as you'll see).

One Too Many Mornings: Back to the 60s with a fine acoustic version of one of my favourites. It was about now that it occured to me that Bob was probably going to ignore his catalogue between Highway 61 and L&T, so when people started calling for songs (there were calls for Hattie Carroll and Masters Of War and some lunatics were actually calling for Silvio), I yelled out for Idiot Wind. You never know. It worked at Titchfield . . .

Hard Rain: Straightforward version of a classic song. What was memorable was how the crowd, which had been mostly quiet, really got into this. The crowd's singing seemed to echo off the walls and ceiling. Yes, still another highlight although I don't know if I can explain why I was moved by this. Maybe it's just I sensed a communion between artist and audience that had been to some extent missing until now. Maybe it was just me.

Don't Think Twice: Another crowd pleaser. I love this song too, but Bob seemed a little shaky and the audience participation was more like a singalong on this one.

Summer Days; A real toe tapper. Even a couple of the statues near me were dancing.

Make You Feel My Love: Tuff Mama and I had been making fun of the Garth Brooks version before the show and now Bob showed how it should be sung. Great song sung well. Highlight number 5 or 6 or something like that.

Wicked Messenger: Yeah, he sang that one too. Either that or Drifter's Escape. The band rocked, but it hard to tell from what he was singing. Maybe he sang Idiot Wind after all.

Rainy Day Woman: Never a favourite of mine and I was kind of hoping he wouldn't do it, but this version really rocked. It was pretty impressive. Then into the band introduction and some soloing (including a wonderful loopy bass solo from Tony) before Bob did the one knee bow and they were off.

The audience went clap clap clap and they came back for the encore.

Honest With Me: I don't know why, of all the songs, Bob picked this as an encore standby instead of Mississippi (or Idiot Wind, for that matter). It's a good song, but I don't know why Bob loves it so much. Still, this version was strong enough to make me want to go back and listen to it again on L&T. Maybe that's why he plays it.

Blowin' In The Wind: Great song. Crowd loved it. The version was okay, but not much more. I would rather have heard LARS (or, come to think of it, Idiot Wind).

Watchtower: When I listen to it on a boot, it never does much for me, but this was different. I don't know whether it was because I was there to see it or if it was just better than usual, but it really clicked for me here. Bob did the one knee bow again and left us shouting for more.

I haven't been to nearly as many shows as a lot of other poolers, so I may have been bowled over by his stage presence or just the chance to see him live, but I thought it was a fabulous concert, one of the best I've ever been to.

After concert stuff:

On the way out, bobdylansflower came over and said hello. We later hooked up with Toomraider and wandered around looking for Henry Porter. Toomraider and I then headed back to Moe's for a pint or two and met some more poolers, all of them buzzing with a post concert high. A fine night.

Posted to the Dylan Pool. Thurs., Aug 15, 2002. Reprinted with permission of David Hanley.

Tuesday, August 13, 2002 --- Corel Centre Ottawa, ON

Set List

	Song	From The Album	Released
1.	Somebody Touched Me (trad.)	–	–
2.	My Back Pages	Another Side of Bob Dylan	Aug. 8, 1964
3.	Tangled Up in Blue	Blood on the Tracks	Jan. 20, 1975
4.	Don't Think Twice, It's All Right	The Freewheelin' Bob Dylan	May 27, 1963
5.	Til I Fell In Love With You	Time Out of Mind	Sept. 30, 1997
6.	Most Likely You Go Your Way and I'll Go Mine	Blonde on Blonde	May 16, 1966

7.	Floater (Too Much To Ask)	Love and Theft	Sept. 11, 2001
8.	High Water (for Charlie Patton)	Love and Theft	Sept. 11, 2001
9.	Masters of War	The Freewheelin' Bob Dylan	May 27, 1963
10.	Visions of Johanna	Blonde on Blonde	May 16, 1966
11.	I Shall Be Released	Bob Dylan's Greatest Hits, Vol. 2	Nov. 17, 1971
12.	Summer Days	Love and Theft	Sept. 11, 2001
13.	Like a Rolling Stone	Highway 61 Revisited	Aug. 30, 1965
14.	Cold Irons Bound	Time Out of Mind	Sept. 30, 1997
15.	Rainy Day Women #12 & 35	Blonde on Blonde	May 16, 1966
	Encores		
16.	Honest With Me	Love and Theft	Sept. 11, 2001
17.	Blowin' in the Wind	The Freewheelin' Bob Dylan	May 27, 1963
18.	All Along the Watchtower	John Wesley Harding	Dec. 27, 1967

The Musicians

Bob Dylan (vocal, guitar & harmonica), Charlie Sexton (guitar, dobro & backup vocals), Larry Campbell (guitar, fiddle, steel guitar, electric slide guitar & backup vocals), Tony Garnier (bass), George Recile (drums & percussion).

Notes

- 104th Bob Dylan concert in Canada; 9th Bob Dylan concert in Ottawa.
- 1-4, 9-11, 17, acoustic with the band.
- 1, 11, 17, Larry Campbell & Charlie Sexton (backup vocals).
- 2, Larry Campbell (fiddle).
- 2, 6, Bob Dylan (harmonica).
- 7, 12, Tony Garnier (standup bass).
- 9, Charlie Sexton (dobro).
- 15, Larry Campbell (steel guitar).
- 16, Larry Campbell (electric slide guitar).
- Canadian live debut of songs 1 & 7.

Reviews

Dylan shows his blues roots

By Bruce Ward, with files from Mike Blanchfield.

Bob Dylan's roots are deep in the blues, and last night at the Corel Centre ol' Zimmie reworked several of his best known songs Chicago-style.

Dressed in a black stetson and a western suit with red trim, Dylan looked a little like Roy Rogers at a funeral when he walked on stage.

And at first he sounded like Roy's sidekick Gabby Hayes – pretty squally.

But once his chain-saw voice warmed up, Dylan was equal to his red-hot band: guitarists Larry Campbell and Charlie Sexton, bassist Tony Garnier and drummer George Ricelli.

After a four-song acoustic set that featured standout versions of the Dylan classics *Tangled Up In Blue*, and *My Back Pages*, the band turned up the amps and made the rock gods smile.

Dylan, 61, was clearly in the mood to play his Stratocaster, trading solos with Campbell and Sexton several times and taking his fair share of lead breaks too.

He revisited his 1967 classic *Blonde On Blonde* album, with a gorgeous acoustic arrangement of *Visions of Johanna* and a ragged-but-right go at *Most Likely You'll Go Your Way and I'll Go Mine*.

These were delights, with Dylan playing harmonica, backed by Campbell on pedal steel guitar.

He also played an assortment from last year's Grammy-winning *Love and Theft* album, in an incendiary version of *High Water*, a lightly swinging M*oonlight*, and a five-minute romp on *Summer Days*.

With the stage lights turned up, Dylan performed *Masters of War* – a subtle reminder that Sept. 11 is on the horizon, and the Americans are thought to be on the brink of invading Iraq.

Two highlights of the show, which appeared to be nearly sold out, were *I Shall Be Released* with chiming harmony singing by the band, and his 1965 classic *Like A Rolling Stone*.

Another standout was Dylan's bluesy shuffle version of *'Til I Fell In Love With You* from the *Time Out Of Mind* album a few years back.

Dylan showed his fans a little body language on stage, twisting his legs and pumping his guitar in time to the music, and if you looked back on his amplifier, you could see the Oscar he won for the soundtrack song *Things Have Changed* from the 2001 movie *Wonder Boys*.

For his encores, Dylan played *All Along the Watchtower* and a hauntingly lovely, version of *Blowin' In the Wind* that brought the crowd to its feet.

Yet the biggest message of the night is that still Dylan delights in reworking his songs, changing the tempos and – horrors – even the lyrics.

If you want dusty relics, there's plenty of museums to visit in Ottawa.

But if you saw Bob Dylan last night, you saw an artist in top form performing his works in progress. That's all any fan can ask.

Dylan packs 40 years of musical history into a single show

By Denis Armstrong, Ottawa Sun.

OTTAWA – Bob Dylan's eternal.

At least, he's as close to musical perpetuity as any of us will ever get.

For a couple of hours at last night's concert, the suburban Corel Centre was one of rock's legendary concert halls, honky-tonks and beer joints, where three generations of music, politics and attitude were forged into someone called Dylan 40 years ago.

Ageless Bob Dylan. His longevity is a logical puzzle worthy of Stephen Hawking. How is it that one of music's true dinosaurs, and I'm only using that in the kindest historical context, performs like the latest thing?

It certainly helps when your repertoire is still as pertinent today as it was in the '60s.

Even at age 61, Dylan remains defiantly indefinable, playing the musician who changes identity as soon as someone invents the label du jour. Dylan just as quickly switched personalities from the original folkie, rocker and bluegrass hillbilly to country crooner, crusty blues down-and-outer and yes, even the snarling punk poet.

After spending most of his life singing on the road, the times they still are a-changing.

KIDS AGAIN

There has to be some rule about Dylan. Every self-respecting concert-goer has to see him at least once in their life and last night, there were a few excited initiates. For the most part, though, the 8,000 ticketholders were old enough to remember Dylan the first time he came around. Hair bleached white by time, they were kids of the Vietnam war. Rebellious and hopeful.

Last night at the Corel Centre, Dylan gave them the chance to be kids again.

He didn't say a word all night. His only communication was sung or mumbled. Looking like a country posse member in black jacket and cowboy hat, Dylan got things going with the gospel-tinged Somebody Touch Me and a bluegrass spin on My Back Pages, arrangements that hinted that the former Robert Zimmerman would not be playing it straight all the way through.

STILL A MYSTERY

Every cover got new threads.

Backed by alt-country acoustic bandmates, Dylan gave Tangled Up In Blue a bluer feel, while going jazz-combo on Don't Think Twice, It's All Right and Subterranean Homesick Blues.

With 43 albums in 40 years, you think you know everything about him. But he's a mystery, a gorgeously difficult, gifted artist who's still bold enough to win last year's Grammy for Love and Theft at an age when most entertainers are playing the casinos.

Sure, his voice suffered in the arena, sometimes sounding more like an angry duck than Dylan. Of course, there are many who would say that that criticism was not fair to the Corel Centre.

Then, Dylan turned it all around with an emotionally uplifting I Shall Be Released and a sexy slow Like A Rolling Stone before a rousing encore of All I Need Is You followed by All Along the Watchtower.

"If you're spiritually open, Dylan opens every door," said Steve, who came from Chicago for the Corel Centre concert. "He touches everyone who's ever loved, or been angry or lonely."

"He's the only artist we can agree on," laughed Barb at David, her husband of 29 years. "He's Eagles and I'm Led Zeppelin, but Dylan does it all, doesn't he."

Yes, last night he did.

JAM! RATING: 4 out of 5

The Ottawa Sun. Wed., Aug. 14, 2002. Reprinted with permission of The Sun Media Corp.

Ottawa 2002

By Shawn Pulver.

I decided on fairly short notice to make the trek down to Ottawa. After seeing Bob at the Corel in 1998, I said I would never go back because the crowd at that show stunk and the security was awful. Four years later, the crowd stunk again, but at least the security was friendly. Things started off strongly with an excellent Somebody Touched Me, with Bob remembering most of the words, and the band following him nicely. Back Pages was nice, but I was a little distracted by the people behind me who were yelling at those standing in the front. I am always amazed that people come to a Bob Dylan show and can't understand why someone might want to stand for a bit in order to have a better view of Bob and the band. Some of these fans on the floor wasted the entire show yelling at people about standing, when they could have simply stood themselves for a bit. Even the security guards didn't have a problem with people standing. Well, enough about that topic.

Tangled was nice, and had a slightly new intro by Larry. However, it still wasn't able to get the crowd off their feet. Don't Think Twice was excellent, and featured some great phrasing in the last verse. As was the case in Worcester, it was the middle electric set that stole the show. Till I Fell in Love With You had the same arrangement from last summer, although Recelli was doing some very funky things on the drums. Bob nailed the lyrics, and the band seemed to be enjoying it. Most likely started off with a nice harp solo, and kept the show's momentum going. Highwater was once again intense, and featured a great bongo intro from George. Floater was, well, Floater. Great sound, weird lyrics and nice a arrangement. Recelli also gets to show off his jazzy side on this song. The middle acoustic set was outstanding, despite the lack of crowd involvement. I told my traveling buddy that I thought the version of Masters was perhaps the best that I ever heard. It was very tight, and I'll have to wait till I hear a recording to see if my recollection.is accurate. Visions was slower than usual, with Larry doing some great finger-picking and Bob delivering the words with real flair. I Shall be Released was a nice surprise, and the backing vocals sounded great. If I recall, it was the first song that really got the crowd off its feet all night. The set then switched back to electric, and we got an outstanding Summer Days with a great mid-song jam that appeared to make Bob (and a select portion of the crowd) very happy. The rest of the set was pretty standard, although it was a little unfortunate that Rolling Stone was added to the main set, at the expense of the "wildcard" slot that has followed Summer Days so far this tour. I did notice that the band has been playing with the arrangement a bit. Larry was playing the brown Fender that is burnt on the end, and Tony was playing a new grey bass that I had never seen. The performance was a little funkier than usual, and fairly effective.

There were a couple of other things that I wanted to mention. First, during the band intros, Bob introduced everyone in the band except for Tony. After a few minutes of jamming, Bob finally went back to introduce him. It was very funny, and Tony seemed to get a kick out of it. Second, during Cold Irons, Bob was very upset during the last verse at someone in the band (not sure who) and the song kind of fell apart, and wasn't jammed out like it normally is. Finally, during Blowing, after each beat, Bob would strum his guitar incredibly loud, to the point where it would drown out the rest of the band. Not sure if he was just trying to play around, or if maybe is he becoming restless after playing the song so much. I guess we will see. Overall, it was a great show with a bad crowd. I can't even imagine how much better this exact show could have been if he had received a more enthusiastic response from those in the audience. Regardless, Bob is in excellent form, and I look forward to seeing what the rest of the tour will bring. Thanks for reading!

Posted to the Dylan Pool. Wed., Aug. 14, 2002. Reprinted with permission of Shawn Pulver.

Friday, August 16, 2002 --- Molson Amphitheatre Toronto, ON

Set List

	Song	From The Album	Released
1.	A Voice From On High (Bill Monroe/Bessie Lee Mauldin)	–	–
2.	Watching the River Flow	Bob Dylan's Greatest Hits, Vol. 2	Nov. 17, 1971
3.	It's Alright, Ma (I'm Only Bleeding)	Bringing It All Back Home	March 22, 1965
4.	Forever Young	Planet Waves	Jan. 17, 1974
5.	Tweedle Dee & Tweedle Dum	Love and Theft	Sept. 11, 2001
6.	Under the Red Sky	Under the Red Sky	Sept. 11, 1990
7.	Floater (Too Much To Ask)	Love and Theft	Sept. 11, 2001
8.	High Water (for Charlie Patton)	Love and Theft	Sept. 11, 2001
9.	Masters of War	The Freewheelin' Bob Dylan	May 27, 1963
10.	Tangled Up in Blue	Blood on the Tracks	Jan. 20, 1975
11.	I Shall Be Released	Bob Dylan's Greatest Hits, Vol. 2	Nov. 17, 1971
12.	Summer Days	Love and Theft	Sept. 11, 2001
13.	Moonlight	Love and Theft	Sept. 11, 2001
14.	The Wicked Messenger	John Wesley Harding	Dec. 27, 1967
15.	Rainy Day Women #12 & 35	Blonde on Blonde	May 16, 1966
	Encores		
16.	Honest With Me	Love and Theft	Sept. 11, 2001
17.	Blowin' in the Wind	The Freewheelin' Bob Dylan	May 27, 1963
18.	All Along the Watchtower	John Wesley Harding	Dec. 27, 1967

The Musicians

Bob Dylan (vocal, guitar & harmonica), Charlie Sexton (guitar, dobro & backup vocals), Larry Campbell (guitar, cittern, mandolin, pedal steel guitar, steel guitar, electric slide guitar & backup vocals), Tony Garnier (bass), George Recile (drums & percussion).

Notes

- 105th Bob Dylan concert in Canada; 30th Bob Dylan concert in Toronto.
- 1, Larry Campbell (mandolin).
- 1-4, 9-11, 17, acoustic with the band.
- 1, 4, 11, 17, Larry Campbell & Charlie Sexton (backup vocals).
- 3, 9, Charlie Sexton (dobro).
- 4, 14, 17, Bob Dylan (harmonica).
- 6, Larry Campbell (pedal steel guitar).
- 7, 12-13, Tony Garnier (standup bass).
- 15, Larry Campbell (steel guitar).
- 16, Larry Campbell (electric slide guitar).
- Canadian live debut of song 1.
- Song 1 has been performed only once in Canada.

Reviews

Back on Track

Reviewed by Bill Reynolds, Special to The Globe and Mail.

Bob Dylan has written innumerable songs, but few remain as timely as *All Along the Watchtower* from his 1967 folk record of religious allegories, *John Wesley Harding*.

Dressed like the Hank Williams of popular song, the reinvigorated bard of American music and his crack band ended their performance on Friday night with guitars ablaze, nodding to the song's popular 1968 version by Jimi Hendrix.

Yet the stinging lyrics could easily be applied to the current regime in the White House: "Businessmen they drink my wine, plowmen dig my earth/None of them along the line know what any of it is worth."

Although Dylan played famous love songs such as *Tangled Up in Blue* with much good humour and aplomb, it was the politically motivated material that resonated. *High Water (Song for Charley Patton)* from his latest album, the much lauded *Love and Theft*, could have been about the floods in Europe as much as the Republicans' distaste for democratic principles.

The slowed-down blues-funk of *Masters of War* put across Dylan's position on the looming war against Iraq: "Like Judas of old/You lie and deceive/A world war can be won/You want me to believe." Another of *John Wesley Harding's* parables, *The Wicked Messenger*, tarted up with a mesmerizing descending electric-guitar figure, ended with the famous head-in-the-sand line: "If ye cannot bring good news, then don't bring any."

On more spiritual inclined material, two members of Dylan's band, guitarists Charlie Sexton and Larry Campbell, combined to provide stellar harmonies. Their vocal chops lifted *Forever Young*, *I Shall Be Released* and *Blowin' in the Wind* to glory, leaving souls melting in their wake.

Even less extraordinary material. Such as the title song on 1990's *Under the Red Sky*, was recast in better light by the band's obvious empathy for their leader's intentions.

If anything, the group provided too many dollops of instrumental passages – a few songs tightly rendered without solos would have varied the arrangements.

But other that that quibble, what else is there to complain about? His master's voice? Sure, it's creaky and craggy, the canyons and peaks of a long life and career having been etched deeply. And it's true that Dylan has played some horrendous shows in Toronto, bulldozing songs indiscriminately with hard-rock fury. His apathy toward his own words was legendary. He became Dylan in code, all but indecipherable.

But that's all in the past: Whereas he used to shun new material in concert, Dylan performed six tunes from *Love and Theft*, and there is no greater indicator of the man's confidence, ease and good nature.

With back-to-back excellent albums of original material and numerous accolades, Dylan is now the fountainhead of American song. He's the Hank Williams who rolls along in the limousine from town to town, rather than the Hank Williams who died in the back seat from an overdose.

As appeared in The Globe and Mail. Mon., Aug. 19, 2002. Reprinted with permission of Bill Reynolds.

Dylan predictably stellar

By Vit Wagner, Pop Music Critic.

Bob Dylan's shows have become so reliably excellent since he rededicated himself to live performance after his near-death experience in the mid-'90s that anyone looking to find fault could only say that the concerts have taken on a predictability that the younger Dylan would have considered almost square.

Even returning recently to the Newport Folk Festival, where he famously caused havoc back in 1965, Dylan apparently resisted the temptation to concoct some new way to scandalize the audience – unless you count that lanky wig he was wearing.

On Friday, a night when the Rolling Stones were stealing some of his thunder with a club gig at Palais Royale, Dylan's Never Ending Tour stopped at the Molson Amphitheatre, his third visit to Toronto in the last two years. And, as on the previous two occasions, the presentation was flawlessly taut.

As he does nearly every night, Dylan played 15 numbers, mixing in some wrinkles but always finishing with "Rainy Day Women # 12 & 35," followed by an encore than builds to "All Along The Watchtower." On this occasion, the audience was treated to a rare rendition of "I Shall Be Released." Not a moment was wasted.

The only interruptions were occasioned by the seamless switches between acoustic and electric instrumentation. Dylan, 61, didn't utter so much as a word of thank-you between songs. Even the introduction of his stellar sideman – Charlie Sexton on guitar, Larry Campbell on guitar, steel pedal and mandolin, Tony Garnier on bass and George Receli on drums – was incorporated into the music.

"High Water" and "Summer Days," from last year's Love & Theft, and "Tangled Up In Blue" emerged as particular standouts, but nothing was less than rock solid.

Nobody is pining for a return to the days when shoddy indifference, rather than stand-up professionalism, was the norm at Dylan's shows. But a little of that old mischief might be fun.

The Toronto Star. Sun., Aug. 18, 2002. Reprinted with permission - Torstar Syndication Services.

... And like a rolling stone

Another music legend graces a T.O. stage

By Derek Tse, Music.

In case you didn't know, the Rolling Stones weren't the only musical legends from the 1960s in town last night.

That's because venerable folk-rock icon Bob Dylan took the stage at a packed Molson Amphitheatre – and while this affair didn't quite generate the same buzz as did Mick, Keith, Ron, Charlie and the rest's impromptu gig, Dylan more than satisfied the massive throng of faithful with a decidedly laidback affair.

Affecting the look of a country gentleman in his dark clothes and white cowboy hat, Dylan was all business, launching from song to song with absolutely no chit-chat.

Which is probably just as well – his now-infamous penchant for mumbling almost incoherently crept into the show throughout the night.

But, luckily, his beautiful guitar-work did much of the talking last night, as much of the setlist allowed Dylan and the band to play their instruments for lengthy stretches.

Dylan was helped immensely by that superb, four-man band – songs like I Shall Be Released, Forever Young and Blowin' In The Wind, which was saved for the encore, were enriched by their strong back-up vocals.

Meanwhile, the singer-songwriter performed a healthy mix of classics and newer material from his Grammy-winning album, 2001's Love And Theft.

Some of the highlights included the honky-tonk of Summer Days, the aforementioned old favourites I Shall Be Released and Forever Young – which got one of the biggest ovations of the night – the slow and smoky Moonlight, the viscerally powerful Masters Of War and a rocking rendition of Tangled Up In Blue.

Sweet-smelling haze

Maybe the concert was a little too laidback, especially in the early going, but you could feel the energy in the crowd growing as the night wore on.

Also growing as the night wore on: The sweet-smelling haze of smoke that rose from many a cigarette (?) butt. By the time Dylan, belting out a stirring version of Rainy Day Women #12 And 35, sang the immortal line "Everybody must get stoned," you could be sure he didn't mean the Rolling kind.

SUN RATING: 3 1/2 out of 5

The Toronto Sun. Sat., Aug. 17, 2002. Reprinted with permission of The Sun Media Corp.

An oldie, then a goodie

By Mike Doherty.

Some musicians are born to reinvent themselves, some achieve reinvention, and others have reinvention thrust upon them. Bob Dylan has belonged to all three categories: He changed with the times in his early years, became willfully wayward in middle age, and now, it seems, has been nudged by Old Father Time in a gentler direction.

Yes, the former "Judas," the scourge of reporters and the forceful voice of a generation has become – of all things – cuddly. On stage, with his graying nest of hair tucked into a white cowboy hat, Dylan bends his spindly legs in quaint shuffling dance moves, hams up his vocals jovially (even in spiteful songs like *Tangled Up in Blue*), and delivers a set of unchallenging summer music that wraps you in a hammock of sound, swings you back and forth and stops just short of actually handing you a book and a bottle of beer.

The fathers and sons in the audience yell "BOB!" together and cheer when Dylan rasps out a pithy (or at least intelligible) line, and also on the infrequent occasions when he picks up his harmonica to blow a plangent solo. Would that he had played that harp more often: With two other guitarists on board, many of his songs devolve into acoustic strum-a-thons or electric janglefests. Occasionaly, things take off a bit: New number *Summer Days* features sprightly and stirring swing-rock guitar interplay, and *All Along the Watchtower* is given a post-Hendrix swirling attack.

But on this last song, as well as some other classics, Dylan's delivery is affected; he rushes his lyrics as if auctioning them off, and abandons his melodies for jagged motifs. Even the chestnut *Blowin' in the Wind* is unrecognizable until the chorus. His philosophical messages may always be relevant, but these days, Dylan doesn't really seem to care.

As appeared in The National Post. Mon., Aug. 19, 2002. Reprinted with permission of Mike Doherty.

Saturday, August 24, 2002 --- Winnipeg Arena
Winnipeg, MB

Set List

	Song	From The Album	Released
1.	I Am the Man, Thomas (Ralph Stanley/Larry Sparks)	–	–
2.	Mr. Tambourine Man	Bringing It All Back Home	March 22, 1965
3.	It's Alright, Ma (I'm Only Bleeding)	Bringing It All Back Home	March 22, 1965
4.	This World Can't Stand Long (Jim Anglin)	–	–
5.	Highway 61 Revisited	Highway 61 Revisited	Aug. 30, 1965
6.	You're a Big Girl Now	Blood on the Tracks	Jan. 20, 1975
7.	You Ain't Goin' Nowhere	Bob Dylan's Greatest Hits, Vol. 2	Nov. 17, 1971
8.	Honest With Me	Love and Theft	Sept. 11, 2001
9.	Masters of War	The Freewheelin' Bob Dylan	May 27, 1963
10.	One Too Many Mornings	The Times They Are A-Changin'	Feb. 10, 1964
11.	Tangled Up in Blue	Blood on the Tracks	Jan. 20, 1975
12.	Summer Days	Love and Theft	Sept. 11, 2001
13.	Make You Feel My Love	Time Out of Mind	Sept. 30, 1997
14.	Cold Irons Bound	Time Out of Mind	Sept. 30, 1997
15.	Rainy Day Women #12 & 35	Blonde on Blonde	May 16, 1966
	Encores		
16.	Like a Rolling Stone	Highway 61 Revisited	Aug. 30, 1965
17.	Blowin' in the Wind	The Freewheelin' Bob Dylan	May 27, 1963
18.	All Along the Watchtower	John Wesley Harding	Dec. 27, 1967

The Musicians

Bob Dylan (vocal, guitar & harmonica), Charlie Sexton (guitar, dobro & backup vocals), Larry Campbell (guitar, cittern, mandolin, pedal steel guitar, steel guitar, electric slide guitar & backup vocals), Tony Garnier (bass), George Recile (drums & percussion).

Notes

- 106th Bob Dylan concert in Canada; 5th Bob Dylan concert in Winnipeg.
- 1, 4, 7, 17, Larry Campbell & Charlie Sexton (backup vocals).
- 1-4, 9-11, 17, acoustic with the band.
- 3, Larry Campbell (cittern).
- 3, 9, Charlie Sexton (dobro).
- 4, Larry Campbell (mandolin).
- 6-7, 10, Larry Campbell (pedal steel guitar).
- 7, 17, Bob Dylan (harmonica).
- 8, Larry Campbell (electric slide guitar).
- 12, Tony Garnier (standup bass).
- 15, Larry Campbell (steel guitar).

Reviews

Dylan sizzles through set and has fun performing

By Morley Walker.

HIS body and voice might be creaking with age, but Bob Dylan proved again last night that his music remains forever young.

Performing with a four-piece country rock ensemble at the Winnipeg Arena – a venue he last played in October 1998 – Mr. Tambourine Man proved to a small but appreciative crowd that he's not ready to roll over and die.

His 125-minute set, consisting of 18 songs, sizzled with a few bluesy numbers from his most recent CD, Love and Theft, commingled with acoustic chestnuts from his vast catalogue.

Dressed in black suit with red trim, a Regis-style silver tie and a black hat (minus the wig and beard he wore at Newport earlier this month), he led his co-guitarists Larry Campbell and Charlie Sexton through a rocking version of Rainy Day Women No. 12 & 35 and a transcendent Tangled Up in Blue.

His voice, believe it or not, sounded sweeter than it has on the last several CDs. Making out the lyrics, mind you, was another matter. He seemed to be enjoying himself and played with a conviction that belied his 61 years.

Altogether, this was a better show than four years ago. Still, anyone who came expecting to hear their favourite songs reproduced with notes and vocal swoops intact would have been disappointed. Several times it was guessing game well past the intro and into the first verse.

The audience, numbering about 4,000, ranged in age from 15 to 65, with the majority being boomers who sat politely on their bums.

As has been the norm for his North American dates this summer, Dylan steered clear of talking to the crowd.

If he felt like congratulating the Bombers for their brilliant overtime victory over Calgary the night before or bringing greetings to his Winnipeg cousins, he chose to keep those sentiments to himself.

As usual, he forbade newspaper photographers from entering the building to snap his craggy countenance.

The Bobster hit the stage at 8:10 p.m., on the tail end of his new introduction, a rambling affair controversial among Dylanheads, which he lifted from the text of an Aug. 9 article in the Buffalo News.

First on the bill was A Voice From on High, an acoustic bluegrass tune with which he has opened several recent shows.

Then came Mr. Tambourine Man and It's Alright Ma, (I'm Only Bleeding). He quickly moved through You're a Big Girl Now and You Ain't Going Nowhere.

He wrapped with a three-song encore, including a magnificent Like a Rolling Stone, a semi-recognizable Blowin' in the Wind and re-phrased All Along the Watchtower.

While Campbell switched between six and 12-string acoustic guitars, a variety of electrics and pedal steel, Sexton manned stage right with a collection of classic axes.

Dylan kept a tight leash on both Campbell and Sexton; he hogged many of the guitar solos for himself, while his two supporting players jingled and jangled beneath, between and behind him.

The beat-keepers, drummer George Receli and bassist Tony Garnier, the latter the longest-serving member of Dylan's touring band, were as steady behind their man as Aline Chretien is behind hers.

* * * * out of five.

Attendance: 4,000.

Another Fine Day at Work

Dylan, Gives a No-Frills, Solid Performance

By Darryl Sterdan.

Things have changed all right.

There was a time when a Bob Dylan concert would have been a landmark event in this city.

Not anymore – or at least not last night. With summer winding down and the free Muddy Rivers Music Festival on downtown, the folk-rock legend drew only a respectable (but hardly impressive) audience of about 4,000 to the Winnipeg Arena.

But if Dylan minded – or even noticed – the sparse turnout, he didn't show it. After all, after several years on his so-called Never Ending Tour, one more concert is hardly an event for him anymore, either. It's just another day at the office, doing a job he loves. And that was the way he treated last night's show, turning in yet another of the no-frills, dependably solid performances that he's become known for lately.

Still sporting that mischievous moustache and nattily outfitted like a stylish gunslinger in black western wear with red piping, Dylan got right down to business, punching in at 8:05 p.m., with a spry version of Bill Monroe's A Voice From on High. Standing well back from the front of a checkerboard-stage backed by thick curtains, he led his road-honed backing quartet through a rootsy, rocking set divided between country-tinged updates of '60s and '70s classics and material from his latest career-rejuvenating disc Love and Theft.

SONGS DID THE TALKING

Audience interaction was nonexistent; Dylan let his songs do all the talking. And they spoke with a twang – when you could get past the typically cavernous Arena sound that did little to help decipher Dylan's already-incomprehensible vocals. Honest With Me – at least we think it was Honest With Me – galloped along to guitarist Charlie Sexton's ringing slide guitar; Summer Days shuffled along to a country-swing backbeat and Tangled Up in Blue was outfitted with a propulsively loping two-step groove.

As he neared the anticipated set-closer Rainy Day Women # 12 & 35 and encores of Like a Rolling Stone, Blowin' in the Wind and All Along the Watchtower, it became obvious that while things like crowd size and musical focus may have changed for Dylan, his commitment to his craft remains impressive as ever.

And even though his shows may no longer be landmarks for him or his audience, those who were loyal or savvy enough to show up last night were treated to a damn fine musical event nonetheless.

**** out of *****

Dylan a master at playing the crowd

By Gerry Krochak.

Here's hoping you caught one of Bob Dylan's Western Canadian shows this past week.

I'm a bit embarrassed – ashamed even – about the fact that I was a late bloomer when it came to Robert Allan Zimmerman. Through my whole life as a music fan, I always had a great deal of respect for the man. Hell, I always knew that he was one of the greatest songwriters who ever lived. I mean, I had *Greatest Hits* and I'd even seen him live once or twice. But I didn't *get* Dylan until I was in my late 20s, maybe even 30.

A great friend who had been a lifetime fanatic hooked me up with a birthday gift a few years back, consisting of what I now call: the essential Bob Dylan starter kit. It included *The Times They Are A-Changin,' Highway 61 Revisited, Blonde On Blonde, Nashville Skyline, Blood On The Tracks* and my personal favorite, *The Freewheelin' Bob Dylan.*

I hold that CD in my hand now and absolutely marvel at the fact that in 1963 this 22-year-old kid put out a record that included "Blowin' In the Wind," "Masters Of War," "Don't Think Twice It's All Right," "A Hard Rain's A-Gonna Fall" and "I Shall Be Free." It still seems incomprehensible. To me, the quality of those songs would define a brilliant songwriting *career*. But they were all on one record!

There's something so pure about Dylan. It's something that can't be explained or articulated even 39 years after *The Freewheelin' Bob Dylan* came out.

I got a brief but very clear snapshot of Dylan's greatness – an iconic epiphany, if you will – just as he was about to leave the stage Saturday night in Winnipeg. He had just finished a set that included "Mr. Tambourine Man," "This World Can't Stand Long," "Highway 61 Revisited," "Tangled Up In Blue," "Cold Irons Bound," and "Rainy Day Woman #12 and 35," as well as an encore of "Like A Rollin' Stone," "Blowin' In The Wind" and "All Along The Watchtower."

After that three-song encore, it hit me hard – this feeling that people must get when they turn from casual fan and concertgoer into hardcore believer. It's a bit scary. We met people at the show who book their holidays based on where and how many shows they can catch. (I wonder if Carla from Florida might be reading this on her way back home).

In any case, this was the moment: in a black cowboy hat and western-style suit, a single bead of sweat dripping down his narrow and slightly weather-beaten face, an acoustic guitar at his side, Dylan stared expressionless into the crowd, at no one in particular, as the cheers grew louder, and louder, and louder.

After about two minutes, he nodded ever so slightly and exited the stage. That was it. It was that simple and that subtle. When people talk about cool, they talk about Miles Davis, but, man, Dylan redefined cool Saturday night. In fact, it's easy to get the impression he does it every night he performs. It's virtually impossible to imagine him having an off-night. Dylan is cool in ways that are way beyond cool in the conventional sense.

One thing that stands out, after a few Dylan concert experiences, is the way he plays the crowd – and how he *always* wins. His set lists differ so drastically every night that it becomes a case of not so much what he *did* do as what he *didn't* do. (Check bobdylan.com for postings of set lists). Every show is unique in that respect.

Dylan reworks each song and keeps his unbelievable band on its toes by incorporating alternate riffs and tempos, often disguising a tune to the extent that it sometimes takes 30 or 40 seconds to figure out which song it is. He always keeps a fan guessing and he always leaves a crowd wanting more. He speaks not a word but goes straight to his work. If he takes a moment to introduce his band, it could be seen as downright gregarious. Yet Dylan says more with his songs than any words he could ever speak.

True greatness can be measured in a lot of different ways, and it speaks volumes that Dylan's last two albums, Time Out Of Mind and Love And Theft, are two of his best. Perhaps greatness is best measured when it's unspoken and understood. It might seem hard to believe, but 40 years after his first record came out, Bob Dylan is at the top of his game.

The Regina Leader-Post. Thurs., Aug. 29, 2002.

Monday, August 26, 2002 --- Saskatchewan Place
Saskatoon, SK

Set List

	Song	From The Album	Released
1.	Somebody Touched Me (trad.)	–	–
2.	It Ain't Me, Babe	Another Side of Bob Dylan	Aug. 8, 1964
3.	It's Alright, Ma (I'm Only Bleeding)	Bringing It All Back Home	March 22, 1965
4.	This World Can't Stand Long (Jim Anglin)	–	–
5.	Solid Rock	Saved	June 19, 1980
6.	Lay, Lady, Lay	Nashville Skyline	April 9, 1969
7.	Honest With Me	Love and Theft	Sept. 11, 2001
8.	Moonlight	Love and Theft	Sept. 11, 2001
9.	Don't Think Twice, It's All Right	The Freewheelin' Bob Dylan	May 27, 1963
10.	Things Have Changed	The Essential Bob Dylan	Oct. 31, 2000

11.	Tangled Up in Blue	Blood on the Tracks	Jan. 20, 1975
12.	Summer Days	Love and Theft	Sept. 11, 2001
13.	Make You Feel My Love	Time Out of Mind	Sept. 30, 1997
14.	Drifter's Escape	John Wesley Harding	Dec. 27, 1967
15.	Rainy Day Women #12 & 35	Blonde on Blonde	May 16, 1966
	Encores		
16.	Like a Rolling Stone	Highway 61 Revisited	Aug. 30, 1965
17.	Blowin' in the Wind	The Freewheelin' Bob Dylan	May 27, 1963
18.	All Along the Watchtower	John Wesley Harding	Dec. 27, 1967

The Musicians

Bob Dylan (vocal, guitar & harmonica), Charlie Sexton (guitar, dobro & backup vocals), Larry Campbell (guitar, cittern, mandolin, pedal steel guitar, steel guitar, electric slide guitar & backup vocals), Tony Garnier (bass), George Recile (drums & percussion).

Notes

- 107th Bob Dylan concert in Canada; 2nd Bob Dylan concert in Saskatoon.
- 1-4, 9-11, 17, acoustic with the band.
- 1, 4, 17, Larry Campbell & Charlie Sexton (backup vocals).
- 2, 14, Bob Dylan (harmonica).
- 3, Larry Campbell (cittern).
- 3, Charlie Sexton (dobro).
- 4, Larry Campbell (mandolin).
- 6, Larry Campbell (pedal steel guitar).
- 7, Larry Campbell (electric slide guitar).
- 8, 12, Tony Garnier (standup bass).
- 15, Larry Campbell (steel guitar).

Review

Rock icon Dylan finds groove at SaskPlace

By Cam Fuller, The StarPhoenix.

Bob Dylan was never more freewheelin' than he was Monday night at SaskPlace, challenging the crowd with new material, making old chestnuts virtually unrecognizable and flitting from genre to genre.

The song-packed, banter-free, two-hour show started, surprisingly, with the country gospel tune Somebody Touched Me. A touch of O, Bob, Where Art Thou? perhaps.

Dylan himself was clad in a black squire's suit, black boots and hat. The music and the look made you wonder if you'd barged into a Stompin' Tom concert by mistake.

There was no mistaking Dylan's spirit of adventure. You couldn't even identify It Ain't Me. Dylan's troll-like voice disguised the lyrics and the melody was absent. Only Dylan would dare.

After a couple more tunes failed to ignite the crowd, you had to wonder if Dylan would live up to the high standard he set four years ago here. Not to worry. As the band warmed up, the concert kept getting better. Greeted with relief as much as appreciation was a fairly straightforward version of Lay Lady Lady, accented nicely by steel guitar.

Next came a thick and crunchy rocker followed, incredibly, by the '30s-style crooner Moonlight from Love and Theft, Dylan's 43rd album.

Before you had time to think, Dylan was back to his roots with Don't Think Twice, done up with some nice acoustic strumming.

Then, mercy, came the highlight of the night – a long, loud, folk-rockin' version of Tangled up in Blue. With baby-faced guitar prodigy Charlie Sextonn digging into his acoustic and the band totally in the pocket, it sounded like Bob Dylan doing John Hiatt doing Bob Dylan. The jam went on for about eight minutes and nobody wanted it to stop.

Dylan doesn't speak or thank the audience or even look up much. The odd hip swivel showed he was into it, and he let the music do the talking. It speaks a variety of languages – the Feel-My-Love romantic ballad, the rockabilly rave-up, the hair-raising nu-Hendrix chemical-inspired rocker and the classic rebel-yell Everybody Must Get Stoned. Amazing.

The crowd pleaded for an encore, and the band made them earn it. Dylan came out with three gems: Like a Rolling Stone, Blowin' in the Wind and All Along the Watchtower.

At that point, you weren't just watching a concert, you were part of history. O, Bob, thou art the man.

The Saskatoon StarPhoenix. Tues., Aug. 27, 2002.

Tuesday, August 27, 2002 --- Skyreach Centre Edmonton, AB

Set List

	Song	From The Album	Released
1.	I Am the Man, Thomas (Ralph Stanley/Larry Sparks)	–	–
2.	The Man in Me	New Morning	Oct. 21, 1970
3.	It's Alright, Ma (I'm Only Bleeding)	Bringing It All Back Home	March 22, 1965
4.	Boots of Spanish Leather	The Times They Are A-Changin'	Feb. 10, 1964
5.	Highway 61 Revisited	Highway 61 Revisited	Aug. 30, 1965
6.	Lay, Lady, Lay	Nashville Skyline	April 9, 1969
7.	Subterranean Homesick Blues	Bringing It All Back Home	March 22, 1965
8.	Cry A While	Love and Theft	Sept. 11, 2001
9.	Mr. Tambourine Man	Bringing It All Back Home	March 22, 1965
10.	Forever Young	Planet Waves	Jan. 17, 1974
11.	Tangled Up in Blue	Blood on the Tracks	Jan. 20, 1975
12.	Summer Days	Love and Theft	Sept. 11, 2001
13.	Not Dark Yet	Time Out of Mind	Sept. 30, 1997
14.	The Wicked Messenger	John Wesley Harding	Dec. 27, 1967
15.	Rainy Day Women #12 & 35	Blonde on Blonde	May 16, 1966
	Encores		
16.	Like a Rolling Stone	Highway 61 Revisited	Aug. 30, 1965
17.	Knockin' on Heaven's Door	Pat Garrett & Billy The Kid	July 13, 1973
18.	All Along the Watchtower	John Wesley Harding	Dec. 27, 1967

The Musicians

Bob Dylan (vocal, guitar & harmonica), Charlie Sexton (guitar, dobro & backup vocals), Larry Campbell (guitar, mandolin, cittern, pedal steel guitar, steel guitar & electric slide guitar & backup vocals), Tony Garnier (bass), George Recile (drums & percussion).

Notes

- 108th Bob Dylan concert in Canada; 5th Bob Dylan concert in Edmonton.
- 1, Larry Campbell (mandolin).
- 1-4, 9-11, 17, acoustic with the band.
- 1, 10, 17, Larry Campbell & Charlie Sexton (backup vocals).
- 2, 6, Larry Campbell (pedal steel guitar).
- 3, Larry Campbell (cittern).
- 3, Charlie Sexton (dobro).
- 4, 14, Bob Dylan (harmonica).
- 7, 8, Larry Campbell (electric slide guitar).
- 12, Tony Garnier (standup bass).
- 15, Larry Campbell (steel guitar).
- Canadian live debut of song 2.
- Song 2 has been performed only once in Canada.

Reviews

Bob Dylan deals a winning hand at Skyreach

Legend still rocks at 61, but it helps to know the words

By Sandra Sperounes, Journal Music Writer.

Bob Dylan is not usually the type to raise eyebrows or spark a flurry of gossip over his choice of stage wardrobe.

He's a musician's musician – one with a catalogue of 30-plus albums and die-hard fans who try to predict his setlists, not his outfits, on pool.dylantree.com.

But ever since Dylan donned a fake wig and a beard at the recent Newport Folk Festival, the rumpled folk veteran now has everyone guessing: "What the heck is he going to wear tonight?"

On Tuesday, at the Skyreach, Dylan was back to his usual wig-free self. Yet he still was dressed like he was playing a part.

Clad in perfect Alberta attire – an all-black outfit topped with a cowboy hat – Dylan looked like a shifty, silent Blackjack dealer from a 19th century saloon, ready to deal a few unpredictable cards to more than 5,500 fans.

True to his look, Dylan didn't say much during his two-hour set. (But the repeated shuffle of his left foot betrayed his enjoyment.) Nor did he give fans any indication where he was going or what voice he was going to use – his nasal twang, his pseudo-Tina Turner growl, his mumbling marble-mouth or his devilish rumbles about love, drugs and politics.

Dylan is known for his penchant for re-interpreting his own songs and Tuesday's night show was no different. *Mr. Tambourine Man* became a stripped-down acoustic number with a prominent bass and a William Shatner-style rap. *Lay, Lady, Lay* turned into a lap-steel guitar tune with devilish overtones. And *Rainy Day Women #12 & #35*, better known as the "Everybody must get stoned" song, was transformed into a smoky, bluesy romp by his jaw-droppingly amazing players – bassist Tony Garnier, drummer George Receli and guitarists Larry Campbell and Charlie Sexton, who often looked to Dylan for approval.

Sexton, nor his bandmates, didn't lack any approval from the audience. Crowd favourites included a swampy version of *Subterranean Homesick Blues*; the swing-meets-'50s rock flavour of *Summer Days* (from 2001's *Love and Theft*); and of course, the encore – which kicked off with *Like A Rolling Stone*.

Dylan didn't actually say a word until right before his encore, when he introduced his players during *Rainy Day Women #12 & #35*.

Even then, he sort of sang their names, so it sounded like he was reciting a few more lyrics.

For those who didn't know the words to every one of Dylan's songs, it was almost impossible to make out his lyrics. (A lot of shoulders tilted constantly as the confused asked their friends: "What did he just say?") In fact, to the untrained ear, one of the verses in *It's Alright, Mama (I'm Only Bleeding)* probably sounded like "Fusha fusha fush HUH."

Huh? Translation: "For them that must obey authority/That they do not respect in any degree."

One thing was crystal clear: Dylan doesn't like having his mug shot. Press photographers weren't allowed in and upon entering the Skyreach, security guards asked fans if they had any cameras on them.

A few amateur shutterbugs didn't want to obey authority and managed to sneak their cameras into the arena. But as soon as their flashes went off, zoom! They were surrounded by guards.

Lighten up, Bob. At 61, you still look great. You play even better.

The Edmonton Journal. Wed., Aug. 28, 2002. Reprinted with the permission of The Edmonton Journal.

Dylan lets his songs do all the talking

He gets to you

By Fish Griwkowsky, Edmonton Sun Freelance.

You just have to think of Bob Dylan as a beautiful old bluesman – it makes everything way easier.

The reason for the qualification: last night's gig in front of 5,500 behind the Gretzky statue. His crowd was twitchy, not quite able to fully understand why, at 61, with a million reasons to not even have a voice at all, Dylan didn't quite sing like a 25-year-old boy, still madly in love with the colours and smells of the world. Because, of course, everyone else who's 61 just loves doing the same thing for 40 years. No, ask them.

So I will put an iron shield up in front of Dylan, here and now. Sure, he had, like, zero rapport with the crowd. But when he opened up with the Stanley Brothers' I Am the Man, a cocky bluegrass song to show off his hot quintet, he got me. Yes, Bob, anything you say, Bob.

Then, later, during a rousing Tangled Up in Blue, he started to verifiably get a lot of others, including himself. The former folk-singer started to smile around then, his dance steps under that black, pinstripe cowboy costume more noticeable, especially through $6 rental binoculars. And man, when he came back for his hit encore with a subdued but SO poignant Like a Rolling Stone and Knockin on Heaven's Door and a spoken-word All Along the Watchtower, he got everyone else, and all the people who doubted, well, they just kept quiet and stood up clapping anyway. As they should.

The breakless set moved from bluegrass to old folk to a couple of hits, spoken as often as sung, like Highway 61 Revisited, Lay Lady Lay off Nashville Skyline and Subterranean Homesick Blues, the original white rap song (well, maybe not).

Mr. Tambourine Man was a quavering shade of the original, mostly just whispered. But when he called out "Everybody must get stoned" in Rainy Day Woman #12 & 35, we sang along.

You know that new album, Love and Theft? Well, good, maybe you can tell me what songs he played off that. That one song he'd done at the Grammys, for sure, when he looked all mean and mad, maybe because someone else won in his category. Maybe not. Maybe he had his own reasons. He's Bob Dylan, he kind of gets to.

The moment that made me actually tear up a little, and forgive me for something highly personal, was Not Dark Yet off Time Out of Mind. It reminded me of waiting at home in Asahi, Japan for my girlfriend to come home, and especially how someone else does that now.

"I know sometimes it looks like I'm moving when I'm standing still," he sang in front of the curtain. "It's not dark yet, but it's getting late." Oh, life. Why are you so hard sometimes? If you really want to get in to Dylan you have to suffer a little, is the lesson. You could see that in his eyes when he sang Forever Young, backed up by the boys in grey flanking him.

A paradox to consider. His guitarist, stage left, looked right off of an episode of Six-Million Dollar Man, all tall, big-haired and mustached. Then he played blues so complex you could barely recognize it as such.

Dylan refused to be photographed, though The Sun managed anyway. The red shirts were gathering cameras like grapes. He really didn't warrant the worry, he looked fine, still with the skinny legs and occasional smiles. One problem with having such an immense catalogue is everyone's going to be disappointed they didn't hear their obscure favourite. Ah, to have such problems.

But really, Bob, it would have been nice if you'd said a SINGLE personal word to us not on the lyrics sheets. Like, you know. One.

He only talked to us to introduce the band, including Charlie Sexton on guitar. But at least he sang. Maybe that's more important than insincerely putting on an Oilers jersey.

MAIN EVENT: Bob Dylan
IN THE SEATS: 5,500 In Skyreach
BEST MOMENT: Not Dark Yet
SOUR NOTE: The Nagging Point of Two Hours Without a 'Hello'
Rating: 3 ½ (out of 5)

The Edmonton Sun. Wed., Aug. 28, 2002. Reprinted with the permission of The Edmonton Sun.

Wednesday, August 28, 2002 --- Pengrowth Saddledome Calgary, AB

Set List

	Song	From The Album	Released
1.	Somebody Touched Me (trad.)	–	–
2.	I Want You	Blonde on Blonde	May 16, 1966
3.	It's Alright, Ma (I'm Only Bleeding)	Bringing It All Back Home	March 22, 1965
4.	This World Can't Stand Long (Jim Anglin)	–	–
5.	Stuck Inside of Mobile with the Memphis Blues Again	Blonde on Blonde	May 16, 1966
6.	Ballad of a Thin Man	Highway 61 Revisited	Aug. 30, 1965
7.	Honest With Me	Love and Theft	Sept. 11, 2001
8.	Lay, Lady, Lay	Nashville Skyline	April 9, 1969
9.	Visions of Johanna	Blonde on Blonde	May 16, 1966
10.	Things Have Changed	The Essential Bob Dylan	Oct. 31, 2000
11.	Tangled Up in Blue	Blood on the Tracks	Jan. 20, 1975
12.	Summer Days	Love and Theft	Sept. 11, 2001
13.	Standing in the Doorway	Time Out of Mind	Sept. 30, 1997
14.	Cold Irons Bound	Time Out of Mind	Sept. 30, 1997
15.	Rainy Day Women #12 & 35	Blonde on Blonde	May 16, 1966
	Encores		
16.	Like a Rolling Stone	Highway 61 Revisited	Aug. 30, 1965
17.	Knockin' on Heaven's Door	Pat Garrett & Billy The Kid	July 13, 1973
18.	All Along the Watchtower	John Wesley Harding	Dec. 27, 1967

The Musicians

Bob Dylan (vocal, guitar & harmonica), Charlie Sexton (guitar, dobro & backup vocals), Larry Campbell (guitar, mandolin, cittern, pedal steel guitar, steel guitar, electric slide guitar & backup vocals), Tony Garnier (bass), George Recile (drums & percussion).

Notes

- 109th Bob Dylan concert in Canada; 5th Bob Dylan concert in Calgary.
- 1-4, 9-11, 17, acoustic with the band.
- 1, 4, 17, Larry Campbell & Charlie Sexton (backup vocals).
- 2, 6, 8, Larry Campbell (pedal steel guitar).
- 3, Larry Campbell (cittern).
- 3, Charlie Sexton (dobro).
- 4, Larry Campbell (mandolin).
- 7, Larry Campbell (electric slide guitar).
- 12, Tony Garnier (standup bass).
- 15, Larry Campbell (steel guitar).
- Canadian live debut of song 13.

Reviews

This old ROCKER still ROLLS

Dylan's show imperfect but awe-inspiring

By Heath McCoy, Calgary Herald.

Bob Dylan performed Wednesday at the Saddledome.
Attendance: About 7,000.

In the history books Bob Dylan is a phenomenon, a musical and cultural revolutionary.

On his records he's been, for most of his career, brilliant.

But live, even some of the hard core fans will tell you, the Bob Dylan experience can be a mixed bag. Some folks invariably walk away raving, like they've seen God. But stories of rambling, incoherent vocals, unidentifiable songs, and an aloof, uncommunicative Bob are also plentiful. Dylan, being the challenging, unpredictable icon he is, moves via his artistic whims – whims that are far too mysterious for us non-geniuses to comprehend.

All of the above criticisms could legitimately be applied to parts of Wednesday's Saddledome show.

That said however, the night had a sense of adventure to it that was reflective of Dylan's powerful revival of late on such fantastic albums as Time Out of Mind and last year's Love and Theft. Indeed, the 61-year-old living legend proved that his recent bout of inspiration is not limited to his recordings, but also carries into his live show.

Dylan hit the stage in a dressy black cowboy suit, appropriate enough since the first segment of his show was hillbilly to the core with Appalachian takes on such numbers as This World Can't Stand Long, Somebody Touched Me and It's Alright Ma (I'm Only Bleeding).

A highlight of this countrified set was a superbly reworked version of the hit I Want You, where a mourning lap-steel guitar took the place of the song's original groovy '60s vibe. During this song Dylan's voice croaked away weakly, which some might interpret as brilliant (it effectively conveys the song's sense of hurt, longing and vulnerability, man!) – while others might just call it bad singing.

Either way, from the first number only one deficiency was evident in the show – no big screen. Maybe we've gotten spoiled in the last decade or so, but for big stadium shows like this one, the big screen is a necessity.

Band had the Dome jumpin'

People didn't only want to hear Dylan, they wanted to see him, and unless you were sitting right up front, that was impossible. But ultimately, a show like this one is better suited to a smoky saloon than an arena anyway.

Still, the night had more than its share of great moments. The night came to life most definitely when Dylan's excellent four-piece band, including hotshot Texas guitarist Charlie Sexton, were able to cut loose. They did so on the lumbering blues cut, Honest With Me off Love and Theft, a song which literally jump-started the evening's excitement level. Even Dylan seemed revitalized on this song, as he wailed compellingly against the insistent beat.

A slinking, jangling take on the recent hit Things Have Changed was another highlight with Dylan throwing himself into the song like a wise, if hoarse, old rocker. A fairly faithful version of Lay Lady Lay was every bit as sexy and beautiful as anyone could expect it to be, drummer George Receli, in fact the whole incredible band, Bob included, gave Tangled Up in Blue a shot of life worthy of Blood On The Tracks, the groundbreaking album from which the song originated.

Then, when it seemed impossible that things could get any more lively (this was, after all, a Bob Dylan show, ferpetesakes) the band launched into the unbelievably hot jump blues of Summer Days, off the new album.

By the time the encore rolled around – a highly crowd-pleasing encore that included a strong version of Like A Rolling Stone, a romantic take on Knockin' On Heaven's Door that was part anthem, part country waltz, and a hard-hitting All Along The Watchtower that was far closer to the Jimi Hendrix version of the tune then Dylan's original – Dylan had the audience eating out of his hand.

Of course, a lot of them were no doubt there before he played a note, but impressively, he lived up to those legendary expectations.

The Calgary Herald. Thurs., Aug. 29, 2002.

Legend Wins Fans with Musical Mastery

Dylan's Alright Ma

By Lisa Wilton, Calgary Sun.

One thing that has always been a constant in Bob Dylan's career is his inconsistent live performances.

Ask any local Dylan fan who has seen him more than once and they'll admit buying a ticket for a Dylan show can be a crapshoot.

Last night, however, the risk paid off. Dylan was in top form, relatively speaking, during his highly anticipated show at the Saddledome.

About 7,000 fans watched the legendary singer-songwriter perform songs culled from his massive canon of work.

The fact is, Dylan has never possessed the strongest, most ear-pleasing voice, but he has certainly sounded worse for wear. His vocals may have been gruff and croaky for most of the evening, but Dylan could also express such a tender wail that it could make your heart bleed.

Such was the case during the breathtaking version of Visions of Johanna from his album Blonde on Blonde.

Clad almost entirely in black, including his trademark cowboy hat, Dylan was his usual cool self – acknowledging the audience with a nod or two, but no stage banter.

Backed by a tight, superb-sounding four-piece band, which included renowned Texas guitar gunner Charlie Sexton – Dylan began his set with a lively, top-tappin' rendition of Somebody Touched Me.

The gospel-like track was a fitting start as it was a prime example of Dylan's mastery of different musical genres.

He then launched into I Want You and It's Alright Ma (I'm Only Bleeding). But it wasn't until the driving Memphis Blues that Dylan and his band hit their stride.

You could say Dylan rocked out, even if his idea of rockin' out is a little hop here and a foot stomp there. This was perhaps the biggest, and maybe the only, flaw with last night's concert.

While musically astonishing, it wasn't much to look at on stage. It's not to say his laid-back stage presence wouldn't work in a more intimate venue, such as the Jack Singer or Jubilee. But he just doesn't have the kind of stage show that reaches to the far end of a big arena like the Saddledome.

Still, Dylan appeared to be rejuvenated. The numbers crackled with energy and slower, bluesier numbers, such as Ballad of a Thin Man, were vibrant.

While some may argue Dylan had his heyday in the 1960s, his impact on popular music has lasted for decades. This was apparent last night, in the diversity of the audience.

Grey-haired couples sat next to teenage girls in low-slung jeans and thirty-something professionals clapped approvingly alongside tie-dye-wearing twenty-somethings.

Despite the age differences, they all knew the words to Lay Lady Lay.

However, with such a wide range of songs to choose from, the crowd was treated to some lesser-known songs when all some of them wanted to hear were his hits, Like A Rolling Stone and Times, They Are A-Changin'. It was obvious people were becoming restless a little more than hour into the show.

As cheesy as the on stage greeting of "hello (insert city name here)" is, it would have been nice to hear Dylan utter a few words. Babblative, he is not.

The simple lighting and stage set up (the only backdrop was a black drape with a hippy eye design, later replaced by a white, pleated theatre curtain) was subtle enough to keep the attention on the man.

For those, like myself, who had never seen Dylan before, the show was a wonderful opportunity to see one of music's most enduring figures. For others, it may go down as his best Calgary performance.

The Calgary Sun. Thursday, August 29, 2002. Reprinted with permission of The Calgary Sun.

Review

By Robert Johnston.

This was my first time seeing Bob Dylan live. I always enjoy going to live performances to get a much better impression of the people that the songs come from. The show was great all night. Bob Dylan is an impressive character to witness.

The first half of the show included a few tunes familiar to me, but all were played out with the appropriate attention and conviction. The slightly altered arrangements of some of the tunes in the second half added to their impact. Tangled Up In Blue was done with some extra zip, and the whole concert seemed to take a leap to a higher energy level after that. It was getting into great guitar duos and (dare I use the phrase) country-rock-hillbilly on a few tunes, and the guitar work with Bob and Charlie Sexton was tremendous.

When the time came for Like A Rolling Stone, I was very impressed with the conviction of the performance....it's a song with a question that makes a very strong challenge to conscience and for those who may be so lucky to have never experienced those kinds of very unfortunate states or moments (at their worst......we all have the rugs pulled out from under us periodically), a chance to take a look around and be more compassionate. It needs to be performed from a forceful and purely authentic frame of mind. Bob projected that clearly. He finds the right way to perform such songs and moments within songs so well.

I came away very impressed with Dylan's sense of conviction, lively spirit, sense of humour and obviously, the incredible list of songs with which he can build a concert from.

Mr. Dylan, you are invited back to Calgary. Annually or more, if it so pleases you.

Posted to Bob Links. Reprinted with permission of Robert Johnston.

2003

Introduction

The Never-Ending Tour circled the globe in 2003. However, there was only one concert in Canada.

The sole Canadian date would mark Bob Dylan's 110th concert in Canada.

The Date

Niagara Falls, ON	Sat., Aug. 23, 2003

The show was Dylan's debut concert in Niagara Falls.

The Musicians

Bob Dylan (vocal, keyboard & harmonica).

Freddie Koella (guitar), Larry Campbell (guitar, mandolin, pedal steel guitar & electric slide guitar), Tony Garnier (bass), George Recile (drums & percussion).

The Songs

Bob Dylan performed a total of 16 songs (all 16 were from albums).

Two songs made their Canadian live debut.

Tombstone Blues	Dignity

Two songs have been played only once in Canada.

Tombstone Blues	Dignity

Bob Dylan performed songs from 10 different albums.

Album	Released	# of Songs Performed by Album
Bringing It All Back Home	March 22, 1965	1
Highway 61 Revisited	Aug. 30, 1965	3
Blonde on Blonde	May 16, 1966	1
John Wesley Harding	Dec. 27, 1967	1
Nashville Skyline	April 9, 1969	1
Planet Waves	Jan. 17, 1974	1
Oh Mercy	Sept. 12, 1989	1
Bob Dylan's Greatest Hits, Vol. 3	Nov. 15, 1994	1
Time Out of Mind	Sept. 30, 1997	1
Love and Theft	Sept. 11, 2001	5

Special Guest

Tommy Morrongiello sat in on guitar for most of the night.

The Venue

It was Bob Dylan's debut concert at the Oakes Garden Theatre.

Saturday, August 23, 2003 --- Oakes Garden Theatre
Niagara Falls, ON

Set List

	Song	From The Album	Released
1.	Tombstone Blues	Highway 61 Revisited	Aug. 30, 1965
2.	Lay, Lady, Lay	Nashville Skyline	April 9, 1969
3.	Tweedle Dee & Tweedle Dum	Love and Theft	Sept. 11, 2001
4.	Make You Feel My Love	Time Out of Mind	Sept. 30, 1997
5.	Dignity	Bob Dylan's Greatest Hits, Vol. 3	Nov. 15, 1994
6.	Highway 61 Revisited	Highway 61 Revisited	Aug. 30, 1965
7.	Shooting Star	Oh Mercy	Sept. 12, 1989
8.	Most Likely You Go Your Way and I'll Go Mine	Blonde on Blonde	May 16, 1966
9.	Cry A While	Love and Theft	Sept. 11, 2001
10.	Mr. Tambourine Man	Bringing It All Back Home	March 22, 1965
11.	High Water (for Charlie Patton)	Love and Theft	Sept. 11, 2001
12.	Honest With Me	Love and Theft	Sept. 11, 2001
13.	Forever Young	Planet Waves	Jan. 17, 1974
14.	Summer Days	Love and Theft	Sept. 11, 2001
	Encores		
15.	Like a Rolling Stone	Highway 61 Revisited	Aug. 30, 1965
16.	All Along the Watchtower	John Wesley Harding	Dec. 27, 1967

The Musicians

Bob Dylan (vocal, keyboard & harmonica), Freddie Koella (guitar), Larry Campbell (guitar, mandolin, pedal steel guitar & electric slide guitar), Tony Garnier (bass), George Recile (drums & percussion).

Notes

- 110th Bob Dylan concert in Canada; Debut Bob Dylan concert in Niagara Falls.
- 1-7, 9, 11-14, 16, Tommy Morrongiello (electric guitar).
- 2, 4, 7-8, 10, 16, Bob Dylan (harmonica).
- 2, 7, Larry Campbell (pedal steel guitar).
- 10, Tommy Morrongiello (acoustic guitar).
- 10, 13, acoustic with the band.
- 12, Larry Campbell (electric slide guitar).
- 14, Tony Garnier (standup bass).
- Canadian live debut of songs 1 & 5.
- Songs 1 & 5 have been performed only once in Canada.
- This concert was added on as the last date of the U.S. Summer Tour.

Reviews

Dylan Magnificent in a Majestic Niagara Falls Setting

Review by Brady J. Leyser.

Bob Dylan brought his Never-Ending Tour to Niagara Falls on Saturday night, the first and only Canadian date scheduled for 2003. The venue was the majestic Oakes Garden Theatre. Built in 1936, the 3,200 capacity outdoor amphitheatre offers a spectacular view of the American Falls as a stage backdrop.

The show was presented by Casino Niagara. Pre-show speculation had faithful followers and odds makers skeptical about whether or not Bob was too road weary to be able to deal a winning hand. After all, this was his 5th consecutive night of performances. But by the time the 62-year-old, revered icon took the stage at 8:25 all bets were off. Dylan had come to play and with his multi-talented, four-piece band did so magnificently throughout the one-hour and forty-five minute, 16 song set that included selections from 10 albums spanning 36 years.

Opening with a rollicking version of "Tombstone Blues" from 1965's "Highway 61 Revisited," you could immediately feel the energy on stage and in the crowd. Dylan seemed to be enjoying himself and having fun bouncing around in front of his piano. Tonight, like previous shows on this tour, Bob would be "tickling the ivories" for the entire evening rather than strumming a guitar.

An absolutely beautiful rendition of "Lay Lady Lay" followed, definitely one of the shows highlights, albeit there were so many – the sheer eloquence of "Make You Feel My Love," the bittersweet honesty of "Most Likely You Go Your Way (And I'll Go Mine)," the striking poignancy of "Mr. Tambourine Man," and the emotional intensity of "Forever Young," – to name a few.

Dylan's song selection appealed to both old and new fans alike. A particular crowd pleaser was the surprising gem "Shooting Star." It was the first time the song had been played on the 2003 tour and thus far 98 different songs have been showcased.

His brilliant 2001 Grammy Award winning album "Love and Theft" was well represented by five tracks skillfully played with "Summer Days" the main set closer.

Seconds into Dylan's first encore, the classic anthem "Like A Rolling Stone," a dazzling fireworks display erupted over the Falls. Even Dylan seemed somewhat amused as he briefly glanced up from his piano to catch a glimpse. It was simply too surreal as the fireworks continued through an electrifying version of "All Along the Watchtower" and as they ended, so to did the show.

The true test of any live performance is what the audience takes away with them. Saturday night's show left the crowd gasping for more and as they filed out of the amphitheatre all you could hear were the numerous comments about what a magnificent show it was. Case in point. Two young teenage girls were given tickets to the show while their parents spent time in the Casino. When asked if they were Bob Dylan fans, they politely and enthusiastically replied, "we weren't, but we are now."

And that is the true essence and enduring power of Bob Dylan's music. Not only does he continuously please his loyal fans, many new fans constantly discover his exquisite and expansive body of work that encompasses over four decades and represents some of the greatest songs written in the 20th century.

As appeared in Y&R Daily Reading. Mon., Aug 25, 2003. Reprinted with permission of Brady J. Leyser.

Bob Rocks the Falls

Review by Dale Gago.

Great show at a great venue! The boys were on again last night at the Oakes Garden Theatre in Niagara. I've seen Bob and the band 5 times since 2000 (I'm only 23, so hopefully many more to come) and this one was definitely one of the most memorable. The small venue was beautiful, lined with plants and shrubs. It was like being in someone's back yard! What made the setting even more incredible was that the stage's backdrop was Niagara Falls. Breathtaking! For sure the best venue I've seen Bob at, with l'Agora du Vieux Port in Quebec City coming a close second.

The band made a late start coming on at around 8:25, entering from directly behind the stage, and opening with a great Tombstone Blues. This was my first show seeing Bob behind the keys, and it was pretty cool to see. That was followed with a nice Lay Lady Lay which was a pleasant surprise. Larry played a sweet pedal steel on this one.

Dignity was strong and fresh sounding (never thought I'd hear that live), and that was followed with a kick-ass extended Highway 61. These were some highpoints of the regular set for me. It was on these tracks where things really started heating up and the chemistry showed with some great jamming. And as it got dark the Falls were lit up with changing colours. The stage and the backdrop were quite a sight. Cry A While was a great surprise also.They were definitely in the groove on that one! High Water was driving and really powerful too. It's great to see such an incredible band like this in action. Forever Young was beautiful with Bob on vocals without any accompaniment on the chorus.

And then, the usual set closer, Summer Days, which was absolutely wonderful. This one just cooks every time! No one could stand still during this one. Everyone was really into it. Freddy was pretty good all night with some shining moments, including on this song where he played some great leads. I think I still kind of miss Charlie though. Bob was really pounding the keys during this one too, really boppin' and bouncing to the groove. It was cool to see people looking on and taking in the show from their hotel rooms which overlooked the Oakes Garden Theatre as well.

Then it was time for the encore, and they broke into Like A Rolling Stone. At this point, security must have removed the ropes which were barriers for the VIP section, because everyone was able to move a lot closer to the stage. They played a great version of the song, and during it fireworks started lighting up the sky behind the stage. It was an incredible sight to remember for sure. Bob Dylan and his band rocking out to LARS with a brilliant fireworks display and Niagara Falls right behind them. Incredible! They closed off the show with a great, rocking All Along the Watchtower. Recile was really pounding the drums on this one.

The whole band was great tonight, showing yet again that they're world-class musicians. Larry Campbell's got to be one of the finest guitar playing sidemen out there. What a band! The fireworks were still going during Watchtower and it was a great close to a fantastic concert and night. And I went with my dad which made it even cooler.

It's always great to see Bob and the band standing up there receiving applause from the crowd after the show. They knew they put on a fine performance. Great times! Thanks for always keeping it fresh Bob.

Posted to Bob Links. Reprinted with permission of Dale Gago.

In The Garden

By Charles Cicirella.

Fierce Fierce Fierce !!! That is precisely the words that continue to come into my mind when I think about Saturday's performance in Niagara Falls, Ontario. I was not fortunate enough to have attended any of the previous shows of this tour though I had heard a number of the performances from out west so I knew Dylan and the best band in the land was becoming ever tighter and Niagara Falls was no exception. Matter a fact I'd even go as far as to say Niagara Falls was the hardest I've ever seen Dylan or his band of hybrid angelic thugs ever go at it and the inclusion of Tommy the guitar tech was pure genius on Senor Dylan's part. When I was first told about Tommy playing from the side of the stage I could not even begin to imagine how this could work and yet every time Dylan gave Tommy the sign and Tommy strapped on Dylan's signature Stratocaster Dylan went into over-drive and that was when things really began cooking. Now don't misunderstand me things were cooking from the very beginning with a Tombstone Blues that rivaled any Tombstone Blues that has come before it so when I say really began cooking I mean things got truly nuts – truly supernatural – truly Buddy Holly rock solid – ass kicking – smoking like a fiend HOT HOT HOT !!! It was like with Tommy there Dylan could focus on him and use that to his advantage to explore the keyboard like only Dylan the mad scientist can leaving the band to really form a womb of pure majestic white light/white heat giving unto the crowd a newborn Spirited type of music predating any of the mechanical crap passed off for music today. Even on the ballads there was an intensity and a searing brave pioneering mysticism that left you in awe as well as on another plane of glorified redemptive existence. "Lay, Lady, Lay", "Make You Feel My Love", and especially "Tambourine Man", were so elegant and personally done you could feel your heart both tearing and mending at the same exact moment in Hank Williams, Jimmie Rodgers, Dock Boggs, Bessie Smith, Billie Holiday, Ralph Stanley, Roscoe Holcomb, Skillet Lickers, Johnny Cash, Charley Patton time. How Dylan can take a song he has already done more than likely a million times plus and again reveals nuances in the song that had not been felt quite this way before is anyone's guess and yet he did it not only once or if you are lucky twice, but over and over and over and over and over again in Niagara Falls. Plus and I know we have all experienced this before he made you feel like he was singing the songs personally to you and only you as the Falls sprayed in the background and fireworks burst in the air. I left, "Shooting Star", out from the songs above because it really deserves to be mentioned by itself first because it isn't one played that often, but also because this particular performance of this rare gem was magic incarnate as Dylan informed us this could be, "the last time you might hear the Sermon on the Mont...", I knew then without any doubt that not only are there an infinite number of voices still crying in the wilderness, but that Dylan's cry is still the most prevalent of lone voices in a wilderness becoming only more expansive and wild as the end of time kicks us in the teeth repeatedly. Which brings us to, "Cry A While", what a surprise and what a ferocious untamed lion version of this wounded unrelenting lament. Especially after a, "Most Likely You Go Your Way", that was possessed. I kid you not especially the verse about the judge walking on stilts which Dylan repeated twice – already having had the song go much longer then expected as Dylan continued to look for Tommy over his shoulder and yet when he repeated the judge stilts verse again and I mean spit out those words like even if there was a tomorrow he could have no part in it you knew he meant business. "Dignity", was as hard driving as the versions from the recent Southern tour and perhaps even harder and more driven. There were so many surprises in the set like for instance a, "Forever Young", that I know could not have left a dry eye in the house (Larry I wish you had stepped up and brought back some of the vocal harmony I miss so much on songs like this one). The show was from beginning to end one of the tightest most consistent sets I have ever heard Dylan and his band deliver and I am thankful I was able to attend (the nineteen hours in the car from Oxford, Mississippi was truly worth every last second – even when we got pulled over at the border) and witness this song and dance man show no signs of slowing down in the least little bit as he pushed beyond the envelope once again. Dignity may have never been photographed, but thank God it has been heard and I do mean heard from in the garden in Niagara Falls, Ontario on a night like this!

Posted to the Dylan Pool. Tues., Aug. 26, 2003. Reprinted with permission of Charles Cicirella.

Additional Review

Dylan delivers memorable performance, by John Law. The Niagara Falls Review. Mon., Aug. 25, 2003. p. A2.

2004

Introduction

The Never-Ending Tour rolled on in 2004 with three concerts in Canada.

These shows would mark Bob Dylan's 111th, 112th, & 113th concert in Canada.

The Dates

Toronto, ON	Fri., March 19, 2004
Toronto, ON	Sat., March 20, 2004
Toronto, ON	Sun., March 21, 2004

The Tour stop was in Toronto for a three night run in three different venues.

The shows would be Dylan's 31st, 32nd & 33rd concert in Toronto.

The Musicians

Bob Dylan (vocal, keyboard & harmonica).

Freddie Koella (guitar, electric slide guitar & violin), Larry Campbell (guitar, cittern, pedal steel guitar & electric slide guitar), Tony Garnier (bass), George Recile (drums & percussion), Richie Hayward (drums & percussion).

The Songs

Bob Dylan performed a total of 50 songs. Of those, 38 were different songs (all 38 were from albums).

One song made its Canadian live debut.

Bye and Bye	–

One song has been played only once in Canada.

Bye and Bye	–

Bob Dylan performed songs from 15 different albums.

Album	Released	# of Songs Performed by Album
The Freewheelin' Bob Dylan	May, 27, 1963	2
Another Side of Bob Dylan	Aug. 8, 1964	2
Bringing It All Back Home	March 22, 1965	2
Highway 61 Revisited	Aug. 30, 1965	5
Blonde on Blonde	May 16, 1966	4
Bob Dylan's Greatest Hits	March 27, 1967	1
John Wesley Harding	Dec. 27, 1967	3
Nashville Skyline	April 9, 1969	2
Bob Dylan's Greatest Hits, Vol. 2	Nov. 17, 1971	2
Blood on the Tracks	Jan. 20, 1975	2
Oh Mercy	Sept. 12, 1989	1
Under the Red Sky	Sept. 11, 1990	1
Time Out of Mind	Sept. 30, 1997	4
The Essential Bob Dylan	Oct. 31, 2000	1
Love and Theft	Sept. 11, 2001	6

Special Guest

Tommy Morrongiello sat in on guitar for Highway 61 Revisited and Summer Days at the Fri. March 19th concert.

The Venues

It was Bob Dylan's debut concert at the Ricoh Coliseum, debut concert at the Phoenix Concert Theatre and debut concert at Kool Haus.

Friday, March 19, 2004 --- Ricoh Coliseum Toronto, ON

Set List

	Song	From The Album	Released
1.	Drifter's Escape	John Wesley Harding	Dec. 27, 1967
2.	It's All Over Now, Baby Blue	Bringing It All Back Home	March 22, 1965
3.	Tweedle Dee & Tweedle Dum	Love and Theft	Sept. 11, 2001
4.	Just Like a Woman	Blonde on Blonde	May 16, 1966
5.	Things Have Changed	The Essential Bob Dylan	Oct. 31, 2000
6.	Highway 61 Revisited	Highway 61 Revisited	Aug. 30, 1965
7.	Ballad of a Thin Man	Highway 61 Revisited	Aug. 30, 1965
8.	Stuck Inside of Mobile with the Memphis Blues Again	Blonde on Blonde	May 16, 1966
9.	Floater (Too Much To Ask)	Love and Theft	Sept. 11, 2001
10.	Most Likely You Go Your Way and I'll Go Mine	Blonde on Blonde	May 16, 1966
11.	Make You Feel My Love	Time Out of Mind	Sept. 30, 1997
12.	Honest With Me	Love and Theft	Sept. 11, 2001
13.	Girl of the North Country	The Freewheelin' Bob Dylan	May 27, 1963
14.	Summer Days	Love and Theft	Sept. 11, 2001
	Encores		
15.	Cat's in the Well	Under the Red Sky	Sept. 11, 1990
16.	Like a Rolling Stone	Highway 61 Revisited	Aug. 30, 1965
17.	All Along the Watchtower	John Wesley Harding	Dec. 27, 1967

The Musicians

Bob Dylan (vocal, keyboard & harmonica), Freddie Koella (guitar & electric slide guitar & violin), Larry Campbell (guitar, pedal steel guitar & electric slide guitar), Tony Garnier (bass), George Recile (drums & percussion), Richie Hayward (drums & percussion).

Notes

- 111th Bob Dylan concert in Canada; 31st Bob Dylan concert in Toronto.
- 6, Freddie Koella (electric slide guitar).
- 6, 14, Tommy Morrongiello (guitar).
- 7, Larry Campbell (pedal steel).
- 9, Freddie Koella (violin).
- 12, Larry Campbell (electric slide guitar).
- 13, acoustic with the band.
- 13, Bob Dylan (harmonica).
- 14, Tony Garnier (standup bass).

Reviews

Hoarse Whisperer

Dylan's voice a 'scratchy, helium-laced croak'

By Mary Dickie, Toronto Sun.

There's a fine line between putting a fresh spin on songs you've been singing for nearly 40 years and altering them – and their presentation, almost beyond recognition. The former is definitely desirable, but the latter can be a little unsettling.

For the first of his three Toronto shows this week – the others are tonight at the Phoenix and tomorrow at the Kool Haus – Bob Dylan chose the latter route. During his entire set at Ricoh Coliseum last night, he stood off to one side of the stage, singing and playing a keyboard and occasionally a harmonica. Not once did he pick up a guitar, move around or take the spotlight. This left a strange blank space at centre stage, with the rest of the band hovering around the double drum kit – yes, there were two drummers.

Meanwhile, new arrangements made many of Dylan's most well-known songs practically unrecognizable until a familiar riff or lyric emerged to set the crowd cheering.

Older folkie songs like Highway 61 Revisited became bluesy slide guitar workouts, while the breathtaking country duet with Johnny Cash, Girl From The North Country, was an entirely different creation – pretty, to be sure, but missing the majesty of the Nashville Skyline version. Others, like Most Likely You Go Your Way And I'll Go Mine, Stuck Inside of Mobile With The Memphis Blues Again, Just Like A Woman and Ballad Of A Thin Man, became simple blues-rock tunes lacking the subtle nuances of the originals.

Of course, such antics are nothing new for someone who's taken so many different tangents over the decades, from going electric to getting religious, and the generationally mixed crowd was more than forgiving of Dylan's whims. That probably had something to do with their appreciation of his magnificent touring band, which included Freddy Koella and Larry Campbell on guitars, bassist Tony Garnier and drummers Richie Hayward and George Recile. The sleek, road-tested group sounded impeccable even in a hockey arena, swinging their way from Nashville country to hard-edged blues-rock to Texas swing/rockabilly.

The same could not be said for Dylan's increasingly peculiar singing voice, which frequently sank into a frighteningly scratchy, helium-laced croak. Newer songs like Tweedle Dee And Tweedle Dum and Summer Days, from 2001's acclaimed Love And Theft album, and Things Have Changed worked well with it, as did the big encores Like A Rolling Stone and All Along The Watchtower. But in others, like It's All Over Now, Baby Blue, it was a distraction.

Still, when you've got such an amazing group of musicians and probably the best songbook of any contemporary singer/songwriter, who cares if you sound like an asthmatic alley cat?

You're Bob Dylan, for heaven's sake.

SUN RATING: 3 out of 5

The Toronto Sun. Sat., March 20, 2004. Reprinted with permission of The Sun Media Corp.

LIVE: Bob Dylan Hides In The Corner

By Elizabeth Chorney-Booth, Chartattack.com.

When you buy a ticket to a Bob Dylan concert, you're taking a gamble. This has nothing to do with Dylan's age or latest disc, 2001's Love And Theft. Since he was a young man, Dylan has refused to give his audience exactly what they want. So, you lay down your $60 and you may get genius, you may get a disaster. Like I said, it's a gamble.

At the first and largest of Dylan's three Toronto appearances over the weekend, the ticket price was a wager that the audience pretty much lost. While Dylan has been putting on some pretty hot performances since beginning his seemingly ever-lasting Love And Theft tour nearly three years ago (he was great at Toronto's Air Canada Centre in the fall of 2001), this Ricoh Coliseum show was weak. As expected, Dylan and his band played in the blues-rock style of Love And Theft – laying that style down on a set that consisted of many of that album's songs as well as a sprinkling of classic hits. Dylan has been reinventing his own songs for decades (check out the live Rolling Thunder Revue live box set for more savory results of this practice) and the blues rock treatment usually involves completely reworking the songs' melodies, making them only recognizable by their garbled lyrics. The retooling worked on some of his songs – namely "All Along The Watchtower" and "Highway 61 Revisited" – but others, like "It's All Over Now, Baby Blue" and "Just Like a Woman" were completely buried in the boogie.

Still, Dylan's penchant for reinventing himself is part of what makes him so fascinating, and his failure to stick to his original melodies or play a larger selection from his back catalogue is not what ruined this particular show. Rather, it was Dylan's outright refusal to connect with his audience that was so bitterly disappointing. Now, Dylan has never been famous for being a particularly friendly fellow, but this time out he was practically despondent. Instead of taking to centre stage and accepting the role of lead man, he crouched behind a keyboard in the corner, neither addressing the audience or even looking directly at them. While it was fitting that the band – complete with two drummers – were at the center of the stage, seeing as their heavy blues grooves were what drove the show, the people didn't come to see a tight white blues band. They came to see Bob Dylan.

Futhermore, while Dylan has never been accused of having a particularly angelic singing voice, his vocals have degraded to the point of being cartoonish. His approach fit with some of the new songs, which were written around his current vocal peculiarities, but again, the older songs suffered. He grunted and wheezed in some spots and phrased nearly every line of "Baby Blue" and "Watchtower" like a question, a technique that got pretty irritating by the end of his two-hour set.

But despite Dylan's sourness, the man is still a genius, and that genius shone through now and again. The highlight of his set was an acoustic version of "Girl Of The North Country," in which the lyrics were not only audible, but actually quite pretty. Dylan also put the audience in its place with his harmonica solos, which far out-dazzled his singing and inconsequential keyboard playing.

Bob Dylan is getting older and maybe even getting weirder, but the beauty of a lousy show like this one is the knowledge that it should in no way serve as an indication that Dylan's next show in Toronto won't be incredible. He's been both disappointing and astounding audiences for 40 years – there's no reason for that to ever change.

Chartattack.com. Mon., March 22, 2004. Reprinted with permission of Chartattack.com/Chart Communications Inc.

Review

By Jerry Tenenbaum.

The band came on promptly at 8 PM and launched into "Drifter's Escape". I was amazed at the sound at this hockey arena. I expected a muted muffled below average noisy barrage (usual at most hockey arenas I attend) but instead got a relatively crisp clear sound. Congratulations to the sound man.

Some of the regular songs already presented at these concerts followed. "Ballad of A Thin Man" was welcomed by all. The new arrangement of "Girl of The North Country" was the highlight for me. What I really liked though was the hard sound of this excellent band. It really complemented the harsh vocal presentation of the rock sounds. I haven't been present for better presentations of "Highway 61Revisited" or "Memphis Blues Again". "Floater" was most enjoyable and Freddy Koella's talents are formidable. There was a 'mystery' guitarist behind Dylan on at least two of the songs. (Who was that masked man?). The novices were concerned about the gruffness of his voice (the seasoned veteran's have come to expect this) and some would have liked the guitar to have appeared with Mr. Dylan front and centre where they felt he belonged. Dylan looked like he enjoyed himself and was decked out in black suit with sidestripe and white cowboy hat. He really seemed to enjoy playing with this band and was obviously highly involved in the music. This was not a man 'going through the motions' but someone who cared about what was being presented. That is refreshing for those of us who still feel that what he is doing is important.

Posted to Bob Links. Reprinted with permission of Jerry Tenenbaum.

Review: Toronto 3/19/04

By Marcus Thunich.

The first of a three night Toronto stand at the recently renovated (this was the first concert in this new building) Ricoh Coliseum proved to be an average, if mundane at times, Dylan gig. By the time the band took to the stage just after 8:00 p.m., the 10K seat building looked to be ~95% full with the g/a floor being (thankfully) only 1/3 filled with bodies. This made it very easy to get close to the stage if you had a floor ticket. Rather than do a song by song breakdown of the entire show, I'm going to just point out a few random things that come to mind:

The sound/mix. Standing 25 feet back dead center on the floor provided an outstanding stereo image with the mix being dialed in superbly from the first note. Hats off to Zimmy's sound crew.

Girl From the North Country. A reworked version with a very different feel. Zimmy's reworking almost gives the tune a strange gospel-like feel. Amazing.

Ballad of a Thin Man. My personal highlight. Nice to see this tune make an appearance. Dylan sang it with great aplomb and the band played their collective asses off.

Floater. Nice interplay between Koella's excellent violin work (the only time he impressed) and Larry's killer work on the Gibson.

The reworked Baby Blue was hideous. Aside from being nearly unrecognizable, Dylan's extreme over enunciation of the lyrics didn't do any favours to this top shelf Dylan classic either. Easily one of the worst re-workings of a Dylan tune by Dylan I think I've ever heard.

Dylan himself. After attending a so-so gig in Niagara Falls last August which featured a seemingly burnt out and bored looking Dylan, it was nice to see Zim back in fine form looking energized and smiling occasionally. He did however, speak not a word the entire night aside from introducing the band.

Larry was definitely the MVP on this night. Killer solos on Summer Days and Highway '61. The man was a force to be reckoned with.

The band looked really BORED while having to play the umpteenth CatsRollingWatchtower show ender. I bet the band (esp Larry and Tony) wishes Dylan would retire the always-the-encore tunes Rolling Stone and Watchtower as much as I would. Shake up those encore tunes Bob!

The second drummer that played probably 2/3 of the show: Why he was there only Zimmy knows. He added *nothing* to the sound and played exactly what George was playing 95% of the time. He seemed really out of place up there staring at Bob the whole night with this goofy grim on his face as if he was thinking "wow am I really onstage with Bob Dylan!"

Freddie Koella still does not impress me at all. In fact I find his tone rather unpleasant and playing to be bar band pedestrian at best. I also don't care for the way he likes to move to centre stage a lot and play rather un-exciting if flashy solos. A poor choice to replace Charlie Sexton, who's loss was *huge* to this band. I surely missed his presence last night.

Toronto blues legend Paul James (who played onstage in Toronto in '01) was side stage the whole night but didn't get the nod from His Zimness to play.

All in all a decent show (and a fun time) but not nearly in the same league as some of the monster shows Dylan played during the Fall of 2001 (a Never Ending Tour (tour) yet to be surpassed IMO). Tonight's gig promises to be special if only for the fact that it's in an 800 capacity club. Here's hoping the intimate surroundings elevate the band to play above and beyond the average-ness of last night's show.

Posted to rec.music.dylan. Sat., March 20, 2004. Reprinted with permission of Marcus Thunich.

2004-03-19 Toronto, ON

By Cory Hawley.

Just got back from the 2 1/2 hour drive to Toronto. Good show, NOT great. Luckily, Ballad of a Thin Man was played, and a great version. The new Just Like A Woman arrangement was good, and Bob's phrasing on it was even better. I don't mind the new Baby Blue arrangement. BUT, Girl of the North Country was horrendous, in my opinion. The guitars are ok, and have a Blackbird sound to them, but the way Bob sang it tonight, and the phrasing, was bad. He went directly into LARS from Cats in the Well and I like the new drums in LARS. A nice subtle change. Now, as far as Freddy Koella goes. The guy is hit or miss. On Floater, he did some great violin work, and a nice solo too on it. But what the hell was he doing on Honest w/ Me? When Larry was playing his usual slide guitar part (like on the studio version), Freddy was banging some god awful shit on his guitar, and was turned up higher than Larry so it sounded just terrible. Did anyone else at this show notice this. Freddy was just playing some choppy shit when Larry was doing that slide part that is found constantly throughout the song. Sometimes Freddy has some great solos, but other times, he plays something, maybe doesn't like it, and then changes to something totally different. It's almost like he's trying too hard on his solos, instead of doing what Larry does with his. Just my opinion.

The 2 drummers? Not bad. Not a heck of a lot of difference, but at times sounded real good. I guess it would depend on the song.

There was one point, I believe right before an average Highway 61, Bob looked over at Tommy, and motioned to him. So Tommy grabbed one of Bob's guitars and started walking towards him. I thought Bob was actually going to play. Bob even leaned towards him as if to grab it, but pointed and most have said play it. So there was no guitar from Bob.

Posted to the Dylan Pool. Sat., March 20, 2004. Reprinted with permission of Cory Hawley.

Saturday, March 20, 2004 --- Phoenix Concert Theatre Toronto, ON

Set List

	Song	From The Album	Released
1.	To Be Alone with You	Nashville Skyline	April 9, 1969
2.	I'll Be Your Baby Tonight	John Wesley Harding	Dec. 27, 1967
3.	Maggie's Farm	Bringing It All Back Home	March 22, 1965
4.	Desolation Row	Highway 61 Revisited	Aug. 30, 1965
5.	Tangled Up in Blue	Blood on the Tracks	Jan. 20, 1975
6.	Million Miles	Time Out of Mind	Sept. 30, 1997
7.	Positively 4th Street	Bob Dylan's Greatest Hits	March 27, 1967
8.	If You See Her, Say Hello	Blood on the Tracks	Jan. 20, 1975
9.	Standing in the Doorway	Time Out of Mind	Sept. 30, 1997
10.	Rainy Day Women #12 & 35	Blonde on Blonde	May 16, 1966
11.	Don't Think Twice, It's All Right	The Freewheelin' Bob Dylan	May 27, 1963
12.	Bye and Bye	Love and Theft	Sept. 11, 2001
13.	Honest With Me	Love and Theft	Sept. 11, 2001
14.	Summer Days	Love and Theft	Sept. 11, 2001
	Encores		
15.	Like a Rolling Stone	Highway 61 Revisited	Aug. 30, 1965
16.	All Along the Watchtower	John Wesley Harding	Dec. 27, 1967

The Musicians

Bob Dylan (vocal, keyboard & harmonica), Freddie Koella (guitar), Larry Campbell (guitar, cittern, pedal steel guitar & electric slide guitar), Tony Garnier (bass), George Recile (drums & percussion), Richie Hayward (drums & percussion).

Notes

- 112th Bob Dylan concert in Canada; 32nd Bob Dylan concert in Toronto.
- 2-5, 11, 15, Bob Dylan (harmonica).
- 2, 6, 13, Larry Campbell (pedal steel guitar).
- 4-5, 11, acoustic with the band.
- 4-5, 11-12, 14, Tony Garnier (standup bass).
- 11, Larry Campbell (cittern).
- 10, 13, Larry Campbell (electric slide guitar).
- Canadian live debut of song 12.
- Song 12 has been performed only once in Canada.

Reviews

Club date with Bob on our side

Reviewed by James Adams.

Club dates can be a source of dread, especially for audiences, say, 40 to 55 years along life's demographic.

Sure, the date gives the fan the chance to experience a beloved artist up close and personal, accompanied by a few overpriced drinks. On the other hand, there's the threat said artist will make his appearance two or even three hours after the doors open, play a 60 minute first set, break for 45 or 60 minutes, then show up at midnight or later for another set. In other words, for an overworked, child-saddled generation of mathematicians and carpenter's wives that now values "good sleep" as highly as it once did good sex, a long night's journey into day is a mixed blessing.

Thank God then for Bob Dylan. The pride of Hibbing, Minn., made a rare club appearance at the Phoenix nightclub Saturday, in the middle of a three-night Toronto stand, that seemed tailor-made to the demands of both his 62 years and those of his largely older fans. Following the playing of Copeland's *Fanfare for the Common Man* and a witty, tongue-in-cheek taped introduction that spoke of the man's discovery of Jesus and his "disappearance into substance abuse in the eighties," His Bobness took the stage with his crack quintet almost precisely at 8:15 p.m. and left it almost precisely two hours, 16 songs and much applause later.

Between the beginning and end, the former Robert Zimmerman spoke nay a word, save to introduce the members of his band before they cranked into the show's finale, a rousing rendition of *All Along the Watchtower* carried by the din of Larry Campbell's and Freddy Koella's electric guitars. There's nothing new there, of course: Dylan has been singularly uncommunicative with his audience for years, choosing instead an occasional smile and widely varying degrees of commitment to his vast catalogue of songs to let his fans "discover where he's at."

The consensus Saturday was that Dylan gave "good Bob." Wearing a black Stetson and a black suit with red flashing, he spent virtually the entire evening stage right, hunkered behind and electric keyboard. On several occasions – *I'll Be Your Baby Tonight* and *Desolation Row* among them – he blew harmonica, but not once did he pick up a guitar or move to centre stage to stand in front of bassist Tony Garnier and drummer George Recile (who was spelled off on three or four numbers by Richie Hayward, of Little Feat/Joan Armatrading fame).

Yet for all this self-effacement, Dylan did appear to be "in the moment" most of the time, and enjoying it, particularly during a majestic reading of *Positively 4th Street*. Admittedly, more often than not he sounded as if he'd gargled that morning with thumbtacks and a Listerine chaser. Moreover, as has been his want in live performance for the past couple of decades, he chose to scat and skim over his lyrics rather than enunciate them. As a result, the packed, mostly adoring crowd ended up responding most vociferously to songs they knew (*Tangled Up in Blue*, *Maggie's Farm*, *Rainy Day Women #12 &35*, *Don't Think Twice*) than to newer material such as *By and By*, a slinky rewrite of the standard *Blue Moon*, and bluesy shuffle of *Million Miles*.

The evening was at its best when the band managed to escape Dylan's own rather clunky and obtrusive keyboard stylings, and get into its own hard-rocking groove, which it did to great effect on the *Highway 61*-ish *Honest with Me* and the pre-encore show closer *Summer Days*, both from Dylan's most recent recording, 2001's *Love and Theft*.

Thirty years ago, a sign reading "Beware of Dog" taped to a guitar rack (as happened Saturday) would have had some Dylanologists pondering its significance for days. Thirty years ago, too, the coincidence of a Dylan concert with an event such as the one-year anniversary of the U.S. invasion of Iraq would have had the audience poring over the set list, looking for allusions to and illuminations of their common predicament. None of this seemed in evidence Saturday. Instead, the crowd got a good, at times brilliant evening of entertainment from an artist who can still summon the energy and the desire to be that icon called Bob Dylan.

The Globe and Mail. Mon., March 22, 2004. Reprinted with permission from The Globe and Mail.

Dylan is still way out there

… to the far left of the stage

By Jane Stevenson, Music.

Torontonians got their Bob Dylan fix this weekend, in sizes ranging from small, medium and large.

The folk-rock-country legend, who turns 63 in May, played three shows in the city: Friday night at Ricoh Coliseum, Saturday night at the Phoenix, and last night at Kool Haus.

Why, you may ask? Because he can, and he has been playing multiple dates in different venues in other cities too.

I was fortunate enough to take in the master songwriter at his most intimate show.

My colleague Mary Dickie expressed astonishment in her Saturday review of Dylan playing keyboards the entire night at Ricoh – he left the guitar-playing to two other accomplished musicians – which helped prepare me for what was about to unfold at the Phoenix. So I wasn't entirely disappointed when Dylan didn't pick up the guitar once over two hours.

Some of his fans might have been perplexed by his guitar-less performance, but truthfully, there didn't seem to be a disappointed person in the dedicated Dylan lot. (Did I mention their dedication? I saw one person with his arm in a sling, and another with his cane raised high in the air.)

When I arrived at the Phoenix, which holds about 1,000 when it's packed to the rafters as it was on Saturday night – there were still people lined up far down the block to get inside. Once you had gained entry, it was a smoky, sweaty, sardine-like atmosphere with a lot of excited anticipation fueling the crowd.

After a ramblng but hilarious introduction that even made reference to his finding Jesus in the late '70s, the man himself took the stage with his four musicans in tow.

Dylan's position, as at the Ricoh, was way off to the left of the stage, as he hunched over his keyboards, decked out in a black cowboy hat and black and red cowboy suit.

From there, it was two hours of pure Bob. Fantastic musicianship, lengthy jams, classic songs like Maggie's Farm, Tangled Up In Blue, Positively 4th Street, Rainy Day Women #12 & 35, Don't Think Twice, It's All Right, or newer tunes like Million Miles or Honest With Me and almost undecipherable vocals in that crazy, nasal delivery of his.

There was also a rather irritating tendency for the house lights to be blasted at the audience between songs while the stage went to black.

A small complaint, since Dylan's neverending tour, which began back in the late '80s and has included multiple visits to Toronto, shows no signs of abating any time soon.

Nor does his commercial ouput. Still to come on March 30 is Bob Dylan Live 1964, while his recent movie, Masked And Anonymous, is out on video.

Wonderfully inventive film-maker Todd Haynes (Far From Heaven, Velvet Goldmine, Safe), has a biopic in the works for which Dylan has licensed rights to his music.

In the meantime, those of us who were at the Phoenix have the thrilling encores of Like A Rolling Stone and All Along The Watchtower to keep us satisfied.

SUN RATING: 3 1/2 out of 5

The Toronto Sun. Mon., March 22, 2004. Reprinted with permission of The Sun Media Corp.

Sunday, March 21, 2004 --- Kool Haus Toronto, ON

Set List

	Song	From The Album	Released
1.	Maggie's Farm	Bringing It All Back Home	March 22, 1965
2.	Lay, Lady, Lay	Nashville Skyline	April 9, 1969
3.	Lonesome Day Blues	Love and Theft	Sept. 11, 2001
4.	I Don't Believe You (She Acts Like We Never Have Met)	Another Side of Bob Dylan	Aug. 8, 1964.
5.	Tweedle Dee & Tweedle Dum	Love and Theft	Sept. 11, 2001
6.	You Ain't Goin' Nowhere	Bob Dylan's Greatest Hits, Vol. 2	Nov. 17, 1971
7.	Cold Irons Bound	Time Out of Mind	Sept. 30, 1997
8.	It Ain't Me, Babe	Another Side of Bob Dylan	Aug. 8, 1964
9.	Watching the River Flow	Bob Dylan's Greatest Hits, Vol. 2	Nov. 17, 1971
10.	Just Like a Woman	Blonde on Blonde	May 16, 1966
11.	Just Like Tom Thumb's Blues	Highway 61 Revisited	Aug. 30, 1965
12.	Honest With Me	Love and Theft	Sept. 11, 2001
13.	Shooting Star	Oh Mercy	Sept. 12, 1989
14.	Summer Days	Love and Theft	Sept. 11, 2001
	Encores		
15.	Cat's in the Well	Under the Red Sky	Sept. 11, 1990
16.	Like a Rolling Stone	Highway 61 Revisited	Aug. 30, 1965
17.	All Along the Watchtower	John Wesley Harding	Aug. 30, 1965

The Musicians

Bob Dylan (vocal, keyboard & harmonica), Freddie Koella (guitar), Larry Campbell (guitar, cittern, pedal steel guitar & electric slide guitar), Tony Garnier (bass), George Recile (drums & percussion), Richie Hayward (drums & percussion).

Notes

- 113th Bob Dylan concert in Canada; 33rd Bob Dylan concert in Toronto.
- 2, 6, 13, Larry Campbell (pedal steel guitar).
- 3, 9, 12, Larry Campbell (electric slide guitar).
- 4, 6, 11, 13, Bob Dylan (harmonica).
- 8, acoustic with the band.
- 8, Larry Campbell (cittern).
- 8, 14, Tony Garnier (standup bass).
- This live version of It Ain't Me, Babe can be heard at www.bobdylan.com under performances.

Reviews

Review

By Jerry Tenenbaum.

Kool Haus – Toronto – formerly the Warehouse and now a standing room bar/entertainment venue. The sound was very good. In front of me... a Leopard Skin Pill-Box hat. Missed the Phoenix but glad I decided to come tonight. Overal hard rock blues the way I like to hear it. And in the smaller venue, very satisfying. The band is gritty and tight as they were Friday at the Ricoh Centre. Highlights were a moderate reworking of "It Ain't Me, Babe" (for me anyway) and a superlative "Tom Thumb's Blues" (how I love that song). "Honest With Me", "Lonesome Day Blues", and "Cold Irons Bound" proved again that my appreciation of Dylan and his blues approach is not misplaced. He is a master of this form and thrived on it tonight. "Lay Lady Lay" was most appealing and certainly was a crowd pleaser for those around me. The extended rocking "Summer Days" was great with the musicians really showing their stuff as a tight and effective rock and roll band. A pleasure to see Bob Dylan in a smaller venue. It really does make a difference.

Joke during band introduction after Rolling Stone: "Freddy Koella eats a lot of chicken. That must be why he's always in a foul mood." They laughed.

Posted to Bob Links. Reprinted with permission of Jerry Tenenbaum.

Bob-Fest

Dylan delights for three nights

Review by Brady J. Leyser.

Bob Dylan brought his Never-Ending Tour back to Toronto over the weekend for not one, not two, but three consecutive sold out shows at three different venues (The Ricoh Coliseum, The Phoenix Concert Theatre and Kool Haus).

Each show offered hard core Dylan fans and casual concert-goers something new as the iconic 62-year-old changed set lists nightly. In total, he played 50 songs (38 different ones).

Both Bob's voice and the overall sound quality consistently improved with each night's performance and peaked on Sunday night at Kool Haus. However, the majority of Dylanologists would categorically state Saturday's Phoenix show offered the best song selection. At all the shows there were moments of sheer brilliance but also moments of mediocrity.

The one constant was Dylan's superb backing band: Larry Campbell (guitar, slide guitar, pedal steel), Freddy Koella (guitar, violin), Tony Garnier (bass), George Recile (drums) and Richie Hayward (drums). The band blended together fine textures of rock, blues, folk and country, often taking some of Dylan's classic songs places they had never been before. This was especially true with their treatments of each night's main set closer "Summer Days" and the last two encores each night "Like a Rolling Stone" and "All Along the Watchtower."

Throughout the three-night stand Bob played piano exclusively, stopping once in a while to blow some harp, never once picking up a guitar. Dressed as a country gentleman in cowboy garb (black) and Stetson hat (white then black then white) he never once spoke to the audience other than to introduce his band. Although Sunday night he did crack a joke, "Freddy Koella eats a lot of chicken. That must be why he's always in a foul mood."

Opening night at the Ricoh Coliseum got off to a shaky start. Dylan's voice was raspier than ever (if you can believe that) and at times it was downright hoarse. It wasn't until the fourth song into the set that he seemed to find his vocal range and launched into a lovely rendition of "Just Like a Woman." Later he found the magic again on "Things Can Change," "Ballad of a Thin Man" and "Girl of the North Country."

Night number two at the intimate Phoenix Concert Theatre everything seemed to gel perfectly with outstanding versions of "I'll Be Your Baby Tonight," "Desolation Row," "Tangled Up in Blue" and "Positively 4th Street."

Closing night at Kool Haus Bob seemed to be in his best spirits. The sound at the venue was also much cleaner and crisper than previous nights. And when all things come together it doesn't get any better than hearing Dylan at his finest especially on "Lay Lady Lay," "You Ain't Going Nowhere," "It Ain't Me Babe" and "Shooting Star."

This past weekend's Bob-Fest will be talked about for years to come. The living legend left fans with much fodder to engage in heated discussions over what show was best or what set list was best. That should keep everybody delightfully satisfied until the Never-Ending Tour stops in Toronto again.

As appeared in Y&R Daily Reading. Mon., March 22, 2004. Reprinted with permission of Brady J. Leyser.

My weekend with Dylan

Rock legend plays three T.O. shows in three nights

He's old, raspy, hard to hear – it was nearly perfect

By Vit Wagner, Pop Music Critic.

On the street outside of the three splendid shows that Bob Dylan gave in Toronto over the weekend, vendors were hawking copies of Bob Dylan Live 1964, the sixth entry in the legendary musician's officially sanctioned bootleg series.

The double CD, which didn't actually arrive in stores until today, brandished a sticker exclaiming "Bob Dylan Unplugged!"

Indoors, the 62-year-old singer and his five breathtakingly accomplished side players were anything but unplugged.

While the set lists posted on Dylan's official Web site indicate that a handful of each night's selections were performed acoustically, the designation is a bit misleading. Freddy Koella, one of two guitarists in the band, rarely relinquished his electric model, frequently using it to augment counterpart Larry Campbell's six- or 12-string strumming. Most of the time, Koella and Campbell were both fully juiced, trading licks in the most electrifying manner imaginable.

For the bulk of the three nights, the only "unplugged" instrumentalist was Dylan, standing off to the side, seemingly content to pound away on an under-mixed and at times virtually inaudible keyboard. He never once picked up a guitar.

Some might consider it a cheat that Dylan, his singing as raspy and unintelligible as ever, has come to rely so heavily on the virtuosity of the musicians who surround him. But it's unlikely that many left the Ricoh Coliseum on Friday, the Phoenix Concert Theatre on Saturday or Kool Haus on Sunday feeling anything but fully exhilarated by what they had just heard.

It is difficult, at this late stage in his career, to imagine a solitary, folk-singing Dylan generating the same enthusiasm. Besides, he wrote the songs. And the songs, no matter how utterly transformed by necessity and invention, remain the main attraction.

Of the 50 tunes played during the Toronto visit, 38 were singular. The band played a dozen numbers at the Phoenix before duplicating anything from the night before. The concluding Kool Haus gig, while replicating songs from both preceding shows, introduced nine additional offerings, including a rendition of "You Ain't Goin' Nowhere," a song written by Dylan but most fondly remembered as the opening track on the Byrds' 1968 classic Sweethearts Of The Rodeo.

The changes in the set lists gave each concert a slightly different flavour. The Phoenix probably provided the most memorable experience, if only because it was the more intimate of the two club shows. But each occasion produced its share of highlights.

The Ricoh Coliseum opener was characterized not only by the arena setting but by the diversity of the audience, which ranged from fans too old to face the rigours of standing for two hours in a club (added to the time spent lined up outside) and too young to gain access to a licensed venue. The moment the lights went down to the recorded Aaron Copland fanfare that invariably heralds Dylan's arrival, the inside of the Ricoh was instantly fogbound by billowing plumes of pot smoke.

Musically, the mood was amplified by "Tweedle Dee & Tweedle Dum," one of four offerings on the night from Dylan's most recent studio recording, 2001's largely buoyant and upbeat Love And Theft. The rollicking approach influenced re-interpretations of older favourites, including "Highway 61 Revisited" and "Stuck Inside Of Mobile With The Memphis Blues Again," stretched out by one of Koella's several jammy insertions and reinforced by the double assaults of drummers George Recile and Richie Hayward. The band reached its apex by closing out the pre-encore portion of the set with a delirious run through "Summer Days," a pattern maintained through the next two nights.

There wasn't room for two full kits on the stage of the Phoenix, leaving Recile to keep the beat for much of the second night, occasionally ceding to the equally adept Hayward. Tony Garnier hauled out the upright bass for "Desolation Row," followed by Campbell's thrillingly acoustic evocation of the opening chords to "Tangled Up In Blue." Other highlights included the harmonica-laced "Maggie's Farm," as well as back-to-back renditions of "Rainy Day Women #12 & 35" and "Don't Think Twice, It's All Right."

Any doubts that the heady experience couldn't possibly be sustained through a third night were immediately dispelled when the band kicked off its Kool Haus set by revisiting "Maggie's Farm," before Campbell, seated at the pedal steel, summoned his cohort to "Lay Lady Lay." Dylan, who had trouble projecting at the Ricoh, turned in his finest vocal performance of the stay, lending his own inimitable magic to "Watching The River Flow" and "Shooting Star," while providing the necessary measure of animation to the "Whoo-ee!" chorus of "You Ain't Goin' Nowhere."

Typically, Dylan – dressed each night in a different black suit and alternating between white and black cowboy hats – saved what is left of his voice for singing. The only time he spoke was to introduce his bandmates between "Like A Rolling Stone" and "All Along The Watchtower," the two songs that closed out all three encores.

It was a transcendent finale each and every time. Trading riffs, Koella and Campbell siphoned the fiery octane of Jimi Hendrix' famous cover of "All Along The Watchtower," without attempting to mimic the guitar great's psychedelic gloss.

"Finally, I'll be able to listen to that song without automatically thinking of Hendrix," said a fan who caught the first and last of the three shows.

Doubtless, the sentiment was widely shared. From now on, when I hear "All Along The Watchtower," I'll be transported back to three glorious nights in March of 2004. And I'll be thinking of Bob.

The Toronto Star. Tues., March 23, 2004. Reprinted with permission - Torstar Syndication Services.

2005

Introduction

The Never-Ending Tour stopped in Canada for the 10th consecutive year. There were six concerts out west in 2005.

These shows would mark Bob Dylan's 114th, 115th, 116th, 117th, 118th & 119th concert in Canada.

The Dates

Victoria, BC	Sun., July 17, 2005
Vancouver, BC	Tues., July 19, 2005
Vancouver, BC	Wed., July 20, 2005
Vancouver, BC	Thurs., July 21, 2005
Kelowna, BC	Fri., July 22, 2005
Calgary, AB	Sun., July 24, 2005

The shows would be Dylan's 2nd concert in Victoria, 11th, 12th & 13th concert in Vancouver, debut concert in Kelowna and 6th concert in Calgary.

The Musicians

Bob Dylan (vocal, keyboard & harmonica).

Stu Kimball (lead guitar), Denny Freeman (guitar), Donnie Herron (banjo, electric mandolin, violin, pedal steel guitar & lap steel guitar), Tony Garnier (bass), George Recile (drums).

The Songs

Bob Dylan performed a total of 96 songs. Of those, 45 were different songs (all from albums).

One song made its Canadian live debut.

Down Along the Cove	–

One song has been played only once in Canada.

Down Along the Cove	–

Bob Dylan performed songs from 19 different albums.

Album	Released	# of Songs Performed by Album
The Freewheelin' Bob Dylan	May, 27, 1963	4
The Times They Are A-Changin'	Feb., 10, 1964	3
Another Side of Bob Dylan	Aug. 8, 1964	1
Bringing It All Back Home	March 22, 1965	1
Highway 61 Revisited	Aug. 30, 1965	4
Blonde on Blonde	May 16, 1966	5
Bob Dylan's Greatest Hits	March 27, 1967	1
John Wesley Harding	Dec. 27, 1967	3
Nashville Skyline	April 9, 1969	2
New Morning	Oct. 21, 1970	1
Bob Dylan's Greatest Hits, Vol. 2	Nov. 17, 1971	1
Blood on the Tracks	Jan. 20, 1975	1
Slow Train Coming	Aug. 20, 1979	1
Oh Mercy	Sept. 12, 1989	1
U the Red Sky	Sept. 11, 1990	2
The Bootleg Series Volumes 1-3	March 26, 1991	1
MTV Unplugged	June 30, 1995	1
Time Out of Mind	Sept. 30, 1997	4
Love and Theft	Sept. 11, 2001	8

The Venues

It was Bob Dylan's debut concert at the Save-On-Foods Memorial Centre in Victoria, debut concert, 2nd & 3rd time playing at the Orpheum in Vancouver, debut concert at Prospera Place in Kelowna and 4th time playing at the Saddledome in Calgary.

Sunday, July 17, 2005 --- Save-On-Foods Memorial Centre Victoria, BC

Set List

	Song	From The Album	Released
1.	Maggie's Farm	Bringing It All Back Home	March 22, 1965
2.	Tonight I'll Be Staying Here With You	Nashville Skyline	April 9, 1969
3.	I'll Be Your Baby Tonight	John Wesley Harding	Dec. 27, 1967
4.	Lay, Lady, Lay	Nashville Skyline	April 9, 1969
5.	Most Likely You Go Your Way and I'll Go Mine	Blonde on Blonde	May 16, 1966
6.	Blind Willie McTell	The Bootleg Series Volumes 1-3	March 26, 1991
7.	Watching the River Flow	Bob Dylan's Greatest Hits, Vol. 2	Nov. 17, 1971
8.	Ballad of a Thin Man	Highway 61 Revisited	Aug. 30, 1965
9.	Highway 61 Revisited	Highway 61 Revisited	Aug. 30, 1965
10.	New Morning	New Morning	Oct. 21, 1970
11.	Stuck Inside of Mobile with the Memphis Blues Again	Blonde on Blonde	May 16, 1966
12.	Positively 4th Street	Bob Dylan's Greatest Hits	March 27, 1967
13.	God Knows	Under the Red Sky	Sept. 11, 1990
14.	Summer Days	Love and Theft	Sept. 11, 2001
	Encores		
15	Don't Think Twice, It's All Right	The Freewheelin' Bob Dylan	May 27, 1963
16.	All Along the Watchtower	John Wesley Harding	Dec. 27, 1967

The Musicians

Bob Dylan (vocal, keyboard and harmonica), Stu Kimball (lead guitar), Denny Freeman (guitar), Donnie Herron (banjo, electric mandolin, pedal steel guitar & lap steel guitar), Tony Garnier (bass), George Recile (drums).

Notes

- 114th Bob Dylan concert in Canada; 2nd Bob Dylan concert in Victoria.
- 1, 5, 7-9, Donnie Herron (lap steel guitar).
- 3-4, Donnie Herron (pedal steel guitar).
- 6, Donnie Herron (banjo).
- 15, acoustic with the band.

Reviews

Grizzled folk-rock hero deconstructs hits

By Adrian Chamberlain, Times Colonist.

In typical fashion, Bob Dylan gave Victorians both more and less than they hoped for this weekend.

After a lengthy introduction painting him as "the poet laureate of rock 'n' roll," Dylan and his five-piece band launched into an rocking, rootsy version of Maggie's Farm.

His voice was strong, his singing surprisingly tuneful. The message was clear: at age 64, Bob is still a potent musical force who, if so inclined, can carry a melody. Of course Dylan, being the artistic contrarian that he is, is not often so inclined.

On Sunday night, this was most apparent when he trotted out his most famous hits for a crowd of about 6,700. Typical was Positively 4th Street, with Dylan subverting the conventional melody by opting to sing certain words high up the octave. The same approach, almost like a child's sing-song, was used for Don't Think Twice, It's All Right – one of two encores.

Certainly no one can fault him for deconstructing the classics, after all, he's been performing these songs since 1965 and 1963 respectively. But it's a sure bet many concert-goers didn't realize they were hearing these Dylan blockbusters until they recognized snatches of lyrics. It was as though he was unearthing ancient relics and bemusedly poking at them with a stick.

Still, it was a fine concert – he certainly seemed more animated and focused than at his last Victoria show 15 years ago at the old Memorial Arena.

No longer the guitar strumming troubadour, Dylan – wearing a white Panama hat and a black suit with white accents – spent most of a two-hour, 16-song show crouched over an electric piano. (On occasion he picked up a harmonica.) Rather than facing the audience, the anti-star was mostly seen in profile. He spoke only once, to introduce his band. This first-rate outfit, clad in matching beige suits, gave the songs a country-tinged rock flavour, thanks in part to a pedal steel player who sometimes switched to banjo.

Seemingly restrained and polished (perhaps too slick) for the first half hour, the band eventually cranked up the volume and truly rocked out. The final encore, All Along the Watchtower, exploded during the instrumental breaks with wild, ear-splitting guitar solos that echoed throughout the sold-out arena. Similarly, Blind Willie McTell – an homage to the influential bluesman – built up to power chords like waves crashing.

An indisputable highlight was Highway 61 Revisited. Prodded along by ZZ Top La Grange-style chording, it was a seriously rocking affair bisected by a stinging, Texas blues guitar solo and roaring pedal steel licks. Dylan, who sneered out the words "Highway 61," hammered out simple piano riffs.

He sang powerfully throughout. Dylan's voice is a weathered, cracked instrument – terribly flawed but oddly splendid, like that ancient leather jacket that's just too cool to throw out. He dug deep into the low notes of Lay Lady Lay ("big, brass be-e-ed"); his voice fractured like a firecracker during Stuck Inside of Mobile With the Memphis Blues Again; it coarsened with emotion for the love song Tonight I'll Be Staying Here With You.

His latter-day work was little in evidence, although we did hear Summer Days from the 2001 Love and Theft album – a rockabilly-style outing that Dylan sang with obvious gusto. He's a legend obviously at war with his iconic status – actually, Dylan has struggled with this almost from the outset of his career.

Kudos to Bob for avoiding the path taken by fellow '60s stalwarts the Rolling Stones, who are little more than a geriatric greatest hits package.

Some will argue – and they are correct – that Dylan's artistic approach to his old material works to subvert rather than reinterpret it. Then again, there's something fascinating about watching this folk-rock hero as he continues his Never Ending Tour, grizzled and defiant to the end.

The Victoria Times Colonist. Tues., July 19, 2005.
Material reprinted with the express permission of: "Victoria Times Colonist Group Inc.", a CanWest Partnership.

Review

By Jerry Tenenbaum & Lucretia van den Berg.

It was with some trepidation that Lucretia and I arrived at the new Save-On Foods Centre this evening. Having just met the "Trainload of Fools" at the local food/bar establishment, Earl's (and a nice bunch they are), our concerns centred upon what type of sound we might encounter in this new sports arena. Our arena experiences in the past had not been the best. Well, we were pleasantly surprised. The sound was crisp and clear. Bob was in great form. His voice was strong. Aside from the sometimes annoying 'upsinging' (a quibbling complaint at best), he sang well and the arrangements were strong. The new catalogue was virtually ignored until the end (a great "Summer Days"). The triumvirate of "Tonight", "I'll Be Your Baby" and "Lay Lady Lay" were stellar. "Blind Willie" was terrific with great solos. "New Morning" was a welcome addition to the set list. "Highway" had superb solos by all. Bob's harp playing was up to its usual high level. This is a really tight band with great guitars on all counts, the usual great Tony bass and drumming that reminded me of the early 90s. Bob looked like he was enjoying himself and the 6700 attendees gave him a number of standing ovations after some of the songs. The band was introduced by Bob near the end. "All Along The Watchtower" finished the show with the strength and dynamism that was characteristic of the entire show. All in all, this show was among the best I have seen in the past 6 or 7 years. Catch this version of Bob and the band if you can.

Posted to Bob Links. Reprinted with permission of Jerry Tenenbaum & Lucretia van den Berg.

2005-07-17 Victoria, BC

By Alan Kollins.

It's been 15 years since I last saw Dylan (a 1990 three show run at the Okeefe Centre in Toronto with the G.E. Smith band). I really didn't know what to expect given the time (and tours) that have passed since then. It should also be noted Dylan has not played Victoria in more than a decade. The audience seemed conservative at best throughout most of the set but as the band loosened up the crowd seemed to follow. Although seated through the entire set, the band received a standing ovation following Summer Days and some folks finally found their way to the stage for the encores. While I found the set list to my liking, some of the arrangements seemed misguided and overly blues based. While it was a treat to hear Positively 4th Street, the band seemed sluggish, Dylan losing himself in his lyrics at one point. Memphis Blues was also illogically arranged as it seemed to stutter at key points. This was an abridged version as only 4 verses were offered. Despite my criticisms there are some fine things to report. Lay Lady Lay was perhaps the finest moment of the evening. The band seemed best suited for this number for whatever reason. Dylan's vocals were superb here. Highway 61, although a standard on this tour, seemed to offer some additional grit that did not always work on the more upbeat tracks. There were certainly other highpoints (Willie McTell, Ballad and Maggie's Farm all rocked in their own way). For reasons unexplained, the sound dude appeared to turn the band up during more upbeat numbers. At times Dylan's vocals were submerged in the amplification. Other notes of possible interest: Dylan did not address the crowd once, though I have only seen him do this in a more intimate venue. His fluid movement towards the final third of the show suggested he was loose and enjoying himself (perhaps the finest thing about this show). At times he appeared to attack the microphone with assurance. His vocals sounded much finer than I expected. Oh, did I mention I found two front row tickets at face value 30 minutes before the show? Only in Victoria.

Posted to the Dylan Pool. Mon., July 18, 2005. Reprinted with permission of Alan Kollins.

Tuesday, July 19, 2005 --- The Orpheum
Vancouver, BC

Set List

	Song	From The Album	Released
1.	Maggie's Farm	Bringing It All Back Home	March 22, 1965
2.	Tonight I'll Be Staying Here With You	Nashville Skyline	April 9, 1969
3.	I'll Be Your Baby Tonight	John Wesley Harding	Dec. 27, 1967
4.	Lay, Lady, Lay	Nashville Skyline	April 9, 1969
5.	Most Likely You Go Your Way and I'll Go Mine	Blonde on Blonde	May 16, 1966
6.	Blind Willie McTell	The Bootleg Series Volumes 1-3	March 26, 1991
7.	Watching the River Flow	Bob Dylan's Greatest Hits, Vol. 2	Nov. 17, 1971
8.	Shooting Star	Oh Mercy	Sept. 12, 1989
9.	Cold Irons Bound	Time Out of Mind	Sept. 30, 1997
10.	John Brown	MTV Unplugged	June 30, 1995
11.	Under the Red Sky	Under the Red Sky	Sept. 11, 1990
12.	Highway 61 Revisited	Highway 61 Revisited	Aug. 30, 1965
13.	Just Like a Woman	Blonde on Blonde	May 16, 1966
14.	Summer Days	Love and Theft	Sept. 11, 2001
	Encores		
15.	Masters of War	The Freewheelin' Bob Dylan	May 27, 1963
16.	Like a Rolling Stone	Highway 61 Revisited	Aug. 30, 1965

The Musicians

Bob Dylan (vocal, keyboard & harmonica), Stu Kimball (lead guitar), Denny Freeman (guitar), Donnie Herron (banjo, electric mandolin, pedal steel guitar & lap steel guitar), Tony Garnier (bass), George Recile (drums).

Notes

- 115th Bob Dylan concert in Canada; 11th Bob Dylan concert in Vancouver.
- 1, 5, 7, 12, Donnie Herron (lap steel guitar).
- 2-3, 5, 7, 11, Bob Dylan (harmonica).
- 3-4, 16, Donnie Herron (pedal steel guitar).
- 6, Donnie Herron (banjo).
- 10, 15, acoustic with the band.

Reviews

Dylan still wows a crowd with his emotion and art

By Kerry Gold, Vancouver Sun.

Bob Dylan has long been on a mission to rework and revitalize his prolific repertoire, and the raspy legend chose to steep the old chestnuts in rollicking jazzy blues at the Orpheum Theatre last night.

The three shows he plays at the acoustically rich venue sold out in record time, a testament to Dylan's enduring, iconic appeal. Fans will have seen Dylan pass through here many times over the years, but without a doubt it's the small venues where he plays best.

Together with his newly revised five-piece band, all studiously devoted to wailing riffs and blues rock solos, Dylan is not an arena act, but an odd pleasure who comes alive close up, in the world weary flesh, with every grimace and gyrating knee move betraying his passion for playing.

The live Dylan experience is a different animal from the recorded version. Only God and Dylan know whatever it is he's mumbling about a lot of the time, especially when he delivers the demented, helium-and-nicotine ravaged vocals, dragging words out luxuriously across his tongue, then rushing them out of his mouth as if they're too hot to handle.

Dylan unceremoniously appeared with the rest of his band, including new members Denny Freeman and Donnie Herron, and settled behind his station at the keyboard and dove into an easy rocking, loping, countrified version of Maggie's Farm. The band looked dapper in grey suits, three of them – including Dylan – in black Stetsons, looking every bit the southern gents.

Dylan's skinny frame was emphasized by a colonel-type black suit with red stripes down the legs, and he seldom left his sideways position on the keyboards except to play a harmonica solo facing the audience at the mic stand. Dylan generated a lot of excitement on these solos, one of the first on Tonight I'll Be Staying Here With You. On I'll Be Your Baby Tonight, Dylan played harmonica with one hand while following a keyboard line with the other, his band following his every move.

Dylan and his superb new line-up were in fine form, and a lot of the highlights of the evening involved the tag team approach between the players, with big, rocking pedal steel solos and light-fingered guitar leads massively winding up, then tempered by Dylan's bluesy harmonica playing. Such dynamic rockers jazzed up songs Most Likely You Go Your Way and I'll Go Mine, Watching the River Flow, Cold Irons Bound, Blind

Willie McTell, and most spectacularly, the finale before the encore, Love and Theft's Summer Days. Highway 61 Revisited got Dylan's legs moving and his head bobbing, which is about as close as he gets to busting a rug. It also got members of the band more animated, with seamless solos and even Dylan tossing in a freewheeling keyboard solo, before building again to a massive, steamrolling blues jam. And Summer Days started off with a loungey, big-band feel with stand-up bass and pedal steel, then ignited halfway through and drove the audience to its feet as it wound up in a firestorm of drums and blues guitar.

Dylan rounded out the evening with an encore set of straightforward versions of Masters of War and Like a Rolling Stone, leaving the audience basically spent. His anti-war message was focused and intentionally clear, and, like a lot of the evening, was Dylan at his most expressive. He must be into the smelling salts because he's never seemed so big on expression, enunciating the details of bittersweet and darkly dramatic songs, the words dragged out and left hanging in the air. It made for an incredibly compelling experience.

His other anti-war song, John Brown, was so wonderfully, horrifically told against a backdrop of banjo playing twang, that it was almost like theatre. And Just Like a Woman was almost unidentifiable in its re-arrangement, not as effective as the original, but a matter of taste, since the playing couldn't be faulted.

Dylan never said a word other than to introduce his band, and it was clear that we were just another tour date lost in the routine of his never ending tour. But at 64, the craggy voiced Dylan has hit another peak, and he's obviously devoted to the art of playing, and that's what made the simple act of a centre-stage harmonica solo a thrill for the sold-out audience.

The Vancouver Sun. Wed., July 20, 2005.

Dylan is taking stock, so Rolling Stone is back

Legend says little, but gets swept up in moment

By Tom Harrison, The Province.

It's tempting to second-guess Bob Dylan. So much has been said about him, so much has been said about his songs.

It's almost impossible to think that maybe he wants to stand up on a stage and just play. To be swept up in the music and just be part of something.

He got that opportunity last night at the Orpheum. It was the first of three sold-out shows.

On display was Country Bob, Blues Bob, Rockin' Bob, Folkey Bob, Boogie Bob. He tried a lot of different songs that someone else might have thought were from his B-List. But from anyone else they'd be A-List.

There were a few surprises. But this shouldn't have been a surprise: He didn't talk between his songs.

He stayed resolutely behind a keyboard – only coming out front once in a while to play harmonica, which he now plays in a way more mellow than as a weapon. And he finished with "Like a Rolling Stone," which he swore he wasn't going to perform.

Perhaps it is because author Griel Marcus has written an entire book about the song. Perhaps because Martin Scorcese will be televising his documentary, No Direction Home, next week. Perhaps because there will be a new compilation based on the show. Perhaps because Starbucks will market a 1963 concert. Perhaps because Dylan has written the first part of his memoirs, Chronicles, Volume One. Perhaps for all these reasons, Dylan is taking stock again.

And so "Like a Rolling Stone" is back.

His perception isn't always accurate.

The new arrangements of old songs we've gotten used to.

But sometimes the exploration, such as the phrasing of "Just Like a Woman," doesn't work.

Sometimes songs begin disastrously, but hold together wonderfully.

And Dylan – clad in a black suit to his five-man band's grey – got as swept away as his audience by the constant give and take.

The metamorphosis of songs such as "Highway 61 Revisited" a high point – goes on.

It is always why there is a temptation to second-guess him.

The Vancouver Province. Wed., July 20, 2005.

Instant Review: Vancouver Night #1 July 19/05

By Marq DeSouza.

This was my first attended Bob show since Seattle of 2002 (the first piano show), though I have heard pretty much every posted show/bit torrent/mp3 since then. Overall probably just an average night in the NET. Still, there's something about seeing the greatest singer/songwriter of all time up on stage doing his thing, singing a cross section of his work from the last 40 or so years. Bob was dressed in black with red trimming on his pants and collar. Looked very good. I think I saw Billy Corgan of Smashing Pumpkins come in the side door with some venue security guys. Could that be possible?

The set list is boring to read, but only tells a fraction of the story...

1. Maggies Farm: I expected Drifters Escape, but this one absolutely rocked. The crowd was right into it. Bob's phrasing was very rhythmic and this was surprisingly a highlight of the night.

2. Tonight I'll Be...: An average performance. The funniest was when Bob walked around to do his mid-stage harp solo. He kept hesitating, as if there were no clear musical entrance for him. He found it though.

3. I'll Be Your...: Average

4. Lay Lady Lay: Average. This is where the upsinging really began, not much of it up to here, and I had my fingers crossed, but alas, it was not to be.

5. Most Likely: This was to me, the highlight of the night. The drums were slamming and the band was ultratight. This is in the middle of the pack of my favorite Bob songs, but tonight it was perfect as a rendition.

6. Blind Willie: A close second to Most Likely as the best song of the night. The acoustics at the Orpheum Theatre are topnotch, and you could hear all George's gorgeous cymbal work. Banjo solo was nice.

7. Watching The River: Bob seemed disconnected from this one. Things picked up in the solo sections though, and it ended better than it began.

8. Shooting Star: The band seemed a little unsure of themselves and had their eyes glued to the roving gambler on the piano, who remained expressionless through the long intro passage. This one was OK, but too much upsinging.

9. Cold Irons: Another highlight. Perfect drumming. The best I've ever heard at a Bob show.

10. John Brown: Faster than any modern version I've heard. It was OK. Not a great song by any means, but a nice song to be 'performed', even if upsung.

11. Under The Red Sky: I love this song, but this version was very tentative, despite some nice guitar interplay.

12. Highway 61: This did rock as I expected it to. A long instrumental breakdown (too long) in the middle.

13. Just Like A Woman: A lowlight. Entirely upsung.

14. Summer Days: I've heard too many boots of this to ever hear it again. Not the song for this band.

15. Masters: Very good.

16. LARS: Also very good.

Back for the next 2 nights. I heard from a source in Victoria that Bob was very visibly unhappy with the show there on Sunday, and shot the band dirty looks all night. Perhaps that's why we got so many repeats tonight. I hope he shakes it up for the next 2 a little.

Posted to the Dylan Pool. Wed., July 20, 2005. Reprinted with permission of Marq DeSouza.

Wednesday, July 20, 2005 --- The Orpheum
Vancouver, BC

Set List

	Song	From The Album	Released
1.	Maggie's Farm	Bringing It All Back Home	March 22, 1965
2.	Tonight I'll Be Staying Here With You	Nashville Skyline	April 9, 1969
3.	I'll Be Your Baby Tonight	John Wesley Harding	Dec. 27, 1967
4.	Lay, Lady, Lay	Nashville Skyline	April 9, 1969
5.	Most Likely You Go Your Way and I'll Go Mine	Blonde on Blonde	May 16, 1966
6.	Blind Willie McTell	The Bootleg Series Volumes 1-3	March 26, 1991
7.	Tweedle Dee & Tweedle Dum	Love and Theft	Sept. 11, 2001
8.	I Want You	Blonde on Blonde	May 16, 1966
9.	High Water (for Charlie Patton)	Love and Theft	Sept. 11, 2001
10.	Absolutely Sweet Marie	Blonde on Blonde	May 16, 1966
11.	Love Sick	Time Out of Mind	Sept. 30, 1997
12.	Highway 61 Revisited	Highway 61 Revisited	Aug. 30, 1965
13.	Desolation Row	Highway 61 Revisited	Aug. 30, 1965
14.	Summer Days	Love and Theft	Sept. 11, 2001
	Encores		
15.	Girl of the North Country	The Freewheelin' Bob Dylan	May 27, 1963
16.	All Along the Watchtower	John Wesley Harding	Dec. 27, 1967

The Musicians

Bob Dylan (vocal, keyboard & harmonica), Stu Kimball (lead guitar), Denny Freeman (guitar), Donnie Herron (banjo, electric mandolin, pedal steel guitar & lap steel guitar), Tony Garnier (bass), George Recile (drums).

Notes

- 116th Bob Dylan concert in Canada; 12th Bob Dylan concert in Vancouver.
- 1, 5, 12, Donnie Herron (lap steel guitar).
- 2-3, 5, 15, Bob Dylan (harmonica).
- 3, 4, 7, 15, Donnie Herron (pedal steel guitar).
- 6, 9, Donnie Herron (banjo).
- 13, 15, acoustic with the band.

Review

Instant Review: Vancouver Night #2 July 20/05

By Marq DeSouza.

I was very upset at the repeat of the first 6 songs, but at least things switched up a little after. I'll be there tomorrow and I get the feeling we're in for the same 6 again (at least). Something is happening here, and from songs 1-6, I know what it is.

Bob was wearing a black suit, the one with stars down the side of the pantleg and arms. No hat tonight, though he did walk over and grab it to carry offstage at the shows end. He looked and sounded much better last night. Last night was more of the wolfman voice, but tonights voice was pinched and garbled. At least the wolfman voice cuts right through everything in the mix. Bob let Stu do WAY MORE of the guitar soloing tonight, which I liked.

1. Maggie's: Not as strong as last night at all. Bob's voice seemed alot weaker and his phrasing not as sure.

2. Tonight: Not as strong as last night, harp solo center stage.

3. I'll Be: Same as last night, harp solo at piano.

4. Lay Lady: Unremarkable.

5. Most Likely: Not as strong as last night. Harp solo at the piano.

6. Blind Willie: Pretty good.

7. Tweedle Dum: The first song not played last night...and it's this!!! I admit I haven't listened to any MP3's of this from this year on purpose. Gotta say, Bob was off the mark on this, screwed up a few lines. There was some nice guitar interplay and the band built it nicely in the musical breaks. Still, if I never hear this song again, I'll be happy. Entirely upsung.

8. I Want You: This was a new arrangement (obviously). It has potential. It reminds me of the first appearance of Shelter From The Storm from earlier this year. It was unfocused, but just the appearance of it was very cool. Upsung alot though. Tony was on upright and Stu on acoustic for this.

9. High Water: The best performance of the night, no question.

10. Absolutely Sweet Marie: The biggest letdown of the night. I was so excited to hear the intro chords. Bob let the middle drag into oblivion. After a decent amount of time, the band rightly assumed to go back to the bridge, but Bob would have none of it and made them play through the main verse pattern and endless number of times. It was pretty funny actually. Bob looked pretty pissed off.

11. Lovesick: Bob blew this one too. It was very messy musically. None of the gloomy menace of versions on previous tours. Meandering.

12. Highway 61: Good, but not as good as last night.

13. Desolation Row: Stu did the exact flamenco style strumming as on the original recording. I wish I could say it was a good version as it was my first time hearing it in person, but it wasn't. It did get much better by the last few verses, which included "Nero's Neptune." The security let everyone rush the front of the stage during this. I thought that was it for the main set.

14. Summer Days: Like Sweet Marie, this dragged on forever. Bob threw this one away.

15. Girl From The: It was alright. I did not think it was humanly possible to upsing in one song this much. It's like he cannot help it. Harp solo at piano.

16. AATW: Rocked fiercely. Very good.

Posted to the Dylan Pool. Thurs., July 21, 2005. Reprinted with permission of Marq DeSouza

Thursday, July 21, 2005 --- The Orpheum
Vancouver, BC

Set List

	Song	From The Album	Released
1.	Maggie's Farm	Bringing It All Back Home	March 22, 1965
2.	Tonight I'll Be Staying Here With You	Nashville Skyline	April 9, 1969
3.	I'll Be Your Baby Tonight	John Wesley Harding	Dec. 27, 1967
4.	Lay, Lady, Lay	Nashville Skyline	April 9, 1969
5.	Most Likely You Go Your Way and I'll Go Mine	Blonde on Blonde	May 16, 1966

6.	Moonlight	Love and Theft	Sept. 11, 2001
7.	Down Along the Cove	John Wesley Harding	Dec. 27, 1967
8.	One Too Many Mornings	The Times They Are A-Changin'	Feb. 10, 1964
9.	Cry A While	Love and Theft	Sept. 11, 2001
10.	Boots of Spanish Leather	The Times They Are A-Changin'	Feb. 10, 1964
11.	Honest With Me	Love and Theft	Sept. 11, 2001
12.	I Believe in You	Slow Train Coming	Aug. 20, 1979
13.	Summer Days	Love and Theft	Sept. 11, 2001
14.	It Ain't Me, Babe	Another Side of Bob Dylan	Aug. 8, 1964
	Encores		
15.	Don't Think Twice, It's All Right	The Freewheelin' Bob Dylan	May 27, 1963
16.	All Along the Watchtower	John Wesley Harding	Dec. 27, 1967

The Musicians

Bob Dylan (vocal, keyboard & harmonica), Stu Kimball (lead guitar), Denny Freeman (guitar), Donnie Herron (banjo, electric mandolin, pedal steel guitar & lap steel guitar), Tony Garnier (bass), George Recile (drums).

Notes

- 117th Bob Dylan concert in Canada; 13th Bob Dylan concert in Vancouver.
- 1, 5, 7, 11, Donnie Herron (lap steel guitar).
- 2-3, 5, 8, 10, 15, Bob Dylan (harmonica).
- 3-4, 14, Donnie Herron (pedal steel guitar).
- 9, Donnie Herron (banjo).
- 8, 10, 14-15, acoustic with the band.
- Canadian live debut of song 8.
- Song 8 has been performed only once in Canada.

Reviews

Stuck inside the Orpheum with the Dylan blues again

By Wayne Moriarty, The Province.

Just who does Bob Dylan think he is? OK, sure, he's Bob Dylan.

But really, does that excuse his coming on stage 25 minutes late, as he did Thursday night at the Orpheum Theatre?

I can't imagine he was stuck on the Port Mann Bridge. And trust me, the extra 25 minutes wasn't spent in wardrobe.

Seriously, the guy must have jumped out of bed, looked at his daytimer and seen one lone item: Concert, Orpheum Theatre, Granville Street, 8 p.m.

So how could he possibly be 25 minutes late?

Rockers have long upheld a checkered tradition of arriving late on stage. At least in the '70s and '80s, when concerts were bloated theatrical operas, the sheer magnitude of these ridiculous shows gave the performers a solid excuse for being late.

After all, someone had to give the dancing elephant an enema. And who is going to argue with the roadie who puts that job off until the last minute?

But Bob didn't have any dancing elephants. He didn't even have a opening act.

The Orpheum stage was set. The instruments were tuned. At 7:57 p.m., the voice in the lobby was saying "go to your seats, the concert starts in three minutes."

So, I go to my seat and sit there for 25.

Tardiness wasn't the only annoyance Thursday night.

Please, if you will, allow me to discuss the show.

As Province rock critic Tom Harrison pointed out in his review of Dylan's Tuesday concert, Bob doesn't talk to the audience. Not a word.

What Tom failed to point out is that Bob doesn't look at the audience either.

I'm sorry, but Stevie Wonder makes more eye contact.

I used to think Michael Jackson would be the first music star to turn into Howard Hughes.

My money is now solidly backing Bob on that dubious carpet ride.

Dylan also chose to rearrange many of his classics.

"Lay Lady Lay," for example, sounded like a bad lounge act on a Monday night at the Last Chance Motel.

Why would he do that to "Lay Lady Lay"?

If Michelangelo went back on tour, do you think he'd slap Ron Jeremy on the Sistine Chapel?

As for the audience, suffice to say they raised the bar so high on sycophancy that even God, fearful of being one-upped, has probably chosen to delay the Second Coming until well after Bob's sleep of reason.

Just how adoring was the crowd, you ask? The man got a standing ovation for playing a harmonica.

A harmonica!

Who knows what might have happened had he whipped out the kazoo?

In fairness, I must point out that a commitment necessitated my leaving a tad early.

I probably missed the last 25 minutes of the show.

Gee, 25 minutes! How unfortunate was that?

Wayne Moriarty is The Province's editor-in-chief. For the record, he is also a big Bob Dylan fan.

The Vancouver Province. Sun., July 24, 2005.
Material reprinted with the express permission of: "Pacific Newspaper Group Inc.", a CanWest Partnership.

Instant Review: Vancouver Night #3 (faith restored) July 21/05

By Marq DeSouza.

Bob rocked the house tonight. Happy to say.

The crowd overall was much more enthusiastic, which must've helped matters. I thought there was less upsinging on the whole, though still far too much. My seat was quite a bit closer too.

1. Maggie: Best of all 3 Van. versions. Bob was actually smiling throughout it. That was the first time we'd seen that. Stu did a kickass guitar solo.

2. Tonight...: There was less upsinging in this than the last 2 nights. It was not a stupendous version, but it had promise in the vocals. He did end it with probably the most go-nowhere harp solo I've ever heard. Harp solo centre stage.

3. I'll Be: Best of all 3 Van. versions. Bob was putting much more sustaining notes into his vocals tonight. He played with the phrasing in this without only resorting to upsinging. This Bob had bite. Harp solo at piano.

4. Lay Lady Lay: I can't believe I'm saying this, but this was good. The crowd roared approval at the opening notes. Bob "downsang" at least every second line and alternated that with upsang final words of lines. It was kinda fun to guess which one he was gonna do. The downsang notes were not pinched off either. They were pronounced, low and sexy. Quite a seductive technique.

Someone in another post mentioned that we only need one of songs 2-4 per night, I'd agree.

5. Most Likely: Very good. I wouldn't mind it if Bob played this every show for awhile, as I wouldn't know what else to compare it to in his canon. Again, a more sustained effort in holding notes in the vocals in this version. Harp solo centre stage.

6. Moonlight: expected Blind Willie. This was alright. The vocal was quite well enunciated and he did well with the words. The sound in the Orpheum was very good. A delicate version. Bob lost a bit of his focus when the crowd applauded one of the solos (I think it was the violin), but the old man came out alright.

7. Down Along...: Rocked as expected. Overall, there was far less meandering musical breaks tonight. Each solo lasted about the right time. Donnie actually smiled very wide during this.

8. One Too Many: Yes, I was surprised. This was great. Far better than I Want You last night. The vocals were nice. Just idiosyncratic enough to be interesting, but not overboard. The band locked in right from the get-go. They followed Bob well as sometimes he added a bar to each change, sometimes didn't. Harp solo centre stage. He repeated the first verse at the end. Alternating up and downsinging. It worked.

9. Cry Awhile: This to me was the performance of this whole 3 show run. They absolutely nailed it. Bob's vocal taking it as far out on the edge as it could go. Damn, it was perfect. The crowd loved it.

10. Boots: Excellent. The band nailed it. The only negative was a terrible solo by Denny. Harp solo at piano.

11. Honest With Me: Yeah, I know, it's boring to 'see' it in the set, but when they kick it into gear, it's something else. George deserves extra props for his playing on this. Bob was bouncing up and down, getting right into it.

The band huddled for a minute, I guess deciding what to do.

12. I Believe In You: Gorgeous. Majestic. A thrill to see him do this song from the neglected gospel years. Upsinging galore, though it didn't bug me.

13. Summer days: The best of all the Vancouver versions (he did it every show). Kept it shorter and tighter than the other night. There was purpose to the middle section that wasn't there before. George and Tony were smiling away. The crowd had rushed the stage and Bob seemed to feed off that energy. He bounced up and down at the piano all throughout it.

14. It Aint Me: I thought the main set was over, but then they busted this out and after Cry Awhile, it was my favorite song of the run. This is my favorite arrangement of this since the Rolling Thunder days. Stu did another great solo. Just a great version. It got quiet, then LOUD.

15. Don't Think...: Always a thrill to hear that opening guitar line. It wasn't the best, but as the show built, it fit in. Upsinging lots, but good despite. Harp solo centre stage.

Bob turned around to walk over to the harp table and kind of tripped on some cables or something.

16. AATW: Better than last night. After they did this, Bob and the band stood centre stage as usual, but tonight Bob talked to Tony for a minute, both smiling the whole time. Then Bob turned around and laughed/pointed to George, who broke out laughing. I thought they may have decided to bust out LARS, but they melted back into the night.

On the way out, I overheard some people talking about how "obscure" the setlist was.

Great show.

Posted to the Dylan Pool. Fri., July 22, 2005. Reprinted with permission of Marq DeSouza.

Friday, July 22, 2005 --- Prospera Place
Kelowna, BC

Set List

	Song	From The Album	Released
1.	Maggie's Farm	Bringing It All Back Home	March 22, 1965
2.	Tonight I'll Be Staying Here With You	Nashville Skyline	April 9, 1969
3.	I'll Be Your Baby Tonight	John Wesley Harding	Dec. 27, 1967
4.	Lay, Lady, Lay	Nashville Skyline	April 9, 1969
5.	Stuck Inside of Mobile with the Memphis Blues Again	Blonde on Blonde	May 16, 1966
6.	Moonlight	Love and Theft	Sept. 11, 2001
7.	Highway 61 Revisited	Highway 61 Revisited	Aug. 30, 1965
8.	Shelter from the Storm	Blood on the Tracks	Jan. 20, 1975
9.	Cry A While	Love and Theft	Sept. 11, 2001
10.	Just Like a Woman	Blonde on Blonde	May 16, 1966
11.	Honest With Me	Love and Theft	Sept. 11, 2001
12.	The Times They Are A-Changin'	The Times They Are A-Changin'	Feb. 10, 1964
13.	Floater (Too Much To Ask)	Love and Theft	Sept. 11, 2001
14.	Summer Days	Love and Theft	Sept. 11, 2001
	Encores		
15.	Like a Rolling Stone	Highway 61 Revisited	Aug. 30, 1965
16.	All Along the Watchtower	John Wesley Harding	Dec. 27, 1967

The Musicians

Bob Dylan (vocal, keyboard & harmonica), Stu Kimball (lead guitar), Denny Freeman (guitar), Donnie Herron (banjo, electric mandolin, violion, pedal steel guitar & lap steel guitar), Tony Garnier (bass), George Recile (drums).

Notes

- 118th Bob Dylan concert in Canada; Debut Bob Dylan concert in Kelowna.
- 1, 7, 11, Donnie Herron (lap steel guitar).
- 2-3, 8, 12-13, Bob Dylan (harmonica).
- 3-4, 16, Donnie Herron (pedal steel guitar).
- 12, acoustic with the band.
- 13, Donnie Herron (violin).

Reviews

2005-07-22 Kelowna, BC

By Don Helling.

...or what a difference a day makes. From the Orpheum to a hockey arena.

I wasn't going to write a review because I wasn't that excited about the show. It's tough seeing Bob at the Orpheum, then Prospera Place twice as far from the stage…and other things noted below put a bit of a negative spin on the experience, but since no one else reviewed it here, I'll do my best:

I planned to make it a Bob show+fishing trip, and it worked out pretty much as planned. I left late and cruised the first 400 kilometers, only to be stuck in a massive traffic jam the 10 K leading to the one lane of traffic across the bridge entering Kelowna (I later found out that there were bunch of accidents that added to the half hour jam). I checked in at the Postill Lake "resort" and just had time to set up my tent and head to the show.

I got there just before 8:00 only to find out that they had moved my seat because they needed the sound mixing area closer to the stage. I figured, okay as long as it's substantially better seating. The ticket guy really lit up and said that I get to sit in the players bench area! Not that I knew what that was, but it sounded important. Needless to say, the seats were directly to the side of my original seat, but the (hockey) players bench area had a bunch of folding chairs and wasn't policed well, so it became a magnet for the nosebleed seat folks. Oh well. I had some nice folks around me and I settled in for the show. (BTW: I get a kick out of pointing out Bob's Oscar to casual fans.)

Okay, after that I was still ready for a great show after seeing the Orpheum show the night before. Bob came out in black and the boys were in grey, looking sharp. The acoustics of the room, tin roof and all, left a lot to be desired, especially compared to the night before.

Maggies-Stu's solo, okay
Tonight– center stage harp, Denny & Donnie solos
I'll Be Your-harp at the piano
Lay Lady – upsing deluxe, plus a bit o' the wolf "see them shiiiiiiiine"
Stuck inside of mobile – Stu on acoustic, solos were average

At this point the crowd near me got distracting. Two loud talkers would alternate between talking about the song (during the song) and anything else that came to mind. Then security decided to oust a dancer who was annoying a bunch of people sitting behind him, and they chose the area directly in front of me to discuss the situation with him. Ughh.

Moonlight. Donny on fiddle, more subdued not as strong.
Hwy 61 – Rocking start, got the crowd going. Weird piano solo by Bob, strong vocal and piano high in the mix. Bob then had a short chat with Tony.

***Shelter from the storm! Great acoustic intro, moderate upsinging, all-in-all Bob's vocals were average on this, but it was my favorite song of the night. Decent solo by Denny. Harp at the piano.

Lights came on the audience after EVERY song. I'm not sure why, but it was annoying.

Cry Awhile. Band wasn't as tight as the night before. Donnie banjo solo again. Another conference followed this one.
Just Like a Woman – A bit boring. Growlin' Wolfy on "just like a little girl"

Here the curtains drew back to the sparkly background, and later in the encore we got the eye curtain. I thought it was kinda funny that this is the extent of Bob's "special effects."

Honest With Me – A little slower tempo than last night. George was really trying hard on this one, but the band just wasn't as tight.

Times they are a'changing – another highlight for me. Harp center stage.

Floater. Also a bit boring, and I like the song. Upsung mightily. Good solo by Donnie on violin. Bob harp at piano.

Summer Days – Tony and George clicked on this one. Tony seemed to be having fun going down low playing the bass. Bob's voice was stronger "Gooooood Luck..." as was his piano work, very active. A nice soft section in the middle of the song. Guitar solos stronger here too. I wasn't close enough to see facial expressions, but with this one exception tonight's show seemed a bit stiff, and more of a rote performance overall.

Encores: average, upsing on Rolling Stone, Watchtower was loud like last night. Echo used for the first time (I noticed it anyway) "distance...istance..."

Sorry for being a bit negative about this show, but that was how I experienced it.

As for the fishing, it was fine and the weather was cooperative. Now it's back to work!

Posted to the Dylan Pool. Tues., July 26, 2005. Reprinted with permission of Don Helling.

Like a groaning drone

By Andre Wetjen, The Okanagan Sunday.

If his Kelowna performance was any indication, perhaps Bob Dylan's "Never Ending Tour" should come to an end.

Although he was the most legendary act to ever grace the Prospera Place stage, many fans in the sold-out crowd left Friday's concert disappointed, his faltering voice and poor stage presence being the biggest contributing factors.

The concert began on a high note, with Dylan's superb band delivering a tight rendition of Maggie's Farm, the master wordsmith growling out the lyrics to the 40-year-old song with intensity and authority. The country-tinged Tonight I'll Be Staying With You and I'll Be Your Baby Tonight followed, warming up the audience for what all believed would be a memorable evening.

An approving roar emanated from the crowd as the band played the opening notes to Lay Lady Lay. Dylan's voice couldn't manage the notes to the new, almost childlike arrangement, destroying what is surely one of his most beautiful love songs. A horrid rendition of Stuck Inside of Mobile With the Memphis Blues Again followed, with Dylan managing to salvage the song just before it ended.

The highlight of the concert came with a rollicking rendition of Highway 61 Revisited. The band cooked, both as a tight unit and with their solos, propelling Dylan along at what was his finest moment of the evening.

Another high point was Dylan's new rendition of Just Like a Woman, which, although growled out in a more guttural manner than the recorded version, maintained the tenderness of the original.

Most of the evening's 17-song set featured Dylan classics, but they were rendered almost unrecognizable by the rearrangements. To his credit, you could tell Dylan was mixing it up, the band members watching his every move to see what he was up to next. All musicians were equal to the task of keeping up to the man who is renowned for changing songs and interpretations on the fly.

The absolute low point of the evening came with a completely rearranged and butchered version of The Times They Are A-Changin'. The most loyal of Dylan fans will argue that new interpretations and his spontaneity should be applauded, not criticized. However, that would be true only if it was for the better, and such was not the case.

Equally irksome to Dylan's poor performance was his lack of rapport with the audience. Not a word was said throughout the entire evening, except for the introduction of band members five minutes before the concert ended.

Liz McKinney, radio morning host for Power 104 in Kelowna, put it rather succinctly.

"Not even a thank you," she said. "I'm very disappointed; he didn't even thank us for coming."

As well, because he no longer slings a guitar and prefers standing behind a keyboard, many in the audience saw only his back throughout the concert. A big screen would have made the show more enjoyable for those sitting on the left side of the stage.

The Dylan line "Don't criticize what you don't understand" looms as this review is being written. After all, how can you knock a musical icon of Dylan's stature?

In the end, though, it is Dylan's inability to carry the notes of his own songs, as well as his apparent disdain for his audience that gives him a failing grade. Even icons falter, and Dylan did so on Friday.

Despite the mostly uneven performance, many in the crowd were on their feet for a number of songs, especially for the two encores, Like A Rolling Stone and All Along the Watchtower.

At the conclusion of the latter, Mr. Zimmerman lined up with his bandmates, gave the crowd an almost quizzical look, motioned to his musicians to leave, and walked off the stage.

The Kelowna Daily Courier. Sun., July 24, 2005. Reprinted with permission of The Kelowna Daily Courier.

Sunday, July 24, 2005 --- Pengrowth Saddledome Calgary, AB

Set List

	Song	From The Album	Released
1.	Maggie's Farm	Bringing It All Back Home	March 22, 1965
2.	Tonight I'll Be Staying Here With You	Nashville Skyline	April 9, 1969
3.	I'll Be Your Baby Tonight	John Wesley Harding	Dec. 27, 1967
4.	Lay, Lady, Lay	Nashville Skyline	April 9, 1969
5.	God Knows	Under the Red Sky	Sept. 11, 1990
6.	Shooting Star	Oh Mercy	Sept. 12, 1989
7.	Lonesome Day Blues	Love and Theft	Sept. 11, 2001
8.	Positively 4th Street	Bob Dylan's Greatest Hits	March 27, 1967
9.	Watching the River Flow	Bob Dylan's Greatest Hits, Vol. 2	Nov. 17, 1971
10.	Can't Wait	Time Out of Mind	Sept. 30, 1997
11.	Highway 61 Revisited	Highway 61 Revisited	Aug. 30, 1965
12.	Tryin' To Get To Heaven	Time Out of Mind	Sept. 30, 1997
13.	A Hard Rain's A-Gonna Fall	The Freewheelin' Bob Dylan	May 27, 1963
14.	Summer Days	Love and Theft	Sept. 11, 2001
	Encores		
15.	Don't Think Twice, It's All Right	The Freewheelin' Bob Dylan	May 27, 1963
16.	All Along the Watchtower	John Wesley Harding	Dec. 27, 1967

The Musicians

Bob Dylan (vocal, keyboard & harmonica), Stu Kimball (lead guitar), Denny Freeman (guitar), Donnie Herron (banjo, electric mandolin, pedal steel guitar & lap steel guitar), Tony Garnier (bass), George Recile (drums).

Notes

- 119th Bob Dylan concert in Canada; 6th Bob Dylan concert in Calgary.
- 1, 9, 11, Donnie Herron (lap steel guitar).
- 2-3, Bob Dylan (harmonica).
- 3-4 Donnie Herron (pedal steel guitar).
- 13, 15, acoustic with the band.

Reviews

The Book of Bob

It's Still Worth Pulling This Classic Off The Shelf

By Mike Bell, Calgary Sun.

Is there a better way to wrap up a weekend of folk music than with a man who is synonymous with the genre?

Can you think of a more apropos capper to four days of classic roots music and the various other genres that have branched off of it than a concert by the individual responsible for those offshoots?

Actually, yeah – yeah, last night could have been better.

Bob Dylan, on the 40th anniversary of his song Like A Rolling Stone hitting the charts, could have been playing on the main stage of Prince's Island Park instead of in the Saddledome.

But because of a number of different factors – scheduling, corporate greed, etc. – the legend performed in front of 7,000 or so fans in a hockey arena with a sometimes sketchy sound system instead of in gorgeous natural surroundings.

Still, however imperfect the setting and the timing of the show, his Bobness was in excellent form last night.

Kicking off with the seminal – only one of many tunes from Dylan you could describe as such – Maggie's Farm, the 64-year-old and his five piece band attacked two hours of his half-century career with an almost workman-like attitude and approach.

While the term workman-like normally denotes a cold detachment to the task at hand, there was an undeniable warmth and even intimacy about the set.

Sure, for much of his career, Dylan has never been one for showmanship, preferring instead to let the depth of the material and skills of himself and whatever players he surrounds himself with sell the show.

And that was definitely the case last night as the man, true to form, had said nothing to the crowd in the first hour and a half except the words which were sung in his charming, nasal mumble.

But in the past decade – since he's become the consummate road warrior on a never-ending tour, he's played himself into a comfortable place.

And onstage, clad in his (these days) signature white cowboy hat and standing mostly in front of his keyboards, that comfort came through and lit up his country-rock treatments of tracks such as Lay, Lady, Lay.

He doesn't have to worry about his material, he doesn't have to worry about his band – if they were any tighter you'd need a shoehorn to tell the sound of one instrument from another – and as you can probably tell from his commercials hawking panties, he doesn't have to worry about his legacy.

He just goes out and plays, seemingly enjoying – you never know, the man defines stoicism – still being able to do it and do it well.

If you've seen him on any of his past tours through town, yes it was pretty much by the book. That book, the book of Bob, albeit ragged, dog-eared and worn, is one still worth taking off the shelf every so often and getting re-acquainted with. The classics usually are.

Dylan delivers a 'Dome dandy

By Heath McCoy, Calgary Herald.

Who would've guessed that at 64, Bob Dylan could pack this much raw blues power?

The folk rock legend played a tremendous show Sunday night at the 'Dome. That might have turned off a few of the purists who would like Dylan to sound as he did on his original records for all eternity.

But then, Dylan has always defied anybody who wanted to pigeon-hole him. For those happy to see the man grow, Dylan put on one of the best shows of the year.

As for worries that the Dylan gig would butt heads with the Calgary Folk Music Festival, which wrapped up at the same time at Prince's Island Park, those worries were swept away.

If there was any doubt before, there's none now. Calgary really is a folk music city.

That is to say, neither gig stole a significant audience from the other, even though both appeal to essentially the same crowd. The Folk Fest attracted about 10,500 fans, which is about right for a day that was only OK weather-wise, and Dylan brought about 6,500 devotees to the 'Dome, which doesn't sound great, but it's about the same size crowd he attracted when he played here last.

You see, while Dylan's legend cannot be questioned, in the live department he's developed a well-deserved reputation for being brilliant one minute and a down-right mess the next.

But Sunday, the scales tipped toward the brilliant.

Looking every bit the country gentleman in a white cowboy hat and black three-piece suit, Dylan and a country-blues quintet that were never less than killer opened up with a gritty, shockingly muscular run through Maggie's Farm.

The bard and his band seldom let up an inch from then on, Dylan laying his distinctive mountain man croak down like a seasoned blues vet on such tracks as a honky-tonk I'll Be Your Baby Tonight, a romantic Lay Lady Lay, and the country-blues lullaby Moonlight, off his latest album Love and Theft. Also unforgettable was a whiskey-drenched, sorrow-at-last-call take on Positively 4th Street.

A blues-rock slam through Highway 61 Revisited was a high point of the evening.

It left little doubt about the power of Dylan's current band and the way they bring the best out of him. The audience noticed it, too.

At press time, just before the encore, 6,500 fans were stomping their feet and yelling, "Bobby! Bobby!"

There's little question that anybody who wrote Dylan off as a legend that is winding down has to eat their words.

Sunday night the king of folk was the king of country-blues, and he set the 'Dome on fire.

Attendance: 6,500.

Other Appearances

Thursday, September 16, 1965 --- Friar's Tavern Toronto, ON

When Dylan got rocked

Folk purist met Levon and the Hawks at the Friar's Tavern on Yonge St. and changed the course of pop music history

By John Goddard, Toronto Star.

Patrons of the downtown Hard Rock Cafe can be forgiven for knowing nothing of its true musical connection.

Eyes are naturally drawn to the memorabilia on the walls – Randy Bachman's guitar from his B.T.O. days, a poster for the Elvis Presley movie Kissin' Cousins, a black leather jacket once worn by Iggy Pop.

Easy to miss are details of the room itself, most prominent among them being the overhead Elizabethan-style beams and tiles.

They formed the original ceiling of the previous occupant, the Friar's Tavern, home to an event that Time magazine once called "the most decisive moment in rock history."

From 1964 to 1976, the Friar's served as one of the most popular nightclubs in the downtown core, and it was there in the early morning of Thurs., Sept. 16, 1965, that Bob Dylan first met Levon and the Hawks, later renamed the Band.

Today, anybody sitting at the Friar's oddly configured bar, now positioned near the cafe's north wall, would be perched roughly where Levon Helm laid into his drum kit to begin rehearsals for Dylan's revolutionary electric-debut world tour.

It opened two weeks later at New York's Carnegie Hall and passed through Toronto's Massey Hall that Nov. 14 and 15 – 35 years ago this week.

"Maybe it would be ignorance," Toronto Hard Rock general manager Tim Eddis says to explain why the historic meeting and rehearsal sessions are nowhere commemorated at the cafe, allowing that neither he nor any of his staff knows the story.

But now there may be a chance to pay tribute, he says. Hard Rock corporate headquarters in Orlando, Fla., is preparing to spend $4 million to $6 million over the next 18 months on renovations to the Yonge St. location, opposite the Eaton Centre.

Tentative plans call for expanding the existing cafe and bar into the entire first floor of the former Friar's club. Dance floors and lounges with live music would take over the upstairs.

"Maybe we could bring that history back to life," Eddis says. "Could you send us more information?"

The story begins in 1963 with the matchmaker, Mary Martin.

She works now as a talent scout in Nashville but she was born in Toronto, went to the Havergal girls' school, and after a brief stint working for a Toronto insurance company, moved to New York's Greenwich Village.

By chance she landed a receptionist's job with Albert Grossman, manager at the time to the hottest acts in folk music – Peter, Paul and Mary; Ian and Sylvia; and Bob Dylan. She kept her connection with Toronto, however, sometimes returning for a couple of months at a time and becoming one of the biggest fans of Levon and the Hawks.

"We would go to drink at the Pilot Tavern near Yonge and Bloor," she says of her and her friends. "Then after several beers, or gin-and-tonics, we'd go down to see the Hawks at 'the Le Coq d'Or.'

"Those boys talked to each other musically," she says. "They had conversations with themselves that were so deeply musical that if you listened, you got to go along. They were the best band that we had ever, ever heard."

The Hawks had formed as backing players to Toronto rockabilly star Ronnie Hawkins, splitting with him in late 1963 to extend their range into early rock 'n' roll songs, bluesy ballads and soulful r 'n' b tunes. In his 1993 autobiography, This Wheel's On Fire, Helm says that the Hawks considered themselves "the undisputed champions of Canadian rock and roll."

But they were still playing bars. In search of something bigger, they started travelling to New York, playing club dates and cutting an unsuccessful single there in early 1964. Some of the members also played on So Many Roads, the third album by solo blues artist John Hammond – "one of the first to see the possibilities of having an electric band," Helm says.

In early 1965, still looking to make a record of their own, the Hawks sent a demo tape to Mary Martin. She was back full time with Albert Grossman by then, and passed a copy to a Grossman assistant.

" 'Miss Martin, we aren't interested in talent of that calibre,' " she recalls him saying – "meaning, I suppose, 'They're a bar band. Who cares?' "

At the same time, Martin noticed that Dylan was becoming agitated. She dates the period to April, 1965, when a new group called the Byrds recorded an electric version of Dylan's "Mr. Tambourine Man."

"He was just sitting in the office sort of shaking his leg and his head, going, 'Golly, what do I do next, huh?' " Martin recalls.

"And what had happened is very simple to explain. Bob Dylan had heard drums, an electric bass and an electric guitar on 'Mr. Tambourine Man' – and for a folk singer that was a giant leap to think, 'Damn, now I'm going to have to get a band.'

"But that's really what he had to ponder. And he did ponder it, and I said, 'Well, go to Toronto and see the Hawks.' "

Dylan did not go right away.

He went to England and Dylan's biographers all agree that he went through some kind of profound dissatisfaction that spring. He was fed up with playing guitar and harmonica alone in front of reverential sold-out crowds, a mood intimately captured in D. A. Pennebaker's film Don't Look Back. At one point before walking onstage, Dylan says, "I don't feel like singing."

In early June, 1965, he returned home. Within days he wrote "Like A Rolling Stone," and on June 15, with an electric band, he recorded it – a six-minute masterpiece that represented, in the words of biographer Paul Williams, "a whole new kind of music."

It wasn't folk. It wasn't rock and roll. It was something else – a rich, stately release, perhaps, of all the restlessness and boredom Dylan had been feeling that spring.

On July 20, "Like A Rolling Stone" was released as a single and five days after that, at the Newport Folk Festival, Dylan made his first controversial stage appearance with an electric group, put together the night before.

Mary Martin was in the audience and says watching Dylan at that now famous concert where fans booed him off the stage stiffened her resolve to play go-between.

"Bob Dylan still needed his own band," she says, "and I really felt that the boys needed to take that other step before they really emerged."

The Hawks were playing all that summer at a teenage nightclub near Atlantic City. Martin persuaded a Grossman scout, Dan Weiner, to check them out. She also told the Hawks about the Newport concert, and in early August she brought Rick Danko an advance copy of Dylan's sixth album, Highway 61 Revisited, with "Like A Rolling Stone."

The Hawks had still barely heard of Dylan. "We had no idea how big Bob Dylan was," Helm says in his book. In their ignorance, they dismissed him as a folkie – a "strummer" they called him – and viewed themselves far more favourably as a hard-edged bar band.

They were worlds apart, but the band's resistance to Dylan still seems astounding given the phenomenon he had become.

At 24 years old, Dylan stood at the centre of a new music that critics were calling folk-rock and that Dylan himself refused to label. Sound, lyrics, and emotion swirled and fit together in his songs in revolutionary new ways.

All that August, "Like A Rolling Stone" rode near the top of the charts, soon followed by "Positively Fourth Street." Other artists scrambled to record Dylan songs and sing in the Dylan style. That month alone, 48 Dylan songs were released by other people, including the Turtles' hit, "It Ain't Me Babe," and Cher's "All I Really Want To Do."

But if the Hawks were not entirely sold on Dylan, neither was Dylan sold on the Hawks. His first choice on guitar was Chicago guitarist Mike Bloomfield, who had played the Newport gig. Only after Bloomfield turned him down for other commitments did Dylan turn to Hawks' guitarist Robbie Robertson.

"(Mary Martin) knew all the bands and singers from Canada," Dylan later told Rolling Stone editor, Jann Wenner, "and she kept pushing these guys the Hawks on me."

Dylan invited Robertson to audition in New York with the beginnings of a band, and Robertson suggested replacing the drummer with Helm, which Dylan did. The other Hawks would continue to play the nightclub, while Robertson, Helm and two other musicians would play two electric concerts with Dylan.

The first took place on Aug. 28, 1965, at New York's Forest Hills Tennis Stadium before 15,000 people – the biggest audience Robertson and Helm had ever played to.

Dylan divided the concert into two sets. In the first, he sang seven numbers by himself with an acoustic guitar and harmonica. Then came the electric set. Before they went on, Helm says, Dylan gathered them together and said, "Just keep playing, no matter how weird it gets."

Boos and catcalls followed. "Yeah, yeah, shake it up, baby." "Scumbag." "Where's Ringo?" A fight broke out. People threw fruit at the band members, although not at Dylan, and at one point a man rushed the stage and knocked keyboard player Al Kooper off his chair.

Six days later, the group repeated the show at California's Hollywood Bowl, after which Dylan proposed to tour. Kooper, however, said he'd had enough. Helm said he would not break up the Hawks.

"Take us all, or don't take anybody," he recalls telling Grossman, and Dylan later replied, "When can I hear the band?"

On Wednesday afternoon, Sept. 15, 1965, Dylan arrived in Toronto by private plane. At midnight, he went to the Friar's Tavern to watch Levon and the Hawks play their final set, and afterward he rehearsed with them until 6 a.m.

The whole next night they rehearsed together, and at one point Dylan gave an interview to Robert Fulford, then a reporter for The Star.

"I know my thing now," Dylan told him. "I know what it is. It's hard to describe. I don't know what to call it because I've never heard it before."

Two months later at Massey Hall, before the Hawks' hometown crowd, Star reviewer Antony Ferry let go one of the harshest attacks of the entire tour.

"Here was a Bob Dylan who once was a purist," he wrote,"electronically hooked up to a third-rate Yonge St. rock 'n' roll band."

Fulford disagreed.

"To me the new Dylan seems the better Dylan – more expressive, more exciting," he wrote in a column later that week.

"The second half of the Massey Hall concert, with that wild rock beat coming from Levon and the Hawks, was a remarkable experience – great waves of sound roaring off the stage in marvellously subtle rhythms, a tremendous roaring hurricane of a style . . .

"I love it."

Hard Rock Café honours Bob Dylan

Toronto restaurant acknowledges 'decisive moment in rock history'

By John Goddard, The Toronto Star.

The first plaque marking a rock 'n' roll historic site in Toronto is to be installed this weekend.

It will commemorate the spot where Bob Dylan first rehearsed with a hard-edged Toronto rock group called Levon and the Hawks, later to become famous as the Band.

"The most decisive moment in rock history," Time magazine once called the event.

It took place in the early hours of Sept. 16, 1965, in what was then the Friar's Tavern and is now the Hard Rock Café on Yonge St., just south of Dundas St.

"The plaque is being prepared in Orlando, Fla. (world headquarters for the Hard Rock Café)," local manager Kirk Thompson said earlier this week.

"We want to embrace the musical history of this building."

Until now, despite numerous guitars and costumes mounted on the walls, nothing in the Hard Rock Café had made reference to the former Friar's or to that seminal event.

Displays instead featured such items as Randy Bachman's guitar from his Bachman-Turner Overdrive days, a black leather jacket once worn by Iggy Pop, and a poster for the Elvis Presley movie Kissin' Cousins.

Then just over a year ago, the restaurant's management twigged to a Saturday feature in The Star that told how Dylan met the Band in Toronto shortly after his chaotic electric debut at the 1965 Newport Folk Festival.

It told how a Toronto music fan, Havergal graduate Mary Martin, persuaded Dylan to hire the Hawks and how they rehearsed for two nights in the club after hours, and how one week later, they set off on a gruelling eight-month tour of North America and Europe. Dylan alienated the loyal folkies in his audiences and unleashed a whole new sound that critics named "folk rock" and that Dylan himself refused to label. Now the Hard Rock has paid tribute in a big way.

The Café recently renovated and expanded to become a two-floor restaurant and nightclub complex, the first completed project of the planned Dundas Square development.

On either side of the interior entrance are giant display cases – one dedicated to Dylan, the other to the Band. Next to the Band display is where the plaque will go.

An early version was installed in time for a public reopening in November, but the text contained errors, which knowledgeable customers and one staff member drew to the management's attention, Thompson said.

Although the rewritten version wasn't ready in time for an invitation-only bash last weekend, guests did receive a special pin tied to the Dylan/Band theme.

The pin is a replica of the wood-varnished Fender Stratocaster guitar Dylan played at Newport, likely the same one he brought with him to the Toronto rehearsals two months later.

Dylan's major recordings with the Hawks/the Band are Bob Dylan Live 1966 (a double CD from that first electric tour, released 1998); The Basement Tapes (1975); Planet Waves (1974); Before The Flood (live double CD, 1974) and; The Last Waltz (album, movie and home video, 1978).

Sunday, July 17, 1972 --- Mariposa Folk Festival Toronto, ON

Dylan surprise Mariposa visitor

By Robert Martin.

Seldom-seen Bob Dylan, an almost legendary figure of folk music, made an unannounced appearance at the Mariposa Folk Festival last night, but was mobbed by an overly-enthusiastic crowd shortly after his arrival and had to return to the mainland on the private launch on which he arrived.

The Mariposa gathering spotted him as he headed to a stage and rushed toward him. Security guards with him led Dylan to the cordoned-off area where he waited behind a steel fence for about 15 minutes until the boat arrived.

Dick Flohill, a Mariposa director, said Dylan had intended to make an event of his visit by performing in public, something he seldom does any more. (His last public performance was in New York at the Concert for Bangladesh a few months ago.)

Dylan showed up with Adam Mitchell, a former member of the Paupers, who had been performing earlier on the weekend at the festival.

All ticket's for yesterday's performances were sold by noon and at 5 p.m. the gates were opened to let in the hundreds of fans who had been waiting outside for hours.

Dylan wasn't the only big-name performer to show up at Mariposa, although the famous names tended at first to just blend with the crowd.

Gordon Lightfoot, wearing a pair of rose colored glasses, sat virtually unnoticed on the grass among a crowd watching a new American folk singer, John Prine, perform.

It's understandable that Lightfoot went unnoticed because Prine kept everyone's eyes strictly on him. He has a voice like the early Dylan, all late nights and cigarette butts, the easygoing delivery of Kris Kristofferson and a repertoire of funny-sad songs about various aspects of losing that are all his own.

Everything was quiet as long as guests passed quietly through the crowds. However, when Joni Mitchell joined her friend Murray McLauchlan for a few songs during his set, people started to go a little crazy.

Their joy at seeing and hearing Joni Mitchell perform live understandable because it is not something she does very often any more, But enthusiasm led to fired-up imaginations and in half an hour, if you listened to the rumor mongers, Woody Guthrie himself had risen from the grave and was at Mariposa.

The announcement that Salome Bey would appear at Stage Four, one of the six stages providing continuous entertainment, started a general stampede in that direction. The event that was supposed to take place then was a workshop on roots and traditions of blues. The size and expectations of the crowd turned it into a group concert which included, besides Miss Bey, who did in fact show up, Bukka White, Roosevelt Sykes and Taj Mahal, all of whom were wildly applauded.

Then the rains came. There had been showers on and off throughout Saturday, but at 5 p.m. the skies opened up as though they intended to wash the island into Lake Ontario. Suddenly whole audiences became wrapped in plastic, Trench coats, yellow slickers, green garbage bags with holes cut for arms and heads and immense sheets of white plastic emerged from picnic hampers and rucksacks.

The hardihood of the crowd was admirable; very few people left, most of them simply huddling under whatever was handy and trying not to get rain down their necks.

But there were not many places to go for shelter: not enough trees on the site to provide cover for 10,000, and catching a ferry could mean a 20-minute wait in the open. So most just sat around until the rain soaked through whatever their protection was, then threw it aside and danced in the puddles.

Many remained in the hope of seeing more superstars. The rumor at the Dave Bromberg concert was that Neil Young was coming. He did not show – at least not until later – but was not missed because Bromberg put on a fine show of his own.

Bromberg is one of a new generation of white blues singers whose sufferings have not made him lose his sense of humor. Songs like You've Got to Suffer if You Want to Sing the Blues were firmly tongue-in-cheek.

When Young showed up for Bruce Cockburn's concert, there was an initial hysterical reaction, then the audience quieted down to listen to him sing a new song, Sugar Mountain, and an old one, Helpless, which he dedicated to the Pickering airport.

Yesterday the sun turned out and so did the same large crowds that came on Saturday. In some areas, the grass had turned to mud, but most of the site was in pretty good shape, if wet.

Generally, the 12th version of Mariposa can be counted a rousing success. The acts were good – many were great – nobody seemed seriously put out by the weather and the festival actually made money for the third time in its history.

Dick Flohill, one of the festival directors, announced on Saturday that the festival had broken even at this point and that Sunday's receipts would all be profit.

This compares favorably with last year's Mariposa which lost $4,000. The new multiple-stage, continuous-entertainment format has been accepted by folk fans and will be continued next year.

The only improvement festival organizers would like to see next year, they say, is three days of sunshine.

Friday, November 28, 1975 --- A Hotel Room
Quebec City, QC

During the Rolling Thunder Revue Tour, Bob Dylan filmed his 4-hour movie Renaldo and Clara. In the movie Dylan is seen singing and playing guitar on House of the Risin' Sun in a hotel room in Quebec City. He was joined by Rob Stoner (vocal & bass), David Mansfield (steel guitar) and Mick Ronson (guitar). The one-minute scene was included in the long version of Renaldo and Clara released on January 25, 1978 and the short version released in late 1978.

Friday, December 5, 1975 --- A Hotel Room
Montreal, QC

During the Rolling Thunder Revue Tour, Bob Dylan filmed his 4-hour movie Renaldo and Clara. In the movie Dylan is seen playing guitar riffs in a hotel room in Montreal. The scene was included in the long version of Renaldo and Clara released on January 25, 1978 and the short version released in late 1978.

Friday, October 10, 1986 --- Warehouse Studio
Toronto, ON

Dylan gives secret 'concert'

By Greg Quill, Toronto Star.

Bob Dylan played in Toronto Friday night, and only 1,000 people knew it.

They were the fortunate few invited by the British-based producers of the $8 million movie Hearts Of Fire to a converted warehouse-studio in the city's west end for "a concert" featuring the legendary American poet-songwriter and pop star Fiona Flanagan.

Dylan and Flanagan arrived here Wednesday and will remain in Toronto for the next five weeks to complete the movie, directed by Richard Marquand (Return Of The Jedi, Jagged Edge.) About two-thirds of the rock 'n' roll love saga will be shot in southern Ontario. The remainder is set in London, England, and has already been completed.

American hometown

The scene that was shot Friday night is the movie's climax, a concert performance in which Flanagan, playing a rock star named Molly, and her band performed the movie's title song before a supposedly American hometown audience. During the final minutes of the song Flanagan was joined onstage by Dylan, playing Billy Parker, a retired rock hero who contributes to Molly's career.

During the first three "takes" last night, Dylan didn't say or sing a word. He picked unenthusiastically at an electric guitar and seemed confused whenever the song demanded more than the three conventional rock 'n' roll chord changes.

Molly's "fans," doused in a chemical fog and impatient after a 2 1/2-hour wait in a makeshift grandstand inside the cold warehouse, sat beneath industrially printed banners that read "We Love You Molly" and "Welcome Home Molly."

No one from the production crew had explained the nature of the "concert" or the responsibilities of the audience, a majority of which was clearly expecting Dylan to perform. The "fans" stifled their boredom with $1.85 hot dogs and lukewarm coffee.

When Flanagan, a singer almost entirely unknown in this country, appeared unannounced on stage at 8.30, she was greeted with fake cheers and a chant. "We love you, Molly!" one section of the audience screamed, then a lone voice asked, "Are you Molly?"

Left the stage

Flanagan left the stage.

Some minutes later Toronto singer-actress Taborah Johnson, who plays a back-up singer in the movie, introduced a production company representative. "Get rowdy!" he yelled. "We want you to cheer when Molly comes out and cheer even more when Bob makes his entrance."

On the second "take" the crowd took to its task with a vengeance. Still, Dylan looked perturbed. Those extra chords still eluded him, even though the five-piece band was miming pre-recorded parts.

During the third take, Flanagan, after some consultation with Marquand, was much more animated. She flailed her arms in imagined rock 'n' roll ecstasy, repeatedly shook her long, black mane and looked genuinely touched when Dylan suddenly appeared beside her.

"Haven't I seen this movie before?" one member of the audience asked a passing production assistant.

"Please take off your jacket," she replied. "We're supposed to be in America and there are maple leafs all over your jacket."

He didn't oblige. He looked as confused as Dylan, who was at that moment less interested in Flanagan's dramatic interplay than he was in finding the pesky fourth chord of "Hearts Of Fire."

Saturday, November 1, 1986 --- Nags Head North
Markham, ON

Bob Dylan joined veteran Toronto bluesman Paul James on stage at the Nags Head North in Markham. He played rhythm and lead guitar on an assortment of standard blues numbers including songs by Muddy Waters, Howlin' Wolf and Elmore James.

Monday, November 10, 1986 --- Hilton Harbour Castle Convention Center
Toronto, ON

Bob Dylan appeared at the 1986 Juno Awards to induct his long time friend, Gordon Lightfoot, into the Canadian Music Hall of Fame. Dylan received a standing ovation as he was introduced by Anne Murray.

The Indexes

Songs Performed

Summary

- Bob Dylan has performed 1,923 songs in Canada that have been documented. He has played 241 different songs (181 songs from thirty-five different albums, 8 unreleased songs and 52 cover and/or traditional songs).
- Seventy-seven songs have been performed only once in Canada.
- The six songs played the most times are: All Along the Watchtower (78), Like a Rolling Stone (65), Highway 61 Revisited (52), Masters of War (47), Blowin' in the Wind (41) and Maggie's Farm (41).
- All Along the Watchtower has been performed at least once in nineteen different years. Like a Rolling Stone, Mr. Tambourine Man and It Ain't Me, Babe have all been performed at least once in sixteen different years.
- Eight different songs made their Canadian live debut in the sixties' and were most recently played in 2005: Girl of the North Country (1964), Don't Think Twice It's All Right (1964), The Times They Are A-Changin' (1964), A Hard Rain's A-Gonna Fall (1964), Ballad of a Thin Man (1965), Desolation Row (1965), It Ain't Me, Babe (1965) and Positively 4th Street (1966).
- Blowin' in the Wind made its Canadian live debut on Mon., July 2, 1962 in Montreal and was most recently played on Mon., Aug. 26, 2002 in Saskatoon.
- Like a Rolling Stone and Stuck Inside of Mobile with the Memphis Blues Again were played at all sixteen concerts in 1990. All Along the Watchtower, Masters of War, Gotta Serve Somebody and Everything is Broken were each played at fifteen different concerts in 1990.
- All Along the Watchtower and Summer Days were played at all eleven concerts in 2002. Rainy Day Women #12 & 35 and Honest With Me were each played at ten different concerts in 2002.
- Eleven songs made their worldwide live debut in Canada: As I Went Out One Morning (1974), Ain't Gonna Go to Hell for Anybody (1980), Cover Down, Break Through (1980), I Will Love Him (1980), She's About a Mover (1988), No More One More Time (1990), Nowhere Man (1990), Unbelievable (1992), You're Gonna Quit Me (1993), Blind Willie McTell (1997) and Hallelujah, I'm Ready to Go (1999).
- Set lists are not available for five concerts and are incomplete for seven concerts.

Song	# of Times Performed	Canadian Live Debut	Most Recent Performance	# of Times Performed by Year
All Along the Watchtower	78	Wed., Jan. 9, 1974 (Toronto)	Sun., July 24, 2005 (Calgary)	1974 (4), 1978 (3), 1981 (4), 1986 (1), 1988 (5), 1989 (3), 1990 (15), 1991 (1), 1992 (7), 1993 (2), 1996 (4), 1997 (6), 1998 (1), 1999 (1), 2001 (1), 2002 (11), 2003 (1), 2004 (3), 2005 (5)
Like a Rolling Stone	65	Wed., Jan. 9, 1974 (Toronto)	Fri., July 22, 2005 (Kelowna)	1974 (4), 1978 (3), 1981 (4), 1986 (1), 1988 (8), 1989 (3), 1990 (16), 1992 (2), 1997 (8), 1999 (1), 2000 (1), 2001 (1), 2002 (7), 2003 (1), 2004 (3), 2005 (2)
Highway 61 Revisited	52	Fri., July 8, 1988 (Montreal)	Sun., July 24, 2005 (Calgary)	1988 (6), 1989 (1), 1990 (13), 1991 (1), 1992 (4), 1993 (1), 1997 (4), 1998 (9), 1999 (1), 2000 (1), 2001 (1), 2002 (3), 2003 (1), 2004 (1), 2005 (5)
Masters of War	47	Tues., Sept. 19, 1978 (Montreal)	Tues., July 19, 2005 (Vancouver)	1978 (3), 1981 (4), 1986 (1), 1988 (3), 1989 (1), 1990 (15), 1996 (2), 1997 (2), 1998 (7), 1999 (1), 2002 (7), 2005 (1)
Blowin' in the Wind	41	Mon., July 2, 1962 (Montreal)	Mon., Aug. 26, 2002 (Saskatoon)	1962 (1), 1974 (1), 1975 (3), 1978 (3), 1981 (4), 1986 (1), 1989 (1), 1990 (9), 1998 (7), 2000 (1), 2001 (1), 2002 (9)
Maggie's Farm	41	Tues., Sept. 19, 1978 (Montreal)	Sun., July 24, 2005 (Calgary)	1978 (3), 1981 (4), 1988 (5), 1990 (8), 1992 (6), 1993 (1), 1996 (3), 1997 (2), 2001 (1), 2004 (2), 2005 (6)
Tangled Up in Blue	39	Tues., Dec. 2, 1975 (Toronto)	Sat., March 20, 2004 (Toronto)	1975 (2), 1978 (3), 1988 (1), 1992 (3), 1993 (2), 1996 (2), 1997 (4), 1998 (9), 1999 (1), 2000 (1), 2001 (1), 2002 (9), 2004 (1)
Don't Think Twice, It's All Right	38	Fri., Nov. 13, 1964 (Toronto)	Sun., July 24, 2005 (Calgary)	1964 (1), 1974 (3), 1981 (1), 1988 (2), 1989 (2), 1990 (7), 1992 (5), 1993 (1), 1996 (1), 1997 (4), 1998 (1), 2000 (1), 2002 (5), 2004 (1), 2005 (3)

Song	# of Times Performed	Canadian Live Debut	Most Recent Performance	# of Times Performed by Year
Mr. Tambourine Man	37	Sun., Nov. 14, 1965 (Toronto)	Sat., Aug. 23, 2003 (Niagara Falls)	1965 (1), 1966 (2), 1975 (1), 1978 (1), 1981 (4), 1988 (4), 1989 (1), 1990 (8), 1991 (1), 1992 (1), 1996 (2), 1997 (3), 1998 (3), 1999 (1), 2002 (3), 2003 (1)
It Ain't Me, Babe	37	Sun., Nov. 14, 1965 (Toronto)	Thurs., July 21, 2005 (Vancouver)	1965 (1), 1974 (3), 1975 (4), 1978 (3), 1981 (2), 1988 (5), 1989 (1), 1990 (2), 1991 (1), 1992 (5), 1997 (2), 1998 (4), 1999 (1), 2002 (1), 2004 (1), 2005 (1)
Rainy Day Women #12 & 35	37	Wed., Jan. 9, 1974 (Toronto)	Sat., March 20, 2004 (Toronto)	1974 (1), 1978 (1), 1986 (1), 1992 (1), 1993 (1), 1996 (3), 1997 (8), 1998 (9), 2001 (1), 2002 (10), 2004 (1)
Gotta Serve Somebody	36	Thurs., April 17, 1980 (Toronto)	Tues., July 18, 2000 (Toronto)	1980 (8), 1981 (3), 1986 (1), 1988 (1), 1990 (15), 1991 (1), 1998 (6), 2000 (1)
Just Like a Woman	34	Wed., Jan. 9, 1974 (Toronto)	Fri., July 22, 2005 (Kelowna)	1974 (2), 1975 (4), 1978 (3), 1981 (3), 1988 (2), 1989 (1), 1990 (2), 1992 (3), 1993 (1), 1997 (2), 1998 (5), 2001 (1), 2002 (1), 2004 (2), 2005 (2)
Stuck Inside of Mobile with the Memphis Blues Again	33	Fri., July 8, 1988 (Montreal)	Fri., July 22, 2005 (Kelowna)	1988 (4), 1990 (16), 1992 (2), 1993 (2), 1996 (1), 1997 (1), 1998 (1), 1999 (1), 2002 (2), 2004 (1), 2005 (2)
It's Alright, Ma (I'm Only Bleeding)	32	Fri., Nov. 13, 1964 (Toronto)	Wed., Aug. 28, 2002 (Calgary)	1964 (1), 1974 (4), 1978 (3), 1981 (3), 1988 (2), 1989 (1), 1990 (10), 1992 (1), 2002 (7)
Ballad of a Thin Man	32	Sun., Nov. 14, 1965 (Toronto)	Sun., July 17, 2005 (Victoria)	1965 (1), 1974 (4), 1978 (3), 1981 (4), 1986 (1), 1988 (3), 1989 (2), 1990 (7), 1991 (1), 1992 (1), 1997 (1), 1998 (1), 2002 (1), 2004 (1), 2005 (1)
Silvio	30	Mon., July 11, 1988 (Hamilton)	Wed., Oct. 21, 1998 (Winnipeg)	1988 (6), 1989 (3), 1992 (2), 1996 (4), 1997 (8), 1998 (7)
I Shall Be Released	29	Sat., Nov. 29, 1975 (Quebec City)	Fri., Aug. 16, 2002 (Toronto)	1975 (4), 1978 (3), 1988 (6), 1989 (1), 1990 (12), 1998 (1), 2002 (2)
Girl of the North Country	28	Sat., Feb. 1, 1964 (Toronto)	Wed., July 20, 2005 (Vancouver)	1964 (1), 1974 (1), 1978 (2), 1981 (4), 1988 (4), 1989 (1), 1990 (4), 1992 (1), 1993 (2), 1996 (3), 1997 (2), 1998 (1), 2004 (1), 2005 (1)
The Times They Are A-Changin'	27	Sat., Feb. 1, 1964 (Toronto)	Fri., July 22, 2005 (Kelowna)	1964 (2), 1966 (1), 1974 (2), 1975 (1), 1978 (1), 1981 (4), 1988 (3), 1989 (1), 1990 (3), 1992 (5), 1997 (1), 1998 (1), 2001 (1), 2005 (1)
Forever Young	25	Wed., Jan. 9, 1974 (Toronto)	Sat., Aug. 23, 2003 (Niagara Falls)	1974 (4), 1978 (3), 1981 (4), 1997 (2), 1998 (7), 2001 (1), 2002 (3), 2003 (1)
Lay, Lady, Lay	23	Wed., Jan. 9, 1974 (Toronto)	Sun., July 24, 2005 (Calgary)	1974 (4), 1990 (3), 1997 (2), 2000 (1), 2002 (5), 2003 (1), 2004 (1), 2005 (6)
Simple Twist of Fate	22	Sat., Nov. 29, 1975 (Quebec City)	Fri., Oct. 30, 1998 (Ottawa)	1975 (2), 1981 (1), 1988 (3), 1989 (1), 1990 (5), 1991 (1), 1992 (5), 1996 (1), 1997 (2), 1998 (1)
Everything is Broken	22	Tues., May 29, 1990 (Montreal)	Sun., April 6, 1997 (Halifax)	1990 (15), 1991 (1), 1992 (3), 1996 (1), 1997 (2)
Summer Days	22	Thurs., Nov. 8, 2001 (Toronto)	Sun., July 24, 2005 (Calgary)	2001 (1), 2002 (11), 2003 (1), 2004 (3), 2005 (6)
Most Likely You Go Your Way and I'll Go Mine	21	Wed., Jan. 9, 1974 (Toronto)	Thurs., July 21, 2005 (Vancouver)	1974 (6), 1989 (2), 1990 (4), 1996 (1), 1997 (1), 2002 (1), 2003 (1), 2004 (1), 2005 (4)
Knockin' on Heaven's Door	20	Wed., Jan. 9, 1974 (Toronto)	Wed., Aug. 28, 2002 (Calgary)	1974 (4), 1975 (4), 1981 (4), 1986 (1), 1988 (4), 1999 (1), 2002 (2)
In the Garden	20	Thurs., April 17, 1980 (Toronto)	Sun., Aug. 12, 1990 (Edmonton)	1980 (8), 1981 (4), 1986 (1), 1988 (3), 1989 (1), 1990 (3), 1999 (1)
It's All Over Now, Baby Blue	19	Sun., Nov. 14, 1965 (Toronto)	Fri., March 19, 2004 (Toronto)	1965 (1), 1966 (1), 1975 (2), 1978 (3), 1988 (2), 1989 (1), 1990 (3), 1997 (1), 1998 (1), 2002 (2), 2004 (1)
Gates of Eden	17	Fri., Nov. 13, 1964 (Toronto)	Sat., Aug. 22, 1992 (Ottawa)	1964 (1), 1965 (1), 1974 (3), 1989 (1), 1990 (9), 1992 (2)
Honest With Me	17	Thurs., Nov. 8, 2001 (Toronto)	Fri., July 22, 2005 (Kelowna)	2001 (1), 2002 (10), 2003 (1), 2004 (3), 2005 (2)

Song	# of Times Performed	Canadian Live Debut	Most Recent Performance	# of Times Performed by Year
Desolation Row	16	Sun., Nov. 14, 1965 (Toronto)	Wed., July 20, 2005 (Vancouver)	1965 (1), 1966 (2), 1990 (6), 1996 (2), 1997 (1), 2000 (1), 2001 (1), 2004 (1), 2005 (1)
I'll Be Your Baby Tonight	16	Thurs., Oct. 29, 1981 (Toronto)	Sun., July 24, 2005 (Calgary)	1981 (3), 1988 (1), 1991 (1), 1992 (2), 1997 (2), 2004 (1), 2005 (6)
Boots of Spanish Leather	16	Fri., July 8, 1988 (Montreal)	Thurs., July 21, 2005 (Vancouver)	1988 (2), 1990 (5), 1992 (6), 1993 (1), 2002 (1), 2005 (1)
The Lonesome Death of Hattie Carroll	15	Sat., Feb. 1, 1964 (Toronto)	Fri., Oct. 30, 1998 (Ottawa)	1964 (2), 1975 (4), 1988 (1), 1989 (1), 1990 (3), 1992 (1), 1993 (1), 1998 (2)
I Don't Believe You (She Acts Like We Never Have Met)	15	Sun., Nov. 14, 1965 (Toronto)	Sun., March 21, 2004 (Toronto)	1965 (1), 1974 (3), 1978 (3), 1989 (1), 1992 (2), 1993 (1), 1996 (1), 1997 (1), 2002 (1), 2004 (1)
I Believe in You	15	Thurs., April 17, 1980 (Toronto)	Thurs., July 21, 2005 (Vancouver)	1980 (6), 1981 (4), 1990 (4), 2005 (1)
Cold Irons Bound	15	Wed., May 13, 1998 (Vancouver)	Tues., July 19, 2005 (Vancouver)	1998 (9), 2002 (4), 2004 (1), 2005 (1)
A Hard Rain's A-Gonna Fall	14	Sat., Feb. 1, 1964 (Toronto)	Sun., July 24, 2005 (Calgary)	1964 (1), 1975 (2), 1981 (4), 1986 (1), 1988 (3), 2001 (1), 2002 (1), 2005 (1)
Subterranean Homesick Blues	14	Fri., July 8, 1988 (Montreal)	Tues., Aug. 27, 2002 (Edmonton)	1988 (8), 1990 (3), 2002 (3)
What Good Am I?	14	Tues., May 29, 1990 (Montreal)	Sun., April 28, 1996 (Toronto)	1990 (6), 1991 (1), 1992 (5), 1993 (1), 1996 (1)
Just Like Tom Thumb's Blues	13	Sun., Nov. 14, 1965 (Toronto)	Sun., March 21, 2004 (Toronto)	1965 (1), 1974 (4), 1988 (1), 1992 (1), 1996 (1), 1997 (1), 1998 (1), 2002 (2), 2004 (1)
Solid Rock	13	Thurs., April 17, 1980 (Toronto)	Mon., Aug. 26, 2002 (Saskatoon)	1980 (8), 1981 (4), 2002 (1)
One Too Many Mornings	13	Fri., Aug. 1, 1986 (Vancouver)	Thurs., July 21, 2005 (Vancouver)	1986 (1), 1988 (2), 1989 (1), 1990 (4), 1997 (1), 1998 (1), 2002 (2), 2005 (1)
Love Minus Zero/No Limit	12	Sun., Nov. 14, 1965 (Toronto)	Sat., Aug. 10, 2002 (Quebec City)	1965 (1), 1966 (1), 1974 (1), 1975 (3), 1990 (4), 2000 (1), 2002 (1)
It Takes a Lot to Laugh, It Takes a Train to Cry	12	Wed., Jan. 9, 1974 (Toronto)	Wed., Oct. 21, 1998 (Winnipeg)	1974 (1), 1975 (1), 1989 (1), 1990 (3), 1992 (1), 1996 (2), 1997 (1), 1998 (2)
Tonight I'll Be Staying Here With You	12	Sat., Nov. 29, 1975 (Quebec City)	Sun., July 24, 2005 (Calgary)	1975 (3), 1996 (1), 1997 (1), 1998 (1), 2005 (6)
Shelter from the Storm	12	Tues., Sept. 19, 1978 (Montreal)	Fri., July 22, 2005 (Kelowna)	1978 (3), 1988 (2), 1989 (1), 1990 (4), 1991 (1), 2005 (1)
When You Gonna Wake Up	12	Thurs., April 17, 1980 (Toronto)	Mon., Nov. 2, 1981 (Ottawa)	1980 (8), 1981 (4)
Man Gave Names to All the Animals	12	Thurs., April 17, 1980 (Toronto)	Mon., Nov. 2, 1981 (Ottawa)	1980 (8), 1981 (4)
I'll Remember You	12	Sun., Aug. 21, 1988 (Vancouver)	Wed., Oct. 21, 1998 (Winnipeg)	1988 (2), 1990 (3), 1991 (1), 1996 (1), 1998 (5)
Watching the River Flow	12	Mon., Aug. 17, 1992 (Toronto)	Sun., July 24, 2005 (Calgary)	1992 (2), 1993 (1), 1996 (1), 1997 (3), 2002 (1), 2004 (1), 2005 (3)
I Want You	11	Tues., Sept. 19, 1978 (Montreal)	Wed., July 20, 2005 (Vancouver)	1978 (1), 1981 (4), 1989 (2), 1997 (1), 1998 (1), 2002 (1), 2005 (1)
Love Sick	11	Wed., May 13, 1998 (Vancouver)	Wed., July 20, 2005 (Vancouver)	1998 (9), 1999 (1), 2005 (1)
She Belongs to Me	10	Sun., Nov. 14, 1965 (Toronto)	Tues., July 18, 2000 (Toronto)	1965 (1), 1966 (1), 1988 (1), 1990 (2), 1992 (2), 1997 (1), 1998 (1), 2000 (1)
Ballad of Hollis Brown	10	Wed., Jan. 9, 1974 (Toronto)	Tues., Aug. 25, 1992 (Sault Ste. Marie)	1974 (4), 1989 (1), 1990 (4), 1992 (1)
Make You Feel My Love	10	Wed., May 13, 1998 (Vancouver)	Fri., March 19, 2004 (Toronto)	1998 (4), 2002 (4), 2003 (1), 2004 (1)
To Ramona	9	Fri., Nov. 13, 1964 (Toronto)	Sun., May 12, 1996 (London)	1964 (1) 1978 (1), 1986 (1), 1988 (3), 1990 (1), 1992 (1), 1996 (1)
Positively 4th Street	9	Sun., Feb. 20, 1966 (Montreal)	Sun., July 24, 2005 (Calgary)	1966 (1), 1990 (1), 1992 (1), 1996 (1), 1997 (1), 1998 (1), 2004 (1), 2005 (2)
My Back Pages	9	Tues., Sept. 19, 1978 (Montreal)	Tues., Aug. 13, 2002 (Ottawa)	1978 (3), 1996 (1), 1997 (1), 1998 (2), 2002 (2)
Saved	9	Thurs., April 17, 1980 (Toronto)	Mon., Nov. 2, 1981 (Ottawa)	1980 (8), 1981 (1)
Are You Ready?	9	Thurs., April 17, 1980 (Toronto)	Sat., Oct. 31, 1981 (Kitchener)	1980 (8), 1981 (1)

Song	# of Times Performed	Canadian Live Debut	Most Recent Performance	# of Times Performed by Year
Absolutely Sweet Marie	9	Mon., July 11, 1988 (Hamilton)	Wed., July 20, 2005 (Vancouver)	1988 (2), 1990 (3), 1997 (2), 1998 (1), 2005 (1)
Little Moses	9	Mon., Aug. 17, 1992 (Toronto)	Thurs., Sept. 2, 1993 Toronto)	1992 (7), 1993 (2)
Til I Fell In Love With You	9	Wed., May 13, 1998 (Vancouver)	Tues., Aug. 13, 2002 (Ottawa)	1998 (8), 2002 (1)
Moonlight	9	Tues., Aug. 6, 2002 (Halifax)	Fri., July 22, 2005 (Kelowna)	2002 (7), 2005 (2)
Mama, You Been on My Mind	8	Sat., Nov. 29, 1975 (Quebec City)	Sat., Aug. 10, 2002 (Quebec City)	1975 (3), 1988 (1), 1996 (1), 1998 (1), 2002 (2)
Ain't Gonna Go to Hell for Anybody	8	Thurs., April 17, 1980 (Toronto)	Fri., April 25, 1980 (Montreal)	1980 (8)
Cover Down, Break Through	8	Thurs., April 17, 1980 (Toronto)	Fri., April 25, 1980 (Montreal)	1980 (8)
Precious Angel	8	Thurs., April 17, 1980 (Toronto)	Fri., April 25, 1980 (Montreal)	1980 (8)
Slow Train	8	Thurs., April 17, 1980 (Toronto)	Fri., April 25, 1980 (Montreal)	1980 (8)
Do Right to Me Baby (Do Unto Others)	8	Thurs., April 17, 1980 (Toronto)	Fri., April 25, 1980 (Montreal)	1980 (8)
Saving Grace	8	Thurs., April 17, 1980 (Toronto)	Fri., April 25, 1980 (Montreal)	1980 (8)
What Can I Do For You?	8	Thurs., April 17, 1980 (Toronto)	Fri., April 25, 1980 (Montreal)	1980 (8)
Tweedle Dee & Tweedle Dum	8	Fri., Aug. 9, 2002 (Saint John)	Wed., July 20, 2005 (Vancouver)	2002 (4), 2003 (1), 2004 (2), 2005 (1)
Leopard-Skin Pill-Box Hat	7	Sun., Feb. 20, 1966 (Montreal)	Fri., Aug. 9, 2002 (Saint John)	1966 (1), 1990 (1), 1996 (1), 1997 (1), 1998 (1), 2000 (1), 2002 (1)
One More Cup of Coffee (Valley Below)	7	Sat., Nov. 29, 1975 (Quebec City)	Sun., Nov. 11, 1978 (Vancouver)	1975 (4), 1978 (3)
Pressing On	7	Thurs., April 17, 1980 (Toronto)	Fri., April 25, 1980 (Montreal)	1980 (7)
You're a Big Girl Now	7	Wed., Aug. 24, 1988 (Edmonton)	Sat., Aug. 24, 2002 (Winnipeg)	1988 (2), 1990 (2), 1997 (1), 1998 (1), 2002 (1)
Shooting Star	7	Mon., Aug. 20, 1990 (Vancouver)	Sun., July 24, 2005 (Calgary)	1990 (1), 1992 (1), 1997 (1), 2003 (1), 2004 (1), 2005 (2)
Man in the Long Black Coat	7	Mon., Aug. 24, 1992 (Sudbury)	Sat., Aug. 10, 2002 (Quebec City)	1992 (3), 1996 (1), 1997 (1), 2002 (2)
Drifter's Escape	7	Fri., April 26, 1996 (Montreal)	Fri., March 19, 2004 (Toronto)	1996 (2), 2000 (1), 2002 (3), 2004 (1)
Crash on the Levee (Down in the Flood)	7	Sun., April 28, 1996 (Toronto)	Tues., April 8, 1997 (Saint John)	1996 (1), 1997 (6)
High Water (for Charlie Patton)	7	Thurs., Nov. 8, 2001 (Toronto)	Wed., July 20, 2005 (Vancouver)	2001 (1), 2002 (4), 2003 (1), 2005 (1)
I Am the Man, Thomas	7	Tues., Aug. 6, 2002 (Halifax)	Tues., Aug. 27, 2002 (Edmonton)	2002 (7)
Seeing the Real You at Last	6	Fri., Aug. 1, 1986 (Vancouver)	Mon., April 7, 1997 (Fredericton)	1986 (1), 1989 (1), 1992 (1), 1996 (1), 1997 (2)
Tears of Rage	6	Sat., July 29, 1989 (Toronto)	Tues., Aug. 18, 1992 (Toronto)	1989 (1), 1990 (4), 1992 (1)
John Brown	6	Tues., June 5, 1990 (Toronto)	Tues., July 19, 2005 (Vancouver)	1990 (2), 1992 (2), 2001 (1), 2005 (1)
Oh Baby It Ain't No Lie	6	Mon., March 31, 1997 (St. John's)	Tues., April 8, 1997 (Saint John)	1997 (6)
Cry A While	6	Thurs., Nov. 8, 2001 (Toronto)	Fri., July 22, 2005 (Kelowna)	2001 (1), 2002 (2), 2003 (1), 2005 (2)
Señor (Tales of Yankee Power)	5	Tues., Sept. 19, 1978 (Montreal)	Tues., Aug. 6, 2002 (Halifax)	1978 (2), 1997 (1), 1998 (1), 2002 (1)
I and I	5	Fri., Aug. 1, 1986 (Vancouver)	Mon., April 7, 1997 (Fredericton)	1986 (1), 1992'(2), 1993 (1), 1997 (1)
Pretty Peggy-O	5	Sun., July 30, 1989 (Ottawa)	Tues., Aug. 25, 1992 (Sault Ste. Marie)	1989 (1), 1992 (4)
God Knows	5	Sun., Aug. 22, 1993 (Vancouver)	Sun., July 24, 2005 (Calgary)	1993 (1), 1997 (2), 2005 (2)

Song	# of Times Performed	Canadian Live Debut	Most Recent Performance	# of Times Performed by Year
Blind Willie McTell	5	Tues., Aug. 5, 1997 (Montreal)	Wed., July 20, 2005 (Vancouver)	1997 (1), 2002 (1), 2005 (3)
This World Can't Stand Long	5	Tues., July 18, 2000 (Toronto)	Wed., Aug. 28, 2002 (Calgary)	2000 (1), 2001 (1), 2002 (3)
Things Have Changed	5	Tues., July 18, 2000 (Toronto)	Fri., March 19, 2004 (Toronto)	2000 (1), 2001 (1), 2002 (2), 2004 (1)
The Wicked Messenger	5	Thurs., Nov. 8, 2001 (Toronto)	Tues., Aug. 27, 2002 (Edmonton)	2001 (1), 2002 (4)
All I Really Want to Do	4	Fri., Nov. 13, 1964 (Toronto)	Sun., Nov. 11, 1978 (Vancouver)	1964 (1), 1978 (3)
Something There is About You	4	Wed., Jan. 9, 1974 (Toronto)	Sat., Jan. 12, 1974 (Montreal)	1974 (4)
When I Paint My Masterpiece	4	Sat., Nov. 29, 1975 (Quebec City)	Thurs., Dec. 4, 1975 (Montreal)	1975 (4)
Romance in Durango	4	Sat., Nov. 29, 1975 (Quebec City)	Thurs., Dec. 4, 1975 (Montreal)	1975 (4)
Isis	4	Sat., Nov. 29, 1975 (Quebec City)	Thurs., Dec. 4, 1975 (Montreal)	1975 (4)
Dark as a Dungeon	4	Sat., Nov. 29, 1975 (Quebec City)	Thurs., Dec. 4, 1975 (Montreal)	1975 (4)
I Dreamed I Saw St. Augustine	4	Sat., Nov. 29, 1975 (Quebec City)	Mon., Aug. 17, 1992 (Toronto)	1975 (3), 1992 (1)
Oh, Sister	4	Sat., Nov. 29, 1975 (Quebec City)	Thurs., Dec. 4, 1975 (Montreal)	1975 (4)
Hurricane	4	Sat., Nov. 29, 1975 (Quebec City)	Thurs., Dec. 4, 1975 (Montreal)	1975 (4)
Sara	4	Sat., Nov. 29, 1975 (Quebec City)	Thurs., Dec. 4, 1975 (Montreal)	1975 (4)
This Land is Your Land	4	Sat., Nov. 29, 1975 (Quebec City)	Thurs., Dec. 4, 1975 (Montreal)	1975 (4)
Gamblin' Man	4	Thurs., Oct. 29, 1981 (Toronto)	Mon., Nov. 2, 1981 (Ottawa)	1981 (4)
Watered Down Love	4	Thurs., Oct. 29, 1981 (Toronto)	Mon., Nov. 2, 1981 (Ottawa)	1981 (4)
Heart of Mine	4	Fri., Oct. 30, 1981 (Montrea)	Mon., Aug. 17, 1992 (Toronto)	1981 (3), 1992 (1)
Barbara Allen	4	Sun., Aug. 21, 1988 (Vancouver)	Tues., June 5, 1990 (Toronto)	1988 (2), 1989 (1), 1990 (1)
Political World	4	Mon., June 18, 1990 (Winnipeg)	Wed., Aug. 15, 1990 (Calgary)	1990 (4)
Visions of Johanna	4	Fri., July 26, 1991 (Toronto)	Wed., Aug. 28, 2002 (Calgary)	1991 (1), 2002 (3)
Cat's in the Well	4	Tues., Aug. 18, 1992 (Toronto)	Sun., March 21, 2004 (Toronto)	1992 (2), 2004 (2)
Unbelievable	4	Sat., Aug. 22, 1992 (Ottawa)	Thurs., Aug. 27, 1992 (Thunder Bay)	1992 (4)
Under the Red Sky	4	Sun., Aug. 22, 1993 (Vancouver)	Tues., July 19, 2005 (Vancouver)	1993 (1), 1997 (1), 2002 (1), 2005 (1)
Alabama Getaway	4	Fri., April 26, 1996 (Montreal)	Sun., May 12, 1996 (London)	1996 (4)
Can't Wait	4	Thurs., Oct. 15, 1998 (Calgary)	Sun., July 24, 2005 (Calgary)	1998 (3, 2005 (1)
Floater (Too Much To Ask)	4	Tues., Aug. 13, 2002 (Ottawa)	Fri., July 22, 2005 (Kelowna)	2002 (2), 2004 (1), 2005 (1)
Am I Your Stepchild?	3	Tues., Sept. 19, 1978 (Montreal)	Sun., Nov. 11, 1978 (Vancouver)	1978 (3)
Changing of the Guards	3	Tues., Sept. 19, 1978 (Montreal)	Sun., Nov. 11, 1978 (Vancouver)	1978 (3)
Driftin' Too Far from Shore	3	Sat., July 9, 1988 (Ottawa)	Fri., Aug. 26, 1988 (Winnipeg)	1988 (3)
Early Mornin' Rain	3	Sat., July 29, 1989 (Toronto)	Wed., Aug. 15, 1990 (Calgary)	1989 (1), 1990 (2)
No More One More Time	3	Tues., May 29, 1990 (Montreal)	Mon., Aug. 13, 1990 (Edmonton)	1990 (3)

Song	# of Times Performed	Canadian Live Debut	Most Recent Performance	# of Times Performed by Year
Tomorrow is a Long Time	3	Tues., June 5, 1990 (Toronto)	Thurs., Aug. 8, 2002 (Moncton)	1990 (1), 1998 (1), 2002 (1)
Wiggle Wiggle	3	Fri., July 26, 1991 (Toronto)	Tues., Aug. 18, 1992 (Toronto)	1991 (1), 1992 (2)
New Morning	3	Fri., July 26, 1991 (Toronto)	Sun., July 17, 2005 (Victoria)	1991 (1), 1992 (1), 2005 (1)
Idiot Wind	3	Mon., Aug. 17, 1992 (Toronto)	Fri., Aug. 21, 1992 (Hamilton)	1992 (3)
To Be Alone with You	3	Sat., Aug. 22, 1992 (Ottawa)	Sat., March 20, 2004 (Toronto)	1992 (2), 2004 (1)
If You See Her, Say Hello	3	Fri., April 26, 1996 (Montreal)	Sat., March 20, 2004 (Toronto)	1996 (1), 1997 (1), 2004 (1)
This Wheel's on Fire	3	Sat., April 27, 1996 (Toronto)	Thurs., Aug. 7, 1997 (Toronto)	1996 (2), 1997 (1)
You Ain't Goin' Nowhere	3	Tues., Aug. 5, 1997 (Montreal)	Sun., March 21, 2004 (Toronto)	1997 (1), 2002 (1), 2004 (1)
Cocaine Blues	3	Tues., Aug. 5, 1997 (Montreal)	Thurs., May 14, 1998 (Vancouver)	1997 (2), 1998 (1)
Million Miles	3	Wed., May 13, 1998 (Vancouver)	Sat., March 20, 2004 (Toronto)	1998 (2), 2004 (1)
Lonesome Day Blues	3	Tues., Aug. 6, 2002 (Halifax)	Sun., July 24, 2005 (Calgary)	2002 (1), 2004 (1), 2005 (1)
Somebody Touched Me	3	Tues., Aug. 13, 2002 (Ottawa)	Wed., Aug. 28, 2002 (Calgary)	2002 (3)
Baby, Let Me Follow You Down	2	Thurs., June 28, 1962 (Montreal)	Sun., Nov. 14, 1965 (Toronto)	1962 (1), 1965 (1)
Talkin' World War III Blues	2	Sat., Feb. 1, 1964 (Toronto)	Fri., Nov. 13, 1964 (Toronto)	1964 (2)
Nobody 'Cept You	2	Wed., Jan. 9, 1974 (Toronto)	Fri., Jan. 11, 1974 (Montreal)	1974 (2)
Never Let Me Go	2	Mon., Dec. 1, 1975 (Toronto)	Thurs., Dec. 4, 1975 (Montreal)	1975 (2)
I'm Ready	2	Tues., Sept. 19, 1978 (Montreal)	Thurs., Oct. 12, 1978 (Toronto)	1978 (2)
Is Your Love in Vain?	2	Tues., Sept. 19, 1978 (Montreal)	Thurs., Oct. 12, 1978 (Toronto)	1978 (2)
Going, Going, Gone	2	Tues., Sept. 19, 1978 (Montreal)	Thurs., Oct. 12, 1978 (Toronto)	1978 (2)
One of Us Must Know (Sooner or Later)	2	Tues., Sept. 19, 1978 (Montreal)	Thurs., Oct. 12, 1978 (Toronto)	1978 (2)
Covenant Woman	2	Sat., April 19, 1980 (Toronto)	Thurs., April 24, 1980 (Montreal)	1980 (2)
I Will Love Him	2	Sat., April 19, 1980 (Toronto)	Wed., April 23, 1980 (Montreal)	1980 (2)
Let It Be Me	2	Thurs., Oct. 29, 1981 (Toronto)	Fri., Oct. 30, 1981 (Montreal)	1981 (2)
Dead Man, Dead Man	2	Thurs., Oct. 29, 1981 (Toronto)	Sat., Oct. 31, 1981 (Kitchener)	1981 (2)
One Irish Rover	2	Sun., July 30, 1989 (Ottawa)	Mon., July 31, 1989 (Joliette)	1989 (2)
I've Been All Around This World	2	Wed., June 6, 1990 (Toronto)	Thurs., June 7, 1990 (Toronto)	1990 (2)
What Was It You Wanted?	2	Wed., June 6, 1990 (Toronto)	Thurs., June 7, 1990 (Toronto)	1990 (2)
Queen Jane Approximately	2	Mon., June 18, 1990 (Winnipeg)	Mon., Aug. 13, 1990 (Edmonton)	1990 (2)
Man of Constant Sorrow	2	Sun., Aug. 19, 1990 (Victoria)	Mon., Aug. 20, 1990 (Vancouver)	1990 (2)
Don't Let Your Deal Go Down	2	Fri., Aug. 21, 1992 (Hamilton)	Tues., Aug. 25, 1992 (Sault Ste. Marie)	1992 (2)
You're Gonna Quit Me	2	Sun., Aug. 22, 1993 (Vancouver)	Thurs., Sept. 2, 1993 (Toronto)	1993 (2)
If Not for You	2	Sat., April 27, 1996 (Toronto)	Tues., April 8, 1997 (Saint John)	1996 (1), 1997 (1)

Song	# of Times Performed	Canadian Live Debut	Most Recent Performance	# of Times Performed by Year
Tough Mama	2	Tues., Aug. 5, 1997 (Montreal)	Thurs., Aug. 7, 1997 (Toronto)	1997 (2)
I'm Not Supposed to Care	2	Wed., May 13, 1998 (Vancouver)	Thurs., Oct. 29, 1998 (Toronto)	1998 (2)
Every Grain of Sand	2	Thurs., Oct. 29, 1998 (Toronto)	Fri., Aug. 9, 2002 (Saint John)	1998 (1), 2002 (1)
Not Dark Yet	2	Fri., June 11, 1999 (Vancouver)	Tues., Aug., 27, 2002 (Edmonton)	1999 (1), 2002 (1)
Tryin' To Get To Heaven	2	Fri., June 11, 1999 (Vancouver)	Sun., July 24, 2005 (Calgary)	1999 (1), 2005 (1)
Standing in the Doorway	2	Wed., Aug. 28, 2002 (Calgary)	Sat., March 20, 2004 (Toronto)	2002 (1), 2004 (1)
Freight Train Blues	1	Thurs. June 28, 1962 (Montreal)	Thurs., June 28, 1962 (Montreal)	1962 (1)
The Death of Emmett Till	1	Mon., July 2, 1962 (Montreal)	Mon., July 2, 1962 (Montreal)	1962 (1)
Stealin'	1	Mon., July 2, 1962 (Montreal)	Mon., July 2, 1962 (Montreal)	1962 (1)
Hiram Hubbard	1	Mon., July 2, 1962 (Montreal)	Mon., July 2, 1962 (Montreal)	1962 (1)
Rocks and Gravel	1	Mon., July 2, 1962 (Montreal)	Mon., July 2, 1962 (Montreal)	1962 (1)
Quit Your Low Down Ways	1	Mon., July 2, 1962 (Montreal)	Mon., July 2, 1962 (Montreal)	1962 (1)
He Was a Friend of Mine	1	Mon., July 2, 1962 (Montreal)	Mon., July 2, 1962 (Montreal)	1962 (1)
Let Me Die in My Footsteps	1	Mon., July 2, 1962 (Montreal)	Mon., July 2, 1962 (Montreal)	1962 (1)
Two Trains Runnin'	1	Mon., July 2, 1962 (Montreal)	Mon., July 2, 1962 (Montreal)	1962 (1)
Ramblin' On My Mind	1	Mon., July 2, 1962 (Montreal)	Mon., July 2, 1962 (Montreal)	1962 (1)
Muleskinner Blues	1	Mon., July 2, 1962 (Montreal)	Mon., July 2, 1962 (Montreal)	1962 (1)
Restless Farewell	1	Sat., Feb. 1, 1964 (Toronto)	Sat., Feb. 1, 1964 (Toronto)	1964 (1)
With God on Our Side	1	Fri., Nov. 13, 1964 (Toronto)	Fri., Nov. 13, 1964 (Toronto)	1964 (1)
If You Gotta Go, Go Now	1	Fri., Nov. 13, 1964 (Toronto)	Fri., Nov. 13, 1964 (Toronto)	1964 (1)
Only a Pawn in Their Game	1	Sat., Feb. 19, 1966 (Ottawa)	Sat., Feb. 19, 1966 (Ottawa)	1966 (1)
Wedding Song	1	Wed., Jan. 9, 1974 (Toronto)	Wed., Jan. 9, 1974 (Toronto)	1974 (1)
As I Went Out One Morning	1	Thurs., Jan. 10, 1974 (Toronto)	Thurs., Jan. 10, 1974 (Toronto)	1974 (1)
Wild Mountain Thyme	1	Tues., Dec. 2, 1975 (Toronto)	Tues., Dec. 2, 1975 (Toronto)	1975 (1)
Baby, Stop Crying	1	Tues., Sept. 19, 1978 (Montreal)	Tues., Sept. 19, 1978 (Montreal)	1978 (1)
Where Are You Tonight?	1	Thurs., Oct. 12, 1978 (Toronto)	Thurs., Oct. 12, 1978 (Toronto)	1978 (1)
She's Love Crazy	1	Sun., Nov. 11, 1978 (Vancouver)	Sun., Nov. 11, 1978 (Vancouver)	1978 (1)
We Better Talk This Over	1	Sun., Nov. 11, 1978 (Vancouver)	Sun., Nov. 11, 1978 (Vancouver)	1978 (1)
It's All in the Game	1	Sat., Oct. 31, 1981 (Kitchener)	Sat., Oct. 31, 1981 (Kitchener)	1981 (1)
Jesus Is the One	1	Mon., Nov. 2, 1981 (Ottawa)	Mon., Nov. 2, 1981 (Ottawa)	1981 (1)
Bye Bye Johnny	1	Fri., Aug. 1, 1986 (Vancouver)	Fri., Aug. 1, 1986 (Vancouver)	1986 (1)
Clean-Cut Kid	1	Fri., Aug. 1, 1986 (Vancouver)	Fri., Aug. 1, 1986 (Vancouver)	1986 (1)

Song	# of Times Performed	Canadian Live Debut	Most Recent Performance	# of Times Performed by Year
Emotionally Yours	1	Fri., Aug. 1, 1986 (Vancouver)	Fri., Aug. 1, 1986 (Vancouver)	1986 (1)
Shot of Love	1	Fri., Aug. 1, 1986 (Vancouver)	Fri., Aug. 1, 1986 (Vancouver)	1986 (1)
That Lucky Old Sun	1	Fri., Aug. 1, 1986 (Vancouver)	Fri., Aug. 1, 1986 (Vancouver)	1986 (1)
I Forgot More Than You'll Ever Know	1	Fri., Aug. 1, 1986 (Vancouver)	Fri., Aug. 1, 1986 (Vancouver)	1986 (1)
Band of the Hand (It's Hell Time Man!)	1	Fri., Aug. 1, 1986 (Vancouver)	Fri., Aug. 1, 1986 (Vancouver)	1986 (1)
When the Night Comes Falling from the Sky	1	Fri., Aug. 1, 1986 (Vancouver)	Fri., Aug. 1, 1986 (Vancouver)	1986 (1)
Lonesome Town	1	Fri., Aug. 1, 1986 (Vancouver)	Fri., Aug. 1, 1986 (Vancouver)	1986 (1)
Across the Borderline	1	Fri., Aug. 1, 1986 (Vancouver)	Fri., Aug. 1, 1986 (Vancouver)	1986 (1)
Shake a Hand	1	Fri., Aug. 1, 1986 (Vancouver)	Fri., Aug. 1, 1986 (Vancouver)	1986 (1)
Hallelujah	1	Fri., July 8, 1988 (Montreal)	Fri., July 8, 1988 (Montreal)	1988 (1)
Lakes of Pontchartrain	1	Fri., July 8, 1988 (Montreal)	Fri., July 8, 1988 (Montreal)	1988 (1)
Joey	1	Sat., July 9, 1988 (Ottawa)	Sat., July 9, 1988 (Ottawa)	1988 (1)
Eileen Aroon	1	Tues., Aug. 23, 1988 (Calgary)	Tues., Aug. 23, 1988 (Calgary)	1988 (1)
She's About a Mover	1	Wed., Aug. 24, 1988 (Edmonton)	Wed., Aug. 24, 1988 (Edmonton)	1988 (1)
Trouble	1	Sat., July 29, 1989 (Toronto)	Sat., July 29, 1989 (Toronto)	1989 (1)
Hey La La (Hey La La)	1	Sat., July 29, 1989 (Toronto)	Sat., July 29, 1989 (Toronto)	1989 (1)
Don't Pity Me	1	Mon., July 31, 1989 (Joliette)	Mon., July 31, 1989 (Joliette)	1989 (1)
Where Teardrops Fall	1	Wed., May 30, 1990 (Kingston)	Wed., May 30, 1990 (Kingston)	1990 (1)
Disease of Conceit	1	Fri., June 1, 1990 (Ottawa)	Fri., June 1, 1990 (Ottawa)	1990 (1)
Tight Connection to My Heart (Has Anybody Seen My Love)	1	Sat., June 2, 1990 (Ottawa)	Sat., June 2, 1990 (Ottawa)	1990 (1)
One More Night	1	Wed., June 6, 1990 (Toronto)	Wed., June 6, 1990 (Toronto)	1990 (1)
Nowhere Man	1	Sun., Aug. 12, 1990 (Edmonton)	Sun., Aug. 12, 1990 (Edmonton)	1990 (1)
The Water is Wide	1	Sun., Aug. 12, 1990 (Edmonton)	Sun., Aug. 12, 1990 (Edmonton)	1990 (1)
Lenny Bruce	1	Fri., July 26, 1991 (Toronto)	Fri., July 26, 1991 (Toronto)	1991 (1)
Trail of the Buffalo	1	Fri., July 26, 1991 (Toronto)	Fri., July 26, 1991 (Toronto)	1991 (1)
Folsom Prison Blues	1	Fri., July 26, 1991 (Toronto)	Fri., July 26, 1991 (Toronto)	1991 (1)
Female Rambling Sailor	1	Mon. Aug. 17, 1992 (Toronto)	Mon. Aug. 17, 1992 (Toronto)	1992 (1)
2 x 2	1	Tues., Aug. 18, 1992 (Toronto)	Tues., Aug. 18, 1992 (Toronto)	1992 (1)
Obviously Five Believers	1	Fri., April 26, 1996 (Montreal)	Fri., April 26, 1996 (Montreal)	1996 (1)
Friend of the Devil	1	Sun., April 28, 1996 (Toronto)	Sun., April 28, 1996 (Toronto)	1996 (1)
Seven Days	1	Sun., April 28, 1996 (Toronto)	Sun., April 28, 1996 (Toronto)	1996 (1)
Born in Time	1	Tues., April 8, 1997 (Saint John)	Tues., April 8, 1997 (Saint John)	1997 (1)

Song	# of Times Performed	Canadian Live Debut	Most Recent Performance	# of Times Performed by Year
Not Fade Away	1	Wed., May 13, 1998 (Vancouver)	Wed., May 13, 1998 (Vancouver)	1998 (1)
Stone Walls and Steel Bars	1	Wed., May 13, 1998 (Vancouver)	Wed., May 13, 1998 (Vancouver)	1998 (1)
Hallelujah, I'm Ready to Go	1	Fri., June 11, 1999 (Vancouver)	Fri., June 11, 1999 (Vancouver)	1999 (1)
The Sound of Silence	1	Fri., June 11, 1999 (Vancouver)	Fri., June 11, 1999 (Vancouver)	1999 (1)
I Walk the Line	1	Fri., June 11, 1999 (Vancouver)	Fri., June 11, 1999 (Vancouver)	1999 (1)
Blue Moon of Kentucky	1	Fri., June 11, 1999 (Vancouver)	Fri., June 11, 1999 (Vancouver)	1999 (1)
Duncan and Brady	1	Tues., July 18, 2000 (Toronto)	Tues., July 18, 2000 (Toronto)	2000 (1)
Song to Woody	1	Tues., July 18, 2000 (Toronto)	Tues., July 18, 2000 (Toronto)	2000 (1)
Country Pie	1	Tues., July 18, 2000 (Toronto)	Tues., July 18, 2000 (Toronto)	2000 (1)
Humming Bird	1	Thurs., Nov. 8, 2001 (Toronto)	Thurs., Nov. 8, 2001 (Toronto)	2001 (1)
Sugar Baby	1	Thurs., Nov. 8, 2001 (Toronto)	Thurs., Nov. 8, 2001 (Toronto)	2001 (1)
Never Gonna Be the Same Again	1	Thurs., Aug. 8, 2002 (Moncton)	Thurs., Aug. 8, 2002 (Moncton)	2002 (1)
If Dogs Run Free	1	Fri., Aug. 9, 2002 (Saint John)	Fri., Aug. 9, 2002 (Saint John)	2002 (1)
A Voice From On High	1	Fri., Aug. 16, 2002 (Toronto)	Fri., Aug. 16, 2002 (Toronto)	2002 (1)
The Man in Me	1	Tues., Aug. 27, 2002 (Edmonton)	Tues., Aug. 27, 2002 (Edmonton)	2002 (1)
Tombstone Blues	1	Sat., Aug. 23, 2003 (Niagara Falls)	Sat., Aug. 23, 2003 (Niagara Falls)	2003 (1)
Dignity	1	Sat., Aug. 23, 2003 (Niagara Falls)	Sat., Aug. 23, 2003 (Niagara Falls)	2003 (1)
Bye and Bye	1	Sat., March 20, 2004 (Toronto)	Sat., March 20, 2004 (Toronto)	2004 (1)
Down Along the Cove	1	Thurs., July 21, 2005 (Vancouver)	Thurs., July 21, 2005 (Vancouver)	2005 (1)

Songs Performed by Album

Summary

- Bob Dylan has performed 181 different songs from thirty-five albums in Canada. In total, these songs have been played 1,796 times.
- The top five albums by the total number of times songs have been played are: Highway 61 Revisited (193), Bringing It All Back Home (182), The Freewheelin' Bob Dylan, (170), Blonde on Blonde (159) and John Wesley Harding (112).
- Dylan has played selections from his most recent album, 2001's Love & Theft, a total of seventy-eight times.
- During the eleven shows in 2002, songs were performed from twenty-three different albums. In 1997 (8 concerts) and 1992 (7 concerts) songs were played from twenty-one different albums. During the most recent 2005 Tour (6 concerts), selections were performed from nineteen different albums. Songs from nineteen different albums were also played in 1998.
- With the exception of Bob Dylan's Greatest Hits and MTV Unplugged, no album has had every song on it performed. However, songs are listed by the album of their first release and only one song each is attributed to those two albums (Positively 4th Street & John Brown).
- The albums with the most individual songs performed from it are: Highway 61 Revisited (8 of 9), Saved (8 of 9), Desire (7 of 9), Slow Train Coming (7 of 9), The Times They Are A-Changin' (8 of 10), Oh Mercy (8 of 10), Time Out of Mind (9 of 11) and Love and Theft (10 of 12).
- Eight different unreleased songs have been performed. In total, these songs have been played 25 times.
- Fifty-two different cover songs and/or traditional songs have been performed. In total, these songs have been played 102 times.
- Some of the covers performed include songs by: The Beatles, Bill Monroe, Chuck Berry, The Clancy Brothers, Gordon Lightfoot, The Grateful Dead, Johnny Cash, Leonard Cohen, Muddy Waters, Paul Simon, Ralph Stanley, Robert Johnson, Van Morrison, Willie Dixon and Woody Guthrie.
- Set lists are not available for five concerts and are incomplete for seven concerts.

Bob Dylan (released March 19, 1962)

Total Number of Songs on the Album (13); Total Number of Different Songs Performed from the Album (5).

Song	# of Times Performed	Canadian Live Debut	Most Recent Performance
Pretty Peggy-O	5	Sun., July 30, 1989 (Ottawa)	Tues., Aug. 25, 1992 (Sault Ste. Marie)
Baby, Let Me Follow You Down	2	Thurs., June 28, 1962 (Montreal)	Sun., Nov. 14, 1965 (Toronto)
Man of Constant Sorrow	2	Sun., Aug. 19, 1990 (Victoria)	Mon., Aug. 20, 1990 (Vancouver)
Freight Train Blues	1	Thurs., June 28, 1962 (Montreal)	Thurs., June 28, 1962 (Montreal)
Song to Woody	1	Tues., July 18, 2000 (Toronto)	Tues., July 18, 2000 (Toronto)
Total Performances	**11**		

The Freewheelin' Bob Dylan (released May 27, 1963)

Total Number of Songs on the Album (13); Total Number of Different Songs Performed from the Album (6).

Song	# of Times Performed	Canadian Live Debut	Most Recent Performance
Masters of War	47	Tues., Sept. 19, 1978 (Montreal)	Tues., July 19, 2005 (Vancouver)
Blowin' in the Wind	41	Mon., July 2, 1962 (Montreal)	Mon., Aug. 26, 2002 (Saskatoon)
Don't Think Twice, It's All Right	38	Fri., Nov. 13, 1964 (Toronto)	Sun., July 24, 2005 (Calgary)
Girl of the North Country	28	Sat., Feb. 1, 1964 (Toronto)	Wed., July 20, 2005 (Vancouver)
A Hard Rain's A-Gonna Fall	14	Sat., Feb. 1, 1964 (Toronto)	Sun., July 24, 2005 (Calgary)
Talkin' World War III Blues	2	Sat., Feb. 1, 1964 (Toronto)	Fri., Nov. 13, 1964 (Toronto)
Total Performances	**170**		

The Times They Are A-Changin' (released Feb. 10, 1964)

Total Number of Songs on the Album (10); Total Number of Different Songs Performed from the Album (8).

Song	# of Times Performed	Canadian Live Debut	Most Recent Performance
The Times They Are A-Changin'	27	Sat., Feb. 1, 1964 (Toronto)	Fri., July 22, 2005 (Kelowna)
Boots of Spanish Leather	16	Fri., July 8, 1988 (Montreal)	Thurs., July 21, 2005 (Vancouver)
The Lonesome Death of Hattie Carroll	15	Sat., Feb. 1, 1964 (Toronto)	Fri., Oct. 30, 1998 (Ottawa)
One Too Many Mornings	13	Fri., Aug. 1, 1986 (Vancouver)	Thurs., July 21, 2005 (Vancouver)
Ballad of Hollis Brown	10	Wed., Jan. 9, 1974 (Toronto)	Tues., Aug. 25, 1992 (Sault Ste. Marie)
Restless Farewell	1	Sat., Feb. 1, 1964 (Toronto)	Sat., Feb. 1, 1964 (Toronto)
With God on Our Side	1	Fri., Nov. 13, 1964 (Toronto)	Fri., Nov. 13, 1964 (Toronto)
Only a Pawn in Their Game	1	Sat., Feb. 19, 1966 (Ottawa)	Sat., Feb. 19, 1966 (Ottawa)

Total Performances **84**

Another Side of Bob Dylan (released Aug. 8, 1964)

Total Number of Songs on the Album (11); Total Number of Different Songs Performed from the Album (5).

Song	# of Times Performed	Canadian Live Debut	Most Recent Performance
It Ain't Me, Babe	37	Sun., Nov. 14, 1965 (Toronto)	Thurs., July 21, 2005 (Vancouver)
I Don't Believe You (She Acts Like We Never Have Met)	15	Sun., Nov. 14, 1965 (Toronto)	Sun., March 21, 2004 (Toronto)
To Ramona	9	Fri., Nov. 13, 1964 (Toronto)	Sun., May 12, 1996 (London)
My Back Pages	9	Tues., Sept. 19, 1978 (Montreal)	Tues., Aug. 13, 2002 (Ottawa)
All I Really Want to Do	4	Fri., Nov. 13, 1964 (Toronto)	Sun., Nov. 11, 1978 (Vancouver)

Total Performances **74**

Bringing It All Back Home (released March 22, 1965)

Total Number of Songs on the Album (11); Total Number of Different Songs Performed from the Album (8).

Song	# of Times Performed	Canadian Live Debut	Most Recent Performance
Maggie's Farm	41	Tues., Sept. 19, 1978 (Montreal)	Sun., July 24, 2005 (Calgary)
Mr. Tambourine Man	37	Sun., Nov. 14, 1965 (Toronto)	Sat., Aug. 23, 2003 (Niagara Falls)
It's Alright, Ma (I'm Only Bleeding)	32	Fri., Nov. 13, 1964 (Toronto)	Wed., Aug. 28, 2002 (Calgary)
It's All Over Now, Baby Blue	19	Sun., Nov. 14, 1965 (Toronto)	Fri., March 19, 2004 (Toronto)
Gates of Eden	17	Fri., Nov. 13, 1964 (Toronto)	Sat., Aug. 22, 1992 (Ottawa)
Subterranean Homesick Blues	14	Fri., July 8, 1988 (Montreal)	Tues., Aug. 27, 2002 (Edmonton)
Love Minus Zero/No Limit	12	Sun., Nov. 14, 1965 (Toronto)	Sat., Aug. 10, 2002 (Quebec City)
She Belongs to Me	10	Sun., Nov. 14, 1965 (Toronto)	Tues., July 18, 2000 (Toronto)

Total Performances **182**

Highway 61 Revisited (released Aug. 30, 1965)

Total Number of Songs on the Album (9); Total Number of Different Songs Performed from the Album (8).

Song	# of Times Performed	Canadian Live Debut	Most Recent Performance
Like a Rolling Stone	65	Wed., Jan. 9, 1974 (Toronto)	Fri., July 22, 2005 (Kelowna)
Highway 61 Revisited	52	Fri., July 8, 1988 (Montreal)	Sun., July 24, 2005 (Calgary)
Ballad of a Thin Man	32	Sun., Nov. 14, 1965 (Toronto)	Sun., July 17, 2005 (Victoria)
Desolation Row	16	Sun., Nov. 14, 1965 (Toronto)	Wed., July 20, 2005 (Vancouver)
Just Like Tom Thumb's Blues	13	Sun., Nov. 14, 1965 (Toronto)	Sun., March 21, 2004 (Toronto)
It Takes a Lot to Laugh, It Takes a Train to Cry	12	Wed., Jan. 9, 1974 (Toronto)	Wed., Oct. 21, 1998 (Winnipeg)
Queen Jane Approximately	2	Mon., June 18, 1990 (Winnipeg)	Mon., Aug. 13, 1990 (Edmonton)
Tombstone Blues	1	Sat., Aug. 23, 2003 (Niagara Falls)	Sat., Aug. 23, 2003 (Niagara Falls)

Total Performances **193**

Blonde on Blonde (released May 16, 1966)

Total Number of Songs on the Album (14); Total Number of Different Songs Performed from the Album (10).

Song	# of Times Performed	Canadian Live Debut	Most Recent Performance
Rainy Day Women #12 & 35	37	Wed., Jan. 9, 1974 (Toronto)	Sat., March 20, 2004 (Toronto)
Just Like a Woman	34	Wed., Jan. 9, 1974 (Toronto)	Fri., July 22, 2005 (Kelowna)
Stuck Inside of Mobile with the Memphis Blues Again	33	Fri., July 8, 1988 (Montreal)	Fri., July 22, 2005 (Kelowna)
Most Likely You Go Your Way and I'll Go Mine	21	Wed., Jan. 9, 1974 (Toronto)	Thurs., July 21, 2005 (Vancouver)
I Want You	11	Tues., Sept. 19, 1978 (Montreal)	Wed., July 20, 2005 (Vancouver)
Absolutely Sweet Marie	9	Mon., July 11, 1988 (Hamilton)	Wed., July 20, 2005 (Vancouver)
Leopard-Skin Pill-Box Hat	7	Sun., Feb. 20, 1966 (Montreal)	Fri., Aug. 9, 2002 (Saint John)
Visions of Johanna	4	Fri., July 26, 1991 (Toronto)	Wed., Aug. 28, 2002 (Calgary)
One of Us Must Know (Sooner or Later)	2	Tues., Sept. 19, 1978 (Montreal)	Thurs., Oct. 12, 1978 (Toronto)
Obviously Five Believers	1	Fri., April 26, 1996 (Montreal)	Fri., April 26, 1996 (Montreal)

Total Performances **159**

Bob Dylan's Greatest Hits (released March 27, 1967)

Total Number of Songs on the Album (10); Total Number of Different Songs Performed from the Album (1).

Note: Positively 4th Street was first released on this album. The other nine songs have all been performed but are included under the album they were first released.

Song	# of Times Performed	Canadian Live Debut	Most Recent Performance
Positively 4th Street	9	Sun., Feb. 20, 1966 (Montreal)	Sun., July 24, 2005 (Calgary)

Total Performances **9**

John Wesley Harding (released Dec. 27, 1967)

Total Number of Songs on the Album (12); Total Number of Different Songs Performed from the Album (7).

Song	# of Times Performed	Canadian Live Debut	Most Recent Performance
All Along the Watchtower	78	Wed., Jan. 9, 1974 (Toronto)	Sun., July 24, 2005 (Calgary)
I'll Be Your Baby Tonight	16	Thurs., Oct. 29, 1981 (Toronto)	Sun., July 24, 2005 (Calgary)
Drifter's Escape	7	Fri., April 26, 1996 (Montreal)	Fri., March 19, 2004 (Toronto)
The Wicked Messenger	5	Thurs., Nov. 8, 2001 (Toronto)	Tues., Aug. 27, 2002 (Edmonton)
I Dreamed I Saw St. Augustine	4	Sat., Nov. 29, 1975 (Quebec City)	Mon., Aug. 17, 1992 (Toronto)
As I Went Out One Morning	1	Thurs., Jan. 10, 1974 (Toronto)	Thurs., Jan. 10, 1974 Toronto)
Down Along the Cove	1	Thurs., Jul 21, 2005 (Vancouver)	Thurs., Jul 21, 2005 (Vancouver)

Total Performances **112**

Nashville Skyline (released April 9, 1969)

Total Number of Songs on the Album (10); Total Number of Different Songs Performed from the Album (5).

Note: The five songs listed below were first released on this album. One other song has been performed but is included under the album it was first released.

Song	# of Times Performed	Canadian Live Debut	Most Recent Performance
Lay, Lady, Lay	23	Wed., Jan. 9, 1974 (Toronto)	Sun., July 24, 2005 (Calgary)
Tonight I'll Be Staying Here With You	12	Sat., Nov. 29, 1975 (Quebec City)	Thurs., Jul 21, 2005 (Vancouver)
To Be Alone with You	3	Sat., Aug. 22, 1992 (Ottawa)	Sat., March 20, 2004 (Toronto)
One More Night	1	Wed., June 6, 1990 (Toronto)	Wed., June 6, 1990 (Toronto)
Country Pie	1	Tues., July 18, 2000 (Toronto)	Tues., July 18, 2000 (Toronto)

Total Performances **40**

Self Portrait (released June 8, 1970)

Total Number of Songs on the Album (24); Total Number of Different Songs Performed from the Album (3).

Note: The three songs listed below were first released on this album. Two other songs have been performed but are included under the album they were first released.

Song	# of Times Performed	Canadian Live Debut	Most Recent Performance
Early Mornin' Rain	3	Sat., July 29, 1989 (Toronto)	Wed., Aug. 15, 1990 (Calgary)
Let It Be Me	2	Thurs., Oct. 29, 1981 (Toronto)	Fri., Oct. 30, 1981 (Montreal)
I Forgot More Than You'll Ever Know	1	Fri., Aug. 1, 1986 (Vancouver)	Fri., Aug. 1, 1986 (Vancouver)

Total Performances **6**

New Morning (released Oct. 21, 1970)

Total Number of Songs on the Album (12); Total Number of Different Songs Performed from the Album (4).

Song	# of Times Performed	Canadian Live Debut	Most Recent Performance
New Morning	3	Fri., July 26, 1991 (Toronto)	Sun., July 17, 2005 (Victoria)
If Not for You	2	Sat., April 27, 1996 (Toronto)	Tues., April 8, 1997 (Saint John)
If Dogs Run Free	1	Fri., Aug. 9, 2002 (Saint John)	Fri., Aug. 9, 2002 (Saint John)
The Man in Me	1	Tues., Aug. 27, 2002 (Edmonton)	Tues., Aug. 27, 2002 (Edmonton)

Total Performances **7**

Bob Dylan's Greatest Hits, Vol. 2 (released Nov. 17, 1971)

Total Number of Songs on the Album (21); Total Number of Different Songs Performed from the Album (6).

Note: The six songs listed below were first released on this album. Fourteen other songs have all been performed but are included under the album they were first released.

Song	# of Times Performed	Canadian Live Debut	Most Recent Performance
I Shall Be Released	29	Sat., Nov. 29, 1975 (Quebec City)	Fri., Aug. 16, 2002 (Toronto)
Watching the River Flow	12	Mon., Aug. 17, 1992 (Toronto)	Sun., July 24, 2005 (Calgary)
Crash on the Levee (Down in the Flood)	7	Sun., April 28, 1996 (Toronto)	Tues., April 8, 1997 (Saint John)
When I Paint My Masterpiece	4	Sat., Nov. 29, 1975 (Quebec City)	Thurs., Dec. 4, 1975 (Montreal)
You Ain't Goin' Nowhere	3	Tues., Aug. 5, 1997 (Montreal)	Sun., March 21, 2004 (Toronto)
Tomorrow is a Long Time	3	Tues., June 5, 1990 (Toronto)	Thurs., Aug. 8, 2002 (Moncton)

Total Performances **58**

Pat Garrett & Billy the Kid (released July 13, 1973)

Total Number of Songs on the Album (10); Total Number of Different Songs Performed from the Album (1).

Song	# of Times Performed	Canadian Live Debut	Most Recent Performance
Knockin' on Heaven's Door	20	Wed., Jan. 9, 1974 (Toronto)	Wed., Aug. 28, 2002 (Calgary)

Total Performances **20**

Planet Waves (released Jan. 17, 1974)

Total Number of Songs on the Album (11); Total Number of Different Songs Performed from the Album (5).

Song	# of Times Performed	Canadian Live Debut	Most Recent Performance
Forever Young	25	Wed., Jan. 9, 1974 (Toronto)	Sat., Aug. 23, 2003 (Niagara Falls)
Something There is About You	4	Wed., Jan. 9, 1974 (Toronto)	Sat., Jan. 12, 1974 (Montreal)
Going, Going, Gone	2	Tues., Sept. 19, 1978 (Montreal)	Thurs., Oct. 12, 1978 (Toronto)
Tough Mama	2	Tues., Aug. 5, 1997 (Montreal)	Thurs., Aug. 7, 1997 (Toronto)
Wedding Song	1	Wed., Jan. 9, 1974 (Toronto)	Wed., Jan. 9, 1974 (Toronto)

Total Performances **34**

Blood on the Tracks (released Jan. 20, 1975)

Total Number of Songs on the Album (10); Total Number of Different Songs Performed from the Album (6).

Song	# of Times Performed	Canadian Live Debut	Most Recent Performance
Tangled Up in Blue	39	Tues., Dec. 2, 1975 (Toronto)	Sat., March 20, 2004 (Toronto)
Simple Twist of Fate	22	Sat., Nov. 29, 1975 (Quebec City)	Fri., Oct. 30, 1998 (Ottawa)
Shelter from the Storm	12	Tues., Sept. 19, 1978 (Montreal)	Fri., July 22, 2005 (Kelowna)
You're a Big Girl Now	7	Wed., Aug. 24, 1988 (Edmonton)	Sat., Aug. 24, 2002 (Winnipeg)
Idiot Wind	3	Mon., Aug. 17, 1992 (Toronto)	Fri., Aug. 21, 1992 (Hamilton)
If You See Her, Say Hello	3	Fri., April 26, 1996 (Montreal)	Sat., March 20, 2004 (Toronto)

Total Performance **86**

The Basement Tapes (released July 1, 1975)

Total Number of Songs on the Album (24); Total Number of Different Songs Performed from the Album (2).

Note: The two songs listed below were first released on this album. Two other songs have been performed but are included under the album they were first released.

Song	# of Times Performed	Canadian Live Debut	Most Recent Performance
Tears of Rage	6	Sat., July 29, 1989 (Toronto)	Tues., Aug. 18, 1992 (Toronto)
This Wheel's on Fire	3	Sat., April 27, 1996 (Toronto)	Thurs., Aug. 7, 1997 (Toronto)

Total Performance **9**

Desire (released Jan. 5, 1976)

Total Number of Songs on the Album (9); Total Number of Different Songs Performed from the Album (7).

Song	# of Times Performed	Canadian Live Debut	Most Recent Performance
One More Cup of Coffee (Valley Below)	7	Sat., Nov. 29, 1975 (Quebec City)	Sun., Nov. 11, 1978 (Vancouver)
Romance in Durango	4	Sat., Nov. 29, 1975 (Quebec City)	Thurs., Dec. 4, 1975 (Montreal)
Isis	4	Sat., Nov. 29, 1975 (Quebec City)	Thurs., Dec. 4, 1975 (Montreal)
Oh, Sister	4	Sat., Nov. 29, 1975 (Quebec City)	Thurs., Dec. 4, 1975 (Montreal)
Hurricane	4	Sat., Nov. 29, 1975 (Quebec City)	Thurs., Dec. 4, 1975 (Montreal)
Sara	4	Sat., Nov. 29, 1975 (Quebec City)	Thurs., Dec. 4, 1975 (Montreal)
Joey	1	Sat., July 9, 1988 (Ottawa)	Sat., July 9, 1988 (Ottawa)

Total Performances **28**

Street Legal (released June 15, 1978)

Total Number of Songs on the Album (9); Total Number of Different Songs Performed from the Album (6).

Song	# of Times Performed	Canadian Live Debut	Most Recent Performance
Señor (Tales of Yankee Power)	5	Tues., Sept. 19, 1978 (Montreal)	Tues., Aug. 6, 2002 (Halifax)
Changing of the Guards	3	Tues., Sept. 19, 1978 (Montreal)	Sun., Nov. 11, 1978 (Vancouver)
Is Your Love in Vain?	2	Tues., Sept. 19, 1978 (Montreal)	Thurs., Oct. 12, 1978 (Toronto)
Baby, Stop Crying	1	Tues., Sept. 19, 1978 (Montreal)	Tues., Sept. 19, 1978 (Montreal)
Where Are You Tonight?	1	Thurs., Oct. 12, 1978 (Toronto)	Thurs., Oct. 12, 1978 (Toronto)
We Better Talk This Over	1	Sun., Nov. 11, 1978 (Vancouver)	Sun., Nov. 11, 1978 (Vancouver)

Total Performances **13**

Slow Train Coming (released Aug. 20, 1979)

Total Number of Songs on the Album (9); Total Number of Different Songs Performed from the Album (7).

Song	# of Times Performed	Canadian Live Debut	Most Recent Performance
Gotta Serve Somebody	36	Thurs., April 17, 1980 (Toronto)	Tues., July 18, 2000 (Toronto)
I Believe in You	15	Thurs., April 17, 1980 (Toronto)	Thurs., July 21, 2005 (Vancouver)
When You Gonna Wake Up	12	Thurs., April 17, 1980 (Toronto)	Mon., Nov. 2, 1981 (Ottawa)
Man Gave Names to All the Animals	12	Thurs., April 17, 1980 (Toronto)	Mon., Nov. 2, 1981 (Ottawa)
Precious Angel	8	Thurs., April 17, 1980 (Toronto)	Fri., April 25, 1980 (Montreal)
Slow Train	8	Thurs., April 17, 1980 (Toronto)	Fri., April 25, 1980 (Montreal)
Do Right to Me Baby (Do Unto Others)	8	Thurs., April 17, 1980 (Toronto)	Fri., April 25, 1980 (Montreal)

Total Performances **99**

Saved (released June 19, 1980)

Total Number of Songs on the Album (9); Total Number of Different Songs Performed from the Album (8).

Song	# of Times Performed	Canadian Live Debut	Most Recent Performance
In the Garden	20	Thurs., April 17, 1980 (Toronto)	Sun., Aug. 12, 1990 (Edmonton)
Solid Rock	13	Thurs., April 17, 1980 (Toronto)	Mon., Aug. 26, 2002 (Saskatoon)
Saved	9	Thurs., April 17, 1980 (Toronto)	Mon., Nov. 2, 1981 (Ottawa)
Are You Ready?	9	Thurs., April 17, 1980 (Toronto)	Sat., Oct. 31, 1981 (Kitchener)
Saving Grace	8	Thurs., April 17, 1980 (Toronto)	Fri., April 25, 1980 (Montreal)
What Can I Do For You?	8	Thurs., April 17, 1980 (Toronto)	Fri., April 25, 1980 (Montreal)
Pressing On	7	Thurs., April 17, 1980 (Toronto)	Fri., April 25, 1980 (Montreal)
Covenant Woman	2	Sat., April 19, 1980 (Toronto)	Thurs., April 24, 1980 (Montreal)

Total Performances **76**

Shot of Love (released Aug. 12, 1981)

Total Number of Songs on the Album (10); Total Number of Different Songs Performed from the Album (7).

Song	# of Times Performed	Canadian Live Debut	Most Recent Performance
Watered Down Love	4	Thurs., Oct. 29, 1981 (Toronto)	Mon., Nov. 2, 1981 (Ottawa)
Heart of Mine	4	Fri., Oct. 30, 1981 (Montreal)	Mon., Aug. 17, 1992 (Toronto)
Dead Man, Dead Man	2	Thurs., Oct. 29, 1981 (Toronto)	Sat., Oct. 31, 1981 (Kitchener)
Every Grain of Sand	2	Thurs., Oct. 29, 1998 (Toronto)	Fri., Aug. 9, 2002 (Saint John)
Shot of Love	1	Fri., Aug. 1, 1986 (Vancouver)	Fri., Aug. 1, 1986 (Vancouver)
Trouble	1	Sat., July 29, 1989 (Toronto)	Sat., July 29, 1989 (Toronto)
Lenny Bruce	1	Fri., July 26, 1991 (Toronto)	Fri., July 26, 1991 (Toronto)

Total Performances **15**

Infidels (released Oct. 27, 1983)

Total Number of Songs on the Album (8); Total Number of Different Songs Performed from the Album (1).

Song	# of Times Performed	Canadian Live Debut	Most Recent Performance
I and I	5	Fri., Aug. 1, 1986 (Vancouver)	Mon., April 7, 1997 (Fredericton)

Total Performances **5**

Empire Burlesque (released May 30, 1985)

Total Number of Songs on the Album (10); Total Number of Different Songs Performed from the Album (7).

Song	# of Times Performed	Canadian Live Debut	Most Recent Performance
I'll Remember You	12	Sun., Aug. 21, 1988 (Vancouver)	Wed., Oct. 21, 1998 (Winnipeg)
Seeing the Real You at Last	6	Fri., Aug. 1, 1986 (Vancouver)	Mon. April 7, 1997 (Fredericton)
Clean-Cut Kid	1	Fri., Aug. 1, 1986 (Vancouver)	Fri., Aug. 1, 1986 (Vancouver)
Emotionally Yours	1	Fri., Aug. 1, 1986 (Vancouver)	Fri., Aug. 1, 1986 (Vancouver)
When the Night Comes Falling from the Sky	1	Fri., Aug. 1, 1986 (Vancouver)	Fri., Aug. 1, 1986 (Vancouver)
Tight Connection to My Heart (Has Anybody Seen My Love)	1	Sat., June 2, 1990 (Ottawa)	Sat., June 2, 1990 (Ottawa)
Never Gonna Be the Same Again	1	Thurs., Aug. 8, 2002 (Moncton)	Thurs., Aug. 8, 2002 (Moncton)

Total Performances **23**

Knocked Out Loaded (released July 14, 1986)

Total Number of Songs on the Album (8); Total Number of Different Songs Performed from the Album (1).

Song	# of Times Performed	Canadian Live Debut	Most Recent Performance
Driftin' Too Far from Shore	3	Sat., July 9, 1988 (Ottawa)	Fri., Aug. 26, 1988 (Winnipeg)

Total Performances **3**

Down in the Groove (released May 19, 1988)

Total Number of Songs on the Album (10); Total Number of Different Songs Performed from the Album (1).

Song	# Times Performed	Canadian Live Debut	Most Recent Performance
Silvio	30	Mon., July 11, 1988 (Hamilton)	Wed., Oct. 21, 1998 (Winnipeg)

Total Performances **30**

Oh Mercy (released Sept. 12, 1989)

Total Number of Songs on the Album (10); Total Number of Different Songs Performed from the Album (8).

Song	# of Times Performed	Canadian Live Debut	Most Recent Performance
Everything is Broken	22	Tues., May 29, 1990 (Montreal)	Sun., April 6, 1997 (Halifax)
What Good Am I?	14	Tues., May 29, 1990 (Montreal)	Sun., April 28, 1996 (Toronto)
Shooting Star	7	Mon., Aug. 20, 1990 (Vancouver)	Sun., July 24, 2005 (Calgary)
Man in the Long Black Coat	7	Mon., Aug. 24, 1992 (Sudbury)	Sat., Aug. 10, 2002 (Quebec City)
Political World	4	Mon., June 18, 1990 (Winnipeg)	Wed., Aug. 15, 1990 (Calgary)
What Was It You Wanted?	2	Wed., June 6, 1990 (Toronto)	Thurs., June 7, 1990 (Toronto)
Where Teardrops Fall	1	Wed., May 30, 1990 (Kingston)	Wed., May 30, 1990 (Kingston)
Disease of Conceit	1	Fri., June 1, 1990 (Ottawa)	Fri., June 1, 1990 (Ottawa)

Total Performances **58**

Under the Red Sky (released Sept. 11, 1990)

Total Number of Songs on the Album (10); Total Number of Different Songs Performed from the Album (7).

Song	# of Times Performed	Canadian Live Debut	Most Recent Performance
God Knows	5	Sun., Aug. 22, 1993 (Vancouver)	Sun., July 24, 2005 (Calgary)
Cat's in the Well	4	Tues., Aug. 18, 1992 (Toronto)	Sun., March 21, 2004 (Toronto)
Unbelievable	4	Sat., Aug. 22, 1992 (Ottawa)	Thurs., Aug. 27, 1992 (Thunder Bay)
Under the Red Sky	4	Sun., Aug. 22, 1993 (Vancouver)	Tues., July 19, 2005 (Vancouver)
Wiggle Wiggle	3	Fri., July 26, 1991 (Toronto)	Tues., Aug. 18, 1992 (Toronto)
2 x 2	1	Tues., Aug. 18, 1992 (Toronto)	Tues., Aug. 18, 1992 (Toronto)
Born in Time	1	Tues., April 8, 1997 (Saint John)	Tues., April 8, 1997 (Saint John)

Total Performances **22**

The Bootleg Series Volumes 1-3 (released March 26, 1991)

Total Number of Songs on the Album (58); Total Number of Different Songs Performed from the Album (8).

Note: The eight songs listed below were first released on this album. Eleven other songs have all been performed but are included under the album they were first released.

Song	# of Times Performed	Canadian Live Debut	Most Recent Performance
Mama, You Been on My Mind	8	Sat., Nov. 29, 1975 (Quebec City)	Sat., Aug. 10, 2002 (Quebec City)
Blind Willie McTell	5	Tues., Aug. 5, 1997 (Montreal)	Wed., July 20, 2005 (Vancouver)
Nobody 'Cept You	2	Wed., Jan. 9, 1974 (Toronto)	Fri., Jan. 11, 1974 (Montreal)
Quit Your Low Down Ways	1	Mon., July 2, 1962 (Montreal)	Mon., July 2, 1962 (Montreal)
He Was a Friend of Mine	1	Mon., July 2, 1962 (Montreal)	Mon., July 2, 1962 (Montreal)
Let Me Die in My Footsteps	1	Mon., July 2, 1962 (Montreal)	Mon., July 2, 1962 (Montreal)
If You Gotta Go, Go Now	1	Fri., Nov. 13, 1964 (Toronto)	Fri., Nov. 13, 1964 (Toronto)
Seven Days	1	Sun., April 28, 1996 (Toronto)	Sun., April 28, 1996 (Toronto)

Total Performances **20**

Good As I Been to You (released Nov. 3, 1992)

Total Number of Songs on the Album (13); Total Number of Different Songs Performed from the Album (1).

Song	# of Times Performed	Canadian Live Debut	Most Recent Performance
You're Gonna Quit Me	2	Sun., Aug. 22, 1993 (Vancouver)	Thurs., Sept. 2, 1993 (Toronto)

Total Performances **2**

Bob Dylan Greatest Hits, Vol. 3 (released Nov. 15, 1994)

Total Number of Songs on the Album (14); Total Number of Different Songs Performed from the Album (1).

Note: Dignity was first released on this album. Eight other songs have all been performed but are included under the album they were first released.

Song	# of Times Performed	Canadian Live Debut	Most Recent Performance
Dignity	1	Sat., Aug. 23, 2003 (Niagara Falls)	Sat., Aug. 23, 2003 (Niagara Falls)

Total Performances **1**

MTV Unplugged (released June 30, 1995)

Total Number of Songs on the Album (11); Total Number of Different Songs Performed from the Album (1).

Note: John Brown was first released on this album. The other ten songs have all been performed but are included under the album they were first released.

Song	# of Times Performed	Canadian Live Debut	Most Recent Performance
John Brown	6	Tues., June 5, 1990 (Toronto)	Tues., July 19, 2005 (Vancouver)

Total Performances **6**

Time Out of Mind (released Sept. 30, 1997)

Total Number of Songs on the Album (11); Total Number of Different Songs Performed from the Album (9).

Song	# of Times Performed	Canadian Live Debut	Most Recent Performance
Cold Irons Bound	15	Wed., May 13, 1998 (Vancouver)	Tues., July 19, 2005 (Vancouver)
Love Sick	11	Wed., May 13, 1998 (Vancouver)	Wed., July 20, 2005 (Vancouver)
Make You Feel My Love	10	Wed., May 13, 1998 (Vancouver)	Fri., March 19, 2004 (Toronto)
Til I Fell In Love With You	9	Wed., May 13, 1998 (Vancouver)	Tues., Aug. 13, 2002 (Ottawa)
Can't Wait	4	Thurs., Oct. 15, 1998 (Calgary)	Sun., July 24, 2005 (Calgary)
Million Miles	3	Wed., May 13, 1998 (Vancouver)	Sat., March 20, 2004 (Toronto)
Not Dark Yet	2	Fri., June 11, 1999 (Vancouver)	Tues., Aug., 27, 2002 (Edmonton)
Tryin' To Get To Heaven	2	Fri., June 11, 1999 (Vancouver)	Sun., July 24, 2005 (Calgary)
Standing in the Doorway	2	Wed., Aug. 28, 2002 (Calgary)	Sat., March 20, 2004 (Toronto)

Total Performances **58**

The Essential Bob Dylan (released Oct. 31, 2000)

Total Number of Songs on the Album (30); Total Number of Different Songs Performed from the Album (1).

Note: Things Have Changed was first released on this album. Twenty-seven songs have all been performed but are included under the album they were first released.

Song	# of Times Performed	Canadian Live Debut	Most Recent Performance
Things Have Changed	5	Tues., July 18, 2000 (Toronto)	Fri., March 19, 2004 (Toronto)

Total Performances **5**

Love and Theft (released Sept. 11, 2001)

Total Number of Songs on the Album (12); Total Number of Different Songs Performed from the Album (10).

Song	# of Times Performed	Canadian Live Debut	Most Recent Performance
Summer Days	22	Thurs., Nov. 8, 2001 (Toronto)	Sun., July 24, 2005 (Calgary)
Honest With Me	17	Thurs., Nov. 8, 2001 (Toronto)	Fri., July 22, 2005 (Kelowna)
Moonlight	9	Tues., Aug. 6, 2002 (Halifax)	Fri., July 22, 2005 (Kelowna)
Tweedle Dee & Tweedle Dum	8	Fri., Aug. 9, 2002 (Saint John)	Wed., July 20, 2005 (Vancouver)
High Water (for Charlie Patton)	7	Thurs., Nov. 8, 2001 (Toronto)	Wed., July 20, 2005 (Vancouver)
Cry A While	6	Thurs., Nov. 8, 2001 (Toronto)	Fri., July 22, 2005 (Kelowna)
Floater (Too Much To Ask)	4	Tues., Aug. 13, 2002 (Ottawa)	Fri., July 22, 2005 (Kelowna)
Lonesome Day Blues	3	Tues., Aug. 6, 2002 (Halifax)	Sun., July 24, 2005 (Calgary)
Sugar Baby	1	Thurs., Nov. 8, 2001 (Toronto)	Thurs., Nov. 8, 2001 (Toronto)
Bye and Bye	1	Sat., March 20, 2004 (Toronto)	Sat., March 20, 2004 (Toronto)

Total Performances **78**

Unreleased Songs Performed

Total Number of Unreleased Songs Performed (8). Total Performances 25.

Song	# of Times Performed	Canadian Live Debut	Most Recent Performance
Ain't Gonna Go to Hell for Anybody	8	Thurs., April 17, 1980 (Toronto)	Fri., April 25, 1980 (Montreal)
Cover Down, Break Through	8	Thurs., April 17, 1980 (Toronto)	Fri., April 25, 1980 (Montreal)
Am I Your Stepchild?	3	Tues., Sept. 19, 1978 (Montreal)	Sun., Nov. 11, 1978 (Vancouver)
I Will Love Him	2	Sat., April 19, 1980 (Toronto)	Wed., April 23, 1980 (Montreal)
The Death of Emmett Till	1	Mon., July 2, 1962 (Montreal)	Mon., July 2, 1962 (Montreal)
Rocks and Gravel	1	Mon., July 2, 1962 (Montreal)	Mon., July 2, 1962 (Montreal)
Jesus Is the One	1	Mon., Nov. 2, 1981 (Ottawa)	Mon., Nov. 2, 1981 (Ottawa)
Band of the Hand (It's Hell Time Man!)	1	Fri., Aug. 1, 1986 (Vancouver)	Fri., Aug. 1, 1986 (Vancouver)

Cover Songs and Traditional Songs Performed

Total Number of Cover Songs and Traditional Songs Performed (52). Total Performances 102.

Song	# of Times Performed	Canadian Live Debut	Most Recent Performance
Little Moses (Bert A. Williams/Earle C. Jones)	9	Mon., Aug. 17, 1992 (Toronto)	Thurs., Sept. 2, 1993 (Toronto)
I Am the Man, Thomas (Ralph Stanley/Larry Sparks)	7	Tues., Aug. 6, 2002 (Halifax)	Tues., Aug. 27, 2002 (Edmonton)
Oh Baby It Ain't No Lie (Elizabeth Cotton)	6	Mon., March 31, 1997 (St. John's)	Tues., April 8, 1997 (Saint John)
This World Can't Stand Long (Jim Anglin)	5	Tues., July 18, 2000 (Toronto)	Wed., Aug. 28, 2002 (Calagry)
Dark as a Dungeon (Merle Travis)	4	Sat., Nov. 29, 1975 (Quebec City)	Thurs., Dec. 4, 1975 (Montreal)
This Land is Your Land (Woody Guthrie)	4	Sat., Nov. 29, 1975 (Quebec City)	Thurs., Dec. 4, 1975 (Montreal)
Gamblin' Man (trad.)	4	Thurs., Oct. 29, 1981 (Toronto)	Mon., Nov. 2, 1981 (Ottawa)
Barbara Allen (trad.)	4	Sun., Aug. 21, 1988 (Vancouver)	Tues., June 5, 1990 (Toronto)
Alabama Getaway (Robert Hunter/Jerry Garcia)	4	Fri., April 26, 1996 (Montreal)	Sun., May 12, 1996 (London)
No More One More Time (Troy Seals/Dave Kirby)	3	Tues., May 29, 1990 (Montreal)	Mon., Aug. 13, 1990 (Edmonton)
Cocaine Blues (trad.)	3	Tues., Aug. 5, 1997 (Montreal)	Thurs., May 14, 1998 (Vancouver)
Somebody Touched Me (trad.)	3	Tues., Aug. 13, 2002 (Ottawa)	Wed., Aug. 28, 2002 (Calgary)
Never Let Me Go (Joseph C. Scott)	2	Mon., Dec. 1, 1975 (Toronto)	Thurs., Dec. 4, 1975 (Montreal)
I'm Ready (Willie Dixon)	2	Tues., Sept. 19, 1978 (Montreal)	Thurs., Oct. 12, 1978 (Toronto)
One Irish Rover (Van Morrison)	2	Sun., July 30, 1989 (Ottawa)	Mon., July 31, 1989 (Joliette)
I've Been All Around This World (trad.)	2	Wed., June 6, 1990 (Toronto)	Thurs., June 7, 1990 (Toronto)
Don't Let Your Deal Go Down (trad.)	2	Fri., Aug. 21, 1992 (Hamilton)	Tues., Aug. 25, 1992 (Sault Ste. Marie)
I'm Not Supposed to Care (Gordon Lightfoot)	2	Wed., May 13, 1998 (Vancouver)	Thurs., Oct. 29, 1998 (Toronto)
Stealin' (trad. arr. Memphis Jug Band)	1	Mon., July 2, 1962 (Montreal)	Mon., July 2, 1962 (Montreal)

Song	# of Times Performed	Canadian Live Debut	Most Recent Performance
Hiram Hubbard (trad.)	1	Mon., July 2, 1992 (Montreal)	Mon., July 2, 1992 (Montreal)
Two Trains Runnin' (McKinley Morganfield)	1	Mon., July 2, 1962 (Montreal)	Mon., July 2, 1962 (Montreal)
Ramblin' On My Mind (Robert Johnson)	1	Mon., July 2, 1962 (Montreal)	Mon., July 2, 1962 (Montreal)
Muleskinner Blues (Jimmie Rodgers/George Vaughan)	1	Mon., July 2, 1962 (Montreal)	Mon., July 2, 1962 (Montreal)
Wild Mountain Thyme (trad.)	1	Tues., Dec. 2, 1975 (Toronto)	Tues., Dec. 2, 1975 (Toronto)
She's Love Crazy (Tampa Red)	1	Sun., Nov. 11, 1978 (Vancouver)	Sun., Nov. 11, 1978 (Vancouver)
It's All in the Game (Carl Sigman/Charles Gates Dawes)	1	Sat., Oct. 31, 1981 (Kitchener)	Sat., Oct. 31, 1981 (Kitchener)
Bye Bye Johnny (Chuck Berry)	1	Fri., Aug. 1, 1986 (Vancouver)	Fri., Aug. 1, 1986 (Vancouver)
That Lucky Old Sun (Haven Gillespie/Beasley Smith)	1	Fri., Aug. 1, 1986 (Vancouver)	Fri., Aug. 1, 1986 (Vancouver)
Lonesome Town (Baker Knight)	1	Fri., Aug. 1, 1986 (Vancouver)	Fri., Aug. 1, 1986 (Vancouver)
Across the Borderline (Ry Cooder/John Hiatt/Jim Dickinson)	1	Fri., Aug. 1, 1986 (Vancouver)	Fri., Aug. 1, 1986 (Vancouver)
Shake a Hand (Joe Morris)	1	Fri., Aug. 1, 1986 (Vancouver)	Fri., Aug. 1, 1986 (Vancouver)
Hallelujah (Leonard Cohen)	1	Fri., July 8, 1988 (Montreal)	Fri., July 8, 1988 (Montreal)
Lakes of Pontchartrain (trad.)	1	Fri., July 8, 1988 (Montreal)	Fri., July 8, 1988 (Montreal)
Eileen Aroon (trad., arr. Clancy Brothers/Tommy Makem)	1	Tues., Aug. 23, 1988 (Calgary)	Tues., Aug. 23, 1988 (Calgary)
She's About a Mover (Doug Sahm)	1	Wed., Aug. 24, 1988 (Edmonton)	Wed., Aug. 24, 1988 (Edmonton)
Hey La La (Hey La La) (McBride)	1	Sat., July 29, 1989 (Toronto)	Sat., July 29, 1989 (Toronto)
Don't Pity Me (?)	1	Mon., July 31, 1989 (Joliette)	Mon., July 31, 1989 (Joliette)
Nowhere Man (John Lennon/Paul McCartney)	1	Sun., Aug. 12, 1990 (Edmonton)	Sun., Aug. 12, 1990 (Edmonton)
The Water is Wide (trad.)	1	Sun., Aug. 12, 1990 (Edmonton)	Sun., Aug. 12, 1990 (Edmonton)
Trail of the Buffalo (trad. arr. Woody Guthrie)	1	Fri., July 26, 1991 (Toronto)	Fri., July 26, 1991 (Toronto)
Folsom Prison Blues (Johnny Cash)	1	Fri., July 26, 1991 (Toronto)	Fri., July 26, 1991 (Toronto)
Female Rambling Sailor (trad.)	1	Mon. Aug. 17, 1992 (Toronto)	Mon. Aug. 17, 1992 (Toronto)
Friend of the Devil (Jerry Garcia/Robert Hunter/John Dawson)	1	Sun., April 28, 1996 (Toronto)	Sun., April 28, 1996 (Toronto)
Not Fade Away (Norman Petty/Charles Hardin)	1	Wed., May 13, 1998 (Vancouver)	Wed., May 13, 1998 (Vancouver)
Stone Walls and Steel Bars Bars (Ray Pennington/Ray Marcum)	1	Wed., May 13, 1998 (Vancouver)	Wed., May 13, 1998 (Vancouver)
Hallelujah, I'm Ready to Go (trad.)	1	Fri., June 11, 1999 (Vancouver)	Fri., June 11, 1999 (Vancouver)
The Sound of Silence (Paul Simon)	1	Fri., June 11, 1999 (Vancouver)	Fri., June 11, 1999 (Vancouver)
I Walk the Line (Johnny Cash)	1	Fri., June 11, 1999 (Vancouver)	Fri., June 11, 1999 Vancouver)
Blue Moon of Kentucky (Bill Monroe)	1	Fri., June 11, 1999 (Vancouver)	Fri., June 11, 1999 (Vancouver)
Duncan and Brady (trad.)	1	Tues., July 18, 2000 (Toronto)	Tues., July 18, 2000 (Toronto)
Humming Bird (Johnnie Wright/Jim Anglin/Jack Anglin)	1	Thurs., Nov. 8, 2001 (Toronto)	Thurs., Nov. 8, 2001 (Toronto)
A Voice From On High (Bill Monroe/Bessie Lee Mauldin)	1	Fri., Aug. 16, 2002 (Toronto)	Fri., Aug. 16, 2002 (Toronto)

Opening Song and Closing Song by Concert

Summary

- Bob Dylan has opened his Canadian concerts with thirty different songs and closed them with twenty-one different songs.
- Gotta Serve Somebody has been the opening song at the most concerts (17).
- Maggie's Farm has been the opening song thirteen times, including six concerts in 2005.
- All Along the Watchtower has been the closing song at the most concerts (27). In fact, it has been the closing song for all but one of the last twenty-two concerts dating back to Thurs., Nov. 8, 2001. All Along the Watchtower did not close the show in Vancouver on Tues., July 19, 2005.
- Rainy Day Women #12 & 35 closed twelve consecutive concerts between Sun., April 28, 1996 and Thurs., May 14, 1998.
- Most Likely You Go Your Way and I'll Go Mine, Maggie's Farm, My Back Pages and Rainy Day Women #12 & 35 have been both the opening and closing song.
- Most Likely You Go Your Way and I'll Go Mine was the opening and closing song at the same concert. This happened twice in 1974. Both times in Montreal.
- Songs not written by Bob Dylan (traditional and/or cover songs) have been the opening song twenty-five times. There have been ten different traditional and/or cover songs that have been the opening song.
- A non Bob Dylan song has been the closing song only once. This happened in Edmonton in 1988. After Knockin' on Heaven's Door, Doug Sahm of the Sir Douglas Quintet joined the band for a rendition of his classic hit, She's About a Mover.
- Opening song and closing song information is not available for eleven concerts. The closing song is counted as the very last song of the concert.

Date	Opening Song	Closing Song
Sat., Feb. 1, 1964 (Toronto)	The Times They Are A-Changin'	Restless Farewell
Fri., Nov. 13, 1964 (Toronto)	The Times They Are A-Changin'	All I Really Want to Do
Wed., Jan. 9, 1974 (Toronto)	Rainy Day Women #12 & 35	Most Likely You Go Your Way and I'll Go Mine
Thurs., Jan. 10, 1974 (Toronto)	Most Likely You Go Your Way and I'll Go Mine	Like a Rolling Stone
Fri., Jan. 11, 1974 (Montreal)	Most Likely You Go Your Way and I'll Go Mine	Most Likely You Go Your Way and I'll Go Mine
Sat., Jan. 12, 1974 (Montreal)	Most Likely You Go Your Way and I'll Go Mine	Most Likely You Go Your Way and I'll Go Mine
Sat., Nov. 29, 1975 (Quebec City)	When I Paint My Masterpiece	This Land is Your Land
Mon., Dec. 1, 1975 (Toronto)	When I Paint My Masterpiece	This Land is Your Land
Tues., Dec. 2, 1975 (Toronto)	When I Paint My Masterpiece	This Land is Your Land
Thurs., Dec. 4, 1975 (Montreal)	When I Paint My Masterpiece	This Land is Your Land
Tues., Sept. 19, 1978 (Montreal)	My Back Pages	Changing of the Guards
Thurs., Oct. 12, 1978 (Toronto)	My Back Pages	Changing of the Guards
Sat., Nov. 11, 1978 (Vancouver)	My Back Pages	Changing of the Guards
Thurs., April 17, 1980 (Toronto)	Gotta Serve Somebody	Pressing On
Fri., April 18, 1980 (Toronto)	Gotta Serve Somebody	Pressing On
Sat., April 19, 1980 (Toronto)	Gotta Serve Somebody	I Will Love Him
Sun., April 20, 1980 (Toronto)	Gotta Serve Somebody	Pressing On
Tues., April 22, 1980 (Montreal)	Gotta Serve Somebody	Pressing On

Date	Opening Song	Closing Song
Wed., April 23, 1980 (Montreal)	Gotta Serve Somebody	Pressing On
Thurs., April 24, 1980 (Montreal)	Gotta Serve Somebody	Pressing On
Fri., April 25, 1980 (Montreal)	Gotta Serve Somebody	Pressing On
Thurs., Oct. 29, 1981 (Toronto)	Gotta Serve Somebody	Knockin' on Heaven's Door
Fri., Oct. 30, 1981 (Montreal)	Gotta Serve Somebody	Knockin' on Heaven's Door
Sat., Oct. 31, 1981 (Kitchener)	Gotta Serve Somebody	Knockin' on Heaven's Door
Mon., Nov. 2, 1981 (Ottawa)	Saved	Knockin' on Heaven's Door
Fri., Aug. 1, 1986 (Vancouver)	Bye Bye Johnny	Knockin' on Heaven's Door
Fri., July 8, 1988 (Montreal)	Subterranean Homesick Blues	All Along the Watchtower
Sat., July 9, 1988 (Ottawa)	Subterranean Homesick Blues	Maggie's Farm
Mon., July 11, 1988 (Hamilton)	Subterranean Homesick Blues	Maggie's Farm
Sun., Aug. 21, 1988 (Vancouver)	Subterranean Homesick Blues	Knockin' on Heaven's Door
Tues., Aug. 23, 1988 (Calgary)	Subterranean Homesick Blues	Knockin' on Heaven's Door
Wed., Aug. 24, 1988 (Edmonton)	Subterranean Homesick Blues	She's About a Mover
Fri., Aug. 26, 1988 (Winnipeg)	Subterranean Homesick Blues	Maggie's Farm
Mon., Aug. 29, 1988 (Toronto)	Subterranean Homesick Blues	Knockin' on Heaven's Door
Sat., July 29, 1989 (Toronto)	Trouble	All Along the Watchtower
Sun., July 30, 1989 (Ottawa)	Most Likely You Go Your Way and I'll Go Mine	All Along the Watchtower
Mon., July 31, 1989 (Joliette)	Most Likely You Go Your Way and I'll Go Mine	All Along the Watchtower
Tues., May 29, 1990 (Montreal)	Absolutely Sweet Marie	Stuck Inside of Mobile with the Memphis Blues Again
Wed., May 30, 1990 (Kingston)	Most Likely You Go Your Way and I'll Go Mine	Highway 61 Revisited
Fri., June 1, 1990 (Ottawa)	Most Likely You Go Your Way and I'll Go Mine	Highway 61 Revisited
Sat., June 2, 1990 (Ottawa)	Subterranean Homesick Blues	Highway 61 Revisited
Mon., June 4, 1990 (London)	Subterranean Homesick Blues	Highway 61 Revisited
Tues., June 5, 1990 (Toronto)	Subterranean Homesick Blues	Highway 61 Revisited
Wed., June 6, 1990 (Toronto)	Absolutely Sweet Marie	Highway 61 Revisited
Thurs., June 7, 1990 (Toronto)	Most Likely You Go Your Way and I'll Go Mine	Maggie's Farm
Sun., June 17, 1990 (Winnipeg)	Most Likely You Go Your Way and I'll Go Mine	Highway 61 Revisited
Mon., June 18, 1990 (Winnipeg)	Absolutely Sweet Marie	Highway 61 Revisited
Sun., Aug. 12, 1990 (Edmonton)	Maggie's Farm	All Along the Watchtower
Mon., Aug. 13, 1990 (Edmonton)	Maggie's Farm	Highway 61 Revisited
Wed., Aug. 15, 1990 (Calgary)	Maggie's Farm	All Along the Watchtower
Thurs., Aug. 16, 1990 (Calgary)	Maggie's Farm	Highway 61 Revisited

Date	Opening Song	Closing Song
Sun., Aug. 19, 1990 (Victoria)	Maggie's Farm	Highway 61 Revisited
Mon., Aug. 20, 1990 (Vancouver)	Maggie's Farm	Highway 61 Revisited
Fri., July 26, 1991 (Toronto)	New Morning	Ballad of a Thin Man
Mon., Aug. 17, 1992 (Toronto)	Wiggle Wiggle	Highway 61 Revisited
Tues., Aug. 18, 1992 (Toronto)	2 x 2	It Ain't Me, Babe
Fri., Aug. 21, 1992 (Hamilton)	Don't Let Your Deal Go Down	It Ain't Me, Babe
Sat., Aug. 22, 1992 (Ottawa)	Rainy Day Women #12 & 35	Girl of the North Country
Mon., Aug. 24, 1992 (Sudbury)	New Morning	It Ain't Me, Babe
Tues., Aug. 25, 1992 (Sault Ste. Marie)	Don't Let Your Deal Go Down	It Ain't Me, Babe
Thurs., Aug. 27, 1992 (Thunder Bay)	Everything is Broken	It Ain't Me, Babe
Sun., Aug. 22, 1993 (Vancouver)	You're Gonna Quit Me	Girl of the North Country
Thurs., Sept. 2, 1993 (Toronto)	You're Gonna Quit Me	Rainy Day Women #12 & 35
Fri., April 26, 1996 (Montreal)	Drifter's Escape	Rainy Day Women #12 & 35
Sat., April 27, 1996 (Toronto)	Drifter's Escape	My Back Pages
Sun., April 28, 1996 (Toronto)	Crash on the Levee (Down in the Flood)	Rainy Day Women #12 & 35
Sun., May 12, 1996 (London)	Leopard-Skin Pill-Box Hat	Rainy Day Women #12 & 35
Mon., March 31, 1997 (St. John's)	Crash on the Levee (Down in the Flood)	Rainy Day Women #12 & 35
Tues., April 1, 1997 (St. John's)	Crash on the Levee (Down in the Flood)	Rainy Day Women #12 & 35
Sat., April 5, 1997 (Moncton)	Crash on the Levee (Down in the Flood)	Rainy Day Women #12 & 35
Sun., April 6, 1997 (Halifax)	Crash on the Levee (Down in the Flood)	Rainy Day Women #12 & 35
Mon., April 7, 1997 (Fredericton)	Crash on the Levee (Down in the Flood)	Rainy Day Women #12 & 35
Tues., April 8, 1997 (Saint John)	Crash on the Levee (Down in the Flood)	Rainy Day Women #12 & 35
Tues., Aug. 5, 1997 (Montreal)	Absolutely Sweet Marie	Rainy Day Women #12 & 35
Thurs., Aug. 7, 1997 (Toronto)	Absolutely Sweet Marie	Rainy Day Women #12 & 35
Wed., May 13, 1998 (Vancouver)	Not Fade Away	Rainy Day Women #12 & 35
Thurs., May 14, 1998 (Vancouver)	Absolutely Sweet Marie	Rainy Day Women #12 & 35
Thurs., Oct. 15, 1998 (Calgary)	Leopard-Skin Pill-Box Hat	Forever Young
Fri., Oct. 16, 1998 (Edmonton)	Gotta Serve Somebody	Forever Young
Sun., Oct. 18, 1998 (Saskatoon)	Gotta Serve Somebody	Forever Young
Tues., Oct. 20, 1998 (Regina)	Gotta Serve Somebody	Forever Young
Wed., Oct. 21, 1998 (Winnipeg)	Gotta Serve Somebody	Forever Young
Thurs., Oct. 29, 1998 (Toronto)	Gotta Serve Somebody	It Ain't Me, Babe
Fri., Oct. 30, 1998 (Ottawa)	Gotta Serve Somebody	Forever Young

Date	Opening Song	Closing Song
Fri., June 11, 1999 (Vancouver)	Hallelujah, I'm Ready to Go	Knockin' on Heaven's Door
Tues., July 18, 2000 (Toronto)	Duncan and Brady	Blowin' in the Wind
Thurs., Nov. 8, 2001 (Toronto)	Humming Bird	All Along the Watchtower
Tues., Aug. 6, 2002 (Halifax)	I Am the Man, Thomas	All Along the Watchtower
Thurs., Aug. 8, 2002 (Moncton)	I Am the Man, Thomas	All Along the Watchtower
Fri., Aug. 9, 2002 (Saint John)	I Am the Man, Thomas	All Along the Watchtower
Sat., Aug. 10, 2002 (Quebec City)	I Am the Man, Thomas	All Along the Watchtower
Mon., Aug. 12, 2002 (Montreal)	I Am the Man, Thomas	All Along the Watchtower
Tues., Aug. 13, 2002 (Ottawa)	Somebody Touched Me	All Along the Watchtower
Fri., Aug. 16, 2002 (Toronto)	A Voice From On High	All Along the Watchtower
Sat., Aug. 24, 2002 (Winnipeg)	I Am the Man, Thomas	All Along the Watchtower
Mon., Aug. 26, 2002 (Saskatoon)	Somebody Touched Me	All Along the Watchtower
Tues., Aug. 27, 2002 (Edmonton)	I Am the Man, Thomas	All Along the Watchtower
Wed., Aug. 28, 2002 (Calgary)	Somebody Touched Me	All Along the Watchtower
Sat., Aug. 23, 2003 (Niagara Falls)	Tombstone Blues	All Along the Watchtower
Fri., March 19, 2004 (Toronto)	Drifter's Escape	All Along the Watchtower
Sat., March 20, 2004 (Toronto)	To Be Alone with You	All Along the Watchtower
Sun., March 21, 2004 (Toronto)	Maggie's Farm	All Along the Watchtower
Sun., Jul 17, 2005 (Victoria)	Maggie's Farm	All Along the Watchtower
Tues., July 19, 2005 (Vancouver)	Maggie's Farm	Like a Rolling Stone
Wed., July 20, 2005 (Vancouver)	Maggie's Farm	All Along the Watchtower
Thurs., July 21, 2005 (Vancouver)	Maggie's Farm	All Along the Watchtower
Fri., July 22, 2005 (Kelowna)	Maggie's Farm	All Along the Watchtower
Sun., July 24, 2005 (Calgary)	Maggie's Farm	All Along the Watchtower

Opening Song and Closing Song Totals

Opening Song	Times Opened
Gotta Serve Somebody	17
Maggie's Farm	13
Subterranean Homesick Blues	11
Most Likely You Go Your Way and I'll Go Mine	9
Crash on the Levee (Down in the Flood)	7
I Am the Man, Thomas	7
Absolutely Sweet Marie	6
When I Paint My Masterpiece	4
My Back Pages	3
Drifter's Escape	3
Somebody Touched Me	3
Rainy Day Women #12 & 35	2
New Morning	2
Don't Let Your Deal Go Down	2
You're Gonna Quit Me	2
Leopard-Skin Pill-Box Hat	2
The Times They Are A-Changin'	2
Saved	1
Bye Bye Johnny	1
Trouble	1
Wiggle Wiggle	1
2 x 2	1
Everything is Broken	1
Not Fade Away	1
Hallelujah, I'm Ready to Go	1
Duncan and Brady	1
Humming Bird	1
A Voice From On High	1
Tombstone Blues	1
To Be Alone with You	1
Totals	**30**

Closing Song	Times Closed
All Along the Watchtower	27
Rainy Day Women #12 & 35	14
Highway 61 Revisited	13
Knockin' on Heaven's Door	9
Pressing On	7
It Ain't Me, Babe	6
Forever Young	6
This Land is Your Land	4
Maggie's Farm	4
Most Likely You Go Your Way and I'll Go Mine	3
Changing of the Guards	3
Girl of the North Country	2
Like a Rolling Stone	2
Restless Farewell	1
All I Really Want to Do	1
I Will Love Him	1
She's About a Mover	1
Stuck Inside of Mobile with the Memphis Blues Again	1
Ballad of a Thin Man	1
My Back Pages	1
Blowin' in the Wind	1
Totals	**21**

Total Number of Songs Performed by Year

Summary

- Bob Dylan performed 295 songs in 1990, the most for any single year. However, there were sixteen concerts that year. In 2002, there were 200 songs performed at eleven shows.
- Of the 295 songs performed in 1990, sixty were different songs. Of the 200 songs played in 2002, sixty-five were different songs. In 1997, of the 118 songs performed, fifty-four were different ones.
- At least one song has made a Canadian live debut in every year there has been a concert.
- Bob Dylan's five-night debut stand in Montreal in 1962 would obviously have more Canadian live debuts in any given year, but only thirteen of the songs performed are known.
- On the 1980 Gospel Tour, eighteen songs made their Canadian live debut. Seventeen songs made their live debut in both 1975 and 1990. There was only one Canadian live debut in 2005.
- Fans in Vancouver, at the single Canadian stop of the True Confessions Tour in 1986 were treated to eleven songs that have been performed only once in Canada.
- Eleven songs played in 1962 have been performed only once in Canada. Again there would obviously be many more if all the songs were known.
- In every year, with the exception of 1965, 1980 and 1993, there has been at least one song performed only once in Canada.
- Between 1962 and 1966, set lists are not available for five concerts and are incomplete for seven concerts.

Year	# of Concerts	# of Songs Performed	# of Different Songs Performed	# of Songs Making Their Canadian Live Debut	# of Songs Performed Only Once in Canada
1962	5	13	13	13	11
1964	2	16	13	13	3
1965	3	11	11	9	0
1966	3	11	9	3	1
1974	4	71	25	14	2
1975	4	85	28	17	1
1978	3	81	35	16	4
1980	8	129	18	18	0
1981	4	107	34	8	2
1986	1	25	25	14	11
1988	8	123	43	15	5
1989	3	47	36	7	3
1990	16	295	60	17	6
1991	1	18	18	6	3
1992	7	125	50	10	2
1993	2	25	19	3	0
1996	4	59	37	9	3
1997	8	118	54	6	1
1998	9	146	47	10	2
1999	1	17	17	6	5
2000	1	17	17	5	3
2001	1	22	22	7	2
2002	11	200	65	11	4
2003	1	16	16	2	2
2004	3	50	38	1	1
2005	6	96	45	1	1

Total Number of Songs Performed by City

Summary

- Bob Dylan has performed 541 songs in Toronto, 277 songs in Montreal, 197 songs in Vancouver and 146 songs in Ottawa.
- There were twenty-eight songs performed in Kitchener on the 1981 Shot of Love Tour, the most songs played in any of the ten cities that have hosted one concert each.
- Thirty-four songs have been performed in both Halifax and Moncton. Out of these, thirty different songs were played in each city. In Saint John, thirty-three songs have been performed in which thirty-one were different.
- Twenty cities have all had at least one song performed making its Canadian live debut.
- Quebec City concert goers have seen fourteen songs make their Canadian live debut and yet there has only been thirty-four different songs performed there. This is because the Canadian leg of the 1975 Rolling Thunder Review Tour kicked off in Quebec City.
- Fans in thirteen different cities lay claim to the fact they saw the only performance in Canada of at least one song.
- Set lists are not available for five concerts and are incomplete for seven concerts.

City	# of Concerts	# of Songs Performed	# of Different Songs Performed	# of Songs Making Their Canadian Live Debut	# of Songs Performed Only Once in Canada
Toronto, ON	33	541	169	104	24
Montreal, QC	20	277	126	46	15
Vancouver, BC	13	197	97	37	21
Ottawa, ON	9	146	75	12	5
Calgary, AB	6	104	60	3	1
Winnipeg, MB	5	87	52	2	0
Edmonton, AB	5	86	51	5	4
Quebec City, QC	2	38	34	14	0
Saskatoon, SK	2	35	31	0	0
Halifax, NS	2	34	30	3	0
Moncton, NB	2	34	30	1	1
London, ON	2	33	28	0	0
Hamilton , ON	2	33	28	3	0
Saint John, NB	2	33	31	3	2
St. John's, NF	2	30	24	1	0
Victoria, BC	2	34	28	1	0
Kitchener, ON	1	28	28	1	1
Kingston, ON	1	20	20	1	1
Thunder Bay, ON	1	18	18	0	0
Sault Ste. Marie, ON	1	18	18	0	0
Sudbury, ON	1	18	18	1	0
Regina, SK	1	17	17	0	0
Niagara Falls, ON	1	16	16	2	2
Kelowna, BC	1	16	16	1	1
Joliette, QC	1	15	15	1	1
Fredericton, NB	1	15	15	0	0

Musicians on Tour

Summary

- Bob Dylan has toured and performed with 65 different band members at his 119 concerts in Canada.
- Current band member Tony Garnier (bass) has played 74 concerts with Bob Dylan in Canada. The most concerts for any of Dylan's various players over the years. His first show was on Sat. July 29, 1989 in Toronto and his most recent show was on Sun., July 24, 2005 in Calgary.
- Larry Campbell (guitar, pedal steel guitar, steel guitar, banjo, electric slide guitar, fiddle, cittern, mandolin, bouzouki & backup vocals) played 35 concerts with Bob Dylan in Canada. His first show was on Mon., March 31, 1997 in St. John's and his most recent show was on Sun., March 21, 2004 in Toronto.
- Bucky Baxter (dobro, mandolin, pedal steel guitar, lap steel guitar, electric slide guitar, concertina & backup vocals) played 30 concerts with Bob Dylan in Canada. His first show was on Mon., Aug. 17, 1992 in Toronto and his most recent concert was on Fri., Oct. 30, 1998 in Ottawa.
- G. E. Smith (guitar, acoustic slide guitar, electric slide guitar & backup vocals) and Christopher Parker (drums), both members of the first Never-Ending Tour band have played 27 shows each.
- Current band member George Recile, (drums & percussion) has played 21 concerts with Bob Dylan in Canada. His first show was on Tues., Aug. 6, 2002 in Halifax and his most recent concert was on Sun., July 24, 2005 in Calgary.

Musician	Total Concerts Played	Debut Concert	Most Recent Concert
Bob Dylan (vocal, guitar, harmonica, keyboard & piano)	119 (8 solo shows)	Thurs., June 28, 1962 (Montreal)	Sun., July 24, 2005 (Calgary)
Robbie Robertson (guitar)	9	Sun., Nov. 14, 1965 (Toronto)	Sat., Jan. 12, 1974 (Montreal)
Garth Hudson (organ & synthesizer)	9	Sun., Nov. 14, 1965 (Toronto)	Sat., Jan. 12, 1974 (Montreal)
Richard Manual (keyboards)	9	Sun., Nov. 14, 1965 (Toronto)	Sat., Jan. 12, 1974 (Montreal)
Rick Danko (bass)	9	Sun., Nov. 14, 1965 (Toronto)	Sat., Jan. 12, 1974 (Montreal)
Levon Helm (drums)	6	Sun., Nov. 14, 1965 (Toronto)	Sat., Jan. 12, 1974 (Montreal)
Sandy Konikoff (drums)	3	Sat., Feb. 19, 1966 (Ottawa)	Sat., March 26, 1966 (Vancouver)
Joan Baez (vocal & guitar)	4	Sat., Nov. 29, 1975 (Quebec City)	Thurs., Dec. 4, 1975 (Montreal)
Scarlet Rivera (violin)	4	Sat., Nov. 29, 1975 (Quebec City)	Thurs., Dec. 4, 1975 (Montreal)
T-Bone J. Henry Burnett (guitar)	4	Sat., Nov. 29, 1975 (Quebec City)	Thurs., Dec. 4, 1975 (Montreal)
Steven Soles (guitar & backup vocals)	7	Sat., Nov. 29, 1975 (Quebec City)	Sun., Nov. 11, 1978 (Vancouver)
Mick Ronson (guitar)	4	Sat., Nov. 29, 1975 (Quebec City)	Thurs., Dec. 4, 1975 (Montreal)
David Mansfield (steel guitar, mandolin, violin & dobro)	7	Sat., Nov. 29, 1975 (Quebec City)	Sun., Nov. 11, 1978 (Vancouver)
Rob Stoner (bass)	4	Sat., Nov. 29, 1975 (Quebec City)	Thurs., Dec. 4, 1975 (Montreal)
Luther Rix (drums & percussion)	4	Sat., Nov. 29, 1975 (Quebec City)	Thurs., Dec. 4, 1975 (Montreal)
Howie Wyeth (piano & drums)	4	Sat., Nov. 29, 1975 (Quebec City)	Thurs., Dec. 4, 1975 (Montreal)
Bob Neuwirth (vocal & guitar)	4	Sat., Nov. 29, 1975 (Quebec City)	Thurs., Dec. 4, 1975 (Montreal)
Roger McGuinn (vocal & guitar)	4	Sat., Nov. 29, 1975 (Quebec City)	Thurs., Dec. 4, 1975 (Montreal)
Ronee Blakley (vocal)	4	Sat., Nov. 29, 1975 (Quebec City)	Thurs., Dec. 4, 1975 (Montreal)
Billy Cross (lead guitar)	3	Tues., Sept. 19, 1978 (Montreal)	Sun., Nov. 11, 1978 (Vancouver)
Alan Pasqua (keyboards)	3	Tues., Sept. 19, 1978 (Montreal)	Sun., Nov. 11, 1978 (Vancouver)

Musician	Total Concerts Played	Debut Concert	Most Recent Concert
Steve Douglas (saxophone & flute)	3	Tues., Sept. 19, 1978 (Montreal)	Sun., Nov. 11, 1978 (Vancouver)
Jerry Scheff (bass)	3	Tues., Sept. 19, 1978 (Montreal)	Sun., Nov. 11, 1978 (Vancouver)
Bobbye Hall (percussion)	3	Tues., Sept. 19, 1978 (Montreal)	Sun., Nov. 11, 1978 (Vancouver)
Helena Springs (backup vocals)	3	Tues., Sept. 19, 1978 (Montreal)	Sun., Nov. 11, 1978 (Vancouver)
Jo Ann Harris (backup vocals)	3	Tues., Sept. 19, 1978 (Montreal)	Sun., Nov. 11, 1978 (Vancouver)
Carolyn Dennis (backup vocals)	4	Tues., Sept. 19, 1978 (Montreal)	Fri., Aug. 1, 1986 (Vancouver)
Fred Tackett (guitar)	12	Thurs., April 17, 1980 (Toronto)	Mon., Nov. 2, 1981 (Ottawa)
Spooner Oldham (keyboards)	8	Thurs., April 17, 1980 (Toronto)	Fri., April 25, 1980 (Montreal)
Tim Drummond (bass)	12	Thurs., April 17, 1980 (Toronto)	Mon., Nov. 2, 1981 (Ottawa)
Terry Young (piano)	8	Thurs., April 17, 1980 (Toronto)	Fri., April 25, 1980 (Montreal)
Jim Keltner (drums)	12	Thurs., April 17, 1980 (Toronto)	Mon., Nov. 2, 1981 (Ottawa)
Clydie King (backup vocals)	12	Thurs., April 17, 1980 (Toronto)	Mon., Nov. 2, 1981 (Ottawa)
Gwen Evans (backup vocals)	8	Thurs., April 17, 1980 (Toronto)	Fri., April 25, 1980 (Montreal)
Mary Elizabeth Bridges (backup vocals)	8	Thurs., April 17, 1980 (Toronto)	Fri., April 25, 1980 (Montreal)
Regina McCrary (backup vocals)	12	Thurs., April 17, 1980 (Toronto)	Mon., Nov. 2, 1981 (Ottawa)
Mona Lisa Young (backup vocals)	8	Thurs., April 17, 1980 (Toronto)	Fri., April 25, 1980 (Montreal)
Steve Ripley (guitar)	4	Thurs., Oct. 29, 1981 (Toronto)	Mon., Nov. 2, 1981 (Ottawa)
Al Kooper (keyboards)	4	Thurs., Oct. 29, 1981 (Toronto)	Mon., Nov. 2, 1981 (Ottawa)
Arthur Rosato (drums)	4	Thurs., Oct. 29, 1981 (Toronto)	Mon., Nov. 2, 1981 (Ottawa)
Madelyn Quebec (backup vocals)	5	Thurs., Oct. 29, 1981 (Toronto)	Fri., Aug. 1, 1986 (Vancouver)
Tom Petty (vocal, guitar & bass)	1	Fri., Aug. 1, 1986 (Vancouver)	Fri., Aug. 1, 1986 (Vancouver)
Mike Campbell (guitar)	1	Fri., Aug. 1, 1986 (Vancouver)	Fri., Aug. 1, 1986 (Vancouver)
Benmont Tench (keyboards)	1	Fri., Aug. 1, 1986 (Vancouver)	Fri., Aug. 1, 1986 (Vancouver)
Howie Epstein (bass & electric slide guitar)	1	Fri., Aug. 1, 1986 (Vancouver)	Fri., Aug. 1, 1986 (Vancouver)
Stan Lynch (drums)	1	Fri., Aug. 1, 1986 (Vancouver)	Fri., Aug. 1, 1986 (Vancouver)
Queen Esther Marrow (backup vocals)	1	Fri., Aug. 1, 1986 (Vancouver)	Fri., Aug. 1, 1986 (Vancouver)
Louise Bethune (backup vocals)	1	Fri., Aug. 1, 1986 (Vancouver)	Fri., Aug. 1, 1986 (Vancouver)
G. E. Smith (guitar, acoustic slide guitar, electric slide guitar & backup vocals)	27	Fri., July 8, 1988 (Montreal)	Mon., Aug. 20, 1990 (Vancouver)
Kenny Aaronson (bass)	8	Fri., July 8, 1988 (Montreal)	Mon., Aug. 29, 1988 (Toronto)
Christopher Parker (drums)	27	Fri., July 8, 1988 (Montreal)	Mon., Aug. 20, 1990 (Vancouver)
Tony Garnier (bass)	74	Sat., July 29, 1989 (Toronto)	Sun., July 24, 2005 (Calgary)
John Jackson (guitar & backup vocals)	14	Fri., July 26, 1991 (Toronto)	Fri., April 26, 1996 (Montreal)
Ian Wallace (drums)	11	Tues., Sept. 19, 1978 (Montreal)	Thurs., Aug. 27, 1992 (Thunder Bay

Musician	Total Concerts Played	Debut Concert	Most Recent Concert
Bucky Baxter (dobro, mandolin, pedal steel guitar, lap steel guitar, electric slide guitar, concertina & backup vocals)	30	Mon., Aug. 17, 1992 (Toronto)	Fri., Oct. 30, 1998 (Ottawa)
Charlie Quintana (drums & percussion)	7	Mon., Aug. 17, 1992 (Toronto)	Thurs., Aug. 27, 1992 (Thunder Bay
Winston Watson (drums & percussion)	6	Sun., Aug. 22, 1993 (Vancouver)	Fri., April 26, 1996 (Montreal)
Larry Campbell (guitar, pedal steel guitar, steel guitar, banjo, electric slide guitar, fiddle, cittern, mandolin, bouzouki & backup vocals)	35	Mon., March 31, 1997 (St. John's)	Sun., March 21, 2004 (Toronto)
David Kemper (drums & percussion)	20	Mon., March 31, 1997 (St. John's)	Thurs., Nov. 8, 2001 (Toronto)
Charlie Sexton (guitar, dobro & backup vocals)	14	Fri., June 11, 1999 (Vancouver)	Wed., Aug. 28, 2002 (Calgary)
George Recile (drums & percussion)	21	Tues., Aug. 6, 2002 (Halifax)	Sun., July 24, 2005 (Calgary)
Freddie Koella (guitar, electric slide guitar & violin)	4	Sat., Aug. 23, 2003 (Niagara Falls)	Sun., March 21, 2004 (Toronto)
Richie Hayward (drums & percussion)	3	Fri., March 19, 2004 (Toronto)	Sun., March 21, 2004 (Toronto)
Stu Kimball (lead guitar)	6	Sun., July 17, 2005 (Victoria)	Sun., July 24, 2005 (Calgary)
Denny Freeman (guitar)	6	Sun., July 17, 2005 (Victoria)	Sun., July 24, 2005 (Calgary)
Donnie Heron (banjo, electric mandolin, violin, pedal steel guitar, & lap steel guitar)	6	Sun., July 17, 2005 (Victoria)	Sun., July 24, 2005 (Calgary)

Opening Acts, Shared Bills & Special Guests

Summary

- Bob Dylan has toured in Canada with 26 different acts, be it opening acts or bands on a shared bill. He has not toured in Canada with an opening act since 1998 or been on a shared bill since 2000.
- The Band (1974) and Tom Petty & the Heartbreakers (1986) were Dylan's backing band at their respected concerts. They also played a selection of their own songs.
- The four concerts on the 1975 Rolling Thunder Revue Tour featured many special guests that were not part of the core band known as Guam. Joan Baez played her own music as well as joining in with Dylan on a few songs. Ramblin' Jack Elliott, Cindy Bullens, Joni Mitchell, Gordon Lightfoot, Ronnie Hawkins and Jack Scott all played their own songs and joined Dylan on stage for the finale of This Land is Your Land. Some members of the core band also played a song or two of their own — Bob Neuwirth, T-Bone J. Henry Burnett, Steven Soles, Rob Stoner, Mick Ronson, Ronee Blakley, and Roger McGuinn. Poet Allen Ginsberg also appeared at the shows.
- Ronnie Hawkins, Tracy Chapman, Doug Sahm, Paul Simon, Paul James, Steve Bruton, and Tommy Morrongiello have all joined Dylan on stage at a concert in Canada.
- On the 1980 Gospel Tour, Dylan's backup singers began the concerts with a half a dozen songs. Clydie King, Gwen Evans, Mary Elizabeth Bridges, Regina McCrary and Mona Lisa Young were accompanied by Terry Young on piano.
- The Sat. Aug. 22, 1992 show in Ottawa featured Bob Dylan with Joe Cocker, The Neville Brothers and Michelle Shocked. The Thurs., May 14, 1998 concert in Vancouver was a triple bill that featured Bob Dylan with Joni Mitchell and Van Morrison.
- Dylan opened the 1999 show with Paul Simon and the 2000 concert with Phil Lesh and Friends.
- Canada's own Sue Medley has opened for Dylan on eighteen different occasions. Fellow Canadian Jann Arden has opened five concerts for Dylan.
- Derek Lamb opened at least one of the four shows at The Pot-pourri in Montreal in 1962.

Opening Act/Shared Bill	Total Concerts Played	Debut Concert	Most Recent Concert
The Band	4	Wed., Jan. 9, 1974 (Toronto)	Sat., Jan. 12, 1974 (Montreal)
Tom Petty & the Heartbreakers	1	Fri., Aug. 1, 1986 (Vancouver)	Fri., Aug. 1, 1986 (Vancouver)
The Alarm	3	Fri., July 8, 1988 (Montreal)	Mon., July 11, 1988 (Hamilton)
Tracy Chapman	3	Sun., Aug. 21, 1988 (Vancouver)	Wed., Aug. 24, 1988 (Edmonton)
Timbuk 3	2	Fri., Aug. 26, 1988 (Winnipeg)	Mon., Aug. 29, 1988 (Toronto)
Steve Earle & the Dukes	3	Sat., July 29, 1989 (Toronto)	Mon., July 31, 1989 (Joliette)
Sue Medley	18	Wed., May 30, 1990 (Montreal)	Tues., Aug. 25, 1992 (Sault Ste. Marie)
Paul James	1	Fri., July 26, 1991 (Toronto)	Fri., July 26, 1991 (Toronto)
Moxy Fruvous	2	Mon., Aug. 17, 1992 (Toronto)	Tues., Aug. 18, 1992 (Toronto)
Junkhouse	1	Fri., Aug. 21, 1992 (Hamilton)	Fri., Aug. 21, 1992 (Hamilton)
Michelle Shocked	1	Sat., Aug. 22, 1992 (Ottawa)	Sat., Aug. 22, 1992 (Ottawa)
The Neville Brothers	1	Sat., Aug. 22, 1992 (Ottawa)	Sat., Aug. 22, 1992 (Ottawa)
Joe Cocker	1	Sat., Aug. 22, 1992 (Ottawa)	Sat., Aug. 22, 1992 (Ottawa)
Wailing Souls	2	Sun., Aug. 22, 1993 (Vancouver)	Thurs., Sept. 2, 1993 (Toronto)
Santana	2	Sun., Aug. 22, 1993 (Vancouver)	Thurs., Sept. 2, 1993 (Toronto)
Aimee Mann	3	Fri., April 26, 1996 (Montreal)	Sun., April 28, 1996 (Toronto)
BR5-49	2	Tues., Aug. 5, 1997 (Montreal)	Thurs., Aug. 7, 1997 (Toronto)
Ani DiFranco	2	Tues., Aug. 5, 1997 (Montreal)	Thurs., Aug. 7, 1997 (Toronto)

Opening Act/Shared Bill	Total Concerts Played	Debut Concert	Most Recent Concert
Ron Sexsmith	1	Wed., May 13, 1998 (Vancouver)	Wed., May 13, 1998 (Vancouver)
Van Morrison	1	Thurs., May 14, 1998 (Vancouver)	Thurs., May 14, 1998 (Vancouver)
Joni Mitchell	3	Thurs., May 14, 1998 (Vancouver)	Fri., Oct. 30, 1998 (Ottawa)
Jann Arden	5	Thurs., Oct. 15, 1998 (Calgary)	Wed., Oct. 21, 1998 (Winnipeg)
Dave Alvin and the Guilty Men	2	Thurs., Oct. 29, 1998 (Toronto)	Fri., Oct. 30, 1998 (Ottawa)
Paul Simon	1	Fri., June 11, 1999 (Vancouver)	Fri., June 11, 1999 (Vancouver)
Phil Lesh and Friends	1	Tues., July 18, 2000 (Toronto)	Tues., July 18, 2000 (Toronto)

Concerts by City

Summary

- Bob Dylan has performed 119 concerts in twenty-six Canadian cities from coast-to-coast. The debut concert was in Montreal (1962) and the most recent show was in Calgary (2005).
- Toronto has played host to the most concerts (33), followed by Montreal (20), then Vancouver (13).
- Ten cities have hosted only one concert each.
- The two concerts in Maple, ON (Sat., July 29, 1989 & Fri., July 26, 1991) are included under Toronto.
- The two concerts in Kanata, ON (Fri., Oct. 30, 1998 & Tues., Aug. 13, 2002) are included under Ottawa.
- The concert in Vancouver on Sat., March 26, 1966 was Bob Dylan's last show in Canada for almost eight years. On Wed., Jan. 9, 1974, he was back performing in Toronto.
- Quebec City has had the longest time span between concerts (27 years). Sat., Nov. 29, 1975 was the debut and Sat., Aug. 10, 2002 was the most recent show. Ottawa went 15 years from Sat., Feb. 19, 1966 until Mon., Nov. 2, 1981 without a concert. Victoria also waited 15 years between concerts with the debut on Sun., Aug. 19, 1990 and the most recent on Sun., July 17, 2005.
- No city has played host to a concert in every single year Bob Dylan has toured Canada.
- In certain years there were concerts in only one city: Montreal (1962), Toronto (1991, 2000, 2001, 2004), Vancouver (1986, 1999) and Niagara Falls (2003). The 1962 shows in Montreal were part of a five-night stand. The 2004 concerts in Toronto was a three-night run in three different venues. The 1986, 1991, 1999, 2000, 2001 and 2003 shows were the only concert in Canada for that year.

City	# of Concerts	# of Concerts by Year	Debut Concert	Most Recent Concert
Toronto, ON	33	1964 (2), 1965 (2), 1974 (2), 1975 (2), 1978 (1), 1980 (4), 1981 (1), 1988 (1), 1989 (1), 1990 (3), 1991 (1), 1992 (2), 1993 (1), 1996 (2), 1997 (1), 1998 (1), 2000 (1), 2001 (1), 2002 (1), 2004 (3)	Sat., Feb. 1, 1964 (CBC TV Studios)	Sun., March 21, 2004 (Kool Haus)
Montreal, QC	20	1962 (5), 1966 (1), 1974 (2), 1975 (1), 1978 (1), 1980 (4), 1981 (1), 1988 (1), 1990 (1), 1996 (1), 1997 (1), 2002 (1)	Thurs, June 28, 1962 (The Pot-pourri)	Mon., Aug. 12, 2002 (Molson Centre)
Vancouver, BC	13	1965 (1), 1966 (1), 1978 (1), 1986 (1), 1988 (1), 1990 (1), 1993 (1), 1998 (2), 1999 (1), 2005 (3)	Fri., April 9, 1965 (Queen Elizabeth Theatre)	Thurs., July 20, 2005 (The Orpheum)
Ottawa, ON	9	1966 (1), 1981 (1), 1988 (1), 1989 (1), 1990 (2), 1992 (1), 1998 (1), 2002 (1)	Sat., Feb. 19, 1966 (Ottawa Auditorium)	Tues., Aug. 13, 2002 (Corel Centre)
Calgary, AB	6	1988 (1), 1990 (2), 1998 (1), 2002 (1), 2005 (1)	Tues., Aug. 23, 1988 (Olympic Saddledome)	Sun., July 24, 2005 (Pengrowth Saddledome)
Edmonton, AB	5	1988 (1), 1990 (2), 1998 (1), 2002 (1)	Wed., Aug. 24, 1988 (Edmonton Coliseum)	Tues., Aug. 27, 2002 (Skyreach Centre)
Winnipeg, MB	5	1988 (1), 1990 (2), 1998 (1), 2002 (1)	Fri., Aug. 26, 1988 (Winnipeg Arena)	Sat., Aug. 24, 2002 (Winnipeg Arena)
Quebec City, QC	2	1975 (1), 2002 (1)	Sat., Nov. 29, 1975 (Quebec City Coliseum)	Sat., Aug. 10, 2002 (l'Agora du Vieux-Port)
Hamilton, ON	2	1988 (1), 1992 (1)	Mon., July 11, 1988 (Copps Coliseum)	Fri., Aug. 21, 1992 (Hamilton Place)
London, ON	2	1990 (1), 1996 (1)	Mon., June 4, 1990 (University of Western Ontario, Alumni Hall)	Sun., May 12, 1996 1990 (University of Western Ontario, Alumni Hall)
Victoria, BC	2	1990 (1), 2005 (1)	Sun., Aug. 19, 1990 (Memorial Arena)	Sun., July 17, 2005 (Save-On-Foods Memorial Centre)
St. John's, NL	2	1997 (2)	Mon., March 31, 1997 (St. John's Memorial Stadium)	Tues., April 1, 1997 (St. John's Memorial Stadium)
Moncton, NB	2	1997 (1), 2002 (1)	Sat., April 5, 1997 (Moncton Coliseum)	Thurs., Aug. 8, 2002 (Moncton Coliseum)
Halifax, NS	2	1997 (1), 2002 (1)	Sun., April 6, 1997 (Metro Centre)	Tues., Aug. 6, 2002 (Metro Centre)
Saint John, NB	2	1997 (1), 2002 (1)	Tues., April 8, 1997 (Harbour Station)	Fri., Aug. 9, 2002 (Harbour Station)

City	# of Concerts	# of Concerts by Year	Debut Concert	Most Recent Concert
Saskatoon, SK	2	1998 (1), 2002 (1)	Sun., Oct. 18, 1998 (Saskatchewan Place)	Mon., Aug. 26, 2002 (Saskatchewan Place)
Kitchener, ON	1	1981 (1)	Sat., Oct. 31, 1981 (Kitchener Memorial Auditorium)	Sat., Oct. 31, 1981 (Kitchener Memorial Auditorium)
Joliette, QC	1	1989 (1)	Mon., July 31, 1989 (Lanaudière Outdoor Amphitheatre)	Mon., July 31, 1989 (Lanaudière Outdoor Amphitheatre)
Kingston, ON	1	1990 (1)	Wed., May 30, 1990 (Kingston Memorial Centre)	Wed., May 30, 1990 (Kingston Memorial Centre)
Sudbury, ON	1	1992 (1)	Mon., Aug. 24, 1992 (Sudbury Arena)	Mon., Aug. 24, 1992 (Sudbury Arena)
Sault Ste. Marie, ON	1	1992 (1)	Tues., Aug. 25, 1992 (Memorial Gardens)	Tues., Aug. 25, 1992 (Memorial Gardens)
Thunder Bay, ON	1	1992 (1)	Thurs., Aug. 27, 1992 (Fort William Gardens)	Thurs., Aug. 27, 1992 (Fort William Gardens)
Fredericton, NB	1	1997 (1)	Mon., April 7, 1997 (University of New Brunswick, Aitken Centre)	Mon., April 7, 1997 (University of New Brunswick, Aitken Centre)
Regina, SK	1	1998 (1)	Tues., Oct. 20, 1998 (Regina Exhibition Park, Agridome)	Tues., Oct. 20, 1998 (Regina Exhibition Park, Agridome)
Niagara Falls, ON	1	2003 (1)	Sat., Aug. 23, 2003 (Oakes Garden Theatre)	Sat., Aug. 23, 2003 (Oakes Garden Theatre)
Kelowna, BC	1	2005 (1)	Fri., July 22, 2005 (Prospera Place)	Fri., July 22, 2005 (Prospera Place)

Concerts by Consecutive Nights in One City

Summary

- Bob Dylan's Canadian debut, five-night stand in Montreal, will undoubtedly remain as the most consecutive concerts he has played in one city.
- His most recent 2005 summer tour of Western Canada stopped in Vancouver for three straight nights.
- In 2004 he played three consecutive nights in Toronto at three different venues.
- The 1980 Gospel Tour stopped in both Toronto and Montreal for four straight nights.
- In 1990 he played three nights in Toronto and two-night stands in Ottawa, Winnipeg, Edmonton, and Calgary.

City	Total Nights	Dates
Montreal, QC	5	Thurs., June 28, 1962 through Mon., July 2, 1962
Toronto, ON	4	Thurs., April 17, 1980 through Sun., April 20, 1980
Montreal, QC	4	Tues., April 22, 1980 through Friday April 25, 1990
Toronto, ON	3	Tues., June 5, 1990 through Thurs., June 7 1990
Toronto, ON	3	Fri., March 19, 2004 through Sun., March 21, 2004
Vancouver, BC	3	Tues., July 19, 2005 through Thurs., July 21, 2005
Toronto, ON	2	Sun., Nov. 14, 1965 through Mon., Nov. 15, 1965
Toronto, ON	2	Wed., Jan. 9, 1974 through Thurs., Jan 10. 1974
Montreal, QC	2	Fri., Jan. 11, 1974 through Sat., Jan. 12, 1974
Toronto, ON	2	Mon., Dec. 1, 1975 through Tues., Dec. 2, 1975
Ottawa, ON	2	Fri., June 1, 1990 through Sat., June 2, 1990
Winnipeg, MB	2	Sun., June 17, 1990 through Mon., June 18, 1990
Edmonton, AB	2	Sun., Aug. 12, 1990 through Mon., Aug 13, 1990
Calgary, AB	2	Wed., Aug 15, 1990 through Thurs., Aug 16, 1990
Toronto, ON	2	Mon., Aug. 17, 1992 through Tues., Aug 18, 1992
Toronto, ON	2	Sat., April 27, 1996 through Sun., April 28, 1996
St. John's, NL	2	Mon., March 31, 1997 through Tues., April 1, 1997
Vancouver, BC	2	Wed., May 13, 1998 through Thurs., May 14, 1998

Concerts by Venue

Summary

- Bob Dylan has performed at sixty-two different venues in Canada. The debut concert was held at the Pot-pourri in Montreal and the most recent show was at the Pengrowth Saddledome in Calgary.
- The most concerts have taken place at the historic Massey Hall in Toronto. "The Venerable Old Lady of Shuter Street" has hosted nine concerts including a show in 1964, a two-night stand in 1965, a four-night run on the 1980 Gospel Tour and back-to-back nights in 1992.
- Maple Leaf Gardens and the Montreal Forum have hosted seven and six concerts, respectively. Both venues are now defunct. They were without a doubt two of the most revered venues in Canada.
- Several other venues are long gone including, The Pot-pourri, The Finjan Club, the Ottawa Auditorium and the CNE Grandstand.
- Thirty-three different venues have hosted only one concert each.
- Toronto audiences have seen Bob Dylan in twelve different venues. Montreal fans have seen him in nine different venues. Vancouver weighs in with eight different venues and Ottawa with five different venues.
- With the trend in the last decade for corporate naming rights to arenas and stadiums many venues have changed names. The Saddledome in Calgary has been called the Olympic Saddledome, the Canadian Airlines Saddledome and now the Pengrowth Saddledome. The Skyreach Centre in Edmonton was formerly known as the Northlands Coliseum and the Edmonton Coliseum.

Venue	Concerts	Year	Debut Concert	Most Recent Concert
Massey Hall (Toronto)	9	1964 (1), 1965 (2), 1980 (4), 1992 (2)	Fri., Nov. 13, 1964	Tues., Aug. 18, 1992
Maple Leaf Gardens (Toronto)	7	1974 (2), 1975 (2), 1978 (1), 1981 (1), 1998 (1)	Wed., Jan. 9, 1974	Thurs., Oct. 29, 1998
Montreal Forum (Montreal)	6	1974 (2), 1975 (1), 1978 (1), 1981 (1), 1988 (1)	Fri., Jan. 11, 1974	Fri., July 8, 1988
The Pot-pourri (Montreal)	4	1962 (4)	Thurs., June 28, 1962	Sun., July 1, 1962
Le Theatre Saint-Denis (Montreal)	4	1980 (4)	Tues., April 22, 1980	Fri., April 25, 1980
The Saddledome (Calgary)	4	1988 (1), 1998 (1), 2002 (1), 2005 (1)	Tues., Aug., 23, 1988	Sun., July 24, 2005
Ottawa Civic Centre (Ottawa)	3	1981 (1), 1988 (1), 1989 (1)	Mon., Nov. 2, 1981	Sun., July 30, 1989
Pacific Coliseum (Vancouver)	3	1988 (1), 1990 (1), 1993 (1)	Sun., Aug., 21, 1988	Sun., Aug, 22, 1993
Northlands Coliseum, Edmonton Coliseum, Skyreach Centre (Edmonton)	3	1988 (1), 1998 (1), 2002 (1)	Wed., Aug. 24, 1988	Tues., Aug. 27, 2002
Winnipeg Arena (Winnipeg)	3	1988 (1), 1998 (1), 2002 (1)	Fri., Aug. 26, 1988	Sat., Aug. 24, 2002
O'Keefe Centre (Toronto)	3	1990 (3)	Tues., June 5, 1990	Thurs., June 7, 1990
Molson Amphitheatre (Toronto)	3	1997 (1), 2000 (1), 2002 (1)	Thurs., Aug. 7, 1997	Fri., Aug. 16, 2002
The Orpheum (Vancouver)	3	2005 (3)	Tues., July 19, 2005	Thurs., July 21, 2005
CNE Grandstand (Toronto)	2	1988 (1), 1993 (1)	Mon., Aug. 29, 1988	Thurs., Sept. 2, 1993
Kingswood Music Theatre (Toronto)	2	1989 (1), 1991 (1)	Sat., July 29, 1989	Fri., July 26, 1991
National Arts Centre Opera (Ottawa)	2	1990 (2)	Fri., June 1, 1990	Sat., June 2, 1990
Alumni Hall (London)	2	1990 (1), 1996 (1)	Mon., June 4, 1990	Sun., May 12, 1996
Centennial Centre Concert Hall (Winnipeg)	2	1990 (2)	Sun., June 17, 1990	Mon. June 18, 1990
Jubilee Auditorium (Edmonton)	2	1990 (2)	Sun., Aug. 12, 1990	Mon., Aug. 13, 1990
Jubilee Auditorium (Calgary)	2	1990 (2)	Wed., Aug. 15, 1990	Thurs., Aug. 16, 1990

Venue	Concerts	Year	Debut Concert	Most Recent Concert
The Concert Hall (Toronto)	2	1996 (2)	Sat., April 27, 1996	Sun., April 28, 1996
St. John's Memorial Stadium (St. John's)	2	1997 (2)	Mon., March 31, 1997	Tues., April, 1, 1997
Moncton Coliseum (Moncton)	2	1997 (1), 2002 (1)	Sat., April 5, 1997	Thurs., Aug. 8, 2002
Metro Centre (Halifax)	2	1997 (1), 2002 (1)	Sun., April 6, 1997	Tues., Aug. 6, 2002
Harbour Station (Saint John)	2	1997 (1), 2002 (1)	Tues., April, 8, 1997	Fri., Aug. 9, 2002
GM Place (Vancouver)	2	1998 (1), 1999 (1)	Thurs., May 14, 1998	Fri., June 11, 1999
Saskatchewan Place (Saskatoon)	2	1998 (1), 2002 (1)	Sun., Oct. 18, 1998	Mon., Aug. 26, 2002
The Corel Centre (Ottawa)	2	1998 (1), 2002 (1)	Fri., Oct. 30, 1998	Tues., Aug. 13, 2002
The Finjan Club (Montreal)	1	1962 (1)	Mon., July 2, 1962	Mon., July 2, 1962
CBC TV Studios (Toronto)	1	1964 (1)	Sat., Feb. 1, 1964	Sat., Feb. 1, 1964
Queen Elizabeth Theatre (Vancouver)	1	1965 (1)	Fri., April 9, 1965	Fri., April 9, 1965
Ottawa Auditorium (Ottawa)	1	1966 (1)	Sat., Feb. 19, 1966	Sat., Feb. 19, 1966
Place des Arts (Montreal)	1	1966 (1)	Sun., Feb. 20, 1966	Sun., Feb. 20, 1966
PNE Agrodome (Vancouver)	1	1966 (1)	Sat., March 26, 1966	Sat., March 26, 1966
Quebec City Coliseum (Quebec City)	1	1975 (1)	Sat., Nov. 29, 1975	Sat., Nov. 29, 1975
Pacific National Exhibition Hall (Vancouver)	1	1978 (1)	Sat., Nov. 11, 1978	Sat., Nov. 11, 1978
Kitchener Memorial Auditorium (Kitchener)	1	1981 (1)	Sat., Oct. 31, 1981	Sat., Oct. 31, 1981
BC Place (Vancouver)	1	1986 (1)	Fri., Aug. 1, 1986	Fri., Aug. 1, 1986
Copps Coliseum (Hamilton)	1	1988 (1)	Mon., July 11, 1988	Mon., July 11, 1988
Lanaudière Outdoor Amphitheatre (Joliette)	1	1989 (1)	Mon., July 31, 1989	Mon., July 31, 1989
Centre Sportif de l'Université de Montréal (Montreal)	1	1990 (1)	Tues., May 29, 1990	Tues., May 29, 1990
Kingston Memorial Centre (Kingston)	1	1990 (1)	Wed., May 30, 1990	Wed., May 30, 19
Memorial Arena (Victoria)	1	1990 (1)	Sun., Aug. 19, 1990	Sun., Aug. 19, 1990
Hamilton Place (Hamilton)	1	1992 (1)	Fri., Aug. 21, 1992	Fri., Aug. 21, 1992
Landsdowne Stadium (Ottawa)	1	1992 (1)	Sat., Aug. 22, 1992	Sat., Aug. 22, 1992
Sudbury Arena (Sudbury)	1	1992 (1)	Mon., Aug. 24, 1992	Mon., Aug. 2, 1992
Memorial Gardens (Sault Ste. Marie)	1	1992 (1)	Tues., Aug. 25, 1992	Tues., Aug. 25, 1992
Fort William Gardens (Thunder Bay)	1	1992 (1)	Thurs., Aug 27, 1992	Thurs., Aug 27, 1992
Verdun Auditorium (Montreal)	1	1996 (1)	Fri., April 26, 1996	Fri., April 26, 1996
University of New Brunswick, Aitken Centre (Fredericton)	1	1997 (1)	Mon., April 7, 1997	Mon., April 7, 1997

Venue	Concerts	Year	Debut Concert	Most Recent Concert
du Maurier Stadium (Montreal)	1	1997 (1)	Tues., Aug. 5, 1997	Tues., Aug. 5, 1997
The Rage (Vancouver)	1	1998 (1)	Wed., May 13, 1998	Wed., May 13, 1998
Regina Exhibition Park, Agridome (Regina)	1	1998 (1)	Tues., Oct. 20, 1998	Tues., Oct. 20, 1998
Air Canada Centre (Toronto)	1	2001 (1)	Thurs., Nov. 8, 2001	Thurs., Nov. 8, 2001
l'Agora du Vieux-Port (Quebec City)	1	2002 (1)	Sat., Aug. 10, 2002	Sat., Aug. 10, 2002
Molson Centre (Montreal)	1	2002 (1)	Mon., Aug. 12, 2002	Mon., Aug. 12, 2002
Oakes Garden Theatre (Niagara Falls)	1	2003 (1)	Sat., Aug. 23, 2003	Sat., Aug. 23, 2003
Ricoh Colisuem (Toronto)	1	2004 (1)	Fri., March 19, 2004	Fri., March 19, 2004
Phoenix Concert Theatre (Toronto)	1	2004 (1)	Sat., March 20, 2004	Sat., March 20, 2004
Kool Haus (Toronto)	1	2004 (1)	Sun., March 21, 2004	Sun., March 21, 2004
Save-On-Foods Memorial Centre (Victoria)	1	2005 (1)	Sun., July 17, 2005	Sun., July 17, 2005
Prospera Place (Kelowna)	1	2005 (1)	Fri., July 22, 2005	Fri., July 22, 2005

Concerts by Province

Summary

- Bob Dylan has performed in nine Canadian provinces.
- The most concerts have been in Ontario (46%). Not very surprising since he has played ten cities in the province and Toronto alone, represents 29% of all concerts in Canada.

Province	# of Concerts	Cities	Debut Concert	Most Recent Concert
Ontario	52	Toronto (33), Ottawa (9), Hamilton (2), London (2), Kitchener (1), Kingston (1), Sudbury (1), Sault Ste. Marie (1), Thunder Bay (1), Niagara Falls (1)	Sat., Feb. 1, 1964 (Toronto)	Sun., March 21, 2004 (Toronto)
Quebec	23	Montreal (20), Quebec City (2), Joliette (1)	Thurs, June 28, 1962 (Montreal)	Mon., Aug. 12, 2002 (Montreal)
British Columbia	16	Vancouver (13), Victoria (2), Kelowna (1)	Fri., April 9, 1965 (Vancouver)	Fri., July 22, 2005 (Kelowna)
Alberta	11	Calgary (6), Edmonton (5)	Tues., Aug. 23, 1988 (Edmonton)	Sun., July 24, 2005 (Calgary)
Manitoba	5	Winnipeg (5)	Fri., Aug. 26, 1988 (Winnipeg)	Sat., Aug. 24, 2002 (Winnipeg)
New Brunswick	5	Moncton (2), Saint John (2), Fredericton (1)	Sat., April 5, 1997 (Moncton)	Fri., Aug. 9, 2002 (Saint John)
Saskatchewan	3	Saskatoon (2), Regina (1)	Sun., Oct. 18, 1998 (Saskatoon)	Mon., Aug. 26, 2002 (Saskatoon)
Newfoundland	2	St. John's (2)	Mon., March 31, 1997 (St. John's)	Tues., April 1, 1997 (St. John's)
Nova Scotia	2	Halifax (2)	Sun., April 6, 1997 (Halifax)	Tues., Aug. 6, 2002 (Halifax)

Concerts by Year

Summary

- Bob Dylan performed the most concerts in 1990. There were sixteen shows in ten cities with multiple nights in five cities.
- In 2002 there were eleven concerts in eleven different cities.
- In 1986, 1991, 1999, 2000, 2001 and 2003 there was only one concert per year.
- For the last ten consecutive years (1996-2005) there has been at least one concert in Canada.
- Consecutive years with concerts: 1962 (1), 1964-1966 (3), 1974-1975 (2), 1978 (1), 1980-1981 (2), 1986 (1), 1988-1993 (6), 1996-2005 (10).
- It has been forty-three years from the debut concert in 1962 and the most recent concert in 2005. During this time there have been concerts in twenty-six different years.
- There were no concerts between Saturday, March 26, 1966 (Vancouver) and Wednesday, January 9, 1974 (Toronto).
- There were no concerts in 1963, 1967, 1968, 1969, 1970, 1971, 1972, 1973, 1976, 1977, 1979, 1982, 1983, 1984, 1985, 1987, 1994 and 1995.

Year	# of Concerts	Concerts by City	Debut Concert	Last Concert
1962	5	Montreal (5)	Thurs., June 28, 1962 (Montreal)	Mon., July 2, 1962 (Montreal)
1964	2	Toronto (2)	Sat., Feb. 1, 1964 (Toronto)	Fri., Nov. 13, 1964 (Toronto)
1965	3	Vancouver, Toronto (2)	Fri., April 9, 1965 (Vancouver)	Mon., Nov. 15, 1965 (Toronto)
1966	3	Ottawa, Montreal, Vancouver	Sat., Feb. 19, 1966 (Ottawa)	Sat., March 26, 1966 (Vancouver)
1974	4	Toronto (2) Montreal (2)	Wed., Jan. 9, 1974 (Toronto)	Sat., Jan. 12, 1974 (Montreal)
1975	4	Quebec City, Toronto (2), Montreal	Sat., Nov. 29, 1975 (Quebec City)	Thurs., Dec. 4, 1975 (Montreal)
1978	3	Montreal, Toronto, Vancouver	Tues., Sept. 19, 1978 (Montreal)	Sat., Nov. 11, 1978 (Vancouver)
1980	8	Toronto (4), Montreal (4)	Thurs., April 17, 1980 (Toronto)	Fri., April 25, 1980 (Montreal)
1981	4	Toronto, Montreal, Kitchener, Ottawa	Thurs., Oct. 29, 1981 (Toronto)	Mon., Nov. 2, 1981 (Ottawa)
1986	1	Vancouver	Fri., Aug. 1, 1986 (Vancouver)	Fri., Aug. 1, 1986 (Vancouver)
1988	8	Montreal, Ottawa, Hamilton, Vancouver, Calgary, Edmonton, Winnipeg, Toronto	Fri., July 8, 1988 (Montreal)	Mon., Aug. 29, 1988 (Toronto)
1989	3	Toronto, Ottawa, Joliette	Sat., July 29, 1989 (Toronto)	Mon., July 31, 1989 (Joliette)
1990	16	Montreal, Kingston, Ottawa (2), London, Toronto (3), Winnipeg (2), Edmonton, (2), Calgary (2), Victoria, Vancouver	Tues., May 29, 1990 (Montreal)	Mon., Aug. 20, 1990 (Vancouver)
1991	1	Toronto	Fri., July 26, 1991 (Toronto)	Fri., July 26, 1991 (Toronto)
1992	7	Toronto (2), Hamilton, Ottawa, Sudbury, Sault Ste. Marie, Thunder Bay	Mon., Aug. 17, 1992 (Toronto)	Thurs., Aug. 27, 1992 (Thunder Bay)
1993	2	Vancouver, Toronto	Sun., Aug. 22, 1993 (Vancouver)	Thurs., Sept. 2, 1993 (Toronto)
1996	4	Montreal, Toronto (2), London	Fri., April 26, 1996 (Montreal)	Sun., May 12, 1996 (London)
1997	8	St. John's (2), Moncton, Halifax, Fredericton, Saint John, Montreal, Toronto	Mon., March 31, 1997 (St. John's)	Thurs., Aug 7, 1997 (Toronto)
1998	9	Vancouver (2), Calgary, Edmonton, Saskatoon, Regina, Winnipeg, Toronto, Ottawa	Wed., May 13, 1998 (Vancouver)	Fri., Oct., 30, 1998 (Ottawa)
1999	1	Vancouver	Fri., June 11, 1999 (Vancouver)	Fri., June 11, 1999 (Vancouver)
2000	1	Toronto	Tues., July 18, 2000 (Toronto)	Tues., July 18, 2000 (Toronto)
2001	1	Toronto	Thurs., Nov. 8, 2001 (Toronto)	Thurs., Nov. 8, 2001 (Toronto

Year	# of Concerts	Concerts by City	Debut Concert	Last Concert
2002	11	Halifax, Moncton, Saint John, Quebec City, Montreal, Ottawa, Toronto, Winnipeg, Saskatoon, Edmonton, Calgary	Tues., Aug. 6, 2002 (Halifax)	Wed., Aug. 28, 2002 (Calgary)
2003	1	Niagara Falls	Sat. Aug. 23, 2003 (Niagara Falls)	Sat. Aug. 23, 2003 (Niagara Falls)
2004	3	Toronto (3)	Fri., March 19, 2004 (Toronto)	Sun., March 21, 2004 (Toronto)
2005	6	Victoria, Vancouver (3), Kelowna, Calgary	Sun., July 17, 2005 (Victoria)	Sun., July 24, 2005 (Calgary)

Concerts by Month

Summary

- Bob Dylan has performed the most concerts in August.
- He has played the least number of concerts in September.

Month	# of Concerts	Debut Concert	Most Recent Concert
January	4	Wed., Jan., 9, 1974 (Toronto)	Sat., Jan. 12, 1974 (Montreal)
February	3	Sat., Feb. 1, 1964 (Toronto)	Sun., Feb. 20, 1966 (Montreal)
March	5	Sat., March 26, 1966 (Vancouver)	Sun., March 21, 2004 (Toronto)
April	17	Fri., April 9, 1965 (Vancouver)	Tues., April 8, 1997 (Saint John)
May	5	Tues., May 29, 1990 (Montreal)	Thurs., May 14, 1998 (Vancouver)
June	12	Thurs., June 28, 1962 (Montreal)	Fri., June 11, 1999 (Vancouver)
July	16	Sun., July 1, 1962 (Montreal)	Sun., July 24, 2005 (Calgary)
August	34	Fri., Aug. 1, 1986 (Vancouver)	Sat., Aug. 23, 2003 (Niagara Falls)
September	2	Tues., Sept. 19, 1978 (Montreal)	Thurs., Sept. 2, 1993 (Toronto)
October	11	Thurs., Oct. 12, 1978 (Toronto)	Fri., Oct. 30, 1990 (Ottawa)
November	7	Fri., Nov. 13, 1964 (Toronto)	Thurs., Nov. 8, 2001 (Toronto)
December	3	Mon., Dec 1, 1975 (Toronto)	Thurs., Dec 4, 1975 (Montreal)

Concerts by Day of the Month

Summary

- Bob Dylan has performed the most concerts on the 29th day of the month (seven times).
- He has played on the 1st day of the month, the 19th & 20th six times each and five times each on the 2nd, 12th, 18th, 21st, 24th, 26th and 30th day of the month.
- Mr. Dylan has never performed in Canada on the 3rd day of the month.

Day of the Month	# of Concerts	Debut Concert	Most Recent Concert
1st	6	Sun., July 1, 1962 (Montreal)	Tues., April 1, 1997 (St. John's)
2nd	5	Mon., July 2, 1962 (Montreal)	Thurs., Sept. 2, 1993 (Toronto)
3rd	0	–	–
4th	2	Thurs., Dec. 4, 1975 (Montreal)	Mon., June 4, 1990 (London)
5th	3	Tues., June 5, 1990 (Toronto)	Tues., Aug. 5, 1997 (Montreal)
6th	3	Wed., June 6, 1990 (Toronto)	Tues., Aug. 6, 2002 (Halifax)
7th	3	Thurs., June 7, 1990 (Toronto)	Thurs., Aug. 7, 1997 (Toronto)
8th	4	Fri., July 8, 1988 (Montreal)	Thurs., Aug. 8, 2002 (Moncton)
9th	4	Fri., April 9, 1965 (Vancouver)	Fri., Aug. 9, 2002 (Saint John)
10th	2	Thurs., Jan. 10, 1974 (Toronto)	Sat., Aug. 10, 2002 (Quebec City)
11th	4	Fri., Jan. 11, 1974 (Toronto)	Fri., June 11, 1999 (Vancouver)
12th	5	Sat., Jan. 12, 1974 (Montreal)	Mon., Aug. 12, 2002 (Montreal)
13th	4	Fri., Nov. 13, 1964 (Toronto)	Tues., Aug. 13, 2002 (Ottawa)
14th	2	Sun., Nov. 14, 1965 (Toronto)	Thurs., May 14, 1998 (Vancouver)
15th	3	Mon., Nov. 15, 1965 (Toronto)	Thurs., Oct 15, 1998 (Calgary)
16th	3	Thurs., Aug. 16, 1990 (Calgary)	Fri., Aug. 16, 2002 (Toronto)
17th	4	Thurs., April 17, 1980 (Toronto)	Sun., July 17, 2005 (Victoria)
18th	5	Fri., April 18, 1980 (Toronto)	Tues., July 18, 2000 (Toronto)
19th	6	Sat., Feb. 19, 1966 (Ottawa)	Tues., July 19, 2005 (Vancouver)
20th	6	Sun., Feb., 20, 1966 (Montreal)	Wed., July 20, 2005 (Vancouver)
21st	5	Sun., Aug. 21, 1988 (Vancouver)	Thurs., July 21, 2005 (Vancouver)
22nd	4	Tues., April 22, 1980 (Montreal)	Fri., July 22, 2005 (Kelowna)
23rd	3	Wed., April 23, 1980 (Montreal)	Sat., Aug. 23, 2003 (Niagara Falls)
24th	5	Thurs., April 24, 1980 (Montreal)	Sun. July 24, 2005 (Calgary)
25th	2	Fri., April 25, 1980 (Montreal)	Tues., Aug. 25, 1992 (Sault Ste. Marie)
26th	5	Sat., March 26, 1966 (Vancouver)	Mon., Aug. 26, 2002 (Saskatoon)
27th	3	Thurs., Aug. 27, 1992 (Thunder Bay)	Tues., Aug. 27, 2002 (Edmonton)

Day of the Month	# of Concerts	Debut Concert	Most Recent Concert
28th	3	Thurs., June 28, 1962 (Montreal)	Wed., Aug 28, 2002 (Calgary)
29th	7	Fri., June 29, 1962 (Montreal)	Thurs., Oct 29, 1998 (Toronto)
30th	5	Sat., June 30, 1962 (Montreal)	Fri., Oct. 30, 1998 (Ottawa)
31st	3	Sat., Oct. 31, 1981 (Kitchener)	Mon., March 31, 1997 (St. John's)

Concerts by Day of the Week

Summary

- Bob Dylan has performed the most concerts on Friday and Saturday nights, respectively.
- He has played the least number of concerts on a Wednesday.

Day of the Week	# of Concerts	Debut Concert	Most Recent Concert
Monday	17	Mon., July 2, 1962 (Montreal)	Mon., Aug. 26, 2002 (Saskatoon)
Tuesday	17	Tues., Dec. 2, 1975 (Toronto)	Tues., July 19, 2005 (Vancouver)
Wednesday	10	Wed., Jan. 9, 1974 (Toronto)	Wed., July 20, 2005 (Vancouver)
Thursday	18	Thurs., June 28, 1962 (Montreal)	Thurs., July 21, 2005 (Vancouver)
Friday	21	Fri., June 29, 1962 Montreal)	Fri., July 22, 2005 (Kelowna)
Saturday	19	Sat., June 30, 1962 (Montreal)	Sat., March 20, 2004 (Toronto)
Sunday	17	Sun., July 1, 1962 (Montreal)	Sun., July 24, 2005 (Calgary)

City Statistics at a Glance

City Statistics at a Glance

Calgary, AB

Number of Concerts	6
Number of Songs Performed	104
Number of Different Songs Performed	60
Number of Songs Performed Making Their Canadian Live Debut	3
Number of Songs Performed Only Once in Canada	1
Number of Venues Played	2

The Concerts

	Year	Date	Day	Venue
1.	1988	August 23	Tuesday	Olympic Saddledome*
2.	1990	August 15	Wednesday	Jubilee Auditorium
3.	1990	August 16	Thursday	Jubilee Auditorium
4.	1998	October 15	Thursday	Canadian Airlines Saddledome*
5.	2002	August 28	Wednesday	Pengrowth Saddledome*
6.	2005	July 24	Sunday	Pengrowth Saddledome*

Note: * Venue changed name.

Edmonton, AB

Number of Concerts	5
Number of Songs Performed	86
Number of Different Songs Performed	51
Number of Songs Performed Making Their Canadian Live Debut	5
Number of Songs Performed Only Once in Canada	4
Number of Venues Played	2

The Concerts

	Year	Date	Day	Venue
1.	1998	August 24	Wednesday	Northlands Coliseum*
2.	1990	August 12	Sunday	Jubilee Auditorium
3.	1990	August 13	Monday	Jubilee Auditorium
4.	1998	October 16	Friday	Edmonton Coliseum*
5.	2002	August 27	Tuesday	Skyreach Centre*

Note: * Venue changed name.

Fredericton, NB

Number of Concerts	1
Number of Songs Performed	15
Number of Different Songs Performed	15
Number of Songs Peformed Making Their Canadian Live Debut	0
Number of Songs Performed Only Once in Canada	0
Number of Venues Played	1

The Concert

	Year	Date	Day	Venue
1.	1997	April 7	Monday	University of New Brunswick, Aitken Centre

Halifax, NS

Number of Concerts	2
Number of Songs Performed	34
Number of Different Songs Performed	30
Number of Songs Performed Making Their Canadian Live Debut	3
Number of Songs Performed Only Once in Canada	0
Number of Venues Played	1

The Concerts

	Year	Date	Day	Venue
1.	1997	April 6	Sunday	Metro Centre
2.	2002	August 6	Tuesday	Metro Centre

Hamilton, ON

Number of Concerts	2
Number of Songs Performed	33
Number of Different Songs Performed	28
Number of Songs Performed Making Their Canadian Live Debut	3
Number of Songs Performed Only Once in Canada	0
Number of Venues Played	2

The Concerts

	Year	Date	Day	Venue
1.	1988	July 11	Monday	Copps Coliseum
2.	1992	August 21	Friday	Hamilton Place

Joliette, QC

Number of Concerts	1
Number of Songs Performed	15
Number of Different Songs Performed	15
Number of Songs Performed Making Their Canadian Live Debut	1
Number of Songs Performed Only Once in Canada	1
Number of Venues Played	1

The Concert

	Year	Date	Day	Venue
1.	1989	July 31	Monday	Lanaudière Outdoor Amphitheatre

Kelowna, BC

Number of Concerts	1
Number of Songs Performed	16
Number of Different Songs Performed	16
Number of Songs Performed Making Their Canadian Live Debut	0
Number of Songs Performed Only Once in Canada	0
Number of Venues Played	1

The Concert

	Year	Date	Day	Venue
1.	2005	July 22	Friday	Prospera Place

Kingston, ON

Total Number of Concerts	1
Number of Songs Performed	20
Number of Different Songs Performed	20
Number of Songs Performed Making Their Canadian Live Debut	1
Number of Songs Performed Only Once in Canada	1
Number of Venues Played	1

The Concert

	Year	Date	Day	Venue
1.	1990	May 30	Wednesday	Kingston Memorial Centre

Kitchener, ON

Number of Concerts	1
Number of Songs Performed	28
Number of Different Songs Performed	28
Number of Songs Performed Making Their Canadian Live Debut	1
Number of Songs Performed Only Once in Canada	1
Number of Venues Played	1

The Concert

	Year	Date	Day	Venue
1.	1981	October 31	Saturday	Kitchener Memorial Auditorium

London, ON

Number of Concerts	2
Number of Songs Performed	33
Number of Different Songs Performed	28
Number of Songs Performed Making Their Canadian Live Debut	0
Number of Songs Performed Only Once in Canada	0
Number of Venues Played	1

The Concerts

	Year	Date	Day	Venue
1.	1990	June 4	Monday	University of Western Ontario, Alumni Hall
2.	1996	May 12	Sunday	University of Western Ontario, Alumni Hall

Moncton, NB

Number of Concerts	2
Number of Songs Performed	34
Number of Different Songs Performed	30
Number of Songs Performed Making Their Canadian Live Debut	1
Number of Songs Performed Only Once in Canada	1
Number of Venues Played	1

The Concerts

	Year	Date	Day	Venue
1.	1997	April 5	Saturday	Moncton Coliseum
2.	2002	August 8	Thursday	Moncton Coliseum

Montreal, QC

Number of Concerts	20
Number of Songs Performed	277
Number of Different Songs Performed	126
Number of Songs Performed Making Their Canadian Live Debut	46
Number of Songs Performed Only Once in Canada	15
Number of Venues Played	9

Note: The set lists for the 2nd, 3rd & 4th concerts in 1962 are unknown. The set lists for the 1st and 5th concerts in 1962 are incomplete as is the set list for the 1966 concert.

The Concerts

	Year	Date	Day	Venue
1.	1962	June 28	Thursday	The Pot-pourri
2.	1962	June 29	Friday	The Pot-pourri
3.	1962	June 30	Saturday	The Pot-pourri
4.	1962	July 1	Sunday	The Pot-pourri
5.	1962	July 2	Monday	Finjan Club
6.	1966	February 20	Sunday	Place des Arts
7.	1974	January 11	Friday	Montreal Forum
8.	1974	January 12	Saturday	Montreal Forum
9.	1975	December 4	Thursday	Montreal Forum
10.	1978	September 19	Tuesday	Montreal Forum
11.	1980	April 22	Tuesday	Le Theatre Saint-Denis
12.	1980	April 23	Wednesday	Le Theatre Saint-Denis
13.	1980	April 24	Thursday	Le Theatre Saint-Denis
14.	1980	April 25	Friday	Le Theatre Saint-Denis
15.	1981	October 30	Friday	Montreal Forum
16.	1988	July 8	Friday	Montreal Forum
17.	1990	May 29	Tuesday	Centre Sportif de l'Université de Montréal
18.	1996	April 26	Friday	Verdun Auditorium
19.	1997	August 5	Tuesday	du Maurier Stadium
20.	2002	August 12	Monday	Molson Centre

Niagara Falls, ON

Number of Concerts	1
Number of Songs Performed	16
Number of Different Songs Performed	16
Number of Songs Performed Making Their Canadian Live Debut	2
Number of Songs Performed Only Once in Canada	2
Number of Venues Played	1

The Concert

	Year	Date	Day	Venue
1.	2003	August 23	Saturday	Oakes Garden Theatre

Ottawa, ON

Number of Concerts	9
Number of Songs Performed	146
Number of Different Songs Performed	75
Number of Songs Performed Making Their Canadian Live Debut	12
Number of Songs Performed Only Once in Canada	5
Number of Venues Played	5

Note: The set list for the 1966 concert is incomplete.

The Concerts

	Year	Date	Day	Venue
1.	1966	February 19	Saturday	Ottawa Auditorium
2.	1981	November 2	Monday	Ottawa Civic Centre
3.	1988	July 9	Saturday	Ottawa Civic Centre
4.	1989	July 30	Sunday	Ottawa Civic Centre
5.	1990	June 1	Friday	National Arts Centre Opera
6.	1990	June 2	Saturday	National Arts Centre Opera
7.	1992	August 22	Saturday	Lansdowne Stadium
8.	1998	October 30	Friday	Corel Centre
9.	2002	August 13	Tuesday	Corel Centre

Quebec City, QC

Number of Concerts	2
Number of Songs Performed	38
Number of Different Songs Performed	34
Number of Songs Performed Making Their Canadian Live Debut	14
Number of Songs Performed Only Once in Canada	0
Number of Venues Played	2

The Concerts

	Year	Date	Day	Venue
1.	1975	November 29	Saturday	Quebec City Coliseum
2.	2002	August 10	Saturday	l'Agora du Vieux-Port

Regina, SK

Number of Concerts	1
Number of Songs Performed	17
Number of Different Songs Performed	17
Number of Songs Performed Making Their Canadian Live Debut	0
Number of Songs Performed Only Once in Canada	0
Number of Venues Played	1

The Concert

	Year	Date	Day	Venue
1.	1998	October 20	Tuesday	Regina Exhibition Park, Agridome

Saint John, NB

Number of Concerts	2
Number of Songs Performed	33
Number of Different Songs Performed	31
Number of Songs Performed Making Their Canadian Live Debut	3
Number of Songs Performed Only Once in Canada	2
Number of Venues Played	1

The Concerts

	Year	Date	Day	Venue
1.	1997	April 8	Tuesday	Harbour Station
2.	2002	August 9	Friday	Harbour Station

St. John's, NL

Number of Concerts	2
Number of Songs Performed	30
Number of Different Songs Performed	24
Number of Songs Performed Making Their Canadian Live Debut	1
Number of Songs Performed Only Once in Canada	0
Number of Venues Played	1

The Concerts

	Year	Date	Day	Venue
1.	1997	March 31	Monday	St. John's Memorial Stadium
2.	1997	April 1	Tuesday	St. John's Memorial Stadium

Saskatoon, SK

Number of Concerts	2
Number of Songs Performed	35
Number of Different Songs Performed	31
Number of Songs Performed Making Their Canadian Live Debut	0
Number of Songs Performed Only Once in Canada	0
Number of Venues Played	1

The Concerts

	Year	Date	Day	Venue
1.	1998	October 18	Sunday	Saskatchewan Place
2.	2002	August 26	Monday	Saskatchewan Place

Sault Ste. Marie, ON

Number of Concerts	1
Number of Songs Performed	18
Number of Different Songs Performed	18
Number of Songs Performed Making Their Canadian Live Debut	0
Number of Songs Performed Only Once in Canada	0
Number of Venues Played	1

The Concert

	Year	Date	Day	Venue
1.	1992	August 25	Tuesday	Memorial Gardens

Sudbury, ON

Number of Concerts	1
Number of Songs Performed	18
Number of Different Songs Performed	18
Number of Songs Performed Making Their Canadian Live Debut	1
Number of Songs Performed Only Once in Canada	0
Number of Venues Played	1

The Concert

	Year	Date	Day	Venue
1.	1992	August 24	Monday	Sudbury Arena

Thunder Bay, ON

Number of Concerts	1
Number of Songs Performed	18
Number of Different Songs Performed	18
Number of Songs Performed Making Their Canadian Live Debut	0
Number of Songs Performed Only Once in Canada	0
Number of Venues Played	1

The Concert

	Year	Date	Day	Venue
1.	1992	August 27	Thursday	Fort William Garden

Toronto, ON

Number of Concerts	33
Number of Songs Performed	541
Number of Different Songs Performed	169
Number of Songs Performed Making Their Canadian Live Debut	104
Number of Songs Performed Only Once in Canada	24
Number of Venues Played	12

Note: The set list for the 2nd concert in 1965 is unknown. The 1964 concert set list is incomplete as is the set list for the 1st concert in 1965.

The Concerts

	Year	Date	Day	Venue
1.	1964	February 1	Saturday	CBC TV Studios
2.	1964	November 13	Friday	Massey Hall
3.	1965	November 14	Sunday	Massey Hall
4.	1965	November 15	Monday	Massey Hall
5.	1974	January 9	Wednesday	Maple Leaf Gardens
6.	1974	January 10	Thursday	Maple Leaf Gardens
7.	1975	December 1	Monday	Maple Leaf Gardens
8.	1975	December 2	Tuesday	Maple Leaf Gardens
9.	1978	October 12	Thursday	Maple Leaf Gardens
10.	1980	April 17	Thursday	Massey Hall
11.	1980	April 18	Friday	Massey Hall
12.	1980	April 19	Saturday	Massey Hall
13.	1980	April 20	Sunday	Massey Hall
14.	1981	October 29	Thursday	Maple Leaf Gardens
15.	1988	August 29	Monday	CNE Grandstand
16.	1989	July 29	Saturday	Kingswood Music Theatre
17.	1990	June 5	Tuesday	O'Keefe Centre
18.	1990	June 6	Wednesday	O'Keefe Centre

	Year	Date	Day	Venue
19.	1990	June 7	Thursday	O'Keefe Centre
20.	1991	July 26	Friday	Kingswood Music Theatre
21.	1992	August 17	Monday	Massey Hall
22.	1992	August 18	Tuesday	Massey Hall
23.	1993	September 2	Thursday	CNE Grandstand
24.	1996	April 27	Saturday	The Concert Hall
25.	1996	April 28	Sunday	The Concert Hall
26.	1997	August 7	Thursday	Molson Amphitheatre
27.	1998	October 29	Thursday	Maple Leaf Gardens
28.	2000	July 18	Tuesday	Molson Amphitheatre
29.	2001	November 8	Thursday	Air Canada Centre
30.	2002	August 16	Friday	Molson Amphitheatre
31.	2004	March 19	Friday	Ricoh Coliseum
32.	2004	March 20	Saturday	Phoenix Concert Theatre
33.	2004	March 21	Sunday	Kool Haus

Vancouver, BC

Number of Concerts	13
Number of Songs Performed	197
Number of Different Songs Performed	97
Number of Songs Performed Making Their Canadian Live Debut	37
Number of Songs Performed Only Once in Canada	21
Number of Venues Played	8

Note: The set list for the 1965 concert is unknown. The 1966 concert set list is incomplete.

The Concerts

	Year	Date	Day	Venue
1.	1965	April 9	Friday	Queen Elizabeth Theatre
2.	1966	March 26	Saturday	PNE Agrodome
3.	1978	November 11	Saturday	Pacific National Exhibition Hall
4.	1986	August 1	Friday	BC Place
5.	1988	August 21	Sunday	Pacific Coliseum
6.	1990	August 20	Monday	Pacific Coliseum
7.	1993	August 22	Sunday	Pacific Coliseum
8.	1998	May 13	Wednesday	The Rage
9.	1998	May 14	Thursday	GM Place
10.	1999	June 11	Friday	GM Place
11.	2005	July 19	Tuesday	The Orpheum
12.	2005	July 20	Wednesday	The Orpheum
13.	2005	July 21	Thursday	The Orpheum

Victoria, BC

Number of Concerts	2
Number of Songs Performed	34
Number of Different Songs Performed	28
Number of Songs Performed Making Their Canadian Live Debut	1
Number of Songs Performed Only Once in Canada	0
Number of Venues Played	2

The Concerts

	Year	Date	Day	Venue
1.	1990	August 19	Sunday	Memorial Arena
2.	2005	July 17	Sunday	Save-On-Foods Memorial Centre

Winnipeg, MB

Number of Concerts	5
Number of Songs Performed	87
Number of Different Songs Performed	52
Number of Songs Performed Making Their Canadian Live Debut	2
Number of Songs Performed Only Once in Canada	0
Number of Venues Played	2

The Concerts

	Year	Date	Day	Venue
1.	1988	August 26	Friday	Winnipeg Arena
2.	1990	June 17	Sunday	Centennial Centre Concert Hall
3.	1990	June 18	Monday	Centennial Centre Concert Hall
4.	1998	October 21	Wednesday	Winnipeg Arena
5.	2002	August 24	Saturday	Winnipeg Arena

The Concerts at a Glance

The Concerts at a Glance

#	Year	City	Date	Day	Venue
1.	1962	Montreal, QC	June 28	Thursday	The Pot-pourri
2.	1962	Montreal, QC	June 29	Friday	The Pot-pourri
3.	1962	Montreal, QC	June 30	Saturday	The Pot-pourri
4.	1962	Montreal, QC	July 1	Sunday	The Pot-pourri
5.	1962	Montreal, QC	July 2	Monday	Finjan Club
6.	1964	Toronto, ON	February 1	Saturday	CBC TV Studios
7.	1964	Toronto, ON	November 13	Friday	Massey Hall
8.	1965	Vancouver, BC	April 9	Friday	Queen Elizabeth Theatre
9.	1965	Toronto, ON	November 14	Sunday	Massey Hall
10.	1965	Toronto, ON	November 15	Monday	Massey Hall
11.	1966	Ottawa, ON	February 19	Saturday	Ottawa Auditorium
12.	1966	Montreal, QC	February 20	Sunday	Place des Arts
13.	1966	Vancouver, BC	March 26	Saturday	PNE Agrodome
14.	1974	Toronto, ON	January 9	Wednesday	Maple Leaf Gardens
15.	1974	Toronto, ON	January 10	Thursday	Maple Leaf Gardens
16.	1974	Montreal, QC	January 11	Friday	Montreal Forum
17.	1974	Montreal, QC	January 12	Saturday	Montreal Forum
18.	1975	Quebec City, QC	November 29	Saturday	Quebec City Coliseum
19.	1975	Toronto, ON	December 1	Monday	Maple Leaf Gardens
20.	1975	Toronto, ON	December 2	Tuesday	Maple Leaf Gardens
21.	1975	Montreal, QC	December 4	Thursday	Montreal Forum
22.	1978	Montreal, QC	September 19	Tuesday	Montreal Forum
23.	1978	Toronto, ON	October 12	Thursday	Maple Leaf Gardens
24.	1978	Vancouver, BC	November 11	Saturday	Pacific National Exhibition Hall
25.	1980	Toronto, ON	April 17	Thursday	Massey Hall
26.	1980	Toronto, ON	April 18	Friday	Massey Hall
27.	1980	Toronto, ON	April 19	Saturday	Massey Hall
28.	1980	Toronto, ON	April 20	Sunday	Massey Hall
29.	1980	Montreal, QC	April 22	Tuesday	Le Theatre Saint-Denis
30.	1980	Montreal, QC	April 23	Wednesday	Le Theatre Saint-Denis
31.	1980	Montreal, QC	April 24	Thursday	Le Theatre Saint-Denis
32.	1980	Montreal, QC	April 25	Friday	Le Theatre Saint-Denis
33.	1981	Toronto, ON	October 29	Thursday	Maple Leaf Gardens
34.	1981	Montreal, QC	October 30	Friday	Montreal Forum
35.	1981	Kitchener, ON	October 31	Saturday	Kitchener Memorial Auditorium
36.	1981	Ottawa, ON	November 2	Monday	Ottawa Civic Centre
37.	1986	Vancouver, BC	August 1	Friday	BC Place
38.	1988	Montreal, QC	July 8	Friday	Montreal Forum
39.	1988	Ottawa, ON	July 9	Saturday	Ottawa Civic Centre
40.	1988	Hamilton, ON	July 11	Monday	Copps Coliseum
41.	1988	Vancouver, BC	August 21	Sunday	Pacific Coliseum
42.	1988	Calgary, AB	August 23	Tuesday	Olympic Saddledome
43.	1988	Edmonton, AB	August 24	Wednesday	Northlands Coliseum
44.	1988	Winnipeg, MB	August 26	Friday	Winnipeg Arena
45.	1988	Toronto, ON	August 29	Monday	CNE Grandstand
46.	1989	Toronto, ON	July 29	Saturday	Kingswood Music Theatre
47.	1989	Ottawa, ON	July 30	Sunday	Ottawa Civic Centre
48.	1989	Joliette, QC	July 31	Monday	Lanaudière Outdoor Amphitheatre
49.	1990	Montreal, QC	May 29	Tuesday	Centre Sportif de l'Université de Montréal
50.	1990	Kingston, ON	May 30	Wednesday	Kingston Memorial Centre
51.	1990	Ottawa, ON	June 1	Friday	National Arts Centre Opera
52.	1990	Ottawa, ON	June 2	Saturday	National Arts Centre Opera
53.	1990	London, ON	June 4	Monday	University of Western Ontario, Alumni Hall
54.	1990	Toronto, ON	June 5	Tuesday	O'Keefe Centre
55.	1990	Toronto, ON	June 6	Wednesday	O'Keefe Centre
56.	1990	Toronto, ON	June 7	Thursday	O'Keefe Centre
57.	1990	Winnipeg, MB	June 17	Sunday	Centennial Centre Concert Hall
58.	1990	Winnipeg, MB	June 18	Monday	Centennial Centre Concert Hall
59.	1990	Edmonton, AB	August 12	Sunday	Jubilee Auditorium
60.	1990	Edmonton, AB	August 13	Monday	Jubilee Auditoirum
61.	1990	Calgary, AB	August 15	Wednesday	Jubilee Auditoirum
62.	1990	Calgary, AB	August 16	Thursday	Jubilee Auditoirum

#	Year	City	Date	Day	Venue
63.	1990	Victoria, BC	August 19	Sunday	Memorial Arena
64.	1990	Vancouver, BC	August 20	Monday	Pacific Coliseum
65.	1991	Toronto, ON	July 26	Friday	Kingswood Music Theatre
66.	1992	Toronto, ON	August 17	Monday	Massey Hall
67.	1992	Toronto, ON	August 18	Tuesday	Massey Hall
68.	1992	Hamilton, ON	August 21	Friday	Hamilton Place
69.	1992	Ottawa, ON	August 22	Saturday	Lansdowne Stadium
70.	1992	Sudbury, ON	August 24	Monday	Sudbury Arena
71.	1992	Sault Ste. Marie, ON	August 25	Tuesday	Memorial Gardens
72.	1992	Thunder Bay, ON	August 27	Thursday	Fort William Gardens
73.	1993	Vancouver, BC	August 22	Sunday	Pacific Coliseum
74.	1993	Toronto, ON	September 2	Thursday	CNE Grandstand
75.	1996	Montreal, QC	April 26	Friday	Verdun Auditorium
76.	1996	Toronto, ON	April 27	Saturday	The Concert Hall
77.	1996	Toronto, ON	April 28	Sunday	The Concert Hall
78.	1996	London, ON	May 12	Sunday	University of Western Ontario, Alumni Hall
79.	1997	St. John's, NF	March 31	Monday	St. John's Memorial Stadium
80.	1997	St. John's, NF	April 1	Tuesday	St. John's Memorial Stadium
81.	1997	Moncton, NB	April 5	Saturday	Moncton Coliseum
82.	1997	Halifax, NS	April 6	Sunday	Metro Centre
83.	1997	Fredericton, NB	April 7	Monday	University of New Brunswick, Aitken Centre
84.	1997	Saint John, NB	April 8	Tuesday	Harbour Station
85.	1997	Montreal, QC	August 5	Tuesday	du Maurier Stadium
86.	1997	Toronto, ON	August 7	Thursday	Molson Amphitheatre
87.	1998	Vancouver, BC	May 13	Wednesday	The Rage
88.	1998	Vancouver, BC	May 14	Thursday	GM Place
89.	1998	Calgary, AB	October 15	Thursday	Canadian Airlines Saddledome
90.	1998	Edmonton, AB	October 16	Friday	Edmonton Coliseum
91.	1998	Saskatoon, SK	October 18	Sunday	Saskatchewan Place
92.	1998	Regina, SK	October 20	Tuesday	Regina Exhibition Park, Agridome
93.	1998	Winnipeg, MB	October 21	Wednesday	Winnipeg Arena
94.	1998	Toronto, ON	October 29	Thursday	Maple Leaf Gardens
95.	1998	Ottawa, ON	October 30	Friday	Corel Centre
96.	1999	Vancouver, BC	June 11	Friday	GM Place
97.	2000	Toronto, ON	July 18	Tuesday	Molson Amphitheatre
98.	2001	Toronto, ON	November 8	Thursday	Air Canada Centre
99.	2002	Halifax, NS	August 6	Tuesday	Metro Centre
100.	2002	Moncton, NB	August 8	Thursday	Moncton Coliseum
101.	2002	Saint John, NB	August 9	Friday	Harbour Station
102.	2002	Quebec City, QC	August 10	Saturday	l'Agora du Vieux-Port
103.	2002	Montreal, QC	August 12	Monday	Molson Centre
104.	2002	Ottawa, ON	August 13	Tuesday	Corel Centre
105.	2002	Toronto, ON	August 16	Friday	Molson Amphitheatre
106.	2002	Winnipeg, MB	August 24	Saturday	Winnipeg Arena
107.	2002	Saskatoon, SK	August 26	Monday	Saskatchewan Place
108.	2002	Edmonton, AB	August 27	Tuesday	Skyreach Centre
109.	2002	Calgary, AB	August 28	Wednesday	Pengrowth Saddledome
110.	2003	Niagara Falls, ON	August 23	Saturday	Oakes Garden Theatre
111.	2004	Toronto, ON	March 19	Friday	Ricoh Coliseum
112.	2004	Toronto, ON	March 20	Saturday	Phoenix Concert Theatre
113.	2004	Toronto, ON	March 21	Sunday	Kool Haus
114.	2005	Victoria, BC	July 17	Sunday	Save-On-Foods Memorial Centre
115.	2005	Vancouver, BC	July 19	Tuesday	The Orpheum
116.	2005	Vancouver, BC	July 20	Wednesday	The Orpheum
117.	2005	Vancouver, BC	July 21	Thursday	The Orpheum
118.	2005	Kelowna, BC	July 22	Friday	Prospera Plcae
119.	2005	Calgary, AB	July 24	Sunday	Pengrowth Saddledome

About the Authors

Brady J. Leyser

Brady J. Leyser was born in Toronto, Canada in 1959. He started listening to the music of Bob Dylan in 1977 and attended his first Dylan concert in 1978.

Mr. Leyser began his career in research in 1985, first as a library technician at a community college, then in government, law, medical and public libraries and later as Director of Information Resources for an advertising agency. He is now a freelance researcher specializing in advertising, marketing and business information.

Brady is the author of Rock Stars/Pop Stars: A Comprehensive Bibliography, 1955-1994 and the former editor of What's New in Advertising and Marketing.

In his spare time Brady enjoys listening to a wide variety of music, is an avid concert attendee, writes concert reviews and enjoys singing karaoke (especially Dylan songs).

Brady has one daughter; Olivia. He currently resides in Toronto, Canada.

Olof Björner

Olof Björner was born in Stockholm, Sweden in 1942. He started listening to the music of Bob Dylan in 1963 and attended his first Dylan concert in 1987.

Mr. Björner began his career in computer sciences in 1963, first as a programmer, then project manager and later as Managing Director for a consulting company. In the late 90's he started his own computer consulting company specializing in security and healthcare applications.

Olof is the web master for "I Happen To Be A Swede Myself" one of the most popular Bob Dylan sites for data on his recording and concert history, as well as songs covered by other artists. His web site can be found at www.bjorner.com.

In addition to music, Olof is also very interested in literature and art. He is the Chairman of the Swedish John Cowper Powys Society and is a member of several other literary societies.

Olof has three children; Axel, Tore and Ylva and five grandchildren; Matilda, Jonas, Joanna, Livia and Herman. He currently resides in Filipstad, Sweden where he operates a book store with his wife Agneta.

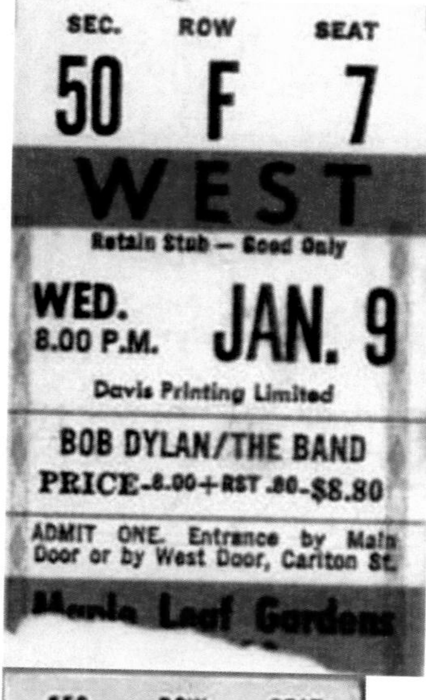

SEC. ROW SEAT
52 G 18
WEST
Retain Stub — Good Only
TUES.
7:00 P.M
DEC. 2
Davis Printing Limited
BOB DYLAN
PRICE-8.00+RST .80-$8.80
ADMIT ONE. Entrance by Main
Door or by West Door, Carlton St.
Maple Leaf Gardens

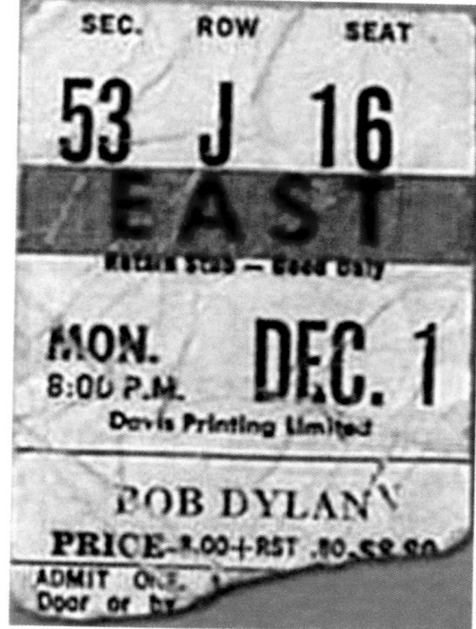

1343 BOX1
35 CENTR
29 FLOOR
FLR1 ADULT
13.64
BOB DYLAN
PRESENTED BY
CHUM & CHUM FM
THU APR 17 1980 8:00 PM
AT
MASSEY HALL
CENTRE FLOOR ADULT
FLR1 D 29 15.00

BOB DYLAN
PRESENTED BY
CHUM & CHUM FM
FRI APR 18 1980 8:00 PM
AT
MASSEY HALL
LEFT FLOOR ADULT
FLR3 D 11 15.00

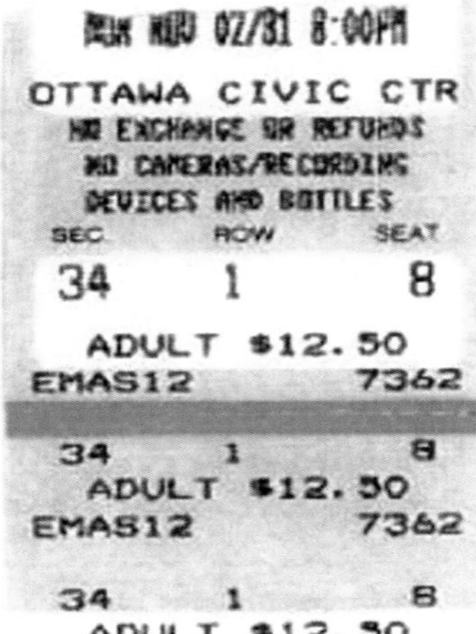

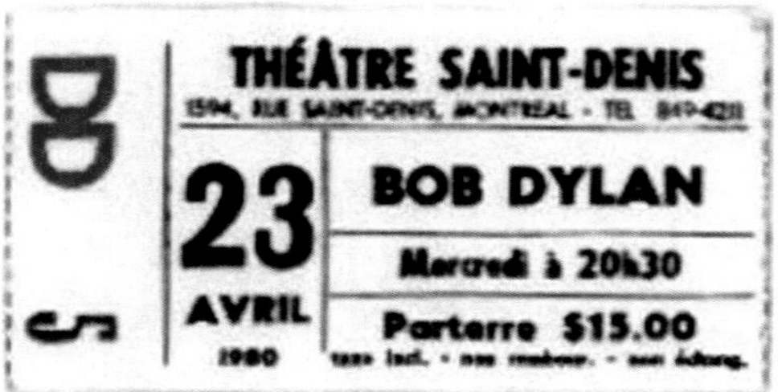

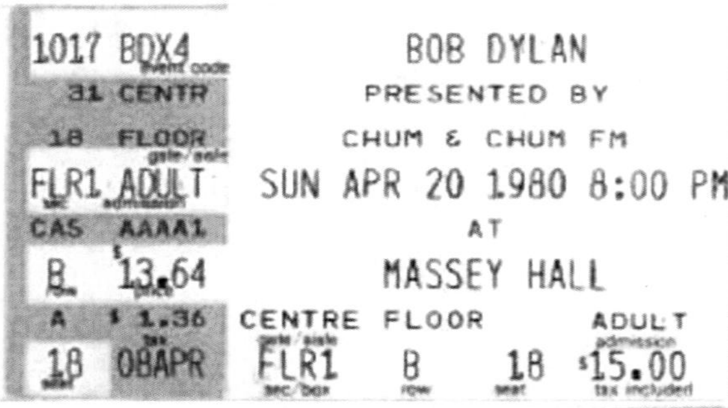

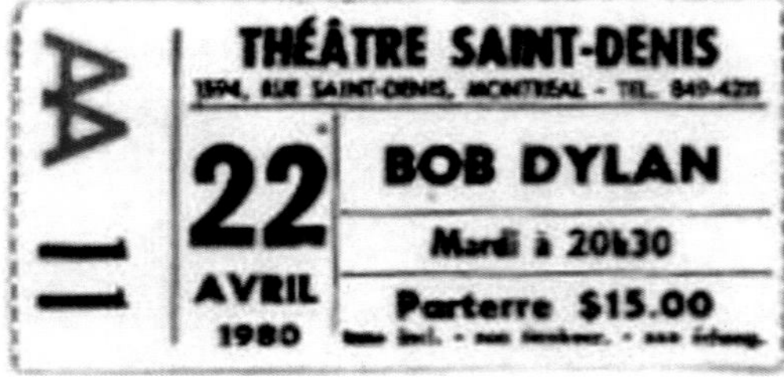

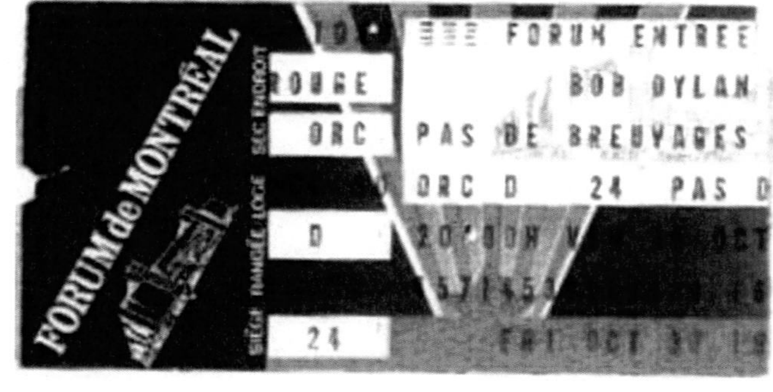

BOB DYLAN
PRESENTED BY
CHUM & CHUM-FM
THU OCT 29 1981 8:00 PM
AT
MAPLE LEAF GARDENS
RED 51 ADULT
RD51 N 7 $12.50

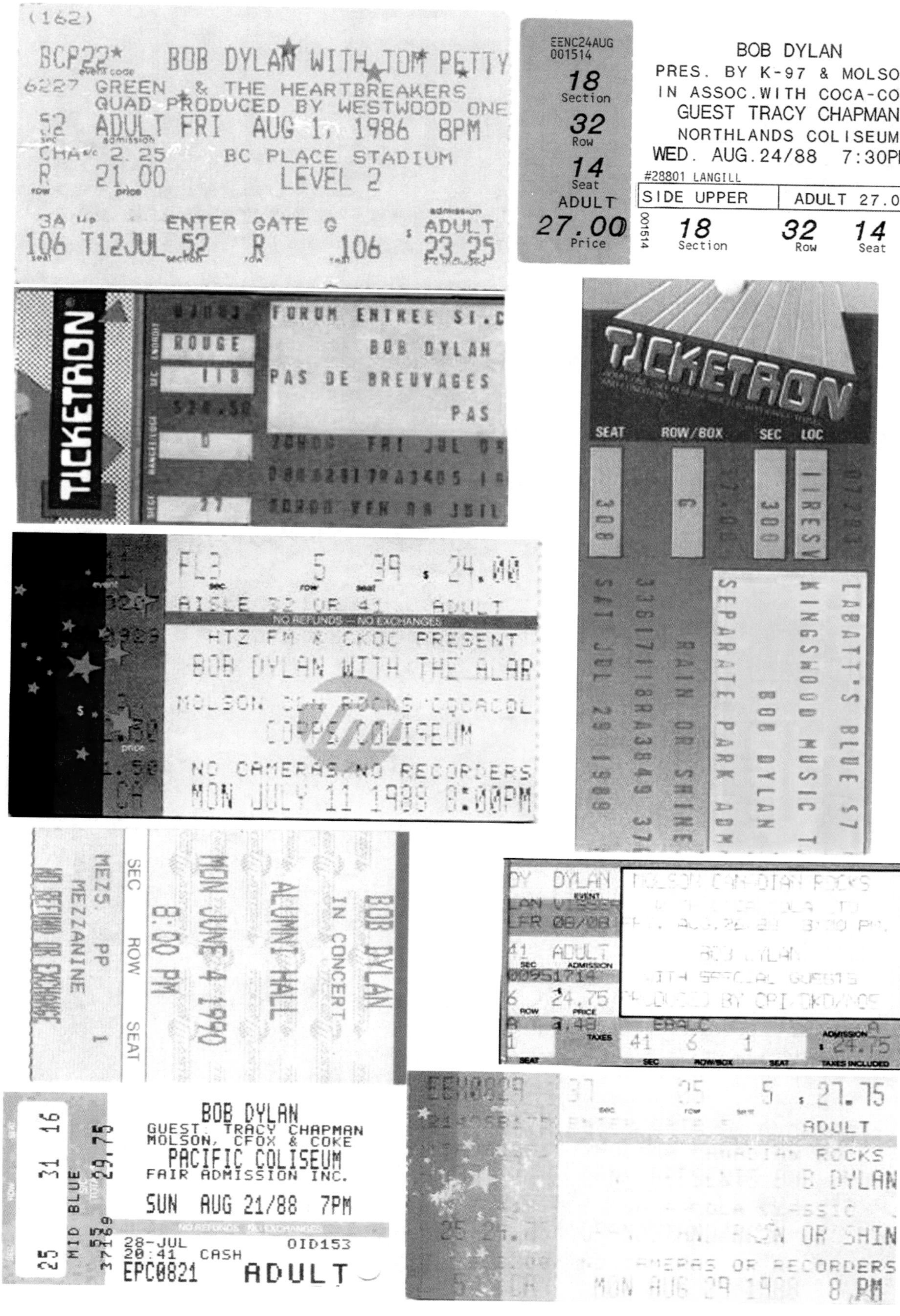
BOB DYLAN WITH TOM PETTY
& THE HEARTBREAKERS
QUAD PRODUCED BY WESTWOOD ONE
ADULT FRI AUG 1, 1986 8PM
BC PLACE STADIUM
LEVEL 2
ENTER GATE G
BOB DYLAN
PRES. BY K-97 & MOLSON
IN ASSOC.WITH COCA-COLA
GUEST TRACY CHAPMAN
NORTHLANDS COLISEUM
WED. AUG.24/88 7:30PM
SIDE UPPER
ADULT 27.00
TICKETRON
FORUM ENTREE ST.C
BOB DYLAN
PAS DE BREUVAGES
NO REFUNDS — NO EXCHANGES
BOB DYLAN WITH THE ALAR
NO CAMERAS NO RECORDERS
MON JULY 11 1988 8:00PM
BOB DYLAN
IN CONCERT
ALUMNI HALL
MON JUNE 4 1990
8:00 PM
MEZZANINE
NO REFUND OR EXCHANGE
BOB DYLAN
GUEST TRACY CHAPMAN
MOLSON, CFOX & COKE
PACIFIC COLISEUM
FAIR ADMISSION INC.
SUN AUG 21/88 7PM
ADULT
MON AUG 29 1988 8 PM

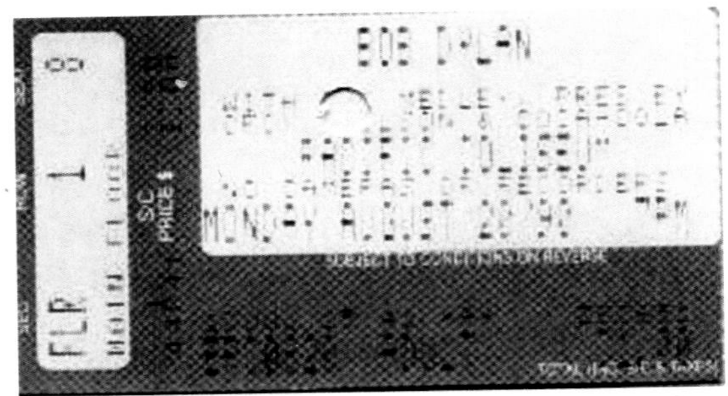

JEN 837
873 MAIN
RC
RC ADULT
CHV WWST1
Y 30.75
A
5 14JUL

BOB DYLAN
WITH SUE MEDLEY
PRESENTED BY K-97
EDM. JUBILEE AUDITORIUM
NO CAMERAS OR RECORDERS
MONDAY AUG. 13/90 8PM
MAIN FLOOR ADULT
RC Y 5 30.75

SUBJECT TO CONDITIONS ON REVERSE

PRESENTED BY Q 100
BOB DYLAN
WITH SUE MEDLEY
****
SUNDAY AUG. 19 1990
8:00 PM
VICTORIA
MEMORIAL ARENA
FLOOR $25.75
(INCLUDES USER FEE)
FLOOR SEAT

42	O	4
SEC.	ROW	SEAT

NO CAMERA/RECORDERS

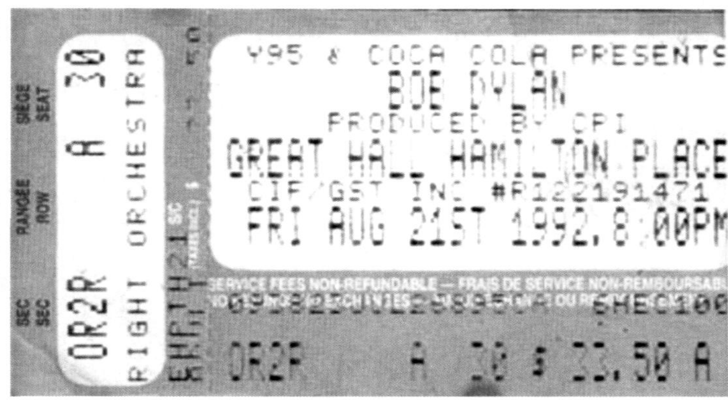

Bob Dylon Concer

8 P.M.

AUG 27 1992

NO REFUNDS OR EXCHANGES

BOB DYLAN
IN CONCERT
SUNDAY
MAY 12 1996
8:00 P.M.
ALUMNI HALL
NO CAMERA/RECORDERS
RESERVED $35.00
ORCH 2-RGHT CTR
RCTR J 7
SEC. ROW SEAT
SUBJECT TO CONDITIONS ON REVERSE
RESERVED $35.00

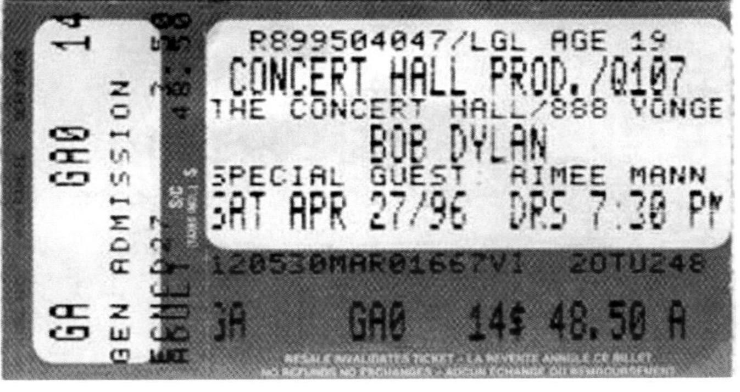

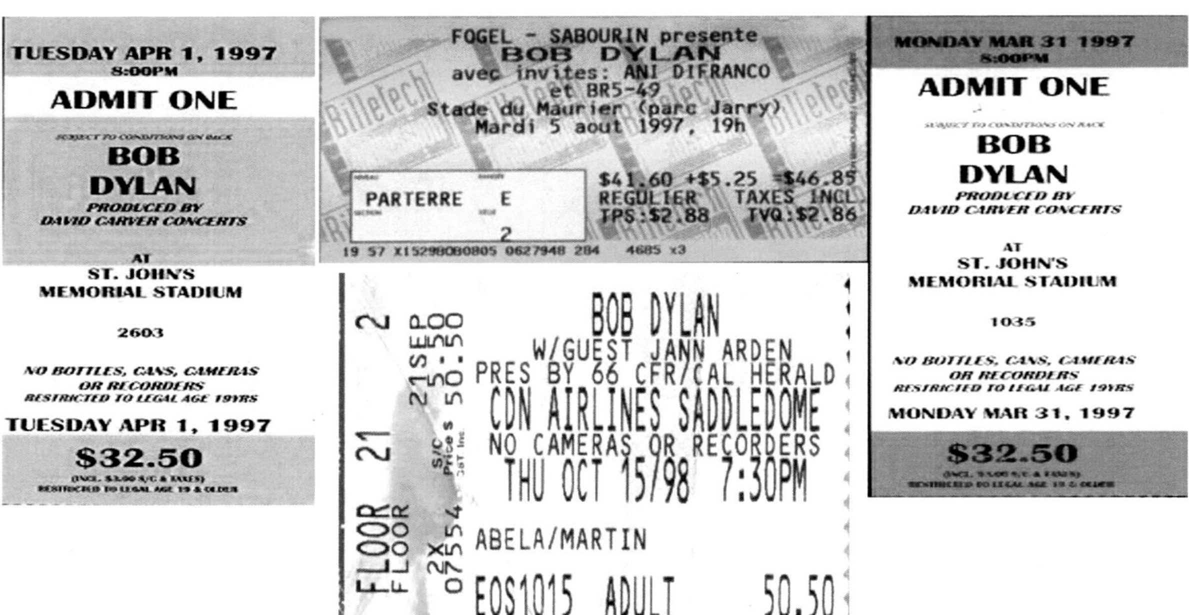
TUESDAY APR 1, 1997
8:00PM
ADMIT ONE
BOB
DYLAN
PRODUCED BY
DAVID CARVER CONCERTS
AT
ST. JOHN'S
MEMORIAL STADIUM
2603
NO BOTTLES, CANS, CAMERAS
OR RECORDERS
RESTRICTED TO LEGAL AGE 19YRS
TUESDAY APR 1, 1997
$32.50
FOGEL - SABOURIN presente
BOB DYLAN
avec invites: ANI DIFRANCO
et BR5-49
Stade du Maurier (parc Jarry)
Mardi 5 aout 1997, 19h
PARTERRE E
2
$41.60 +$5.25 =$46.85
REGULIER TAXES INCL
TPS:$2.88 TVQ:$2.86
19 57 X152980B0805 0627948 284 4685 x3
BOB DYLAN
W/GUEST JANN ARDEN
PRES BY 66 CFR/CAL HERALD
CDN AIRLINES SADDLEDOME
NO CAMERAS OR RECORDERS
THU OCT 15/98 7:30PM
ABELA/MARTIN
EOS1015 ADULT 50.50
FLOOR 21 2
FLOOR
21SEP
50.50
MONDAY MAR 31 1997
8:00PM
ADMIT ONE
BOB
DYLAN
PRODUCED BY
DAVID CARVER CONCERTS
AT
ST. JOHN'S
MEMORIAL STADIUM
1035
NO BOTTLES, CANS, CAMERAS
OR RECORDERS
RESTRICTED TO LEGAL AGE 19YRS
MONDAY MAR 31, 1997
$32.50

DAVID CARVER CONCERTS
Presents
BOB DYLAN
Sunday April 6 1997 7hr30pm
No Bottles,Cans,Cameras,Recorders
$29.50 Plus Ticket Service Charge
No Refunds Or Exchanges
AITKEN CENTRE-UNB
$29.50 +$1.25 =$30.75
ORCHESTRA 1
REGULAR
ALL TAXES INCLUDED
42

THE MIX / UNIVERSAL
BOB DYLAN
RAIN OR SHINE/R126007780
THE MOLSON AMPHITHEATRE
A PORTION TO CHARITY
THU AUG 7 1997 8:00PM
101727JUN25162MC 100BA200
203 N 10 47.00A
203 N 10
LVL200 AISLE 3
47.00

BOB DYLAN / JONI MITCHELL
AND VAN MORRISON
PRESENTED BY CFMI & CKNW
GENERAL MOTORS PLACE
NO CAMERAS/RECORDERS/VIDE
THU MAY 14/98 7:30PM
27MAR 10:58 *A* OTM400
EGM0514 ADULT 89.75
108 15 108
CLUB-GATE 10
89.75

ONE SPECIAL EVENING
WITH
BOB DYLAN
THE RAGE-750 PACIFIC BLVD
NO CAMERAS/RECORDERS
WED MAY 13/98 DRS 8PM
9MAY 11:59 CASH OTM40
ERG0513 ADULT 54.50
GA GA5 85
NO MINORS
54.50

BOB DYLAN
WITH GUEST JANN ARDEN
JOURNAL/MIX 96
EDMONTON COLISEUM
NO CAMERAS/RECORDERS
FRI. OCT 16/98 7:30PM
ABELA/MARTIN
ENC1016 ADULT 51.00
FLR 23 10
FLOOR SEATING
20SEP
51.00

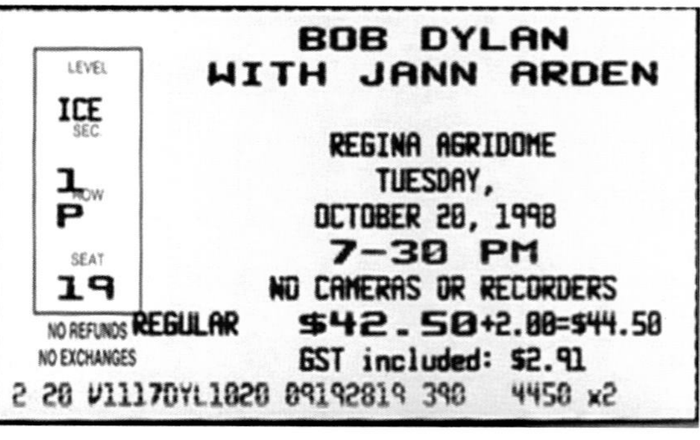
BOB DYLAN
WITH JANN ARDEN
REGINA AGRIDOME
TUESDAY,
OCTOBER 20, 1998
7-30 PM
NO CAMERAS OR RECORDERS
ICE
1
P
19
REGULAR
$42.50+2.00=$44.50
GST included: $2.91
NO REFUNDS
NO EXCHANGES